H E
SERVICE MANAGEMENT

HEALTHCARE SERVICE MANAGEMENT

Marie Muller
Marthie Bezuidenhout
Karien Jooste

JUTA
AND COMPANY LTD

PO Box 24309
Lansdowne 7779
Cape Town, South Africa

Healthcare Service Management

ISBN 07021 71638

Project manager: Sarah O'Neill
Editor and proofreader: Ethné Clarke
Cover design: WaterBerry Design
Index: Jeanne Cope
Designed and typeset in 11/13 Berkley Book Old Style by MckoreGraphics
Printed and bound in the Republic of South Africa by Paarl Print

Preface

Rationale for the book

This book is primarily a replacement of the book *Dimensions of Nursing Management* but is concerned with the management of healthcare organisations by any healthcare service manager and leader amidst the existing dynamic challenges. The main thrust of the book is the coherent portrayal of all the dimensions of management and leadership within the professional, ethical and legal context of healthcare service delivery in South Africa, but with transferability of the management and leadership principles elsewhere in healthcare organisations.

Purpose and aims of the book

The general purpose of the book is to present the best practice guidelines related to the management of a healthcare organisation in the Southern and Eastern African regions. This handbook was written by an interdependent team of three authors, based on our collective experience of management and leadership practice, research and education in the healthcare service context, who worked together to ensure a coherent and holistic product.

Target group

This book serves as a source of reference on healthcare service management to any practising healthcare service manager – general and specialised/functional – and to any lecturer, researcher, senior or post-graduate student involved in healthcare service management. The book is also meant to assist healthcare managers preparing for regional, national or international accreditation or certification of the healthcare organisation.

The individual chapters

Although the chapters could be seen as stand-alone chapters – and thus may be read separately and independently from one another – the sequence of the chapters follows a particular logic commencing with the general principles of management and concluding with the principles of continuous quality improvement resulting in total quality management. The approach of this handbook is based on the belief that quality management and leadership should be practised at every level of the healthcare organisation. The five levels of leadership to take an organisation from good to great described by Jim Collins (2001:19–22) have been applied in selected chapters.

A particular format of contextualisation was used: the context, the relevant role-players involved in healthcare service management, the purpose and process related to that particular dimension of management, as well as the underlying dynamics or critical success factors impacting on this dimension of management, are described. This framework should assist researchers to contextualise a theoretical framework for healthcare service management. The book is divided into 20 chapters.

Chapter 1 was written by Marie Muller and sets the scene for healthcare service management within the particular business ownership context (public, private or mixed). Selected forces impacting on healthcare service management are highlighted. In addition to the legal and professional context, the principles of corporate governance are described in great detail. The levels (corporate, middle and operational) and types of management (strategic, general and functional) are delineated and the management process is described as planning, organising, leading and control. The author continues to give a detailed description of each of these four managerial activities. The underlying dynamics impacting on the success of healthcare service management are briefly discussed, focusing on the macro-environmental and institutional determinants.

Chapter 2 (written by Marie Muller) focuses on strategic management that is contextualised as the continuous positioning or repositioning of the organisation, based on strategy analysis (external and internal environmental assessment), strategy development (determination of the organisation's mission, vision, values, goals and related key performance areas and strategic actions required to achieve the goals), strategy execution (the implementation or deployment of the strategy by translating the corporate goals and strategy into achievable objectives and action plans that cascade down to departmental, unit/area and individual levels), and strategy review (evaluation of organisational, departmental, unit/area and individual performance in accordance with the outcomes and indicators determined).

Chapter 3 describes selected management models, such as participative management, centralisation versus decentralisation, the systems approach, chaos and complexity theories, as well as Ubuntu.

Chapter 4 attempts to explore selected dimensions of functional management, focusing on decision-making and problem-solving (including the consensus problem-solving process) in a healthcare organisation, the principles of project management and performance management (the latter is also described in Chapter 12). All three authors contributed to these two chapters.

Chapter 5 analyses the dynamic complexities of change management in a healthcare organisation, focusing on the following levels of change: individual, organisational development, transitional change management and transformation management. The change management process is also contextualised as change strategy analysis, strategy development, strategy execution and strategy review, in accordance with the different levels of change. Only a few change models were briefly described: ecological change, rational-purposive change, evolutionary organisational life-cycle change, cognitive change, as well as the Good-to-Great model described by Jim Collins. Marie Muller is the author of this chapter with significant input by Karien Jooste.

Chapter 6 discuuses communication management, with specific reference to formal internal communication, informal internal communication, public relations, information management, tele/electronic medicine, the management of patient records, as well as knowledge management. An attempt was made by the two authors (Marie Muller and Karien Jooste) to highlight the best practice standards related to the above dimensions of communication management in a healthcare organisation.

Chapter 7 was written by Karien Jooste and explores the principles of marketing as applied to a healthcare organisation. The marketing process focuses on the strategy analysis (a situation analysis of the market environment), development of a marketing strategy (description of the service, statement of mission, listing of the target group and the marketing methods to be utilised), strategy execution and strategy audit.

Chapter 8 (also written by Karien Jooste) describes the principles and process related to the planning and commissioning of a healthcare service. This process description discusses the application and approval, briefing, design, construction and commissioning of a new service or expansion of an existing service.

Chapter 9 describes the management of HIV and AIDS. The author (Marie Muller) attempts to briefly explore the global and national guidelines that direct the management of HIV and AIDS, focusing on the establishment of workplace programmes and the principles of clinical governance.

Chapters 10 to 15 are about human resource management (authored by Marthie Bezuidenhout). In *Chapter 10* the nature and scope of human resource management are delineated, focusing on the conceptual framework related to the forthcoming chapters. Emphasis is also placed on the employment relationship and strategic human resource management. The planning and provision of human resources are described in *Chapter 11*, exploring the principles of job analysis (job description and job specification), job evaluation and recruitment, selection and appointment. In *Chapter 12* maintenance principles of human resources are described, focusing on occupational health and safety, as well as the quality of work life and productivity. *Chapter 13* is about the optimal utilisation of human resources. The conceptual framework is described, relating to communication, lateral relations, staffing allocation, nursing delivery systems, absenteeism and turnover of staff. In *Chapter 14* the author describes the principles and process related to performance management and the development of human resources. The focus is on performance appraisal, human resources development, motivation, career management, supervision and job design. The principles of fair labour practice are described in *Chapter 15*. The applicable labour-related perspectives, processes and practices are explored. The legal and professional dynamics of human resource management, as applied to the South African context, are highlighted throughout these chapters on human resource management.

In **Chapter 16** Karien Jooste describes leadership in healthcare service management. Selected leadership theories and leadership styles are highlighted, as well as selected components of the leadership process, such as influencing, leadership development, executive leadership, cultural issues, leadership communication and empowerment. The last four chapters were written by Marie Muller. Financial management is described in **Chapter 17**. The process of financial management is divided into budgeting, expenditure control and financial risk management. These principles and processes are described in relation to the type of business ownership (public, private or mixed) of healthcare organisations. Great emphasis is placed on the principles of corporate governance related to financial management. Risk management in a healthcare organisation is described in **Chapter 18**. The generic conceptual framework of strategy analysis, strategy development, strategy execution and strategy review is utilised for the application of risk management. The dimensions of risk management in this chapter focus on corporate governance, business continuity management, disaster management, occupational health and safety, environmental management and adverse event management.

The last two chapters concern quality management. **Chapter 19** explores selected models of quality improvement: international standardisation organisation (ISO), business excellence, balanced scorecard and accreditation. The author attempts to highlight the thrust of each model, as applied to a healthcare organisation. Continuous quality improvement (CQI) in a healthcare organisation is described in **Chapter 20**. The systems-based conceptual framework (strategy analysis, development, execution and review) is once again applied. The CQI cycle (standard setting, monitoring, assessment and evaluation, as well as remedial/corrective action), clinical governance, consumer satisfaction and total quality management (TQM) are highlighted.

Expression of appreciation

The authors would like to sincerely thank the team members who took care of the linguistic, artistic, editorial and secretarial aspects of the book. We would also like to thank Juta Publishers who made this book a reality. In conclusion, we would like to acknowledge with sincere appreciation the understanding and support of those people in the close environments of the three authors during the writing of the book.

Marie Muller
September 2005

Contents

1 Management of a healthcare organisation

KEY CONCEPTS

Management
Planning
Organising
Leading
Control

SPECIFIC OUTCOMES

After studying this chapter, you should be able to:

- Interpret the legal, professional-ethical and healthcare **context** with reference to general forces impacting on healthcare service delivery, the constitution, common law, general national legislation, health-related legislation and directives, corporate governance, professional, ethical and legal context of the healthcare practitioners, business ethics and business ownership
- Analyse and debate the **purpose** of management in a healthcare organisation with reference to organisational goals and impact on healthcare indicators
- Identify the different **role-players** involved in the management of a healthcare organisation, that is legislative authorities, board of directors, managers, community, recognised trade unions and other stakeholders
- Interpret the roles and responsibilities of the different role-players involved in the management of healthcare organisations
- Describe the **management process** as applied to healthcare service management, that is the levels and types of management, as well as the management process (planning, organising, leading and control)
- Critically explore and debate the **underlying dynamics** impacting on healthcare service management, that is macro-environment and institutional determinants.

1.1 INTRODUCTION

This is the introductory chapter of a textbook that introduces learners to the applied science on the management of a healthcare organisation. Selected forces impacting on the management of healthcare organisations are highlighted. The context with reference to the management of a healthcare organisation is described, followed by a description of the purpose of management, the role-players and their subsequent responsibilities, and the process of management. The underlying dynamics that impact on the success or failure of healthcare service management are also elucidated.

1.1.1 Forces impacting on healthcare service management

There are many *forces* impacting on the management of healthcare organisations. The following are briefly discussed: economic, health culture/perspective, competence and experience, value for money (excellence), consumerism, social responsibility and business ethics.

Economic forces

Among the most powerful extraneous determinants are the prevailing economic climate, the economic system of the country, and specific economic factors. A country's particular modes of economic production, distribution and consumption, as well as its patterns of ownership, economic control and the distribution of resources and wealth, directly affect the healthcare organisations and traditions in the healthcare system. Obviously a country's economic ability, economic prosperity, levels of economic development and industrialisation, economic growth and dependence on international economic aid, as well as the national and international economic trends and crises, have a pronounced effect on the healthcare system and the quality of management in the healthcare system and organisations.

Any organisation or business is therefore a component of the economic system, and is also subject to the economic principle. This economic principle consists of the human endeavour to satisfy unlimited needs with limited resources. All economic systems are subject to it. According to the economic principle, a business/organisation always has to endeavour to obtain the highest possible output (product and services) at the least possible input (lowest cost). All businesses/organisations are subject to this principle, regardless of the type and complexity of business ownership. The task of management is therefore to examine the factors, methods and principles that enable a business or organisation to maximise its profits/utilisation of resources, and achieve its objectives (De J. Cronjé, Du Toit, Motlatla & Marais, 2004:27). The healthcare organisation is no exception – unlimited resources need to be maximised to achieve the maximum results and outcomes in a very complex healthcare context.

Health culture or health perspective

Every clientele has or maintains a distinctive health culture or health perspective, that is all those conceptions, beliefs and superstitions, knowledge and skills, values and customs which people share in respect of health, disease and care. Health culture obviously holds important consequences for both the health status and the health behaviour of the clientele, as well as for the nature and organisations of health systems and the management of the healthcare organisations. The health knowledge, health beliefs and health attitudes are important forces impacting on the management of a healthcare organisation. Modernised (Western) scientifically based healthcare as opposed to traditional African-based, as well as complementary and alternative healthcare service delivery are important forces on contemporary healthcare service delivery in various African countries today.

Competence and experience

Successful management of a healthcare organisation is dependent upon the competence of individual and team/corporate managers, clinical practitioners and all non-clinical practitioners. The principle of industry experience – especially with reference to healthcare managers – is also of utmost importance. Managers fulfil different roles and require general and specialised abilities (knowledge, skills, attitudes and values).

The following key abilities are identified as prerequisites for sound management: conceptual, interpersonal and technical abilities:

- *Conceptual abilities*. These include the mental capacity to view the business/organisation in a gestalt/holistic manner. This ability mainly relates to thinking, analytical and planning skills. Locus of control – the deliberate decision to make the best of the situation – also impacts on the competence of the manager.
- *Interpersonal abilities*. These abilities include the people-skills required to lead, enable and motivate the employees towards goal achievement in the organisation, in accordance with the predetermined strategies, plans, standards and indicators.
- *Technical abilities*. These include the application of several sciences (i.e. clinical and management sciences) in the healthcare organisation by utilising and integrating operational information (i.e. information management, technology management) to facilitate the quality of service delivery and management of the healthcare institution.

Value for money (excellence)

The knowledge, beliefs and attitudes related to health in a community will influence the clients'/patients' perceptions and expectations on value for money or excellence.

Consumerism

Consumerism is a social force that protects consumers against unsafe products and malpractices by exerting moral and economic pressure on businesses and organisations. There is often a national consumer union that acts as the watchdog for consumers.

Social responsibility

The social responsibility of an organisation is a concept that originated in media revelations of malpractices by businesses and the resultant insistence of society on restricting such malpractices through regulation. Historically, social responsibility has been measured by the contribution of an organisation towards employment opportunities and its contribution to the economy. Many other factors are, however, important today, such as assessing the social performance of the organisation/ business, safe workplace, community engagement, concern about health issues and environmental safety, HIV and AIDS in the world of work (refer to Chapter 9, Management of HIV and AIDS) and optimal utilisation of environmental resources (i.e. recycling). Social responsibility has been included in the principles of corporate governance and all healthcare organisations need to adhere to this.

Business ethics

Business ethics is closely related to social responsibility, except that business ethics focuses specifically on the ethical behaviour of managers and executives in the business world. Managers, in particular, are expected to maintain high ethical standards. At issue here are the integrity of managers and other practitioners, and the degree to which their decisions conform to the norms and values of society. Business ethics revolves around the trust that society places in people in businesses, and the obligations the latter have towards society. Factors such as greed, the exploitation of workers and consumers, and the abuse of positions of trust have often resulted in the business ethics of managers and practitioners being deplored.

Figure 1.1 illustrates the visual presentation of the various components of healthcare management.

1.2 CONTEXT

The context of healthcare service management refers to the global, legal, professional-ethical, corporate governance and business ownership environment in which the management of a healthcare organisation is practised. A description of the context is given with reference to the following:

- global context
- constitutional context
- common law
- general national legislation
- national health-related legislation
- corporate governance
- business ethics
- professional, ethical and legal context: practitioners
- business ownership.

1.2.1 Global context

Globalisation is rapidly and irrevocably reshaping virtually all spheres of human endeavour – the politico-legal, socio-cultural, economic, environmental, demographic and health spheres. Globalisation is the process of making the world smaller, more integrated, and more compressed in terms of space, time, entities, happenings,

Figure 1.1 Visual presentation of management in a healthcare organisation

Context	Global context Constitution Common law General national legislation National health-related legislation Corporate governance Professional, ethical and legal context: practitioners Business ethics Business ownership
Purpose	Organisational goal achievement Impact on healthcare indicators
Role-players	Legislative authorities and officials Board of directors Managers Community Recognised trade union(s) Other stakeholders Subordinates
Management process	Levels of management Types of management Process of management: planning, organising, leading and control]
Underlying dynamics	Macro-environment Institutional determinants

relationships and consequences. Simultaneously with the accelerating snow-balling of globalisation, the nature, dynamics and impact thereof have become some of the most contested issues in intellectual debates and the actions by various lobby groups.

Organisations worldwide have no choice but to address the impact and the reality of globalisation if they want to survive in the 'global village'. This implies that companies and organisations are striving towards 'world-class' status or achieving a position of optimum competitiveness. It is, however, also a well-known fact that there are two streams of thinking regarding this striving of companies in the 'global village'. On the one hand, there is a school of thinking that believes that globalisation and companies ascend to 'world-class' status, resulting in more job opportunities, economic growth and prosperity. On the other hand, there is a group of people who think that the globalisation process causes poverty, loss of jobs and the exploitation of under-privileged people by powers of superior knowledge and capital. Companies cannot operate successfully outside the mainstream of globalisation – but companies are also embedded in the broader community. This implies that companies have a responsibility towards the socio-economic empowerment of the broader community in order to ensure stability and community wellness. Therefore, community engagement and investments should be part of the overall business strategy of companies.

Converging trends in healthcare service delivery around the world inevitably hint at the globalisation of health, health policy and healthcare. In general, globalisation represents a set of processes that is heading for the following:

- Unprecedented interconnectedness and increasing interdependence (economic, political and social)
- Blurring of a variety of boundaries
- Transforming the nature of human interaction across a wide range of spheres
- Resulting in the emergence of a global community and internationalisation.

In the health sphere, globalisation means that the health and healthcare of the world's population is more and more linked to and determined by global developments, less and less so by events of local geographical importance. This trend is facilitated by the acceleration of communication across national borders, and manifests in the transmission of information and technology across national borders, the worldwide diffusion of scientific findings, devices and drugs, and the cross-national borrowing of health policies and care strategies.

Businesses/organisations today are exposed to a number of revolutionary global forces: technological change, demographic change and trends towards a service society and the information age. Organisations have to be responsive, flexible and capable of competing in a global and 'borderless' market. To be able to do this, management experts have predicted the 'new' organisation to reflect the following:

- Flatter organisational structures with increased accountability by individual employees for collaborative goal attainment
- Knowledge-based management and abilities (knowledge, skills, attitudes and values) of employees as the basis of power, with intensification of performance management, as opposed to job titles and traditional mediocre performance by individuals
- Managers having primarily to become agents of change
- The rendering of healthcare services in the context of the Southern African Development region will also pose many challenges to those countries and healthcare organisations that reflect the 'power' to render 'borderless' services to those less empowered countries.

1.2.2 Constitutional context

The Constitution (South Africa, 1996) established three distinctive but interrelated spheres of government: national, provincial and local. A key feature of this framework is the spirit of cooperative governance. This requires that the spheres of government coordinate their actions and legislation, and exercise their powers in a manner that does not encroach in another sphere. The various spheres of government have an obligation to make every effort to avoid legal proceedings against each other. The Bill of Rights – and subsequent health-related rights – is also included in the Constitution.

1.2.3 Common law

Although the constitution of the country, health-related and generic legislation serve as the major legal reference for the management of a healthcare organisation, the implications of common law should not be ignored.

1.2.4 General national legislation

The general legislation that relates to all spheres of management – public service legislation, financial legislation (refer to Chapter 17, Financial management of a healthcare organisation), provincial and local government legislation, human resource management legislation (see also Chapter 10, Nature and scope of human resource management), occupational health and safety, as well as environmental management legislation (see Chapter 18, Risk management in a healthcare organisation), are taken into consideration during the management of a healthcare organisation. In addition to these, there are general laws affecting business activity, such as those related to insolvency, pension funds, income tax, protection of business, competition, promotion to access of information, etc.

1.2.5 National health-related legislation and directives

The National Health Act and other service-related directives are briefly highlighted.

National Health Act

The National Health Act, 2003 (Chapters 3–5) deliniates the national health system of South Africa, classified into the national, provincial and district health system. Other healthcare facilities, referred to as health establishments, are legislated in terms of Chapter 6 of the National Health Act. The National Health Act also stipulates the regulation of other health-related matters, such as human resources and the regulation of health professionals.

Service delivery

The Patient Rights Charter, as well as the Batho Pele principles of service delivery, are briefly discussed.

The South African Patient Rights Charter

A National Patient Rights Charter was introduced (Department of Health, 1999), focusing on the following:

- **A healthy and safe environment.** This is to ensure physical and mental health or well-being, and would include a safe and therapeutic environment in the healthcare organisation.

- **Access to healthcare**. Access is achieved by making provision for timely emergency care, treatment and rehabilitation, special needs of vulnerable groups, adequate counselling, palliative care, and adequate and appropriated healthcare information.
- **Confidentiality and privacy**. This applies to the disclosure of information based on legal principles.
- **Informed consent**. Appropriate and adequate information must be supplied by the healthcare provider to enable informed consent by the patient or guardian.
- **A second opinion**. Patients must be allowed to seek a second opinion at any stage should it be considered necessary.
- **To exercise choice in healthcare**. This includes choice of healthcare service provider or health facility for treatment, including the utilisation of preferred healthcare.
- **Continuity of care**. This includes all the healthcare practitioners involved in the treatment/caring of the patient.
- **To complain**. Patients/guardians should be free to complain when treatment is being experienced as unacceptable.
- **To participate in decision-making**. This should include active involvement of the patient in treatment regimens.
- **Treatment by a named healthcare provider**. This applies to transparency of service providers.
- **To refuse treatment**. This right is based on appropriate and adequate information related to this decision by the patient/guardian.
- **Knowledge of healthcare insurance/medical aid scheme**. Patients are entitled to detailed and accurate information, especially related to the disclosure of information of all services not covered by the insurance.

The rights and duties of the healthcare user are also confirmed by means of legislation, as stated in the National Health Act (2003:chapter 2).

Batho Pele

Batho Pele refers to 'people first' and is a regulated policy that is concerned with service delivery in the public sector of South Africa (South Africa, 1997). These principles should be converted into a strategy in the healthcare organisation to facilitate compliance:

- **Consultation**. Community engagement should take place with reference to the level and quality of healthcare service delivery.
- **Service standards**. These should be applied to the type and scope of service delivery in the healthcare organisation.
- **Access**. Citizens should have equal access to service delivery.
- **Courtesy**. Citizens should be treated with courtesy and consideration.

- **Information**. Citizens should be given full, accurate information about the healthcare services they are entitled to receive.
- **Openness and transparency**. This refers to the type/scope of service delivery rendered, the running/management of the organisation, and the cost thereof.
- **Redress**. Corrective actions should be taken to address unsatisfactory service delivery.
- **Value for money**. Public services should be provided economically and efficiently in order to give citizens the best possible value for money.

1.2.6 Corporate governance

Background

(a) *From exclusive to inclusive*

In decades past, if people had gathered in order to establish a company to produce goods, they would have applied to a regulator for a licence, hired premises, bought plant and proceeded to manufacture without much regard to the impact on the environment, or the interests of other stakeholders. This approach was known as the 'exclusive approach'. The permission from the regulator to manufacture the goods would have been the 'licence to operate'. Today, the licence to operate a company is much more complex. Boards have to consider not only the regulatory aspect, but also industry and market standards, industry reputation, the investigative media, and the attitudes of customers, suppliers, consumers, employees, investors, and communities (local, national and international), ethical pressure groups, public opinion, public confidence, political opinion – the inclusive approach. The inclusive approach recognises that stakeholders, such as the community in which the company operates, its customers, its employees and its suppliers, need to be considered when developing the strategy of a company. The relationship between a company and these stakeholders can be contractual or non-contractual. The inclusive approach requires that the purpose of the company is defined, and the values by which the company will carry on its daily life should be identified and communicated to all stakeholders. The stakeholders relevant to the company's business should also be identified. These three factors must be combined in developing the strategies to achieve the goals of the company. The relationship between the company and its stakeholders should be mutually beneficial.

(b) *Corporate governance*

The key challenge for good corporate citizenship is to seek an appropriate balance between enterprise (performance) and constraints (conformance), so taking into account the expectations of the relevant stakeholders. Conformance to corporate governance standards results in constraints on management. Boards have to balance this with performance for financial success and the long-term sustainability of the company. Corporate governance principles were developed, among others, because investors, with the era of the professional manager, were worried about the excessive concentration of power in the hands of management.

Corporate governance in South Africa was institutionalised by the publication of the King Report on Corporate Governance in November 1994. This report was known as the 'King Report 1994'. The King Committee on Corporate Governance was formed in 1992, under the auspices of the Institute of Directors and chaired by Mr Mervyn King, to consider corporate governance, of increasing interest around the world, in the context of South Africa. This coincided with profound social and political transformation at the time with the dawning of democracy and the re-admission of South Africa into the community of nations and the world economy. The purpose of the King Report 1994 was, and remains, to promote the highest standards of corporate governance in South Africa. Unlike its counterparts in other countries at the time, the King Report 1994 went beyond the financial and regulatory aspects of corporate governance in advocating an integrated approach to good governance in the interests of a wide range of stakeholders having regard to the fundamental principles of good financial, social, ethical and environmental practice. In adopting a participative corporate governance system of enterprise with integrity, the King Committee in 1994 successfully formalised the need for companies to recognise that they no longer act independently from the societies and the environment in which they operate (King Report on Corporate Governance for South Africa 2002 – Executive Summary, 2002:7).

The King II Report's Code of Practice is applicable to the following business enterprises:

- All companies with securities listed on the Johannesburg Stock Exchange (JSE) (that would include certain private hospitals/health establishments)
- Banks, financial and insurance entities as defined in legislation
- Public sector enterprises and agencies that fall under the Public Finance Management Act and the new Local Government: Municipal Finance Management Bill
- All companies should give due consideration to application.

Characteristics of good corporate governance

The characteristics of good corporate governance relate to the following (King Report on Corporate Governance for South Africa 2002 – Executive Summary, 2002):

(a) *Discipline*

Corporate discipline is a commitment by the senior management of a company to adhere to behaviour that is universally recognised and accepted to be correct and proper. This encompasses a company's awareness of, and commitment to, the underlying principles of good governance, particularly at senior management level.

(b) *Transparency*

Transparency is the ease with which an outsider is able to make meaningful analysis of a company's actions, its economic fundamentals and the non-financial aspects pertinent to that business. This is a measure of how good management is making necessary information available in a candid, accurate and timely manner – not only the audit data but also general reports and press releases. It reflects whether or not investors obtain a true picture of what is happening inside the company.

(c) *Independence*
Independence is the extent to which mechanisms have been put in place to minimise or avoid potential conflicts of interest that may exist, such as dominance by a strong chief executive or large shareowner. These mechanisms range from the composition of the board, to appointments to committees of the board, and external parties such as the auditors. The decisions made, and internal processes established, should be objective and not allow for undue influences.

(d) *Accountability*
Individuals or groups in a company, who make decisions and take actions on specific issues, need to be accountable for their decisions and actions. Mechanisms must exist and be effective to allow for accountability. These provide investors with the means to query and assess the actions of the board and its committees.

(e) *Responsibility*
With regard to management, responsibility pertains to behaviour that allows for corrective action and for penalising mismanagement. Responsible management would, when necessary, put in place what it would take to set the company on the right path. While the board is accountable to the company, it must act responsively to and with responsibility towards all stakeholders.

(f) *Fairness*
The systems that exist in the company must be balanced in taking into account all those that have an interest in the company and its future. The rights of various groups have to be acknowledged and respected. Minority shareowner interests must receive equal consideration to those of the dominant shareowner(s).

(g) *Social responsibility*
A well-managed company will be aware of, and respond to, social issues, placing a high priority on ethical standards. A good corporate citizen is increasingly seen as one that is non-discriminatory, non-exploitative, and responsible with regard to environmental and human issues. A company is likely to experience indirect economic benefits such as improved productivity and corporate reputation by taking those factors into consideration.

Code of Corporate Practices and Conduct

The Code of Corporate Practices and Conduct relates to at least the following:

- *Board of directors.* This includes composition of the board, the role and function of the board and other office bearers, board committees, appraisal business judgement rule, etc.
- *Risk management.* This includes responsibility, assimilating risks to the control environment, and the application of risk management.
- *Internal audit.* This includes the status of the internal audit, the role and function of the internal audit and the scope of the internal audit.
- *Integrated sustainability reporting.* This includes the scope of review, stakeholder relations, ethical practices and organisational integrity, safety, health and environment (SHE), social and transformation issues, including Black Economic Empowerment (BEE), and human capital.
- *Accounting and auditing.* This includes auditing, non-audit services, legal backing for, and the monitoring of, compliance with accounting standards and the accessibility of financial information.
- *Compliance and enforcement.* This consists of the legal mechanisms, the enforcement of existing remedies, principles of disclosure, the role of the media, encouraging shareowner activism, the role of organised business and the enforcement in other jurisdictions.

1.2.7 Business ethics

Business ethics refer to the principles, norms and standards that the organisation promotes for the guidance and conduct of its activities, internal relations and interactions with external stakeholders, in accordance with its corporate values (PricewaterhouseCoopers, 2003:34). Business ethics therefore relates to the ethical dimensions of economic activity. This ethical aspect is constituted by the impact of economic activity on individuals, society and the natural environment. Ethics is concerned with what is good or right in human interaction. Consequently it revolves around three basic concepts, namely the good, the self and the other. Ethical behaviour is being conceived of as behaviour that not only considers what is good for oneself, but also what is good for others. Business ethics therefore relates to the impact of ethical behaviour on economic activity (Rossouw, 2002:2–3). The King II Report (King Committee on Corporate Governance, 2002) requires that every organisation should demonstrate its commitment to organisational integrity by codifying its standards in a code of ethics. Commitment to such a code of ethics will be demonstrated by at least the following dimensions of business ethics management (PricewaterhouseCoopers, 2003:34–35):

- Creating systems and procedures to introduce, monitor and enforce its code of ethics
- Assigning high-level individuals to oversee compliance with the code of ethics
- Assessing the integrity of new appointees in selection and promotion procedures

- Exercising due care in delegating discretionary authority
- Communicating with, and training, all employees regarding the ethical values, standards and compliance procedures of the organisation
- Providing, monitoring and auditing safe systems for reporting of unethical or risky behaviour (i.e. a 'whistleblowing' system)
- Enforcing appropriate discipline with consistency
- Responding to offences and preventing re-occurrence.

1.2.8 Professional, ethical and legal context

The professional practitioners involved in healthcare service delivery – the clinical as well as the non-clinical professional practitioners – are regulated in accordance with the specific professional-ethical legislation (i.e. medical practitioners, nurses, financial auditors). Healthcare service management is therefore also exercised in the context of these practitioners' education, practice and licensing. (Refer to Chapters 10–15 on human resource management).

1.2.9 Business ownership

Business ownership is divided into two main types of ownership: public and private, with sometimes a mixed combination of the two. The public classification of public healthcare organisations is delineated in the National Health Act (2003) as national, provincial and district healthcare organisations. These organisations are managed in accordance with the national, provincial and district-related legislative and regulatory framework.

Although private healthcare organisations are also regulated by the National Health Act (2003) – and referred to as health establishments – there are different forms of private healthcare organisations, based on the general classification of private businesses. Four types of private business ownership are presented: the sole proprietorship, partnership, close corporation and company (De J. Cronjé, et al., 2004:59–68). The formation of a Trust as a private business is not discussed in this chapter.

Sole proprietorship

The sole proprietorship is a business that is owned and managed by one owner. It does not have an independent legal personality, and consequently cannot exist independently of the owner. The assets of the business belong to the owner alone, and the owner is also personally liable for all the debts and claims against the business. In the healthcare context, an example of sole proprietorship is the private clinical practitioner (such as the general practitioner, private midwife and psychiatric nursing consultant).

Partnership

A partnership can exist between individuals by means of a written partnership contract. A partnership does not have a legal personality, and it is the partners in their personal capacity who are jointly and severally liable for all claims against the partnership, regardless of who was responsible for bringing about the claim. The partnership contract can be verbal, in writing, or tacit (that is, through certain behaviour). However, it is customary and preferable for the contract to be in writing. The contract must comply with all the requirements for a valid contract, in accordance with legal and professional-ethical principles. There are many forms of partnerships in clinical health service delivery (medical, physiotherapy, psychiatric nursing consultants, etc).

Close corporation

A close corporation can be formed and registered as a business with a legal personality, in accordance with the legal provisions of such a business ownership. The close corporation is created by the registration of a founding statement, which contains details such as the proposed name of the corporation, the nature of the business, the personal details of members and their interests in the corporation. The founding statement can be compared with a memorandum of association of a company. The close corporation does not have to appoint/contract an auditor, but has to appoint an accountant. Specified financial statements need to be drawn up and approved by all the members of the close corporation. An association agreement could be entered into by the members, to regulate the internal matters of the corporation in accordance with legal provisions.

Company

A company can be formed in accordance with legislative requirements pertaining to companies. The company has a legal personality and is subject to many legislative requirements, such as a constitution/memorandum of association, registration of the company, board of directors, annual general meetings, financial practices and tax liability. There are many forms of companies, such as companies with a share capital (private or public companies), or companies limited by guarantee (i.e. not-for-gain). A company is regulated by means of company-specific legislation (South Africa, 1973). Many examples of private healthcare companies exist.

1.3 PURPOSE OF MANAGEMENT

According to the economic principle, a business organisation always has to endeavour to obtain the highest possible output (product and services) at the least possible input (lowest cost). Based on the type of business ownership, the purpose of management is summarised as follows:

- Achievement of organisational goals
- Impact on health indicators/outcomes.

1.4 ROLE-PLAYERS

The role-players involved in the management of a healthcare service are the legislative authorities, board of directors, the manager, community, recognised trade union(s), and other stakeholders, as well as the subordinates in the organisation.

1.4.1 Legislative authorities

Many legislative authorities and officials are involved in the scope of healthcare service management, such as the national, provincial and local/district legislators and subsequent officials, occupational health and safety inspectors and department of labour officials. These role-players exercise their responsibilities in accordance with the appropriate legislation and subsequent regulations.

1.4.2 Board of directors

The board of directors (i.e. hospital board) has a collective responsibility to provide effective corporate governance. As such, it must be in a position to lead, monitor and control the activities of the organisation. The key attribute for a director/board member is to make a meaningful contribution to the board's deliberations.

Board members should display at least the following (PricewaterhouseCoopers, 2003:27):

- Integrity
- Independence of thought and the courage to express it
- A grasp of the business/organisational operations (core business)
- An understanding of the changes taking place regionally, nationally and internationally
- An understanding of business and financial language.

The King II Report delineates the King Code of Corporate Practices and Conduct:

- The application of the Code
- The Board of Directors: the Board, composition thereof, directors and their remuneration
- Board functioning: meetings, committees, evaluation of performance, secretarial support, etc.
- Risk management: responsibility, application and reporting
- Internal audit: status, role and scope of internal audit
- Integrated sustainability reporting: sustainability reporting, organisational integrity and code of ethics
- Accounting and auditing: services, information and audit committee
- Relations with shareowners/stakeholders
- Communication.

1.4.3 Managers

There are several levels of healthcare delivery (refer to 1.5.2), in accordance with the type of business ownership. Healthcare managers are appointed in different types of posts, also in accordance with the type of business ownership, the level of management, as well as the nature and size of the organisation. Healthcare managers are responsible for the continuous assessment and evaluation of the factors/variables, methods and principles that enable a healthcare organisation to function as efficiently and productively as possible in order to maximise its value contribution to the patients and the community at large. In the case of a private organisation, the additional responsibility is to maximise its profits. The following roles, duties and responsibilities are highlighted: Mintzberg roles, duties in accordance with the principles of corporate governance, and general responsibilities.

Mintzberg roles

Three overlapping roles of managers have been distinguished by Mintzberg (1987), and are commonly referred to in the practice of management – the interpersonal role, information role and decision-making role:

- **Interpersonal role**. This role means to act as the representative figure at internal and external events, to exercise leadership and to maintain relationships in the organisation, as well as externally.
- **Information role**. This applies to the accessing, monitoring and analyses of appropriate and trustworthy information. This role also implies the dissemination of the information at the various points of service delivery for, among others communication, decision-making and negotiation purposes.
- **Decision-making role**. This role involves the appropriate utilisation and application of information in the interest of the relevant stakeholders and to facilitate the attainment of pre-determined goals, outputs, indicators, etc.

Corporate governance duties

The following duties (also applicable to managers and members of any constituted committee in the healthcare organisation) are described in the King II Report (PricewaterhouseCoopers, 2003:45–48) – duty of care, fiduciary duty and a duty to act in their powers and authority.

Duty of care

A duty of care, meaning the requirement to exhibit the degree of care, diligence and skill that may reasonably be expected from individuals with their knowledge and experience. It involves ensuring that they:

- Make sufficient time available for the exercise of their role
- Understand the company's business and familiarise themselves with the financial, social and political environment in which the company operates

- Are in a position to make informed decisions, based on awareness of issues that could have a material impact on the company and its operations
- Diligently prepare for meetings by reviewing all information provided to them in advance
- Actively solicit information in cases where they do not feel the information provided to them is sufficient for their deliberations and seek clarification where required
- Attend board meetings and actively participate in deliberations, applying the knowledge, expertise and experience for which they were appointed.

Fiduciary duty
The requirement to act in good faith and in the company's interest, ensuring that they:
- At all times act in good faith in the company's best interests
- At all times act independently of any outside influence or instruction, impartial to any vested interest or sector of shareholders
- At all times act with disregard for any personal, ulterior or improper purpose, such as their own personal gain
- Avoid and, if unavoidable, declare any conflict of interest between personal and company interests
- Diligently execute all actions delegated to them for completion
- Maintain confidentiality with respect to information acquired about the company's operations and affairs in their capacity as director that is intended to be treated with discretion
- Respect the privilege that they have as directors and ensure that opportunities arising from the knowledge they acquire of certain sensitive information on the course of their activities are not misappropriated
- At all times act legally, and with honesty and integrity in their dealings with, and on behalf of, the company.

Duty to act in powers of authority
The duty to act in their powers of authority involves that they purport to act on behalf of – and commit – the company only to the extent permitted by the powers and authority conferred upon them by:
- The law
- The company statutes or legislation/regulations
- The company's shareholders, and
- Their fellow directorates and managers.

General responsibilities

In addition to the Mintzburg (1987) roles of managers and the duties in accordance with the principles of corporate governance, the following responsibilities are highlighted:

- The manager is accountable, in accordance with the pre-determined level of management, for the core business-related attainment of goals and the management of resources as delegated and duly authorised.
- The manager is responsible for the execution of the management roles and elements of management (planning, organising, leading and control) in accordance with the authorised level and type of management (general and/or functional).
- The manager is accountable for the attainment of performance goals and indicators in accordance with the predetermined key performance areas and subsequent indicators.
- The manager should exhibit a strong internal locus of control – a purposeful decision to be in charge of your destiny (successful management of the assigned portfolio); a belief that the outcome of the event is determined by their personal deliberate goals and actions to make a success thereof.

1.4.4 Community

The principle of community engagement is important. Community engagement entails the deliberate and purposeful engagement of the community by means of consultation (during strategic planning, development of core business strategies, transformation management, assessment of service delivery, leadership representation on hospital boards or as a non-executive director on the board of directors, etc.). The community is represented in a formal or non-formal manner and is mainly engaged with the management of the organisation by means of the following methods:

- Community consultation forums
- Consumer unions
- Environmental safety structures/committees
- Other formalised structures.

1.4.5 Recognised trade unions

The role of the recognised trade union is in accordance with the national labour legislation, focusing mainly on the collective representation of employees (refer to Chapters 10 to 14 on Human resource management).

1.4.6 Other stakeholders

Other stakeholders could be involved in the management of the organisation, such as the board of directors, the institutional forum and shareholders. The inputs of these stakeholders vary according to the level of management concerned and the method of participation (i.e. attendance of an Annual General Meeting, advice to the board of directors, consultation and negotiation).

1.4.7 Subordinates

The clinical and non-clinical subordinates constitute the healthcare service delivery team, with reference to the clinical core business service delivery, the management of the organisation, the technical support team, as well as the members of the 'hotel' service delivery system. Refer to Chapters 10 to 14 on human resource management.

1.5 MANAGEMENT PROCESS

The management process is described with reference to the following: introduction, the levels and types of management, and the management process consisting of planning, organising, leading and control.

1.5.1 Introduction

Management is defined as a process whereby human, financial, physical and information resources are employed in order to achieve the goals and objectives of the organisation, by applying the fundamental management activities of planning, organising, leading and control. The management process and the four elements that it comprises are encountered at all levels of management in the healthcare organisation. The management process is illustrated as a logical sequence of actions. It is, however, important to realise that the functions of management do not occur in a tidy step-by-step order. At any given time a manager is likely to be engaged in several management activities simultaneously. Figure 1.2 illustrates the process of management with reference to the four elements in relation to the fundamental management activity of each.

Figure 1.2 Fundamental management activities

Fundamental management activity	Element
Management decides *what* should be done	Planning
Management decides *how* it should be done	Organising
Management *facilitates* and *enables* the how and when it should be done	Leading
Management ascertains *whether* and *how* it has been done	Control

Planning entails the determination of the vision and mission of the organisation, and the subsequent goals – including the ways in which the goals are to be reached in the long, medium and short term, and the resources required for goal attainment. It includes determining the future position of the organisation, and guidelines or plans on how that position is to be reached (refer also to Chapter 2, Strategic management of a healthcare organisation). Assessment strategies/methods for goal achievement and outcomes are also part of planning. Refer to 1.5.4.1.

Organising is concerned with the allocation of the resources (human, financial, physical and information) required for goal achievement. Organising includes the development of an action framework according to which the core business of the organisation is structured and executed. Refer to 1.5.4.2.

Leading (also referred to as directing) is aimed at the facilitation of goal achievement by applying the principles of enablement and leadership in the organisation. Refer to 1.5.4.3 and Chapter 16, Leadership in healthcare service management.

Control means that managers should constantly establish whether the goals have been achieved by monitoring the progress of goal achievement, supporting and empowering employees to comply with performance strategies and indicators, and the continuous monitoring and evaluation of organisational outputs and outcomes. Control also enables managers to detect any deviations from the plans/strategies and to correct them. It also obliges management to constantly reconsider its goals and plans/strategies. Refer to 1.5.4.4.

1.5.2 Levels of management

Management is traditionally divided into three levels: corporate management (also referred to as top management), middle management and operational or lower management. *Top or corporate management* comprises the relatively small group of executives that is ultimately accountable for the performance of the organisation, and is therefore mainly concerned with the strategic management of the healthcare organisation, as well as with the general management at corporate level. *Middle management* is responsible for the execution of the organisational strategies, plans and policies. Traditionally, middle management consists of functional managers, such as the clinical, financial and human resource manager. Middle management is therefore responsible for total quality management in the organisation in accordance with the strategic plan and also monitors environmental influences that may affect its sphere of operations and compliance with standards and indicators. *Lower or operational management* is responsible for supervising the execution of the core business (clinical and non-clinical) of the organisation, in accordance with the pre-determined strategies, standards and indicators. Figure 1.3 illustrates the levels of management.

Although only three levels of management have been distinguished, in practice the number of levels is determined largely – though not exclusively – by the size of the organisation and the complexity of service delivery. In healthcare management, this is further conceptualised in accordance with the business ownership. The National Health Act (2003) delineates several levels of public healthcare services (national, provincial, district and local) as described in the context of this chapter.

Figure 1.3 Levels and types of management

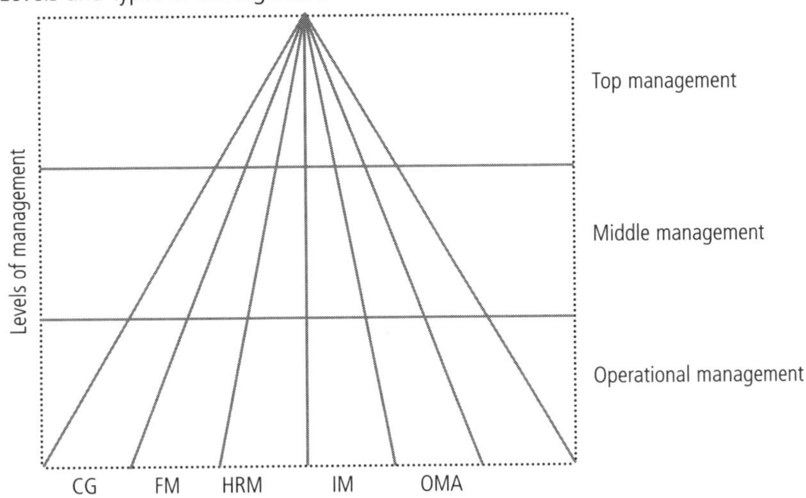

(CG = Clinical governance; FM = Financial management; HRM = Human resource management; IM = Information management; OMA = Other management areas)

Private hospitals tend to structure their levels of management in accordance with the type and size of the business ownership:

- national or corporate managers
- provincial and/or regional managers (general and/or functional)
- organisational managers
- departmental managers
- unit or area managers.

1.5.3 Types of management

In addition to the levels of management, there are different types of management, irrespective of the level: strategic, general and functional management.

1.5.3.1 Strategic management

Strategic management refers to the continual long-term re-positioning and management of the organisation by means of formulating vision, mission and value statements, as well as the development of subsequent goals and strategies, based on the environmental (external and internal) analysis (assessment and evaluation) of the factors (opportunities, threats, strengths and weaknesses) impacting on the core business of the organisation. Strategic management is discussed in Chapter 2.

1.5.3.2 General management

General management is the integration of all spheres of management and is therefore the overriding management function that controls the management process and the general principles of management as applied by top management. General management is exercised by all managers, regardless of the level of management concerned. The international criteria of excellence with reference to general management in the healthcare organisation were developed by the International Society for Health Care (ISQua) and relate to the following:

- **Facility management systems**. This includes all spheres of healthcare management and administration.
- **Patient management and care systems**. These systems are designed to facilitate compliance with access, patient rights, continuum of care, clinical support, continuous quality improvement, etc.
- **Technical support systems**. These systems provide facility maintenance, medical and life-support equipment management, health and safety management, etc.
- **Hotel system**. This system includes food and dietetic services, laundry, housekeeping, etc.

In addition to the international criteria of excellence, the dimensions of general management are determined in accordance with the type of business ownership and the nature and scope of service delivery, based on the strategic focus and subsequent regulatory framework.

1.5.3.3 Functional management

Functional management refers to the specialised area of management, such as financial management, marketing, communication management, information management, project management, human resource management, hotel service management, and defined clinical management (i.e. surgical, critical care and nursing).

1.5.4 Management process activities

The management process is described in accordance with the conceptual definition and includes planning, organising, leading and control.

1.5.4.1 Planning

Planning is the fundamental element of management that predetermines what the business/organisation proposes to accomplish, and how this is to be accomplished. Planning determines the mission and goals of the healthcare organisation, including the ways in which the goals are to be reached and the resources required for the attainment of the goals. It includes determining the existing and future positioning of the organisation, and guidelines/plans on how that position is to be reached. Planning is therefore mainly concerned with the following:

- **The determination dimension**. Here the core business of the organisation (who they want to be and what they want to accomplish) is identified.
- **The decision-making dimension**. This refers to deciding on how the goals

will be accomplished (action plans) and the resources required for goal attainment.
- **The future dimension**. This refers to the intention to cope with change in the business or organisational environment, resulting in proactive interaction with its external environment.

The following aspects of planning are briefly described: the importance of planning, the levels of planning, the planning process, the attributes of plans and the development of a business plan.

Importance of planning

The importance of planning relates to at least the following:
- **Planning gives direction**. Goals and action plans ensure that the organisation is doing the 'right thing'.
- **Promotion of coordination**. This is to ensure a focused contribution of all the different departments and units to facilitate goal attainment.
- **Future orientation**. Planning eliminates crisis management by obliging future-oriented management to anticipate threats and obstacles in the environment, thus ensuring a prosperous sustainability of the organisation.
- **Planning ensures cohesion in the organisation**. Planning focuses the various interdependent functional departments/units on the whole organisation, to not only attain departmental goals, but to attain organisational goals in the interest of the health of the people and the improvement of healthcare indicators of the community at large.
- **Promotion of stability**. Planning encourages proactive management in a dynamic and ever-changing internal and external environment.

Levels of planning

Planning comprises many levels, depending on the nature, size and type of business ownership: strategic, operational, action and project planning. The characteristics of each level are listed.

(a) *Strategic planning*
- Long term
- Vision and mission statements (direction and how to get there)
- Developed by top management led by Corporate Executive Officer/Director.

(b) *Operational planning*
- Medium term
- Detailed objectives and allocation of resources
- Developed by senior management and approved by top management.

(c) *Action planning*
- Short term
- Used to unfold medium- and short-term plans, to define responsibilities and detailed time frames, used to make things happen
- Developed by operational/activity managers (i.e. clinical interventions required).

(d) *Project planning*
- Short term (varied time frames)
- Can be used to implement aspects of strategic and operational plans or to implement new things
- Developed by the project manager or line management and approved by senior management.

The planning process

Planning consists of the following steps: goal setting, development of action plans and implementation strategies, as well as the development of the evaluation strategy to assess the achievement of goals and outcomes. The planning steps/activities relate to the specific levels of management (corporate, middle and operational), as well as the type of management (general or functional). This process is illustrated in Figure 1.4.

In addition to the planning process, the attributes of plans, as well as the business plan (reasons for a business plan and the contents thereof), are explained.

Attributes of plans

Plans should reflect the following attributes:
- Plans are achievable, quantifiable and time-bound, and also form part of the financial management process.
- Plans describe what success will look like, that is, they define outputs and outcomes which determine actual service delivery and resources required.
- Success is measured by performance measures defined in the planning phase, not as an add-on after the fact.
- Managers at all levels of the organisation are acquainted with the plan and exhibit commitment to it.
- Everyone knows how their own responsibilities and objectives relate to the plan.
- At all levels the plan is recognised as the constant point of reference for assessing performance.
- Managers at all levels see the planning process as an aid to successful attainment of goals and outputs.

Business plan

A business plan is a written description (game plan) of the nature and purpose of the business opportunity/venture, the operational service delivery intended, key variables impacting on service delivery, resources required and possible risks. Any venture, especially a new venture, needs to have a business plan to answer any questions that various stakeholders in the venture may raise. The reasons for a business plan and the contents of the business plan are briefly highlighted (De J. Cronjé, et al., 2004:69–77).

Figure 1.4 The planning process

Level of management	Goal setting	Action plans	Implementing strategy	Evaluation strategy
Corporate/top management	Vision, mission and value statements Strategic goals Long term Positioning and sustainability of the organisation	Strategic plans Organisational core business or focus areas Utilisation of opportinities and challenges Counteraction of threats and obstacles	Organisational strategy Organisational resource allocation Organisational policies and procedures Outcome-focused	Corporate performance indicators Planned outcomes
Middle management	Functional departmental goals Specialised focus Medium term How to achieve the strategic goals	Operational plans Functional and specialisation Specified core business area plans	Operational strategy Deployment of specialised resources	Departmental indicators and planned outcomes Planned assessment strategies, ie clinical auditing
Lower or operational management	Operational goals Short term Operational goals Unit/area specialised focus Performance goals and indicators	Operational plans Performance-focused plans	Operational unit/ area strategies Performance strategies	Unit strategies Planned assessment strategies

Reasons for writing a business plan

The reasons for the writing of a business plan are as follows:

- To sell the business/venture: to not only convince the founders (yourself/ partners), but also the other stakeholders
- To obtain financing
- To obtain investment funds, the so-called ticket of admission
- To arrange strategic alliances
- To obtain contracts as a service provider

- To attract key employees
- To motivate and focus the management team(s).

Contents of the business plan

The depth and detail in the business plan depend on the size, scope and complexity of the venture. The format of the business plan needs to be considered (appearance, brief or comprehensive, logical, easy to read and understand, and based on solid facts). The business plan should consist of at least the following, as illustrated in Figure 1.5: executive summary, general business/company description, products/service delivery, marketing plan, management plan, operating plan and the financial plan.

Figure 1.5 Content of a business plan

Executive summary	A summarised description of the business plan, highlighting the significant points and creating excitement to read through the whole plan
Company description	Name and location Nature and primary service delivery of the business Current status (startup, buyout, expansion, etc) Legal form of the business/organisation
Service delivery	Description of products and/or service delivery Superior features of advantages relative to competing services in the area/region Available legal protection: patents, copyrights, trademarks, branding Dangers of technical or style obsolescence
Marketing plan	Analysis of target market and profile of target customers/consumers Identification and attraction of customers/consumers Marketing strategy/approach Service delivery costing to consumers/customers
Management plan	Management team profile and qualifications/experience Other investors and/or directors and their profiles External resources and relevant profiles Recruiting and training of employees and contractors
Operating plan	Service delivery plan: nature/scope Description of operating facilities Quality assurance/improvement strategy Sources of supply and purchasing procedures
Financial plan	Revenue projections for three years Expense projections for three years Necessary financial resources Potential and actual sources of financing

1.5.4.2 Organising

Organising is the second step in the management process and is concerned with the implementation of the plan. After goals and plans have been determined, the core business of the organisation needs to be structured, and the resource allocation (human, financial, physical and information-based resources) deployed in a logical and formalised way to facilitate optimal utilisation and the attainment of goals and outputs. *Organising* refers to:

- The logical and orderly structuring and arrangement/distribution of the core business (i.e. the grouping of clinical services into departments and units)
- The logical and orderly structuring of teams and groups to perform the activities that will convert the plan into accomplished goals
- The logical deployment, combining and coordination of resources (i.e. a centralised pharmacy or a decentralised approach with different pharmaceutical service points in the healthcare organisation)
- The facilitation of optimal attainment of goals, outputs and outcomes, quality, effectiveness and efficiency.

Organising is discussed with reference to the following: the importance of organising, factors influencing organising and the process of organising.

Importance of organising

Organising, like planning, is an integral and indispensable component of the management process. Organising is important for the following reasons:

- Organising ensures a systematic and structured focus on the execution of the plans and strategies with reference to the core business of the organisation.
- Organisational structuring results in a mechanism that coordinates the core business activities of the whole organisation.
- Organisational unity (wholeness) and harmony (interaction between departments and units) are facilitated.
- Organising promotes the productive deployment and utilisation of resources.
- It ensures the logical and fair arrangement and distribution of workload to facilitate productivity.
- The logical grouping of core business dimensions (i.e. surgical or medical services), facilitates functional or specialised management and subsequent measurement of collective and individual performance outputs and outcomes.

Factors influencing organising

The following factors are briefly highlighted:

- The type of business ownership and subsequent legislative framework
- The size and nature of service delivery (i.e. national academic, regional or community public hospitals as opposed to a hospice as a healthcare establishment)
- Strategic plans that can direct the organisational design and other organising

dimensions. The strong relationship between the organisational strategy and the organisational structure is important – structure always follows strategy
- The external environment in which the business/service delivery operates: stable, turbulent or technologically dominated environment
- The internal environment, that is, the strategic intent and the organisational culture will impact on the nature of the organisational structure (formal or less formal).

Process of organising

The process of organising is illustrated in Figure 1.6, in accordance with the levels of management: organisational structure design, designing posts, assigning authority, establishing a command structure and establishing coordinating mechanisms.

Figure 1.6 The process of organising

Level of management	Organisational structure design	Designing posts	Assigning authority	Establishing command structure	Establishing coordinating mechanisms
Corporate/ top management	Organisational organogram	Management posts at top and middle levels	Top management strategic accountability and responsibilities	Middle management reporting lines to top management	Corporate governance committees
Middle management	Departmental organogram	Departmental general and functional posts	General and functional management accountability and responsibilities	Departmental reporting lines to middle management	Departmental committees and decision-making structures
Lower or operational management	Unit/area organogram	Clinical and non-clinical posts within units/areas	Operational DTRs	Unit-specific reporting lines to general and functional departments and support structures	Operational committee and decision-making structures

Organisational structure design

The organisational structure refers to the logical grouping of the core business into divisions, departments, operational units/service delivery points (core business distribution). The logical grouping of the core business activities is also referred to as departmentalisation. The following principles are taken into consideration during the design of an organisational structure of the healthcare organisation:

- The type of business ownership (i.e. public or private) and the subsequent legislative framework and organisational culture plays an important role.
- The scope and location of the healthcare organisation(s) are taken into account.
- The size and complexity of the healthcare organisation are important factors.
- The abilities (knowledge, skills, values and attitudes) of employees and envisaged managers are important.
- The organisational structure can be designed according to the location (national, provincial, regional, local, etc.), the specialised functional areas (non-clinical and clinical), the type of service delivery, also referred to as customer departmentalisation.
- The organisational structure is designed in accordance with the strategic plan of the organisation (core business areas) and the subsequent logical grouping of these core business areas into the various non-clinical functional management departments (i.e. finance, marketing, human resources, maintenance, dietetic/ food services, housekeeping, etc), and the clinical specialised departments (i.e. surgical, medical, obstetrics or paediatrics). It is therefore directed by the strategic plan of the organisation (structure follows strategy).
- The levels of management are determined in accordance with the location (national, provincial, regional, etc.), size and type of business ownership of the organisation. A hospital could be structured in the following way: Hospital manager, followed by the non-clinical and the clinical managing directors, specialised departmental managers (i.e. surgical, medical or pharmaceutical services), as well as the non-clinical departmental managers, such as financial, marketing or human resources.
- Once the core business areas are grouped or classified into manageable departments or zones, the operational units or service delivery areas are determined in each department or zone. The nature and size of these units/areas are influenced by the nature and size of the healthcare organisation and the type of business ownership and subsequent organisational culture.
- A structure can also be designed for specific projects. In this case the design is terminated on completion of the project. The typical matrix organisational structure is most suitable to enable the devolution of authority (simplification of decision-making).
- The vertical and horizontal organisational structure of the healthcare organisation is reflected in the form of an organogram (see Figure 1.7).

Designing posts

Post or job design is the determination of posts in accordance with the organisational structure. General and functional managers' posts are designed, as well as general and specialised operational level posts. Once the posts have been designed (refer

Figure 1.7 Example of an organogram

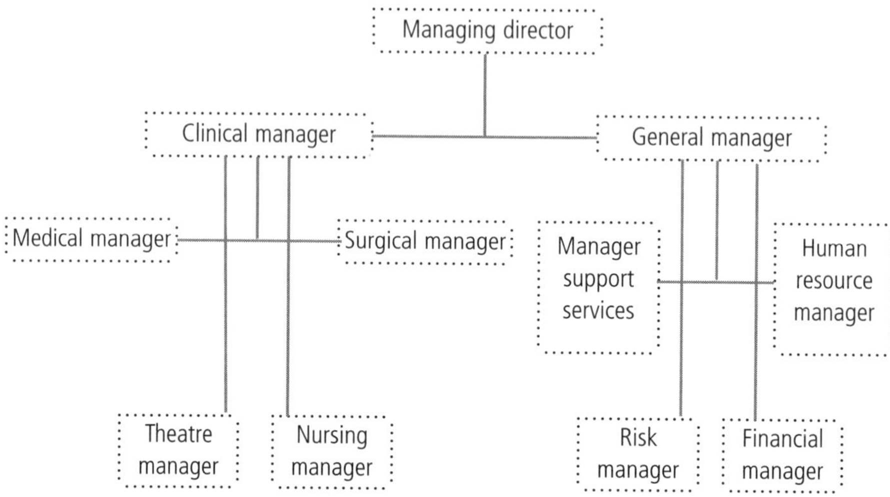

to Chapter 11, Planning and provision of human resources), the relevant job specification and responsibilities (job description) are developed.

Assigning responsibilities and authority

Once the post structure has been designed, the assignment of responsibilities and authority to each post in the organisational structure follows. This entails the creation of organisational relations, that is, stipulating the persons from who subordinates receive directives/instructions, to whom they report, and to whom and for what they are responsible. The following authority types are relevant:

(a) *Line authority*

Line authority is delegated down through the line of command and is usually visually reflected in the organogram by means of an uninterrupted line from senior post level to lower post level.

(b) *Staff authority*

Staff authority is an indirect and supplementary authority, usually by managers at the same post level or by functional managers (i.e. marketing). Staff authority is characterised by giving advice, assisting and making recommendations to other line managers.

Establishing a command structure

A further fundamental organising activity is the establishment of reporting lines among departments and positions in departments. This entails determining who will report to whom, also referred to as the establishment of the chain of command.

Secondly, the span of management needs to be determined: the number/scope of subordinates who report directly to a manager, based on the complexity of the service delivery in that department and the abilities of the manager and subordinates.

Establishing coordinating mechanisms
Coordination refers to the process of linking and integrating the activities of the various departments into a single integrated unit to facilitate attainment of the organisational goals and outcomes. Coordinating is an indispensable part of organising – it is the synthesis of separate parts into a unity, and as such it is the binding factor in the managerial process. The greater the independence between departments, the more coordination is required. Hence, coordination is an endeavour by management to develop congruency (harmonisation of goals) through organising.

Coordination is achieved by means of the following mechanisms:
- General and specialised meetings (i.e. nursing unit managers, surgical or medical)
- Corporate committees in accordance with the strategic intent and core business of the organisation (i.e. audit committee, risk management committee or quality improvement committee)
- Departmental and unit/area committees (i.e. occupational health and safety, quality improvement or finance)
- Formal and informal consultation and negotiation structures (i.e. community forum, trade union or institutional forum)
- Formal coordinating structures in the organisation should be legitimised by means of a Charter or Terms of Reference, in accordance with the principles of corporate governance (PricewaterhouseCoopers, 2003:22), complying with at least the following criteria:
  - Name of the committee
  - Purpose and objectives, aligned with that of the organisation's vision, mission and value statements
  - Composition of the committee
  - Lifespan (term of office)
  - Role and functions
  - Scope of authority, including extent of power to make decisions and/or recommendations
  - Meeting procedures
  - Reporting mechanism.

1.5.4.3 Leading

Leading is the third management activity and is concerned with the dynamic interaction between the leader and the followers – aimed at the facilitation of organisational goal attainment – by means of leadership principles and strategies. Leadership refers to the influencing and directing of the behaviour of followers, in such a way that they willingly strive to accomplish the goals and objectives of the business/organisation. Because the influence exerted by leaders on followers has such an important effect on the performance of a business/organisation, several attempts have been made to determine precisely what it is that enables leaders to influence their followers in this way. Against this background, leadership is clearly seen to be a complex management activity. In order to appreciate the complex process of leadership, one has to understand the aspects of authority, power, influence, delegation, responsibility and accountability (De J. Cronjé et al., 2004:177–178):

- Authority denotes the right of a leader to make decisions with subsequent expectations related to the behaviour of the followers.
- Power denotes the ability of a leader to influence the behaviour of others without necessarily using authority.
- Influence refers to the ability to use authority and power to move the followers to action.
- Delegation occurs when a leader transfers authority to a subordinate. It involves splitting up the task and entrusting part of it, together with the necessary authority, to a subordinate for execution on the leader's behalf.
- Responsibility rests on a leader carrying out a given task in accordance with instructions, and being held accountable for the execution of all tasks by him/her and subordinates/followers.

Jim Collins describes the five levels of leadership to take an organisation from good to great (Collins, 2001:19–22), and these levels will be applied in selected chapters:

- **Level 1: Highly capable individual**. He/she makes productive contributions through talent, knowledge, skills and good work habits.
- **Level 2: Contributing team member.** He/she contributes individual capabilities to the achievement of group objectives and works effectively with others in a group setting.
- **Level 3: Competent manager**. He/she organises people and resources toward the effective and efficient pursuit of pre-determined objectives.
- **Level 4: Effective leader.** He/she catalyses commitment to and vigorous pursuit of a clear and compelling vision, stimulating higher performance standards.
- **Level 5: Executive**. He/she builds enduring greatness through a paradoxical blend of personal humility and professional will.

Leadership has been widely researched and is discussed in Chapter 16, on Leadership in healthcare service management.

1.5.4.4 Control

Control is the last of the four fundamental management activities. It is the final step in the management process, where the assessment of actual performance against planned performance initiates a new cycle of planning, organising, leading and control. The following dimensions of control are discussed: the importance of control, the focus of control, classification of control, the attributes of control and the process of control. The attributes of an effective control system are also highlighted.

Importance of control

The importance of control is summarised as follows:

- Control is intimately linked to planning, organising and leading – it concludes the process of management.
- There is a continuous dynamic impact of the underlying dynamics – internal and external forces – on businesses and healthcare organisations.
- Control therefore enables management to cope with the continuous change and uncertainty.
- Human error occurs because managers and subordinates are capable of making poor decisions and committing errors. An effective control system should be able to detect such errors before they become critical.
- Adequate delegation does not guarantee adequate performance.
- Control is applied to ensure that the resources of the organisation are adequately deployed to ensure efficiency and effectiveness to facilitate goal attainment.
- Control should result in better quality.

Focus of control

The focus of control relates to at least the following:

- The core business of the healthcare organisation is focused in accordance with the strategic intent and subsequent strategies and plans.
- The physical resources include factors such as equipment and inventory control, maintenance of buildings, structures and vehicles.
- Quality control refers to the execution of the core business activities, that is, clinical performance (refer also to Chapter 19, Quality improvement models in a healthcare organisation and Chapter 20, Continuous quality improvement in a healthcare organisation).
- Financial control relates to compliance with the financial principles of corporate governance (refer to Chapter 17, Financial management of a healthcare organisation).
- Control of information relates to the appropriate access of core business-related information, and the subsequent adequate environmental scanning, market and economic forecasting, etc.
- Control of human resources includes performance, labour turnover, absenteeism and the composition of the labour force.

Classification of control

Control is classified into three types of control: proactive, continuous and reactive control (refer also to Chapter 20, Continuous quality improvement in a healthcare organisation):

- Proactive control is concerned with the setting of standards derived from the goals reflected in the corporate/strategic, departmental and unit/service area plans of the healthcare organisation.
- Continuous control will focus on the monitoring and measuring of actual performance against these standards. Deviations from performance standards (performance gaps) are evaluated. In a healthcare organisation, continuous control is not only exercised in accordance with the assessment dates of the quality improvement programme, but on a day-to-day basis by the operational managers. The Balanced Scorecard principles can be integrated to assess the progress of compliance with performance standards. Refer also to Chapter 4, Dimensions of functional management in a healthcare organisation and Chapter 19, Quality improvement models in a healthcare organisation.
- Reactive control relates to rectifying the deviations by taking appropriate remedial or corrective actions. The intent is to improve the quality of healthcare service delivery and to mitigate the risks involved.

Attributes of an effective control system

The following attributes of an effective control system are highlighted (De J. Cronjé, et al., 2004:274):

- **Integration**. This means that a control system is more effective when it is integrated with planning, and when it is flexible, accurate, objective/trustworthy, timely and not unnecessarily complex. Control complements planning, because deviations highlight the need to review plans and even goals. Data related to results, outputs or outcomes should therefore be accessible, meaningful and user-friendly, such as infection rates, adverse events and patient compliance with medication.
- **Flexibility**. This is the ability to accommodate change. Timely adjustments in objectives or plans should not be regarded as deviations, but as revised objectives or plans, and the control system should be able to adjust to such revision – in limits.
- **Accuracy**. This means that a control system should be designed in such a way that it provides an objective and accurate picture – the truth value (trustworthiness) of the results should therefore be high.
- **Timeliness**. This means that timely control data should be supplied regularly, as needed. A sensible approach is one based on the principle of timeliness.
- **Unnecessary complexity.** This means that unnecessary complex systems are often an obstacle because they can have a negative influence on the sound judgement of competent managers. A system that is too complex is often negated by managers – leading to disempowerment of the manager.

Figure 1.8 Process of control

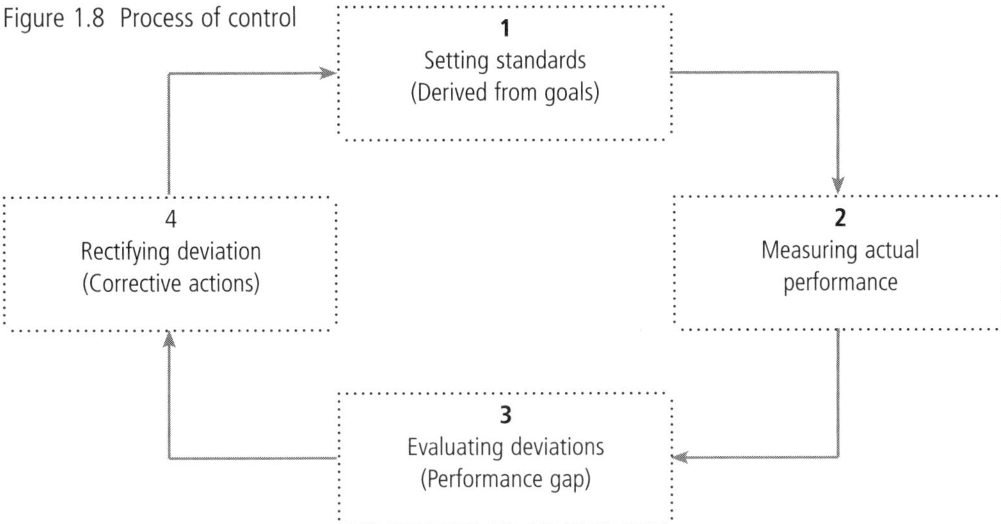

Process of control

Control is the process by which management ensures that the organisation's goals are accomplished and/or that actual performance compares favourably with the predetermined standards. This process comprises four steps: setting of standards, measuring actual performance against these standards, evaluating deviations that might occur, and taking steps to rectify deviations. The process of control is illustrated in Figure 1.8. (Refer also to Chapter 20, Continuous quality improvement in a healthcare organisation.)

Setting standards

The first step in the control process is the setting of standards, related to the core business areas, in accordance with the strategic plan of the healthcare organisation. A performance standard is a written statement of the desired level of performance, and is classified into structure, process and outcome standards (refer to Chapter 4, Dimensions of functional management in a healthcare organisation; Chapter 17, Financial management of a healthcare organisation, Chapter 18; Risk management in a healthcare organisation; Chapter 19, Quality improvement models in a healthcare organisation and Chapter 20, Continuous quality improvement in a healthcare organisation). Standards should be relevant, realistic, attainable and measurable. Standards are a function of the goals that are set in the planning phase, and they enable management to monitor the progress of strategies and attainment of goals. The different level managers (corporate, middle and operational) are responsible for the setting of standards, in accordance with the strategic goals and plans and the focus areas of control.

Measuring actual performance
Management information is collected, collated and presented to indicate the disparities between performance standards and actual performance, and to enable management to concentrate on deviations and problem areas. The data should be valid, quantifiable and absolutely reliable. The collection of information and reporting on actual performance are continuous activities. The type of performance standard determines the type of information that needs to be collected and how this information should be collected. There are different methods of data collection (i.e. financial statements, observation of clinical performance and patient satisfaction surveys), requiring the most suitable instruments and data collection systems. Refer to the Chapter 4, Dimensions of functional managementin a healthcare organisation; Chapter 18, Risk management in a healthcare organisation; Chapter 19, Quality improvement models in a healthcare organisation and Chapter 20, Continuous quality improvement in a healthcare organisation).

Evaluating deviations (performance gap)
This step comprises the determination of the performance gap between the performance standard and actual performance. Disparities should be reliable. It is important to know why a standard has only been matched – and not exceeded – or even why performance has been much better that the standard. The following principles are important:
- The deviations/disparities should be trustworthy (reflect truth value).
- The extent of the deviation or non-compliance should be determined and evaluated with reference to its impact (i.e. the impact on legality, patient safety and organisational resources).
- The contributory factors should be investigated to guide the nature and scope of corrective/remedial action required.
- It should be determined or decided whether the extent of the deviations requires or justifies further investigation.

Rectifying deviations
The final step in the control process is to determine the need for corrective or remedial action and to ensure that deviations do not recur. The remedial action strategy is in accordance with the focus of control (clinical performance, physical, financial, human resources, etc.), and implies the development of a risk management strategy in the particular area of performance. Refer to Chapter 18, Risk management in a healthcare organisation and Chapter 20, Continuous quality improvement in a healthcare organisation.

1.6 UNDERLYING DYNAMICS

Many variables have an impact on the quality of management of a healthcare organisation, of which the ever-changing environment is but one of them. Change implies any variation of the status quo – from a condition of stability to one of instability, a shift from the predictable to the unpredictable, or one from the known to the unknown. If this change cannot be measured, it causes insecurity. No single factor can be held responsible for it, and in particular places and communities it occurs in different ways and at a different rate. Moreover, the rate of change often has greater effect on the environment than the direction of the change. Change is therefore a process of constant renewal and regeneration in every conceivable sphere of society. Therefore businesses/organisations, as the central component of the business environment, are naturally also subject to change. Worldwide, business organisations are restructuring, outsourcing and trimming workforces. The business/organisation must be able to align itself with the realities of the changing external environment. And without adapting to these changes, they will not be fit to compete or render a service in the global economy. Successful management of a healthcare organisation is therefore influenced by many external and internal underlying dynamics.

The business/organisational environment is usually divided into three sub-sections: the micro-environment in the organisation, the market environment and the macro-environment (De J. Cronjé et al., 2004:85–87). The quality of healthcare service management is dependent on the managers' ability to analyse the environments, in particular the macro-environment, and to timeously adapt to the factors impacting on the quality of management.

Throughout this book, specific underlying dynamics with reference to a specialised area of management are briefly described. Therefore, an overview is given of the underlying dynamics impacting on the management of a healthcare organisation, focusing on the macro-environment and the institutional determinants.

1.6.1 Macro-environment

The macro-environment is external to both the organisation and the market environment, and consists of several distinct components:

- **Technological environment**. This continuously brings change and innovation, requiring constant realignment of organisations in this regard.
- **Economic environment**. Factors such as inflation, exchange rates, recessions, and monetary and fiscal policy influence the prosperity of the business/organisation.
- **Social environment**. Consumer lifestyles, habits and values, formed by culture, make certain demands on the business/organisation, particularly through consumerism. Urbanisation, the level of education and the changing role of women are important social environmental factors. The principles of social responsibility and business ethics also form part of the social environment and should be taken into consideration.
- **Physical environment**. This consists of natural resources such as mineral wealth, flora and fauna, and manufactured improvements such as roads/infra-structure.
- **Institutional environment**. The government and its political and legislative

involvement are the main components. Management decisions are continually affected by the course of politics, especially the political pressures exerted by the ruling administration and authorities.

- **International environment**. Local and foreign political trends and events affect the business organisation (micro-environment), as well as the market environment. The individual business organisation has very little or no control over the macro-environment, and its influence on these variables is negligible. The new economic order that is taking shape worldwide is indicative of the increasing globalisation of the world economy. Globalisation and the trend towards a borderless world continually affect businesses and organisations in new and different ways. There is a shift from manufacturing jobs to service-based jobs. This trend is likely to continue and impacts on the business world, as new products are demanded and the new 'knowledge' workers are developing new ways of managing organisations. The typical business of this century will be knowledge and not labour-based. This will result in a growing emphasis on human capital – the knowledge, training, skills and expertise of an organisation's workers. The rate of migration in the globalised scenario further complicates the management of a healthcare organisation.

1.6.2 Institutional determinants

Various institutional determinants have an impact on the quality of healthcare service management:

- The economic support system, the nature and scope of resources available, the type of healthcare programmes and level of service delivery, the leadership and management framework, as well as cultural determinants, have an impact on the quality of management.
- An organisational culture and environment that fosters organisational performance and better service delivery should have a positive impact on the quality of management. This means having clear strategic and operational objectives that are implemented.
- A reliable and accurate information technology system is required – to ensure optimal utilisation of the operational, middle and strategic management system.
- Competence with regard to healthcare service management is required: a good understanding of how to use existing systems to apply the principles of management and to continuously monitor the progress of goal achievement and compliance with planned performance indicators and outputs.
- A management commitment to understanding the internal and external dynamics impacting on the quality of management – this requires a shift from old management practices to modern and dynamic management practices.
- Organisational structure should foster an alignment of all the managerial activities and accountability by all the managers and practitioners related to their area of responsibility.

- Effective management should be practised before moving to performance management – the information management system should be utilised well, and inputs should be monitored before moving on to the auditing of inputs in relation to outputs.
- Leadership and human resource capacity with regard to healthcare service management and clinical performance is required.
- Many ethical challenges face the healthcare organisation today, such as the management of information – to disclose or not disclose – and the related rights of the consumer and other stakeholders, health research ethics, etc.
- Accountable and justifiable business ethics practice is important.

1.7 CONCLUDING STATEMENTS

The following concluding statements are relevant:

- Many forces have an impact on the management of a healthcare service: economic, health culture or health perspective, competence and experience, value for money and consumerism, social responsibility and business ethics.
- The management of a healthcare organisation is practised in the context of the following: the global context, the constitution, common law, general national legislation as applied to a healthcare organisation, national health-related legislation, the principles of corporate governance, the professional, ethical and legal context of the clinical and non-clinical practitioners, business ethics and the type of business ownership.
- The purpose of management is to facilitate goal achievement, and to make a positive contribution toward the healthcare indicators of the country.
- The main role-players concerned with the management of a healthcare organisation constitute at least the following: the legislative authorities and subsequent officials, the board of directors, the managers (top, middle and operational), the community, the recognised trade union(s), other stakeholders, as well as the subordinates.
- Healthcare managers need to reflect a variety of competencies to enable effective practice of their interpersonal, information and decision-making roles. They also need to execute important corporate governance duties.
- Management is classified into three types of management: strategic, general and functional.
- Management relates to a process of planning, organising, leading and control.
- Planning consists of goal setting, development of strategies/action plans, implementation strategies, as well as strategies to assess goal achievement and outcomes.
- Organising is concerned with organisational structure design, the designing of posts, assigning of responsibilities and authority, establishing a command structure, and establishing coordinating mechanisms to facilitate unity of management in the organisation.

- Leading is concerned with the purposeful and dynamic interaction between the leader and the followers to influence performance and subsequent goal achievement and compliance with the planned outcomes.
- Control refers to the assessment of actual performance against planned performance, and is classified as following: proactive, continuous and reactive control.
- The quality of healthcare service management is influenced by the macro-environment and the institutional determinants.

Seven things could destroy us:
Wealth without work
Pleasure without conscience
Knowledge without character
Business without morality
Science without humanity
Religion without sacrifice
Politics without principle.
(Gandhi)

Self-assessment

(1) Formulate management performance standards for your healthcare organisation in accordance with your chosen type of service delivery and level of management (corporate, middle or operational level) with reference to the following:
   (a) Management and governance of the healthcare organisation
   (b) Administrative support management system
   (c) Patient care and treatment management system (access, patient and family rights, admission, treatment/care and discharge)
   (d) Management of patient information
   (e) Hotel services.

(2) Compile performance standards for the healthcare service manager, in accordance with the type of business ownership and the type of service delivery (e.g. clinical departmental manager: surgical services of a district public hospital).

(3) Compile a Code of Ethics for your healthcare organisation (at corporate, or departmental or operational level).

(4) Develop an instrument to assess the healthcare organisation's compliance with the principles of business ethics.

(5) Develop an instrument to assess the healthcare organisation's compliance with the principles of corporate governance, in accordance with the King II requirements.

2 Strategic management of a healthcare organisation

KEY CONCEPTS

Strategic management
Strategy analysis
Strategy development
Strategy execution
Strategy review

SPECIFIC OUTCOMES

- Interpret the legal, professional-ethical and health **context**, with reference to the strategic management of a healthcare organisation: macro-environment, national and organisational context, as well as corporate governance
- Analyse and debate the **purpose** of strategic management in the healthcare organisation with reference to strategic positioning and re-positioning, contribution to healthcare service delivery, impact on healthcare indicators, survival or sustainability, and to increase efficiency or profit
- Identify the **role-players** and interpret their roles and responsibilities in strategic management: leaders and managers, board of directors, organisational consultation representatives and the community
- Describe and apply the **process** of strategic management: strategy analysis, strategy development, strategy execution and strategy review
- Debate the **underlying dynamics** that could impact on the strategic management of a healthcare organisation, with reference to selected institutional key success factors, as well as the 'Good-to-Great' leadership hierarchy described by Jim Collins.

2.1 INTRODUCTION

Strategic management is the continuous positioning or repositioning of the organisation, based on *strategy analysis* (external and internal environmental assessment), *strategy development* (determination of the organisation's mission, vision, values, goals and related key performance areas and strategic actions required to achieve the goals), *strategy execution* (the implementation or deployment of the strategy by translating the corporate goals and strategy into achievable objectives and action plans that cascade down to departmental, unit/area and individual levels), and *strategy review* (evaluation of organisational, departmental, unit/area and individual performance in accordance with the outcomes and indicators determined). Figure 2.1 reflects the visual presentation of strategic management in a healthcare organisation.

Figure 2.1 Visual presentation of strategic management in a healthcare organisation

Context	Macro-environment National context Organisational context Corporate governance
Role-players	Leaders and managers Board of directors Organisational consultation representatives Shareholders and other stakeholders Community
Purpose	Positioning and re-positioning Contribute/add value to healthcare service delivery Positive impact on healthcare indicators Survival or sustainability Increase efficiency or profit
Process	Strategy analysis Strategy development Strategy execution Strategy review
Underlying dynamics	Institutional critical success factors: Quality of strategic leadership Quality of strategic management Level of organisational commitment: ownership and motivation Institutional capacity 'Good-to-Great' leadership

2.2 CONTEXT

Strategic management of a healthcare organisation is determined by the type and nature of business ownership (refer to Chapter 1), and influenced by the macro-environment.

2.2.1 Macro-environment

The macro-environment is external to both the organisation and the market environment, and consists of several distinct components:

- **Technological environment**. This continuously brings change and innovation, requiring constant realignment of organisations in this regard.

- **Economic environment**. Factors such as inflation, exchange rates, recessions, and monetary and fiscal policy influence the prosperity of the business/organisation.
- **Social environment**. Consumer lifestyles, habits and values, formed by culture, make certain demands on the business/organisation, particularly through consumerism. Urbanisation, the level of education and the changing role of women are important social environmental factors. The principles of social responsibility and business ethics also form part of the social environment to be taken into consideration.
- **Physical environment**. This environment consists of natural resources such as mineral wealth, flora and fauna, and manufactured improvements such as roads and infra-structure.
- **Institutional environment**. Here the government and its political and legislative involvement are the main components. Management decisions are continually affected by the course of politics, especially the political pressures exerted by the ruling administration and authorities.
- **International environment**. Local and foreign political trends and events affect the business organisation (micro-environment), as well as the market environment. The individual business organisation has very little or no control over the macro-environment and its influence on these variables is negligible. The new economic order that is taking shape worldwide is indicative of the increasing globalisation of the world economy. Globalisation and the trend towards a borderless world continually affect businesses and organisations in new and different ways.

2.2.2 National context

Strategic management of healthcare organisations is first and foremost based on the strategic framework and subsequent priorities of the national department of health. *The Strategic Framework for 2004–2009 of the South African Department of Health (2004)* focuses on the following: the vision and mission, introduction, priorities for the next five years, situational analysis, followed by the priorities with subsequent key activities. This is based on a review conducted of the period 1999–2004 to determine what work is outstanding and what new work is needed to provide the necessary stewardship of the South African health system.

Vision and mission of the national department of health

Vision: To provide an accessible, caring and high-quality health system

Mission: To improve health status through prevention and promotion of healthy lifestyles and to consistently improve the healthcare delivery system by concentrating on access, equity, efficiency, quality and sustainability.

Priorities

The priorities for the next five years were generated from discussions on the assessment of the achievements of the past 10 years, the regional and international obligations and work that remains to strengthen the national health system (NHS).

The following priorities were approved:

- Improve the governance and management of the NHS.
- Promote healthy lifestyles.
- Contribute towards human dignity by improving the quality of care.
- Improve management of communicable diseases and non-communicable illnesses.
- Strengthen primary healthcare, Emergency Medical Services (EMS) and hospital service delivery systems.
- Strengthen support services.
- Undertake human resource planning, development and management.
- Prepare and implement legislation.
- Strengthen international relations.

This strategy and the subsequent key activities obviously impact on the strategic management of the public and private healthcare organisations. In addition to this strategy, there are many national legislative and policy frameworks that have an impact on the management of healthcare organisations and which necessitate transformation and strategic re-direction of organisational service delivery.

2.2.3 Organisational context

The organisational context is based on the type of business ownership (public or private) and subsequent legislative and service delivery framework, the nature and size of the organisation, and other related internal determinants. There are several key elements of strategic decisions that are related primarily to the organisation's ability to add value and/or to compete in the market place (De Bruyn, 2004:4–5):

- **Sustainability** relates to the long-term sustainability or survival of the organisation.
- **Development of processes** relates to the delivery of strategy, resulting in innovative ways to execute the core business of the organisation.
- **Competitive advantage** means that a sustainable strategy is more likely if the strategy delivers sustainable competitive advantage over its actual or potential competitors.
- **Utilisation of linkages between the organisation and its environment** refers to links that cannot be easily duplicated and will contribute to superior performance.
- **Vision** refers to the ability to move the organisation forward in a significant way beyond the current reality, with the likelihood to result in innovative strategies.

2.2.4 Corporate governance

The principles of corporate governance are related to the sustainability of the company or organisation and also direct the strategic management of healthcare organisations.

2.3 PURPOSE

The purpose of strategic management is to:

- Position or re-position the healthcare organisation in the context of the external and internal determinants
- Meaningfully contribute/add value to healthcare service delivery
- Positively impact on the healthcare indicators of the population
- Facilitate survival or sustainability of the organisation
- Increase efficiency and, in the case of a private healthcare organisation, to increase the profit of the organisation in a competitive industry.

2.4 ROLE-PLAYERS

The role-players mainly relate to the leaders and managers, the board of directors, organisational consultation representatives, shareholders and other stakeholders, as well as the community.

2.4.1 Leaders and managers

Strategic leadership and management are exercised by all level managers in the healthcare organisation in accordance with the level of accountability concerned, as illustrated in Figure 2.2. Strategic management and transformation management are closely linked. Refer to Chapter 5 on Change management, with reference to the 'Good-to-Great' leadership model described by Jim Collins (2001).

2.4.2 Board of directors

The board should review and agree on the company's purpose and strategy, including its vision, mission, long-term corporate goals and short-term business objectives. The board should also make a periodic determination of the areas of business that the company should be in, based on an evaluation of recognised quantitative measurements of the external environment and surrounding circumstances. The board should ensure that the company adopts the appropriate legal form and organisational structure for the optimal allocation, disposition and utilisation of its assets, both financial and intellectual, in pursuit of strategic objectives. The company's articles of association (in the case of a private healthcare company) will set out the powers reserved to the board for the governance of the company. The standard articles of association allow for the delegation of powers by the board to a chief executive officer and to board committees for certain purposes. The general role and functions of the board of directors are, among others, to:

Figure 2.2 Involvement of level managers in strategic management

Management level	Strategy analysis	Strategy development	Strategy execution	Strategy review
Corporate	Strategic focus	Strategic vision, mission, goals and strategy Focus on organisational performance indicators	Corporate performance management Corporate strategic leadership and strategic management strategies	Corporate performance review National comparison of outcomes and indicators
Departmental	Departmental focus and alignment with strategic focus	Alignment with corporate strategy Focused departmental strategy and performance	Departmental performance management Departmental leadership and management systems	Departmental performance review and contribution to corprate performance Internal comparison
Unit/area	Alignment with departmental focus and deployment to individual focus	Alignment with departmental strategy Focus on unit and individual KPAs and indicators	Operational execution strategies and performance management Operational leadership and management Individual performance management	Operational performance review Individual performance review

- Position the organisation by determining the vision, mission and value statements in accordance with the core business and related service delivery of the organisation
- Determine the company's purpose and goals
- Adopt the strategic plan of the organisation
- Determine the company's strategy to achieve the purpose and to implement its values, in order to ensure that it survives and thrives
- Determine organisational policy and processes to ensure the integrity of the company's risk management and internal controls
- Exercise leadership, integrity and judgement in directing the organisation to achieve continuing prosperity

- Ensure that policies, procedures and practices are in place to protect the company's assets and reputation
- Monitor and evaluate the implementation strategies, policies, management performance and business plans
- Ensure that the organisation complies with the relevant laws, regulations and codes of best business practice.

(PricewaterhouseCoopers, 2003:31–32)

2.4.3 Organisational consultation representatives

Strategic management entails a process of participative management and involvement to facilitate ownership of the strategic plan and the execution thereof at all levels. The corporate strategy needs to be aligned with and cascaded down to departmental and unit/area levels. Furthermore, the principles of performance management need to be integrated – not only at all the management levels – but also to individual performance levels. It is therefore necessary to constitute and utilise the most appropriate consultation structures, such as a Corporate Sounding Board, the Institutional Forum, recognised trade unions, etc.

2.4.4 Shareholders and other stakeholders

Shareholders and other relevant stakeholders are identified, in accordance with the business ownership of the healthcare organisation, and invited to participate in selected dimensions of strategic management.

2.4.5 Community engagement

The principle of community engagement is important, not only during strategy analysis and strategy development, but also during the strategy review phase. The most appropriate community engagement structures (i.e. consumer unions, community leadership structures, community representative forums, and the Annual General Meetings of private companies) should be utilised or created.

2.5 PROCESS

Strategic management is the continuous positioning or repositioning of the organisation, based on the following process (refer to Figure 2.3):

- **Strategy analysis**. This consists of the assessment of external factors (environmental changes, opportunities and threats) and internal factors (quality of service delivery, strengths and weaknesses) – referred to as environmental scanning – impacting on the core business of the organisation and its performance in this regard.
- **Strategy development**. This relates to the development of the organisation's vision, mission and value statements, and formulation of goals – focusing mainly on the long-term goals – and the development of subsequent implementation plans, strategies and performance indicators.

- **Strategy execution**. This consists of implementing the strategy and aligning it with other methods/tools, such as the Balanced Scorecard.
- **Strategy review**. This refers to the assessment of compliance with goal achievement and planned outcomes.

Figure 2.3 Process of strategic management

The process of strategic management is presented with reference to the prerequisites of strategic management, strategy analysis, strategy development, strategy execution and strategy review.

2.5.1 Prerequisites for successful strategic management

Strategic management is based on the following prerequisites:

- A desire and commitment by all level managers to move from 'good to great'
- Participative management to facilitate ownership of the corporate strategy and the optimal integration/cascading to departmental/functional and unit levels
- The implementation of an integrated purpose-driven and focused strategic management programme
- Commitment by all level managers
- An absolute pursuit of excellence, linked to visible management and the will to apply the principles of change/transformation management
- Application of purposeful time management
- Embracing a visionary approach.

2.5.2 Strategy analysis

Strategy analysis consists of the internal (organisational profile analysis) and external environmental (scanning, monitoring, forecasting and assessing) analyses.

2.5.2.1 SWOT analysis

The SWOT analysis could be used as a method to assist with the strategy analysis, and consists of the following:

- **Strengths**. This relates to the analysis of the internal organisational strengths that could be enhanced to the benefit of strategic management. It entails a rational process of resource analysis through benchmarking. Strengths could relate to physical resources and assets, organisational assets (performance management system, quality improvement structure and system, etc.), human resource abilities, intangible assets (image, reputations, branding, etc.), alliances, special achievements or awards.

- **Weaknesses**. This refers to the identification and counteraction of the internal organisational weaknesses related to resources, type and extent of core business service delivery, quality of service delivery, etc. The organisation's internal weaknesses could also relate to a negative incident resulting in negative media coverage, requiring purposeful reputation management.
- **Opportunities**. This includes the identification and utilisation of external opportunities to improve the strategic positioning of the healthcare organisation in terms of meeting the needs and addressing the competitive edge in the market.
- **Threats**. This relates to the identification of internal and external threats that could have a negative impact on the survival or sustainability of the healthcare organisation.

2.5.2.2 Organisational profile analysis

By applying the principles of the SWOT analysis, the organisation is able to start compiling the profile for the purposes of strategic management. The organisational profile analysis should focus on at least the following:

- **Financial profile** means that a thorough analysis of the financial position, as reflected in the financial statements and annual reports, is required.
- **Core business** refers to the nature and scope of service delivery, the quality of the service delivery as reflected in external peer reviews, client/patient satisfaction surveys, performance indicators and outputs, etc.
- **Management performance** relates to an analysis of the management systems processes and holistic performance based on industry-related benchmarking (comparisons with other similar healthcare organisations, annual health review, etc.). Success with transformation management and compliance with business ethics, corporate governance criteria of excellence, and external peer reviews are measured.
- **Research contribution** refers to the organisation's ability to make a meaningful contribution towards knowledge generation and service improvement by means of research participation and subsequent outputs.
- **Human resources** applies to the nature and scope thereof, abilities/ competencies, special awards, credibility in the organisation, as well as external peer group positioning, staff turnover and retention profile, level of motivation and achievement.
- **Strategic management performance** relates to the profile of previous strategic management reviews – the attainment of goals and performance indicators.

2.5.2.3 Environmental scanning

Scanning entails the study of all segments in the general environment. Through scanning, the organisations identify early signals of potential changes and trends. Environmental scanning has been found critically important for effective performance of companies operating in a dynamic and volatile environment. Environmental scanning refers to the process of monitoring, assessment, measurement, forecasting/ projection and evaluation of change in the different environmental variables impacting on the management of the organisation. The business environment – and therefore the health-sector environment – is divided into three sub-sections: micro-environment, market environment and macro-environment (De J. Cronjé et al., 2004:85–113). These types of environment have been briefly discussed in Chapter 1. The degree to which the environment influences the management of a business depends largely on the type of business and the core business activities. Moreover, environmental influences differ from one management area to the next, and even at different levels of management. Clinical operational management is often influenced to a greater extent by the operational technological changes, and corporate management is often influenced to a greater extent by political directives. Therefore, the importance, scope and method of environmental scanning – that is the process of measurement, projection and evaluation of change in the different environmental variables – differ from one organisation to the other.

The **importance** of environmental scanning may be summarised as follows (De J. Cronjé et al., 2004:114):

- The environment is constantly changing – therefore purposeful monitoring is necessary to keep abreast of change.
- Scanning is necessary to determine what factors and patterns in the environment pose threats to the present strategy of a business.
- Scanning is also necessary to determine what factors in the environment present opportunities for the more effective attainment of the goals and objectives of a business.
- Businesses that systematically scan the environment are more successful than those that don't.

The **scope** of environmental scanning is determined by the following factors (De Cronjé et al., 2004:114):

- The nature of the environment in which the bussiness operates, and the demands made by the environment on a business are important. The more unstable the environment, and the more sensitive the business is to change, the more comprehensive the scanning has to be. Increasing instability usually means greater risk.
- The basic relationship between a business and its environment plays an important role.

- The source and extent of change are important. The impact of change is rarely so compartmentalised that it affects only one or two areas of an organisation. Change has an interactive and dynamic effect on several aspects of a business.
- Environmental scanning focuses on at least the following remote forces – economical, social, political, ecological, technological and legislative.

The scope of the environmental scanning is therefore determined by general private business ownership factors, as well as the factors impacting on public healthcare service delivery. Obviously, the national, provincial and local policy directives and key priority areas reflected in the subsequent healthcare delivery strategies (i.e. the Strategic Priorities for the National Health System of the Department of Health), form part of the scope of environmental scanning in the context of the strategic management of a healthcare organisation.

The environmental scanning process is a much-debated subject. The following are a few guidelines (De J. Cronjé et al., 2004:114–115):

- Relevant secondary or published information must be updated and is obtainable from a wealth of sources, such as the media, professional publications, financial journals, statistics, associates in other organisations, research institutions and the website of the specific governmental department.
- The more advanced form of scanning is the addition of primary information, or special investigations on particular trends/aspects of the environment. Such investigations can be carried out by members of the organisation's own staff or external consultants.
- Scanning at a much more advanced level is the establishment of a scanning unit in the business that monitors a range of environmental variables and makes forecasts about certain of these trends. Economic predictions by economists using a number of models, assessments of the market and of competition by market researchers, and technological predictions by industrial analysts, are a few examples. Such a scanning unit is usually located in the planning department of the organisation.
- A formalised information or communication system is necessary to filter the information and to disseminate the relevant information to the appropriate managers.

In addition to the above guidelines, *due diligence and feasibility studies* can be conducted to scientifically assess the strategic positioning or re-positioning (or dynamic transformation) directives related to the internal and external factors and dynamics. Refer to Chapter 5 on Change management.

2.5.3 Strategy development

Strategy development is based on a process of trustworthy consultation with all internal and external stakeholders involved. This results in the drafting of the strategy (with or without an external facilitator/strategy development consultant), and the refinement of the strategy based on the sequential process of consultation as negotiated. Strategy development consists of the following elements:

- Examination of strategy assessment results: description of the organisational profile and the external environmental scan, as well as the strategic choices based on these results
- Formulation of the vision, mission and value statements
- Formulation of strategic goals
- Development of key priorities and subsequent action plans
- Development of master strategy
- Integration with the Balanced Scorecard.

2.5.3.1 Formulation of vision, mission and value statements

A **vision** is a written statement or affirmation relating to the future intent, aspiration(s), uniqueness and identity of the organisation – what we believe we can be. The vision gives direction to the positioning or re-positioning of its core business and related service delivery.

The **mission** is the statement of core business-related service delivery to concretise the vision of the organisation – what we believe we can do. The mission should reflect the nature of the core business, the unique identity of the organisation and alignment with the vision.

Organisational **values** reflect the organisational beliefs, principles and moral statements that guide behaviour during the execution of the strategy and related core business activities. The values usually relate to the social orientation of the organisation, quality, client/customer and output orientation. Examples of value statements are accountability, honesty and excellence.

2.5.3.2 Formulation of strategic goals

An organisational strategic goal is a written target to aim for, in accordance with the core business of the organisation – a process that assists to direct the organisation's future and the development of the organisational strategy. Goal formulation is based on the external and internal environmental analyses, and the strategy selection (determination of key priority areas in relation to the core business elements of service delivery).

Attributes of goals

- Goals are SMART – specific, measurable, achievable, realistic and time-bound.
- Goals are formulated in affirmation form.
- Goals should be different from the current reality or status quo to create a 'thirst' (motivation due to a feeling of dissonance) towards goal attainment.

- Goals should stimulate creativity and energy to achieve them (adventurous as opposed to paralysing).
- Goals are sequenced with due regard of time limits (long-, medium- or short-term).
- Goals are acceptable due to the participatory process of consultation and goal setting.
- Goals are aligned and cascaded down to all management levels in the organisation – corporate goals are translated into departmental goals; departmental goals are cascaded down to the units/areas, which ultimately results in performance indicators at individual level. This results in 'goal-cooperation' of all team players.
- Ongoing modification during the process of strategy execution at departmental or operational level could be necessary to facilitate purpose-driven performance.

2.5.3.3 Development of the action plans

The action plans relate to the following:

- A list of the strategic goals that have been formulated is drawn up.
- The key priority areas – also referred to as Key Performance Areas (in accordance with the core business elements of the organisation) – are selected in relation to each of the strategic goals formulated.
- The formulated objectives for each Key Performance Area (KPA) are drawn up.
- The activities or actions required for each KPA and the attainment of the subsequent objectives, that is the development and adoption of corporate policies and procedures, initiation of quality improvement programmes, establishment of external relationships, and strengthening of existing communication and identity are listed. When developing the action plans, several options need to be assessed, based on the principles of rational decision-making.
- Accountability and subsequent duties, tasks and responsibilities (DTRs) related to each KPA are assigned.
- Due dates for attainment of each KPA objective and execution of the action plan(s) are given.

There are different types of plans – long-term strategic plans, medium-term functional plans and short-term operational plans. The plans should be viable, based on rational assessment of the various strategy options to achieve the goals and objectives related to the key priority areas:

- **Strategic long-term plans**. The strategic long-term plans focus on the core business elements of the healthcare organisation.
- **Medium-term functional plans**. These relate to the departmental general or specialised functional goals (i.e. clinical specialisation plans, such as medical, surgical, critical care; or non-clinical functional plans, such as financial plans, marketing, maintenance, laundry service).

- **Short-term operational plans**. These plans focus on the execution activities related to the execution of the core business at unit/area or operational levels.

2.5.3.4 Master strategy

The master strategy is presented and published:

- The organisational vision, mission and value statements
- Strategic goals, key priority/performance areas and related objectives, action plans and, if appropriate, the designated accountable manager
- Implementation plans: the departmental and operational plans for putting the master plan into operation
- Performance outcomes and indicators.

2.5.3.5 Integration of the strategy with Balanced Scorecard

Once the strategy has been developed, the operational execution thereof is enhanced by integrating the strategy with the Balanced Scorecard (refer to Figures 2.4 and 2.5). Robert Kaplan (2000), the well-known founder of the Balanced Scorecard (refer to Chapter 19, Quality improvement models in a healthcare organisation), describes the principles of a strategy- focused organisation as follows:

- Translate the strategy to operational terms: develop strategy maps and develop Balanced Scorecards.
- Align the organisation around the strategy: define corporate roles, create business unit synergies and develop support unit synergies.
- Make strategy everyone's job: create strategic awareness, develop personal scorecards, develop balanced performance output rewards.
- Make strategy a continuous process: link budgets and strategies with one another, close the loop with strategic learning and empowerment, and develop analytic and information systems.
- The strategy should focus on the four key perspectives reflected in the Balanced Scorecard: financial perspective, customer perspective, internal processes perspective and learning, and growth perspective.

2.5.4 Strategy execution

Strategy execution refers to the implementation or deployment of the strategy/strategic plan. The basic principles related to strategy execution are as follows:

- **Institutionalise the strategy**. Make the master strategy known to everyone (i.e. utilising the Balanced Scorecard), marketing and communication of the strategy (placement on departmental websites, utilising every-day-reminder methods).
- **Build organisational structure to accommodate the strategy**. This means the strengthening of existing organisational structures and/or creation of new structures.

Figure 2.4 Integration of individual and organisational Balanced Scoreboards

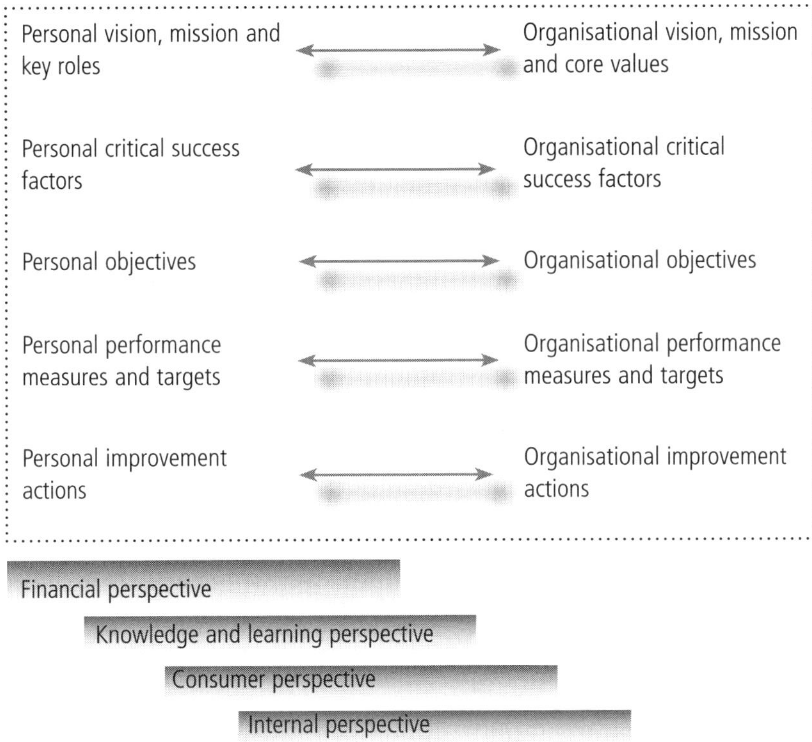

Figure 2.5 Personal Balanced Scorecard

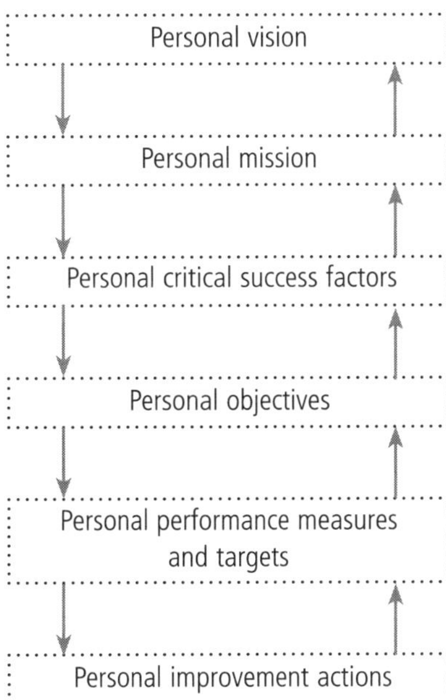

- **Allocate resources and focus on objectives**. This refers to the allocation of resources, application of project management principles for the risk-related priorities, general capacity building (physical, financial, human resources, etc.) to accommodate the execution of the strategy.
- **Exercise strategic leadership**. This is necessary to facilitate the implementation of the master strategy.
- **Create support systems and strategies**. Policies and procedures are required to facilitate repetitive decision-making with the functional departments.
- **Assign key strategic priorities (KPAs)**. These priorities should be assigned to designated managers/leaders in the organisation.
- **Align with performance management strategy and system**. Alignment takes place in the organisation to facilitate commitment of all employees.

2.5.5 Strategy review

Strategy review is the process of strategic control, by which management ensures that the organisation's strategic goals are accomplished and/or that actual performance compares favourably with the predetermined performance standards. This process comprises four steps: setting of standards, measuring actual performance against these standards, evaluating deviations that might occur, and taking steps to rectify deviations (refer also to Chapter 1 Management of a healthcare organisation and Chapter 20 Continuous quality improvement in a healthcare organisation). The integration of the Balanced Scorecard and subsequent Performance Management System could facilitate this process of strategy evaluation.

Strategy review is summarised as follows:

- Determine the critical strategic control points in the parameters of the organisation's strategy (vision, mission, goals, key priority areas/KPAs and subsequent objectives).
- Compile the strategic control plan with reference to the KPAs that require continuous monitoring and evaluation or control by exception.
- Formulate performance standards accordingly.
- Monitor and evaluate performance against these standards.
- Take corrective actions according to the degree of deviations when appropriate.
- Undertake continuous evaluation of progress with reference to the execution of the strategy, compliance with due dates and attainment of sequential objectives.
- Undertake continuous modification of objectives and time limits according to capacity problems and needs, and changes in the current reality.
- Build resilience in the event of non-compliance and temporary setbacks.
- Undertake performance management at individual, team, unit and departmental levels.
- Perform a final evaluation of attainment of goals and performance indicators at the end of the term of office.

2.6 UNDERLYING DYNAMICS

There are obviously many underlying dynamics that have an impact on the quality of strategic management in a healthcare organisation. A few critical institutional success factors are highlighted:

- The quality of strategic leadership capacity will determine the quality of strategy analysis, development, execution and evaluation. This implies the ability to diligently and innovatively apply their minds – in the interest of the organisation and healthcare service delivery – with honesty, determination and commitment.
- The quality of strategic management capacity will influence the strategy execution and evaluation: the ability to apply the principles of participative management, organisational change, the management of diversity, performance management, as well as the ability to build resilience when necessary.
- The level of organisational commitment to the strategy, based on buy-in and acceptance of ownership at all levels of management and operational practice, is important.
- The level of organisational commitment to the strategy, based on the degree of motivation, is an important factor: the drive by all employees to strive towards goal achievement, because this is who and what we really want to be – and I want to be part of it.
- Institutional determinants related to capacity are required: human resources and staff mix, structures, systems, policies, financial resources, etc.
- Finally – Jim Collins describes the five levels of leadership to take a company from good to great (Collins, 2001:19–22):
  - *Level 1: Highly capable individual*. He/she makes productive contributions through talent, knowledge, skills and good work habits.
  - *Level 2: Contributing team member*. He/she contributes individual capabilities to the achievement of group objectives and works effectively with others in a group setting.
  - *Level 3: Competent manager*. He/she organises people and resources toward the effective and efficient pursuit of pre-determined objectives.
  - *Level 4: Effective leader.* He/she catalyses commitment to and vigorous pursuit of a clear and compelling vision, stimulating higher performance standards.
  - *Level 5: Executive*. He/she builds enduring greatness through a paradoxical blend of personal humility and professional will.

2.7 CONCLUDING STATEMENTS

The following concluding statements are made:

- Strategic management is the continuous positioning or re-positioning of the healthcare organisation by applying the principles of strategy analysis, strategy development, strategy execution and strategy review.
- Strategic management is determined by the type and nature of the business

ownership and influenced by the macro-environment related to the technological, economic, social, physical, institutional and international environment context, as well as the context related to national, organisational and corporate governance.

- The purpose of strategic management is to position or re-position the organisation, to meaningfully contribute or add value to healthcare service delivery, to positively impact on the healthcare indicators of the population, to facilitate survival or sustainability of the organisation and to increase efficiency or profit.
- The role-players involved in strategic management focus on the following: the strategic leaders and managers, as well as all level managers in the healthcare organisation, the board of directors, organisational consultation representatives, shareholders and other stakeholders and community representatives.
- The process of strategic management is classified into strategy analysis, strategy development, strategy execution and strategy review.
- Strategy analysis consists of SWOT analysis, organisational profile analysis, and the principles of environmental scanning.
- Strategy development is derived from the strategy analysis, focusing on the drafting and finalisation of the master strategy, reflecting the following: vision, mission and value statements, organisational goals, key priorities or key performance areas (KPAs), development of subsequent objectives and action plans related to each KPA, publication of the final master strategy, and finally, integration with the Balanced Scorecard.
- Strategy execution refers to the implementation or deployment of the master strategy or strategic plan. This involves a series of implementation strategies, such as allocation of resources, the exercising of strategic leadership and management, alignment with performance management, etc.
- Strategy review is the process of strategic control, by which management ensures that the organisation's strategic goals are accomplished and/or that actual performance compares favourably with the predetermined performance standards. This process comprises four steps: setting of standards, measuring actual performance against these standards, evaluating deviations that might occur, and taking steps to rectify deviations.
- Several key success factors impact on the quality of strategic management: the quality of strategic leadership and management, the level of organisational commitment to the strategy, based on acceptance of ownership and internal motivation, as well as other institutional determinants such as capacity. Finally, five levels of leadership to move a company from good to great are required, as described by Jim Collins.

Good is the enemy to great
(Jim Collins)

Self-assessment

Compile an evaluation instrument to measure the quality of a healthcare organisation's strategic plan. Access any healthcare organisation's strategic plan and evaluate the strategy accordingly, focusing on the quality of the:
(a) Strategy analysis
(b) Strategy development
(c) Strategy execution
(d) Strategic review.

3 Selected management models

KEY CONCEPTS

Management models
Participative management
Centralisation and decentralisation
Systems theory
Chaos theory
Complexity theory
Ubuntu

SPECIFIC OUTCOMES

After studying this chapter, you should be able to:

- Interpret the legal, professional-ethical and healthcare **context**, with reference to the selection and application of selected management models
- Analyse and debate the **purpose** of applying different management models
- Identify the **role-players** in the application of management models
- Describe and apply the **dimensions** of selected management models in a healthcare organisation: participative management, centralisation versus decentralisation, systems theory, chaos theory, complexity theory and Ubuntu
- Debate the **underlying dynamics** that could impact on the selection and application of management models.

3.1 INTRODUCTION

Healthcare organisations are dynamic entities that are continuously engaged with their environments and exposed to natural growth and development stages to greater levels of complexity and sophistication. This requires a fine balance between focusing on external demands and internal developmental challenges, and requires an equally careful and considered organisational focus, which will determine how and where energy will be channelled and therefore where and how organisational resources will be allocated. Many management models and theories have been developed – the challenge is to find the balance between centralised control and decentralised freedom with responsibility and accountability. This chapter highlights the following dimensions related to management: participative management, centralisation versus decentralisation, the systems theory and subsequent chaos and complexity theories. The conceptual framework related to this chapter is illustrated in Figure 3.1.

Figure 3.1 Visual presentation of conceptual framework on selected management models in a healthcare organisation

Context	Business ownership: public, private or mixed Generic business environment: interrelated environmental variables, instability, uncertainty and complexity
Role-players	Healthcare service managers
Purpose	Facilitate quality healthcare service delivery
Dimensions	Participative management Centralisation versus decentralisation Systems approach Chaos theory Complexity theory Ubuntu
Underlying dynamics	Manager's cognitive ability Breaking out of the environmental comfort zone

3.2 CONTEXT

The context in which a healthcare organisation operates, as described in Chapter 1, is relevant. The type of business ownership (public, private or mixed), will influence the choice of management models applied. The nature and scope of healthcare service delivery, as well as the size and location of the healthcare organisation (size, shape and function), will impact on the complexity of the organisation and consequently also on the type of management. A few characteristics of the business environment impacting on the management of the organisation are highlighted (De J. Cronjé et al., 2004:88–89):

- **The environmental factors or variables are interrelated**. A change in one of the external variables may cause a change in the micro-environment and, similarly, a change in one external variable may cause a change in the other external variables impacting on the management of the healthcare organisation.
- **Increasing instability**. One of the consequences of interdependence in the environment is increasing instability and change. Although the general rate of change in the environment accelerates, environmental fluctuation is greater for some organisations than for others.
- **Environmental uncertainty**. Uncertainty about the environment is, of course, a function of the amount of information about environmental variables, and of the confidence that management has in such information. If the value of the information is suspect, the uncertainty of management about the environment will increase.

- **The complexity of the environment**. This indicates the number of external variables to which the organisation has to respond, as well as variations in the variables themselves.

3.3 PURPOSE

The most suitable and appropriate management model is selected to facilitate quality healthcare service delivery and attainment of the organisational goals and pre-determined performance indicators.

3.4 ROLE-PLAYERS

The healthcare service manager is the main role-player, in accordance with the type of business ownership and the nature and scope of healthcare service delivery. The healthcare manager is responsible for the continuous assessment, evaluation and interpretation of the variables impacting on the management of the organisation, and selecting the most suitable management model for application.

3.5 SELECTED MANAGEMENT MODELS

The following management models are described: participative management, centralisation versus decentralisation, the systems theory – including the chaos and complexity theories – and Ubuntu.

3.5.1 Participative management

Participative management (see Figure 3.2) is a process of dynamic interactive decision-making and problem-solving, shared governance, ownership and accountability, organisational transformation and empowerment, as well as applicable communication (Muller, 2002:109–115).

Interactive decision-making and problem-solving

Interactive decision-making and problem-solving are based on the principles of involvement/engagement and participation of line managers and other group members – to a lesser or greater extent – who are affected by the decision and/or problem. The general principles of decision-making and problem-solving are applied – based on a continuum of involvement – by using the different strategies determining the degree of involvement or engagement (from a low degree of involvement to an extremely high degree of involvement/engagement): selling, testing, consultation, consensus decision-making and problem-solving, and negotiation.

- **Selling**. An idea or decision/solution is sold to the subordinates, by illustrating or describing the benefits and disadvantages to them.
- **Testing**. An idea or decision/solution is presented to the subordinates, followed by debate and feedback whether they think it will work or not.

Figure 3.2 Participative management

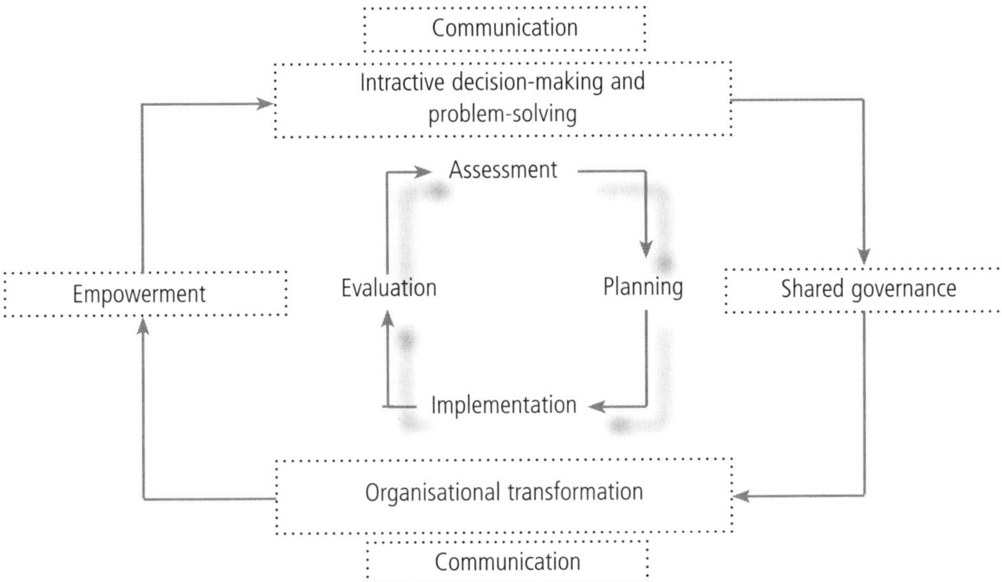

- **Consultation**. A formal or informal process of consultation with the subordinates (or representatives) is activated by means of purposeful engagement. Inputs on a draft idea (i.e. policy) are invited. Once the inputs have been received, they are considered for possible amendment of the decision or draft presentation.
- **Consensus decision-making**. The problem is discussed and meaningful debate is encouraged. The group puts proposals on the table on how to address the issue/problem. Debates in favour of or against the proposals are conducted, and the final proposal is accepted – in the original or amended format – based on the principle of consensus decision-making.
- **Negotiation**. Decisions are reached based on the agreement (mutual acceptance) by two or more parties in a formalised manner (refer to Chapter 10, Nature and scope of human resource management).

Shared governance

Shared governance is the second element of participative management. It refers to the devolution of management (planning, organising, leading and control) to the lowest possible level of operational management and unit/area level where the execution of the core business of the organisation takes place. The devolution of management – and the subsequent authority to manage – is in accordance with the abilities (knowledge, skills, attitudes and values) of the operational managers and subordinates to manage the situation. Shared governance is also based on a relationship of trust between the manager and the subordinates, resulting in co-ownership of the consequences/

results or outcome of the managerial actions. The manager, however, retains ultimate accountability for the outcomes of the devolved management practices.

Organisational transformation

Organisational transformation is the logical consequence of the preceding principle of shared governance, resulting in a flat organisational structure in the organisation. The design of posts and subsequent job descriptions are amended to allow for the principle of shared governance. A matrix organisational structure, focusing on various functional divisions of management, is therefore more advisable.

Empowerment

Empowerment refers to the purposeful process of personal and professional development of the managers and operational decision-makers to accomplish the abilities (knowledge, skills, attitudes and values) related to participative management. This not only entails the general principles of management and decision-making, but also the principles of total quality management, critical and creative thinking, and the enforcement of internal locus of control.

3.5.2 Centralisation versus decentralisation

Healthcare organisations are dynamic and complex systems (refer to 3.5.3), which impact on the selection of management models utilised by the manager. As mentioned previously, the size, shape and function of the organisation are important variables to take into consideration during the management of the healthcare organisation. The principle related to general management and functional management (refer to Chapter 1) will also determine the nature and scope of centralisation and decentralisation in the healthcare organisation. Of particular concern is the specialised nature of healthcare service delivery, necessitating the application of specialised functional management – and in particular clinical governance in the organisation.

The major difference between centralised and decentralised authority is influenced by who makes the important decisions in the organisation. Centralisation and decentralisation thus pertain to the hierarchical level of authority at which decisions are made in the organisation. *Centralisation* means that decision-making authority is located in top management who makes the important decisions. *Decentralisation*, on the other hand, allows for the devolution of decision-making at operational levels where the core business of the organisation is executed.

Decentralisation enables delegating authority and facilitates the empowerment of employees by giving them the right to make decisions that pertain to their work area or division with regard to matters such as the allocation of resources, work schedules, operational directives, policies and procedures. By decentralising power and authority, the principles of participative management can be practised.

In deciding to centralise or decentralise authority, Smit and De J. Cronjé (2002:199–200) suggest that the following factors be considered:

- **The external environment**. The more complex and uncertain the environment is, the greater the tendency to decentralise.
- **The history of the organisation**. As organisations tend to continue doing what they have been doing in the past, there is a tendency to follow the history of the organisation when it comes to centralisation and decentralisation.
- **The strategy of the organisation**. The strategy of the organisation determines the types of market, technological development and competition. In cases where diversification is relevant, a decentralised structure is used. Enterprises doing business in more predictable industries become increasingly more centralised.
- **Skills of lower-level managers**. If the lower-level managers are well qualified and have the skills, top management could benefit by decentralising authority. However, in the case where these managers lack the necessary knowledge and skills, decision-making in the organisation would be more centralised.
- **The nature of the decision**. The more risky the decision and the higher the costs involved, the more pressure there will be to centralise decision-making.
- **The size and growth rate of the organisation**. The larger and more complex an organisation is, the greater the need for decentralisation, as it is impossible to manage a very large organisation without decentralising authority.

3.5.3 Systems theory

A system is defined as a set of objects, the relationships between these objects, and the attributes of the objects (Van Tonder, 2004:37). Systems theory is considered to be the dominant perspective in current thinking about organisations and the management thereof. Systems theory allows us to develop a better understanding of the organisation and its relationship with its environment. Systems theory was present during the earlier stages of organisational thinking, primarily as a closed-system theory. This has since given way to an open-systems theory and more recently network theory, complex and chaos systems theory, and in particular, the emergence of the 'learning organisation' (refer to Figure 3.3).

The concepts related to the systems approach originated in the 1930s and 1940s, when an object or entity viewed in a holistic manner came to be thought of as a system consisting of parts, which in turn were referred to as subsystems. From this perspective virtually all objects and entities were interrelated by virtue of a hierarchy of systems: a system that consisted of subsystems (or parts) in itself formed a subsystem of a larger system referred to as a supra-system. A system was considered to be substantially more than simply the sum of the various subsystems, as there was substantial interaction between the parts or subsystems, which exerted a reciprocal influence on one another. It was this reciprocal-influence relationship among subsystems (parts) that elevated an entity to a system status and allowed it to be conceived of as a whole, substantially beyond the sum total of the parts or subsystems (Stacey, Griffin & Shaw, 2000).

Development of systems

The development of systems theory proceeded along certain pathways: general systems theory (related to the closed and open systems), cybernetic systems and systems dynamics (Stacey et al., 2000; Van Tonder, 2004:37–45). Refer to Figure 3.3.

Figure 3.3 Evolution of systems theory

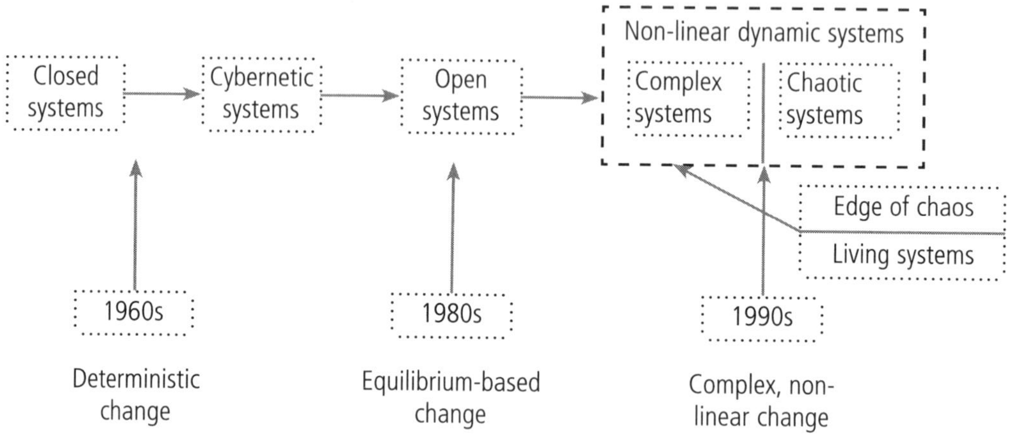

General systems theory

The general systems theory focused on and highlighted the general features of systems, that is the constant pursuit of equilibrium or homeostasis; the progression towards order and stability; and the notion of boundaries as an important defining attribute. Both closed and open systems were described.

Cybernetic systems

Cybernetic (cyclic) systems are self-regulated and adaptive systems, but purposeful in their adaptation to the environment, they are temperature control systems, and in fact include most systems that monitor performance in accordance with a set purpose and introduce corrective action on the basis of output, outcomes and feedback. Examples of cybernetic systems described in this book are:

- The process of management, which includes planning, organising, leading and control
- The process of strategic management and the process of change management, which includes strategy analysis, strategy development, strategy execution and strategy review
- The continuous quality improvement cycle, which consists of setting of standards, monitoring and assessment of actual performance against these standards, followed by corrective action
- The performance management and the integration with the Balanced Scorecard, consisting of collect, create, cultivate, cascade, connect and confirm.

Systems dynamics

Systems dynamics views the relationship (cause-and-effect) between the system and its environment as non-linear and recursive, and draws on complex mathematical models of a system. Unlike general systems and cybernetic systems, these conceptualisations of a system incorporate both negative and positive feedback, and because of the circularity of the cause-and-effect relationship between the system and the organisation (non-linear), they can result in unexpected and unintended outcomes. System dynamics therefore relates to complex systems and chaotic systems.

Attributes of systems

The following primary attributes related to systems are highlighted (Van Tonder, 2004:39):

- The reciprocal process consists of input, throughput and output of both matter and energy (also referred to as import, conversion and export).
- The achievement and maintenance of steady states (homeostasis) occur to the extent that the intrusion of outer energy will not disrupt internal form and order.
- An increase in order over time occurs due to an increase in complexity and differentiation of the parts of the system over time.
- The relationship between the system and its environment is not simply a matter of intake and output of matter and energy, but of extensive transactional commerce.
- All systems are characterised by differentiation and integration processes that occur simultaneously and on a system-wide basis. Differentiation and integration processes in one system/subsystem will impact on related systems and subsystems.
- The system develops from a relatively unstructured and unsophisticated state to progressively structured and sophisticated states.
- Increasing differentiation is continuously re-integrated in increasingly more complex or higher level functioning units. Optimal differentiation does not, however, imply optimal integration, and consequently these processes could become unsynchronised.
- Effective integration is visible in the adaptive capability of the system. When interaction of interdependent system components is aligned and continuous, optimal integration occurs.

The healthcare organisation as a system

The healthcare organisation is a system, consisting of the following (adapted from Van Tonder, 2004:37–38):

- **Open system**. This implies that the organisation is in constant interaction with its environment.
- **A system with several purposes or functions**. This refers to the multiple interactions between the organisation and various facets of the environment.

- **Consisting of many subsystems**. These subsystems, in keeping with general systems, are in dynamic interaction with one another. The subsystems are to varying degrees interdependent, and consequently changes in one subsystem (i.e. finance department) are likely to affect the behaviour of the other subsystems.
- **Being embedded or existing in an environment**. The environment comprises a number of other systems that may be larger or smaller than the organisation. These environments place demands upon and constrain the organisation and its subsystems in a number of different ways, resulting in constant change and re-direction of the organisation.

It is therefore important to comprehend the principles of a systems theory due to the complexity of healthcare organisations.

3.5.4 Chaos theory

Chaos refers to 'order disguised as disorder' (Van Tonder, 2004:42). The chaos theory is based on the systems dynamics principle (refer to Figure 3.3). It focuses on the way in which order originates from the interaction of the different parts of the whole system. It sees a system as continuously transforming itself to a higher level of complexity, making changes that are irreversible and thus evolutionary. The general systems approach has the viewpoint that anything that threatens the existing status quo should be worked against and eliminated in order to maintain order. However, because of an ever-changing environment, organisations no longer have a stable or dynamic equilibrium. The chaos theory is based on the premise that organisations need to be more open, flexible and adaptable, and that they need to function at the edge of chaos. This is of particular importance during Type II change in an organisation (refer to Chapter 5, Change management in a healthcare organisation).

The chaos theory is based on the principle that successful organisations are complex, adaptable systems. Though a dynamic system may appear to be chaotic, its identity, history and sense of purpose ('strange attractors') define its boundaries and guide its evolution and growth. The 'strange attractor' stabilises the system while its natural growth process simultaneously propels it into chaos. Chaos theory views all dynamic systems as self-organising in the way they order and structure themselves and how they grow and change. Self-organisation refers to emergent order, self-generation and co-evolution with the greater environment. A system creates its own order and natural growth by integrating transformations into its identity and thus ensuring continual growth at a higher level of being.

The word 'chaos' in organisational terms implies disorder, loss of control and crisis. In a chaotic state the organisation can no longer maintain stable patterns of behaviour because of an environment that is in a constant state of flux – especially during a period of disruptive Type II change in the organisation. A chaotic phase is said to be evolving from order to disorder and through to a new order. A new relationship is established between the organisation's internal and external environments and itself. The following sequence of events occurs:

- Organisations are forced to reorganise themselves all the time in order to adapt to these changes.
- The structures of an organisation thus changes on a regular basis, which leads to instability. The organisation then responds to the demands of the external environment.
- The organisation functions as a complex network that coordinates its activities in such a way that it can reach a desired outcome.
- The smaller networks rearrange themselves on a constant basis in order to keep pace with changes in the environment.
- The organisation as a system then becomes self-organised as it learns through positive feedback. What is learned becomes part of the organisation's structure.
- People who form part of these networks change and adapt their behaviour based on what they have learned and learn new behaviour that can accommodate new changes.
- Continuous learning gives rise to high levels of professionalism and competence inside the organisation.

Chaotic principles and assumptions

The application of chaotic principles can constitute change management (especially during Type II change) in various ways by substituting the communication process. The following principles and assumptions are applicable (refer to Chapter 5 Change management in a healthcare organisation):

- Ability for self-renewal and self-organisation
- Fragmentation and interdependence
- Butterfly effect and bifurcation
- Non-linearity, scale and holism
- Strange attractors (behaviours)
- Diversity and creativity
- Positive feedback.

Ability for self-renewal and self-organisation

There is always a recognisable structure that maintains the system in a changing environment. This structure forms part of the whole organisation and is not seated in a sub-unit. The system uses its own energy to change itself into a new form that is better equipped to handle the new situation. Too much control from management often hinders the natural flow of the organisation, inhibiting the organisation's ability to renew itself. Renewal is the result of internal guidelines and when people are allowed to participate in the functioning of the organisation, they will have the insight to know when to change and adapt their own behaviour in order to fit new and changing circumstances. Self-organisation means not only emergent order and self-generation but also co-evolution with the greater environment.

The principle of ability for self-renewal and self-organisation (order through fluctuation), therefore consists of two-way symmetrical communication and is both positive and negative. Positive can consist of informative information and negative might be, for example, a budget shortcoming. Communication is the basic tool to control interactions but too much control restrains the natural flow of information in the organisation. Employees need to participate in order to become familiar with the chaotic environment to minimise feelings of confusion and uncertainty. Therefore it is the task of management to foster a learning organisation and facilitate learning.

Fragmentation and interdependence

One can be misled if one were to study the individual parts of the organisation in isolation. This concept leads to the fragmentation of the organisation into smaller interdependent systems or networks. Each system is unique in its own way and contributes towards to the organisation as a whole. An attempt should be made to find certain fragments that show certain resemblances to each other, in order to identify patterns. There are certain bindings between fragments, and the stronger these bindings, the easier the system will be able to maintain it when it is not in a state of equilibrium. Communication is the core function between these fragmented and interdependent systems. The organisation is more flexible to new opportunities and can respond more quickly because the boundaries are not fixed.

Butterfly effect and bifurcation

The butterfly effect spells out that flexibility and the ever-changing nature of chaotic organisations result in small variations (causes) leading to big changes (effects). Bifurcation can be defined as the place of branching or forking. This means that all the elements or systems in an organisation are inter-dependable and that one can change the direction, character and structure of the organisation by thinking out of the box. The system forks (bifurcates) whenever it reorganises itself around a new underlying order, which can differ dramatically from the previous order. A bifurcation point can usually be predicted, but the end result cannot. Therefore a need for a knowledge culture arises so that they can make a contribution to the organisation that might save it from disaster. Bifurcation points can cause sudden changes in direction, character or structure and permanently redefine a system in new and unexpected ways.

The butterfly effect offers the opportunity to consider systematic change in a way consistent with the administrative strategy of devolution of authority and in the context of accepting the disequilibrium and unpredictability that are manifested in the current reality of the organisation, for example the merging of two organisations. Successful and enduring initiatives often spread through an entire organisation; with networks of communication lines made up of people from every facet of the organisation and its much larger environment. In this way if opportunities are seized and communicated along the naturally occurring networks, initiatives can spread even to a whole healthcare system.

Non-linearity, scale and holism

The chaos theory states that cause-effect relationships are difficult to predict, and the slightest change can influence the organisation dramatically. The non-linear concept (e.g. systems in which relationships between cause and effect are not constant) assumes that changes are difficult to foresee. Because a system is nonlinear, small changes in initial stages can amplify exponentially and greatly impact on the pattern of the system's growth and evolution.

The scale of observation is difficult because the sum is greater than the whole and patterns are therefore difficult to observe. Sometimes this makes the organisation appear to be out of control. The complexity of the system cannot be determined by focusing on a single scale of observation. If you want to understand the underlying structures of the organisation, you also have to study the way in which the organisation has evolved. One must have a picture of the whole situation before one can make assumptions about parts of it. If the picture as a whole can be seen when looking back on the change effect, it means that the right decisions were made and the process was successful.

Using strange attractors (behaviours) to keep organisations together

These strange attractors could be some of the elements that were formed during the communication process, for example vision and mission. It can also include the core values of the organisation and the corporate culture. If there is order and clarity on these elements, the work force might feel more confident if changes occur. It is important to realise that when a system is no longer stable, it does not mean that a lack of structure and coherence exists. Even non-linear systems have underlying structures that direct the system – known as the strange attractor. The strange attractor is usually related to the principles and values of the organisation, an inherent condition to which the organisation always returns and it serves as an anchor in the midst of chaos.

A new policy could be the attractor because the controversies generated by its content principles generated the controversial self-referential debate into which all the staff members were drawn for debate. The term 'attractor' could be viewed as a state of more acceptable or changed behaviour. The ideal reality embedded in the policy content was a set of value-laden characteristics that recognised the individual ideal professional employee in his/her ideal and unique context. It was this ideal state to which a healthcare organisation then evolved closer and closer in appearance and behaviour.

Diversity and creativity

This allows the chaotic organisation to be a learning organisation and holds it own source of control. Diversity of members leads to a variety of creative thinking minds which is perfect for constituting change.

Positive feedback

Positive feedback causes the organisation to destabilise, and it brings new patterns into the system. Everything that deviates from the norm is no longer seen as something that needs to be rectified, but rather something that the organisation needs to adapt to. The organisation thus becomes less stable, but more adaptable and flexibility becomes the norm. Feedback also modulates the system, either to maintain the system stability (negative feedback) or to amplify deviations and anomalies, destabilise the existing state, and introduces new patterns into the system (positive feedback). A system betters itself, creates its own future, and continuously adapts to its environment based on its intelligence and information. With the freedom of operating in an open flow of information, it stays connected to its simultaneously evolving environment and enhances its ability to handle environmental changes.

The role of the manager in the chaos theory

Managing organisations should be viewed as a more participative process, and leaders and managers should be more responsible for creating vision and culture (values) in which consistent change can flourish. Participation can give rise to adequate information, shared responsibility and governance, an increase in transparency and trust, and good interpersonal relationships. Information should flow freely during times of chaos. When adequate information is available, employees will become aware that they cannot control it, but will develop transformed knowledge that is flexible. Chaos theory assumes that a system creates its own order and natural growth by integrating transformations into its identity, thus ensuring continual growth at a higher level of being. When fluctuations cause turbulence, the system transforms the rules for how it operates so it can better handle the changing environment.

3.5.5 Complexity theory

This theory is a new systems science that builds on chaos. The underlying principle is that managers need to keep their organisations in the complexity zone where learning takes place, rather than in stability or chaos. Basic rules that govern all behaviours in an organisation need to be identified, and it requires enormous investment in cultural change. Complexity theory is essentially about concentrating on how employees in the health organisation interact, because if this interaction changes, the whole organisation changes, as well as the culture.

Complexity is defined as the zone between stability and predictability, on the one hand, and chaos and unpredictability on the other (Van Tonder, 2004:45; Verwey &

Du Plooy-Cilliers, 2003:45). In the complexity zone, systems adapt, learn and grow. The maximum potential for growth lies between stability and chaos. The following assumptions are made:

- Too little innovation results in an organisation that becomes rigid, totally predictable, that only acts through tried and established methods.
- If the organisation becomes too stable, change and a degree of freedom need to be introduced to facilitate some disequilibrium to bring the organisation back to a state of complexity.
- If there is too much change and the organisation is threatening to melt down, restraint and discipline may have to be reinforced.
- Too much change and freedom in the organisation can lead to chaos.

After direction in an organisation has been established, management should focus on both the formal and informal rules that are understood and agreed on, that govern interaction between employees in the organisation. Governing a health organisation is an art, and the system needs to be monitored all the time in order to determine where it is going. The focus should be on the individual skills and understanding, interpersonal skills and interactions. Complexity theory is essentially about concentrating on how employees in the health organisation interact, because if this interaction changes, the whole organisation changes, as well as the culture.

3.5.6 *Ubuntu*

Ubuntu is a metaphor that describes the significance of group solidarity, on survival issues, that is so central to the survival of African communities, who as a result of poverty and deprivation have to survive through brotherly and sisterly group care, and not individual self-reliance. It is in the spirit of Ubuntu, with its emphasis on working together and respecting human dignity, that a way forward can be found. The spirit of Ubuntu may help define a new critical path towards the new South Africa. If companies are going to be competitive, they will need to develop a tradition of working together on survival and competitive issues (Mbigi & Maree, 1995:9).

Ubuntu is an African view of life and worldview that represents African Humanism. It takes seriously the view that the individual is basically a social being reflected by the central opinion that 'I am because you are' or, '... a person is a person through other people'. It represents a collective consciousness, which implies that the individual is considered a dignified social being. Ubuntu involves compassion and social responsibility, which are expressed in caring for the less privileged, the poor and the orphans, it means being sensitive to the needs of others and alms-giving, and demonstrating an attitude of sympathy, consideration, patience and kindness. Empathy, as directed to putting oneself in the shoes of a person in need, entails that each person must be viewed holistically by focusing on his/her physical, emotional, social and spiritual needs. And the ultimate expression of regard for another is by showing spontaneous concern, and by voluntary assuming a self-imposed sense of duty towards the needy, destitute or bereaved; nobody should be condemned as worthless.

Ubuntu management approach

Mbigi and Maree (1995:9–10) proposed that an innovative way to manage South Africa, based on the collective experience and lessons learnt in the struggle, should be found. This new way must be a package of solutions that would address the survival challenges of global competition, as well as reconstruction and development. These authors proposed that the Ubuntu management approach should have the following outcomes:

- **The development of cooperative and competitive people**. This is acquired by addressing poor education systems, through a holistic training and development strategy which includes generic education focused on the strategic and economic issues facing the organisation and the country.
- **The development of cooperative and competitive paradigms and perspectives**. The shifting of perceptions and mindsets is the most difficult aspect of understanding transformation in Africa. A passion is needed to add value and create wealth at every level in the organisation. A competitive spirit and attitude needs to be developed in order to rise above the country's historical circumstances.
- **The development of cooperative and competitive practices**. It is imperative for organisations to have a passion to create value throughout the organisation. It is important to not only meet the customers' requirements by creating user-friendly products and service, but that it constantly and creatively amazes the customer. Respect should be created for 'made in South Africa' rather than focus on the status of imported goods.
- **The development of cooperative and competitive processes**. A poor country which has few accumulated assets can only compete through efficient transformation and production processes. The management lessons for South Africa is that if our organisations are going to compete on a global scale, unique competitive processes should be developed that are suitable for its people and market.
- **The development of cooperative and competitive policies and procedures**. The challenge for organisations that are operating in a chaotic environment characterised by rapid change, is to remain focused on operational events. If there is not time for reflection, the reality is that one does not manage the opportunities, instead, only problems and crisis situations are recognised, thus negating the opportunities that come their way.
- **The development of cooperative and competitive values and institutions**. There is a need for managers to democratise their institutions by developing inclusive and collaborative managerial practices. The issue of institutional innovation underpinned by bottom-up processes is a critical managerial issue for African managers.

The Ubuntu concept marks the departure from the confrontational approach in this country's labour relations to a more cooperative and competitive approach of managing survival issues. Encouraging a creative and competitive dialogue between management and employees should facilitate finding solutions. The collective solidarity of various groups in the organisation should be respected and enhanced, and the rights of the individual groups should be respected. Then the solidarity spirit of Ubuntu will have found expression in the management practices of our organisations.

Developmental (Ubuntu) model of human resources

In southern Africa it is essential to adapt Western management concepts to address the daunting management challenges. The assumption of the developmental model is that Africa is a poor continent facing tremendous development challenges, therefore, any effective management practices, processes and systems have to focus on development issues.

The focus of the Developmental Human Resources Model is holistic development. It strives for continuous improvement and development of people, products, systems, structures, markets, productivity, quality and performance. Business and economic transformation in Africa has to be driven by people and not technological innovation, because Africa does not have the resources. South Africa's economic transformation will start with the development and empowerment of its people, as well as their collective efforts towards continuous improvement and wealth creation (Mbigi, 1992:24).

Under the developmental model, the HR practitioners would be guided by four cardinal principles, for which Mbigi (1992:24) has given the acronym MIST: morality, interdependence, spirit of humankind and totality. These principles have been derived from the values of the African tribal village community, which is essentially Ubuntu. Translated, it means 'a man is a man', he is therefore entitled to unconditional respect and dignity. The following principles are highlighted:

- **The principle of morality.** This is the belief that no organisation can attain its highest potential without touching its moral base. The purity of both motives and behaviour is critical to effective strategic implementation and is evident in living the code of trust.
- **The principle of interdependence**. This is based on the belief that the task of optimisation of wealth creation in a world of want and poverty requires the collective cooperation of all the stakeholders in the enterprising community, which can only be achieved by acknowledging interdependence of all concerned.
- **The principle of the spirit of humankind**. This principle recognises that humankind is the creator and benefactor of all wealth; therefore people are entitled to unconditional respect and dignity. Humankind is seen as the purpose of all organisations and as such, should be dealt with in the spirit of service and harmony.

- **The principle of totality**. The task of wealth creation is a highly complex process and requires the attention and continuous improvement of everything in the organisation, by every member of the organisation. As a building is made of thousands of bricks, so does a world-class organisation require a thousand little improvements by everyone in the organisation. The building of a great organisation must start with little improvements, in the manner in which each employee does his/her work, and in terms of the following five concepts: relationships, quality, quantity, cost and timing, which are considered the mutual essence of value adding and Ubuntu. This, in turn, will affect management issues such as communication, coordination, competence, competitiveness and compassion (Mbigi, 1992:24).

The Ubuntu ways of conduct in a group are characterised by actions of kindness, compassion, caring, dignity and integrity and aims of working for a common good, and will contribute to teamwork and cooperation in building a common vision.

3.6 UNDERLYING DYNAMICS

Managers find it difficult to comprehend the dynamic complexities of organisations, as applied to the systems theory and the related evolution of the systems theory (and theories) as depicted in Figure 3.3. The following two critical success factors are highlighted:

- **The cognitive abilities of the managers**. This refers to the ability to adequately assess, interpret, understand and comprehend the systems' complexities in the healthcare organisation and to adequately respond by selecting and applying the most suitable management model at a given time.
- **Environmental comfort zone**. We also love to stay in the environmental comfort zone – the place or environment in which we feel comfortable; the kind of environmental conditions to which we have become accustomed, which enables the manager and group members to function without fear or uneasiness. This feeling of comfort will not create energy or dissonance for organisational improvement and change. The challenge therefore is to break out of this comfort zone – to break with traditional management practices and models that just don't work anymore.

3.7 CONCLUDING STATEMENTS

The following concluding statements are made:

- Participative management is a process of dynamic interactive decision-making and problem-solving, shared governance, ownership and accountability, organisational transformation and empowerment, as well as applicable communication.
- Centralisation is the pooling of decision-making power and authority at top management level, as opposed to decentralisation that implies the devolution of

authority to the lowest possible management and decision-making levels in the organisation.

- The systems theory has evolved from traditional closed and open systems to complex systems, focusing on chaos and complexity theories.
- The chaos theory relates to the creation of order in a highly dynamic and complex system – functioning at the edge of chaos. Chaotic principles and assumptions are applied, especially during dynamic transformation (Type II change) in the organisation – the ability for self-renewal and self-organisation, fragmentation and interdependence, butterfly effect and bifurcation, non-linearity, scale of holism, strange attractors, diversity and creativity, as well as positive feedback.
- Complexity theory relates to the zone between stability and predictability on the one hand and chaos and unpredictability on the other hand in the systems approach.
- Ubuntu relates to African Humanism, focusing on solidarity and respect for human dignity. The principle of cooperative management is emphasised.
- The critical success factors relate to the cognitive abilities of the manager and to break out of the environmental comfort zone of traditional management practices.

Self-assessment

(1) Analyse the current systems reality in your organisation (based on the evolution of systems theory as reflected in Figure 3.3). Develop management guidelines that would be most suitable in this systems reality.

(2) The local district hospital is being converted into a clinic for Antiretroviral Therapy. Design a transformational management strategy, based on the principles of the chaos theory, for application during this period of transformation.

(3) Reflect on your current practice and contemplate whether you incorporate the values and principles of Ubuntu in dealing with colleagues, customers and commitment to your employer.

4 Dimensions of functional management in a healthcare organisation

KEY CONCEPTS

Decision-making and problem-solving
Project management
Performance management

SPECIFIC OUTCOMES

After studying this chapter, you should be able to:

- Interpret the legal, professional-ethical and healthcare **context**, focusing on the type of business ownership of the organisation and the professional-ethical legislation of practitioners
- Analyse and debate the **purpose** of the various dimensions of functional management
- Identify the **role-players** and interpret their roles and responsibilities in decision-making, problem-solving, project management and performance management
- Describe and apply the **processes** related to decision-making and problem-solving, project management and performance management
- Debate the **critical success factors** impacting on decision-making and problem-solving, project management and performance management.

4.1 INTRODUCTION

This chapter focuses on selected dimensions of functional management in a healthcare organisation:

- Decision-making and problem-solving
- Project management
- Performance management.

4.2 CONTEXT

Dimensions of functional management are practised within the legal and policy framework of the healthcare organisation, in accordance with the business ownership of the healthcare organisation (public, private or mixed), and the nature and scope

Figure 4.1 Visual presentation of conceptual framework related to selected dimensions of functional management in a healthcare organisation

Context	Legal and policy framework: business ownership Professional-ethical and legal framework of decision-makers and other functional managers
Role-players	Decision-makers and problem-solvers Project manager Human resources manager
Purpose	To facilitate quality service delivery
Dimensions of functional management	Decision-making and problem-solving Project management Performance management
Underlying dynamics	Leadership abilities

of healthcare service delivery. The professional-ethical and legal frameworks of functional managers (i.e. financial managers) and clinical healthcare practitioners are of significant importance. The contextual framework of healthcare service delivery as described in Chapter 1, Management of a healthcare organisation, is applicable.

4.3 PURPOSE

This chapter focuses on selected dimensions of functional management practice that would facilitate the quality of service delivery (by means of project management) and human resources management (by means of performance management).

4.4 ROLE-PLAYERS

The following main role-players are highlighted, with specific reference to the content of this chapter: decision-maker and problem-solver, the project manager and the human resources manager.

4.5 DIMENSIONS OF FUNCTIONAL MANAGEMENT

This chapter focuses on the following dimensions:

- Decision-making and problem-solving
- Project management
- Performance management.

4.5.1 Decision-making and problem-solving

Introduction

Decision-making and problem-solving are both crucial management abilities (knowledge, skills, attitudes and values) required by all leaders, level managers and practitioners (clinical and non-clinical) within the healthcare organisation. Decision-making and problem-solving are almost synonymous – they both relate to the cognitive processes of:

- purposeful selection of the most suitable alternative
- related to a course of action/intervention
- that is most likely to facilitate optimal attainment of goals, outputs and outcomes.

Problem-solving is focused on finding a solution to a particular problem, as opposed to decision-making that could – in addition to finding solutions to problems – also focus on proactive dimensions of management, such as the development of plans, strategies, policies and standards. A problem can be defined as an undesirable gap between an expected and observed state that hinders a worker's ability to complete the task. Problems occur frequently in organisations and are often reflected as faulty systems or procedures that, if changed, could result in organisational improvement. How employees respond to problems encountered on the job is a critical factor in facilitating the quality of service delivery and attainment of outcomes. Part of the solution to empowering employees and having them become potential problem-solvers could be to use a common problem-solving process throughout the organisation. Typically, most organisations are structured in the usually hierarchical pyramid fashion and problems encountered are 'pushed up' the decision-making line of authority within the organisation and not being dealt with where it occurs. Employees should be trained in the use of a common problem-solving process and create an environment where they routinely solve the problems in their work situation.

Decision-making is the most significant activity that managers and practitioners engage in – at levels of management and service delivery. Decision-making and problem-solving are inherent in every interrelationship of healthcare professionals, healthcare systems, materials and technology. Decisions cannot be made in a vacuum and a number of elements are always present. These elements are:

- the problem at hand
- the abilities (knowledge, skills, attitudes and values) and personality of the decision-makers
- the process that is to be implemented in making the decision
- the environment in which the decision has to be taken and executed.

Managers and practitioners need to know the type of decision at hand in order to make and implement it to the advantage of the total healthcare organisation. Decisions can be classified based on the following set of three factors (Harrison & Pelletier, 2000:464):

- **Content of the decision**. The question should be asked if the decision is significant or inconsequential, complex or routine.

- **Frequency of the decision**. Does the decision occur regularly or irregularly, on an ad hoc basis or periodically?
- **Outcome of the decision**. Is the expected result fairly certain or somewhat uncertain?

There are many levels of decision-making and problem-solving, such as the individual or practitioner-based decisions, unit or area-based, departmental and organisational, as well as the national- or provincial-based decisions. Organisational decisions focus on the constant refinement of the organisational direction, based on the environmental dynamics and demands. This process provides opportunities for participative management styles that give healthcare professionals the responsibility of professional decision-making and problem-solving.

The characteristics of strategic decisions taken in a healthcare organisation are the following:

- Strategic decisions must be directed towards defining the healthcare organisation's relationship to its environment.
- The decision must take the healthcare organisation as a whole as unit of analysis.
- Decisions must be multi-functional in character in that it depends on input from a variety of primary functional areas.
- The decision must provide direction for and constraints on administrative and operational activities throughout the healthcare organisation.
- The decision must be important for the success of the organisation (refer to Chapter 1, Management of a healthcare organisation and Chapter 2, Strategic management of a healthcare organisation).

Types of managerial decisions

In general, the decisions made by managers exist on a continuum of being programmed or non-programmed.

Programmed decisions

Decisions are programmed to the extent that they are repetitive and routine in nature, they thus occur regularly. There are set ways of obtaining a solution, and the situation does therefore not have to be investigated anew each time it occurs. Programmed decisions are usually handled by means of policies, standard operating procedures and rules. Examples of programmed decisions include registering students or allowing them examination entrance in a learning institution, the admission and discharge of patients or processing payroll vouchers in an organisation.

Non-programmed decisions

Non-programmed decisions have not occurred before, and there is no established method of dealing with them, they are thus new and complex and require logical thinking and creative problem-solving skills such as brainstorming and quality circles. Examples of non-programmed decisions are changing the workflow procedures or patterns, adjusting work shifts or dealing with an unproductive employee.

Factors that influence decision-making

Several factors exist that can influence decision-making adversely, and management's awareness of these factors can facilitate appropriate proactive responses in a quest to make optimal decisions. Factors influencing decision-making are as follows:

- The type of healthcare organisation and the evolutionary phase with reference to the complexity of the system (life-cycle) as described in Chapter 5, Change management in a healthcare organisation
- Political factors
- Time pressures
- Contingency factors
- Crisis situations
- Insufficiency of available information
- Uniqueness of the situation
- Abilities (knowledge, skills, attitudes and values) of the decision-maker
  - Cognitive
  - Flexibility
  - Intuition
  - Confidence
  - Resistance
  - Fear
  - Preferences.

Decision-making conditions

Once the type of decision has been identified, and the conditions under which the decision needs to be taken are clear, then the manager is in a position to make better decisions. The conditions under which decisions can be made are certainty, risk and uncertainty (Smit & De J. Cronjé, 2002:153–154).

Certainty

A decision is made under conditions of certainty when the available options and the benefits or costs associated with each are known in advance. Under conditions of certainty, managers are simply faced with identifying the consequences of available options and selecting the outcome with the greatest potential benefit. Unfortunately, managers rarely make decisions under conditions of certainty, because the future is an unknown entity without perfect reliability. However, making a fixed investment at a set interest rate will deliver a pre-determined amount of profit and is thus considered a condition of certainty.

Risk

When making a decision under the condition of risk, the manager does not know the outcome of each alternative in advance, but can assign a probability to each outcome. Probability falls into two categories:

- Objective probability is based on historical evidence. It refers to the likelihood that a particular state of things will occur, based on hard facts and figures. Even though one cannot be sure that certain events will occur, one can determine the likely outcome of the event based on previous records and statistics. For instance, in flipping a coin, the probability of obtaining heads or tails has a risk, but will have a 50% chance of succeeding.
- Subjective probability is dependent upon the decision-maker's personal estimate and belief, as there is no historical evidence available. Not knowing for certain what the outcome will be, one must decide whether, for instance, to have a life-threatening operation or face the risk of becoming paralysed.

Uncertainty

A decision is made under conditions of uncertainty when there is a lack of information, in as much as that the outcome of each alternative is unpredictable and managers cannot determine the probabilities. Decisions made under these circumstances are unquestionably the most difficult as the manager has no knowledge on which to base an estimate of the likelihood of various outcomes. No historical data is available from which to infer probabilities, or circumstances are so novel and complex that it is impossible to make comparative judgements. The most common occasions for making decisions under conditions of uncertainty are those involving the introduction of new technology or new markets, where managers rely on their 'gut feeling'.

Decision-making process

In most situations where decisions need to be made, people go through a number of steps that guide them through the problem and assist in developing alternative solutions, such as investigate the subject/theme or problem, develop alternatives, evaluate the alternatives, select and implement the best alternative, evaluate and control the outcome thereof.

Investigate the situation

Problems are not always what they appear to be, therefore a problem needs to be studied carefully within a particular context or situation, in order to address it more effectively. Relevant information needs to be gathered to support or substantiate variables within the situation. There are three main requirements to deal with when investigating the situation, namely:

- Define the subject/theme or problem
- Identify the decision-making objectives
- Diagnose the causes or related underlying assumptions.

Develop alternatives

Develop several alternatives with the assistance of colleagues/groups by means of brainstorming or group discussions, without eliminating any, before proper evaluation of each has been accomplished. Innovation and creativity play a major role in generating various courses of possible action. The availability of information and technology could enhance the process.

Evaluate alternatives

The advantages and disadvantages, strengths and weaknesses, and benefits and costs of each alternative should be determined before comparing the alternatives with one another. Because each alternative is likely to have both positive and negative features, most evaluations involve balancing anticipated consequences. Guidelines that may be useful in the evaluation process are that the quality of the solution be such that the objectives of the institution can be achieved, that the solution be acceptable to those affected by it, and that an alternative be evaluated in terms of the consequences for the institution.

Select the best alternative

In this step the aim is to select the best alternative with the most benefits and least detrimental effects for the organisation and people involved. This is achieved by arranging the alternatives in order of importance with regard to the realisation of the objectives of the institution. The final decision is often a synergy between the different factors that have been considered. It is important to note that the manager's own values and preferences should not play a significant role in selecting the best alternative; however, it is not unusual for the manager's experience and internal politics to affect the decision of a specific alternative.

Implement the selected alternative

Once the choice of alternative has been made, appropriate action should be taken to ensure that it is properly implemented. Resources are allocated, budgets are drawn up and responsibilities are allocated. Decisions should be explained in such a way that all the relevant parties understand the reason and focus of the planned action. Continual monitoring of the course and result of the decisions should be exercised by the manager to handle any problems or obstacles that may arise.

Evaluate and control

Once a decision has been set in motion, evaluation is necessary to provide feedback on its outcome. Adjustments are invariably required to ensure that the actual results compare favourably with the planned outcomes. If necessary, modifications can be made and further options could be identified and evaluated. There are two requirements for this evaluation, namely:

- A set of quantifiable, measurable objectives that serve as standards against which performance can be compared
- A management information system that makes performance data available so that a comparison can be made in accordance with the standards.

Common problem-solving process for the organisation

In addition to the afore-mentioned decision-making process that has been described, the common problem-solving process is also described.

A common problem-solving process for all employees in the healthcare organisation is part of the solution to empowering employees and having them become potential problem solvers. Typically, most organisations are structured in the usual hierarchical pyramid fashion and problems encountered will be 'pushed up' the organisation and not dealt with where they occur. This results in management getting overloaded with problems and leads to a large number of problems being unresolved or sometimes inappropriate solutions applied. The solution is to train employees in the use of a common problem-solving process and create an environment where they routinely address problems encountered. The basic steps in a typical problem-solving process are:

- Identify and select the problem
- Conduct a root cause analysis
- Determine the best potential solutions
- Plan and implement the solution
- Evaluate the results
- Follow through goal attainment: assess what else needs to be done to facilitate sustainability.

The consensus problem-solving process

For many individuals and teams, reaching consensus-based decisions during problem-solving remains an elusive goal. Consensus decision-making can be defined as a problem-solving method in which decisions are reached when, after full discussion, the team members unify behind the best solution that seems possible for the team at that time (refer also to Chapter 3, Selected management models, with reference to the principles of participative management). The consensus problem-solving model places values at the core position; it assists team members with a principle-centred vision to encourage inspired solution finding. Because the model provides a discipline for the alternate suspension and use of critical judgement, it tends to constructively channel the expression of diverse viewpoints and defuse negative conflict. The simpler and less controversial the problem being addressed, the more loosely the team members can follow the steps of the problem-solving model. In following the steps, team members suspend critical judgement during the even-numbered steps and apply critical judgement during the odd-numbered steps. To suspend critical judgement refers to creating an environment in which ideas are allowed to emerge, develop and grow. The steps of the consensus problem-solving model of Harley (1995:26–34) are as follows:

- Make the transition to team status.
- Identify the problem.
- Agree on the problem.
- Identify the facts.
- Agree on the facts.
- Identify the principles/values involved.
- Agree on the principles/values involved.
- Identify the solutions.
- Agree on the solutions.
- Identify implementation steps.
- Agree on the implementation steps.

Step 1: Make the transition to team status

Members should be assisted to let go of negative mind sets and to move consciously from a preoccupation with individual action to one of interdependence and collective action. Members should be more sensitive to the other members and move towards an attitude of service to the team. Team members should view the team as a problem-solving instrument with a collective life of its own. Members should be trained in the key consensus problem-solving process concepts to ensure the most effective use of the model.

Step 2: Identify the problem (suspend critical judgement)

In practice, the problem that members could be working on different problems simultaneously should be addressed. A verbal or written request for a meeting could probably have indicated a specific problem, but the assumption could be made that members had not yet agreed on the problem. The facilitator reminds the member to suspend critical judgement and ask for their ideas on how the problem could be articulated. An open uninterrupted flow of ideas of how the problem should be articulated takes place. Members acknowledge that all of the ideas regarding the problem are recorded.

Step 3: Agree on the problem (apply critical judgement)

Agreement should be reached on the problem statement. The facilitator reads (for example from a flip chart) all of the ideas regarding the problem and members challenge each idea. Deletions or revisions are made to ideas to achieve consensus on the problem statement. Ideas are gradually condensed and combined down to a single statement of the problem to which all agree. All members are now coming from the same point of departure.

Steps 2 and 3 entail agreement on the problem, which is the cornerstone of the structure of consensus problem-solving.

Step 4: Identify the facts (suspend critical judgement)

In identifying facts, input regarding the situation surrounding the problem is looked into. Different opinions, perceptions and feelings, as well as scientific verifiable data, are accepted. When the team begins generating the facts relating to a given problem, members could become aware of the following two aspects:

- that quite a few facts are held in common
- that quite a few are not held in common.

Every member gains by hearing perspectives different from their own which brings out dimensions of the problem of which they were unaware. This step of the problem-solving process is an educational dimension where the withholding of critical judgement forces members to listen to one another without the possibility of direct contradiction. Members tend to challenge facts but should learn to articulate an opposing fact rather than disagreement. Facts could be placed on a flip chart and when the team members cannot think of any other facts, this step is completed.

Step 5: Agree on the facts (apply critical judgement)

The facilitator again reads each fact to the team members, followed by a pause. If members are in agreement with the facts, the members thus agree on the following two aspects:

- the facts are accurate as stated
- the facts are relevant to the problem.

Further discussion is needed when there is no agreement on either or both of these two points. Consensus could be reached by editing the facts. Every possible fact is not necessarily identified during step 5 and could also be added to the list of facts during a later stage.

In steps 4 and 5 all members:

- have opportunities to articulate the facts as they initially see them
- hear the facts as other members articulate them
- see the full complexity of the issues
- achieve consensus on the facts with which the team moves forward to the next step.

Agreement on the facts relating to the problem is the foundation of the structure of consensus problem-solving and the next step can then focus on values and principles.

Step 6: Identify the principles/values involved (suspend critical judgement)

Members could feel inclined to seek immediate solutions to a problem. Members should rather identify the values and principles they want to try to live by which they believe are related to the problem. Initially members may feel awkward to identify values and principles but the facilitator can overcome this by the phrases 'We value ...' or 'We should ...'.

Once these values held in common are identified for a given problem, they tend to serve as unifying principles which harmonise the diversity within the team. The ideas on values and principles will typically reflect the diversity of the team and may contain contradictory elements. Critical judgement is absent and when no more values and principles are forthcoming the next step is followed.

Step 7: Agree on the principles/values involved (apply critical judgement)

Critical judgement applies in this step, as in steps 3 and 5. The facilitator reads each value/principle and silence in response to reading the list indicates consensus on the following two aspects:

- the value as stated is one that we want to live by in our workplace
- the value is relevant to the problem and/or the agreed on facts.

The team seeks to achieve consensus by discussing the issues, and deleting, revising or/and replacing the value/principle. The following is an example of how a value can be redefined:

Value before critical thinking:
'We value risk-based decision-making as long as it does not sacrifice public health and/or the natural environment.'

Consensus value after application of critical thinking:
'We value incorporating flexibility in our decision-making as long as it does not jeopardise public health and/or the natural environment.'

The values and principles we want to live by are related to our personal beliefs. The purpose of steps 6 and 7 is not to change one another's beliefs and values, but to make conscious the relevant values and principles each of us wants to have guiding our lives and to see if any are shared by the other members. If after a full discussion on the values, the team is unable to reach consensus on a value, it drops out. When this happens, the value in question will still remain a personal value of one of the team members but it is simply not a team value.

The articulation and agreement of values and principles tend to increase the team's motivation in its search for solutions and implementation ideas and shed light on the path to goal attainment. Agreement on values and principles represents the pillars and beams making up the superstructure of the consensus problem-solving process.

Step 8: Identify the solutions (suspend critical judgement)

At this stage the energies of team members have been coordinated and channeled and the consensus problem-solving process has kept the team members continuously in focus. The team now generates solution ideas ranging from fragmentary solutions to comprehensive solutions. Solution ideas are written on, for example, flip charts and the facilitator identifies areas for additional exploration suggested by the agreed on facts and values/principles. Brainstorming takes place, including reversing of ideas and prompting by the facilitator.

Step 9: Agree on the solutions (apply critical judgement)

In reaching agreement on solutions, we are building the interior walls and furnishing of the structure of the consensus problem-solving process. Agreements on solutions are driven by the team's sense of moving-as-one, by the energy emanating from a unified focus on the problem and by coming from common values. The team sifts and modifies the solutions. The facilitator slowly reads through the list of solutions and assumes agreement on the solutions unless someone speaks up to the contrary. Discussions may provoke a new idea not thought of in the previous step and listed on the solution sheet. Some solutions are deleted; others are left intact while still others are modified to reflect the consensus emerging from the discussions. The team has now reached consensus on solutions, but probably does not yet have a sense of closure. For that the team should turn to steps 10 and 11. One of the purposes of steps 10 and 11 is to integrate and orchestrate the bundle of solutions so that they become a single solution.

Step 10: Identify implementation steps (suspend critical judgement)

The team suspends critical judgement and generates as many implementation step ideas as it can.

Step 11: Agree on the implementation steps (apply critical judgement)

The implementation ideas agreed on represent the walls, door and hallways of the structure of the consensus decision-making process. They connect the problem-solving structure to the outside world (the context of the problem) and establish connectedness and relationship between the elements of the solution. This is accomplished when the team decides how the solution will be carried out, sequences the solution ideas, assigns responsibility for the solution elements and establishes deadlines for their accomplishment. The agreement of values in step 7 should inspire and inform the search for the most effective implementation steps. The exact nature of steps 10 and 11 depends on the nature and complexity of the problem being addressed and the solutions agreed on. For simple problems, step 10 may be eliminated and the team will simply keep critical judgement engaged and agree on who will do what and in what manner. The implementation steps surviving the application of critical judgement represent the team's implementation plan.

Techniques for improving decision-making

Various techniques can be used to enable managers to make effective decisions. A number of them will be briefly explained according to the views of Smit and De J. Cronjé (2002:1161–168):

Decision tree

A decision tree is a graphic display of the available alternatives, the outcomes, risks and information needs for a specific problem over a period of time. The problem and each alternative decision are graphically displayed in conjunction with the probable consequences of each alternative. As the sequence of the major decision is drawn, the resulting diagram resembles a tree with branches. The process starts with a primary decision that has at least two alternative solutions. The outcome of each solution should be considered. The manager can base her/his decision on a consideration of various alternatives and their probable consequences and should realise that subsequent decisions may be dependent on future events (see Figure 4.2).

Figure 4.2 A decision tree

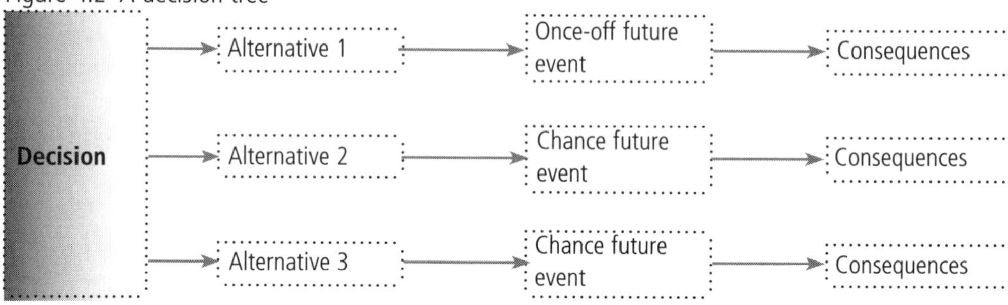

Cause-and-effect diagrams

This device is also referred to as the fishbone diagram, because the completed diagram resembles a fish skeleton, with the problem as the head of the fish, and major causes as fish fins and tail. The aim of this diagram is to analyse relationships among multiple problem factors. The one-level cause and effect diagram can be expanded to include minor factors that predispose to the major problem causes.

Linear programming

Linear programming is a quantitative tool used for optimally allocating scarce resources among competing uses to maximise benefits or minimise losses. The resources may be human, financial, physical or informational. Linear programming is, for instance, capable of determining which route is the shortest or least costly to follow.

Queuing theory

Queuing theory is a quantitative tool for analysing the costs of waiting lines. The objective of queuing theory is to achieve an optimal balance between the cost of increasing service and the amount of time individuals, apparatus or materials must wait for service. The problem is to determine the best balance between the cost of upgrading service potential and the amount of time users of a service must wait in line. In such situations, the queuing theory can be applied to identify an optimal solution for maximising service while minimising costs.

Probability analysis

The term 'probability' refers to the estimated likelihood, expressed as a percentage, that an outcome will occur. In this analysis, a mathematically calculated figure can indicate to management the value, in monetary terms, of each alternative. The manager considers objective and subjective options according to her/his own optimistic and pessimistic philosophy and guesses which alternative will render the most desirable results.

Pay-off matrix

The pay-off matrix is a technique for establishing possible pay-offs, or returns, from pursuing different courses of action. Each option is pursued under different states of nature, or circumstances beyond the control of the decision maker.

Break-even analysis

Break-even analysis is a financial technique which is designed to calculate the point at which a specific project covers costs and begins to show a profit. It requires a forecast of the sales volume and the cost of production.

PERT and CPM

Programme Evaluation and Revision Technique (PERT) and the Critical Path Method (CPM) are methods of network analysis. They are useful in the planning of large and complex projects and help to ensure that all steps are completed in the correct order and time.

In the review technique (PERT) the key events are identified, and may be numbered and/or labelled on a flow chart (Figure 4.3). The actions that cause the progress from one event to another are indicated with arrows showing the direction of the work flow. A formula is used to indicate the optimistic time (t^{o}) to complete the project/action without any complications, the most likely time (tm) to complete the actions with normal problems and the pessimistic time (tp) which estimates the completion time with numerous problems. The calculation that is made is as follows:

$$\text{te (the expected time)} = \frac{t^{o} + 4(tm) + tp}{6}$$

On the other hand, the CPM calculates a single time estimate for each activity. A cost estimate is done for both normal operating conditions (least-cost method), as well

Figure 4.3 Visual presentation of PERT

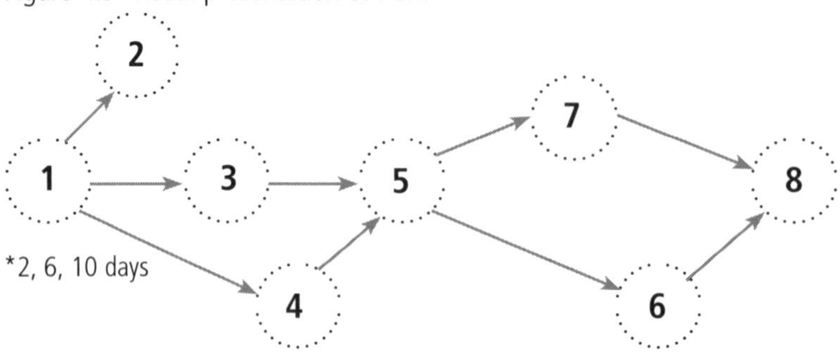

* The entry of 2, 6, 10 days indicated between step 1 and 4 indicates the recording of the optimistic, pessimistic and expected times for the activities between step 1 and 4. Times should be indicated between all steps in such a model

as conditions in less than normal time. A manager can observe the critical path and compare the progress to the projected dates.

Group decision-making
Part of decision strategy is to decide who should make a particular decision. When the leader lacks the required knowledge or skill, or subordinates' commitment is essential to successful outcome, an employee group should be involved in making the decision. When time is available for discussion, a group decision is usually superior to an individual decision because a group possesses broader experience and greater variety in problem approach. By discussing alternative actions and voting for preferred action, members also become committed to the decision that they must later implement.

The setting of goals and the generation of alternatives during the first steps of the decision-making process rely heavily on creativity and innovation. Group decision-making can enhance this process, especially in the case of non-programmed decisions where there is usually a great deal of uncertainty about the outcome.

Groups are subject to social factors when making decisions, which could include social conformity, inter-group dynamics, levels of communication skill, and dominance by a specific group member. According to Smit and De J. Cronjé (2002:159–160), groups often make better decisions than those made by the average group member, however, their decisions consistently fall short of the quality of decisions made by the best individual member. Group decision-making therefore has certain advantages and disadvantages. The advantages of group decision-making are as follows:

- A variety of skills and specialised knowledge can be used to define and solve a problem or recognise an opportunity.
- Multiple and conflicting views can be taken into account.
- Beliefs and values can be transmitted and aligned.

- More members of the organisation will be committed to decisions, since they have participated in the decision-making process.
- Participation in problem-solving and decision-making will improve the morale and motivation of employees.
- Allowing participation in problem-solving and decision-making will facilitate empowerment in the development of group decision-making and problem-solving.

The potential disadvantages of group decision-making are:
- The process may be more time-consuming and lead to slower decision-making.
- Some groups exert strong social pressure for conformity, thereby decreasing the probability of innovative decisions.
- An exceptionally strong member may dominate the discussion, preventing the free give-and-take necessary for high-quality decisions.
- One group member, or a sub-group, may dominate and nullify the group decision.
- Often decisions by consensus are of lower quality than individual decisions, because the solution most acceptable to the group is simply a compromise between best and worst alternatives.
- It may inhibit creativity and lead to conformity and 'groupthink' (Smit & De J. Cronjé, 2002:160).

Group techniques

Methods that promote group decision-making include the following:
- **Brainstorming**. This is aimed at generating as many creative solutions to a problem by a group of people without anybody's idea being evaluated by others. During idea generation, participants are encouraged to build on, but not to criticise ideas produced by others.
- **Nominal group technique**. This is a structured group decision-making technique, which restricts discussion and communication during the solution generation process. Within small groups, a leader is selected and each member of the group independently writes down his/her views and solutions for the problem. The leader then systematically gathers one idea from each group member at a time, until all the ideas have been listed. The ideas are clarified through guided discussion within the group, after which the alternatives are voted into order of priority by the group members.
- **Delphi technique**. The Delphi technique is a decision-making technique that does not require the physical presence of the participants. It involves experts in different geographical areas and makes use of confidential questionnaires to refine a solution. The problem is identified and members are asked to provide potential solutions through a series of carefully designed questionnaires. As the questionnaires are returned and the data is collated, the participants are

requested to respond to the latest results and provide further solutions. The results typically trigger new solutions or cause changes in the original positions.

Decision-making and problem-solving models and theories

A vast number of decision-making and problem-solving models and theories are available. It is not the intention with this chapter to describe any of these models. The following psychological types of problem-solving are, however, briefly discussed: sensing and feeling, sensing and thinking, intuitive thinking and intuitive feeling.

Sensing and feeling

Decisions are approached from a factual point of departure. Decision-makers feel oriented, tactful and highly receptive to the approval of others. A trusting relationship exists with others and managers have favourable expectations of one another, thus promoting a team spirit environment. The focus is on human relationships whereby inadequate performances are tolerated longer than warranted and disciplinary measures are avoided.

Sensing and thinking

Managers tend to focus on the issue rather than people and do not delegate effectively. Managers are conscientious in carrying out their duties and responsibilities through short-term planning and the related managerial functions.

Intuitive thinking

Managers act objectively and impersonally while focusing on the changes and new opportunities. An entrepreneurial focus is displayed, and complex and unstructured problems are addressed. Enthusiastic managers act as visionary leaders who become over-involved in the strategic concerns of the organisation and could lose sight of the operational functioning of the organisation. Excellence is expected from employees; however, praise is often forgotten.

Intuitive feeling

The manager focuses on changes and possibilities from a personal point of view. With their good communication skills, they conceptualise and apply the principles of participative management. They tend to over-delegate without implementing control to oversee that delegated tasks have been accomplished, and limit their disciplinary role.

4.5.2 Project management

Project management refers to an event/endeavour to accomplish a specific objective through a unique set of interrelated tasks and the effective utilisation of resources within a limited life-span. Project management means planning the work and then working the plan. The principles of project management are summarised, based on the framework described by Gido and Clements (2003), focusing on the attributes of projects, the project management process (proposal preparation, planning, project performance, project finalisation, and termination and project review).

Figure 4.4 Project management

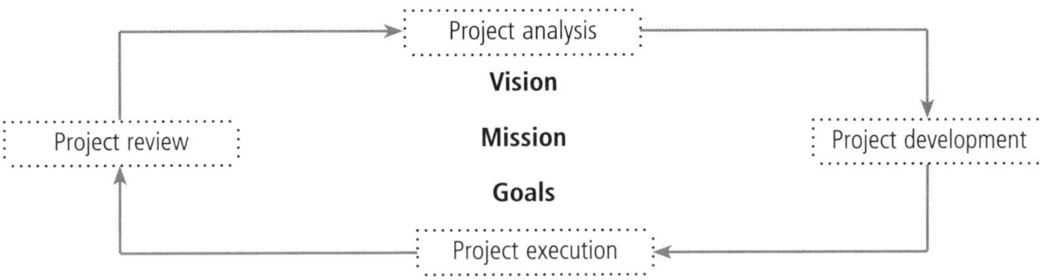

Attributes of projects

Projects generally reflect the following attributes:

- There is a well-defined objective, usually in terms of the scope of the project (specified deliverables), the schedule (timetable) and the cost (agreed-upon budget or tender) in accordance with the project agreement and subsequent business plan.
- Devolution of authority occurs within a matrix organisational structural design to facilitate urgent decision-making, with ultimate accountability by the project manager.
- A project is carried out through a set of independent tasks, that is, a series of non-repetitive tasks that need to be accomplished in a certain sequence to achieve the objective.
- A variation of external resources is utilised, for example caterers and printers.
- The project has a specific time frame or definite lifespan.
- The project reflects definite phases, for example a request for proposal (RFP), submission and acceptance of the proposal by means of an agreement, execution of the project and finalisation/termination of the project.
- Projects reflect unique and customer-designed and customer-driven events.
- Projects reflect a degree of uncertainty, based on assumptions and estimates.

Project management process

The project management process consists of preparation of the proposal, project planning, project performance, finalisation and termination of the project, and project review.

Preparation: Request for Proposal (RFP)

There are different types of projects – those activated internally (i.e. the development of clinical guidelines for a particular clinical intervention), or those projects requested by external organisations, either formally or informally. In the case of external formal projects, a process of invitation (by means of an expression of interest or based on the tender process) is followed. The extreme examples are projects of a major magnitude (i.e. hosting of an international congress or sports event) where the formal process of 'bidding' is followed. A simplified process is described in this chapter. A request for a proposal is prepared, focusing on the following:

- **Needs analysis**. This means analysing the needs and opportunities according to the alignment with the core business and goals of the organisation.
- **Project selection**. This involves assessing the advantages and disadvantages (value added) if the project is selected. Both quantitative and qualitative analyses can be conducted to assess the organisation's capacity and abilities to perform.
- **Project proposal**. The project proposal is prepared, focusing on the project management approach, the deliverables that will be provided, the envisaged work schedule reflected in a network diagramme, the project team's experience, staffing details (project manager, field experts, etc.), as well as the costs.
- **Project solicitation process**. Once the RFP has been prepared, the customer solicits proposals by notifying potential contractors that the RFP is available. Specific assessment criteria are used (i.e. credibility and reputation, capacity, risk factors, alignment with vision, mission and core business of the organisation) when considering the different proposals.
- **Entering into an agreement**. The agreement is prepared and signed, reflecting at least the following:
  - parties involved and representative (project leader) of each party
  - formal relationship agreements
  - type of financial agreement (fixed-price or cost-reimbursement)
  - notice of schedule delays
  - approval of contractors and sub-contractors
  - disclosure of project-related information
  - termination of the project (including verification of results/outcomes)
  - terms of payment
  - final reporting and feedback.

Project planning

Project planning refers to the general planning activities, scheduling, developing the schedule control (quality) plan, resource considerations, cost planning and performance.

Planning relates to determining what activities need to be done, who will be responsible for them, and in what sequence they will be carried out. **Scheduling** deals with estimating the durations for all activities and developing a detailed project schedule that states when each activity should start and finish. **Schedule control** entails monitoring the progress of the project and re-planning and updating the project schedule accordingly. **Resource considerations** focus on the incorporation of resource requirements and constraints into the project plan and schedule. **Cost**

planning and performance include estimating project costs, developing a project budget, analysing project cost performance, and forecasting total costs at project completion (refer also to Chapter 1, Management of a healthcare organisation, with specific reference to the development of a business plan).

Project planning is summarised as follows:

- Clearly define the **project objective**. The definition must be agreed upon by the customer and the individual or organisation that will perform the project.
- Divide and sub-divide the **project scope** in major work packages. Although major projects may seem overwhelming when viewed as a whole, one way to conquer even the most monumental endeavour is to break it down. A Work Breakdown Structure (WBS) is a hierarchical display of work elements or items accomplished by the project team during the project. The work breakdown structure usually identifies the organisation (contractor) or individual (team member) responsible for each group of classified activities or work package (i.e. marketing of the congress).
- Define the specific activities that need to be performed for each work package in order to accomplish the project objective.
- Graphically portray the activities in the form of a network diagram. This diagram shows the necessary sequence and interdependence of activities to achieve the project objective. Different network planning techniques could be used, i.e. Programme Evaluation and Review Technique or Critical Path Method (refer to the principles of PERT and CPM in this chapter).
- Make a time estimate for how long it will take to complete each activity and plan the **work schedule**.
- It is also necessary to determine which types of resources and how many of each resource are needed for each activity to be completed within the estimated duration.
- Make a cost estimate for each activity. The cost is based on the types and quantities of resources required for each activity.
- Calculate a **project schedule and budget** to determine whether the project can be completed within the required time, with the allocated funds and with the available resources. An achievable and realistic baseline plan (a roadmap for accomplishing the project scope on time and within budget) is established.
- The project termination process is also reflected in the baseline plan: record-keeping of all documents and payments, filing system, etc.
- Develop a quality plan. The **project quality plan** should focus on at least the following:
  - the development of job descriptions for each responsible and accountable team member (or contractor)
  - acceptance of the job description by the team members by means of an agreement (preferably signed)

- the development of Key Performance Areas and subsequent performance indicators for each team member (or contractor)
- development of the monitoring and measurement system to determine compliance with performance indicators
- agreement on a code of conduct by all role-players involved
- documentation and filing systems.

- Information Management System and software: identify the needs related to an information management system and software required for the project to facilitate quality management.

Project performance/execution

Project performance refers to the execution of the project, based on the project plan. The following principles are adhered to:

- **Project leader**. The project leader is responsible and accountable for the project, in accordance with the job description.
- **Project team members**. The team members (including contractors) execute their responsibilities according to their job descriptions and performance indicators.
- **Proactive and continuous project control**. This consists of the development of standards and performance indicators, measuring actual performance against pre-determined standards and indicators, and taking corrective action when appropriate.
- **Project reporting methods, format and dates**. These must be determined.
- **Project plan in accordance with the Work Break Structure**. This must be executed digilently.
- **Progress monitoring**. Progress must be continuously monitored to ensure that everything is going according to plan. This implies measuring and analysing current project status with the actual schedule and budget.
- **Frequent meetings with team members**. These are held to analyse project progress: status review meetings, problem-solving meetings and technical design review meetings. Analyses of the reports and interim outputs/results and any changes to the project scope, schedule and budget must be done.
- **Corrective actions**. These must be activated if necessary if the project progress is inadequate, for example adjustment of the project plan (scope, budget, schedule and quality interventions).

Project finalisation and termination/closure

- Finalise the project once the project goals have been achieved to the satisfaction of the stakeholders involved.
- Verify all the deliverables with the stakeholders or external customer concerned.
- Collect the performance evaluation data as stated in the quality plan (i.e. customer satisfaction questionnaires, recommendations for future improvements and complaints).

- Analyse and interpret the performance data and provide feedback to the various team members, contractors and customers.
- The project manager compiles a final report for submission to the accountable authority.
- The customer could request a formal presentation on the completed project.

Project review

Project review after termination should focus on at least the following:

- Technical performance relates to work scope, quality and managing changes:
  - assessment of how the final scope of the work compared with the scope of the work at the start of the project
  - the nature and scope of work changes and the management of these changes
  - impact thereof on the end result/outcomes
- Cost performance involves comparing the final costs with the initial costing of the project.
- Schedule performance relates to the accuracy of scheduling and the relationship between work packages and schedule performance.
- Project planning and control includes:
  - the adequacy or lack of detail planning and the timely updating and management of amended plans
  - whether actual performance was compared with planned performance and Key Performance Areas
  - the accuracy and timeliness of data-collection related to performance management.
- Team relationships include the nature of team dynamics and the impact thereof on the output and outcome of the project.
- Communication includes:
  - the nature, scope and impact of communication with team members and other role-players or stakeholders involved in the project
  - the adequacy of communication methods and strategies, for example meetings and electronic communication.
- Problem identification and resolution include:
  - the mechanisms in place for the identification of problems
  - the management of problems.
- Recommendations for future projects are based on the commendations and limitations identified by the project team members.

Critical success factors in project management

The success of project management is based on at least the following:

- Planning and communication are critical to successful project management. They prevent problems from occurring or minimise their impact on the achievement of the project objective when they do occur. Idealistic planning could fail the project.

- Projects conducted within the organisation (the customer is within the organisation) are dependent upon top management support and leadership commitment.
- Taking the time to develop a well-thought-out plan before the start of the project is critical to the successful accomplishment of any project.
- A project should have a well-defined objective – an expected result, defined in terms of scope, schedule and cost, and agreed upon by the customer.
- The customer should be involved as a partner in the successful outcome of the project through active participation.
- Achieving customer satisfaction requires ongoing communication with the customer to keep the customer informed and to determine whether expectations have changed.
- The key to effective project control is measuring actual progress and comparing it to planned progress on a timely and regular basis and taking corrective action immediately, if necessary.
- After conclusion of the project, the project performance should be evaluated to learn what could be improved if a similar project were to be done in the future. Feedback should be obtained from the customer and the project team.
- The project manager should have leadership and management abilities (including crisis management abilities).
- Change management should take place within the project performance or execution period.
- Time management should be observed by all concerned, for example the ability to meet pre-determined due dates.
- Stress management techniques should be adopted by all concerned.
- Project team members should monitor individual and collective performance in accordance with the key performance areas agreed upon.

4.5.3 Performance management

Performance management is the translation of strategic organisational goals, objectives and outcomes to departmental and unit/area objectives and outcomes, and ultimately into individual performance objectives and outcomes, also referred to as key performance areas and indicators. It is an orderly and formalised sequential process of cascading organisational performance (goals, objectives and outcomes) down to operational unit and individual performance levels (key performance areas and indicators), with resultant measuring of performance and outcome within a given Performance Management Framework/System. A performance management framework or system describes the performance management cycle and processes of the organisation related to performance planning, monitoring, measurement, review and reporting, in accordance with the organisation's strategic plan or Integrated Development Plan and subsequent Balanced Scorecard.

Performance management is summarised as follows:
- Performance management is a means of getting better results from the organisation, team and individuals within an agreed framework of goals and standards.
- Performance management serves to clarify goals and in doing so motivates people to perform well.
- It is a way of translating corporate goals into achievable objectives that cascade down the organisation to individual performance level to produce optimum results.
- It aims to improve strategic focus and organisational effectiveness through continuously securing improvements in the performance of individuals and teams.

Purpose of performance management

The purpose of performance management is to align organisational goals and indicators with the performance of individual employees to facilitate a purpose-driven bottom-up approach of goal achievement and organisational success.

Context

The context is determined by the type and nature of the healthcare organisation's business ownership (refer to Chapter 1, Management of a healthcare organisation) and the legal authorities at national, provincial and local levels of public healthcare service delivery. The financial management legislation (South Africa, 1999) requires a periodic performance financial management review, in accordance with the process of public financial management. At local government level, measurable performance objectives for revenue from each source and for each vote in the budget are required, based on the municipality's Integrated Development Plan (IDP). This has resulted in the concept of performance management being implemented, especially at local government level, in accordance with several local government legislative requirements (Municipal Systems Act, Local Government Structures Act, Regulation, Municipal Finance Act, etc.).

Within the South African local government context, a comprehensive and elaborate system of monitoring performance of municipalities has been adopted and developed. The system is designed to continuously monitor the performance of municipalities in fulfilling their developmental mandate. Central to the system is the development of key performance areas and indicators, as well as instruments to assess compliance with the performance indicators. These indicators assist to translate complex socio-economic development challenges into quantifiable and measurable constructs. They are therefore crucial if trustworthy assessment of the impact of government in improving the quality of life of all is to be achieved. The

South African Local Municipal Systems Act (2000) requires municipalities to develop performance monitoring systems that are intended as strategic management tools to enable municipalities to monitor and measure their own performance, and to improve efficiency, effectiveness, quality and accountability in delivery of services. The Local Government Municipal Planning and Performance Management Regulation (South Africa, 2001) therefore acts as the local regulatory context for performance management – which also includes the delivery of healthcare services as local level. A local Performance Management System must comply with at least the following:

- Set appropriate performance indicators, including outcome and impact
- Set measurable targets
- Monitor performance
- Measure and review performance management at least annually
- Aim to improve performance
- Establish a process of regular reporting
- Determine the frequency of reporting and the lines of accountability for performance
- Relate organisational performance to employee performance.

Focus of performance management

Performance management focuses on:

- Outcomes, outputs, process and inputs
- Planning, measurement and review
- Continuous improvement and development
- Consultation with stakeholders
- Continuous and adequate communication at all levels.

The process of performance management

The organisational strategic plan is used as the point of departure. These organisational objectives are translated into departmental or divisional objectives, followed by the cascading and alignment with the unit/area objectives. The unit objectives are translated into individual objectives. The individual objectives are translated into performance standards and outcomes, reflected in the form of key performance areas (KPAs). Training, coaching and support as needed are supplied, followed by monitoring and periodic review. Formal appraisal is conducted at the end of the period and feedback is given.

Performance management should be integrated with the Balanced Scorecard system within the organisation. Chang and Morgan (2000) developed the principle of Performance Scorecards, by applying the principles of the Balanced Scorecard (refer to Chapter 19, Quality improvement models in a healthcare organisation), consisting of the following steps: Collect, Create, Cultivate, Cascade, Connect, and Confirm.

Collect
'Collect' is the first step in developing a Performance Scorecard for the organisation or department within the organisation. The organisational strategies define what should be measured. The following items are collected (Chang & Morgan, 2000:19–3):
- Obtain top-level objectives, measures and targets (in accordance with the organisation's strategy)
- Identify customer's key requirements
- Define the core process chains (sequence of work activities that provides service to customers)
- Document high-level process flows
- Gather existing measurement data
- Plan the Performance Scorecard development session and agenda.

The outcome of this first step – the Collect Phase – results in a snapshot of the core business process chains, high-level flow charts of core processes, inputs and agenda for the Scorecard development sessions (Chang & Morgan, 2000:20).

Create
Create is the second phase in the development of the Performance Scorecard, and consists of the following steps (Chang & Morgan, 2000:39–53):
- Review the Scorecard development planning inputs
- Define key result areas
- Relate business objectives to key result areas
- Brainstorm potential measures
- Select the key indicators for the Performance Scorecard
- Define the key indicators
- Develop action plans for compiling and reviewing the key indicators.

At the end of this phase, the following outcomes should be clear (Chang & Morgan, 2000:53):
- Team objectives
- Scorecard measures linked to corporate goals, business objectives and customer requirements
- Action plans to develop measures.

Cultivate
Cultivate is the third phase in the development of the Performance Scorecard. This phase consists of the following (Chang & Morgan, 2000:57–78):
- Gather, display and analyse historical data
- Conduct performance reviews
- Determine appropriate targets

- Develop improvement action plans
- Strengthen horizontal and vertical linkages.

The outcomes of this phase should be:
- Shorter, more effective performance reviews
- Appropriate and challenging targets for Scorecard measures
- Specific measurable improvement actions
- Stronger Scorecard links.

Cascade

The fourth phase relates to Cascade and contains the following steps (Chang & Morgan, 2000:83–102):
- Determine Scorecard measures for the next level in the cascade
- Verify cascaded measures are at the appropriate levels
- Establish and affirm linkages and alignment
- Clarify targets
- Establish summary measures as needed
- Refine steps for gathering, reporting and reviewing results.

The outcome of this phase should reflect the following:
- A balanced and linked set of Scorecard measures
- Appropriate feedback measures for each level of accountability.

Connect

The Connect phase reflects the following steps (Chang & Morgan, 2000:109–124):
- Review the performance management process
- Develop an individual performance plan
- Conduct coaching sessions
- Provide evaluation summaries
- Review links and outcomes.

Outcomes of the Connect Phase (Chang & Morgan, 2000:124):
- Individual contributions linked to Scorecard outcomes and business results
- Indications of where the Scorecard should be refined or adjusted.

Confirm

Confirm the Scorecard as the last step (Chang & Morgan, 2000:129–149):
- Evaluate the Scorecard
- Prioritise and act on improvements
- Identify and resolve measurement issues
- Establish a process to refine the Scorecard continually.

Critical success factors

Critical success factors to support the principles and process of performance management are summarised as follows:

- Develop a strategic approach to the management of people and performance – aligned with the key performance/priority areas of the organisation's strategic plan.
- Articulate and promote key human resource management principles and values, in accordance with the values of the organisation as reflected in the strategic plan of the organisation.
- Raise the profile of training, coaching and development as a key performance area of strategic human resource management.
- Ensure conditions of employment and working arrangements supporting the goals of high performance management.
- Invest in monitoring and evaluation of human resource management practices and programmes of reform.
- Ensure that the human resources management division has the capacity to conduct performance management.
- Note that the key elements of a successful performance management system are that it is a business process, it creates a shared understanding, responsibility and accountability in achieving the organisational goals and outcomes, it is an approach to managing people, it increases the probability or organisational success and sustainability, and it is driven by competencies.
- Utilise international best practice guidelines.

4.6 UNDERLYING DYNAMICS

The underlying dynamics were described within each dimension, and are summarised as follows:

- Quality functional management is dependent upon the quality of leadership, with reference to the levels of leadership as described by Jim Collins (2001:19–22):
  - **Level 1: Highly capable individual**. He/she makes productive contributions to the various dimensions of functional management through talent, knowledge, skills and good work habits.
  - **Level 2: Contributing team member**. He/she contributes individual capabilities to the achievement of group objectives – with reference to the various dimensions of functional management in the healthcare organisation – and works effectively with others in a group setting.
  - **Level 3: Competent manager**. He/she organises people and resources toward the effective and efficient pursuit of pre-determined objectives related to the dimensions of functional management.
  - **Level 4: Effective leader**. He/she catalyses commitment to and vigorous pursuit of a clear and compelling vision, stimulating higher performance standards.

  - **Level 5: Executive**. He/she builds enduring greatness through a paradoxical blend of personal humility and professional will.
- The abilities (knowledge, skills, attitudes and values) of the leaders, managers and team members impact on the quality of functional management-related dimensions.
- Internal organisational determinants related to capacity include human resources and staff mix, structures, systems, policies, financial resources, etc. and will impact on the quality of functional management.
- Application of the logical process of management are planning, organising, leading and control, integrated with the process of 'functional management strategy' analysis, development, execution and review.
- Idealism should be balanced with the facts related to the current reality.

4.7 CONCLUDING STATEMENTS

The following concluding statements are made:

- Decision-making and problem-solving are purposeful cognitive processes, based on the selection of the most suitable alternative related to a particular course of action or intervention, that is most likely to facilitate optimal attainment of goals, outputs and outcomes.
- Decision-making differs from problem-solving in that is focuses on subjects, themes, etc. in addition to problems.
- There are different levels and types of decisions, different factors and conditions that influence decision-making.
- Decision-making and problem-solving could be simplified by a few steps (assessment of alternatives, selection and implementation of the alternatives, and review of the outcome), or based on a complicated multi-step process.
- Different tools/aids and types of decision-making exist, as well as many models and theories.
- Project management is a short-term event to accomplish a set of goals and outcomes within a specific framework of internal or external customer needs.
- Project management is based on the following process: preparation of proposal, project planning and project performance/execution, project termination/closure and project review.
- Performance management is the translation of organisational goals, objectives and outcomes to departmental, and ultimately to individual performance objectives, KPAs and outcomes.
- The process of performance management is based on the integration of the organisational, departmental, unit and individual KPAs and outcomes with the Balanced Scorecard related to collect, create, cultivate, cascade, connect and confirm.

Self-assessment

(1) Develop an instrument to assess the quality of project management, with reference to at least the following criteria: completeness of work scope, quality of work, schedule performance, financial management performance, communications, customer relations and overall performance.
(2) Assess your organisation's readiness to implement a performance management system.

5 Change management in a healthcare organisation

KEY CONCEPTS

Change
Organisational development
Change management
Organisational change
Transformation management
Mergers

SPECIFIC OUTCOMES

After studying this chapter, you should be able to:

- Interpret the legal, professional-ethical and healthcare **context**, with reference to change and transformation in a dynamic healthcare environment
- Analyse and debate the **purpose** of change management, that is, alignment to internal and external environmental forces, quality organisational development and change, as well as sustainability and/or profitability of the organisation
- Identify the **role-players** and interpret their roles and responsibilities in change management, with specific reference to the manager as a change agent
- Describe and apply the **process** of change management in the healthcare organisation, with reference to organisational development, change and transformation management, in accordance with the type and level of change and change models/paradigms
- Debate the **underlying dynamics** that could impact on change management in the healthcare organisation with reference to environmental turbulence, unanticipated consequences of evolutionary development of organisational life cycles, inappropriate managerial decision-making and inadequate organisational cognition, as well as the underlying theoretical assumptions related to change management.

5.1 INTRODUCTION

A business/organisation and the environment in which it operates, including the community it serves, depend on each other for survival or sustainability. Together they form a complex business environment where change in the environmental variables continually determines the success or failure of the business. Because these variables are often beyond the control of management, it is management's task to adapt the organisation to change in the environment. At times, management acts proactively by anticipating events, thereby also accelerating change and transformation. Knowledge of a changing environment by means of sustained environmental scanning is a prerequisite for taking advantage of opportunities as well as averting threats. On the other hand, there are many direct external forces, such as legislative and subsequent national policy changes, that impact on change and transformation. Healthcare managers therefore need to have the abilities (knowledge, skills, attitudes and values) to adequately manage change by means of strategy analysis, development, execution and review.

A wide array of terms and concepts are often used interchangeably in change management. The original meaning of the word 'change' refers to 'bend' or 'turn' (and even 'break'). Lewin – the well-known change theorist of the 1950s – described change as a sequence of activities that emanate from disturbances in the stable force field that surrounds the organisation (or object, situation or person), and tends to focus on the role of context, stability as preferred state, and the onset of a chain reaction of events when the force field is disturbed. Change – in the context of an organisation – is defined as follows by Van Tonder (2004:4–5): An initiative which alters critical organisational processes, which in turn influence individual behaviours, and which subsequently impact on organisational outcomes.

Change management refers to the management of developmental change (organisational development), transitional change (Type I change management) and transformational change in the organisation (Type II transformation management), by means of strategy analysis, strategy development, strategy execution and strategy review. Figure 5.1 depicts the conceptual framework of this chapter.

5.2 CONTEXT

The context description of this chapter will focus on the business context only, keeping in mind that all the dimensions of the context – as described in Chapter 1, Management of a healthcare organisation – are relevant.

5.2.1 Global context

The signs of worldwide change are all too evident. We find ourselves in the midst of a rapid evolving society that is no longer characterised by the apparent stability of the 1950s and 1960s. The features of this society include increasing global competition, technological innovation, and declining resources. Change is also evident in the shifting sense of value (business ethics) in the global business context. At the organisational level, the turbulence and rate of change and innovation experienced in the operating context of organisations are equally evident. Organisations have been subjected to a state of constant change since the early 1990s, and consequently

Figure 5.1 Visual presentation of change and transformation management in a healthcare organisation

Context	Global context National, provincial and local context Business ownership Environmental dynamics
Role-players	**Change agents** Individual practitioners (clinical and non-clinical) Team members Managers Leaders Executive
Purpose	Alignment of organisation with internal and external environmental forces and dynamics Facilitation of quality organisational development, transition and transformation Facilitation of sustainability of service delivery
Process	**Levels of change** Individual Developmental (organisational development) Transitional (change management) Transformational (transformation management) **Change management process** Strategy analysis, strategy development, strategy execution and strategy review in accordance with the levels of change **Selected models** Ecological change Rational-purposive change Evolutionary organisational life-cycle change Cognitive change Good-to-Great
Underlying dynamics	Environmental turbulence Unanticipated consequences of evolutionary organisational life-cycle stages Inappropriate managerial decision-making Inadequate organisational cognition Inadequate management of change

institutional change has been considered one of the most salient features of the last decade (Van Tonder, 2004:4).

5.2.2 National, provincial and local context

Change management takes place in the national, provincial and local context, based on the legislative framework, policy directives and healthcare service delivery framework.

5.2.3 Types of business ownership

Business ownership, with reference to healthcare organisations, is first and foremost determined by the national health-related legislation that delineates the levels of public service delivery (national, provincial and local) and other private healthcare organisations or establishments. The size of a private healthcare organisation is also determined by the type of business ownership (refer to Chapter 1, Management of a healthcare organisation), varying from the sole proprietor to a company. Therefore the business environment also varies from a simplified to a complex situation.

5.2.4 Characteristics of the business environment

The following are a few of the main characteristics of the business environment, based on the principles of a system (De J. Cronje, et al., 2004:88–89) that could impact on the demand for change and transformation in the healthcare organisation:

- **The environmental factors or variables are interrelated**. A change in one of the external variables may cause a change in the micro-environment and, similarly, a change in one external variable may cause a change in the other external variables impacting on the management of the healthcare organisation.
- **Increasing instability**. One of the consequences of interdependence in the environment is increasing instability and change. Although the general rate of change in the environment accelerates, environmental fluctuation is greater for some organisations than for others.
- **Environmental uncertainty**. Uncertainty about the environment is, of course, a function of the amount of information about environmental variables, and of the confidence that management has in such information. If the value of the information is suspect, the uncertainty of management about the environment will increase.
- **The complexity of the environment.** This indicates the number of external variables to which the organisation has to respond, as well as variations in the variables themselves.

5.3 PURPOSE

The purpose of change management is summarised as follows:

- To timeously align the healthcare organisation with the internal and external environmental forces and dynamics

- To facilitate continuous purpose-driven quality organisational development, transitional organisational change (Type I change) and transformational organisational change (Type II)
- To facilitate sustainability (and in the case of private healthcare organisations, profitability) of the healthcare organisation.

5.4 ROLE-PLAYERS

The role-players are presented in the context of the 'Good-to-Great' model described by Jim Collins (2001:17–40) and his team of researchers. The role-players are reflected in a hierarchical format – from levels one to five:

- **Level 1 Highly capable individual**. He/she makes productive contributions through talent, knowledge, skills and good work habits in the context of change.
- **Level 2 Contributing team member**. He/she contributes individual capabilities to the change management-related achievement of group objectives and works effectively with others in a group setting.
- **Level 3 Competent manager.** He/she organises people and resources toward the effective and efficient pursuit of pre-determined objectives related to change management.
- **Level 4 Effective leader.** He/she catalyses commitment to and vigorous pursuit of a clear and compelling vision with regard to change, stimulating higher performance standards as a result of the change and transformation.
- **Level 5 Executive**. He/she builds enduring greatness through a paradoxical blend of personal humility and professional will in the context of change and transformation.

Role and responsibilities of the manager as change agent

All these role-players act as change agents in the healthcare organisation. The responsibilities of the manager as change agent are highlighted:

- Purposefully manage developmental and transitional change (Type I change) by means of change strategy analysis, strategy development, strategy execution and review (strategic management).
- Manage transformational change (Type II change) by applying the principles of chaos and complexity theory-based transformational management.
- Identify and manage the potential negative views/perceptions on change by employees, for example potentially harmful or dangerous, an injustice (perceived or experienced as unfair), a blockage of personal goals, a source of uncertainty (i.e. restructuring and possible downsizing).
- Identify and manage the experience of employees during change, for example traumatic, catastrophic or disastrous, a loss (i.e. support or disempowerment).
- Identify and manage organisational consequences of change (both negative and positive), for example resistance to change, new opportunities and benefits.

- Adequately manage the institutionalisation phase by entrenching the change.
- Maintain a continuous and balanced focus, designed to secure optimal external and internal alignment of the healthcare organisation to enable gradual and adaptive Type I change. A discontinuous focus, or disproportionate over- or under-emphasis of either external or internal alignment, rapidly increases the probability of Type II change.

5.5 PROCESS

The process description will focus on the following:

- Levels of change
- Types of change
- Shape and size of change
- Determinants of successful change
- Process of change management (Type I change), that is, strategy analysis, development, execution and review
- Process of change management (Type II transformational change)
- Classification of models
- Selected dimensions of organisational change, for example organisational development and mergers.

5.5.1 Levels of change

Change can take place at individual or organisational level. At organisational level, there are also different levels and degrees of change – individual, developmental, transitional and transformational (Van Tonder, 2004:5–6; 160–161):

- **Individual change**. A gradual and progressive form of human change which reflects both affective (emotional) and cognitive (mental) acceptance; or as attempts to coming to terms on an intrapersonal level with environmental changes that impact on the person. An acceptance at emotional level of the inevitability of the change, and enabling an alteration of meaning structures at the cognitive level.
- **Developmental change**. This refers to an improvement of what is in existence – also referred to as organisational development.
- **Transitional change**. This refers to the implementation of a known new state, and change management of the interim transition state over a controlled period of time, also known as Type I change.
- **Transformational change**. This refers to the emergence of a new state out of the remains of the old state, which is unknown until it takes shape (Type II change). The time period (duration) of the change is not easily controlled. This form of change is also referred to as chaotic or complex change.

5.5.2 Types of change

Change is described by change theorists in terms of two qualitatively different and clearly differentiated change types or categories: Type I and Type II (Van Tonder, 2004:157):

- **Type I change**. This change is a steady-state; incremental or step-by-step sequential change which generally evolves over an extended period of time, does not have a disruptive influence on the system and is generally perceived to be in the control of the system.
- **Type II change**. This change is a major, disruptive, unpredictable, paradigm-altering and system-wide change, which has a very sudden onset and escalates rapidly to a point where it is perceived as being beyond the control of the system. The principles of transformation management, with reference to the chaotic and complexity theories (see Chapter 3, Selected management models), are applicable.

A continuous and balanced focus, designed to secure optimal external and internal alignment, will enable Type I change: gradual, adaptive change. This also relates to the principle of strategic management. A discontinuous focus, or disproportionate over- or under-emphasis on either external or internal alignment, rapidly increases the probability of Type II change (Van Tonder, 2004:157).

5.5.3 Shape and size of change

Change in organisations reflects the following systemic and organisational attributes (Van Tonder, 2004:96):

- **The degree of complexity.** This ranges from simple, single-level to complex, multilevel and multifaceted change.
- **The scope of the change**. This ranges from a relatively limited and isolated impact to system-wide reconfigurations and ramifications.
- **The rate or pace of change**. This ranges from relatively slow to rapid change.
- **The progression or progressive unfolding of the change**. This ranges from incremental and step-wise to quantum leaps.
- **The degree of control over the change**. This ranges from complete control by the organisation and its officials to no control.
- **The extent to which the change can be visualised**. This ranges from clearly predictable outcomes with a high probability of occurrence to completely unpredictable outcomes.
- **The role of the organisation**. This ranges from reactive and responding to proactive and initiating.
- **The ultimate impact of the change**. This ranges from minor, superficial impact in terms of peripheral features of the organisation, to alteration of the core or fundamental features and core business activities of the organisation.

5.5.4 Determinants of successful change

The determinants of successful change are described by Van Tonder (2004:212–213) as follows:

- Avoid non-alignment of the organisation with external and internal forces by focusing on the following:
  - recognising the current dominant paradigm of the organisation, and pursuing a more appropriate and enabling concept of organisation
  - adopting a mindset that will enable the detection, recognition and acknowledgement of different change paradigms.
- Ensure a more informed perspective on change and, consequently, an improved potential for:
  - dealing effectively with unanticipated change
  - limiting unnecessary and avoidable Type II change
  - initiating appropriate change interventions with a greater likelihood of sustainability and 'success'.
- Ensure effective implementation, which typically translates into securing the final change outcomes.
- Ensure efficient implementation, for example remaining in the cost, time and/or quality parameters, in accordance with the change initiative.
- Ensure employee acceptance of the change and by implication minimal or minimised resistance.
- Ensure compliance with specific process steps or content elements in the organisation's change management model, for example articulating the change need, establishing a change vision, and the like.
- Recognise and attend to the so-called critical success factors, which often assume the character of guiding principles, for example senior management support or involvement of all affected stakeholders (refer to the section on Underlying dynamics in this chapter).
- Ensure the sustainability of the change over the medium to long term, which implies institutionalisation of the change.

5.5.5 Process of change management Type I change

The process of change management (Type I change) is simplified as follows: strategy analysis, strategy development, strategy implementation and strategy review (see Figure 5.2).

Strategy analysis

The principles related to strategy analysis, as described in Chapter 2, Strategic management of a healthcare organisation, are applicable – an analysis of the internal (organisational profile analysis) and external environmental (scanning, monitoring, forecasting and assessing) analyses. Additional principles are as follows (Van Tonder, 2004:50–51):

Figure 5.2 Process of change and transformation

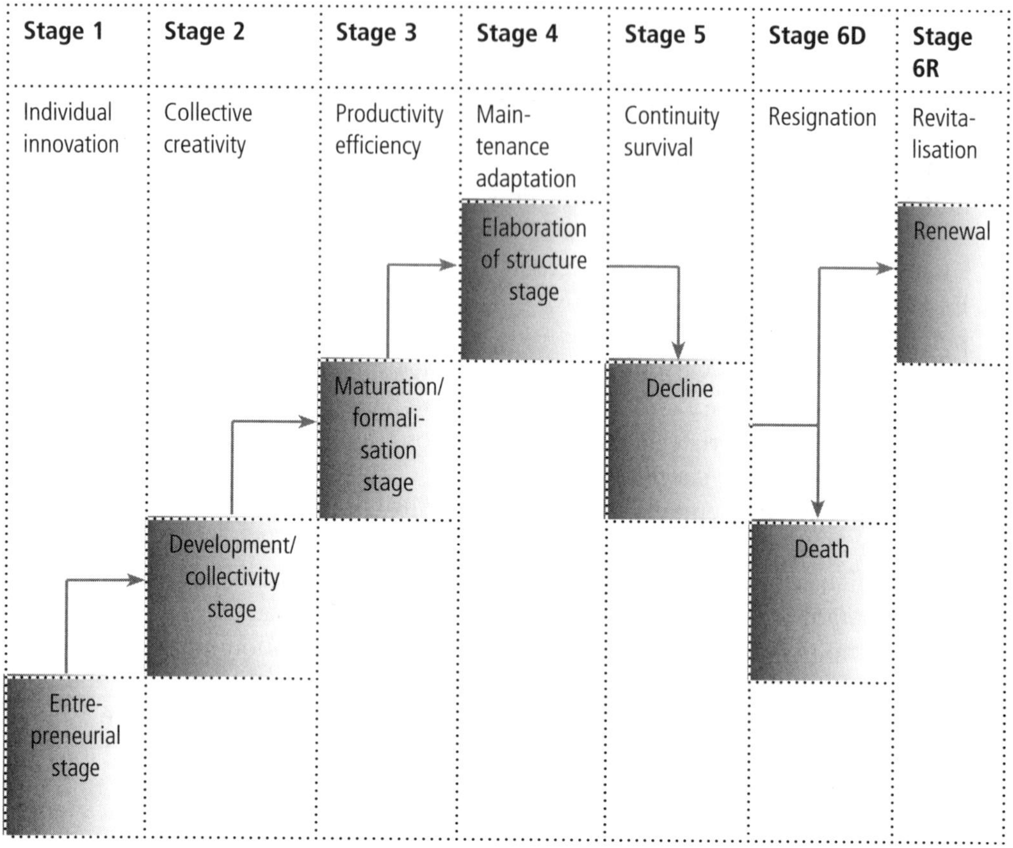

- Analysis of the current reality and need for change (pre-change status) and desired or future (post-change state) of the organisation to the extent that is possible, based on good research, is required.
- Adequate data collection of both the external environment (environmental scanning) and the internal environment (organisational profile analysis) is necessary (refer to Chapter 2, Strategic management of a healthcare organisation).
- An acknowledgement of the social and collective context and content of organisational change and the need to engage change from this perspective, also taking into account the emotional sub-text of change are necessary.
- A realisation that, regardless of whether change is initiated or responded to, alignment between the organisational operating context (internal environment) is at the root of organisational adaptation and survival 'fit alignment'; alignment with the organisation's objectives.
- Employee participation in strategy analysis should be ensured.
- Client (patient and community) input is obtained and incorporated.
- A reasonable balance between risk and cost-benefit analyses is maintained.

- In view of the increasing complexity of the change context and territory, access to appropriate and relevant information, but more importantly, the ability to make sense of this information. This will be core to change and the appropriateness of the organisation's change response.
- A sense of urgency needs to be established.
- Powerful and positive individuals (champions) to embrace the change need to be secured.

Strategy development

The change strategy for the particular type and degree of change is developed, based on the principles described for strategy development in Chapter 2, Strategic management of a healthcare organisation. This entails at least the following:

- Development of the change management plan (draft proposal for consultation purposes), aligned with the identity and core business of the healthcare organisation
- Employee participation in strategy development should be ensured: consultation on the draft proposal (change vision and objectives), continuous and consistent communication to secure acceptance and ownership of the vision and objectives
- Clarification and development of a vision of the change end-state, which is aligned with the organisation's culture, exciting, secured through broad participation and structured around clear goals and objectives
- Development and establishment of an action plan and the 'roll-out' of the change strategy
- Ensuring that the strategy includes the communication strategy, and the strategy to manage negative perceptions/views of employees, potential negative experiences and the institutionalisation of the change.

Strategy execution

The change management strategy is executed, based on the principles described for strategy execution in Chapter 2, Strategic management of a healthcare organisation. In addition to these principles, the following are relevant:

- The piloting of the change plan, depending on the content of the plan and the feasibility of a pilot project
- The execution of the change strategy by all level managers in the organisation, based on training/empowerment, continuous support and facilitation teams if necessary
- The continuous monitoring of progress and the impact of change dynamics
- The execution of the communication strategy, including information related to the unfolding of the change process
- The management of employee perceptions, experience and other challenges:
  - the **implementation time** usually exceeds the original time allocated to or envisaged for the change initiative
  - the **coordination** of the implementation strategy is often experienced as very problematic

- the **capacity (abilities)** of the employees involved in the implementation of the change strategy and subsequent change processes often prove inadequate
- **unexpected and unplanned problems** surface during the implementation phase, for example staff turnover and systems failure
- **training and instruction** are often not adequately focused to deal with all the change dynamics
- **competing activities** and crises often distract the attention and focus from the implementation process
- **external environmental issues** that are uncontrollable, such as disasters and changes in national policy directives
- **employee resistance** due to numerous reasons, for example additional workload, negative perceptions and experiences during the execution phase
- **inadequate leadership** at all levels of management due to lack of abilities (knowledge, skills, attitudes and values) or commitment
- communication failures due to inadequate capacity to deal with the communication demands
- organisational culture, which is also related to resistance to change, due to the changes in the operational environment.

Strategy review

This entails the process of change management control by which management ensures that the organisation's change management goals are accomplished and/or that actual performance compares favourably with the predetermined performance standards. A few attributes/principles are highlighted:

- Assess the process of change and methodology deployed (the quality of the strategy analyses, strategy development, and strategy execution based on the lessons learned during the change management process.
- Compare the actual realisation of change/transformation results, outputs and outcomes with the intended strategy.
- Measure the output and outcomes relative to the stated goals and intended outcomes.
- Consider the benefits/gains that could be used for the reinforcement of stability and the institutionalisation of the change.
- Review the status or organisational change and development and compare with the criteria of excellence in this regard (refer to the section on organisational development in this chapter).
- Institutionalise the change – entrenching the change through performance management, celebrating the success, publicising and marketing of the success, rewarding of staff.

5.5.6 Process of change management (Type II transformational change)

Transformation management is concerned with the management of transformational change at Type II level of change, which implies a disruptive and 'quantum leap' paradigm-altering and system-wide change and adjustment of the current reality or existing state of the organisation. The following principles of transformation management are applicable:

- The general principles of strategy analysis, strategy development, strategy execution and strategy review are utilised if the onset of the change is not so sudden (i.e. the merging of two institutions).
- During transformational change based on a sudden and disruptive onset, self-organisation could take place, for example the emergence of order, self-generation and co-evolution with the greater environment. The system (which is very complex and almost unmanageable), could create its own order and natural growth by integrating transformations into its identity and thus ensuring growth and a high level of performance.
- The underlying assumptions of the chaos theory (Van Tonder, 2004:42) with reference to the following (see also Chapter 3, Selected management models) are applicable:
  - ability for self-renewal and self-organisation
  - fragmentation and interdependence
  - butterfly effect and bifurcation
  - non-linearity, scale and holism
  - strange attractors
  - diversity and creativity
  - positive feedback.
- Allow the process of transformation to unfold and to create its own substantial structure, based on the core values and core purpose of the organisation, and the intellectual capacity and experience in the organisation.
- 'Enduring great companies preserve their core values and purpose while their business strategies and operating practices endlessly adapt to a changing world. This is the magical combination of 'preserve the core and stimulate the progress' (Collins, 2001:195).

5.5.7 Classification of major change paradigms/models

Kurt Lewin led the way with his classic change management model in 1951, which recognised that change is the consequence of a disturbance in the force field surrounding an entity or organisation and that the objective should be to re-establish a situation of balance or equilibrium. He conceptualised the model in three stages: unfreezing, changing and refreezing. Many new approaches to change and change management have emerged, due to the unpredictable nature of the environment and the complexity of systems and organisations today.

This chapter will focus on the description of the following models: ecological change, rational-purposive change, the evolutionary organisational life-cycle model, cognitive change and Jim Collin's (2001) 'Good-to-Great' model.

Ecological change model

Ecologically informed change focuses on a population of organisations that go through an evolutionary process of change. With its primary focus on populations of organisations (i.e. healthcare institutions), this perspective attempts to account for the many different kinds of organisations in existence, and does so by investigating how environmental conditions influence the rate at which new organisational forms are created (founding rates), become extinct (organisational dissolutions or 'mortality' rates) and the rates of change in organisational forms (Van Tonder, 2004:60). A few attributes are highlighted:

- Organisations with the same founding characteristics (i.e. hospitals) follow a similar pattern of change, due to 'similar' internal and external environmental forces and dynamics.
- The sustainability of the organisation is primarily determined by the external environmental dynamics, i.e. new health-related legislation and policy directives and financial legislation and subsequent dynamics.
- The healthcare organisations therefore tend to follow the same pattern of change, in accordance with the type of business ownership and other contextual dynamics. The degree and complexity of change (Type I or Type II change) vary accordingly.

Rational-purposive change model

Rational-purposive change relates to all forms of change that follow from rational, conscious, and/or purposeful considerations or actions (Type I change). It includes all forms and manifestations of what is traditionally referred to as 'planned change'. Planned or 'managed' change efforts are the most obvious form of organisational change and virtually without exception the change responses and change initiatives recognised and found in organisations resort in this approach to change. Rational-purposive change is associated with organisational development and strategic management (Van Tonder, 2004:70). The following attributes of rational-purposive change are summarised:

- This paradigm assumes that control of change in the organisation resorts with the organisation itself. Conscious decisions are taken in the organisation and change is therefore internally controlled, based on the rational assessment of the organisation's current reality and the external environmental dynamics.
- It reflects a formalised sequential and planned process of strategy analysis, strategy development, strategy execution and strategy review.
- A strategic choice is made based on the environmental (internal and external) dynamics and forces.
- There is an intended goal and plan related to purposeful organisational development.

- Deliberate and planned problem-solving is conducted to counteract the limitations (capacity in relation to organisational structure, processes/systems and employee abilities).
- Situation-specific (organisation-relevant) change is facilitated, based on the current reality of the organisation (capacity, etc.).
- Organisational strengths are utilised during the process of change management.
- Organisational development takes place.

The rational-purposive change model is – however – dependent of the following (Van Tonder, 2004:71):
- The rationality of those engaged in the process of change management
- The cognitive capabilities of those engaged in the process of change management
- Pre-existing organisational cognitions (structures of meaning or schemata) which, if inappropriate, may significantly compromise change attempts.

Evolutionary organisational life-cycle model

The life-cycle model is a depiction of a theory that describes commonly occurring characteristics and activities during different stages of an organisation over its lifespan. This change model is based on the premise that organisational change tends to follow a life-cycle pattern. An integrated model of the organisational life-cycle of organisations is presented in Figure 5.3 (adapted from Van Tonder, 2004:64).

The following attributes related to the different organisational life-cycles are highlighted (Van Tonder, 2004:65):
- **Entrepreneurial stage**. This is essentially a creative stage, with high-powered individuals, limited formalised management (planning, organising, leading and control), proactive, idea-rich, more individualised and informal.
- **Development/collective stage**. Here the focus is on teamwork and collaboration, sense of collectivity and high commitment among staff, experiencing a high success rate with sustained growth and direction.
- **Maturation/formalisation stage.** In this stage the organisation is becoming more centralised, formal and structured with institutionalised rules, policies and procedures; the focus is on efficiency, maintenance and outputs.
- **Elaboration of structure stage**. Here stagnation, change resistance, decline of resources, narrowing of core business domain, too centralised, overly complex, failing to anticipate, recognise or adapt, impairment or marginal resistance, inappropriate action-taking and death struggle occur.
- **Decline or death stages**. This is a stage where expansion of strategic domain and growing structure, decentralisation due to complexity, diversification of core business, maintenance and adaptation, slowing growth and multi-purpose sub-systems occur.

Figure 5.3 An integrated model of the organisational life-cycle

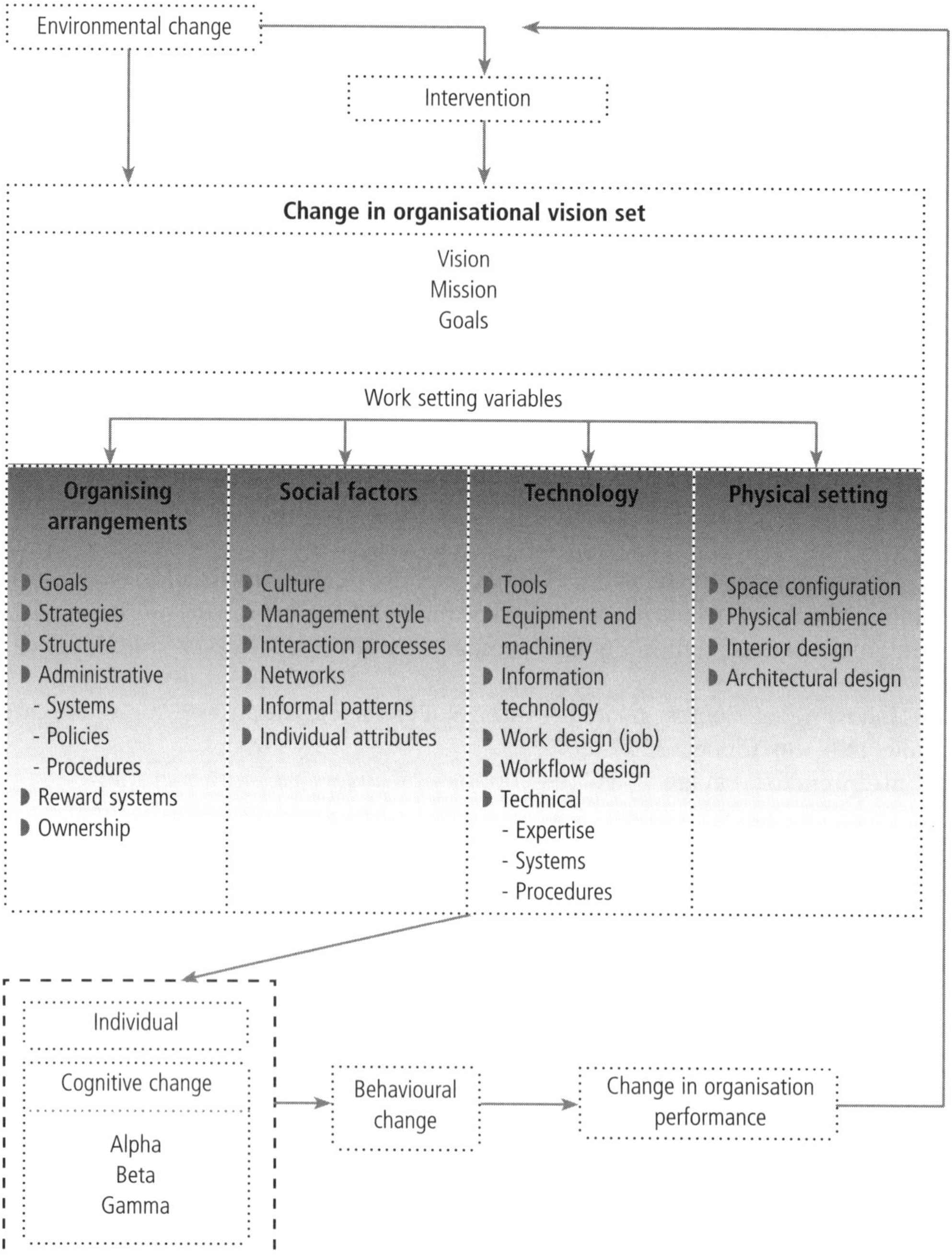

- **Renewal stage**. This is the stage of stabilisation, employee empowerment, increased capacity for change, transforming systems, executive succession, interorganisational frameworks and alliances, intense teamwork and pressure for information.

Cognitive change model

This change paradigm is based on the premise that the future is unpredictable – more so with the accelerating pace of change, which has become a hallmark of contemporary organisational life – and secondly, the inability of prevailing knowledge, experience and established success formulae to assist managers with new adaptive challenges arising from their changing operating context. A few attributes of this model are highlighted (Van Tonder, 2004:118–122):

- Cognitive change is the modification or replacement of pre-existing cognitions that are typically ordered in the form of meaningful structures, also referred to as schemata. Schemata (as a result of learning) are therefore the core structures and smallest units to which the process of cognition change can be reduced.
- Change and survival are dependent upon continuous learning at both individual and organisational levels.
- Ongoing learning is the best and probably the only preparation for an uncertain future.
- Cognitive change is based on the emergence of the complexity systems theory (see Chapter 3, Selected management models).
- The information-based society results in quantum advances in information and communications technology which are producing an overload of information.
- The organisation's ability to create meaning or make sense of information (i.e. about its environment) or more specifically as the process of changing its interpretive or cognitive schemata.
- Cognitive change is therefore at the core of attempts to avoid misinterpretation of emerging or gradually developing situations of non-alignment and taking of inappropriate or even disastrous decisions and actions.
- The healthcare service manager(s) should therefore reflect the cognitive abilities to adequately interpret the environmental forces and dynamics to facilitate timeous change in the organisation.
- The principles of Knowledge Management should be applied (refer to Chapter 3, Selected management models).

Good-to-Great model: Jim Collins

Background

This model (Collins, 2001) is based on the premise that good is the enemy of great. It is based on rigorous research conducted over a five-year period, investigating several international companies that complied with the population description (critical success factors) and subsequent sample criteria, based on the question: Can a good company become a great company and, if so, how? A total of 11 'great' companies were included in the sample. Comparison companies (control group) were also selected. A longitudinal combined quantitative and qualitative research design and related methods were applied. The results were used to describe the companies (and subsequent model) that moved from 'good to great'.

Model description: Good-to-Great

The model consists of the following dimensions: Level 5 Leadership; First who – then what; confront the brutal facts; hedgehog concept; a culture of discipline; and technology accelerators. Lastly, the 'flywheel and the doom loop' is explained.

(a) *Level 5 Leadership*

The five levels of leadership are reflected in a hierarchical format, from levels one to five: highly capable individual, contributing team member, competent manager, effective leader and the executive. The executive builds enduring greatness through a paradoxical blend of personal humility and professional will (Collins, 2002:17–40).

- Every good-to-great company had Level 5 Leadership during the pivotal transition years.
- Level 5 refers to a five-level hierarchy of executive capabilities, with Level 5 at the top. They are ambitious, to be sure, but ambitious first and foremost in the interest of the company, not themselves.
- They set up their successors for even greater success in the next generation.
- They display a compelling modesty, are self-effacing and understated.
- The level 5 leaders are fanatically driven, infected with an incurable need to produce sustained results. They are resolved to do whatever it takes to make the company great, no matter how big or hard the decisions.
- They display a workmanlike diligence; attribute success to factors other than themselves and when things go poorly, they look in the mirror and blame themselves, taking full responsibility; they disregard personal greatness.

(b) *First who – then what*

This dimension is based on the premise that you first need to get the right people on the bus (and the wrong people off the bus) before you figure out where to drive it. The following principles are relevant (Collins, 2001:41–64):

- The good leaders commenced the transformation by first getting the right people on the bus (and the wrong people off the bus) and then figured out where to drive it; they therefore focus on the 'who' questions before asking the 'what' decisions – before vision, before strategy, organisation structure, and tactics.
- The good-to-great leaders were rigorous – not ruthless – in people decisions; they did not rely on layoffs and restructuring as a primary strategy for improving performance.
- Three practical principles were applied: when in doubt, keep looking; when you know you need to make a people change – act! Put your best people on your biggest opportunities, not your biggest problems.
- The management teams consisted of people who debate vigorously in search of the best answers, yet who unify behind decisions, regardless of parochial interests.
- Compensation was used not to motivate the right behaviours from the wrong people, but to get and keep the right people in the first place; therefore: people are not your best asset – the right people are; the right person has more to do with character traits and innate capabilities than with specific knowledge, background, or skills.

(c) *Confront the brutal facts*

The path to greatness is refined with the brutal facts of reality (Collincs, 2001:65–89):

- The path to greatness begins by confronting the brutal facts of the organisation's current reality, based on an honest and diligent effort to determine the truth.
- The need to create an organisational climate that reflects the following: people are given an opportunity to be heard and therefore – for the truth to be heard.
- This involves four basic practices: lead with questions, not answers; engage in dialogue and debate, not coercion; conduct autopsies, without blame; and build red-flag mechanisms that turn information into information that cannot be ignored.
- Hit the realities of the situation head-on, retain absolute faith that you can and will prevail in the end.
- Charisma could be more of a liability than an asset – as the strength of this leadership personality can deter people from bringing you the brutal facts.
- Leadership does not begin just with vision – it begins with getting people to confront the brutal facts and to act on the implications.
- Spending time and energy to motivate people is a waste of time – if you have the right people, they will be self-motivated. The key principle is not to de-motivate them. One of the primary ways to de-motivate people is to ignore the brutal facts of reality.

(d) *Hedgehog concept*

Are you a hedgehog or a fox? This concept (Collins, 2001:90–119) is based upon an ancient Greek parable: 'The fox knows many things, but the hedgehog knows one big thing.' Foxes pursue many ends at the same time and see the world in all its complexity. They are 'scattered or diffused, moving on many levels'. Hedgehogs, on the other hand, simplify a complex world into a single organising idea, a basic principle or concept that unifies and guides everything. It doesn't matter how complex the world, a hedgehog reduces all challenges and dilemmas to simple – indeed almost simplistic – hedgehog ideas. They understand that the essence of profound insight is simplicity. The Hedgehog Concept is a simple, crystalline concept that flows from deep understanding about the intersection of the following three circles: what you can be the best in the world at; what drives your economic engine, and what you are deeply passionate about. Good-to-Great companies focus on those activities that ignite their passion. The following key points are relevant with regard to the hedgehog concept:

- The key is to understand what your organisation can be the best in the world at, and equally important, what it cannot be the best at.
- If you cannot be the best in the world at your core business, then your core business cannot form the basis of your Hedgehog Concept.
- The 'best in the world' understanding is a much more severe standard than your core competence. You might have a competence but not necessarily have the capacity to be truly the best in the world at that competence.
- To gain insight into the drivers of your economic engine, search for the one denominator that has the single greatest impact.
- Set the goals and strategies based on understanding not bravado.
- Good-to-great companies know 'one big thing' and stick to it.

(e) *Culture of discipline*

Highly successful ('great') organisations rely on self-disciplined people to enable freedom and responsibility in the organisational framework (Collins, 2001:120–143):

- Sustained good results depend on building a culture full of self-disciplined people who take disciplined action, fanatically consistent with the three circles (best at the world at, what drives the economic engine, and what you are deeply passionate about).
- A culture of discipline involves a duality. On the one hand, it requires people who adhere to a consistent system; yet, on the other hand, it gives people freedom and responsibility in the framework of that system.
- A culture of discipline is about getting disciplined people who engage in disciplined thought and who then take disciplined action.
- People display extreme diligence and stunning intensity.
- Fanatical adherence to the Hedgehog Concept and the willingness to shun opportunities that falls outside the three circles.

(f) *Technology accelerators*
The challenge is how to use technology in the interest of the organisation (Collins, 2001:144–163):

- Avoid technology fads and bandwagons – become pioneers in the application of carefully selected technologies.
- The key question about technology is: does it fit directly with your Hedgehog Concepts? If yes, then you need to become a pioneer in the application of that technology.
- Use technology as an accelerator of momentum, not a creator of it.
- How a company responds to technological change is a good indicator of its inner drive for greatness versus mediocrity.
- 'Crawl, walk, run' can be a very effective approach, even during times of rapid and radical technological change.

(g) *The flywheel and the doom loop*
To become a great company, you need to capitalise on the momentum (Collins, 2001:164–187):

- Revolution means turning the wheel.
- Persistent effort of 'pushing the wheel' in a consistent direction – creates energy and momentum. Then, at some point – breakthrough is achieved.
- Consistent collective effort is required – until the wheel's own heavy weight starts working for you.
- Tremendous power exists in the fact of continued improvement and the delivery of results – the build-up of momentum is irreversible.
- Sustainable transformation follows a predictable pattern of build-up and breakthrough.
- The opposite is the doom loop: rather than accumulating momentum, companies reflecting the doom loop pattern try to skip build-up and jump immediately to breakthrough, resulting in disappointing results and failing to maintain a consistent direction.

Good-to-great leaders do not spend energy and time trying to create alignment, motivate the troops or manage the change. Under the right conditions of commitment, alignment and motivation, change largely takes care of itself. Alignment principally follows from results and momentum, not the other way around.

5.5.8 Selected dimensions of organisational change

The principles of organisational development are briefly described, as well as the management of a merger.

Organisational development

Organisational development refers to the deliberate and purposeful process of developmental change, resulting in the improvement of the healthcare organisation's service delivery, in accordance with the global, national, provincial and local standards and benchmarks.

Process of organisational development

The process of planned change is followed, consisting of strategy analysis, strategy development, strategy execution and lastly, strategy review.

Categories of organisational development

Four categories of organisational development are highlighted (Van Tonder, 2004:94): tuning, adaptation, reorientation and re-creation.

- **Tuning**. This refers to organisational development related to system-compatible changes of an incremental nature and generally of a limited scope. This therefore implies that the health organisation pays attention to the improvement of systems (or in some cases the development of a new system) in the organisation, that is, information management system, knowledge management system, a system to accommodate Clinical Governance and an integrated system to accommodate risk management in the healthcare organisation, both clinical and non-clinical.
- **Adaptation**. This refers to incremental changes in a step-by-step mode that are undertaken by the organisation in response to external dynamics, such as internal restructuring and new quality initiatives. The introduction of performance management (including performance-based budgeting) is an example in the South African context – especially the local government sphere.
- **Reorientation**. This is also referred to as 'frame-bending changes', that relate to major changes that will fundamentally affect the organisation, but not in a manner that will break with the past; continuity of core business delivery is maintained. These changes are anticipated and usually emanate from strategic planning sessions. The principle of intensified community engagement in healthcare service delivery, is a good example of reorientation in a healthcare organisation.
- **Re-creation**. This is also referred to as 'frame-breaking changes', which are significant in terms of the nature and scope of change. This affects the core attributes of the organisation (i.e. leadership, strategy and organisational culture), and could also result in a change of the core business. Re-creation is a high-impact change that is usually associated with trauma. The implementation of the South African Employment Equity Act, as well as the principle of Black Economic Empowerment (BEE) are examples of re-creation at organisational level.

Focus of organisational development

Based on the afore-mentioned categories, organisational development should reflect at least the following in the healthcare organisation:

- Employee-based development by means of a formalised Skills Development Programme, as well as Continuous Professional Development of the clinical staff
- Performance management of employees (refer to Chapter 4, Dimensions of functional management in a healthcare organisation) to improve the quality of clinical and non-clinical performance
- Physical structures include a formalised maintenance, replacement and expansion programme to meet the needs of the healthcare organisation in accordance with the type of business ownership and healthcare service delivery
- Equipment includes a formalised maintenance, replacement and expansion programme to meet the clinical engineering needs of healthcare service delivery
- Systems development and improvement include maintenance and upgrading of existing systems (or introduction of new systems when required) in accordance with the needs identified
- Process development consists of improvement of processes and the quality of outputs and outcomes
- Continuous Quality Improvement programmes and subsequent benchmarking (refer to Chapter 20, Continuous quality improvement in a healthcare organisation).

Attributes of successful organisational development

The attributes of successful organisational development are summarised as follows (Van Tonder, 2004:23–24):

- A recognition of, and sensitivity to, the organisational environment and continuous adaptation to the environment
- A culture of innovation, entrepreneurship, experimentation and risk-taking reflecting a culture of learning
- A talented and unified staff complement. An enhanced focus on people that recognises that talented, quality staff are crucial and need to be developed, extensively trained and retained at all management and operational levels
- Quality service delivery that is value-adding
- Conservative and transparent financial practices – which include a lean staff complement, wise use of corporate assets and a long-term perspective
- A simplified organisational design and a tendency towards decentralised decision-making
- A focus on core business
- A strong sense of identity – reflected in the vision and mission statements
- A quality management approach and style that demonstrates participative management
- Sustainable change requires an acknowledgement of the presence and influence of the different change paradigms operating in the organisation at any time.

The management of a merger

A merger refers to the integration of two or more independently functioning institutions to become a newly transformed organisation. The merger decision is based on a voluntary or forced basis, the latter most probably being a political governmental decision to address the issue of equity, access and redress.

Motives

The motives for a merger are as follows:

- To facilitate equity and political redress
- Improvement of access to healthcare organisations
- Increased efficiency and economies of scale
- Expansion of bargaining power
- Increased responsiveness to societal interest and needs
- Improvement of organisational governance
- Improvement of institutional competitiveness.

Management of a merger

A merger is a highly disruptive Type II level change, with the emergence of a new state out of the remains of the old state(s), which is unknown until it takes shape. The time period (duration) of the change is not easily controlled. This form of change is also referred to as chaotic or complex change and should be based on the principles of transformation management.

A merger is usually divided into three different stages: pre-merger phase, transition phase and post-merger phase. In the case of a forced merger by governmental authorities, a central merger office is usually established to provide leadership and guidance to merging organisations, to monitor the progress, and to act as facilitators (or mediators in the case of conflicting events). A summary of the following dimensions is presented: general principles, pre-merger phase, transition phase and post-merger phase.

(a) *General principles*

The following general principles are applicable during a merger:

- The principles of strategic management, as described in Chapter 2, Strategic management of a healthcare organisation, with reference to strategy analysis, strategy development, strategy execution and strategy review
- The principles of change management (Type I and Type II) as described in this chapter
- The principles of corporate governance (see Chapter 1, Management of a healthcare organisation), with due regard to the following:
  - characteristics of good corporate governance: discipline, transparency, independence and inter-dependence, accountability, responsibility, fairness, social responsibility (business ethics)

- corporate governance duties: duty of care, fiduciary duty and duty to act in powers of authority
- compiling a formal Memorandum of Understanding or a formal Agreement between the merging parties (with due consultation, acceptance based on sufficient consensus, and duly confirmed/ratified in accordance with the business ownership requirements, that is, approved by the Board of Directors)
- composition and establishment of a Strategic Merger Committee and subsequent project teams and other working groups, in accordance with formally established charters/terms of references for each committee, project team and working group
- adequate and appropriate reporting of progress, contributing factors or deadlocks.

(b) *Pre-merger phase*

The pre-merger phase is focused on the following:

- Strategy analysis means conducting a very thorough internal profile analyses of both (or more) merging organisations with reference to at least the following: financial profiles and performance, the nature and scope of service delivery, the quality of service delivery (with due regard to benchmarking indicators), human resources, strategic general management performance, functional management performance (clinical and non-clinical).
- The strategy analyses should be complemented with advanced and extensive research methods being deployed, such as feasibility and due diligence studies.
- Lessons should be learned by other organisations that have merged by accessing published information and by means of institutional visits.
- Strategy development should consist of at least the following:
  - the vision, mission and value statement of the new organisation
  - strategic goals and subsequent action plans
  - leadership and management development plans for the transition and post-merger phases
  - development (alignment) of strategic policies and procedures for the transition phase
  - corporate culture plan (branding, marketing, organisational culture, etc.)
  - the reconfiguration of the core business service delivery and subsequent designs and systems
  - organisational design aligned with the reconfigured core business service delivery and subsequent support services
  - systems support which refers to the alignment of information management systems for the interim transition period and for the post-merger phase
  - risk management strategy for the transition and post-merger phases
  - continuous quality improvement strategy for the transition and post-merger phases

  - communication strategy for the pre-merger phase, as well as for the transition phase
  - contingency plan for the management of unpredicted internal and external challenges and threats.
- Many interactive decision-making and problem-solving techniques are used (consultation, conflict management, group dynamics, negotiations, etc.).
- The progress and management of pre-merger challenges and conflicts should be monitored.
- Of crucial importance in restructuring healthcare provision is the management of professional leadership and relationships, as well as the impact of teamwork and coordination as a determining factor for success.
- The leadership roles of the different general and functional managers are vital and propose that stakeholder analysis is an essential tool in understanding and reconciling objectives at different stages of the merger process.
- Strong leadership stresses the importance of a balance between the desire for complete participation, the necessity of coordination, communication and supporting activities during transition.
- Effectively addressing the people issues and actively involving all the key stakeholders is a priority in the merging process.
- Closure or termination of the 'old organisations' during the last stages of the pre-merger phase (i.e. finalisation of legal personality responsibilities).
- Setting the stage means creating excitement and anticipation for the new organisation.

(c) *Transition phase*

This phase entails the institutionalisation of the merger strategy (see also the principles of strategy execution related to strategic management and change management):

- Execute the merger strategy.
- Celebrate the transformation by means of a launch, publicity, etc.
- Gradually 'phase out' existing pre-merger practices (i.e. old policies, procedures and stationery).
- Exercise strategic leadership to reinforce the merger strategy.
- Create support systems and structures to facilitate the process of change.
- Apply the principles of diversity management where and when applicable.
- Apply the principles of transformation management with reference to the chaos theory.

(d) *Post-merger phase*

Apply the principles of Strategy Review (described in Chapter 2, Strategic management of a healthcare organisation, and in this chapter on Type I change management). The post-merger phase should focus on at least the following:

- Reviewing of the merger strategy for compliance with intended outputs and outcomes
- Management through goal achievement – the celebration of the successes and re-design or modification strategies for the less successful outputs/outcomes, management of the organisation from 'good-to-great'
- Continuous modification of objectives and time limits according to capacity problems and needs, and changes in the current reality
- Building resilience in the event of non-compliance and temporary setbacks
- Performance management at individual, team, unit and departmental levels
- Final evaluation of attainment of goals and performance indicators at the end of the post-merger period as determined
- Evaluation of the quality of healthcare service delivery, based on the principles described in Chapter 20, Continuous quality improvement in a healthcare organisation), consisting of standard setting, monitoring and evaluation of compliance with predetermined standards, and corrective action where appropriate
- Publishing your lessons learned and making yourself available to assist other merging organisations.

5.6 UNDERLYING DYNAMICS

The following underlying dynamics and critical success factors are highlighted: non-alignment of change and inadequate change management, as well as the underlying theoretical assumptions related to change management.

5.6.1 Non-alignment of change

- Environmental turbulence and change – sudden, unpredictable turbulence or change in the operating environment of the organisation
- Unanticipated consequences of evolutionary development – unanticipated consequences of organisational life-cycle stages, which often stem from limited awareness or knowledge
- Inappropriate managerial decision-making – inappropriate managerial change decisions and the selection of a course of action that will not redress the perceived imbalance or non-alignment
- Inadequate or inappropriate organisational cognition – inappropriate interpretation and sense-making of the signs approaching non-alignment. Ineffective managerial cognition is therefore instrumental in exacerbating non-alignment (gradual drift) and hastening the onset of Type II change. Cognitive change is therefore at the core of attempts to avoid misinterpretation of emerging or gradually developing situations of non-alignment and taking of inappropriate or even disastrous decisions and actions.

5.6.2 Inadequate change management

- Inadequate change management with reference to the levels of change with reference to organisational development, transitional change and transformational change
- Inadequate change management performance with reference to strategy analysis, strategy development, strategy execution and strategy review.

5.6.3 Theoretical assumptions related to change and change management

The following underlying theoretical assumptions related to organisational change and change management will impact on the success and quality of change management in an organisation (Van Tonder, 2004:159–161):

- Organisations are dynamic entities that are continuously engaged in a battle for survival and as a result need to assimilate and adapt to changes in their environments, while at the same time navigating through natural growth and development stages to greater levels of complexity and sophistication. This requires a fine balance between focusing on external adaptation challenges and internal developmental challenges, and requires an equally careful and considered organisational focus, which will determine how and where energy will be channelled and therefore where and how organisational resources will be allocated.
- Organisations naturally drift towards situations of non-alignment, or, through abrupt and marked changes in the operating environment, may be confronted by sudden and more elaborate and challenging situations of non-alignment. Organisations attempt to re-establish alignment through rational action of management, which in turn is premised on management's understanding and interpretation of the environmental and developmental adaptive challenges that the organisation faces. Rational change initiatives by managers may not be sufficient, on occasion, in which event the organisation's internal dynamics should inevitably prompt 'corrective' change, failing which, the organisation could cease to exist (i.e. bankruptcy or takeover).
- Whether the realignment of the organisation is a matter of rational choice (i.e. under managerial control) or not, change processes in organisations unfold in either Type I or Type II change mode(s), where the former entails a gradual, incremental and systematic yet time-intensive form of adaptive change. The Type II mode is of an intensely disruptive and system-wide nature – often experienced as being beyond the control of the organisation. Organisations in effect pass through sequences or cycles of both types that are best described as a dynamic equilibrium (Type I change), punctuated by a burst of Type II change mode. Complexity theory (see Chapter 3, Selected management models) further illuminates this dynamic, proposing that Type I and Type II change are inextricably linked. These two core change types characterise change processes irrespective of where they originate, and describe change types observed in each

of the major change paradigms (i.e. ecological, rational-purposive, life-cycle, or cognitive change at the organisational level). Both Type I and Type II changes bring about a different condition and/or state in an organisation. This change in condition or state occurs through:
- replacing the pre-change condition or state
- contradicting the pre-change condition or state (i.e. introducing opposition)
- combining (merging or incorporation) the pre-change condition or state.

- Because people populate organisations, we recognise that organisational change is ultimately reducible to pooled or collective change, although its collective nature further increases the complexity of dealing with change. At its most fundamental level, individual change comprises change in individual schemata and the emotion or effect associated with these schemata. Successful or sustainable individual change entails the permanent alteration of both schemata and their associated effect. Individual change requires an acceptance at the emotional level of the inevitability of the change, enabling an alteration of meaning structure or schemata at the cognitive level.
- Chaotic or complex change, which suggests that the magnitude and intensity of the energy build-up from forces for and against change (i.e. through resistance), and more specifically the difference between forces for and against change, will determine the intensity and magnitude or energy dissipation, that is, change.
- In practice, however, organisations typically fail to recognise that dealing appropriately with change, regardless of whether it is induced by external environmental conditions or internal rational or development considerations, and regardless of whether it is reactive or proactive, will entail a change of shared organisational schemata with their associated effect. Organisations similarly fail to recognise that:
  - the dissemination of information is an inadequate approach to changing entrenched schemata
  - ignorance (or neglect) of the emotional content exacerbates resistance to change initiatives, the cost of which in financial, social and human terms is seldom recognised
  - in essence, sustainable change entails recognising the nature and demands of personal (individual) change.

5.7 CONCLUDING STATEMENTS

The following concluding statements are made:

- Change is defined as an initiative which alters critical organisational processes, which in turn influence individual behaviours, and which subsequently impact on organisational outcomes.
- Change management refers to the management of developmental change (organisational development), transitional change (Type I change management) and transformational change in the organisation (Type II transformation

management), by means of strategy analysis, strategy development, strategy execution and strategy review.

- Change management is practised in the dynamic context of external and internal environmental forces.
- Two types of change are differentiated: Type I (gradual and adaptive) and Type II (a major disruptive and paradigm-altering organisational-wide change).
- The purpose of change management is to timeously align the healthcare organisation with the internal and external environmental forces and dynamics, to facilitate continuous purpose-driven organisational development, transitional organisational change and transformational organisational change, lastly to facilitate sustainability and profitability of the organisation.
- The managers act as the main change agents in the organisation.
- There are different levels of change in the organisation – individual, level, organisational development, transitional change, as well as transformational change.
- A continuous and balanced focus designed to secure optimal external and internal alignment will enable Type I (gradual and adaptive) change.
- A discontinuous focus, or disproportionate over- or under-emphasis on either external or internal alignment, rapidly increases the probability of Type II change.
- A steady-state, incremental or step-by-step sequential change which generally evolves over an extended period of time, does not have a disruptive influence on the system and is generally in the control of the system and organisation.
- A major, disruptive, unpredictable, paradigm-altering and system-wide change which has a very sudden onset and escalates rapidly to a point where it is perceived as being beyond the control of the system and organisation.
- Change management is influenced by various models/paradigms, such as ecological change, rational-purposive, evolutionary organisational life-cycle, cognitive change, and the good-to-great model.
- Organisational development is concerned with tuning, adaptation, reorientation and re-creation with reference to employee-based development, performance management, the maintenance, replacement and expansion of physical structures and equipment, systems development, process development, as well as continuous quality improvement.
- Organisational mergers are based on the formalised process of Type II change, with reference to the pre-merger phase, the transition phase, and the post-merger phase.
- The critical success factors (underlying dynamics) impacting on the quality of change management focus on the following: environmental turbulence, unanticipated consequences of evolutionary organisational development, inadequate managerial decision-making and inadequate organisational cognition. The theoretical assumptions related to change management are also applicable.

Self-assessment

(1) Compile an organisational development strategy for your healthcare organisation.

(2) Your local district hospital has to be converted into a clinic for the roll-out of the Antiretroviral Therapy regime. Compile a change management strategy for this Type II change in the organisation.

6 Communication management in a healthcare organisation

KEY CONCEPTS

Communication process
Communication management
Communication strategy
Public relations management
Information management
Tele/electronic medicine
Management of patient records
Knowledge management

SPECIFIC OUTCOMES

After studying this chapter, you should be able to:

- Interpret the legal, professional-ethical and healthcare **context**, with reference to the management of communication in a healthcare organisation: general and functional dimensions of communication management
- Analyse and debate the **purpose** of communication management in a healthcare organisation
- Identify the **role-players** and interpret their roles and responsibilities in communication management
- Describe the following **dimensions** of communication management: formal internal communication, informal internal communication, public relations, information management, tele/electronic medicine, the management of patient records and knowledge management
- Debate the **underlying dynamics** that could impact on the quality of communication management in a healthcare organisation.

6.1 INTRODUCTION

All the clinical and non-clinical members/practitioners in a healthcare organisation are involved in formal and informal, internal and external communication with one another, patients and their family members and visitors, the community stakeholders, the media and other members of the public on a daily basis. It is therefore crucial to have a trustworthy system of communication (general and specialised or functional dimensions of communication) in the healthcare organisation. It is important to understand the process, the nature and scope of communication and to effectively manage all the specialised functional dimensions of communication in the healthcare organisation, for example the management of patient records, clinical-related information management and knowledge management.

The intention of this chapter is not to re-write the process of general communication – but to rather focus on the management of specialised dimensions of communication in the healthcare organisation. This chapter therefore focuses on the following (Figure 6.1 reflects the conceptual framework of this chapter):

- A brief overview of the communication process with reference to the nature, scope and modes of communication
- Communication management in the healthcare organisation related to the following: the process of communication management and dimensions of communication management in a healthcare organisation, which consists of formal internal communication, informal internal communication, public relations, information management, tele/electronic medicine, the management of patient records and knowledge management.

6.2 CONTEXT

Communication management in a healthcare organisation is determined by the type and nature of business ownership (refer to Chapter 1, Management of a healthcare organisation), and influenced by the macro-environment, the national, provincial and local environment, organisational context, professional-ethical and legal framework of practitioners and corporate governance.

6.2.1 Macro-environment

The macro-environment is external to both the organisation and the communication environment, and consists of several distinct components:

- **Technological environment**. This continuously brings change and innovation, requiring constant realignment of organisations and subsequent communication management strategies and practices in this regard.
- **Economic environment**. Factors such as inflation, exchange rates, recessions, and monetary and fiscal policy influence the prosperity of the business/organisation and subsequent communication framework, strategy and systems.
- **Social environment**. Consumer lifestyles, habits and values, formed by culture, make certain demands on the business/organisation. The internal and external organisational profile (refer to Chapter 2, Strategic management of a healthcare organisation) impacts on the nature and scope of communication, and the modes and channels of communication utilised in the organisation.
- **International environment**. Local and foreign political trends and events affect the business organisation (micro-environment), as well as the communication environment. The individual business organisation has very little or no control

Figure 6.1 Visual presentation of communication management in a healthcare organisation

Context	Macro-environment National, provincial and local context Organisational context Professional-ethical and legal framework of practitioners Corporate governance
Role-players	General communication: sender and recipient Functional communication managers
Purpose	To facilitate the quality of internal and external communication
Dimensions of communication management	Communication process Communication management: strategy analysis, strategy development, strategy execution and strategy review Dimensions of functional communication management ▸ Formal internal communication ▸ Informal internal communication ▸ Public relations ▸ Information management ▸ Tele/electronic medicine ▸ Management of patient records ▸ Knowledge management
Underlying dynamics	Institutional determinants 'Fit-for-purpose' communication strategy Leadership and management commitment to specialised, functional communication management Existence and management of communication barriers

over the macro-environment and its influence on these variables is negligible. The new economic order that is taking shape worldwide is indicative of the increasing globalisation of the world economy. Globalisation and the trend towards a borderless world continually affect businesses and organisations in new and different ways, resulting in innovative communication practices.

6.2.2 National, provincial and local context

Communication management in the healthcare organisation is first and foremost influenced by the national, provincial and local legislative framework and subsequent formal external communication network. Legislation related to the access of information is also applicable.

6.2.3 Organisational context

The organisational context is based on the type of business ownership (public or private) and subsequent legislative and service delivery framework, the nature and size of the organisation, and other related internal determinants. The internal organisational culture – also influenced by the human resource profile – determines many communication practices in the organisation.

6.2.4 Professional-ethical and legal framework of practitioners

The professional-ethical and legal framework of practitioners – especially related to clinical practitioners – is crucial for the determination of specialised communication management systems, for example clinical documentation, financial documentation and reporting.

6.2.5 Corporate governance

The principles of corporate governance related to the board of directors and subsequent Code of Corporate Practices and Conduct, also direct the nature of communication management in healthcare organisations (refer to Chapter 1, Management of a healthcare organisation). Minimum reporting principles on certain aspects of corporate governance are also stipulated and applicable to all healthcare organisations that are governed by the national financial management legislation.

6.3 PURPOSE

The purpose of communication management is to facilitate the quality of internal and external communication, in accordance with the core business practice of the healthcare organisation, to attain the pre-determined goals and outcomes.

6.4 ROLE-PLAYERS

The role-players in communication management are first and foremost the sender of the message and the recipient thereof. In addition to these role-players, there are many functional communication managers (i.e. public relations officer and knowledge manager), as well as the internal and external stakeholders, in accordance with the various communication management structures and systems in the healthcare service.

6.5 DIMENSIONS OF COMMUNICATION MANAGEMENT IN THE HEALTHCARE ORGANISATION

A brief discussion is given on the following: review of the communication process, general overview and communication management, formal internal communication management, informal internal communication management, public relations, information management, tele/electronic medicine, the management of patient records and knowledge management.

6.5.1 Review of the communication process

A brief review of the communication process is given, with specific reference to the definition of communication, the types of communication, interpersonal communication and communication barriers.

Definition of communication

Communication is a two-way process whereby information (the message) is sent from one person (sender) through a mode or channel to another (the receiver or recipient) who in turn responds by interpreting the message and responding, with due regard of many communication barriers (Van Staden, Marx & Erasmus-Kritzinger, 2002:12–14). Refer to Figure 6.2 and the Glossary at the end of this book.

Types of communication

Communication can take place internally in the organisation or externally with members of the governing authority, the media, stakeholders, or the public/community. Communication is furthermore classified as formal or informal – communication can only be effective if the sender makes use of an appropriate

Figure 6.2 The process of communication

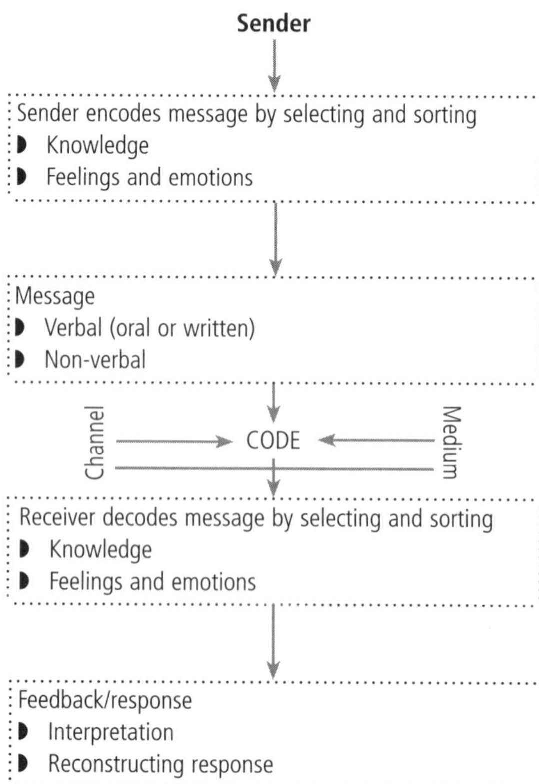

formal or informal channel to get the message across. Organisational success demands that information flows up, down and across the organisation – from the boardroom to the operational floor and from one department/unit to the other. Therefore communication channels include vertical, horizontal and diagonal channels (refer to the Glossary). The type of channel chosen affects the quality of communication. Channel richness refers to the amount of information that can be transmitted during a communication episode. Selection of the appropriate channel depends on the nature of the message. Routine messages convey data that is easily understood and does not necessarily require a very rich channel. Non-routine messages, which are more likely to be misinterpreted, require richer channels. Communication is used not only to convey information, but to also persuade and/or influence people. Communication can take place between two people, but often takes place between communication teams (small or large teams), depending on the organisational design of the healthcare organisation. The principles of group dynamics should therefore also be taken into consideration.

Interpersonal communication

In addition to the afore-mentioned, the principles of interpersonal communication are also important. Interpersonal communication can be verbal or non-verbal, in informal or formal communication circumstances.

Communication barriers

A communication barrier relates to any factor that could distort or confuse the message, competes against communication or prevents a message from being received. The most common barriers relate to physical, physiological, psychological, perceptual and semantic barriers:

- **Physical barriers**. These refer to structural or system-based obstructers, such as noise, indistinct telephone line, inadequate image on television ('snowy image') and disconnection of the electronic system.
- **Physiological barriers**. These refer to physical impairments, such as hearing, vision/eyesight and vocal cord obstruction. Extreme temperature variations in a room could impact on the physiological sensing abilities.
- **Psychological barriers**. These include anger, depression, fear, distrust, etc.
- **Perceptual barriers**. Perceptual differences, based on cultural, biological and other differences, could impact on the interpretation (nature and scope) of the message. Perceptions are often influenced by employee background, gender, culture and ethnic variables, age, religion, level of education and training, intelligence, occupation, interests, needs, and interpretation and judgemental abilities.
- **Semantic barriers**. These include language proficiency, different words (especially abbreviations used in healthcare service delivery), slang, jargon, accent, etc.

Figure 6.3 The process of communication management

6.5.2 General overview of communication management

Communication management refers to a process of strategy analysis, strategy development, strategy execution and strategy review (refer to Figure 6.3), focusing on formal and informal internal communication, public relations and dimensions of functional or specialised communication management in the healthcare organisation, such as information management, tele/electronic medicine, the management of patient records and knowledge management.

The process of communication management

- **Communication strategy analysis**. Conduct an internal organisational profile analysis (see Chapter 2, Strategic management of a healthcare organisation), as well as an external (economic, social, technological and physical) environment analysis. The communication capacity of the healthcare organisation, as well as the employee desires, needs and preferences, with due regard of the nature of the organisational design and the organisational culture, should be taken into consideration. The organisation's strategic plan (vision, mission, goals and the subsequent action plans) should also direct the nature and scope of the communication strategy.
- **Communication strategy development**. All the formal and informal internal and external communication needs are aligned with the nature and scope of the healthcare organisation's core business and subsequent strategic plan. The communication vision, goals, objectives, values and related action plans are developed. The communication strategy should therefore contain the formal internal and external communication strategy, as well as the informal internal communication strategy. Of particular importance are the information management system, telemedicine, the management of patient records, as well as knowledge management. Strategies to counteract the barriers related to communication – especially cultural-based barriers – should also be reflected in the communication strategy.
- **Strategy execution**. The organisation's communication strategy is executed, with continuous risk management and adjustment of the strategy, and monitoring of compliance with the predetermined standards.

- **Strategy review**. The communication strategy is reviewed for goal attainment and compliance with the predetermined performance indicators and outcomes. Lessons learned are documented and taken into consideration for the renewal of the strategy.

6.5.3 Formal internal communication management

Formal internal communication is communication between the employees themselves: managers and practitioners (clinical and non-clinical). Internal formal communication has a very specific function – the command, relationship and ambiguity-management functions (Van Staden et al., 2002:16):

- **The command function.** This includes the delegation of duties, tasks and responsibilities (DTRs) and the subsequent execution of these DTRs, in accordance with the organisational strategy, values and professional-ethical and legal framework.
- **The relationship function**. This refers to creating and maintaining good interpersonal relationships with the healthcare organisation.
- **The ambiguity-management function**. This means getting the job done while showing concern for the needs and feelings of employees.

Standards for the formal internal communication strategy

The formal internal communication strategy complies with at least the following:

- There is an organisational policy on formal internal communication with reference to the modes (policies and procedures, memoranda, newsletters, circulars, etc.), as well as the format of such communication methods.
- Corporate decision-making and consultation structures are formalised, in accordance with the organisational design and subsequent coordinating structures and mechanisms in the organisation (see Chapter 1, Management of a healthcare organisation).
- Departmental (middle management) and operational (unit/area) decision-making and consultation structures are formalised in accordance with the principles of corporate governance (PricewaterhouseCoopers, 2003:22).
- Each decision-making and consultation structure (i.e. board of directors and corporate committees) is constituted and legitimised with an approved Terms of Reference or Charter, in accordance with the principles of corporate governance (PricewaterhouseCoopers, 2003:22), complying with at least the following criteria: name of the committee, purpose and objectives, aligned with that of the organisation's vision, mission and value statements, composition of the committee, lifespan (term of office), role and functions, scope of authority, including extent of power to make decisions and/or recommendations, meeting procedures and reporting mechanism.
- There are policies and procedures related to statuary and non-statuary decision-making, consultation (i.e. annual general meeting) and reporting.

- There is a formal process by which top/corporate management considers the reports (monthly/quarterly and annual) submitted by the various decision-making structures in the healthcare organisation.
- There is a formal process by which middle and operational management considers the reports (monthly/quarterly and annual) submitted by the various decision-making structures in the healthcare organisation.
- There is a formal process whereby the level managers give feedback to the subordinates on the reports and other formal communication received.
- There is a policy and subsequent procedures for the disclosing of relevant information to the stakeholders, for example interactive website and annual published report.
- There is a policy and/or code of conduct on the accessing and utilisation of electronic communication modes, for example Internet and personal cell/mobile phones, in the organisation.
- There are ethical communication standards (ethical code of conduct) on internal formal communication, focusing at least on trustworthiness of the facts, transparency, fairness, accountability and social responsibility (refer to Chapter 1, Management of a healthcare organisation, with reference to the principles of corporate governance).
- The organisational skills development strategy reflects at least the following with reference to communication:
  - general formal communication skills
  - conducting of meetings: the roles and responsibilities of the convenor/chairperson and other committee members
  - the writing of minutes, memorandums, reports, etc.
  - interpersonal relationship skills
  - telephone etiquette
  - how to deal with clients (patients and/or significant others) with reference to client interaction, client expectations and satisfaction with service delivery, patient/client anger and patient fear
  - cultural diversity, for example ethnocentricity, stereotyping and prejudice, cultural differences
  - group dynamics
  - consultation skills
  - negotiating skills
  - information management
  - the management of patient records
  - knowledge management in the organisation.
- There is a strategy/plan to counteract communication barriers in the organisation.

Critical success factors related to formal internal communication in the organisation

The following critical success factors are highlighted:

- Communication routes should constantly be kept open.
- Staff at lower levels should always be able to gain access to their superiors.
- Upward communication in the organisation should be encouraged.
- Messages should not pass through too many intermediaries before reaching their final destination.
- There should be the fewest possible management levels and the shortest possible chain of command.
- There should be purposeful organisational development to accommodate the demands related to formal internal communication.
- The suitability of the selected communication channel(s) should be investigated in accordance with the level of communication – rather use more than one channel in the case of general information, such as salary issues.
- Information overload should be avoided through a specific chosen communication channel.
- Staff should be mindful of the various communication barriers and initiate strategies to mitigate these barriers.
- Purposeful skills development of employees on the various communication strategies and abilities (knowledge, skills, values and attitudes) should take place.
- The principles of positive interpersonal skills should be applied during formal internal communication (i.e. during meetings).
- There should be adequate conflict management.
- Communication-related leadership abilities should be encouraged.

6.5.4 Informal internal communication management

There are many internal communication types and modes in the healthcare organisation (Van Staden et al., 2002:23–25):

- **Phatic communication**. This refers to the daily informal conveying of feelings and showing good manners, personal interest and respect, such as casual greetings: how are you? have a nice weekend, how was your weekend? are you coping? This form of communication contributes to a culture of openness, cooperation, respect, etc. between employees.
- **Informal social groupings**. This refers to the natural forming of social groups based on commonalities, shared interests, etc.
- **The grapevine**. This refers to the informal and unofficial system of communication in which information is based on casual communication and rumours.

Informal communication strategy

The informal communication strategy reflects at least the following:

- Code of conduct on informal internal communication in the organisation (i.e. zero tolerance for abusive and foul communication)
- Guidelines, value statements, and/or policies on social groupings and social gatherings
- Open-door policy by managers, in accordance with the nature and scope of core business and the subsequent service delivery
- Utilisation of the grapevine to the benefit of the healthcare organisation:
  - rumours are activated due to inadequate or incorrect information, requiring immediate interaction and provision of the right information
  - identify certain informants and utilise them to inform the managers of grapevine messages
  - utilise the grapevine to reinforce positive information.

Critical success factors related to internal informal communication

A few critical success factors are highlighted:

- Be aware of different frames of reference – the way people think about people and their world, their particular world views and their preferences.
- Apply the principles of unconditional acceptance during informal internal communication with colleagues/employees.
- Be (or become) acquainted with the organisational culture, with due regard of cultural diversity and social dynamics in the organisation.
- Apply the principles of positive interpersonal skills during informal internal communication.

6.5.5 Public relations management

Every business or organisation has to interact with its environment, and included in this environment are role-players that could have a significant influence on the fortunes of the organisation. This influence could be to the benefit or detriment of the organisation. Sound public relations and the protection of the healthcare organisation's reputation and credibility are important. The objective is to be proactive in the management of the interactions with the role-players that could impact on the reputation of the healthcare organisation. The main task is to create and maintain a favourable public opinion of the organisation. This requires the management of public relations. In managing public relations, the principles of business ethics and social responsibilities, in accordance with the principles of corporate governance, are important (refer to Chapter 1, Management of a healthcare organisation).

Public relations management is defined as a deliberate, planned and sustained process of communication between a business and its publics for the purpose of obtaining, maintaining or improving good strategic relations and mutual understanding between the organisation and its various publics – both internal and external (De J. Cronjé, 2004:354). Public relations management is therefore concerned with the following (De J. Cronjé, et al., 2004:352–354):

- It facilitates a favourable corporate image of the organisation.
- It acts as an interface between a business/organisation and its environment: it interprets the mission, programmes and operations of management to its publics.
- It monitors trends in the business environment and the public perception of the business for management.
- It gives support to the marketing and other functions of the business.
- It helps management in its endeavour to satisfy the need for social responsibility.

Advantages of a favourable corporate image

A favourable corporate image has the following advantages:

- Service providers (such as credible healthcare practitioners) more readily support the organisation.
- Consumers and patients more readily support the organisation.
- Suppliers more readily give credit for longer periods to the business/ organisation.
- People like to work for such an organisation, resulting in a favourable human resource investment and a lower staff turnover.

Criteria of excellence related to public relations management

The following criteria of excellence are highlighted:

- Public relations management is reflected as a separate functional dimension of management in the healthcare organisation.
- There is a formalised public relations management organisational design/ structure with a designated functional manager and support system (i.e. researchers and environmental scanners).
- There is a public relations management strategy (vision, mission, goals, action plans and performance indicators) – based on the principles of strategy analysis, strategy development, strategy execution and strategy review – and aligned with the organisational strategic plan.
- The public relations management strategy reflects an integration with reference to the total quality management of the healthcare organisation, with due regard to the fact that the quality of service delivery, business ethics and social responsibilities, is everyone's business.
- There are subsequent policies and procedures in the healthcare organisation related to public relations.
- There is a policy with subsequent procedures to deal with the media and press conferences.
- There is a skills development programme for employees on how to deal with the public and in particular the 'client' – regardless of who the client is.

- Patient Satisfaction Indices (PSI) are determined, in accordance with the type of business ownership, the nature and scope of the core business rendered by the healthcare organisation and the organisation's Continuous Quality Improvement strategy (refer to Chapter 20, Continuous quality improvement in a healthcare organisation). Appropriate corrective measures are undertaken in the case of negative PSIs.

6.5.6 Information management

Information management refers to the constructive management of information in the interest of quality decision-making with reference to the management of the healthcare organisation's core business. The management of information in the healthcare service is therefore a crucial aspect of communication management. Over time, organisations have become more effective in:

- Identifying information needs
- Designing information management systems to accommodate these needs
- Defining and capturing data and information that could add value to decision-making and the outcome of healthcare service delivery
- Analysing data and transforming it into information
- Transmitting and reporting data and information
- Integrating and using data.

Although computerisation and other technologies improve efficiency, the principles of good information management apply to all methods, whether paper-driven or electronic. Information technology refers to the hardware, software, telecommunication, database and other information-related resources in the organisation, used to store data and to make it available in the form of information for organisational decision-making. The following questions are relevant to facilitate the quality of information management:

- What information should be collected as opposed to what is in fact being collected?
- How is the information collected and collated?
- What does the flow of the information entail?
- How is the information utilised by the managers and practitioners?

In addition to the patient and clinical information management required, the principles of corporate governance are also applicable. The King II Report 2002 requires disclosure of at least the following statutory reports of listed companies and those public institutions governed by the public finance legislation (PricewaterhouseCoopers, 2003: 40–43; 93):

- Annual financial statements: balance sheet, income statement, statement of changes in equity, cash flow statement, director's report and auditor's report
- Complete and meaningful corporate disclosure, targeted at a wide range of stakeholders and management's stewardship

- Quarterly and annual reports of committees and subsequent meetings
- Risk management and internal control (refer also to Chapters 17, Financial management in a healthcare organisation, and Chapter 18, Risk management in a healthcare organisation).

Information, knowledge and wisdom are more than just simply collections. Rather, the whole represents more than the sum of its parts and has a synergy of its own. When we encounter a piece of data, we attempt to find a way to attribute meaning to it. We do this by associating it with other things. The implication here is that when there is no context, there is little or no meaning. A collection of data for which there is no relation between the pieces of data is not information. The pieces of data may represent information; it depends on the knowledge of the interpreter. Information is quite simply an understanding of the relationships between pieces of data, or between pieces of data and other information. While information entails an understanding of the relations between data, it generally does not provide a foundation for why the data is what it is, nor an indication as to how the data is likely to change over time. Information is a relationship between data with great dependence on context for its meaning. Pattern embodies both a consistency and completeness of relations which, to an extent, creates its own context. When a pattern relation exists amidst the data and information, the pattern has the potential to represent knowledge. It only becomes knowledge, however, when one is able to realise and understand the patterns and their implications. A pattern that represents knowledge also provides, when the pattern is understood, a high level of reliability or predictability as to how the pattern will evolve over time, for patterns are seldom static. Patterns that represent knowledge have completeness to them that information simply does not contain. Wisdom arises when one understands the foundational principles responsible for the patterns representing knowledge being what they are. And wisdom, even more so than knowledge, tends to create its own context. So, in summary the following associations can reasonably be made:

- **Information** relates to description, definition, or perspective (what, who, when, where).
- **Knowledge** comprises strategy, practice, method, or approach (how).
- **Wisdom** embodies principle, insight, moral, or archetype (why).

Figure 6.4 demonstrates the process of decision-making as associated with the concepts of the data gathering, information and knowledge. Refer also to the section on knowledge management in this chapter.

Standards for a management information system

The following standards are highlighted:

- There is a 'fit-for-purpose' management information system (MIS) in accordance with the internal and external information management and reporting needs of the healthcare organisation.

Figure 6.4 The relationship between data, information and knowledge

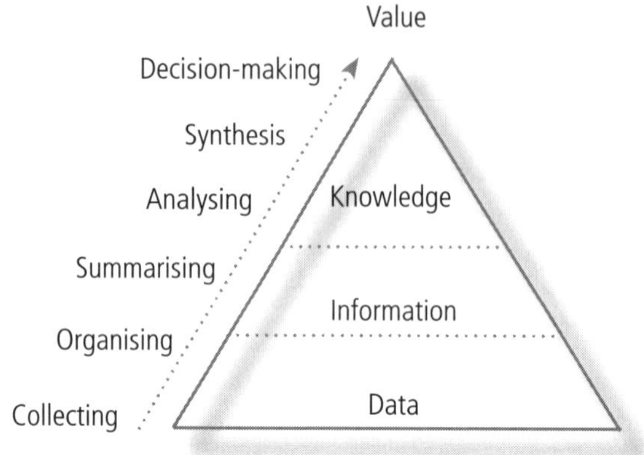

- There is a functional manager who is responsible and accountable for the management information system.
- The information management system is compliant with the professional-ethical and legal requirements.
- There are policies and procedures to ensure confidentiality, security and integrity of data and information with reference to at least the following: control of access, the user's obligation to keep data and information confidential, and disciplinary measures in the case of transgressing the policy.
- There is a process to aggregate data.
- The aggregation of data is used to support decision-making at operational, middle management and corporate management levels.
- The management information system is compliant with the short- and long-term needs for internal and external reporting, in accordance with legal and quality requirements.
- The storing and retrieval of data are in accordance with legal requirements.
- There is a maintenance and replacement system in place to ensure business continuity management.

6.5.7 Management of patient records

Patient records refer to the paper-evidence of the administrative (biographical detail, admission data, etc.) and the clinical data reflected in the patient record. Providing patient care is a complex endeavour that is highly dependent on accurate or trustworthy information. To provide, coordinate and integrate healthcare service delivery, healthcare organisations rely on information about the science of care, individual and collective patient care provided, including the individual and collective results and outcomes of the care rendered, as well as their own individual and collective performance. Patient data is a resource that requires specialised management, in accordance with the administrative and discipline-based professional legal and ethical frameworks. In addition to the principles of information management already discussed, the following standards for the management of patient records are highlighted.

There is a trustworthy patient management information system, based on at least the following needs:

- The needs of the various service providers and multi-disciplinary practitioners
- The needs of the various accountable corporate and legislative authorities, in accordance with the type of business ownership (public/private and level of service delivery) for reporting and accounting purposes
- Professional-ethical and legal requirements of the various professional councils
- Organisational and operational general and clinical management needs.

The patient management system ensures that at least the following security and trustworthy measures are met:

- Adequate and appropriate technological data/records support system and infrastructure
- Policies and procedures to manage authorisation of entries by administrative staff and clinical multi-disciplinary practitioners only
- Patient confidentiality in accordance with legislative and professional-ethical requirements, including the requirements stipulated in the Patients' Rights Charter
- Access control of patient records
- Sustainability of data integrity (i.e. risk management systems and procedures)
- Adequate and safe storage of patient records (including contracted outsourcing)
- A record retrieval management system
- Ethical clearance systems and methods for utilisation of data for research purposes.

There is an adequate and appropriate system to aggregate data for user needs:

- There is a process to aggregate data for internal organisational management requirements: to support quality management programmes and general management decision-making (i.e. average of hospital stay and bed occupancy rates), as well as clinical decision-making (clinical indicators, etc.).
- There is a process to aggregate data for external organisational purposes, required by law or for the purpose of national, provincial and local decision-making, management and benchmarking.
- The system makes provision to comply with the legal requirements on the promotion of access to information (South Africa, 2000).

General legal requirements are adhered to:

- There is a clinical record for each patient, which contains sufficient/substantial information to identify the patient and his/her record accordingly, support the diagnosis, justify the care and treatment prescribed and rendered, documentation on the execution of care and treatment by the different members of the multi-disciplinary team, and to promote continuity of care among the different care providers.

- All entries are legible.
- Every entry is reflected against a date and time.
- There is a signature of the clinician and relevant qualification or professional registration level for each entry.
- Only authorised abbreviations (by the relevant professional regulatory bodies) are used.

Clinical recordkeeping is in accordance with the legal and professional-ethical requirements (laid down by the professional regulatory bodies), with reference to:
- Clinical assessment data
- Planned diagnostic, treatment and care interventions
- Evidence of the implementation and execution of the planned interventions by the various multi-disciplinary clinical practitioners
- Multi-disciplinary referrals and interventions reflected in the patient record
- The outcome of care (continuous and final assessment and evaluation) recorded by the designated multi-disciplinary clinical practitioners
- The prohibition of transcribing of prescribed medicine.

There is a formal auditing system in place to assess the quality of patient record keeping, compliant with at least the following:
- The auditing procedure is formalised by means of an auditing committee with a charter or terms of reference in accordance with the corporate management principles in this regard.
- The auditing system is compliant with the principles of validity and reliability.
- The dissemination of auditing results is in accordance with the requirements reflected in the healthcare organisation's quality improvement programme in this regard.
- The results of auditing are used to improve the quality of patient recordkeeping in the healthcare organisation, including the continuous professional development of all service providers concerned.

6.5.8 Tele/electronic medicine

Telemedicine or electronic medicine refers to the utilisation of electronic systems to supply healthcare information to the public or other clinicians, or to assist in the treatment of illnesses. A few standards are highlighted, if this service is provided by the healthcare organisation:
- There is a functional manager who is responsible and accountable for the management of the system and allocation of assistants, to ensure the trustworthiness of the system and the assistants, for example clinicians providing telephonic healthcare information to the members of the public phoning in.
- A quality system is in place to ensure frequent updating of abilities (knowledge, skills, values and attitudes), credentialing, and privileging (refer to Chapter 20,

Continuous quality improvement in a healthcare organisation) of those providing the tele/electronic service.

- The system is compliant with the professional-ethical and legal requirements related to healthcare service delivery and the management of information.
- There is a system of indemnity insurance to protect the healthcare organisation against malpractice or incorrect information provided by the clinicians, who are accountable for their own professional acts and omissions, in accordance with the relevant professional-ethical and legal framework.

6.5.9 Knowledge management

Knowledge is seen as an important resource and asset of an organisation – it is regarded as a new form of capital in what is referred to as the 'knowledge economy'. At the strategic level the organisation needs to be able to analyse and plan its business in terms of the knowledge it currently has and the knowledge it needs for future business processes. At the tactical level (middle level) the organisation is concerned with identifying and formalising existing knowledge, acquiring new knowledge for future use, archiving it in organisational memories and creating systems that enable effective and efficient application of the knowledge in the organisation. At the operational level knowledge is used in everyday practice by professional practitioners – especially with reference to what is seen as best practice – who need access to the right knowledge, at the right time, in the right location. Healthcare organisations therefore need to share and manage knowledge as a valuable resource. Organisations that suffer from an anti-knowledge culture reflect the following:

- Project failures are not addressed or challenged.
- Assumptions about new projects and ventures are not challenged due to an inadequate knowledge database.
- Lessons learned from previous positive or negative business-related experiences are not identified and utilised for future projects or interventions.
- Individual knowledge ownership is protected with no or little sharing or transfer of knowledge in the interest of the patient care.
- There is lack of entrepreneurship in the healthcare organisation.

Knowledge management is the process of identifying, collecting, storing and transforming data and information into an intellectual asset that is available to all staff members. It aims to develop a solid base of intellectual capital by gathering and sharing the knowledge of individual staff members (De J. Cronjé et al., 2004:586). Knowledge management is a field that is inevitably multidisciplinary and multicontextual – it is a field that is both a practical science of management and a theoretical science of manageability. It is the process through which healthcare organisations generate value from their intellectual and knowledge-based assets. Most often, generating value from such assets involves sharing them among employees, departments and even with other health-related institutions in an effort to devise best practices. While knowledge management is often facilitated by information technology, technology by itself is not knowledge management. Knowledge management in healthcare services is all about cultural reformation along with a little technology (www.knowledgemanagementnetwork.com/whatis.htm). Knowledge management is the acquisition and use of resources to create an environment in which information is accessible to individuals and in which individuals acquire, share and use that information to develop their own knowledge base and are encouraged and enabled to apply their knowledge for the benefit of the organisation. In its simplest form, knowledge management is about encouraging people to share knowledge and ideas to create value-adding products and services.

A brief summary of knowledge management is given, based on the following: the advantages of knowledge management, the difference between knowledge and data/information, the purpose of a knowledge management system (KMS), the process of knowledge management (De J. Cronjé et al., 2004:587–589) and a few criteria of excellence in the management of knowledge.

Advantages of knowledge management

The advantages of knowledge management are as follows:

- To increase workplace efficiency, and to retain, re-use and exchange knowledge as a resource to facilitate quality, productivity, effectiveness and sustainability of core service delivery, and time management
- To foster innovation by encouraging the free flow of ideas
- To improve service delivery by increasing response time
- To enhance employee retention rates by recognising their intellectual capacity and property
- To assist with organisational development, restructuring and transformation with due regard of the 'expertise mix'
- To make employees 'all-knowing'.

The difference between knowledge and data/information

- Knowledge arises from direct perceptions of the world and nothing is real that is not knowable in this way.
- Data and information represent facts and the classification thereof with no interpretative or relational significance (i.e. the signs and symptoms of a patient are listed), as opposed to knowledge that reflects the collation of data and information into a meaningful application and/or judgement of the data presented, for example cause and effect relationship statements inferred from the data and information.
- Data and information have no meaning on their own, whereas knowledge applies the data and information to give meaning and to facilitate the interpretation and judgement thereof in a context-related reality, that is, to make a clinical diagnosis and to prescribe the subsequent treatment and care regimen.

The purpose of a knowledge management system

The purpose of a knowledge management system is as follows:

- To know what particular expertise resides in the healthcare organisation
- To know what expertise is lost when employees leave
- To know which individuals have particular expertise to add value as a project team member
- To understand how knowledge flows in the healthcare organisation
- To track the loss or acquisition of a particular competency or proficiency
- To locate expertise, documents and other media on particular topics
- To assist in planning for training and education (skills development)
- To assist in planning for the recruitment of staff.

The process of knowledge management

Knowledge management consists of the following process:

- **Identify existing knowledge**. This includes the collection of existing knowledge as reflected in resource files, clinical guidelines and protocols, quality improvement programmes, reports, strategic plans and related strategies, policies and procedures, etc.
- **Reflect on existing knowledge**. This refers to the nature and scope of the existing knowledge, as well as the quality and transferability thereof between departments and operational units/areas.
- **Redistribute the knowledge**. Develop a knowledge capital management system and disseminate/distribute the knowledge, for example an electronic system on the organisational and departmental website(s).
- **Apply the knowledge**. This refers to the application and/or amendment thereof to suit the nature and scope of the specialised area (current reality).

Criteria of excellence related to knowledge management

A few criteria of excellence are highlighted:

- There is a knowledge management strategy or programme in accordance with the internal profile analysis of the healthcare organisation in relation to the core business service delivery.
- There is a knowledge management system to accommodate the strategy.
- A functional manager is responsible and accountable for the knowledge management system.
- Knowledge management teams/committees are constituted to assist with the process of knowledge management.
- Knowledge management ownership practices are in place to ensure the protection of intellectual property of individuals and groups, with the appropriate incentives involved to facilitate the transfer and sharing of knowledge.
- There is a designated knowledge management centre with focal points for knowledge management and the facilitation of knowledge flow.

- There is an interactive intranet portal – a 'one-stop-shop' that gives quick access to explicit knowledge, as well as connections to experts for validation purposes to ensure the trustworthiness of the knowledge.
- Life-cycle management of knowledge is executed: knowledge has a life-cycle and therefore outdated knowledge should be replaced or updated on a continuous basis to mitigate the risk of inappropriate knowledge application. A key challenge is to reach a strategic balance between stability and innovation.
- The afore-mentioned therefore necessitates a risk management strategy to mitigate the risk and possible liabilities when using outdated knowledge.
- The different types of knowledge are appropriately managed:
  - *kernel knowledge* is a project-generic form of knowledge that is applied to all the projects in the healthcare organisation. Thus a key issue is to ensure the consistency of the application of kernel knowledge in the interest of sustainability and quality of service delivery. Kernel knowledge needs to be nurtured to sustain high project performance in the long-term
  - *ephemeral knowledge* is project-related knowledge that is applicable for a specific project only, therefore with low transferability to other projects and with a low probability of being used again. It is only active and useful during the lifetime of that specific project.
  - *tacit knowledge* is the personal, embedded, nebulous form of knowledge that is nevertheless essential for effective operations; knowledge experts are needed in the creation and diffusion of tacit knowledge.
- The knowledge management system is exposed to frequent review and continuous quality improvement.

Critical success factors related to knowledge management

The quality and usefulness of knowledge management are influenced by at least the following:

- There should be corporate support and commitment to the principle of knowledge management with subsequent accommodation thereof in the organisation's strategic plan, organisational design and allocation of resources.
- Knowledge management should be focused on those knowledge domains that offer direct service benefits and add value to the core business service delivery.
- The knowledge database should be accessible and visible to all the relevant stakeholders – including those at operational level – and not just set aside for corporate leadership only. This implies that there should be buy-in at all levels in the healthcare organisation.
- The knowledge ownership and intellectual property should be protected by applying the legal principles in this regard and making provision for appropriate incentives for the knowledge creators.
- Risk management strategies should exist to ensure trustworthiness of the knowledge base.

6.6 UNDERLYING DYNAMICS

Various critical success factors have been highlighted in the various dimensions of communication management. The following underlying dynamics are summarised:

- The quality of communication in the healthcare organisation is dependent upon the institutional determinants, such as the organisational culture, the type, nature and scope of core business service delivery, and the capacity to deal with complicated communication structures and strategies.
- The 'fit-for-purpose' of the communication strategy is important to suit the organisational structure, size and culture.
- Leadership and management commitment, especially with reference to the principle of functional or specialised communication management in the organisation, are important.
- The existence of and management of communication barriers in the healthcare organisation are essential.

6.7 CONCLUDING STATEMENTS

A few concluding statements are made:

- 'Communication is the lubricant that makes it possible for change to take place in an atmosphere of understanding and acceptance. The need for effective communication has never been more pressing' (De J. Cronjé et al., 2004:359).
- Communication management is a process of strategy analysis, development, execution and review, focusing on formal and informal internal communication, the management of public relations, information management, tele/electronic medicine, the management of patient records and knowledge management in the healthcare organisation.
- Communication is practised in a context reflecting complexity, according to the nature and scope of the core business service delivery of the healthcare organisation.
- Many role-players are involved in the process and management of communication. In addition to the sender and recipient of the message, there are several functional communication managers, such as information manager, public relations officer and knowledge manager.
- The purpose of communication management is to facilitate the quality of internal and external communication, in the interest of quality healthcare service delivery.
- Communication management in the healthcare organisation can be divided into several specialised or functional management dimensions, such as public relations management, information management, and knowledge management.
- There are many communication barriers that have to be identified and appropriately managed.
- The quality of communication management is influenced by various underlying

dynamics, such as institutional determinants, the communication strategy's 'fitness-for-purpose', leadership and management commitment towards specialised or functional communication management.

Self-assessment

(1) Compile a formal internal communication strategy for your department or healthcare organisation.
(2) Compile an informal internal communication strategy for your department or healthcare organisation.
(3) Assess the quality of public relations management in your healthcare organisation.
(4) Compile an instrument to assess the quality of the management of patient records in your healthcare organisation, based on the standards described in this chapter.
(5) Conduct an internal organisational profile analysis on the capacity of intellectual capital. Draft a knowledge management strategy, based on this internal profile analysis and the type/nature of the core business in your organisation.

7 Marketing of a healthcare organisation

KEY CONCEPTS

Marketing
Market analysis
Market research
Market strategy
Market segmentation
Marketing mix
Internal marketing
Market audit

SPECIFIC OUTCOMES

After studying this chapter, you should be able to:

- Interpret the legal, professional-ethical and healthcare **context**, with reference to the market analysis, research, strategy, segmentation and mix, and market auditing processes that are implemented in a healthcare environment
- Analyse and debate the **purpose** of the marketing process in the healthcare setting
- Identify the **role-players** and interpret their roles and responsibilities in the effective implementation of the marketing process
- Describe and apply the **processes** of market analysis, market research, market strategy, market segmentation and mix, and market auditing in a healthcare institution
- Debate the **underlying dynamics** that could have a positive or negative impact on the marketing process of a healthcare entity.

7.1 INTRODUCTION

The healthcare market has altered dramatically in recent years. However, many healthcare organisations have not yet transformed their marketing strategies in response to a changing market. Marketing is the process of planning and exacting the conception, pricing, promotion and distribution of ideas, goods and services to create exchange and satisfy organisational objectives (Morgan, 1996:20).

Table 7.1 Healthcare service marketing framework

Monitoring the changing market environment A situation analysis • Internal and external environment • Market analysis
Market research
Market strategy • Mission statement
Market segmentation and target market • Marketing mix • Strategic plan
Market audit/evaluation

The essence of marketing is a transaction or exchange that consists of activities designed to generate and facilitate exchanges intended to satisfy human needs or wants. Marketing is a total system of business activities designed to plan, price, promote and distribute want-satisfying products to target markets to achieve organisational objectives. The entire healthcare organisation's activities (planning and operations) should be client-oriented because the needs of clients must be recognised and satisfied. Marketing should start with an idea about a want-satisfied product and should only end when the needs of the client are completely satisfied, which may be after the services have been delivered (Stanton, Etzel & Walker, 1994:5–6). All marketing activities in the healthcare organisation should be coordinated. Marketing efforts should be designed and combined in a coherent, consistent way and the marketer should have overall authority and responsibility for the marketing activities. Customer-oriented, coordinated marketing is essential to achieve the performance objectives of the healthcare organisation.

Marketing forms the *link between society's needs/desires/expectations* and the health service's *response/reaction* to these needs, therefore *balancing a situation* and creating a *supply/demand* scenario. The process of marketing is therefore to *analyse, plan and control exchanges in order to develop relationships with clients, suppliers, partners, the public, employers and the media.*

Marketing is the process of understanding and influencing healthcare markets that has two facets. First, it is a philosophy, an attitude, a perspective or a management orientation that stresses client satisfaction. Secondly, it is a set of activities used to implement this philosophy. Marketing can be defined as a systematic process of planning and executing the conception, pricing, promotion and distribution of ideas, goods and services to create exchanges that satify individual and organisational goals (Lamb, Hair & McDaniel, 2004:6).

Marketing provides for a link between the service and the community to render a service as a response/reaction to the society's needs/desires/expectations. It takes into consideration the balancing between supply of services and the demand therefor. The marketing process analyses, plans and controls exchanges in order to develop relationships with clients, suppliers, partners, public, employers and the media. For purposes of this chapter, marketing will be viewed as a process entailing the steps set out in Table 7.1.

7.2 CONTEXT

There are many drivers for the need for changes in marketing strategies. Some of these drivers include increased consumerism, an aging society, managed care penetration, clinical benchmarking availability, competition for market share, quality as a business strategy and new technologies (Byers, 2001:94).

Various environmental forces influence a healthcare organisation's marketing activities. Some forces are *external* to the organisation and are largely uncontrollable by the organisation. *Demographic* conditions are one of these macro-influences. Another is *economic* conditions, such as the inflation and interest rates. Management must be aware of the various types of *competition* and the competitive structure in which the healthcare organisation operates. *Social and cultural forces*, including cultural changes, are another factor with which to contend. *Political* and *legal forces*, along with *technology*, are also part of the group of external environmental influences. The environmental factors, such as suppliers, marketing intermediaries and the *market* itself, also form part of the external environment. However, these elements are part of the organisation's marketing system and can be controlled to some extent by the organisation. At the same time, a set of non-marketing resources *internal* to the organisation, namely production facilities, personnel, finances, location, research and development, and the image of the organisation, influences its marketing system. These variables generally are controllable by management.

From an organisational perspective, marketing requires to be viewed as both a strategic and operational level management function. At the strategic level responsibility for marketing is seen as being the responsibility of senior management, specifically the strategic planning function, while at the operational level responsibility lies with the relevant functional areas, for example finance or quality control (Laing & McKee,1998:585).

Healthcare organisations should also instill an ethical orientation and ethical guidelines in the marketing environment. One dimension of creating an ethical environment is to make sure that the demands on employees to perform are reasonable. Another important facet of an ethical orientation is communicating clearly what the organisation's standards are. Healthcare professionals should on a continuous basis be reminded of the importance of ethical behaviour and their codes of conduct.

A marketing philosophy should be formulated in the context of a customer orientation, integrated organisational effort and profit direction. An example of such a philosophy is: 'We place a major emphasis on the analysis of target market needs and wants and deliver the desired satisfactions more efficiently and effectively than competitors.'

7.3 PURPOSE

Marketing can be vital to an organisation's success. Marketing can be useful to individual healthcare professionals, particularly in reference to career opportunities. Under the marketing concept, the healthcare sector must find a way to discover unfulfilled client needs and identify market products that satisfy those needs. The process of doing so can be modeled in a sequence of steps, for example the situation is analysed to identify opportunities, the strategy is formulated for a value proposition, tactical decisions are made, the plan is implemented and the results are monitored.

7.4 ROLE-PLAYERS

Management leaders are highly qualified to influence their organisation's approach to marketing. Providing and marketing quality patient care services are integral to nurse executives' professional obligations both in their healthcare organisation and in the community. Characteristics of nurses that make them well qualified to be a marketing spokesperson from the consumers' perspective include their patient care quality focus, ability to translate medical terminology into lay language, and consumer trust.

Patient care operations staff, medical staff, call centre staff, member services, information services and administration should all provide input into marketing plans. Other stakeholders to consider including are past or potential patients, case managers and performance improvement staff. This group would be able to look at both the healthcare provider and patient experience perspectives in addition to being able to prioritise and implement performance improvement activities.

The nature of marketing requires marketing managers and professionals to work together on all aspects of marketing. It is common for the marketing manager to be at the centre of a set of activities being worked on by people in the company (sales force, promotion manager, product development teams, etc.) and outside the company (ad agencies, consultants, marketing research health services, etc). Thus marketing managers must spend considerable time in consultation and collaboration with other people.

Marketing managers play many roles, and we can describe them with words that begin with the letter D:

- **Detective**. The marketer is charged with understanding markets, and thus must spend considerable time learning about consumers, competitors, clients and conditions in the markets. This learning takes many forms: formal marketing

research studies, analysis of market data, market visits, and discussions with people in the markets. The result of these studies includes insights about market conditions, and the identification of problems and opportunities in the various markets.
- **Designer**. Once a problem or opportunity has been identified, the marketer turns her/his attention to designing marketing programmes that solve the problems and/or capture the opportunities.
- **Decision-maker**. Marketing is a group process that involves many different people, each of whom may be designing marketing programmes and events. Thus the marketer must make decisions about which programmes to execute.
- **Decision influencer**. Marketers exist in corporate structures that require higher level executives to approve the marketing plans, programmes and events that come out of the marketing group's work. Thus the marketer must influence the decisions of these senior executives.
- **Diplomat**. Marketers design marketing events that others must execute: the sales force must execute the sales plan, the advertising agency must execute the advertisements, etc. These units do not usually 'report to' the marketing managers, and they are undertaking tasks given to them by multiple marketing managers. Thus, each manager must play a diplomatic role while inducing these units to execute his/her progamme in a timely and high-quality way.
- **Discussant**. All of these roles require considerable discussion among many parties in and outside the company. Thus the marketing manager spends most of his/her time in discussions with others.

The successful **marketing auditor** needs not only technical skills in marketing, but also skills in managing client relationships and organisational behaviour. An effective marketing auditor:
- Is a careful listener and accepts data without contradicting what clients state
- Subjects data to careful consideration from various perspectives from a pool of informants
- Takes time to assess the problem and summarises accurately what clients say
- Takes a positive approach to the situation.

Other marketing competencies that are desirable for effective marketing decision-making are vision, creativity, leadership, communication, motivation, initiative, intuition, adaptability, analytical thinking, judgement, organisational ability, knowledge and networking (Hill, McGowan & Maclaran, 1998:74).

7.5 MARKETING PROCESS

7.5.1 Monitoring the changing market environment: A situation analysis

Situation analysis

The marketing process explores the capabilities of the healthcare service and matches them to user needs. The foundation of the process is knowing what the purpose of the service is in the community.

A thorough analysis of the situation in which the healthcare service finds itself serves as the basis for identifying opportunities to satisfy unfulfilled client needs. In addition to identifying the client needs, the healthcare service must understand its own capabilities and the environment in which it is operating.

The situation analysis thus can be viewed in terms an analysis of the external environment and an internal analysis of the healthcare service itself. The external environment can be described in terms of macro-environmental factors that broadly affect many healthcare services, and micro-environmental factors closely related to the specific situation of the healthcare service (internal non-marketing resources that surround the marketing programme).

The situation analysis should include past, present and future aspects. It should include a history outlining how the situation evolved to its present state and an analysis of trends in order to forecast where it is going. Good forecasting can reduce the chance of spending a year bringing a product to market only to find that the need no longer exists.

If the situation analysis reveals gaps between what consumers want and what currently is offered to them, then there may be opportunities to introduce products to better satisfy those consumers. Hence, the situation analysis should yield a summary of problems and opportunities. From this summary, the healthcare service can match its own capabilities with the opportunities in order to satisfy client needs better than the competition.

A situation analysis involves analysing where the marketing programme of the organisation has been, how it has been doing and what the future helds. A situation analysis also considers the clients served by the organisation, the strategies used to satisfy them and key measures of marketing performance. As part of the situation analysis the organisation identifies and evaluates its most significant strengths, weaknesses, opportunities and threats.

There are several frameworks that can be used to add structure to the situation analysis:

- **5 C analysis**. This includes company, clients, competitors, collaborators and climate. The organisation (company) represents the internal situation; the other four cover aspects of the external situation.
- **PEST analysis.** This refers to macro-environmental political, economic, societal, and technological factors. A PEST analysis can be used as the 'climate' portion of the 5 C framework.

- **SWOT analysis.** This analysis can be used to condense the situation analysis into a listing of the most relevant problems and opportunities and to assess how well the healthcare service is equipped to deal with them. Strengths, weaknesses, opportunities, and threats – for the internal and external situation are therefore determined.
- **Assessment**. The healthcare service capabilities are assessed with a marketing audit that is an internal assessment.
- **Analyses**. The internal/external environment is assessed.

Dynamic external forces have considerable influence on the marketing system of a healthcare organisation. These forces are related to the following:

- **Demography**. The study of human population and its distribution is of special interest to marketing executives because people constitute markets. Aspects of importance are the aging population, the rapid growth of certain population groups, and the large and growing lower class population in southern Africa. Marketing executives should realise that they must target their products and advertisements at a diverse population.
- **Economical conditions**. A marketing programme is affected by for example the current anticipated stage of the business cycle of the organisation, as well as inflation and interest rates. A rise in the prices of goods and services has an impact on the costs of healthcare.
- **Competition**. Marketing executives should monitor all aspects of competitors' marketing activities, such as their healthcare products, pricing, distribution systems, and promotional programmes. To compete in the ever-changing environment, some healthcare organisations can merge and form alliances or partnerships.
- **Social and cultural forces**. Cultural patterns such as lifestyles and social beliefs are changing rapidly. More emphasis is placed on quality of life and consumers are seeking value, quality and safety in healthcare delivery. Recognising the growing economical power and changing lifestyles of people, marketing programmes should be adapted to address the healthcare needs of clients. An increased interest in health and physical fitness in recent years seems to have cut across most demographic and economic segments of our society. The latter has an influence on for example the dietary needs of clients utilising healthcare services. Another factor to take into consideration is that people want services that are convenient, readily available and easy to access. Marketing executives should be aware that the marketing programme is affected by consumers' need and desire for convenience.
- **Political and legal forces**. Political and legal forces stem from legislation and policies established by goverment institutions. Marketing systems are affected by for example the level of goverment spending on healthcare services and tax legislation. Governmental relationships with the health sector play a role through

subsidies and goverment deregulation. Marketers should be aware of any legislation related specifically to the marketing process of a healthcare institution.
- **Technology**. Technology has a tremendous impact on lifestyles, consumer patterns and economical well-being. Technological breakthroughs are expanding the healthcare horizons. These breakthroughs can affect the healthcare market by stimulating new procedures and processes.
- **The market**. The market is the demand made by the community for quality healthcare delivery. In this market there are three things to consider, namely the needs of the community, their capability to afford healthcare services and their behaviour towards using the available healthcare services.

The marketing system of an organisation is also shaped by internal forces that are controllable by management. These internal influences include the facilities, financial and personnel (human resources) activities of a healthcare organisation. Other non-marketing forces are the location of an organisation, its research and development strength, the overall image from its projects and services to the public.

Market analyses

Management should know what their services and resources can offer and what the strengths and weaknesses of the organisation are. The *market analysis* entails evaluation of the *product* (quality healthcare services), the *real/potential consumers* and their *needs/desires/expectations* regarding healthcare delivery. An *analysis of the competitors* is made and decisions should follow on how to distinguish the product of the organisation from competitors. The organisation should strive to position the image of its product in relation to directly competitive products.

The *consumer analysis* addresses the different wants and needs of internal and external consumers. Internal consumers or audiences include volunteers, staff, administrator's medical staff, shareholders (partners) or the board of directors, maintenance services, patients (patient satisfaction) and general complaints of consumers. External audiences fall into two general categories. The first category represents the stakeholders that influence contracts, revenue and referral, for example healthcare payers, managed care contractors, indemnity providers, employers, healthcare business coalitions and physicians. The second category represents potential or previous customers, for example community leaders, consumers and the media.

A *self-assessment of the internal organisation* is essential to determine the indicators of resources, the effectiveness of activities and the availability of support groups.

The market analysis could point out that certain changes are needed for the provider, as listed below:

Promoting an out-patient service focus due to the trend of managed care
- Expanding home care
- Recruiting primary healthcare staff

- Downsizing hospital beds and costs
- Increasing productivity.

Promoting provider incentives

- Forming partnerships
- Investing in information systems
- Following a multi-disciplinary approach, and more focus on the family
- Using technology to improve patient care.

Market research: needs and desires

Marketing research includes all the activities that enable a healthcare organisation to obtain the information it needs to make decisions about its environment, its marketing mix, and its present or potential customers and consumers. It can be done by the organisation's own personnel or by outside researchers.

What do your users want from you? Which services or resources do you have but need to promote, which do you need to acquire or create? Market research takes many forms (e.g. surveys, focus groups, observation). Other sources of information are the marketing information reports through regular scheduled reports to managers and the decision support system, which permits managers to interact directly with data through personal computers to answer specific questions. Results help you to select a target user group (market segment), choose a specific product to promote, or a problem on which to focus.

Marketing research is the development, interpretation, and communication of decision-oriented information to be used in the strategic marketing process.

Marketing strategy

The mission statement (demand/supply link service). An organisation's mission states what clients it serves, what needs it satisfies, and what type of product it offers. A mission statement indicates in general terms the boundaries for the activities of an organisation. The marketing concept is expressed in the mission in customer-oriented terms. Marketers should think about the wants they are satisfying and the benefits they are providing.

Also of importance is the determination of marketing objectives that should be closely related to the goals and strategies of the organisation. Each objective should be assigned a priority based on its urgency and potential impact on the marketing area and, in turn, the organisation.

Key questions should be asked about the marketing programme of the organisation:

- Is the organisation directing marketing messages only to the medical and scientific community?
- Is the organisation competing in a limited healthcare niche while other competitors are marketing more broadly?

MARKETING STRATEGY

1 Description of service delivery/service
- Type of service delivery/nursing care
- Patient profile/specialisation
- Personnel profile

2 Statement of mission
- Type/nature of service delivery
- Commitment: quality
- Geographical location/community

3 Target group/market
- Primary target group
- Secondary target group
- Other multi-target groups
- Complete description: target groups

4 Marketing methods
- Accreditation of services
- Open days
- Managed healthcare
- Total quality management
- Advertising
- Utilisation: community opportunities
- Media
- What is being marketed? Product
- Value/price of the product
- Who is the potential client/consumer?
- How will I sell/market? Promotion

- Is the organisation's marketing programme conservative and based on what is 'risk free' from a legal perspective?

A positive response to these questions will indicate that the organisation's strategies are not in line with the current healthcare environment. Successful marketing strategies are collaborative and flexible. Before developing any marketing strategies, it is important to incorporate techniques for success of the marketing message. The following techniques are of importance:
- The goal of the marketing message should be clear and the communication of the message should be proactive. The media should be alerted the first time a

new cutting-edge procedure is performed. Marketing messages should also address the appropriate target audience.

- Branding assists the public to identify with the healthcare organisation. Branding should be aligned with the mission and vision of an organisation and characterise what the organisation stands for. Branding strategies are outlined in the box below.
  - Marketing strategies should differentiate the organisation from competitors based on positive aspects of care, such as access, efficient patient flow, specialities services, the philosophy of the service to be family inclusive, spirituality focused, customer focused or to provide personal attention.

Branding strategies

Develop a brand personality that reflects your organisation and its uniqueness.
Ensure that the brand logo is memorable and pronounceable.
Use branding in all internal and external communication.
Make facilities and signage visible, including logo.
Use the power of employees as a sales force through internal marketing communication.
Provide consistent service quality excellence.
Develop ongoing marketing initiatives.
Market to specific consumer groups.
Organise community events such as fundraisers.

Once the best opportunity to satisfy unfulfilled client needs is identified, a strategic plan for pursuing the opportunity can be developed. Market research will provide specific market information that will permit the health service to select the target market segment and optimally position the offering in that segment. The result is a value proposition to the target market. The marketing strategy then involves:

- Segmentation
- Targeting (target market selection)
- Marketing mix
- Positioning the product in the target market
- Value proposition to the target market
- The marketing plan.

A marketing strategy is also the set of conscious decisions a marketer makes in determining who is going to be offered a particular product or service, referred to collectively as the target market, and how the chosen target market will be reached.

Market segmentation

Before target markets can be selected, they must be identified and described through the process that is called *market segmentation*.

Market segmentation is a process of dividing the total market for a service into several smaller groups, such that the clients of each group are similiar with respect to the factors that influence demand. Segmentation is customer-oriented where the needs of the customers are identified in a submarket and then decided if it is practical to develop a marketing mix to satisfy those needs. The goal of segmentation is therefore to divide a market so that each segment responds to a different marketing mix. The following conditions help marketers to attain effective segmentation:

- Measurable characteristics should describe what segments customers fall into, for example the age of customers, financial income, education, occupation.
- The market segment should be accessible through, for example advertising media, with a minimum of cost and wasted effort.
- Each segment should be large enough to be profitable.

The consumer market can be divided into further segments using geographic (population distribution, urban and rural distribution), demographic (gender, age, family lifecycle, income, social class), psychological (personality, lifestyle) and behavioural (benefits desired, usage rate) characteristics.

The new conceptualisation of 'segment-based mass customisation' is a strategy aiming at the desired markets or one target market; practically operating on the smallest segment size which maximises the profit or other utility from mass customisation; that is, it does not necessarily assume the perfect heterogeneity of the customers, but strategically focuses on the needs and wants of the smallest unit of the market (Fiang, 2000:217).

Target market

The group of customers for whom the organisation designs a particular marketing mix is a target market. The target market is a well-defined set of existing and/or potential customers the marketer aims to satisfy with a particular product offering (the product or service). Target markets are usually defined in terms of their geographical location, their demographics and psychographic characteristics. Marketers should identify potential target markets, examine any changes in the characteristics of its target markets and alternative markets. Management should decide to what extent and in what manner to divide up to all markets and then pursue only those markets that show the best potential for successful marketing.

Four guidelines govern the selection of target markets:

- Target markets should be compatible with the goals and image of the organisation.
- The market opportunity represented in the target markets should match the resources of the organisation.

- The selection of a target market should result in an organisation that generates a profit to survive.
- An organisation should seek a market where there are the least and smallest competitors.

Target markets such as *primary target groups* and *secondary groups* must be selected on the basis of opportunities. The total market could be treated as a single unit or the total market could be viewed as consisting of several smaller segments with differences to be addressed by separate services or programmes. To analyse the opportunities, an organisation must forecast demand in its target markets. The results of demand forecasting will indicate whether the targets of the organisation are worth pursuing or whether alternatives need to be identified.

Marketing mix

In reaching and influencing the chosen target market the marketer uses what is known as the *marketing mix*. The basic elements of the marketing mix are *product* (quality care), *price* (value), *place* (distribution) and promotion. These four elements are known as the controllable variables of the marketing strategy. The marketing mix is a subtle blend of these elements into a workable set of objectives and activities, which is referred to as the *marketing plan*. *Promotion*, the fourth element of the marketing mix, consists of six elements: advertising, personal selling, sales promotion, direct marketing, public relations and sponsorship (Koekemoer, 2001:1–2).

Managing the marketing mix

Marketing managers can control or influence four aspects of the healthcare service's output: its products, promotions, prices, and the places that all of these are offered.

- **Product: quality healthcare**. A product is a set of tangible and intangible attributes, including quality and brand, plus the services and reputation of the organisation. Product management involves the design of the physical product along with its packaging and warranties, the positioning of that product in terms of the benefits it delivers, and the development of the brand identity of the product.
- **Promotion**. It is generally not true that consumers will beat a path to your door if you have a superior product; they must be told about it and induced to buy it ... thus the need for promotion. Promotion includes personal selling, advertising, sales promotions and public relations.
- **Price and value**. Pricing strategies and tactics must be determined for the product, and then followed to set prices for all the sizes and variants of the product. The result is usually a price schedule that includes the regular price, volume discounts, payment terms, seasonal prices, introductory prices, etc.
- **Place**. Marketing managers are involved in decisions about where the product is offered to the consumer in terms of the channels of distribution.

Detailed tactical decisions are made for the controllable parameters of the marketing mix. The action items include:

- Product development – specifying, designing, and producing the product/service
- Pricing decisions
- Distribution contracts
- Promotional campaign developments.

Implementation and control of the marketing mix

At this point in the process, the marketing plan has been developed and the product has been launched. Given that few environments are static, the results of the marketing effort should be monitored closely. As the market changes, the marketing mix can be adjusted to accommodate the changes. Often, small changes in consumer wants can be addressed by changing the advertising message. As the changes become more significant, a product redesign or an entirely new product may be needed. The marketing process does not end with implementation – continual monitoring and adaptation are needed to fulfil client needs consistently over the long term. Monitoring of the producer, consumer, consumer market, product (quality nursing care), price/value and promotion of the product through, for example advertisement, should continue.

During the implementation of the marketing process a set of professional ethics for healthcare marketing professionals should be developed that address the following aspects:

- Respect for the primacy of the patient's and customer's welfare
- Ensuring competiveness of the healthcare organisation
- Providing communication that informs and persuades but does not deceive
- Comparing competitive offerings in a fair way
- Never enter a relationship that constitutes a conflict with existing client interests
- Respect the privacy and confidentiality of patients
- Acknowledge the right of access to information.

Positioning the product in the target market

Effective use should be made of the media. The market communication mix is a careful blend of advertising, personal selling, sales promotion, direct marketing, public relations and sponsorship. Methods of marketing include for example storyboards, newsletters, oral presentations, radio, television media, Internet and advertisements.

When focusing on *advertising* the specific healthcare organisation, the available budget and image of the organisation should be kept in mind, to produce a quality advertisement. Advertising has three main purposes, namely to *inform* the target audience about a new product, to *persuade* the target audience that the product/ service is superior to those of competitors and to *remind* the target population about the service. The following aspects should be addressed in the message:

- The name of the healthcare organisation should be recognisable.
- The message should be directed to consumer services.
- Specifications of the type of service offered, technology available, cost and quality of the service should be given.
- There should be physician referral for clients.
- The service should have geographical appeal and be locally accessible.
- Satellite locations with community involvement should be available.

Other means of marketing the service are through the following:
- **Personal selling**. This takes place as a person-to-person process by which the service provider learns about the customer's wants and seeks to satisfy them by offering quality services, for example availability and distribution of business cards.
- **Sales promotion**. This takes place as any activity that offers incentives for a limited time period to induce a desired response from those who are targeted, for example at open days to introduce the community to services.
- **Direct marketing**. This takes place as an interactive system of marketing that uses one or more advertising media to effect a measurable response at any location, for example mailed information, visiting important customers, networking with community leaders and distributing brochures.
- **Public relations**. Communication of perceptions and strategic relationships between an organisation and its internal and external stakeholders is important, for example through image building, explaining current initiatives to customers and consumers, outlining future plans to consumers of the service, personal appearances of service providers, publicity outwards through speeches by staff, winning the public's trust, through speaking of limitations and positive aspects of healthcare delivery.
- **Sponsorship**. This is a marketing communications activity whereby a sponsor contractually provides financial or other support to an organisation or individual in return for rights to use the sponsor's name and logo in connection with the sponsored event, for example at health symposia.

The overall marketing function consists of three overlapping sets of activities (modes) whereby the marketers seek to manage the demand for their offerings. The marketing concept (basic offer mode fulfills the marketing concept) embodies the notion that the marketer adapts the services of the organisation to the customers' needs and wants. The promotion concept (accommodated by the persuasive communication and promotional inducements modes) attempts to adapt the customer to the needs and wants of the market. Examples of the three modes of marketing are outlined briefly in the box below.

Modes of marketing

Basic offer

- The product itself
- Terms of services
  - availability and delivery
  - price of services
  - credit terms, guarantees or warranties

Persuasive communication

- Non-personal verbal messages
  - publicity
  - measured advertising: radio, television, newspaper, magazine
  - unmeasured advertising: direct mail, catalogue, Internet
- Personal verbal messages
  - personal selling messages
  - word-of-mouth support
- Non-verbal messages
  - packing of type of services rendered

Promotional inducements

- Character of basic offer
  - free services rendered
- Price related
  - buy-back allowances to equipment dealers
- External to basic offer
  - promotions, e.g. free gift in a pack
  - free offers to customers, e.g. influenza injections

Value proposition to the target market

Recruitment and retention of staff are of utmost importance. The following aspects are considered important in this regard:

- A shift in job security could be experienced due to the managed care approach.
- A change of skills mix and nurse/patient ratios could occur.
- Experience and education should be more important in determining salaries.
- New opportunities exist in the team approach.
- Staff redesign, productivity and creativity should be acknowledged.
- Distribution of nurses may change.
- Outsourcing/session workers could be needed.
- Life-time employment is no longer a reality.
- The need for staff with acute care skills, case management, home care, ambulatory surgery and insurance utilisation reviews are trends in healthcare.

A marketing approach to recruitment of healthcare professionals should focus on the needs of the prospective employee as a customer. It should focus on factors such as job profile, organisational culture, working conditions, location of employment, reputation of the organisation, and compensation (Swansburg, 1996:127).

Marketing plan

A marketing plan serves several purposes:

- It summarises the marketing strategies and tactics that will be used to achieve specified objectives and is the 'how-to-do-it' document that guides persons involved in marketing.
- The plan points to what needs to be done with respect to the steps in the management process (implementing and evaluating) of the marketing programme.
- The plan outlines who is responsible for which activities, when they are to be carried out, and how much time and money can be spent.

The contents of an annual marketing plan could outline the following:

- **Executive summary.** The thrust of the plan is described and explained.
- **Situation analysis.** The service covered by the plan is examined in the context of pertinent past, present and future conditions.
- **Objectives**. The objectives are more specific than those stated in the strategic marketing plan and should help achieve the organisational goals and strategic marketing goals.
- **Strategies**. These should indicate which target markets are going to be satisfied through a combination of product, price, distribution and promotion.
- **Tactics**. Specific activities or action plans (see Table 7.2) for each major strategy should answer the questions of the what, who and how of the marketing efforts.
- **Finances**. The amount of resources dedicated to different activities should be indicated.
- **Timetable**. The timetable indicates when the various marketing activities will be carried out.
- **Evaluation**. Performances are measured against goals and lead to adjustments in the strategies and/or tactics of the plan, or even the objectives to be achieved.

General principles in marketing healthcare

The role of the healthcare service manager is as follows:

- To understand the essence of marketing as the analysis, planning and control of exchanges in order to develop and hold relationships with priority clients, suppliers, partners and relevant publics, such as employers, other healthcare providers and the media.
- To be proactive for future marketing that will produce more collaboration among

Table 7.2 Example of the structure of a marketing plan

Objective	Method	Duties	Tasks	Responsibilities	Target date

insurers and providers, prevention efforts and targeting of specific types of consumers.
- To use market research to identify client needs, serving those needs, understanding competitive and environmental dynamics, and developing strategies in the organisation's mission and objectives (Dienemann, 1998:61).

Internal marketing

Internal marketing is an important activity in developing a customer-focused organisation. Fundamental aims of internal marketing are to develop internal and external customer awareness and remove functional barriers to organisational effectiveness.

Internal marketing is a structured approach to strategy implementation, to the diffusion of innovation, to recruitment and retaining service-minded staff, to creating a service culture, or to increasing internal service delivery.

A number of current managerial issues require strategic management with internal marketing:

- The retention of skilled people in the organisation, by counteracting declining management standards and providing clear corporate and personal direction
- Relationships with the management team who share the objectives, experience, and skills to build, release and to mobilise individual motivation for economic recovery
- The proper understanding and need for quality for competitive service delivery in a changing environment
- Building a corporate brand that appeals to both customers and organisational members
- Communication management with a clear strategy based on research and evaluation, and personal skills development and responsibility
- Productivity through participation requiring leadership, processes and commitment from all (Varey & Lewis, 1998:926).

The following principles should be followed in internal marketing:

- Organisation jobs and employment conditions are products to be marketed and the manager should think like a manager when dealing with people.
- Employees should change their needs and should understand the position of the employer as they respond to the market.
- Internal marketing is aimed at the attraction, retention and motivation of 'service-minded', 'customer-conscious' employees to aid the perceived service quality and effective external marketing of the organisation as a way to competitive advantage.
- Information should be disseminated to and from all internal groups involved or affected by the marketing activities for the efficient implementation of marketing decisions.
- Incentive and motivation systems should be developed and maintained to reward marketing performance.

Market audit: evaluation

Market audit is a systematic examination of the marketing objectives, strategies, organisation and performance of an organisation (Brownlie, 1999:88).

The marketing audit is widely regarded as a valuable diagnostic device in marketing planning. In theory it should be the starting point for any considered course of managerial action in action. Its primary purpose is to identify underachieved marketing resouces and to generate recommendations about how those resources could be put to more effective use.

Four requirements should be borne in mind in terms of planning the marketing audit process:

- Deciding which issues are relevant
- Knowing where or from whom to obtain information on those issues
- Interpreting the data collected in the light of client needs
- Translating findings into conclusions and recommendations for actions.

The audit plan establishes which issues to investigate, how to collect data and from whom, in what time span, at what cost and what management needs to do to communicate an appropriate context for the audit (Brownlie, 1999:89–90).

Steps in the auditing process

The steps in the process are to:

- Clarify and agree on the broad audit
- Establish clear reporting links to the prime source of authority and legitimacy in the client organisation
- Collect relevant background documentation and preliminary options
- Revise broad objectives and clarify and agree on specific audit objectives

- Eliminate all non-application sections from checklist template, delete all non-relevant questions and add/amend where necessary
- Answer all questions in the capability of the auditor, with recommended courses of remedial action
- List other client personnel who need to be consulted for their views and insight
- Decide whether to accept individual or group suggestions and ideas
- Identify which questions will be asked of which person
- Decide how participants will respond, for example by means of self-questionnaire, questionnaire, personal interview or group discussion, and set up an administrative mechanism for the data collection phase, for example personal interview arrangements
- Brainstorm remedial courses of actions and test these on clients
- Extract all action points and categorise them according to urgency, likely cost and ease of implementation
- In discussion with the client allocate each task by name, schedule it by date and elapsed time, agree on a monitoring system.

Audit process considerations

The process considerations are:

- An initial visit to the client organisation to meet management and to discuss the plan how the auditor will go about the marketing audit and what commitment is needed from the host
- Further visits to consult documentation, report marketing activities and procedures, to establish perceived marketing needs and identify suitable benchmark organisations
- Interview with managers to establish perceived marketing effectiveness using checklists
- Development of a suitable battery of benchmarks against which to judge marketing procedures
- Evaluation of marketing procedures on the basis of those benchmarks
- Development of alternatives for improving the marketing of the organisation and the formulation of a draft report
- Discussion of the preliminary findings with the client and recording of feedback and recycling where necessary
- Preparation of the final report and other representations of findings.

Before proceeding with the marketing audit, the consultant requires a knowledge of the client organisation, its products, services, markets, systems, procedures and personnel. The expectations of the client will commit the consultant to deliver an audit report, as well as presenting this report to top management.

The marketing audit information deliverables are:

- An inventory of the client's marketing resources, assets and distinctive competencies
- A statement of the client's marketing needs and problem areas as defined by the sponsor, typically top management, taking into account the views of operational staff who 'own' the various processes that interact with customers and support the delivery of service quality
- A review of the client's relationships with its customers, competitors, suppliers and other influential stakeholder groups
- An analysis of the client's strengths and weaknesses in marketing
- An evaluation of the client's current marketing activities
- An inventory of the marketing resources, assets and competencies which the consultant believes to be desirable for the client to obtain
- Recommendations as to a course of action by means of which the client could go about acquiring the desired marketing approach and expertise and to what expected effect.

7.6 UNDERLYING DYNAMICS

The lack of effective senior management support for marketing has a major impact on the ability of marketing managers to drive and direct the marketing process.

Market research can be influenced by the fact that researchers are often production-oriented when they should act marketing-oriented, poor communication can exist between researchers and managers, and managers do not treat marketing research as a continuous process.

Marketing managers undertake all marketing activities in various constraints, all of which start with the letter C. None of these constraints are under the direct control of the marketing managers; some can be influenced; all can be understood.

- **Competition**. Other companies are competiting for the same consumers and channels of distribution.
- **Channels**. Retail stores, electronic markets, communications media exist to serve the marketer. In the short run, they must be accepted as constraints; in the long run, the marketer can exert some control over them ... even vertically integrate into the channels.
- **Consumers**. Consumers have needs and wants. The marketers must understand those needs before they can design marketing programmes aimed at impacting consumer wants.
- **Conditions**. Markets are not static but in constant evolution under the influences of the economy, changing tastes and fashions, population dynamics, etc.
- **Company**. Company policies, procedures, practices and cultures place constraints upon the marketing resources and programmes that the marketer can deploy.

7.7 CONCLUDING STATEMENTS

- The current level of competition in the healthcare marketplace requires a more sophisticated and strategic marketing plan.
- More savvy healthcare consumers, an aging population with greater healthcare needs, and rapidly developing technology must be considered when constructing marketing messages.
- Nursing leaders have an opportunity to play a critical role in designing and implementing corporate marketing plans given their deep knowledge of healthcare services, understanding of patient needs, and access to clinical outcome data.
- In many health organisations, clinical and marketing departments function independently, leading to uncoordinated communication and missed opportunities to combine talents, develop new messaging tactics and explore new business opportunities.
- Involving expert nurses in communicating internal and external messages can give meaning and depth to marketing initiatives, as well as achieve a level of trust and compassion with the targeted audience.

Self-assessment

Activities

(1) Compile a marketing strategy for a nursing service of your own choice. Demonstrate critical, analytical and reflective abilities (knowledge, skills, values and attitudes) in compiling the marketing strategy of a healthcare service of your own choice by addressing the following aspects:

- Healthcare service: type/nature of service delivery (business) and location
- Target groups: primary and secondary target groups
- Product that needs to be marketed
- Marketing methods
- Marketing plan (operational plan in table format)
- Evaluation strategy: success of marketing.

(2) Evaluate the quality of marketing in the healthcare service in accordance with the standards described in the table below.

There is evidence of a marketing strategy to facilitate accessibility, credibility and visibility of the healthcare service:				
	0,0 NC	0,5 PC	1,0 C	– NA
The community and other relevant marketing sources are identified and described.				
The marketing strategies are identified and described.				
There is an operational/business plan for the execution of the marketing strategy.				
The marketing strategy is evaluated in terms of goal achievement: accessibility, credibility and visibility of the healthcare service.				
There is evidence of appropriate remedial actions to manage under- or over-utilisation of the service.				
Consumer-satisfaction is monitored and evaluated.				
The healthcare service manager is a member of the healthcare organisation's marketing committee.				

Questions

- Describe and debate the marketing responsibilities of the nursing service manager.
- Identify and describe the essential elements of a marketing plan.
- Identify and debate the different marketing methods applicable for/in a healthcare service.
- Describe and debate:
  - What is to be marketed? (Product)
  - Value of the product? (Price)
  - Who is the potential client? (Potential)
  - How will I market? (Promotion).
- Identify and describe the healthcare service's target groups (primary and secondary).
- Identify and describe the different methods to be utilised by the healthcare service manager in the marketing of the healthcare service.

8 Healthcare service planning and commissioning

KEY CONCEPTS

Healthcare facility planning
Healthcare facility commissioning
Market analysis
Strategic healthcare planning
Application and approval
Briefing
Building design
Construction
Commissioning

SPECIFIC OUTCOMES

After studying this chapter, you should be able to:

- Interpret the legal, professional-ethical and healthcare **context**, with reference to the planning and commissioning of a new or expansion of an existing healthcare facility
- Analyse and debate the **purpose** of the planning and commissioning of a new or expansion of an existing healthcare facility
- Identify the **role-players** and interpret their roles and responsibilities in the phases of the planning and commissioning process of a healthcare facility
- Describe and apply the **processes** of application and approval, orientation, design, construction and commissioning during planning and commissioning of a healthcare facility
- Debate the **underlying dynamics** that could have a positive or negative impact on the planning and commissioning of a healthcare facility.

8.1 INTRODUCTION

A healthcare facility (i.e. hospital) should be viewed as a service, not a building. Therefore a manager should start with a vision and the end result in mind. Most facilities are planned and commissioned with the assumption that they will deliver comprehensive healthcare services. Owing to this perspective it is necessary that local doctor involvement, as well as community involvement, should be viewed as a priority. In the planning and commissioning of a healthcare facility, the provision of the various general and functional healthcare service managers should already foresee how the established healthcare service will incorporate community programmes and new healthcare trends, such as managed healthcare.

Commissioning can be described as bringing the building and equipment of a healthcare facility to a state of readiness, for operational use, with an adequate number of trained staff members to function according to systems, as designed. This chapter focuses on the planning and commissioning of a healthcare facility (see Figure 8.1).

Figure 8.1 Visual presentation of conceptual framework related to planning and commissioning of a healthcare organisation

Context	Legal and policy framework: WHO and national principles Professional-ethical and legal framework of members of the planning and commissioning team
Role-players	Health planners, functional planners, financial planners, physical planners Building specialists Architects Engineers (civil, mechanical and sanitary) Quantity surveyors Financial managers Staff responsible for procurement of supplies Staff members such as doctors, nurses, and clients/users
Purpose	A multidisciplinary endeavour to plan and design a new healthcare facility to provide quality healthcare to the community
Dimensions of planning and commissioning	Planning Construction Commissioning Evaluation
Underlying dynamics	Abilities, roles, activities, contributions of members of team

8.2 CONTEXT

Planning and commissioning of healthcare services occur in the international and national arena of healthcare service delivery, in accordance with the national legislative and regulatory framework.

The type of existing or new facilities that are involved in the planning and commissioning process could be:

- Community healthcare centres
- Community hospitals
- Regional/district hospitals
- Academic hospitals.

Nationally, a country has a strategic healthcare plan that influences the mission, philosophy, values, strategic objectives, strategies and service plans for both public and private healthcare facilities. Ongoing audits of healthcare buildings in the public sector are used to direct maintenance and capital expenditure on these buildings.

8.3 PURPOSE

The planning and commissioning of healthcare services in an environment of increasing pressures on financial management of healthcare organisations refer to the creative management of people to run a established healthcare facility, extend an operation, redevelop an existing healthcare institution or plan and commission a new healthcare facility. The aim is to develop a balanced, functional building for patients and staff members alike.

8.4 ROLE-PLAYERS

Projects in the public sector are approved by the Minister of Health, the treasury and the provincial executive committee versus the board of directors in the private sector. In the public sector, strategic planning will involve the relevant authority, for example top-level provincial authority with the local regional management team, and their motivation will be submitted to the appropriate committee of the Department of National Health and Population Development. After approval, a commissioning team is established who works collaboratively with the hospital management team and the project and design teams.

The commissioning team designs the human resources plan in close liaison with medical, nursing, administrative and other members of the hospital and project teams. Table 8.1 on page 188 outlines the human resources planning in relation to commissioning. A multidisciplinary approach (see box on page 187) is followed and all the stakeholder groups should be involved through the planning phase to make a significant contribution in the design and facilities of the health service.

Each member of the team has a role to play. The *health planner* establishes the need for the hospital, its role in the community and the services it will offer. The *functional planner* establishes the functioning of the different departments and of the hospital as a whole. The *financial planner* is involved with the financial feasibility of the project and is responsible for identifying and earmarking the funds for the project. The *physical planner* establishes the relation of the hospital to the town and the community it serves. The *architect* and the *engineering consultants* provide professional planning, design and supervision of construction. The *construction manager* manages people and resources on site to ensure that the project is completed on time in the budgeted amount. The *building contractor* produces the hospital in its physical form using materials, labour and construction equipment. The *procurement staff* and the personnel staff form part of the commissioning team which prepares the hospital for operation by procuring material and recruiting staff. The *client/user* is the owner and final user of the hospital.

Some important role players in the planning and commissioning phases

Planners (such as health planners, functional planners, and building specialists, agronomists)
Building developers
Building designers or consulting design team, e.g. project manager
Building contractor
Construction/space/engineering experts
Building consumers
Architect, engineers, interior designer
Quantity surveyor
Healthcare providers
Financier: state/private
Client:

- Policy-makers e.g. owner, developer, planning division, medical, nursing, administrative staff
- Healthcare consumer (users), of the current facilities and representatives from clinical and support services

Manufacturers and suppliers

Input in the planning phase is needed from all categories of staff, including the nursing staff, medical representatives, other heads and people working in various departments/units, hospital management and policy-makers, support and maintenance services (e.g. domestic and porters), administrative staff and other professionals with appropriate experience, to form a planning and commissioning committee/unit. These experts (planners) should participate throughout the planning phase as they are the persons with the detailed knowledge of the functions, services and equipment needed in the clinical practice. Planners should be able to analyse clinical and management functions and should have the necessary ability and authority to make decisions and recommendations at the appropriate levels. Any category of the healthcare team can therefore be designated in each department to draw up documents for approval by the general manager of the facility. The design team members may include members from the briefing stage to assist with continuity in the planning process.

8.5 PLANNING, CONSTRUCTION AND COMMISSIONING PROCESS

An investigation and forecasting process will involve drawing up a mission statement and setting objectives, an external and internal environmental analysis and determining the required physical facilities, equipment and posts (workforce plan) along with the financial estimates thereof.

Planning, construction and commissioning phases

PHASE 1: PLANNING
Market analysis
Strategic healthcare planning
Application and approval
Briefing
Design

PHASE 2: CONSTRUCTION

PHASE 3: COMMISSIONING

Table 8.1 Human resource planning in relation to commissioning

Human resource planning activities	**Description of planning activities**
PHASE 1: Establishing the commissioning team	
Develop the human resources plan	Set human resources objectives Plan strategies, schedules, posts, finances
PHASE 2: Building and preparation period	
◗ Design staff systems and organisational structures ◗ Prepare staffing schedules ◗ Consult and prepare recruitment plan ◗ Make advance appointments of senior staff members	◗ When the building has commenced, include the creation of operational policies and management systems, documentation and planning equipment and supplies ◗ Design staffing schedules ◗ Consult departmental heads to gain consensus and to develop detailed schedules with costing for each department ◗ Ensure effective advertisement, set criteria for selection, plan dates for appointment
PHASE 3: Completion of buildings and handover	
◗ Undertake recruitment, advertising, selection and appointment of staff ◗ Arrange staff transfers ◗ Provide orientation, induction and training	Plan an effective recruitment strategy and programme and evaluate it

8.6 PLANNING PHASE

In the planning phase certain main principles should be adhered to:

- **Government policies** regarding healthcare services direct the restructuring of healthcare services and one of the main objectives of countries is to create a National Health System for its citizens. The government can, for example, prescribe certain free services to certain categories of the population and can prescribe an essential drug list to manage the access, distribution, availability and cost of essential drugs in all healthcare sectors.
- Healthcare services should address the **public health profile** of the community through the national health services facilities plan structure, from providing basic subsistence needs (e.g. safe drinking water), providing health education, primary healthcare, community hospital services, regional hospital services and academic hospital services. Coordination between local, provincial and national levels should be promoted by the relevant bodies that have been put in place by government.
- It is important to have adequate **financial and human resources** available to run effective healthcare services that serve the community appropriately. Available resources should be utilised in the most efficient manner and client satisfaction, as well as staff satisfaction, should be ensured.
- The **attitudes and perceptions** of the public regarding the healthcare services should be kept positive and the services rendered to the community should strengthen a trusting relationship between service provider and service consumer.
- The focus of healthcare service delivery should be on the general **social development of the community**, in strengthening the health of all citizens of the country.

The planning phase consists of a sequence of steps (see box below).

Steps in the planning phase

Market analysis
Strategic healthcare planning
Application and approval
Briefing
Design

Market analysis

Hospitals differ and can be classified by considering the degree of care (primary to tertiary); levels of services provided (general to specialised); and population base (urban to rural). On the degree of care continuum, hospitals fall on or between *primary care*, that could be defined as for example under 100 beds and offering basic services, and *tertiary care* that can be defined as offering services up to and including open heart surgery. This affects those strategic decisions concerning facilities, vertical integration, processes and technologies. Facilities are directly affected by the number of beds and complexity of care required, and vertical integration is a function of services offered (outpatient services, specialisations, etc.).

Urban facilities are defined as those existing in a metropolitan statistical area. Rural facilities are defined as existing in non-metropolitan statistical areas with a total population of, for example, less than 50 000. Availability and cost of labour typically differ across this range, with labour generally being more sparse and sometimes less expensive in the more rural environment. Additionally, the rand amount of governmental reimbursement for medical services differs across this continuum, and the situation could be that rural facilities receive fewer rands for identical procedures. Levels of competition decrease generally as the environment becomes more rural and it can be argued that quality perceptions differ across this range, with expectations rising as the environment becomes more urban.

Another factor is the types of service offered, from generalised to specialised. This covers the range from general acute care hospitals to specialty facilities, such as children's and rehabilitation hospitals. Facilities, human resources and technologies differ across this continuum, based on the level of demand, specific care requirements and expense of treatment.

On the other hand, ownership status (public or private) should be considered. The general mission differs by ownership status. For example, for those that are either fully or partially supported by the government, the hospitals' mission would be more philanthropic based on an obligation to care for a percentage of indigent patients. Even management decisions regarding layoffs or reducing services might be partially mandated by government entities. Investor-owned hospitals have primary responsibilities to the stockholders, which might call for completely different management decisions than publicly funded groups in dealing with issues of profitability and efficiencies.

The implications of the above-mentioned factors are that strategies of planning, constructing and commissioning of services will differ. After a hospital's position has been evaluated, a mission can be developed for the hospital.

Internal environment analysis

The hospital board must begin by a realistic evaluation of the underlying values on which the existence of a hospital is based. Values drive mission statements, and the mission of each type of hospital can be clearly different.

At the earliest stage, a needs assessment team involving the planners, hospital staff and the community establishes an overall plan of the needs, range of services to be provided, the target population, the financial feasibility of the project with cost-benefit analysis and the scale of the hospital.

The planning process for capital projects starts with the *identification of needs, desires and expectations* of the community. A *community profile* serves us a motivation for the need of a project. These will determine the level and type of healthcare function (primary, secondary, tertiary), space needed in a specific place, as well as the costs involved.

Certain guidelines and *norms* (need norms, space norms and cost norms) set a framework in which planners must satisfy needs and should be adhered to. These norms are, for example, published in documents such as a National Plan and Norms for Health Service Facilities or Hospital Norms for a specific country. Need norms refer to the need (objective) for the healthcare service that is envisaged, whilst space and cost norms define the maximum amounts of space and expenditure allowed for a building, needed to provide the healthcare service. The following principles are important:

- The public sector must confirm to certain hospital norms and different norms apply to academic and regional hospitals, community healthcare centres and staff accommodation.
- Norms are instruments for measuring the funds that are allocated for the achievement of given healthcare objectives in affordable limits (see box below for an example of the steps involved in the need, cost and space norm calculation of a clinic).
- The need norm either uses existing patient statistics to determine the 'planning units' (beds, rooms) or the population to be served (constantly changing) to determine the required staff.
- The number of planning units is used to calculate the space/area guidelines and cost limits of the facilities in which the services will be provided.

An example of the steps in the need, cost and space norm calculation of a clinic

Step 1: Establish the population to be served, e.g. 20 000 people
Step 2: Calculate expected visits per patient/per year, e.g. 40 000 visits
Step 3: Calculate number of visits per day
Step 4: Determine how many patients one nurse can see per day
Step 5: Determine how many patients the medical practitioner can see per day
Step 6: Calculate the total number of nurses and medical practitioners
Step 7: Provide one examination room per staff member
Step 8: Use the area guideline for one examination room (e.g. 12 m^2) and determine the total area for all the staff members
Step 9: Determine the cost limit (budget) for the staff

With this information, appropriate healthcare service goals and the strategies for meeting these goals can be formulated.

A fundamental choice must be made in the selection of services that can be expected and provided in the epidemiological and resource profile of a given community. One has to decide how sophisticated the service should be, whether equipments needed can be operated and maintained, and whether staff can be found to run it. *Services made available to the community should have adequate manpower*.

When existing facilities have to be extended or developed the difference between the allowed area (according to norms) and the existing space should be calculated because the existing space should not exceed the norm allowed. In the process of requiring additional facilities in a service the need norm must first be applied to establish if any increases are possible.

Table 8.2 Examples of how norm application takes place (fictitious norms and values are used)

Department	Planning unit	Need norm	Area m^2	Cost norm
Outpatient unit	Patients in 3-hour peak period	Determine likely number of patients per 3-hour period	430 m^2 for 60 patients plus 100 m^2 for each additional 50 patients	R400/m^2
High care unit	Bed	5% of total general acute beds	40 m^2	R20 000

External environment analysis

Hospitals are faced with the challenges of providing quality care at competitive prices. It is important that efficiencies of the production process be controlled, while constantly monitoring effectiveness of services, in order to attain a competitive advantage, or, in some circumstances, in order to survive. The hospital's mission, therefore, must establish the services to be offered while considering pricing and delivery of those services in a reasonable level of profitability.

There are three regions of considerations that must be addressed prior to discussing the primary operational activities. These are defined as the remote region, the operating region and the infrastructure region.

The remote region is defined in terms of legal, regulatory, economic, religious and social issues. This includes activities associated with changes in the economic situation of the country; *political factors* and *legislative enactments*; religious and *social* issues such as abortion. *Authority policies* should be known and complied with on a continuous basis.

The operating region is defined in terms of those activities that directly affect the hospital industry. These activities include: the labour market, technology market, capital market, supplier market, customer market and payor market. The customer market differs for the traditional firm in terms of its relationship to the product. Physicians are considered primary customers because they often select the product (or supplier of the product) for a secondary customer known as the patient. Furthermore, as a result of certain programmes, business and industry are also considered customers because of the part they play in selecting the product. The payor market is defined in terms of those entities that have a part in paying for the services; these include medical aids, health maintenance organisations, physician provider organisations and insurance companies. Again, this differs from the traditional firm in that payment for the service is generally made by a third party.

The infrastructure region is defined in terms of support activities that include activities that are specific to hospitals; these include human resources management, finance, reimbursement, marketing and development, purchasing, and non-technical and technical support.

In drawing up a profile of the community as mentioned under the internal environment analysis, the following factors should be taken into account:

- Demographics such as morbidity, migration and population growth
- Health profile of the community
- Availability, accessibility and affordability of existing health services
- Extent, nature and quality of existing healthcare delivery
- Availability, training and competencies of nurses, medical practitioners and paramedical personnel
- Availability of capital and operating finances
- Policies, relevant regulations, procedures of the healthcare service
- Public transport and access to healthcare services
- The public's image and attitudes towards using specific healthcare services.

Application and approval

Government *policies and regulations* should be followed to approve new facilities. It should be noted that applications should *comply with the specified norms* set by government authorities before admission. Different bed norms do apply, for example in urban (4:1 000) and rural areas (2:1 000) of a country. The healthcare manager should not be an expert in calculation norms but should have insight in the established norms and guidelines for applying for new facilities.

After developing briefing documents (plan) and the design, it should be approved by all heads of the different departments/units and the head of the service.

In the *public sector* the management of a healthcare facility identifies a need for new services and writes a motivation for the project. The motivation is provided to the planning division of the authority that verifies the need by visiting the facility, confirming the appropriate statistics, calculating the planning units (space), and applying the area and cost norms. If the project is possible and approved, in terms of the need and space norms, the capital and running costs are calculated, as well as the effect of the project on present facilities (if present). The planning division then forwards the motivation to the controlling authority at provincial level. At this stage it is ensured that the authority has the funds and the means (e.g. staff and funds for running costs) to carry out the project. The project should be in line with the strategic health plan of the country and the overall healthcare priorities. The application serves before, for example the regional health coordinating committee, which consists of all relevant healthcare role-players in the region that makes recommendations by consensus. Further approvals could be needed if the project exceeds the norms, it is a new facility or the project is very costly. The relevant authority then applies to the relevant department, for example the Department of National Health and Population, for approval that ensures that the project conforms to national norms. The Health Services and Works department then prioritises the project and manages the project through appointing consultants and putting the project out for tender. It could take one year for the project to be approved.

In the *private sector* a similar process is followed. However, the identification of a need for facilities may be done by any person with or without healthcare experience, for example a private developer or group of medical practitioners. The process can be viewed in Figure 8.2.

Briefing

A *temporary planning committee or briefing team* is appointed to take the project to the design stage. After the needs and the size of the hospital have been determined, the team sit together to prepare the design brief which translates the requirements into functions, activities and space distribution. The designers of the project and

Figure 8.2 The process of application and approval

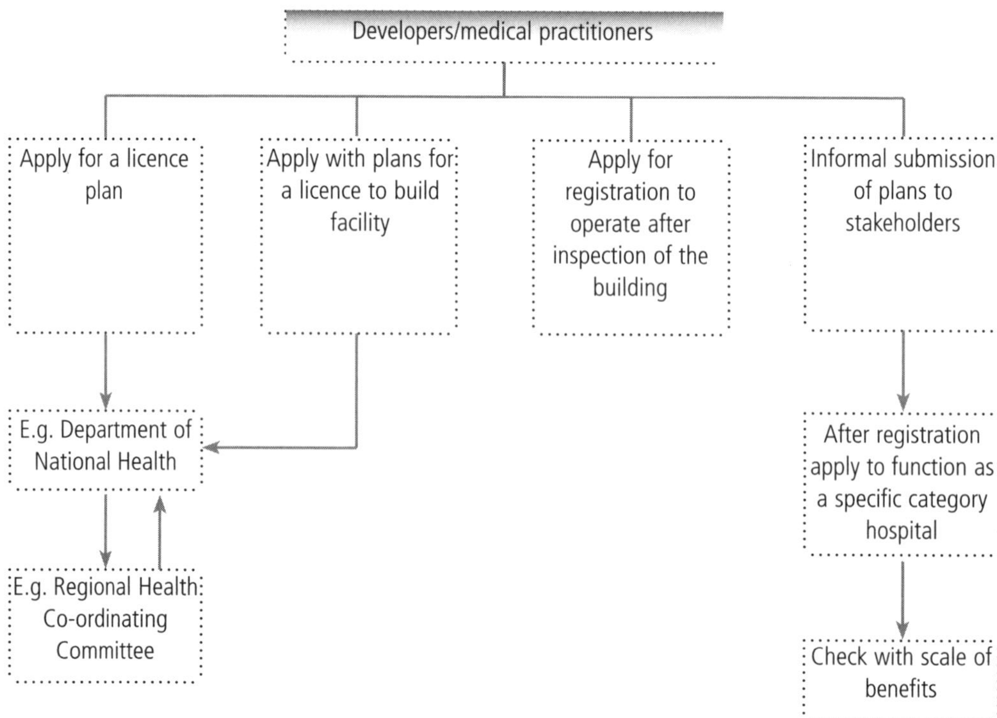

committee members (including healthcare and all service providers, architects, engineers, community leaders) develop a structured key document and influence the design and functioning of the building at this stage. The brief presents a written expression and clear picture of the intentions of the client. The hospital is viewed as a whole and the holistic brief will be used as a checklist once plans have been drawn and during the design stage.

The briefing documents comprise the following:

- **Schedule of accommodations: area/space/rooms/departments**. The schedules refer to the list of all rooms and spaces and their proposed sizes per department, the type and number of occupants, and the sizes and activities performed in them. The total gross area of the hospital or healthcare facility may not exceed the space norms (maximum space allowed) specified for the facility by government. The total gross area refers to the total area occupied by the whole facility, including wall thickness, corridors and staircases. The nett area is the area of the floor calculated to the interior of the containing walls and is the total area in all the listed rooms. The nett areas are calculated first and a grossing factor of between 25% and 45% is added to arrive at the gross area. To establish the recommended space in for example a medical private room, one can use an existing room with the existing furniture, then identify an absolute minimum space. Allowance can be made for more working space if additional space is available.

  The architect is allowed certain flexibility with the transfer of space between departments (in space norms) and together with the policy-makers (coordinators between architect and users) they can consult with the individual departments (users) to adapt space usage. The schedule of accommodation is a guideline and room sizes may change as the design develops.
- **Data sheet: description of room functions**. The room descriptions outline the:
  - functions to be performed in each type of room
  - services, fittings and equipment needed to fulfil the functions in the different rooms.

Table 8.3 Example of an item in a room description

Procedure/function	Facilities, fittings, equipment needed to perform function
Hand washing	Basin with elbow-operated taps Soap and towel dispenser Pedal action bin

Detailed descriptions of the requirements for every room in each department/unit must be provided. Firstly the functions performed in a room should be noted. The functions will lead to identifying the facilities needed to fulfil the functions. Facilities could be equipment, sanitary ware, fixtures such as mirrors, fittings, mechanical and electrical devices, finishes (e.g. floor coverings). A master set of room descriptions could be drawn up as a point of departure to assist departments to complete their room descriptions. The brief also assists in the commissioning phase to develop the operating policies and manuals for every department/unit.

- **Operational narrative**. This narrative describes how a department/facility is intended to function. It outlines the overall concept and the purpose of the facility as well as the:
  - functional content
  - philosophy/objectives of the service
  - planning principles namely policy/programmes of the services
  - workload
  - staffing
  - functional relationships
  - financial aspects.

All aspects are considered in order to decide whether to continue with current practices or to introduce changes.

Writing an operational narrative

In writing an operational narrative the following should apply:

- The **functional content** should indicate the size and content of departments, such as the number of operating theatres and the number of beds in wards.
- The **philosophy and objectives** of the service should give a concise description of the aims, activities and workload of the service, what the departments will and will not do.
- The **planning principles, policies and procedures** of the hospital should outline the:
  - population involved and provide relevant statistics of the consumers of the service
  - staffing principles, namely number and types of staff, peak periods of work, hours of work for different categories of healthcare professionals
  - admission and referral policies
  - functional relationships, namely external (between different departments/ wards) and internal relationships (e.g. relationships between the rooms such as the ward entrance, storeroom, nurses station, beds, dressing room in a general ward)
  - flow patterns and movement of patients, staff, supplies, food and refuse
  - support services such as catering, cleaning, portering, laundry and food
  - supply delivery, disposal of used goods
  - communication, mechanical, electrical services and specific needs per room

- specific physical environmental needs or equipment, or levels of temperature in specific departments
- staff categories, numbers and facilities required
- environmental factors and engineering with regard to fire protection, electric supply, sterilising and sterile supply, security, heating and ventilation, lighting, emergency alarm system, medical gases and vacuum, etc.

- The **workload**, namely the number of hours and the time that the hospital departments will work, the shifts, maintenance time and overtime.
- **Staffing** entails the number and types of staff, and peak periods of work.
- The **functional relationships** should be stipulated between departments and between rooms in a department.
- The **financial aspects** include the budget and possible sources of funds. The budget should include the costs of, for example, construction, professional services, fixed equipment, furniture and movable equipment, professional procurement and installation of equipment, site investigation and development (purchasing of land), insurance, legal counsel, and taxes. Possible sources of funds could be from central government, donations or grants, money generated by hospital activities prior to construction or money to be repaid from future activities.
- **Services and systems** are identified and only described in detail in the design phase. Hospitals and clinics may have any combination of clinical disciplines and services may be rendered at a general practitioner or specialist level of inpatients and/or outpatients. The following services and systems could be identified:
  - medical (e.g. general medical, cardiology, dermatology, haematology, neurology and immunology)
  - surgical (e.g. general surgery, urology, ophthalmology, neurosurgery, thoracic surgery and orthopaedics
  - intensive services (e.g medical emergency, trauma, paediatrics, burns unit, labour ward and renal dialysis)
  - obstetrics and gynaecology (infertility, labour, family planning, etc)
  - alternative medicine (e.g. chiropractor, traditional healer)
  - anaesthetics (e.g. pain clinic)
  - oncology
  - psychiatry
  - clinical support services (e.g. dental clinic, radiology, pathology, occupational therapy, social work, dietetics, community health)
  - general support systems (e.g. catering, linen handling, waste handling, pharmacy, central sterile supplies, infection control)
  - medical and electrical services (e.g. boilers, medical gas, lifts, communication, fire detection and protection)
  - auxiliary services (e.g. education and training, crèche, chapel, banks, post office, public telephones, library).

The outlined systems above should be finalised through the combined efforts of the briefing and design teams that represent as many relevant disciplines as possible. The schedules and narratives for each department should be developed alongside one another to be in balance with one another. The completed narrative guides the planners in the various medical, nursing and other functions to be performed and the requirements in terms of space, fixtures and equipment needed to carry out these functions.

The preparation for planners to participate consists of the following:

- Appointment of appropriate staff
- Reading critically
- Visiting other facilities
- Analysing current healthcare practices
- Anticipating trends.

The appointment of appropriate staff for the briefing team entails the following:

- The multidisciplinary team must have regular meetings chaired by for example a head of a department.
- Representatives of the different units should keep staff in their units updated about the process.
- Every member of the committee at operational level should be known with their functions and be provided with a format for drawing up the briefing documents.
- Management at middle level should draw up an integrated brief for the project.
- Community leaders with appropriate skills could be employed to participate in the planning, design and building phases.

Members of the briefing team should be encouraged to read about hospital and clinic planning in general. In this way lessons can be learned and mistakes avoided. Assistance should be utilised of authority documents and research institutes that describe requirements and solutions for the briefing phase.

Visits to similar services can be a learning situation by listening to the experience of others and documenting valuable information and mistakes to avoid. The visit should be characterised by concentrating on the specific area the team is planning and interviewing different categories of staff and patients. Records should be investigated with the focus on for example their special features and advantages. A report should be drawn up after the visit and the content of the report should be circulated to the relevant stakeholders.

An *analysis* of current healthcare practices and functions should be done to change and streamline work processes. Current facilities and equipment should be evaluated for their purposes.

Committee members should consider *expected developments and trends* in the healthcare setting. New buildings should be planned with the idea of remaining functional for as long as possible. Research findings should be studied for new trends and facilities and equipment needed to implement new trends. Leading manufacturers should be contacted for new products and their implications on space, finances, and staff training.

The coordination between the briefing and designing phases is very important in developing a plan that meets the need of the service. The meetings for the development of the brief lead to design meetings where plans are discussed. This multidisciplinary team could in the design phase continue with its duties but include design members such as architects and engineers. The brief should be thoroughly assessed and verified through discussions between the briefing and design teams.

Designing phase

The briefing team should become part of the design team for continuity in building the hospital that includes engineers, architects, quantity surveyors, hospital staff, the community and the approving authority. The layout and design is now completed and the method of construction is determined for approval by the relevant authorities. The design team produces the instruments for implementing construction, starting from preliminary investigation to the final designs with technical specification, tendering documents and detailed working drawings and estimates of cost.

The design stage is characterised by the *master plan, sketch plan* and *working drawing* stages, after which the latter is *verified with all the role-players*.

Master plan

After a careful analysis of the brief, a master plan is developed, that consititutes a proposal for the intended design of the building. The master plan indicates:

- The interdepartmental relationships
- The flow of patients, visitors, staff and goods in vertical and horizontal patterns
- The site development such as parking and traffic needs
- The other facilities, for example laundry on the building site
- The possibilities for future changes and expansions
- The costs involved for building the hospital or clinic.

Certain priorities are set, such as:

- The flow patterns, urgency and frequency of access between departments/units
- The urgent access between units such as ICU, neonatal nursery, labour ward and theatre.

Sketch plan

Changes regarding the layout of the hospital and individual departments/units should not be made after approval of the sketch plan stage. The first step is the schematic drawings that are developed to indicate the layout of each department and the relationship and size of each room in the department. These drawings reflect the schedules of accommodation and the operational narrative. The second step is drawing room layouts that are plans of individual rooms and indicate for example built-in equipment, wall thickness, and door and window openings. The sketch plan is completed when the room layouts are integrated with the initial line drawings.

Working drawing

Completed sketch plans are further developed into working drawings for the building contractor and have all the necessary information to carry out the project. The drawing includes the correct and detailed sizes and specifications of the architectural, mechanical and electrical services such as building materials, plumbing and lighting. Schedules that describe the doors, windows and furniture are also developed.

Clients give minimum input in developing the work drawings, however, their input in the approval of fixtures and fittings is needed.

The building is drawn on a small scale, for example 1:100 metres, and clients should understand and relate to the scale of the drawing. The working drawings include plans that are drawn as a horizontal section through the building and indicate internal and external walls, the positions of windows and doors, the position of all fittings (e.g. basins) and fixtures (e.g. built-in cupboards). Plans show width and length of the building. Elevations show the height and width of walls, position, size and shape of windows and doors, and the roof or overall profile of the building as seen flat. Sections indicate the vertical view through the building and show foundations and basements below ground level, the internal height of rooms, and ceilings and roof construction. The site plan on a small scale shows the position of the building, in block form, on the site with all roads, paving and other external features. A perspective shows the building design in three-dimensional format. The full set of sketch plans comprises plans (including site plan), elevations, sections and perspective of the building.

8.7 THE CONSTRUCTION PHASE

Building of service according to plan
Continuous monitoring

The main participants in the construction phase are the management team and the construction team. The building contractor, along with sub-contractors, suppliers of materials and equipment, designers, architects and specialists, should complete the project/hospital in accordance with the documentation. The construction team implements the design from the approved drawings and technical specifications in the prescribed time and cost. The client does not deal directly with the contractor. The architect supervises and performs site visits to the building project.

8.8 THE COMMISSIONING PHASE

The purpose of the commissioning stage is to ensure that construction work is completed according to the specific drawings so that the buildings become fully functional on handover to the client. The commissioning team is responsible to staff of the hospital, commissions and procures the equipment, furniture and supplies and prepares it for operation. The stakeholders in this process are the management team and the commissioning team (ideally the previously established planning team).

- Marketing
- Staffing
- Equipment
- Orientation
- Occupying the service
- Opening
- Evaluation

Commissioning becomes a formal process during construction. The community and healthcare professionals should be notified about the new hospital or clinic. Therefore the marketing process should be implemented at a reasonable time before the occupation of the building. The marketing and development function encompasses both the means of getting the patient to the hospital and future service development. Physician recruitment, relationships with insurance carriers and relationships with business and industry are all part of the marketing process. Development activities include packaging hospital services into programmes, such as ambulatory care and women's medicine. Different types of nursing units could be established (see Table 8.4).

This phase also includes the creation of *staff* posts. Staff are recruited, appointed and trained to use the systems and programmes in the new building correctly. *Orientation* of staff in this new environment is essential. Staff members are orientated to operational policies and procedures in the facility, as well as their job description. Senior staff members and key briefing team members are recruited at an early stage in the planning phase of the building. Because labour costs account for the major operating expenses in hospitals, activities associated with recruiting, hiring and retaining employees are of paramount concern. While this function does not differ greatly from other industries, the availability of some labour categories will vary across the rural-urban continuum because of the specialised nature of the work.

The purchasing function includes the procurement of medical, dietary, pharmaceutical supplies and custodial supplies. The ordering, receipt, checking, storage and placement of equipment should take place according to specific procedures and criteria (see box below). Contractors install equipment and services while the engineers and architect monitor the process. Planning should already have been made regarding acquiring new technology.

Table 8.4 Different types of nursing units

Type of unit	Description of unit
Florence Nightingale	Open 30–40 beds Visibility/supervision high Duty room/station far
Continental	Duty room central More patient privacy 1–4 beds per sub-unit
Duplex	More duty rooms More accessibility Promotes team nursing Team wards/units
Racetrack	Double corridor Promotion of compactness 50–60 beds
Courtyard	Natural light/environment Economical space utilisation
Cluster	Better vision/visibility Short distances
Radial	Utilisation of space Shorter distances

If the building is completed it can formally be handed over and opened. The handover process involves room-to-room inspection of the facility by the designers, owners and the contractor. Procedures for the handover should be followed and the retention period specified. During the retention period the building and equipment are checked for reparations.

The healthcare service manager has a role to play in research-based decisions regarding the commissioning process by reading relevant literature regarding the process, visiting similar settings for ideas and avoiding making mistakes in the commissioning process, having interviews with the relevant provider/consumers of the service. The healthcare service manager should promote teamwork during the whole process.

In commissioning of units certain criteria should be taken into consideration (see box below).

Purchasing and purchasing criteria of equipment

Assessment of equipment needed
Type/quantity of equipment
Research into the best possible equipment according to criteria
Manufacturers/types of equipment and prices

Purchasing criteria

- Cost
- Durability
- Service contract
- User friendliness and practical utilisation value
- Aesthetics/culture sensitivity
- Ordering/delivery system to use
- Storage: place/venue and security
- Inventory system
- Maintenance of equipment
- Procedure and policy
- Staff orientation
- Type and operating of equipment

Criteria: Clinical units

General aspects

- Efficiency/economical
- According to type of service delivery
- Utilisation of space
- Productivity
- Adaptability
- Appearance/market value
- Positioning in the services

Patient

- Privacy
- Safety
- Noise control
- Ventilation/light/air

Location of convenience facilities
Location supplementary services
Culture sensitivity taken into consideration

Evaluation instruments such as the Programme Evaluation Review Technique (PERT) are used to evaluate that the project is completed on time. The PERT is a timetable that indicates the chronological steps and time duration of the steps in building a new facility.

Evaluation of the new facility

It is important to monitor and evaluate the performance of a new facility after it has been operational for about a year and to continue to do so at regular intervals. Evaluation may reveal defects in operation of the hospital that can be corrected quickly and easily. For instance, the facilities may not be used as intended, or defects in building design might be overcome by changing methods of use.

Evaluation may reveal defects in the design that can be overcome by changing equipment, relocating activities or redirecting traffic. It will reveal where the design is giving trouble in practice and where it is working well. This will indicate where changes are needed and avoid change for the sake of change.

Evaluation comprises five steps:

(1) Deciding the objectives of the evaluation
(2) Setting up the necessary organisation
(3) Gathering the required information
(4) Analysing the information
(5) Communicating the findings.

The factors that should be evaluated are:

- Performance in use, as perceived by the users, both staff and patients
- Basic records that indicate the known advantages and drawbacks of the buildings with regard to the activities of the users
- Objective observations of performance on site, including the activities in relation to the physical layout, the effect of the layout and siting on the activities in relation to the community, and the activities and work needed to keep the facility functioning
- Objective observation of the performance of the hospital as a building, in terms of layout and siting of buildings, structure, finishes and equipment
- Information on maintenance and running costs for comparison with the planned costs and previous annual recurring costs
- Examination of the extent to which the building fulfils the brief given to the designers and whether it is being used in the way intended at the time the brief was prepared
- Review of the planning decisions that led to the preparation of the brief, examination of the relationship between the objectives and the physical conditions observed in the facilities
- Consideration of the adaptability of the facility to meet future demands and to cope with changing needs.

8.9 UNDERLYING DYNAMICS

The following dynamics are some factors that can hinder or promote the planning and commissioning process:

- Government regulations and policies directing the whole process
- The adequate knowledge and expertise of all stakeholders to effectively implement the process
- Financial resources to implement the process of planning and commissioning appropriately and effectively
- Human resources available in offering a quality service to the community.

8.10 CONCLUDING STATEMENTS

- A hospital should be viewed as a service not a building.
- Commissioning can be described as bringing a hospital building and equipment to a state of readiness, for operational use, with an adequate number of trained staff members to function according to systems, as designed.
- Human resources planning is an essential part in relation to commissioning.
- The aim of the planning and commissioning process is to develop a balanced, functional building for patients and staff members alike.
- Steps in the planning phase are market analysis, application and approval, briefing and design.
- The construction phase entails the building of a service according to plan and continuous monitoring.
- The commissioning phase includes the processes of marketing, staffing, equipment, orientation, occupying the service and the opening of the service.

Self-assessment

Activities

(1) Design a strategy for purchasing new equipment for a new healthcare service.
(2) Design an instrument with appropriate decision-making criteria for the purchasing of new equipment.

Questions

(1) Describe and debate the national principles of planning and commissioning of healthcare services.
(2) Identify and describe the types of healthcare services in your country.
(3) Describe and interpret the healthcare service manager's responsibilities in the planning and commissioning of healthcare services.

➜

(4) Describe and debate the phases of healthcare service planning and commissioning:
- Application and approval
- Orientation
- Design
- Construction
- Commissioning

(5) Describe and interpret the process of staffing in the nursing service to ensure cost-effective utilisation of staff during the planning and commissioning phases.

9 Management of HIV and AIDS

KEY CONCEPTS

HIV and AIDS
Workplace programme
Clinical governance

SPECIFIC OUTCOMES

After studying this chapter, you should be able to:

- Interpret the legal, professional-ethical and healthcare **context**, with reference to the global context (global and business response, ILO code of practice, ISO standards and other international organisations), the constitution, corporate governance, national code of good practice, and human resource-related legislation
- Analyse and debate the **purpose** of HIV and AIDS management, with reference to the mitigation and management of HIV and AIDS
- Identify the main categories of **role-players** (employer and employee in the workplace context, and clinical role-players) and interpret their roles and responsibilities in the management of HIV and AIDS
- Describe and apply the **process** (dimensions) of HIV and AIDS management with reference to the establishment of workplace programmes and the clinical management of HIV and AIDS
- Debate the **underlying dynamics** that could impact on the quality of HIV and AIDS management, focusing on management's commitment, economic and social forces, as well as selected ethical challenges.

9.1 INTRODUCTION

HIV and AIDS have brought about a pandemic far more extensive than what was predicted approximately a decade ago. Still rapidly growing, the pandemic is reversing development gains, obliterating millions of lives, widening the gap between rich and poor, and undermining social and economic security. It has become a major cause of disease burden in sub-Saharan Africa and South Africa in particular, and – arguably – the single most important phenomenon that will shape future demographic, health and development trends in most of Africa. The pandemic impacts mainly on the following sectors: health, education, business/industry, households and the community.

Factors impacting the spread of HIV and AIDS

The following factors are fuelling the spread of HIV and AIDS:
- Poverty and economic marginalisation
- Inter-country and intra-country migration and mobility
- Gender inequity and female subordination
- Sexual violence, abuse and exploitation of women
- Ignorance, denial, myths and cultural beliefs
- High prevalence of STIs and associated HIV infection.

9.2 CONTEXT

The context is elucidated, focusing on the global context, the constitution, corporate governance, the national code of good practice, and human resource-related legislation.

9.2.1 Global context

The global context is described with reference to the International Labour Organisation (ILO), the International Standardisation Organisation's Standards for HIV/AIDS Management System (ISO, 2003: AMS, 16001:2003), and other international organisations, such as the World Health Organisation and The United Nations Children's Fund.

9.2.1.1 Global and business response

The global response to the HIV and AIDS pandemic in the world of work is manifold. The ILO established a programme in 2001, and drafted a Code of Practice the same year to guide response to the pandemic as a workplace issue. Several countries have drafted enlightened legislation in the form of revised or new laws that can play an important role in mitigating the impact of HIV and AIDS in the workplace and protecting the rights of persons who are living with HIV and AIDS. There are efforts in numerous countries in a range of response areas focusing on both prevention and treatment that include developing national sectoral policies, community efforts to reduce stigma and discrimination, private-sector initiatives to promote prevention, behavioural change communication for workers, and, finally, treatment programmes in the workplace, which are increasingly seen by a range of enterprises as the least costly option to maintain profitability and ensure growth (ILO, 2004:xii).

The main responsibilities are described by the ILO (2004:34–35) in the context of specific policy implications with regard to the establishment of a policy and legal framework, development of a research strategy, sustaining educational and training capacity, focusing on poverty, integrating development strategy and sustaining employment.

Figure 9.1 Visual presentation of the Management of HIV and AIDS in a healthcare organisation

Context	Global and business response ILO code of practice ISO standards Other international organisations Constitution Corporate governance National code of good practice Human resource-related legislation
Purpose	Reduce the threat of the spread of HIV and AIDS Mitigate the impact of HIV and AIDS Manage the impact of HIV and AIDS in an ethical and socially responsible manner Foster sustainability of the workforce in organisations Facilitate quality clinical management of HIV and AIDS
Role-players	Employer and employee in the workplace Clinical role-players in the clinical management of HIV and AIDS
Process	**Establishment of workplace programmes**: • Leadership and management framework • Prevention and awareness programmes • Care and support programmes **Clinical governance** • Management and leadership • Human resource management • Administrative support • Access to care • Patient and family rights • Information management • Health and safety • Prevention and control of infection • Medical and surgical care • Obstetric/maternity care • Voluntary Counselling and Testing (VCT) • Antiretroviral therapy • Quality management and improvement
Underlying dynamics	Management's commitment Economic forces Social forces Ethical challenges

Establishing a policy and legal framework

It must be determined whether a framework of policy and of law exists to protect the rights of all persons and workers living with HIV and AIDS, to promote prevention, and to provide care and support in both formal and informal workplaces. Where gaps are identified, it will be important to identify the obstacles to filling them in. As HIV and AIDS have far-reaching effects on sustainable development, it is critical to move beyond the immediate effects of the epidemic and review how social sector plans integrate HIV and AIDS. It is also important to assess whether governments are taking account of the effects of the pandemic on human capital in their public expenditure and development plans, and whether government and major employers understand and plan to address its labour market and employment implications (ILO, 2004:34).

Developing a research strategy

There is a scarcity of qualitative and quantitative information relating to the impact of HIV and AIDS on labour markets. This can be remedied only through a programme of applied research focusing on the needs of policy- and decision-makers to identify what is currently happening to labour supply and labour demand in different labour markets, and the implications of these trends for development processes (ILO, 2004:35).

Sustaining educational and training capacity

Loss of human capital is a result of HIV and AIDS that burdens the capacities of all training institutions in unpredictable ways. It is essential that capacity be sustained if countries are to move towards fulfilment of the Millennium Development goals and their specific targets. Human capital audits can help support the planning of educational supply relative to demand (ILO, 2004:35).

Focusing on poverty

There is a crucial need for applied research to identify what is happening to rural poverty and food insecurity, and what can be done to strengthen policy and programme assistance for affected populations. It is clear that an expansion of food support will be necessary and that children will require targeted health and nutrition programmes. The latter are critical to enabling the future labour supply of the country to benefit from access to educational and other programmes relating to skills development, which ultimately enhances productivity (ILO, 2004:35).

Integrating development strategy

The workload of women is already excessive and HIV and AIDS increase demands made on women who are themselves often HIV-positive. It is essential that the greater constraints that face both agriculture and informal economic activities be urgently addressed, and that programmes be rapidly developed to relieve such constraints. It is evident from country experience in sub-Saharan Africa that relatively small-scale investment with a focus on women's labour can significantly reduce labour constraints (ILO, 2004:35).

Sustaining employment

The labour force will consist of younger and less well-educated persons – a fact that will make it more difficult to create and sustain employment growth. It may well be that the new conditions cannot be left to market processes alone to address. A deliberate programme aimed at enhancing labour skills through vocational education and training is probably essential, requiring public investment in building human and organisational capacity. It will be possible to tackle employment growth only under conditions where the labour supply has the skills requested by public and private employers (ILO, 2004:35).

9.2.1.2 ILO Code of Practice

In addition to the global and business response to the pandemic, the ILO Code of Practice is also relevant. Every organisation/company has a responsibility to establish workplace programmes. These programmes should comply with the global, national and regional/local policy frameworks and directives. The ILO Code of Practice (ILO, 2001) reflects an international framework for the management of HIV and AIDS in the world of work. The Code sets out fundamental principles for policy development and practical guidelines from which concrete responses to HIV and AIDS can be developed at enterprise, community and national levels. It promotes a comprehensive approach to workplace programmes, including:

- The protection of workers' rights, including employment protection, gender equality, entitlement to benefits and non-discrimination
- Prevention through education, gender-aware programmes, and practical support for behavioural change
- Care and support, including reasonable accommodation of access to benefits, confidential voluntary testing and counselling, and treatment in settings where local healthcare systems are inadequate.

The Code contains ten fundamental principles for policies at national and enterprise levels, and practical guidance for workplace programmes. Workplace programmes should therefore reflect the ten principles in accordance with the International Labour Organisation's (2001) Code of Practice: HIV/AIDS in the world of work.

Recognition of HIV and AIDS as a workplace issue

HIV and AIDS are a workplace issue because the conditions affect workers and enterprises – cutting the workforce (by up to 30% in some countries), increasing labour costs and reducing productivity. They should be treated like any other serious illness/condition in the workplace: this statement aims to counter discrimination and also the fears and myths that surround HIV and AIDS. The workplace has a role to play in the wider struggle to limit the spread and effects of the pandemic.

Non-discrimination

There should be no discrimination against workers on the basis of real or perceived HIV-positive status. Non-discrimination is a fundamental principle of the ILO and is at the heart of the response of the ILO to the pandemic. The principle of non-discrimination extends to employment status, recognised dependants, and access to health insurance, pension funds and other staff entitlements. Discrimination and stigmatisation of people living with HIV and AIDS inhibit efforts aimed at promoting HIV and AIDS prevention: if people are frightened of the possibility of discrimination, they will probably conceal their status and are more likely to pass on the infection to others. Moreover, they will not seek treatment or counselling. All successful prevention initiatives have been part of a wider approach that included establishing an atmosphere of openness, trust and a firm stand against discrimination.

Gender equality

The gender dimensions of HIV and AIDS should be recognised. Women are more likely to become infected and are more often adversely affected by the HIV and AIDS pandemic than men, for biological, socio-cultural and economic reasons. It is, therefore, important that HIV and AIDS programmes respond to the circumstances and needs of men and women separately, as well as together – both in terms of prevention and social protection – to mitigate the impact of the pandemic.

Healthy work environment

The work environment should be healthy and safe, as far as is practical, for all concerned parties. This includes the responsibility of employers to provide for information and education on HIV transmission, and appropriate first-aid provisions in the event of an accident. It does not, however, give employers the right to test employees for HIV in the interest of public health, because casual contact at the workplace presents no risk of HIV transmission. A healthy work environment facilitates adaptation of work to the capabilities of workers, in light of their physical and mental health, thereby mitigating the impact of AIDS on workers and the enterprise alike.

Social dialogue

The successful implementation of an HIV and AIDS policy and programme requires cooperation and trust between employers, workers and their representatives and government, where appropriate: this is not only fundamental to the way the ILO works, but is very practical in that any policy is more likely to be implemented effectively if it has been developed with the full participation of all concerned parties.

No screening for purposes of exclusion from employment or work processes

HIV and AIDS screening should not be required of job applicants or persons in employment. HIV testing not only violates the right to confidentiality, but is impractical and unnecessary. At best, an HIV test result is a 'snapshot' of someone's infection status. It is no guarantee that he/she will not become infected tomorrow, or next month. It should also be remembered that people with HIV may remain perfectly fit and healthy for many years.

Confidentiality

There is no justification for asking job applicants or workers to disclose personal HIV-related information. Nor should co-workers be obliged to reveal such personal information about fellow workers. The right to confidentiality does not, of course, apply only to HIV and AIDS; rules of confidentiality apply to all workers.

Continuation of employment relationship

HIV infection is not a cause for termination of employment. As with many other conditions, persons with HIV-related illnesses should be encouraged to work for as long as medically fit in available, appropriate work. This principle is based on the fact that being HIV-positive is not the same as having AIDS and a number of possible opportunistic infections. Reasonable accommodation to help workers continue in employment can include rearrangement of working time, special equipment, opportunities for rest breaks, time off for medical appointments, flexible sick leave, part-time work and return-to-work arrangements.

Prevention

HIV infection is preventable. Prevention of all means of transmission can be achieved through a variety of strategies – guidelines and examples are given in succeeding sections of the Code. Prevention can be furthered through a combination of information, participatory education (including personal risk assessment and life skills), practical support for behavioural change (such as condom distribution), and treatment for sexually transmitted infections.

Care and support

Solidarity, care and support should guide the response to HIV and AIDS in the world of work. Prevention, care and treatment should be seen as a continuum, rather than separate elements, of a workplace programme. The availability of treatment encourages confidential voluntary testing, making it easier to provide care and encouraging prevention. Care and support include the provision of voluntary testing and counselling; treatment for opportunistic infections, especially tuberculosis (and antiretroviral therapy, where affordable); workplace accommodation; employee and family assistance programmes; and access to benefits from health insurance and occupational schemes.

9.2.1.3 ISO standards

The ISO (AMS 16001:2003) standards for the Management of HIV/AIDS in the workplace specify requirements for an HIV/AIDS management system, to enable an organisation to manage its HIV/AIDS-related risks and improve its sustainability and business performance. The standards focus on the following:

- An organisational management HIV/AIDS system, principles and elements
- Management commitment and HIV/AIDS management policy
- Planning of HIV/AIDS management system
- Identification of HIV determinants and evaluation of related risks
- HIV/AIDS-related legal and other requirements
- HIV/AIDS management objective and targets
- HIV/AIDS management plans
- Structure and responsibility
- HIV/AIDS management awareness, education and competence
- HIV/AIDS documentation system
- HIV/AIDS management document control
- Operational controls and management of HIV/AIDS management system
- Emergency response and control.

9.2.1.4 Other international organisations

There are many other international organisations, such as the World Health Organisation and UNICEF. The World Health Organisation provides international leadership in the consultation, research and guidelines on the prevention, mitigation and management of HIV and AIDS. Various international strategies – such as the UNICEF 'Fighting HIV/AIDS Strategies for Success 2002–2005' – also provide international guidelines.

9.2.2 Constitution

The Constitution (South Africa, 1996) makes provision for the Bill of Rights, with reference to the following:

- **Equality**. This is to protect infected employees and people living with AIDS (PLWA) against unfair discrimination.
- **Freedom and security of the person**. This is for protection against coercion, for example testing for HIV without informed consent in accordance with the national regulation/policy in this regard (South Africa, 1999).
- **Privacy and confidentiality.** This relates to the disclosure of status.
- **Labour relations.** This confirms the right to fair labour practice.
- **Access to healthcare**. This ensures access regardless of HIV and AIDS status.

9.2.3 Corporate governance

Companies have several social responsibilities, which include the management of HIV and AIDS in the workplace. Matters requiring specific consideration with regard to the principles of integrated sustainability reporting include the following: the nature and extent of strategy, plan and policies adopted to address and manage the potential impact of HIV and AIDS on the company's activities (PricewaterhouseCoopers, 2003:85). In addition to this, Bendell (2003) suggests international corporate governance practice with reference to reporting by listed private companies. At a minimum, a group-level corporate policy should aim to ensure that all subsidiaries and group companies go through a process of assessing:

- The current and potential impact of critical illnesses such as HIV and AIDS on their workforce, customer base, and stakeholder relations, as well as their financial performance
- Whether their current policies, programmes and practices on various issues, such as occupational health, human resources, industrial relations, marketing and external relations, are compatible with best practice guidelines on critical illnesses such as HIV and AIDS and, therefore
  - what additional prevention measures they can take to reduce exposure to critical illness vectors such as HIV infection – rather than just reducing their immediate exposure to additional costs
  - what additional mitigation measures they can take to manage and reduce the impact of critical illnesses, such as AIDS – rather than just reducing their immediate exposure to additional costs
- How their normal course of business, including all functions such as tax management, lobbying and strategy, affect critical illnesses such as HIV and AIDS through impacts on poverty and inequality, and the capacity of governments
- How they might adjust their strategy, policy and practice to improve their contribution to poverty and inequality reduction and capacity of governments
- How they are supporting or undermining a sector-wide response to the direct and indirect causes of critical illnesses such as HIV and AIDS, particularly factors influencing the capacity of non-private actors to address this
- Whether they have appropriate monitoring, evaluation and reporting processes in place for their policies, programmes and practices that may affect critical illnesses such as HIV and AIDS.

9.2.4 National Code of Good Practice on key aspects of HIV and AIDS and employment

The National Code of Good Practice with regard to the employer-employee relationship (with reference to HIV and AIDS), is applicable. This Code is a policy and encourages employers to develop their own HIV and AIDS policies to:

- Prevent unfair discrimination at work on the basis of employees' HIV status
- Encourage people living with AIDS (PLWA) to be open about their HIV status without fear
- Create a balance between the rights and responsibilities of everyone at work.

9.2.5 Human resource-related legislation

There is various human resource-related legislation that protects staff against discrimination, unfair labour practices and occupational health and safety hazards: Employment Equity Act (South Africa, 1998), Labour Relations Act (South Africa, 1995), Basic Conditions of Employment Act (South Africa, 1997), as well as other related legislation/regulations.

9.2.6 National strategies

Various national strategies (according to the ministerial directorates, i.e. health and education), give direction to the management of HIV and AIDS. The South African Department of Health (2000) has published its strategy for 2000–2005. This strategy represents the national strategy against the pandemic. The strategic plan is built around the following dimensions: prevention, treatment, care and support, human and legal rights, and monitoring, research and surveillance. It lays emphasis on effective and culturally appropriate information, education and counselling, increasing acceptability of Voluntary Counselling and Testing (VCT), improving management of STDs and promoting condom use to reduce sexual transmission of the virus, and improving the care and treatment of people living with HIV and AIDS. The strategic plan provides a framework for developing operational plans with set indicators for monitoring the success of the country in response to the pandemic. A national coordinating body has been established (the South African AIDS Council) to facilitate inter-sectoral integration and collaborative management of the problem.

9.3 PURPOSE

The purpose of HIV and AIDS management is as follows:

- To reduce the threat of the spread of HIV and AIDS
- To mitigate the impact of HIV and AIDS
- To manage the impact of HIV and AIDS in an ethical and socially responsible manner
- To facilitate quality clinical management of HIV and AIDS in the healthcare organisation
- To foster sustainability of the workforce in the organisation.

9.4 ROLE-PLAYERS

The role-players in the management of HIV and AIDS are briefly highlighted with reference to the employer-employee relationship, and the clinical role-players.

9.4.1 Employer and employee

The employer-employee relationship is based on the national and international principles of workplace practice, focusing on at least the following:

- Sustaining employment

- Recognition of HIV and AIDS as a workplace issue
- Non-discrimination
- Gender equality
- Healthy work environment
- Social dialogue
- No screening for purposes of exclusion from employment or work processes
- Confidentiality
- Continuation of employment relationship
- Prevention
- Care and support.

9.4.2 Clinical role-players

The clinical role-players are those clinical managers and clinicians responsible for the implementation of the clinical management regimes, in accordance with the national, provincial and district/local strategies, policies and performance indicators.

9.5 PROCESS

The process is described with reference to workplace programmes and clinical governance.

9.5.1 Workplace programme

A workplace programme refers to a formalised programme for employees with HIV and AIDS, focusing on at least the following: leadership and structure, awareness, prevention, care and support, employee assistance, as well as employee benefits. The objectives of a workplace programme are to:

- Establish, maintain and improve an HIV and AIDS management system
- Mitigate and manage the impact of HIV and AIDS on the organisation's workforce
- Ensure a safe and supportive working environment for all employees
- Develop capacity amidst the impact of the epidemic in an organisation
- Comply with the international and national standards and codes of practice/ conduct.

The workplace programme should address at least the following: leadership and management framework, prevention and awareness programmes, as well as care and support programmes.

Leadership and management framework

The leadership and policy framework should consist of:

- Designated leadership or manager (institutional officer), with a defined role, responsibility and authority, to manage HIV and AIDS in the workplace
- HIV and AIDS management structure – functional HIV and AIDS manager in the

human resources management department, HIV and AIDS Committee, support groups and social dialogue sessions
- HIV and AIDS policy, in accordance with the international (ILO and ISO) and National Code of Practice/Conduct, including information management and the confidentiality thereof
- HIV and AIDS strategy – HIV/AIDS determinant identification and risk assessment, mitigation and management (goals, objectives, targets, plans, implementation strategies, monitoring and evaluation of conformance methods, etc.)
- HIV and AIDS audit system to determine compliance with the organisational strategy and the impact of AIDS on the organisation
- Appropriate HIV and AIDS information management system (including documentation control)
- Updated HIV/AIDS-related legal and other requirements
- Conditions of Service to benefit employees living with AIDS – reflecting reasonable accommodation of access to benefits, such as opportunities for rest breaks, time off for medical appointments, flexible sick leave, part-time work and return-to-work programmes
- Appropriate HIV and AIDS-related workplace procedures
- Appropriate risk management programmes for occupational and non-occupational exposures (proactive, continuous and reactive)
- Appropriate communication structures and strategies
- Research programmes and/or the support thereof
- Annual reporting, in accordance with the principles of corporate governance – nature and extent of strategy, plan and policies adopted to address and manage the potential impact of HIV and AIDS on the company's activities (PricewaterhouseCoopers, 2003:85)
- HIV and AIDS management system review.

Prevention and awareness programmes

Prevention and awareness programmes focus on at least the following:
- Education and awareness programmes in the workplace, utilising the model for Science Education for New Civic Engagements and Responsibilities (SENCER)
- Skills development programmes to ensure competence in the prevention, mitigation and management of HIV and AIDS in the workplace
- Participatory education programmes, referred to as Peer Group Education
- Programmes to facilitate behavioural change
- Condom distribution
- Voluntary Counselling and Testing (VCT) programmes, crucial to all employees, who should be encouraged to use testing services to determine their status in a context of informed consent, confidentiality and non-discrimination
- Occupational health and safety programmes.

Care and support programmes

Care and support programmes in the workplace should focus on at least the following:

- Wellness management, such as Employee Assistance Programme for employees living with AIDS, including psychosocial support
- Access to treatment and drugs, both therapeutic and palliative, such as antiretroviral therapy and treatment for opportunistic infections and STIs
- Nutritional support for PLWA.

9.5.2 Clinical governance

Healthcare organisations are also responsible for the clinical management of HIV and AIDS as part of their core business (in accordance with the business ownership of the healthcare organisation). The following standard dimensions are highlighted (COHSASA, 2004: service element 42):

(1) Management and leadership

- The establishment of a specialised HIV and AIDS clinical department, with designated clinical leadership and a strategic plan, in accordance with the pre-defined level of service delivery (primary healthcare, etc.)
- All the specialised services are available (VCT services, ARV treatment, etc.), in accordance with the pre-defined level of service delivery
- Specific HIV and AIDS management policies and procedures are developed, in accordance with the national, provincial and local guidelines
- Appropriate community engagement is reflected
- Collaborative management practice with other service providers are evident
- Referral services are identified and adequately utilised
- Alignment with the national, provincial or local strategy is reflected.

(2) Human resource management

- Human resource management is in accordance with generic national legislation and subsequent related regulations
- Human resource management is in accordance with the national and provincial policies and guidelines for HIV and AIDS specialisation (minimum qualifications related to the clinical management of HIV and AIDS)
- Clinical project leaders are assigned where and when appropriate
- Appropriate staffing and staff mixes of the relevant clinical practitioners involved in the implementation or roll-out of the HIV and AIDS clinical management programmes and strategies
- Performance management is exercised in accordance with national, provincial and district authorities' guidelines and policies
- Human resource management is in accordance with the organisational strategy, policy and specialised clinical management of HIV and AIDS

- Continuous professional development of clinical practitioners is in accordance with the national department of health requirements, as well as the profession's regulatory requirements.

(3) Administrative support

- There is adequate administrative support to facilitate effective and efficient implementation of the national, provincial and local HIV and AIDS management strategies
- General management and administration systems are in place to accommodate and support the clinical programmes and special projects (financial management, information management, etc.)
- Adequate communication structures and systems are in place to facilitate efficient and quality service delivery.

(4) Access to care

- Patients have access to the healthcare organisation for general HIV and AIDS-related treatment and care
- Patients have access to specialised treatment (i.e. antiretroviral therapy) in accordance with the international (WHO) and national protocols and guidelines in this regard (defining the stage of the disease and the clinical condition of the patient)
- Inter-sectoral/institutional treatment/referral systems are in place, and facilitate access to care
- Follow-up care policies and procedures are available
- Appropriate palliative care systems are established or activated.

(5) Patient and family rights

- There are adequate systems and processes in place to ensure compliance with patient and family rights
- Family-care participation strategies are in place
- Patient confidentiality is protected in accordance with the various clinical professions' codes of ethics
- The principles of international and national research ethics are adhered to, with evidence of the appropriate formalised and accredited ethical clearance structures
- Patient rights are protected in accordance with international standards and the national charter(s) in this regard.

(6) General and clinical information management

- There is a general and clinical information management system in accordance with international and national practice standards
- Clinical record-keeping is in accordance with the regulatory and ethical requirements of the various professions

- An individual clinical care plan is developed for each patient
- Compliance with national legislative requirements is illustrated (i.e. access to information legislation), by developing and implementing related policies and procedures
- Policies and procedures related to data entry, clinical assessment and evaluation of patient progress, modification of care plans or treatment regimes, and discharge authorisation, are developed, adhered to and continuously reviewed and updated
- There is a system to ensure trustworthy practitioner exchange, storing and retrieval of clinical patient records.

(7) Health and safety

- The healthcare organisation's occupational health and safety programme is executed
- Special occupational health and safety measures are in place to prevent or mitigate HIV transmission to staff and other patients
- There is a system to make provision for the procurement, distribution and management of post-exposure prophylaxis settings (i.e. needle-stick injuries and bodily fluid contamination).

(8) Prevention and control of infection

- The organisation-wide infection control programme is executed
- HIV-infected patients are protected from opportunistic nosocomial infections
- Opportunistic infections of patients with HIV and AIDS are treated in accordance with the national guidelines and protocols
- Universal precautions are intensified during the clinical care of patients with AIDS
- Immunisation of children infected with HIV or living with AIDS is in accordance with the national protocols/guidelines
- Referral pathways for infections associated with HIV and AIDS are in accordance with the national guidelines
- Drugs specified by national guidelines for the prophylaxis of common opportunistic infections are available.

(9) General medical and surgical care

- The delivery of medical and surgical services is integrated and coordinated during all phases of care
- Clinical practitioners involved in medical and surgical services of patients with HIV and AIDS are appropriately trained in accordance with the HIV and AIDS training requirements of the national department of health
- Clinical practice guidelines for the diagnosis and management of HIV and AIDS – and related problems – are in accordance with national, provincial and local policies, protocols and guidelines

- Nutritional assessment is performed and the appropriate nutritional support is given to patients with HIV and AIDS
- Exchange of information in clinical records is subject to the voluntary informed consent or informed assent of the patient and/or guardian concerned, in accordance with national regulatory requirements.

(10) Obstetric/maternity care

- All public obstetric healthcare organisations are adequately equipped (including MTCT drugs) for the management of HIV obstetric management
- All obstetric patients are offered VCT
- There are policies and procedures for the management of obstetric care of mothers infected with HIV, in accordance with national, provincial and local guidelines
- There are policies and procedures to address Mother-to-Child-Transmission (MTCT), in accordance with national, provincial and local guidelines (i.e. mode of delivery, minimisation of obstetric interventions, drug treatment and breastfeeding)
- All HIV-infected obstetric patients are offered Mother-To-Child-Transmission (MTCT) prophylactic measures in accordance with national guidelines
- Follow-up testing of infants born to mothers with HIV is in accordance with national guidelines
- All HIV-infected mothers are referred to defined HIV services following delivery.

(11) Voluntary Counselling and Testing (VCT)

- The VCT site is accredited in accordance with the national guidelines
- VCT staff are appropriately trained and qualified in accordance with the national guidelines and programme accreditation requirements
- VCT management is in accordance with the national guidelines (informed consent, pre- and post-test counselling, execution of the test, as well as referrals when applicable).

(12) Antiretroviral (ARV) therapy

- ARV management is in accordance with the national roll-out strategy
- ARV therapists (clinical practitioners, counsellors, etc.) are adequately trained in accordance with national requirements
- ARV systems are in place to ensure procurement, storage and sustainable supply of drugs, prescription and dispensing, in accordance with national requirements
- ARV laboratory support systems and equipment are in place, in accordance with the national, provincial and local management regimes
- ARV management is in accordance with the provincial, national and international guidelines (selection of patients, administration of drugs, monitoring and assessment of side-effects and appropriate interventions accordingly)

- The clinical management of ARV is in accordance with the local, provincial and national guidelines, taking into consideration the immunologic, clinical and virological indicators/markers
- Patients on ARV therapy are monitored in accordance with the protocol-defined intervals, utilising clinical, immunological and virological indicators/parameters, as stipulated in local, provincial and national guidelines
- Failure of ARV therapy is diagnosed and investigated according to the local, provincial and national guidelines
- Patients are continuously counselled on expected outcomes, side-effects and adherence to issues related to the ARV programme
- ARV agents are administered in the context of a robust treatment literacy campaign for patients, and in a system to monitor patients defaulting programme appointments and ARV pharmacy refills.

(13) Quality management and improvement

- There is a formalised quality improvement management system in place, focusing on the relevant clinical and non-clinical HIV and AIDS management-related interventions and activities
- There is a written quality improvement programme in place, compliant with the principles of trustworthiness (validity, methods of data-collection and analyses, and reliability of results)
- There is evidence of the full quality improvement cycle being implemented, consisting of setting of standards, monitoring and evaluation of compliance with standards, and remedial action taken accordingly (refer to Chapter 19 Quality improvement models in a healthcare organisation)
- Performance indicators (clinical and non-clinical) are developed, monitored and evaluated
- There is a system for the monitoring of adverse events (negative incidents) in the management of HIV and AIDS.

9.6 UNDERLYING DYNAMICS

A few underlying dynamics, impacting on the quality of HIV and AIDS management, are highlighted:

- Management's (including the board of directors, where applicable) commitment to deal with the problem in a moral and socially acceptable manner
- Economic forces – the institutional capacity (physical resources, finance, human resources, etc.) to cope with the financial demands related to the offering of exceptional fringe benefits, antiretroviral therapy to employees, and other 'reasonable accommodation' activities

- Social forces – the social expectations and demands placed on healthcare organisations to comply with international standards with reference to workplace programmes and the clinical treatment of HIV and AIDS
- There are many ethical challenges related to the management of HIV and AIDS. Many of these challenges reflect a paradox between moral views, fears and expectations of various role-players. The ethical challenges mainly relate to clinical (confidentiality or disclosure of status, informed consent and end-of-life issues), social (sustaining production and productivity, social programmes, support and benefits, gender equality, care, treatment and support), political (impact of HIV and AIDS on business activity versus the impact of the business on HIV and AIDS, access to ARV treatment, compliance with national and international codes of practice, etc.) and research (protection of vulnerable groups versus knowledge generation responsibilities) challenges.

9.7 CONCLUDING STATEMENTS

The destructive power of the HIV and AIDS pandemic on the social and economic development of South Africa creates a dark and gloomy image. In economic terms, the decline in productivity will impact negatively on the country's Human Development Index. Poverty alleviation efforts will be reversed, therefore exacerbating socio-economic inequalities and restricting economic growth. Concluding statements with reference to the conceptual framework are briefly made:

- The context was elucidated, focusing on the following: global and business response, the ILO code of practice, ISO standards, other international organisations providing frameworks and guidelines, the constitution, corporate governance, the National Code of Good Practice and human resource-related legislation
- The purpose of HIV and AIDS management is to reduce the threat of the spread and to mitigate the impact of HIV and AIDS, to foster sustainability of the workforce in healthcare organisations, and to facilitate quality clinical management of HIV and AIDS
- Only two categories of role-players were identified, as being the employer and employee in the workplace, and the clinical role-players responsible for the execution of the clinical management programmes
- The discussion of underlying dynamics was limited to management's commitment, economic and social forces, as well as ethical challenges related to the clinical, social, and political and research dimensions of HIV and AIDS management.

Self-assessment

(1) Compile a workplace programme for employees with HIV and Aids in your healthcare organisation.
(2) Download the UNAIDS Tools for Evaluating HIV Voluntary Counselling and Testing 2000 – Best Practice Collection – and assess your healthcare organisation's VCT programme accordingly (www.unaids.org).
(3) Compile an education programme for your staff on HIV and AIDS, based on the SENCER education model.
(4) Plan and organise a 'Candlelight Memorial' for your organisation, based on the USAIDS Toolkit in this regard: (www.candlelightmemorial.org).
(5) Compile a Peer Group Education Programme (HIV and Aids) for your staff, based on Internet resources accessed in this regard.

10 Nature and scope of human resource management

KEY CONCEPTS

Human resource management
Employment relationship
Psychological contract
Strategic management
Strategic human resource management

SPECIFIC OUTCOMES

After studying this chapter, you should be able to:

- Interpret the legal and professional-ethical (and subsequent regulations, codes and circulars) human resource management **context** with reference to public and private (type of business ownership) healthcare organisations and their relevant healthcare practitioners or clinicians in terms of the following legislation:
  - Constitution of the Republic of South Africa, 1996 (Act 108 of 1996)
  - Labour Relations Act, 1995 (Act 66 of 1995)
  - Basic Conditions of Employment Act, 1997 (Act 75 of 1997)
  - Occupational Health and Safety Act, 1992 (Act 85 of 1993)
  - Skills Development Act, 1998 (Act 97 of 1998)
  - Skills Development Levies Act, 1999 (Act 9 of 1999)
  - Employment Equity Act, 1998 (Act 55 of 1998)
  - The Compensation for Occupational Injuries and Diseases Act, 1993 (Act 130 of 1993)
  - Unemployment Insurance Act, 2001 (Act 63 of 2001)
- Identify and describe the **role-players**, such as the state, employers, employees and organised labour and interpret their roles and responsibilities in human resource management in a healthcare organisation
- Analyse and debate the **purpose** of human resource management in the context of a healthcare organisation

- Analyse and debate the **process** of human resource management in the context of a healthcare organisation, with specific reference to the fundamental principles of planning and provision, maintenance, utilisation, performance management and development of human resources, as well as fair labour practice
- Debate the **underlying dynamics** that could impact on the human resource management of a healthcare organisation, with specific reference to constituents responsible for funding, labour rights, institutional determinants and external factors impacting on human resources.

10.1 INTRODUCTION

Successful chief executive officers (CEOs) see human resources (HR) as an asset that needs to be managed more conscientiously and in tune with their proposed business outcomes if their organisations are to be competitive. The nature of managing human resources engages all line managers and refers to activities undertaken to attract, develop and maintain an effective workforce in an organisation. The relationship between management and HR emphasises the achievement of organisational goals through the efforts of the employed human resources. Employment relationships are focused on economic, legal, social and psychological contingencies requiring management to be conscientiously transparent and fair in their management of people and the way in which they deal with employee aspirations. Strategic management is closely interwoven with strategic human resource planning and management, as people are required to implement the plans generated during strategic planning so that the organisational goals can be achieved.

This chapter will highlight the following components (see Figure 10.1):

- The **context** of human resource management (HRM) refers to the legal and professional-ethical environment.
- The **purpose** of HRM is to enable integrated decisions about the employment relationship which affects the effectiveness of both the employees and the organisation.
- The different **role-players** in HRM, are described with specific reference to the state, employers, employees and organised labour.
- In describing the nature and scope of HRM, the **process** is divided into the nature of HRM, management and HRM, the employment relationship, HRM functions and strategic HRM.
- The **underlying dynamics** impacting on HRM in a healthcare organisation refer to the management of people dynamics and cultural diversity, the working relationship between different categories of healthcare personnel, financial and economic pressures and the available pool of professional healthcare practitioners, as well as business ethics.

Figure 10.1 Visual presentation of the nature and scope of human resource management in a healthcare organisation

Context	Constitution of the Republic of South Africa, 1996 (Act 108 of 1996) Labour Relations Act, 1995 (Act 66 of 1995) Basic Conditions of Employment Act, 1997 (Act 75 of 1997) Occupational Health and Safety Act, 1993 (Act 85 of 1993) Skills Development Act, 1998 (Act 97 of 1998) Transformation Decreased financial resources
Purpose	HR is a vital resource HR is required to effect organisational goals and growth Optimal utilisation of HR Acquiring and retaining qualified personnel
Role-players	State Employers Employees Organised labour
Process	Nature of human resources management Management and human resources management Employment relationship Human resources management functions Strategic human resources management
Underlying dynamics	People dynamics Business ethics Financial and economic pressures Availability of healthcare practitioners

10.2 CONTEXT

The context refers to all the external forces that exist outside the boundary of the organisation and have the potential to affect work organisations and in turn shape human resource management strategy, policies and practices. Managing people at work does not take place in a vacuum. Wider economic, technological, political and social forces influence and shape human resource management practices. So global and local economic development sometimes have an indirect or multiplier effect. For instance, corporate mergers, downsizing and the transformation of services have a pervasive impact on the human resources of such enterprises. Much attention is usually focused on the financial packages developed to effect the changes, but little thought and regard is given to the impact of such major occurrences on the psychological well-being of employees and the human resource management implications of restructuring (Belohlav & LaVan, 1989:1). Organisations often try to reap quick benefits from rationalising and redesigning organisational processes through cost reduction obtained by reducing the number of employees. Understanding fully the strategic role of human resource management requires an understanding of external contexts and their dynamic realities of context and its causal effects with HRM, as shown in Figure 10.2.

Two imperatives reflect the critical relevance of a strategic approach to HR in South Africa. First, to address the discriminatory legacy of apartheid in removing unfair discrimination in the workplace and enhancing representation of Africans, Coloured people, Indians and women. This is achieved by the legislated processes of transformation, affirmative action, employment equity and black empowerment. The second strategic imperative is formulating HR strategies at both

Figure 10.2 A model of the external contexts of HRM

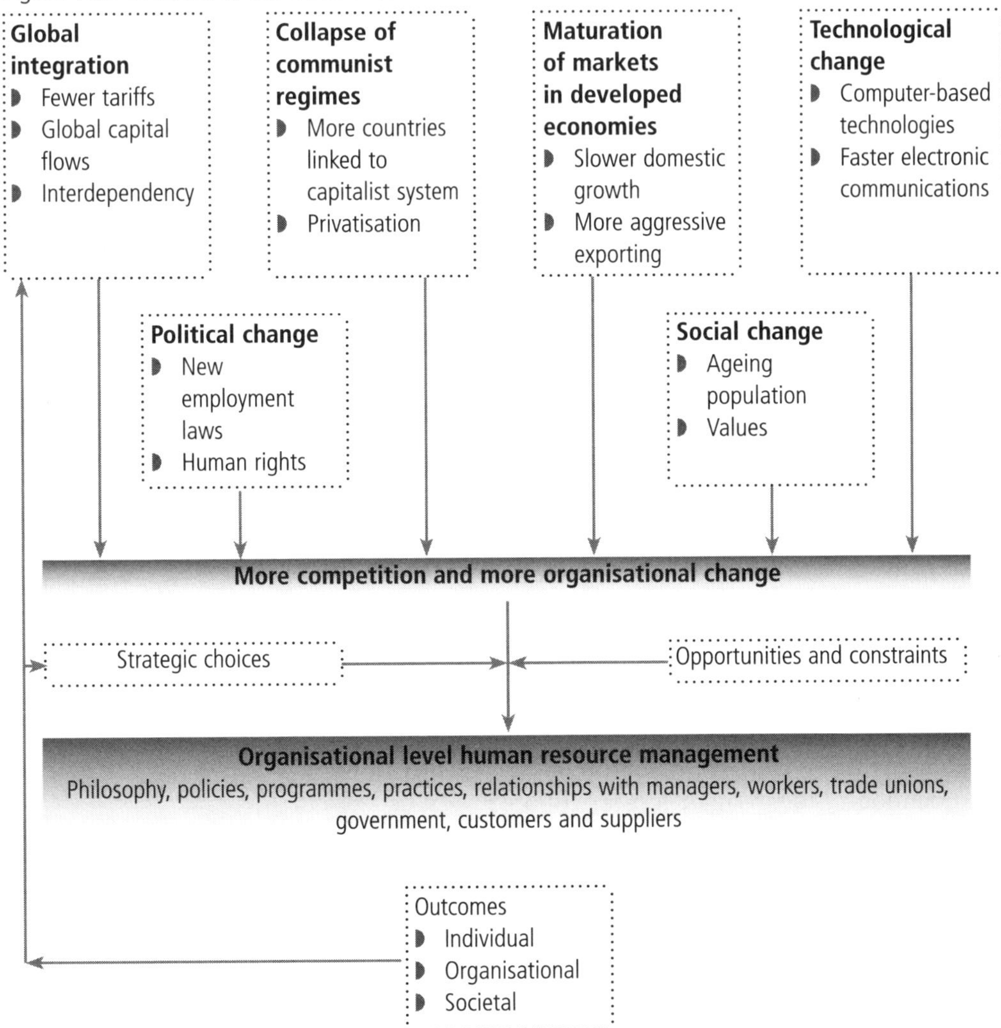

Source: Bratton & Gold, 2003:79

national and organisational levels to enhance competitiveness and performance improvement. Human resources practitioners in South Africa see the most important workplace challenges as performance improvement, employment equity, training and development, and managing trade union expectations (Kamoche, Debrah, Horwitz & Muuka, 2004:3).

The healthcare industry has been going through some radical changes in recent years. There has been a growing interest in increasing the participation of employees in decision-making processes, and improving their level of psychological development and commitment in the organisation. Concepts such as quality circles and total quality management (TQM) are being implemented, and possibilities of the value of corporate culture in helping healthcare service organisations in its efforts for high performance, are being explored.

However, financial and economic pressures on the healthcare organisation have resulted in these institutions becoming more concerned about maintaining the market share, improving their competitiveness, achieving internal efficiencies, and maximising reimbursements. The drive for financial performance often forces health institutions to take actions like reducing their workforce through termination, curtailing spending on employee development, postponing compensation increases, and to make other short-term decisions that are not conducive to a quality of work life for their employees such as flexible working hours, during which employees are sent home if there is not sufficient work and are requested to come back when it suits the employer (Siddiqui & Kleiner, 1998:2). It is also known that especially where nursing human resources are concerned, that healthcare organisations redefine their skill mix to increasingly make use of nurses who have undergone shorter training programmes than the professional nurse as a means of decreasing the personnel budget.

Another factor affecting the provision of healthcare in South Africa is the emigration of medical staff, and especially doctors and nurses to countries abroad, which places severe constraints on the provision of healthcare services. The direct results of a shortage of professional nurses include the closure of hospital wards and/or clinics, reducing the available healthcare services; leading to long waiting lists at healthcare facilities. The major indirect result of such shortages revolves around the increased workloads experienced by the remaining healthcare personnel and the consequential remedies management has to seek for retaining the overworked staff members, often without any means for consideration of their quality of work life (Ehlers, Oosthuizen, Bezuidenhout, Monareng & Jooste, 2003:25).

Human resource management is described in the context of a healthcare organisation, with specific reference to the Constitution, professional, ethical and legal framework for healthcare practitioners and labour management related legislation.

10.2.1 Constitution

According to the Constitution of the Republic of South Africa, 1996 (Act 108 of 1996), every South African is entitled to respect for human dignity and every employee deserves to be treated as an individual in his/her own right and should enjoy the right to fair labour practice.

10.2.2 Professional, ethical and legal framework for healthcare practitioners

The clinical practice of healthcare practitioners is governed by the respective professional, ethical and legal frameworks, such as legal registration with professional statutory bodies, through which the clinical function of practitioners is regulated by the respective scopes of practice regulations. These scopes of practices should be taken into consideration when appointing and placing personnel. HRM in healthcare organisations should focus on acquiring appropriately qualified staff, to train and develop them, and to retain the qualified workers by means of fair treatment and remuneration.

10.2.3 Labour management-related legislation

Labour-related legislation pertains, among others, to the following Acts, which strive to ensure fair and just treatment of employees, and create measures to focus on their safety and development:

- Labour Relations Act, 1996 (Act 66 of 1996)
- Basic Conditions of Service Act, 1997 (Act 75 of 1997)
- Occupational Health and Safety Act, 1993 (Act 85 of 1993)
- Skills Development Act, 1998 (Act 97 of 1998)
- Skills Development Levies Act, 1999 (Act 9 of 1999)
- Employment Equity Act, 1998 (Act 55 of 1998)
- The Compensation for Occupational Injuries and Diseases Act, 1993 (Act 130 of 1993)
- Unemployment Insurance Act, 2001 (Act 63 of 2001).

10.3 PURPOSE

Human resource management is understood in the broadest sense of the term, as encompassing all management decisions and actions that affect the nature of the relationship between the organisation and the employees, its human resources. The effective management of an organisation's human resources is vital for the successful implementation of strategies and plans. The purpose of HRM is to enable integrated decisions about the employment relationship that will influence the effectiveness of the employees and the organisation, ensuring organisational growth, employee productivity and stronger financial performance. Keating and Thompson (2004:595) postulate that the globalisation of business has resulted in the increasing recognition of the value of a well-managed workforce and the evolution of the human resource function from being viewed as a support function to one of strategic importance. The purpose of HRM is to plan and provide for adequately trained HR, to maintain and sustain these resources by means of acceptable terms and conditions of service, to utilise them appropriately, assess their performance and to develop them when necessary. And throughout all theses processes fair labour practice should be maintained.

10.4 ROLE-PLAYERS

HRM is imperative to employers who require labour to produce their product or deliver their service, and thus employ people to do the work. This takes place in a specific context being affected by the environment, legislation and collective action. The main role-players in the HRM situation are consequently the state, the employer, its employees and their representative trade unions. Human resource managers are usually subordinate to top management and are functional as mid-level management.

10.5 PROCESS

It is argued that as organisations become increasingly aware that people are among their most valuable strategic assets, they are reappraising the way in which they manage their human capital. The emphasis is on shifting from *personnel management* to the wider, strategic concept of *human resource management*, in which human resource policies and activities, including training and development, are linked more closely to business strategy. Human resource specialists who wish to develop a more strategic approach to people management must establish credibility with top management as key figures in the achievement of successful results (Handy, Barham, Panter & Winhard, 1989:1). The process of HRM in this chapter, as an overview chapter, incorporates a description of the nature of HRM, the management of human resources, employment relationships, HRM functions and strategic HRM. The section on HRM, consisting of five chapters, deals more comprehensively with HR concepts, such as:

- Planning and provision of HR
- Maintenance of HR
- Utilisation of HR
- Performance management
- Development of HR
- Fair labour practice.

10.5.1 The nature of human resource management

Human resource management is considered the way an organisation manages its staff, helps them develop, and concerns itself only with people who contribute to the economy as workers in formal organisations, large or small, private or public. HRM is defined by Bratton and Gold (2003:3) as a strategic approach to managing employment relations which emphasises that leveraging people's capabilities is critical to achieving sustainable competitive advantage, this being achieved through a distinctive set of integrated employment policies, programmes and practices.

It is generally assumed that HRM has a set of core activities, and that there is a body of good practice associated with each of them:

- **Human resource planning**. This refers to the group of techniques which enables managers to plan the staffing of an organisation. Organisations, especially large ones, need to forecast their staffing needs.
- **Job analysis.** This is complementary to HR planning, being carried out at the level of the individual job or group of jobs. It refers to the group of techniques which is used to determine the content of the jobs (job description) and the knowledge, skills and abilities that job holders require to carry out the required tasks (job specification).
- **Managing pay**. Deciding how much and in what way employees should be paid is based on job evaluation methods which determine the value of one job in comparison with others in the organisation.
- **Recruitment and selection**. Once the job description, job specification and salary structure are in place, the organisation can proceed to recruit staff to fill the identified jobs. During the recruitment stage candidates are attracted to apply for the jobs, and during the selection stage, the best person among the attracted candidates is selected to fill specific positions.
- **Performance management and appraisal**. Once the best person has been identified and has started work, organisations usually monitor performance by way of a formal annual review, which is known as the performance appraisal.
- **Learning and training**. It recognises that staff need to develop new skills, both for their own development and to meet the organisation's needs. In many countries it has now become a legislated responsibility.
- **Employee relations.** This deals with the management of the relationship between the organisation and the staff as a whole. In many organisations the employees are represented by trade unions who seek to collectively bargain on behalf of their members.
- **Job reduction**. It is a fact of life that organisations either grow or contract, due to times of recession, mergers and/or financial difficulties. This results in a need to reduce a number of jobs, which in turn often leads to the retrenchment of employees.

The emerging trend in HRM is clearly toward the adoption of the human resource approach through which organisations benefit in two ways; an increase in organisational effectiveness and the satisfaction of employees' needs. Rather than addressing the organisational goals and employee needs as two separate entities, the human resource approach holds that organisational goals and human needs are mutual and compatible (Carrell, Elbert & Hatfield, 2000:6). One set of needs need not be gained at the expense of the other.

In recent times, HRM has assumed new prominence because of continuing concerns about global competition, the internationalisation of technology and the productivity of labour. It is argued that these market imperatives require managers to change the way in which they manage the employment relationship in order to allow for the most effective utilisation of human resources (Bratton & Gold, 2003:4).

Current managerial practice suggests the need for restructuring towards flatter hierarchical structures, an enlargement of job tasks with greater employee autonomy, and managerial leadership to shape the more intangible aspects of the workplace, for example pertaining to beliefs, norms and values. Contemporary HRM is associated with a set of distinctive best practices that aim to recruit, develop, reward and manage people in ways that create a sustainable dedication to high commitment management, or what is also called high-performing work systems.

10.5.2 Management and human resource management

Human resources management underlines a belief that people really make a difference, as people are the only resource that has the capacity to generate value. It follows from this premise that human knowledge and skills are a strategic resource that needs to be managed skilfully. HRM should be integrated with the organisational strategy by means of a coherent set of employment policies, programmes and practices. It follows therefore, that if the workforce is so critical for organisational success, the responsibility for HRM activities rests with all line managers and should not be left to HR specialists only.

HRM consists of three parts, firstly, all managers are human resource managers, as each manager is expected to pay attention to the development and satisfaction of his/her subordinates. However, successful organisations are those that combine the experience of line managers with the expertise of HR specialists, and even though they both strive to address people-related issues of the organisation, the functions of HR managers are different from that of line managers. They typically are responsible for:

- **Advising and counselling**. Managers and executives are advised and counselled on issues such as HR policies, labour agreements, past practices and the needs of employees.
- **Providing a service**. HR managers engage in a number of activities such as HR planning, recruitment, selection, training and compensation.
- **Policy formulation and implementation**. HR managers generally propose and draft new policies or revise existing ones to deal with recurring problems or prevent anticipated ones.
- **Employee advocacy**. HR managers listen to employees' concerns and represent their needs to management (Cronjé, Du Toit, Marais & Motlatla, 2004:194).

Secondly, employees are viewed as an asset, as it is only the employees, not buildings or machinery, that give a company a competitive advantage. In today's competitive business environment, how a company manages its workforce may be the single most important factor in sustained competitive success. And thirdly, human resource management is a matching process, integrating the organisation's goals with employees' needs, as employees should receive satisfaction equal to that of the company (Daft, 2000:394).

10.5.2.1 The meaning of human resources

The organisation's human resources are its employees. Human beings become a human resource or human capital by virtue of the roles they assume in the work organisation. People as employees of an organisation set overall strategies and goals, design work systems, produce goods and services, monitor quality, allocate financial resources, and market products and services. Employment roles are defined and described in a manner designed to maximise employees' contributions to achieving the organisational goals.

In management terms, human resources or human capital refers to the traits people bring to the workplace; intelligence, aptitudes, commitment, tacit knowledge and skills, and the ability to learn. However, the open-ended nature of people often makes their contribution to the organisation variable and unpredictable. Several factors have been identified that drive people's behaviour at work, these could be ability, motivation, role perception, situational contingencies, control and commitment (Bratton & Gold, 2003:8). Human capital differs from other resources, partly because individuals are endowed with various levels of ability, aptitudes, skills and knowledge, with differences in personality traits, gender, role perception and experience, and partly as a result of differences in motivation and commitment. They therefore differ from other resources because of their ability to assess and question management's actions, while their commitment and cooperation always have to be won. In addition, employees have the capacity to form groups and trade unions to defend or further their own economic interest.

10.5.2.2 The meaning of management

The term 'management' may be applied to either a social group or process. A manager is an organisational member who is institutionally empowered to determine and regulate certain aspects of the actions of others (Willmott, 1984 in Bratton & Gold, 2003:0). Managers are usually differentiated horizontally by their functional activities and vertically by the level at which they are located in their organisational hierarchy. Management has been conceptualised as a system of authority and administration, which coordinates and controls production or service activities with the aim of providing direction in the achievement of organisational goals and objectives.

In recent times, the academic journals and bestselling business books have awakened managers to new views of the nature of work, people at work and changing work values. Though difficult to define, the new perspective has triggered the need for deep-rooted transformation and the emergence of strikingly different approaches to people management (Pennington, 2001:iii). Organisations have replaced the harsh, dictatorial managers of the past with a new brand of leaders who openly and earnestly believe in, and practise more caring and benevolent employee relations. The edges of top-down styles have begun to soften, and the mechanistic model of organisational design seems to be changing into less rigid forms. Less structured teams have become more commonplace, and people skills have become the distinguishing characteristic of a good leader. Catch words and phrases such as empowerment, transformation, teams, putting people first and human capital have become commonplace.

10.5.3 The employment relationship

The employment relationship describes dynamic interlocking relations that exist between individuals and their work organisations. These relationships can be oriented towards economic, legal, social and psychological aspects in the place of work (Bratton & Gold, 2003:11–13).

- The **economic** relationship embraces the exchange of pay for work. When individuals enter the workplace they enter into a pay-effort bargain, which places an obligation on both the employer and employee; in exchange for a wage paid by the employer, the employee is obligated to perform a certain amount of physical or intellectual labour at the standards set by the employer.

  Conflict is inherent to the employment relationship as the payment of one party is a cost to the other. In the capitalist labour market, people sell their labour and seek to maximise their pay, while wages and salaries are a cost to the employer which reduces profit and therefore needs to be minimised.

  The performance or effort side of the contract also generates tensions and conflict because its nature is imprecise and indeterminate. The employment contract permits the employer to buy a potential level of physical and intellectual labour, the task of management is thus to transform this potential into actual value-added labour. Human resource practices are designed to narrow the gap between employees' potential and actual performance.
- The second component of the employment relationship relates to the **legal** relationship. A contract of employment can be entered into informally or formally, and it is subject to the general contractual rules of common law (Selwyn 2000 in Bratton & Gold, 2003:12). It thus has a network of common law and statutory rights and obligations affecting both parties to the contract. There are many pieces of legislation that impact on the employer-employee relationship, for instance those that determine the right to manage, the right to fair treatment, the right to belong to a trade union, the right not to be unfairly dismissed and so forth.
- The **social** relationship is the third distinguishing component of the employment relationship. The social dimension of the employment relationship relates to the issue of power in the workplace. Both members of management and the employee group are members of social groups responding to social norms and values which influence their actions in the workplace. Human behaviour is an important facet affecting the employment relationship. Normally the

employment relationship involves an uneven balance of social power between the employer and employee. And unless there is collective (trade union) or statutory intervention, the employer as the most powerful party, can impose an agreement with force.

- The fourth component of the employment relationship involves a dynamic mutual exchange of perceived promises and obligations between employees and their organisation, known as the psychological contract. The psychological contract captures a wide variety of mainly unwritten expectations and understandings of the two parties about their mutual obligations. Two important factors affecting the **psychological contract** are ineffective communication practices; when the organisation does not always communicate with one voice, and the promissory exchange of offers and mutual obligations where it is found that managers often fail to keep their promises.

10.5.4 Human resource management functions

In the organisational framework, the human resources functions are manifested in the human resources department. This department is aimed at providing the organisation with labour in sufficient numbers and of the correct skill mix. Human resources management encompasses a body of knowledge and a set of policies and practices that shape the nature of acquiring and retaining personnel and regulating the employment relationship, the functions emanating from HRM are depicted in Figure 10.3 (Bratton & Gold 2003:15; Gerber, Nel & Van Dyk 1998:15–16):

10.5.5 Strategic human resource management

The notion that people management can be a key source of sustained competitive advantage calls for the integration of HRM and business strategy and emphasises the relationship between strategic management and employee relations. Karami, Analoui and Cusworth (2004:60) conclude that increasing core competencies of the enterprise, in particular HR, is one of the key elements to the success of the performance of an enterprise and that HR involvement in the development and implementation of business strategy leads to organisational effectiveness. The premise behind strategic HRM is that HR decisions that match the organisational conditions positively affect performance with encouraging outcomes for the organisation. The purpose of human resource strategy is to help guide managers' personnel decisions and thereby affect the success of the organisation.

In the fast-paced global economy, change is the norm. Environmental factors such as social, technological, legal, skills and personnel shortages, and balancing work and family issues result in long-term planning being risky, but absolutely essential. Through strategic planning, decisions are made by top management that define the overall mission, determining the most effective utilisation of its resources, and crafting and executing the strategy in ways that produce the intended results. Strategic decisions involve choices, and these choices shape human resource decisions. If one

Figure 10.3 Functional components of HRM in a healthcare organisation

Planning and provision of HR	◗ Human resource planning ◗ Job analysis ◗ Job evaluation ◗ Recruitment, selection and appointment
Maintenance of HR	◗ Occupational health and safety ◗ Quality of work life and productivity
Utilisation of HR	◗ Communication ◗ Lateral relations ◗ Staffing allocation ◗ Absenteeism and turnover
Assessment and development of HR	◗ Appraisal and performance management ◗ Human resources development
Fair labour practice	◗ Perspectives ◗ Labour relations processes ◗ Practices

views human resources as any organisation's most valuable asset, then the most important task becomes finding and keeping the people who will contribute value to the organisation's bottomline (Carrell, Elbert & Hatfield, 2000:8). Identifying the type of employees needed should only be done after defining the desired business results. Once the results are clearly defined, identification of the business strategies by which the results can be attained follows, and from there it becomes easier to identify the kind of employees and their skills, competencies, and experiences required to implement the strategy (see Figure 10.4). However, it must be noted that just as the business strategy shapes human resources decisions, so, too, do human resource decisions affect strategic choices, for instance the selection of chief executives and top managers. Since these people are so involved in formulating strategies, changes in their ranks can have significant effects on the whole organisation.

Strategic human resource management is the process of linking the human resource function with the strategic objectives of the organisation in order to improve performance. In the management context, 'strategy' implies a specific pattern of decisions and actions undertaken by top management of an organisation to accomplish performance goals and to sustain a competitive advantage through people. Strategic management is considered to be a continuous activity that requires a constant adjustment of three major interdependent components, namely the values of senior management, the environment and the available resources (see Figure 10.5).

Figure 10.4 Personnel requirements are driven by business results

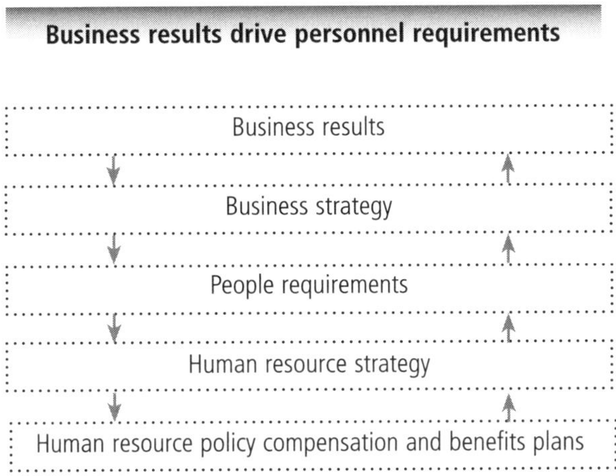

Source: Adapted from Carrell et al., 2002:9

Figure 10.5 The three components of a strategic plan

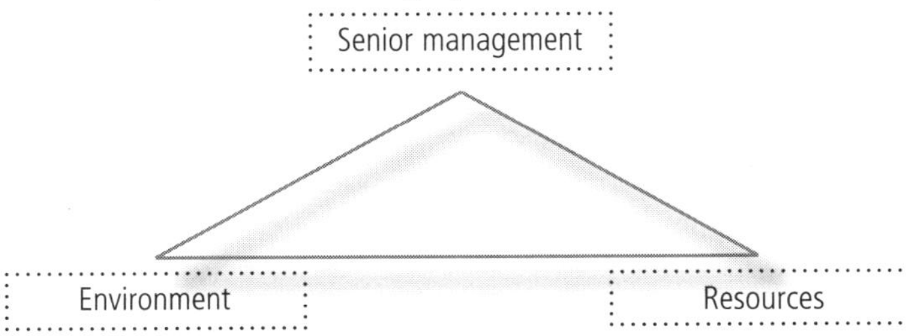

Source: Adapted from Bratton & Gold, 2003:39

10.5.5.1 Strategic management in view of HRM

Strategic management is the set of decisions and actions used to formulate and implement strategies that will provide a competitively superior fit between the organisation and its environment so as to achieve organisational goals. Also refer to Chapter 2, Strategic management of a healthcare organisation, however, it is necessary to briefly describe the strategic management process in order to apply it to HRM. Superior organisational performance is determined by the choices managers make. Top executives use strategic management to define an overall direction for the organisation, which is called the organisation's grand strategy (Daft, 2000:235). The strategic management process is typically broken down into the following five steps:

(1) **Mission and goals**. These express management's philosophy and values as a guiding element for the whole process.
(2) **Environmental analysis**. This determines internal and external strengths and weaknesses, opportunities and threats (SWOT) so that focus areas can be established.

(3) **Strategic formulation**. This consists of formulating strategies at corporate, business and functional levels with the aim of realising the goals.
(4) **Strategy implementation**. This encompasses leadership, structure, control systems and human resources.
(5) **Strategy evaluation**. This means assessing the operating and financial performance in relation to goal achievement and operational problems.

Once the corporate strategy has been determined, a HR strategy is implemented to support the chosen competitive strategy, matching the philosophy, policies, programmes, practices and processes in a way that will stimulate and reinforce the different employee role behaviours appropriate for each competitive strategy. The concept of integrating corporate HR strategies implies the:

- Support and steadfast commitment of management
- Linking HR policies and practices with the strategic management process of the organisation
- Internalisation of the importance of HR on the part of line managers
- Commitment of the workforce with the strategic goals.

10.5.5.2 Dimensions of strategic human resources management

Strategic HRM implies getting all the employees of an organisation in a position, with the necessary structures, to work towards achieving the goals of the organisation. Researchers have identified a number of important themes associated with the concept of strategic human resources management (Bratton & Gold, 2003:59–60), as follows:

- **Human resource practice and performance**. It is assumed that an alignment between business strategy and HR strategy will improve organisational performance and competitiveness.
- **Re-engineering and strategic human resource management**. The re-design of work organisations encompasses a flattened hierarchy, decentralised decision-making to line managers and work teams, enabling information technology, strong leadership and a set of HR practices that make employees' behaviour more congruent with the organisation's culture and goals.
- **Leadership and strategic human resource management**. A leadership style is required that would develop the organisation's human endowment, cultivate commitment, flexibility, innovation and change by empowering employees at all levels.
- **Workplace learning and strategic human resource management**. From a managerial perspective, formal and informal learning can strengthen an organisation's core competencies and thus act as a lever to sustainable competitive advantage. Having the ability to learn faster than one's competitors is thus required.
- **Trade unions and strategic human resource management**. Due to the

collectivist culture of employees creating the 'them' and 'us' attitude, the HRM goals of high employee commitment and the individualisation of the employment relationship are not always in a positive correlation.

10.6 UNDERLYING DYNAMICS

The underlying dynamics in the HRM sphere are closely related to human behaviour, commitment and aspirations. However, management's strategies, foresight, planning and open and fair treatment of all their employees are crucial to a stable, content workforce. The determinants affecting the process of HRM are described below.

The management of people dynamics

The most important underlying dynamics in HRM is the management of people dynamics and unexpected issues due to cultural diversity:

- The scope and quality of diversity management
- Issues due to cultural diversity
- Conflict management
- Transformation management and issues.

Consistency of business ethics

Business ethics relates, among others, to the ethical dimensions of HRM. The way in which human interaction, practices and procedures are handled and dealt with in view of what is right for all concerned constitutes the ethics of an organisation. This is particularly relevant to the following:

- The working relationship between different categories of healthcare personnel
- The presence, or lack of, mutual respect between different groups of healthcare personnel
- Unconditional acceptance of the professional roles and contributions of the different healthcare practitioners.

Financial and economic constraints

Decreased budgets and costly healthcare have pressurised healthcare organisations into becoming more concerned with improving their competitiveness and internal efficiency. Of relevance here are:

- Reducing their work force
- Postponing compensation increases
- Redefining the skill mix of healthcare workers

Available pool of healthcare practitioners

A serious factor affecting the provision of healthcare is the mobility of healthcare workers and especially their emigration to other countries. This has resulted in the following:

- Closure of hospital wards and clinics
- Increased workloads for the remaining members of staff
- Decreased quality of work life for healthcare personnel.

10.7 CONCLUDING STATEMENTS

The following concluding statements are relevant to the conceptual framework of HRM:

- Human resource management occurs in the legal and professional-ethical context, in accordance with the business ownership of the particular healthcare organisation, with reference to the Constitution, labour-related legislation and ethical codes of the different professions.
- The major role-players in HRM are the state, employers, the human resource manager, and organised labour encompassing the employees and their trade unions.
- Human resource management refers to activities undertaken to acquire, develop and maintain an effective workforce in an organisation. The purpose of HRM is to enable integrated decisions about employment relationships that will influence the effectiveness of the employees and the organisation, ensuring organisational growth, employee productivity and stronger financial performance.
- The process of HRM relates mainly to the nature of HRM, management and human resources, the employment relationship, HRM functions and strategic HRM. The managing of people should take precedence over other resources in the workplace as they are the only resource that can add value in the organisational context.
- HRM builds a cognitive construct concerned with developing a reciprocal commitment and obligation between each of the parties, thus, managing the psychological contract is an important task for managers in the contemporary workplace.
- Strategic HRM follows after the organisational strategies have been developed and the outcomes have been identified, only then can the appropriate employees be found, appointed and managed.
- The dimensions of strategic HRM incorporates HR practices and performance, re-engineering, leadership, workplace training and trade unions.
- Various underlying dynamics, such as the management of people dynamics, cultural diversity, adherence to business ethics, financial and economic constraints and the availability of healthcare practitioners affect the management of human resources.

Self-assessment

(1) Go to the website of the 1998 Workplace Employee Relations Survey: www.dti.gov.uk/er/emar/1998WERS.htm for data on the job responsibilities for HR managers.

(2) Visit www.ipm.co.za and click on the accreditation and/or the certification button. Using the information you find, compare the practices HR professionals are formally accredited to undertake, with the practices in your work environment.

(3) What are the most critical challenges facing HR managers today? What changes have been instrumental in reshaping the HR role in society and in organisations?

11 Planning and provision of human resources

KEY CONCEPTS

Human resource planning
Job analysis
Job description
Job specification
Job evaluation
Recruitment
Selection

SPECIFIC OUTCOMES

After studying this chapter, you should be able to:

- Interpret the legal and professional-ethical human resource management **context** with reference to public and private (type of business ownership) healthcare organisations and their relevant healthcare practitioners or clinicians in terms of the following legislation:
  - Labour Relations Act, 1995 (Act 66 of 1995)
  - Basic Conditions of Employment Act, 1997 (Act 75 of 1997)
  - Occupational Health and Safety Act, (Act 85 of 1993)
  - Employment Equity Act, 1998 (Act 55 of 1998)
- Identify the **role-players** and interpret their roles and responsibilities in the planning and provision of human resource in a healthcare organisation
- Analyse and debate the **purpose** of human resource planning and provision in a healthcare organisation
- Describe and apply the **process** of planning for, and the provision of human resource in the context of a healthcare organisation, with reference to job analysis, recruitment, the contract of employment and induction of new employees
- Debate the **underlying dynamics** that could impact on the planning and provision of human resource for a healthcare organisation, with specific reference to economic, equity and scarcity factors related to the provision of HR.

11.1 INTRODUCTION

Human resource planning is the process of anticipating and making provision for the movement of people into, in, and out of the organisation. Its purpose is to deploy the resources as effectively as possible, when and where they are needed, in order to accomplish the goals of the organisation. Other more specific aims of human resource planning include anticipating labour shortages and surpluses, providing more employment opportunities for women, disabled people and other designated groups. In fact, human resource planning serves as a launching point for most of the activities that are subsumed under HRM.

Once the HR planning function is fulfilled, the staffing of the organisation must be completed through the recruitment process. However, for recruitment to take place some advance preparation should have been done by means of a job analysis which brings forth a job specification and job description; both are necessary for advertising and selection purposes. Information gathered during the job analysis process is also utilised in doing a job evaluation, which is the process of determining the relative worth of jobs in order to establish the pay allocated to different jobs in a specific organisation.

Recruitment is the process of attracting individuals with the appropriate qualifications in sufficient numbers, so that the best candidates can be selected from them for employment and placement in the organisation. Once appointed, all new employees need to be introduced to the goals and culture of the organisation by means of an induction and orientation programme so that they can function effectively and optimally, while the employee expects to be treated in a fair and just manner according to the terms and conditions of employment and the set remuneration arrangements.

This chapter will highlight the following (refer to Figure 11.1):

- The **context** of human resource planning and provision with reference to the legal and professional-ethical environment
- The **purpose** of planning in order to provide HR for a specific healthcare institution
- The different **role-players** in the planning and provision of HR, with specific reference to the state in terms of legislation, top management, the HR department and organised labour
- The **process** of planning and the provision of HR, consisting of components such as the planning process, job analysis, job evaluation and recruitment, selection and appointment
- The **underlying dynamics** impacting on the planning for and provision of human resource in a healthcare organisation such as budgetary provision, equity requirements and the availability of suitable candidates.

Figure 11.1 Visual presentation of the planning and provision of human resource in a healthcare organisation

Context	• Constitution of the Republic of South Africa, 1996 (Act 108 of 1996) • Labour Relations Act, 1995 (Act 66 of 1995) • Basic Conditions of Employment Act, 1997 (Act 75 of 1997) • Employment Equity Act, 1998 (Act 55 of 1998) • Health-related legislation • Transformation • Affirmative action • Decreased financial resources • Decreased pool of available personnel
Purpose	• Identify future HR demands • Appoint the best candidate for the job • Decrease excessive turnover • Invest in human resource
Role-players	• State • Top management • HR department • Organised labour
Process	• HR planning • Job analysis • Job evaluation • Recruitment, selection and appointment
Underlying dynamics	• Type and level of healthcare service • Economic factors • Available pool of adequately trained personnel • Equity requirements

11.2 CONTEXT

Environmental change factors that are lending human resource planning greater importance are legislation and social pressure in support of affirmative action, equal employment opportunities, and the demand for occupational health and safety. Transformation, restructuring and downsizing of organisations often lead to fear of retrenchment and consequent unemployment. The high rate of unemployment, skills shortages and the migration of healthcare professionals to other countries, contribute to difficulties in realising the HR plans developed for healthcare institutions. The aging population who is still able to perform satisfactorily, the general expansion and diversification of organisations, and trends toward multi-national operations are affected by difficulties in transferring workers, and in operating and staffing in foreign countries.

Specific legislation which guides the planning and provision of human resource are:

- Constitution of the Republic of South Africa, 1996 (Act 108 of 1996)
- Labour Relations Act, 1995 (Act 66 of 1995)
- Basic Conditions of Employment Act, 1997 (Act 75 of 1997)
- Employment Equity Act, 1998 (Act 55 of 1998)
- Health-related legislation.

11.3 PURPOSE

A major purpose of HR planning and provision is to identify future human resource demands and to develop programmes to eliminate any discrepancies, in the best interests of the individual and the organisation. HR planning can also reduce expenses associated with excessive turnover and absenteeism, low productivity and unproductive training programmes.

Another compelling reason for HR planning is the investment an organisation makes in its human resource. Human assets, as opposed to some other resources, can increase in value due to training, development and experience that enables the acquisition of skills and abilities. Because an organisation makes an investment in its personnel either through direct training or job assignments, it is important that employees are utilised effectively throughout their careers.

11.4 ROLE-PLAYERS

During the phase of planning and providing human resource for the purpose of realising the organisational goals and objectives, different role-players are involved in the process. Top management sets the strategic goals and employment criteria, the human resource department attends to the processes of recruitment, establishing selection panels and appointing successful applicants, all the while taking cognisance of the legalities of each step. Potential candidates from in and external to the organisation become involved when they apply for the advertised positions.

11.5 PROCESS

The management of people in the workplace is a line function that should be carried out by line management, supported by the human resource department. As organisations grow in size and complexity, the human resource department should be staffed with qualified personnel who are able to perform the necessary functions and tasks.

11.5.1 Human resource planning

Figure 11.2 depicts the components dealt with under the human resource planning process.

Figure 11.2 Components dealt with in this chapter relating to human resource planning and provision

Human resource planning	◗ Phases of human resource planning ◗ Human resource planning in the context of change
Job analysis	◗ Job description ◗ Job specification
Job evaluation	◗ Gather data ◗ Select compensable factors ◗ Evaluate the job ◗ Assign pay to the job
Recruitment, selection and appointment	◗ Recruitment ◗ Selection ◗ Appointment and placement ◗ Induction and orientation

Human resource issues are a major part of any change effort, however, changes in how an organisation manages human resource seldom occur in isolation. HR issues are necessarily considered in the context of issues related to other tangible or intangible resources, including finances, technology, physical resources and the current and desired reputation of the organisation. HR planning refers to the efforts of organisations to identify human resource implications of the key issues posed by the changing environment, in order to align their human resource with needs resulting from these issues (Jackson & Schuler, 2000:184–185).

Human resource planning is the process of systematically reviewing human resource requirements to ensure that the required number of employees, with the required skills, are available when they are needed. It is the process of matching the internal and external supply of people with job openings anticipated in the organisation over a specified period of time. The changing labour pool, rapid technological change, globalisation and the mobility of people all have a serious effect on a potential labour force.

Strategic planning, which considers both the external and internal environment, precedes human resource planning (see Figure 11.3). Strategic planning is the determination of overall organisational purposes/goals and objectives and how they can be achieved. After organisational strategic plans have been formulated, human resource planning can be undertaken. Strategic plans are reduced to specific quantitative and qualitative human resource plans.

11.5.1.1 Phases of human resource planning

The human resource planning process must consider both the long-term and short-term HR implications of organisational changes. Using the process of HR planning

Figure 11.3 The human resource planning process

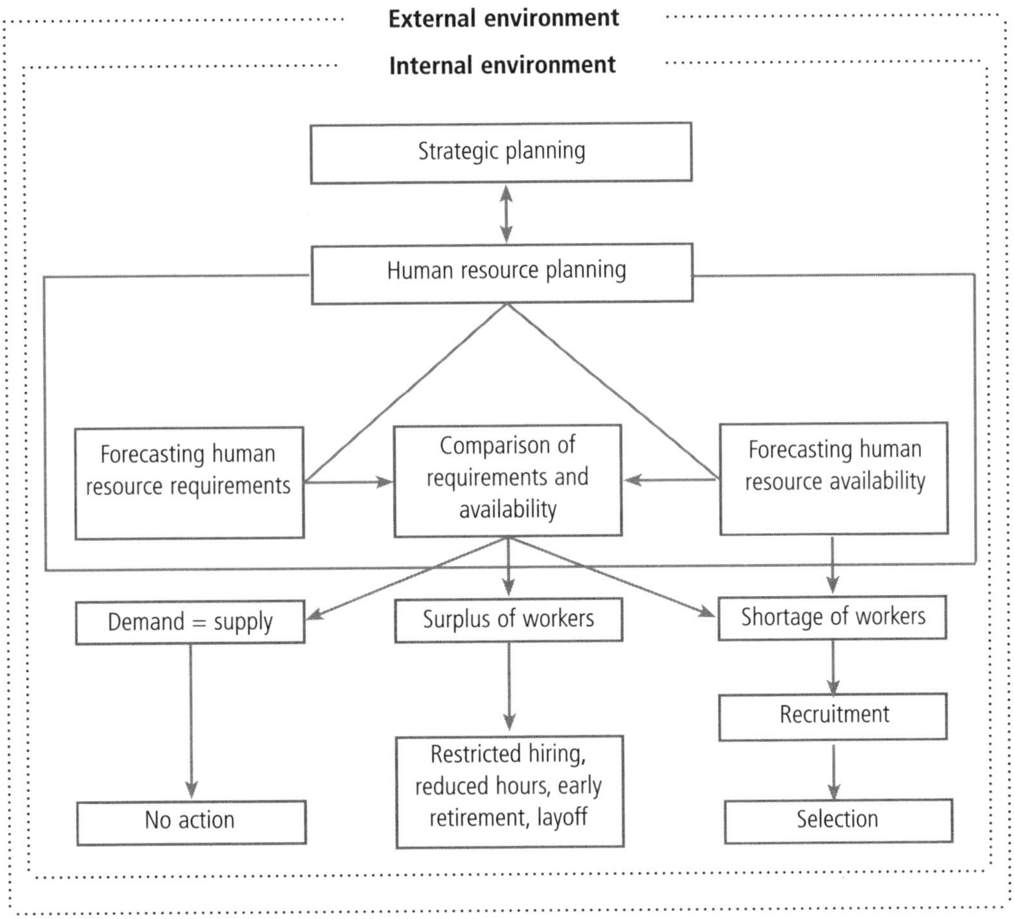

Source: Adapted form Mondy & Noe, 1993:147

helps ensure that the human resource implications of organisational changes and key business issues are dealt with systematically and thoroughly. Regardless of the time horizon or the issues at stake, the HR planning process has five phases (Schuler & Jackson, 1996:137–141) as described below.

Phase 1: Identify the key business issues

In the first phase of human resource planning, data is gathered to learn about and understand all aspects of the organisation's environment. This enables the organisation to anticipate and plan for issues arising from both stable and dynamic conditions. For example, planning for increased global competition based on cost could involve assessing current labour productivity, if the company wants to expand its revenue by

10% over the next five years, it may need more employees. On the other hand, due to technological advances it might require fewer employees in future.

The organisational structure also needs to be examined. In view of future developments, is the distribution of positions at top, middle and lower levels of the organisation appropriate for the organisation of tomorrow? Which functional areas or specific activities can be expected to undergo particularly severe growth or contraction? Considering globalisation and the new less structured working environment, where will employees be located, in a central location, abroad, at regional offices or at home?

Phase 2: Determine the human resource implications

The aims of the second phase are twofold, firstly, to develop a clear understanding of how the information gathered in the first phase affects the *demands* of the organisation, and secondly, to develop an accurate picture of the current *supply* available internally.

Forecasting human resource demands. A variety of forecasting methods can be used to determine an organisation's demand for human resource. The type of forecast applied depends on the time frame and the type of organisation, the size and dispersion of the organisation, and the accuracy and certainty of available information.

Forecasting involves approximations and depends on the accuracy of information and the predictability of events. The shorter the time span, the more predictable the events and the more accurate the information. Two classes of techniques can be used by line managers to determine their organisation's projected demand for human resource, they are *judgemental forecasts* and *statistical projections*.

- *Judgmental forecasts*. Judgemental approaches to demand forecasts involve the use of human judgement, rather than a manipulation of numbers, and employs the inputs of experts. When using judgemental methods, participants must make certain assumptions regarding the future of the organisation and its environment, taking cognisance of the organisation's strategic plans involving new products, programmes or expanding markets. The following are common judgemental methods of predicting human resource demands:
  - *Managerial estimates*. These are based on experience and familiarity with employee productivity rates and can be done by top managers using the brainstorming process. Alternatively, the review process can commence at lower levels of management and be communicated upwards for refinement. Useful information in this process includes current and projected productivity levels, market demand for service delivery or products, sales, current staffing levels and mobility statistics.
  - *The Delphi technique*. This technique involves experts presenting their forecasts and assumptions to other expert members of the group, members of

the group then make revisions to their forecasts. This combination process is continuous until a viable composite forecast emerges.
- *The Nominal Group technique*. This technique enables a group of people to independently list their ideas on a sheet of paper, after which each member in succession has an opportunity to forward their best ideas until all ideas have been exhausted. The ideas are then listed and grouped on a flip chart, after which the whole group participates in prioritising the ideas so that consensus is reached about the best forecast.

- *Statistical projections*. Using a statistical approach, an organisation predicts the required workforce size on the basis of business factors. A business factor is an attribute of the business, such as sales volume or market share, which closely relates to the size of the needed workforce. For instance, a hospital could use the business factor of projected patient load to predict the number of nurses it would need at some point in time.

  A statistical approach to demand forecasting is typically used when an organisation functions in a stable environment, where a business factor can be predicted with some form of certainty. For example, a statistical approach may be appropriate for a hospital located in an area with little population growth. Whereas hospitals operating in less stable environments (an area experiencing explosive growth and change) would more likely rely on the judgemental approach.

  The most commonly used statistical methods of demand forecasting are trend, ratio and regression analysis (Kleiman, 2000:58):
  - In *trend analysis*, the future demand for human resource is projected on the basis of past business trends regarding a business factor, for instance the relationship between sales volume and workforce size.
  - *Ratio analysis* is the process of determining future HR demand by computing an exact ratio between the specific business factor and the number of employees needed. An example could be the ratio of tutors to number of students, it thus provides a more precise estimate than trend analysis.
  - *Regression analysis* requires that a scatter diagram be drawn depicting the relationship between the business factor and workforce size. This process then calculates a regression line, which is a line that cuts right through the centre of the points on the scatter diagram. By inspecting the regression line, one can see how many employees are needed at each value of the business factor.

Forecasting human resource supplies. Internal sources of supply are generally the focus of this stage of planning although forecasted supply can be derived from both internal and external sources of information. As with forecasting demand, two basic techniques help forecast internal labour supply, namely judgemental and statistical. Once made, the supply forecast can be compared with the human resource demand forecast to help determine action programming for identifying human resource talent and balancing the supply and demand forecasts. Often the forecasting of labour supply is short-range with the emphasis on budgeting and the controlling of costs.

Two judgemental techniques used by organisations to make supply forecasts are replacement planning and succession planning. Planning for five years or more usually needs to address the company's need for managerial replacements.

Replacement planning. This involves developing replacement charts to show the names of the current and potential occupants of positions. Potential promotions can be estimated by the performance levels of employees currently in jobs and their developmental needs. Individuals likely to fill potential vacancies are listed directly under the incumbent.

Succession planning. This is similar to replacement planning except that it is usually based on longer-term projections and involves more developmental inputs. Succession planning is becoming a greater priority as companies recognise that good leadership is essential for survival in today's competitive business environment. Thus, organisations are increasingly designing developmental activities to make sure the right people are available with the right skills at the right time.

Phase 3: Develop human resource goals and objectives

With the completion of phase 2, a great deal of descriptive information is available about current and future conditions pertaining to the organisation. The next phase involves interpreting this information and using it to establish priorities and to set goals and objectives.

With short-term planning, as is often the case when downsizing is adopted, the goals are often easy to state in quantifiable terms. Examples of short-term HR objectives include increasing the number of people who are attracted to the organisation and apply for jobs, attracting a different mix of applicants (such as different skills or different locations), improving the qualifications of new hires, increasing the length of time that desirable employees remain with the company, or decreasing the time that undesirable employees stay with the organisation, and assisting current and newly hired employees to quickly develop the required skills.

The issues of total quality management and diversity management usually involve adopting intermediate- and long-term time frames for setting goals and objectives. Thus, whereas short-term objectives include attracting, assessing, and assigning employees to jobs, intermediate-term objectives are more likely to include adjusting employees' skills, attitudes and behaviour to fit major changes and needs of the organisation, as well as adjusting human resource practices to fit changes in the needs of employees.

Longer-term goals might include creating a major change in corporate culture, or could be to position the organisation to compete in totally new areas of application.

Phase 4: Design and implement human resource policies, programmes and practices

Whereas the activities of phase 3 established what had to be accomplished, phase 4 addresses how these objectives should be accomplished. The policies, programmes and practices necessary to achieve the stated objectives now have to be formulated. These could include diversity programmes to make the organisation more attractive for a broader array of applicants. Programmes to downsize or extend the organisation, such as early retirement incentives and generous severance packages to complement the normal attrition rate, programmes to improve loyalty and socialisation efforts so that good employees will want to remain with the organisation, and programmes to empower and involve employees in order to ensure success in a change process, for instance, to total quality management.

Phase 5: Evaluate, revise and refocus

In this phase the objectives set in phase 3 come into play again, for these objectives define the criteria that need to be used in evaluating whether a programme or initiative is successful or needs revision. The goal and its relevant objectives will determine the amount of information to be collected, and from whom, in order to measure outcome status. Interviews, checklists, questionnaires and audits are some of the means that can be applied to collect data for analysis and evaluation purposes.

Where less than ideal conditions are found, management meets with the relevant employees to develop a plan of action for improvement. The evaluation phase can also be considered the data analysis stage for the next round of planning. Evaluation of HR plans and programmes is an important process for determining the effectiveness of HR planning but also demonstrates the significance of both HR activities and the HR department in the organisation as a whole.

11.5.1.2 Human resource planning in the context of change

The five phases of human resource planning discussed above are relevant to times of relevant environmental stability. However, because the environment is changing organisations so dramatically, human resource planning has become a more dynamic, volatile issues game. According to Jackson and Schuler (2000:185) HR planning still involves numbers but in addition, it now also involves:

- Crafting and communicating missions and value statements
- Ensuring that managers and other employees understand and buy into the process of change
- Systematically designing and aligning HR activities to address the concerns of multiple stakeholders
- Developing methods to monitor the effects of change
- Being alert to signs that plans should be reconsidered or modified
- Integrating all of these activities with other change efforts in areas such as finance, marketing, and operations.

Figure 11.4 Job analysis and its relationship with HRM components

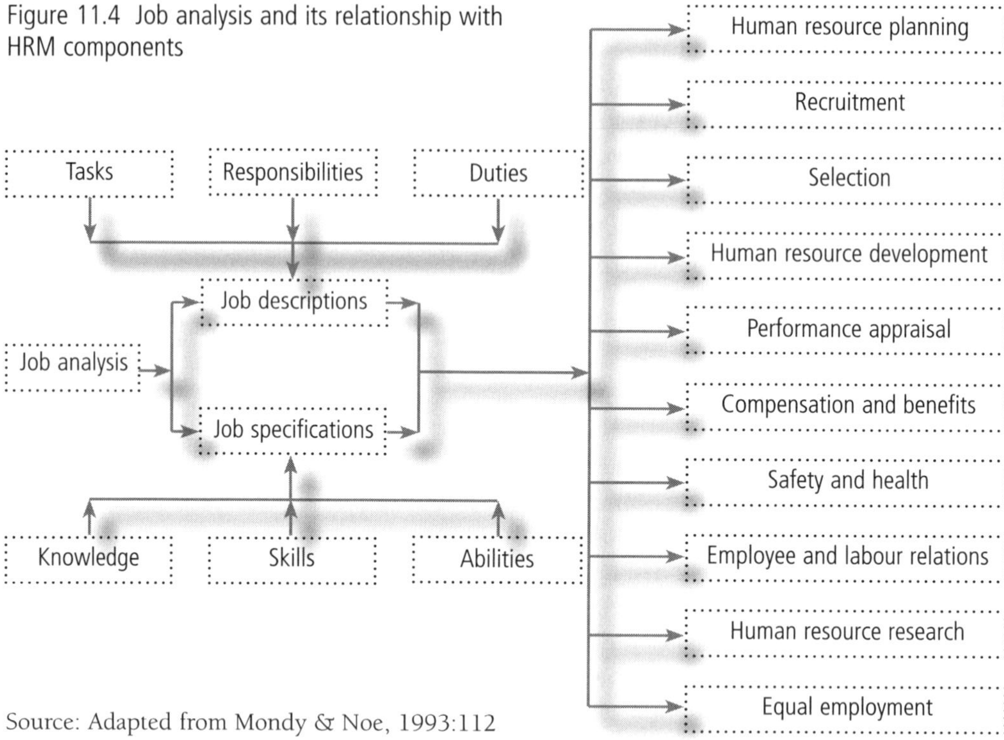

Source: Adapted from Mondy & Noe, 1993:112

Effective human resource planning considers change from both long- and short-term perspectives, corresponding with the typical cycles for business planning, always keeping in mind the strategic vision, mission and goals.

11.5.2 Job analysis

Job analysis is often called the cornerstone of HRM because the information it collects serves many HRM functions, as indicated in Figure 11.4. Job analysis is the process of systematically obtaining information about jobs by determining what the duties, tasks and responsibilities of those jobs are in the context of a specific job. The basic premise underlying job analysis is that jobs are more likely to be described, differentiated and evaluated consistently if accurate information is available to managers.

Much of what happens to individuals at work depends on the job they currently hold or the ones they aspire to. For example, recruitment procedures, selection methods, performance management, training programmes, and compensation are all designed around the demands of the job. For these HRM practices to be effective, the jobs must be clearly understood by both the organisation and the jobholders, a proper job analysis provides this understanding.

The process of job analysis consists of two main stages, firstly, data collection and secondly, the application of this data by the preparation of job descriptions, job specifications and job standards. Collecting the information involves three tasks

– identifying the jobs to be analysed, developing a job analysis questionnaire, and collecting the data. Questionnaires are helpful tools in gathering information on the duties, responsibilities, human abilities and performance standards of the job investigated. However, other methods and sources of information such as interviews, diaries, document research, employee reports and observation can also be used in combination, acquiring information from current job incumbents, supervisors and customers.

Job analysis information is then used to develop two basic documents required to select applicants, and to inform them of their job content:

- **A job description** is a written statement that explains the purpose, scope, duties and responsibilities of a specified job.
- **A job specification** is a detailed statement of the human characteristics involved in the job, including aptitudes, skills, knowledge, physical demands, mental demands and the experience required to perform the job.

11.5.2.1 Job description

Often the most immediate use of job analysis results is preparing job descriptions. In several ways, the job description serves as part of the written contract that governs the employment relationship. Employees use their job descriptions as guides to their behaviour and performance, directing their energies to the components of the job that seems the most important. While supervisors use job descriptions in evaluating performance and providing feedback, job descriptions also minimise misunderstandings that occur between managers and their subordinates concerning job requirements. Job descriptions also establish management's right to take corrective action when the duties covered are not performed as required (Sherman, Bohlander & Snell, 1996:138). Consequently, a job description should represent a complete and accurate picture of all job duties and responsibilities.

Since there is no pre-required standard format for job descriptions, they tend to vary in appearance and content from one organisation to another, yet most job descriptions will contain at least the following sections: the job title section which also contains the job identification information, a job statement and the essential duties and responsibilities (see Figure 11.5).

- **Job title**. Selecting a job title is important for a number of reasons, and should be formulated with its effect on the incumbent in mind. First, the job title is of psychological importance, providing status to the employee. Second, if possible, the title should provide some identification of what the duties of the job entail. Third, the job title should also indicate the relative level occupied by its holder in the organisational hierarchy.
- **Job identification**. The job title is followed by the job identification section which includes items such as post level, personnel number, departmental location of the job, the person to whom the incumbent reports and the date the job description was last revised.

Figure 11.5 Job description for an employment assistant

Job identification

Job title: Employment assistant
Division: Southern area
Department: Human resource management
Job analyst: Virginia Sasaki
Data analysed: 12/3/05
Wage category: Exempt
Report to: HR manager
Job code: 11-17
Date verified: 12/17/05

Brief listing of major job duties

Job statement
Performs professional human resource work in the areas of employee *recruitment* and *selection, testing, orientation, transfers*, and maintenance of employee human resource files. May handle special assignments and projects in *EEO/Affirmative Action, employee grievances, training*, or *classification and compensation*. Works under general supervision. Incumbent exercises initiative and independent judgement in the performance assigned tasks.

Essential functions and responsibilities

Essential functions
1 Prepares recruitment literature and job advertisements for applicant placement.
2 Schedules and conducts personal interviews to determine applicant suitability for employment. Includes reviewing mailed applications and résumés for qualified personnel.
3 Supervises administration of testing programme. Responsible for developing or improving testing instruments and procedures.
4 Presents orientation programme to all new employees. Reviews and develops all materials and procedures for orientation programme.
5 Coordinates division job posting and transfer programme. Establishes job posting procedures. Responsible for reviewing transfers applications, arranging transfer interviews, and determining effective transfer dates.
6 Maintains a daily working relationship with division managers on human resource matters, including recruitment concerns, retention or release of probationary employees, and discipline or discharge of permanent employees.
7 Distributes new or revised human resource policies and procedures to all employees and managers through bulletins, meetings, memorandums, and/or personal contact.
8 Performs related duties as assigned by the human resource manager.

Job specifications and requirements

Employee requirement
1 Four-year college or university degree with major course work in human resource management, business administration, or industrial psychology; OR a combination of experience, education, and training equivalent to a four-year college degree in human resource management.
2 Considerable knowledge of principles of employee selection and assignment of personnel.
3 Ability to express ideas clearly in both written and oral communications.
4 Ability to independently plan and organise one's own activities.
5 Knowledge of human resource computer applications desirable.

Source: Adjusted from Sherman, Bohlander and Snell, 1996:135–6

- **Job statement**. The job statement provides an overall view of what this specific job entails and serves to distinguish the job from other jobs, something the job title might fail to do.
- **Essential functions and responsibilities**. Statements pertaining to job duties are usually arranged in order of importance, and should indicate the weight, or value of each duty. The essential functions and responsibilities can also be categorised under Key Performance Areas (KPAs), and their related duties, in which case the employees' expected time expenditure on each of the KPAs is indicated as a percentage of the total working time. These statements should stress the responsibilities all the duties entail and the results they are to accomplish. It is general practice to indicate the tools and equipment used by the employee in performing the job.

11.5.2.2 Job specifications

The personal qualifications, attributes, experience, abilities and manual dexterities required of an individual in order to perform the duties and responsibilities contained in a job description are compiled in a job specification. The physical demands of a job refer to how much walking, standing, reaching, lifting or talking must be done on the job, the condition of the physical work environment, as well as the hazards employees may encounter. If the job specifications are not prepared as a separate document, they are usually contained in the concluding section of the job description, as indicated in the given example.

11.5.3 Job evaluation

Job evaluation is important when organisations are concerned about establishing internal equity among the different jobs in the organisation. Job evaluation involves the systematic, rational assessment of jobs to determine their relative internal worth. Internal worth reflects the importance of a job or its contribution to the overall attainment of organisational objectives. By design, job evaluation focuses internally on the structure of the organisation, it does not take into account market forces, individual skills, or individual performance (Jackson & Schuler, 2000:417). After jobs are formally evaluated, they are grouped into classes or grades. In each class, jobs are then arranged in order of importance, and ranges of pay are established with the aid of wage surveys.

Job evaluation is closely related to job analysis, but they have different outcomes. Obtaining information through a job analysis is an essential prior step to job evaluation. Job evaluation focuses on what the relative value of different jobs, with diverse contents and responsibilities requiring the use of different competencies, are for the organisation in terms of monetary value.

As a means to ensure justice, the corporate philosophy should include the belief that the job evaluation process is the foundation of a sound compensation system.

Therefore the job evaluation process must satisfy the following requirements:

- Provide a consistent measure of job worth that is easily understood by everyone concerned
- Involve managers from its inception through its administration and subsequent revision
- Protect employees from favouritism, bias and resultant internal pay inequities
- Measure the job and not the performance of employees doing the job
- Apply to broad clusters in functional groups (Mondy & Noe, 1993:453).

According to Bratton and Gold (2003:300–303) the job evaluation process comprises four steps, they are to:
(1) Gather the data
(2) Select compensable factors
(3) Evaluate the job
(4) Assign pay to the job.

11.5.3.1 Gather data

Information is gathered by means of a job analysis, in relation to job duties and responsibilities and about employee requirements for successful performance of the job, ensuring that validity is the guiding principle in all aspects of data collection.

11.5.3.2 Select compensable factors

The second step is deciding which factors will be used to evaluate the job, they are the factors the organisation chooses to reward through differential pay. These factors are like yardsticks used to measure the relative importance of jobs. The most typical factors are skill, effort, knowledge, accountability, problem-solving ability, responsibility and physical demands. Once the compensable factors have been determined, their relative importance needs to be defined. The relative importance is reflected in differential points or weights assigned to each of these factors.

11.5.3.3 Evaluate the job

There are four fundamental methods of job evaluation: ranking, job-grading, factor comparison and the point method. Brief descriptions will be given of these four methods.

- **Ranking jobs**. In this method jobs are ordered from the least to the most valued in an organisation based on a subjective evaluation of relative value. This method is convenient when only a few jobs need to be evaluated, when all the jobs are different from each other, and when one person is familiar with them all. Obvious disadvantages of the ranking method are that it is crude and entirely subjective, the results are therefore difficult to uphold and legal challenges may be difficult to defend.
- **Job-grading**. This is also called job classification and is similar to the ranking

method, except that classes or grades are established and the jobs are then placed into the classes. It is decided in advance how many grades of pay will be created, the jobs are then placed into grades based on the degree to which the jobs possess a set of compensable factors. The lowest grade will be described as containing jobs that require little skill and need to be closely supervised. With each successive grade, skills, knowledge and responsibilities increase. A disadvantage of this method is that complex jobs are difficult to fit into the system, as a job may seem to have characteristics of two or more grades.

- **Factor comparison**. This is a quantitative method that evaluates jobs on the basis of a set of compensable factors. Jobs are compared with each other across several factors, such as mental effort, skills, responsibility, physical effort and working conditions. For each job, the compensable factors are ranked according to their relative importance in each job. After each benchmark job has been ranked on each factor, the job evaluator allocates a monetary value to each factor. This is achieved by deciding how much of the pay rate for each benchmark job is associated with mental ability, how much with skill requirement and so on across all the compensable factors. The main disadvantage of this approach is that it is complex, especially translating factor comparison into actual pay rates is a cumbersome process.
- **Point method**. This is the most widely used method of job evaluation. Similar to the factor comparison method, the point method develops separate scales for each compensable factor in order to establish a hierarchy of jobs, but instead of using monetary values, points are allocated. A range of points are allocated to each compensable factor and each factor is weighted, which is an assessment of how important one factor is in relation to another. The point value allocated to each compensable factor is then added to arrive at the overall worth of a job, placing it in a hierarchy. The jobs at the top of the hierarchy would then deserve a higher wage rate than those lower down. This is a relatively stable system over time but has the disadvantage of high administrative costs, making it unfeasible for smaller organisations.

11.5.3.4 Assign pay to the job

The end result of any job evaluation exercise is to have a hierarchy of jobs in place according to their relative value to the organisation. A policy decision needs to be taken with regard to pricing the pay structure, taking into account the organisation's pay levels in comparison with other similar institutions. The compensation tool used to help set wages is the *wage and salary survey*. The wage and salary survey is a survey of the wages paid by employers in an organisation's relevant labour market, locally, regionally, or nationally, depending on the job. The labour market is frequently defined as that area from which employers obtain certain types of workers. It is the wage and salary survey which permits an organisation to maintain external equity, that is, to pay its employees wages equivalent to the wages similar employees earn in other establishments.

Subsequent to the job analysis process, job descriptions and their job specifications can be developed, to determine who should be appointed and what this person's task would be. The job evaluation process enables the allocation of a monetary worth to each specific job. After all this initial planning has been completed, the process of providing human resource can commence.

11.5.4 Recruitment, selection and appointment

Recruitment is the process used by an organisation to locate and attract job applicants in order to fill a position, after which selection takes place, when a person who is believed to be the most likely to succeed in the job is chosen from the pool of applicants.

Recruitment and selection have always been critical processes for organisations. In recent times, there has been growing evidence that the formation of a positive psychological contract with employees provides the basis for a positive outcome in terms of organisational commitment and motivation. According to Bratton and Gold (2003:222) recruitment and the subsequent selection of new employees are vital stages in the formation of the expectations that form such a contract, on which employees select an organisation and the work on offer as much as employers select employees. Thus, employers need to view the attraction and retention of employees as part of the developing employment relationship, based on a mutual and reciprocal understanding of expectations and trust.

11.5.4.1 Recruitment

Recruitment is the process of attracting individuals on a timely basis, in sufficient numbers and with appropriate qualifications, and encouraging them to apply for jobs in the organisation. Unless a sufficient number of qualified prospects apply, a firm cannot have a truly selective employment system. However, in many developing countries where unemployment is high, it is often found that the number of candidates applying for jobs is so high that there can be a long delay in processing all the applications.

Due to the conditions in the labour market, with its supply and demand sides, HR managers often understand that able candidates, especially for specialist jobs, are at a premium, and that some jobs will be hard to fill. In a loose labour market, the employer can afford to pick and choose from among applicants, while in a tight labour market the employer needs to make an effort to attract applicants. Another variable in relation to attracting sufficient applicants is the area in which the work is situated, it may be remote or have an unpleasant climate, where many job seekers do not want to live, despite a relative availability of jobs.

Often, employers are not sufficiently sensitive to labour market conditions. They may continue to assume that they will have a steady stream of candidates even when the demand for such candidates from the private sector has risen as a consequence

Figure 11.6 Relationships and components of recruitment

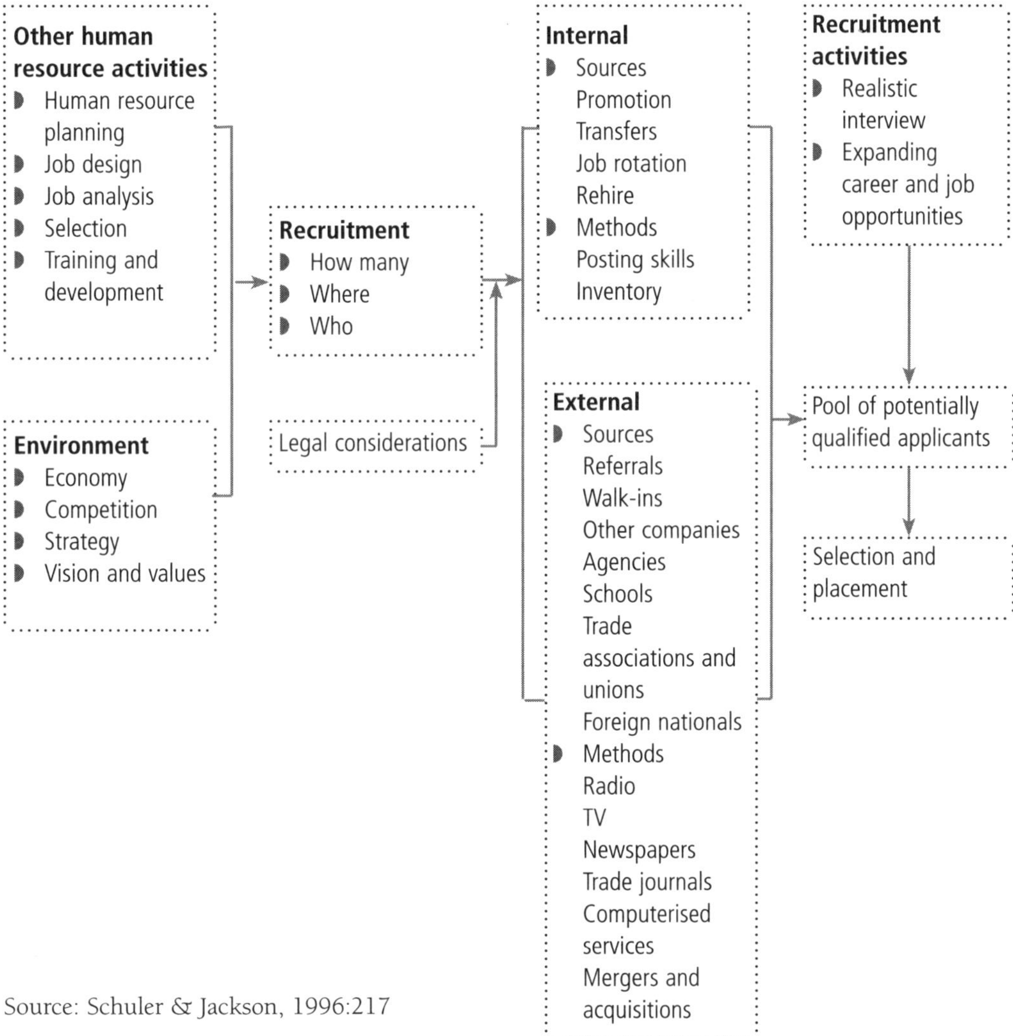

Source: Schuler & Jackson, 1996:217

of economic liberation. Alternatively, a civil service may continue to operate a system of guaranteed entry to public sector employment long after the supply of qualified applicants in the form of secondary school or university graduates has far outstripped demand, as was the case until recently in certain sub-Saharan African countries (McCourt in McCourt & Eldrige, 2003:176).

Figure 11.6 provides the relationships and components of recruitment, while the key activities that are part of the recruitment process and which need to be accomplished in a legal context, include:

- Determining the organisation's long- and short-term needs by job title and level in the organisation

- Staying informed of labour market conditions
- Developing effective recruitment materials
- Developing a systematic and integrated programme of recruitment in conjunction with other human resource activities and with the cooperation of line managers and employee representatives (trade unions)
- Obtaining a pool of qualified job applicants
- Recording the number and quality of job applicants produced by the various sources and methods of recruiting
- Following up on applications, those hired and those not hired, in order to evaluate the effectiveness of the recruitment effort (Schuler & Jackson, 1996:215–6).

Sources and methods for obtaining job applicants

Because of the high cost of recruiting, organisations need to utilise the most productive recruitment sources and methods available. Recruitment sources refer to avenues where qualified individuals can be found, whereas recruitment methods are the specific means by which potential employees can be attracted to the organisation. When designing a recruitment programme, the first step is establishing the objectives. What are the characteristics of the ideal recruit, do you need long- or short-term commitment, should the applicants have well-developed skills or should they be capable and eager to learn, is affirmative action required or is diversity sought after? Once the objectives of recruitment have been stated, the next step is to determine where and how to recruit people.

Internal sources

Internal sources include current employees who become candidates for promotions, transfers and job rotations, as well as former employees who are available for rehiring and recall.

- *Promotions*. Existing employees are encouraged to apply for positions at a higher level, thus enabling them to move upward in the organisation. Employees are likely to feel more secure and to identify their long-term interests with an organisation that provides them the first choice of job opportunities and progression on their career ladder.
- *Transfers*. Transfers occur when current employees are moved laterally to different types of jobs, this is often done to provide developmental opportunities for the individual. Or, transfers in the same job to another location may also be required if the need arises.
- *Job rotations*. Similar to transfers, job rotation can be used to expose employees to various aspects of organisational life. Job rotation has also been applied to relieve job burnout for employees in high-stress occupations.
- *Rehires and recalls*. Thousands of employees are temporarily laid off from work in times of financial difficulties and some are recalled to their former jobs when the

organisation's financial status has improved. Rehiring former or retrenched employees is a relatively inexpensive and effective method of internal recruiting, as the organisation already has information about their performance, attendance and safety records. In addition, these former employees are familiar with job responsibilities and may be better performers than recruits from other sources.

Internal recruitment methods

Identification of applicants for job vacancies can be achieved by posting a notice on bulletin boards, word of mouth, examining personnel records, perusing promotion lists based on performance, checking seniority lists and obtaining ratings from assessment activities (Schuler & Jackson, 1996:224):

- *Job posting.* These display current job openings in an organisation to all employees on bulletin boards, newsletters and on e-mail. These postings serve to:
  - Provide an opportunity for employee growth and development
  - Provide equal opportunity for advancement to all employees
  - Create an openness in the organisation as opportunities are made known to all employees
  - Increase staff awareness about salary grades, job descriptions, transfer and promotion procedures and what constitutes effective job performance
  - Communicate the organisational goals and objectives, allowing individual employees an opportunity for mobility in the organisation.

  There are, nonetheless, some potential problems related to job posting, which can have a negative aftermath:
  - Conflict can arise if an 'heir apparent' is passed over in favour of another candidate from another department or division
  - Credibility may be lost if it appears that the successful candidate has been identified in advance and that managers are only going through the motions of considering other candidates
  - Choosing between more than one equally qualified internal candidate may be difficult and can have serious political consequences
  - Set-back in the morale of unsuccessful candidates may occur if feedback is not handled properly.

- *Computerised career progression system.* This is also known as a skills inventory and includes any data that can be quantified and coded. Information usually included in the skills inventory are the employee's name, employment number, job classification, prior jobs, prior experience, and salary levels. The results of formal assessments, the employee's job interests, geographic preferences, and career goals should be included. Skill inventories are only as good as the updated data they contain, as people's skills and interests change over time. This method of identifying employees helps ensure fairness because they make it easier to identify and consider all internal candidates with the necessary qualifications for a position.

- *Supervisor recommendations.* Supervisors can identify internal candidates if they are asked to nominate people for consideration, they will typically indicate individuals whose work capabilities are well known to them. This is a very subjective process and is susceptible to bias and possible discrimination, resulting in qualified employees being overlooked in order to get 'favourites' promoted, or because the supervisors are simply unaware of the capabilities possessed by some individuals (Kleiman, 2000:112).

External recruitment methods

External recruitment has a number of advantages, including bringing in people with new ideas. It also supplies temporary employees who give the organisation more flexibility to expand or contract its workforce. A variety of methods can be used to recruit candidates externally:

- *Employee referrals.* Employee referral programmes are in fact word-of-mouth advertisements through which current employees notify and refer applicants from outside to the organisation. Applicants referred by employees tend to perform better and remain with the company longer than applicants recruited by other means. This could be because employees know the work environment and portray a balanced view of organisational life.
- *Applicant-initiated recruitment.* This is also known as walk-in applicants. Organisations often receive unsolicited applications or résumés from people who are interested in working for the company. This is often the case where the organisation enjoys a reputation of being a good place to work in terms of compensation policy, working conditions, employee relations, and/or participation in community activities (Kleiman, 2000:115).
- *Advertisements.* The best-known method of notifying applicants of job openings is by means of advertisements. The appropriate media for placing an ad depends primarily on the geographic recruitment area. For instance, for a specific geographical area, the local newspaper, radio or billboards might be appropriate, while a national newspaper, the Internet or professional journals would be more effective for recruiting over a broader geographic area.
- *Employment agencies.* In this case the employer initiates the recruitment process by contacting the appropriate employment agency, informing it of the type of person and qualifications required for the position. The agency then assumes the tasks of attracting and screening applicants, after which applicants are referred to the employer for further screening and possible selection. Kleiman (2000:117) informs that three types of employment agencies have experienced remarkable growth in the past decade:
  - *Public employment agencies.* In the USA, federal law requires that individuals

who receive unemployment compensation must register for work with the public agency of their state. This method is efficient because jobs can be filled fairly quickly as potential applicants are already registered with the state agency and are available to start work immediately because they are unemployed. With these agencies, some employers are concerned about the applicant's motivation level, as they may be applying for work simply to keep their eligibility for unemployment compensation.
 - *Private employment agencies*. Candidates register voluntarily with the agency and may thus be more committed to accept a job offer than in the case of a public agency. The agency charges a fee for its services, usually paid by the company when higher level positions are filled. Clerical and blue-collar candidates may be required to pay the fee themselves. Because private employment agencies relieve an organisation of the administrative burden of finding, contacting and prescribing applicants, they are especially useful when many individuals are expected to apply for a job or when qualified applicants are hard to find.
 - *Executive search firms*. These are also known as 'head-hunters' and specialise in the recruitment of mid- and senior-level managers. Executive search firms can locate successful executives working elsewhere, who are not actively seeking a new job. These agencies can charge employers large fees for their services, which may be due even if none of the firm's candidates are hired.
- *Campus recruiting*. This involves an organisation's representatives visiting college and university campuses to recruit people for positions requiring a college or university qualification. Campus recruitment is used to provide for specialised, entry-level jobs such as engineering, finance, accounting, computer science, law and supervisory management (Kleiman, 2000:119).
- *On-line recruiting*. This is the latest approach to external recruiting. The Internet is used to advertise jobs and find résumés of job seekers. Compared to newspaper advertisements, on-line recruiting is much faster and reaches a much larger audience simultaneously. Within minutes of posting, the job vacancy can be viewed by millions of people over a wide geographical area.

Recruitment of protected groups

In meeting their legal obligations to provide equal employment opportunities, employers often develop formal Employment Equity (EE) policies and procedures. In South Africa employment equity is legislated by means of the Employment Equity Act, 1998 (Act 55 of 1998). An essential part of any EE policy must be an affirmative effort to recruit members from protected groups or classes. These groups normally include women, men from traditionally women held jobs (such as secretaries, phone operators, flight attendants, and nurses), minorities, specific races and disabled people.

11.5.4.2 Selection

The recruiting process typically yields quite a number of applicants whose qualifications must be measured against the job specifications. Selection is the process of obtaining and using information about job applicants in order to determine who should be hired for long- or short-term positions.

Increasingly, greater attention is being given to the selection process than ever before. With the emphasis being placed on the human side of competitiveness, making correct selection decisions is of crucial importance to most organisations. Those individuals hired after thorough screening, against carefully developed job specifications, learn their job tasks readily, are productive, and generally adjust to their jobs with a minimum of difficulty. As a result, both the individual and the organisation benefit from a careful and honest selection process (Sherman, Bohlander & Snell, 1996:190).

Selection was once the exclusive concern of management, but has now become a matter with many role-players, requiring attention to be given to equal opportunity, affirmative action, protected groups, trade union demands and long time-consuming procedures. Where the job tenure of employees is protected by a union agreement or by civil service regulations, there is an additional incentive for management to have sound selection policies and procedures, since it is usually more difficult to discharge unsatisfactory employees who have such protection.

Selection process

The number of steps in the selection process and their sequence may vary, not only in different organisations but also with the type and level of jobs to be filled. Organisations usually have an employment policy and procedure specific to their needs and circumstances. Each step should be evaluated in terms of its contribution. Normally the basic steps are completion of the application form, short listing followed by the selection interview. An example of the steps that typically make up the selection process are shown in Figure 11.7. Not all applicants will go through all of these steps, an applicant may be rejected after any step in the process.

Several different means are used by organisations to obtain information about applicants. These include application forms, interviews, tests, medical examinations and background investigations. Regardless of the methods used, they must be in line with legal requirements, and should conform to accepted ethical standards, including privacy and confidentiality, a further requirement is that the information obtained must be sufficiently reliable and valid.

Employment interview

Of all the techniques used in selection, the interview is the oldest and most widely used along with the application form. Yet interviews are often not predictors of future job performance due to low validity, low reliability and untrained interviewers. Often the final hiring decision rests on the interview, and to conduct successful interviews, the manager should:

Figure 11.7 The selection process

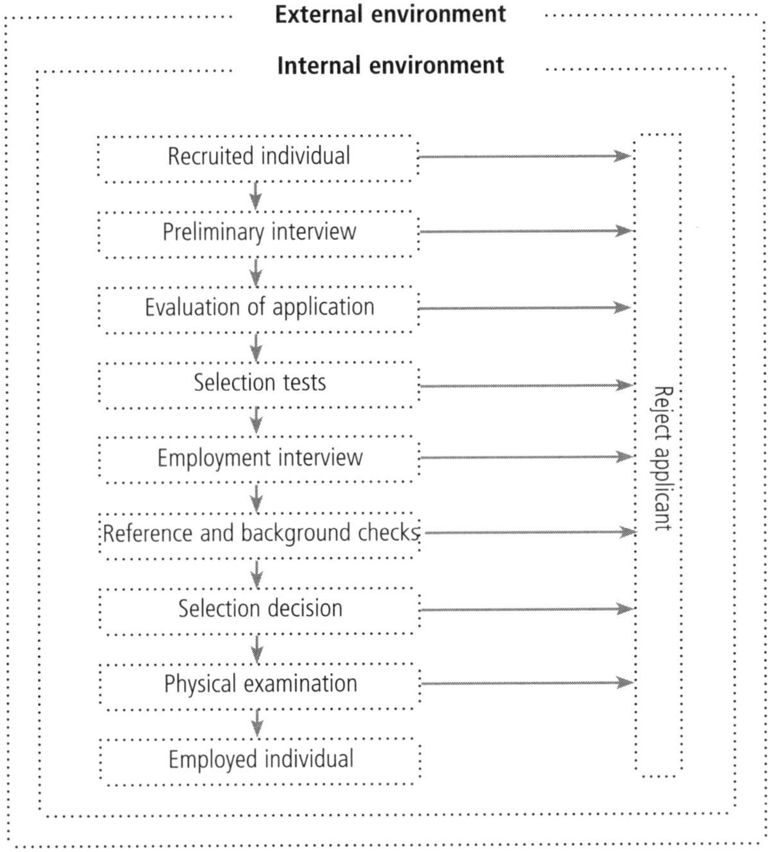

- Use an interview committee of two or three people to increase reliability
- Use a structured approach, to increase consistency of information gained and double the validity
- Avoid vague questions, instead ask behavioural questions which require the candidate to give specific job-related samples of their experience and knowledge
- Use four types of questions: situational questions, job knowledge questions, job sample/simulation questions, and worker requirement questions
- Consistently follow the same procedures in all instances to ensure that each applicant has exactly the same chance as every other applicant
- Let the candidate do most of the talking (80% of the time)
- Ensure that the process is documented for future reference and in case of legal challenge (Sherman et al., 1996:207; Carrell et al., 2000:204).

Conducting an objective interview is primarily a two-phase process. The first is to create a good interview setting before the applicant arrives and to prepare for the interview. The aim of the second phase is to establish a useful questioning frame during the interview, which will generate information to base sound decisions upon.

11.5.4.3 Appointment and placement

While all the steps in the selection process are important, the most critical step is the decision to accept or reject applicants. Because of the cost of placing a new employee on the payroll, the short probationary period in some organisations, equity and affirmative action considerations, and the long-term implications for the organisation, the final decision must be a sound one. It is useful to make use of a summary form or a checklist to ensure that all of the pertinent information has been included in the evaluation of applicants.

Once a decision about the desired candidate has been made, a job offer is extended to the successful applicant. Kleiman (2000:157) argues that the following two principles are important in making a job offer:

- The offer should not be perceived as a gift; it must be sold to the candidate.
- The offer should not remain open awaiting response for too long, which would preclude making an offer to another candidate.

It must be noted, that if the selectee has serious reservations about the job, he/she should not be oversold. Candidates should be given realistic information about the job so that they can decide for themselves whether they and the position are suitably matched. When the applicant has accepted the offer, a letter of appointment with a contract of employment should be issued to the new employee.

Contract of employment

The contract of employment is a stipulation of the terms and conditions of employment, and serves to inform both parties of their reciprocal obligations in view of the applicant taking up employment with the organisation. The typical provisions which should be incorporated in any contract of employment should include at least the following (Bezuidenhout, Garbers & Potgieter, 1998:93–98):

- *The parties.* The employer and employee must be accurately described.
- *Nature of the agreement.* It must be clearly stated that the agreement is in fact a contact of employment.
- *The job.* Aspects of the job such as job title, duties, location, times and hours of work, mealtimes and work on public holidays must be stated.
- *Induction, probation and evaluation.* Indication must be given of when and where induction will take place, whether the employee is appointed on probation and its implications, and how evaluation relates to probationary and permanent employees.
- *Remuneration.* The actual salary scale at the commencement of employment, the basis on which payment will take place, for example weekly or monthly, allowances, overtime and public holiday payment, annual bonus and deductions must be stated.

- *Duration of contract.* When it commences, the duration of the contract and the prescribed retirement age must be specified.
- *Relocation.* If the appointment of an employee involves a relocation of the employee, particulars of the employee's contribution, if any, to the relocation should be stated, and it should be stated how transfers will be effected and who will bear the cost of such a transfer.
- *Benefits.* The employee's entitlement to any of the following should be stated: pension, medical aid, life insurance, housing and housing allowance, car or transport allowance, subsistence allowance and expense account.
- *Leave.* All aspects regarding the different types of leave entitlement must be addressed, such as how much is granted, when it may be taken, how the leave accrues during a given cycle, whether leave may be accumulated, and whether payment in lieu of leave may take place.
- *Protection of the employer.* This deals with mainly three concepts, namely restraint of trade, disclosure of confidential information and the obligation not to compete with the employer.
- *Copyright and patents.* Who will be the owner of any inventions or original work developed by the employee while in the employment of the employer must be specified.
- *Termination.* The ways in which an employee's services can be terminated and how notice will be given, acknowledging the legal prescriptions, must be stated.
- *Dispute resolution.* Provision should be made for how disputes about the interpretation or application of the agreement should be resolved. Provision should also be made for the resolution of other disputes.
- *The incorporation of standard terms and conditions of service.* It is clear that the incorporation of the above-mentioned aspects would lead to a very bulky document. Therefore, a clause is often found in the contract of employment, which simply incorporates these policies by way of reference and which leaves it to the employee to familiarise him-/herself with the contents thereof.

Placement

Given the wide variation among personalities and among jobs, an important responsibility of managers is to try to match employee and job characteristics so that the work is done by people who are well suited to do it. This requires that managers should be clear about what they expect employees to do. Placement is concerned with matching individuals to jobs, based on the demands of the job and the knowledge, skills, abilities, preferences, interests, and personality of the individual. The extent to which a person's ability and personality match the requirements of a job is called the person-job-fit. When hiring and leading employees, managers should try and accomplish the best person-job-fit, so that employees are more likely to contribute because they feel comfortable and satisfied in the job responsibilities allocated to them.

11.5.4.4 Induction and orientation

The new employee needs to be welcomed and oriented towards the work environment. The first few days are crucial in facilitating a feeling of belonging and creating an association with the goals of the organisation. Assisting the new employee to feel welcome, acknowledged and valued are crucial to successful integration of newly appointed people with the goals and functions of the institution.

Induction

Induction is considered the first step in the orientation process and has as its aims to:

- Reduce anxiety and uncertainty
- Save time for supervisors and fellow workers
- Create a positive attitude towards the employer
- Assist the employee to become fully productive as soon as possible
- Assist in creating realistic employee expectations.

Induction training is usually the responsibility of the human resource department, and is presented as the first section of the employee's orientation programme. All categories of new employees are subjected to the same content during the induction period, and this normally deals with (Booyens, 1998:382):

- An overview of the organisation, describing the philosophy, explaining the history, goals, products and services, culture, norms and standards, as well as communication procedures and an introduction to the names and offices of executive members of management and other important authority figures
- The physical and geographical layout of the institution, indicating safety measures, such as emergency exits, fire extinguishers, and disaster care plans
- Conditions of service and benefits, such as salary scales, overtime payment, leave arrangements, night duty, weekend and public holiday duty policies, and recreational activities
- Policies and procedures, such as work schedules, grievance and disciplinary procedures, uniform allowance, leave of absence (sickness, study, maternity and compassionate leave), and registration with professional bodies
- Facilities available to personnel such as cloak rooms, canteen and gymnasium or employee assistance programmes.

Orientation

Orientation is the personalised training and support the individual employee receives in the specific place of work, enabling the person to become aware of the requirements of the job itself. The aim is to achieve effective and productive work performance in the rules and procedures of the institution at functional level, as soon as possible. The newcomer is introduced to his/her fellow workers, the supervisor, work environment and job responsibilities.

The direct supervisor is responsible for orienting new staff members to their specific duties and responsibilities. Clinical supervisors and middle management are usually jointly responsible for presenting and assessing the orientation programme. Despite the training that novice healthcare professionals receive, and their specialist knowledge of their subject, they often find the integration of theory and practice difficult. This is where a sympathetic, understanding manager and direct supervisor can help the new employee to cope with the difficulties of actual practice.

Taking a new job involves not only new job tasks but also new interpersonal relationships. The new person comes into an ongoing social system which has evolved a unique set of values, ideals, frictions, conflicts, friendships, coalitions and all other characteristics of work groups. If left alone, the new employee must cope with the new environment in ignorance, but if given assistance, guidance and support, he/she can cope more effectively.

The orientation programme will differ in different departments or units. As an example, the following aspects should be covered when a nurse is oriented to a hospital ward or unit (Booyens, 1998:382–384):

- Physician-related aspects:
  - the allocation of beds to doctors and consultants
  - routine and emergency admission days
  - days and times of consultants' rounds
  - theatre days
  - procedures for referring patients to outpatients and other departments
  - procedures for calling doctors in terms of patient consultations
  - taking instructions from doctors
  - conducting rounds with doctors
  - taking doctors' instructions over the phone
- Unit administration aspects:
  - job descriptions of different categories of personnel
  - unit routine, such as meal, medicine administration and visiting times
  - routine ordering of supplies, diets and equipment
  - routine and emergency maintenance of equipment
  - porter service
  - messenger service
  - procedures for admission, transfers and discharge of patients
  - communication channels and procedures
  - routine records and reports
  - operation of the patient-call-system
  - managing and handling drugs and the key to the drug cupboard
  - rules for duty rosters and requests for off-duties.
- Clinical nursing aspects:
  - standard nursing care plans for the most frequently treated illnesses
  - documentation and patients' care records

- checking emergency trolley supplies
- checking, maintenance and use of resuscitation equipment, e.g. ambubag, oxygen, suction apparatus and ventilator
- handling soiled linen
- isolation nursing policy
- incident reporting.

- Environmental aspects:
  - control of noise
  - control of unpleasant odours
  - maintenance of a comfortable temperature and level of humidity
  - disinfection measures.

The more time and effort spent in helping new employees feel welcome, the more likely they are to identify with the organisation and become valuable members of it. Orientation is designed to develop in employees a particular attitude about the work they will be doing and their role in the organisation. It defines the philosophy behind the organisation's rules and provides a framework for job-related tasks. A properly planned induction programme, followed by job-related orientation in the work environment, ensures that new staff members feel welcome, have the confidence to ask about things they don't understand, and become productive members of the healthcare team in the shortest possible time.

11.6 UNDERLYING DYNAMICS

The planning and provision of human resource for organisations are not only determined by the needs of the organisation but are affected by legislation emphasising equal opportunity, affirmative action, empowerment of designated groups and the transformation of institutions. Forces in the labour market also have a direct effect on the availability of sufficient numbers of well-qualified candidates. Of special reference here are the following factors:

- The type of healthcare organisation and level of healthcare service provision, for example an academic hospital or a primary healthcare clinic, play a role.
- Economic factors determine the available budgetary resources, of which the personnel budget often requires the highest percentage.
- Availability of human resource pool and skills mix requirements. The migration of large numbers of healthcare personnel has a significant impact on HR planning and provision, as it affects the meeting of needs for certain competencies, scarce skills and high tech requirements.
- The impact of equity legislation often results in the best candidate not being selected due to requirements that jobs should be allocated to specific groups.

11.7 CONCLUDING STATEMENTS

The following concluding statements are relevant to the planning and provision of HR:

- Human resource planning and provision occur in the legal and professional-ethical context, in accordance with the business ownership of the particular healthcare organisation, with reference to the Constitution, as well as labour and health-related legislation.
- The major role-players in HR planning and provision are the state, top management, the human resource managers and organised labour.
- Human resource planning and provision refer to activities undertaken to determine the future HR needs of the organisation, and to recruit and appoint the best candidates for the job.
- The process of HR planning and provision relates mainly to the HR planning process which incorporates the activities of job analysis and job evaluation, recruitment, selection and appointment.
- As organisation's plan for the future, top management and strategic planners must realise that the strategic decisions affect and are affected by HR functions. HR planning strives to make sure that the correct number and type of employees are available to implement the plans of the organisation.
- HR planning is a systematic process that involves forecasting demand for labour, performing supply analysis, and balancing supply and demand considerations. Forecasting demand aims to identify the number and type of people needed to meet organisational objectives, whereas supply analysis involves determining if sufficient employees are available in the organisation to meet the demand, and also to establish whether potential employees are available on the job market. Matching supply and demand requires a host of activities, including internal and external recruitment.
- Job analysis is a process of identifying all the relevant factors pertaining to a particular job to enable the compilation of a job description and a job specification. The job analysis information also serves the process of performing a job evaluation, which is the method of determining the monetary value of a position by comparing it with similar jobs in the organisation.
- Various recruitment sources and methods are available for implementation, depending on who the target population is from which candidates are envisaged to be drawn.
- Once a person is appointed and placed in an organisation it becomes necessary to orientate the new employee about the philosophy, goals and culture of the organisation, and to familiarise him/her about the existing regulatory guidelines in the form of policy, procedure and processes. This is achieved by means of the initial induction period followed by the longer orientation process.
- Various underlying dynamics, such as the type of healthcare organisation, economic factors, the availability of an HR pool of practitioners with the

appropriate competencies and skills, and equity requirements, affect the provision of HR for a healthcare institution.

Self-assessment

(1) Clearly differentiate between job analysis, job description, job specification and job evaluation.
(2) What basic steps are normally followed in the selection process?
(3) Briefly describe the objectives of the selection interview.
(4) As a project, prepare a description of a job at which you are currently working. Develop specifications listing minimum qualifications required for the job and assess how your qualifications and experience compare with the job specifications. Are you underemployed or overemployed?
(5) How would an employer prove to you that it is seeking to develop a positive psychological contract? Go to the BP Career Centre at www.bpfutures.com and determine whether BP is a progressive human resource management employer.
(6) Think about an organisation you would like to work for. What images, values and information related to that organisation come to mind?
(7) Visit the Monster www.monster.co.uk and StepStone www.stepstone.com/workthing/index.htm websites and examine the services they offer job-seekers.

12 Maintenance of human resources

KEY CONCEPTS

Health and safety
Employee assistance programmes
Quality of work life
Participative management
Quality circles
Management by objectives

SPECIFIC OUTCOMES

After studying this chapter, you should be able to:

- Interpret the legal and professional-ethical human resource management **context** in view of maintaining human resources with reference to public and private (type of business ownership) healthcare organisations in terms of the following legislation:
  - Labour Relations Act, 1995 (Act 66 of 1995)
  - Basic Conditions of Employment Act, 1997 (Act 75 of 1997)
  - Occupational Health and Safety Act, 1993 (Act 85 of 1993)
  - The Compensation for Occupational Injuries and Diseases Act, 1993 (Act 130 of 1993)
  - Unemployment Insurance Act, 2001 (Act 63 of 2001)
- Identify and describe the **role-players**, such as the state, managers, employees, safety representatives, safety committees and inspectors, and interpret their roles and responsibilities in the maintenance of human resources in a healthcare organisation
- Analyse and debate the **purpose** of maintaining human resources in the context of a healthcare organisation
- Analyse and debate the **process** of human resource maintenance in the context of a healthcare organisation, with specific reference to occupational health and safety, physical and psychological hazards in the workplace and quality of work life

- Debate the **underlying dynamics** that could impact on the maintenance of human resources of a healthcare organisation, with specific reference to the impact of organisational culture and climate, top and middle management's valuing of their personnel and business ethics.

12.1 INTRODUCTION

Maintenance of human resources refers to management's input in taking care of their workforce as individuals in terms of providing a safe working environment, recognising the value of people and acknowledging their potential in making greater inputs into the realisation of organisational goals.

Once employees have been recruited, selected and placed in the enterprise, they are incorporated into the organisation by the induction an orientation programmes. Their socialisation in the organisation takes place through their interactions with existing employees, preceptors and mentors. The philosophy and management style of managers and supervisors have a strong influence on whether employees consider the institution to be a caring one, or not, and whether they experience quality of work life.

The quality of work life indicates the degree to which employees are able to satisfy their personal needs by working in an institution. Quality of work life means different things to different people, it may mean a fair day's pay, safe working conditions, being treated with dignity, opportunities for advancement, creative tasks, or a successful career, depending on the personal needs and development level of the employee.

Occupational health and safety refers to the physiological and socio-psychological conditions of an organisation's workforce resulting from elements in the work environment. If an organisation takes effective health and safety measures, fewer of its employees will suffer harm and the enormous costs that result from inadequate health and safety conditions in terms of monetary and human costs should be reduced. Especially, the elimination of causes of stress are extremely important, because the pace and workload that most clinical practitioners are subjected to in the healthcare environment tend to lead to burnout in the long run.

This chapter will highlight the following components (see visual presentation in Figure 12.1):

- The **context** of human resource management refers to the legal and professional-ethical environment of a particular service.
- The **purpose** of maintaining human resources is to take care of and value employees as individuals, and to foster an environment in which they feel safe and recognised.
- The different **role-players** in maintaining human resources are the state through its legislation, top and middle management, safety committees and inspectors, as well as the employees and organised labour.

- In describing the **process** of maintaining the human resources of an organisation, emphasis is placed on the health and safety of employees, their quality of work life and productivity.
- The **underlying dynamics** impacting on the maintenance of human resources in a healthcare organisation are, among others, the organisational culture and climate, the management and leadership styles of superiors, the commitment of staff and business ethics.

Figure 12.1 Visual presentation of the maintenance of human resources in a healthcare organisation

Context	◗ Labour Relations Act, 1995 (Act 66 of 1995) ◗ Basic Conditions of Employment Act, 1997 (Act 75 of 1997) ◗ Occupational Health and Safety Act, 1993 (Act 85 of 1993) ◗ The Compensation for Occupational Injuries and Diseases Act, 1993 (Act 130 of 1993) ◗ Unemployment Insurance Act, 2001 (Act 63 of 2001)
Purpose	◗ Value HR as individuals ◗ Maintain health and safety in the workplace ◗ Prevent workplace hazards ◗ Meet employees' higher level needs
Role-players	◗ State ◗ Top and middle management ◗ Safety committees and inspectors ◗ Employees ◗ Organised labour
Process	◗ Occupational health and safety ◗ Quality of work life and productivity
Underlying dynamics	◗ Organisational culture and climate ◗ Management and leadership styles ◗ Commitment of staff ◗ Business ethics

12.2 CONTEXT

Employers are required by law to provide working conditions that do not impair the health and safety of their employees. Therefore employers must ensure a work environment that protects employees from physical hazards, unhealthy conditions, and unsafe acts by other personnel. Through legislation in the form of occupational health and safety Acts and effective health and safety programmes, the physical and emotional wellbeing, as well as the economic security of employees, may be preserved and even enhanced. The following Acts are relevant in this regard:

- Labour Relations Act, 1995 (Act 66 of 1995)
- Basic Conditions of Employment Act, 1997 (Act 75 of 1997)
- Occupational Health and Safety Act, 1993 (Act 85 of 1993)
- The Compensation for Occupational Injuries and Diseases Act, 1993 (Act 130 of 1993)
- Unemployment Insurance Act, 2001 (Act 63 of 2001).

While the laws safeguarding employee's physical and emotional wellbeing are an incentive, many employers are motivated to provide desirable working conditions by virtue of their sensitivity to human needs and rights. In addition, cost associated with sick leave, disability payments, replacement of employees who are injured or killed, and workers' compensation far exceed the cost of maintaining a health and safety programme.

12.3 PURPOSE

With a mandate to be more cost effective and to play a more significant role in the management of human resources, managers can prove their value by concerning themselves with occupational health and safety in their organisations, indeed many HRM functions are related to health and safety in the workplace, and neglect can result in substantial costs to the organisation and the individual employee, which may be compounded by inputs from organised labour. A more humanised work environment helps to meet workers' higher level needs. Quality of work life programmes are designed to facilitate the best fit between the individual, technology, job and the work environment, and in achieving this, allowing the individual employee greater autonomy and participation in management affairs.

12.4 ROLE-PLAYERS

The Occupational Health and Safety Act, 1993 (Act of 1993) is designed to ensure, as far as possible, safe and healthy work environments. It must be emphasised that both the employer and employee have a responsibility for adhering to health and safety regulations and policy. Management, the employee, safety representatives, safety committees and inspectors all play a role in the achievement and maintenance of a safe and healthy work environment.

12.5 PROCESS

In the process of maintaining human resources, two components are important as they specifically affect the physical and psychological wellbeing of employees and thus serve to provide employees, who feel safe and secure in their place of work and who realise that management is concerned about their welfare as individuals, acknowledging the contributions they can make at higher levels. These components are health and safety in the work environment, and the quality of work life, the latter being linked to productivity. Refer to Figure 12.2 for an outlay of this chapter's content.

Figure 12.2 Outlay of components dealt with under the maintenance of human resources

Occupational health and safety	The importance of health and safety Occupational health hazards and issues Managing health and safety Employee assistance programmes
Quality of work life and productivity	Quality of work life defined Enhancing the quality of work life Strategies to improve the quality of work life

12.5.1 Occupational health and safety

Occupational health and safety are concerned with the identification and control of hazards associated with the physical workplace environment (refer also to Chapter 18 Risk management in a healthcare organisation). These hazards, which range from technological, physical and chemical agents to psycho-social disorders, such as workplace stress, shape objective patterns of interaction, behaviour and process and also subjective feelings about the employment relationship (Bratton & Gold, 2003:149).

It is important to realise that concerns about health and safety are no longer limited to areas of industrial work. Office workers, managers and professionals are increasingly anxious about repetitive strain injuries, sick building syndrome, work-related stress, work-place violence and second-hand smoke. Common occupation-caused physiological maladies include cardiovascular disease, various forms of cancer, emphysema, and actual loss of a limb or life. Leukemia, lung disease, sterility, central nervous system damage and chronic bronchitis are other physical conditions that may occur. Common harmful socio-psychological conditions which may be causes of low quality of work life, include stress, dissatisfaction, apathy, withdrawal, tunnel vision, forgetfulness, inner confusion about roles, mistrust of others, inattentiveness, irritability, procrastination, and a tendency to become distraught about insignificant matters (Dolan & Schuler, 1996:443–444).

Those characteristics of the work environment associated with injuries are known as **safety risks**. To avoid accidents, these risks must be removed and managed by means of protective clothing, shielding dangerous apparatus, safe procedures and a continuous awareness of safety measures among employees. On the other hand, health risks are those work-related characteristics that are associated with diseases among employees. These risks are often more difficult to identify and manage as they are more subtle and may take a long time to surface.

12.5.1.1 The importance of health and safety

There are strong economic, legal, psychological and moral reasons why managers should earnestly attend to health and safety issues in their domain of command (Bratton & Gold, 2003:153–156):

Economic considerations

The enormous costs that result from inadequate health and safety conditions, both in monetary and human terms, are enough to justify workplace improvement programmes.

When considering the economics of an unhealthy and unsafe workplace, it is necessary to distinguish between the direct costs falling upon the organisation and those carried by government-funded bodies such as hospitals. An accident is defined as an unforeseen or unplanned event that results in an injury and/or material damage or loss. The direct economic costs of a work-related accident can be determined by using the following criteria:

- Cost of wages paid for the time spent by uninjured employees (assisting the injured person, sympathy, curiosity)
- Cost of material or equipment damaged
- Cost of injured worker's time lost
- Supervisor's time spent assisting, investigating, reporting, assigning work, training or instructing a replacement and making other necessary adjustments
- Wage cost of decreased output by injured worker after return to work
- Medical cost to the company
- Cost of time spent by administration staff and specialists on investigations or in the processing of compensation questions.

Thousands of working hours are lost in South African healthcare services every year because employees feel unwell, fall ill or are involved in accidents at work. When this happens, the system loses in terms of direct cost of the worker's wages, decreased productivity and decreased quality (because of staff shortages). This results in slower patient recovery and additional increase in the cost of healthcare.

Legal considerations

With respect to workplace health and safety, the legal rights of employees can be divided into two broad categories, namely individual and collective rights. **Individual rights** evolve from common law, in which case every employer has a vicarious common law duty to provide a safe working environment for his/her employees. (Also refer to Chapter 18, Risk management in a healthcare organisation).

Occupational health and safety in South Africa is regulated by the Occupational Health and Safety Act, 1993 (Act 85 of 1993) (OHSA). This Act protects people's health and safety at work in terms of the use of operating equipment and machinery, against threats to their health and safety arising from work activities, and is also concerned with the health and safety of the general public who may be affected. The OHSA regulates the establishment of an Advisory Council for Occupational Health and Safety and related matters. According to Gerber et al. (1998:251–255) health and safety in the workplace are regulated and administered by the following structures:

- The Advisory Council for Occupational Health and Safety
- Health and safety representatives within the organisation
- Safety committees appointed by the employer
- Inspectors from the Department of Labour
- The National Occupational Safety Association of South Africa (NOSA) is a public, not-for-gain body, which focuses on the prevention of occupational accidents by means of guidance and training.

The main source of **collective health and safety rights** arises from the negotiated collective agreements between union and management. Incorporated in these agreements are the following three rights: the right to refuse dangerous work without penalty, the right to participate in identifying and correcting health and safety problems, and the right to know about hazards in the workplace.

Psychological considerations

It is recognised that, going beyond the legal requirements of due diligence, a healthy organisation can have a strong positive affect on the psychological contract by strengthening employee commitment, motivation and loyalty. At a collective level, it is argued that union-management relations are improved when employers take greater responsibility in satisfying their employees' health and safety needs, and that employees may take a less militant stance during wage bargaining if management pays attention to housekeeping.

Moral considerations

Employers have a moral obligation to provide a safe and healthy work environment for their employees, as those who contribute to the causation of work-related diseases and injuries (such as asbestosis and lung cancer), and who do so knowingly can be held both causally and morally responsible for their action.

In addition to the legislation, regulations and codes of practice, economic and moral reasons dictate to the employer that a safe and healthy work environment must be created for its employees, and HR managers have taken on the role of advising managers on the content and legal obligations of this aspect.

12.5.1.2 Occupational health hazards and issues

Human resource managers today have to deal with complex problems that threaten the health of employees. The following health problems will briefly be mentioned: sick building syndrome, stress, alcohol and drug abuse, smoking, and human immunodeficiency virus and acquired immune deficiency syndrome (HIV/AIDS).

Sick building syndrome

In 1982, sick building syndrome (SBS) was recognised by the WHO as occurring where a cluster of work-related symptoms of unknown cause are significantly more prevalent among the occupants of certain buildings in comparison to others. The causes of SBS can be attributed to a lack of fresh air supply, inadequate ventilation, unsuitable lighting, airborne pollutants and, at a more general level, low morale. Typical symptoms of SBS include eye, nose and throat irritation, a sensation of dry mucous membranes and skin, skin rash, mental fatigue, headaches, a high frequency of airway infection and cough, nausea, dizziness, hoarseness and wheezing (Bratton & Gold, 2003:163). SBS increases labour costs due to absenteeism and undermines relationships as managers resort to disciplinary measures to reduce time taken off work.

Workplace stress

Stress is any demand on the individual that requires coping behaviour. Stress comes from two basic sources: physical activity and mental or emotional activity. Two types of stress have been identified, namely **eustress**, which is considered positive stress that accompanies achievement and exhilaration, and the second being **distress**, which is harmful stress characterised by a loss of feelings of security and adequacy.

Causes of job-related stress are numerous and may not have the same effect on all employees, but a few common sources of stress are disagreements with supervisors or colleagues, conflict, role ambiguity, feeling trapped in a job for which the person feels ill-suited to, workplace violence and harassment, lack of privacy in offices, unappealing music, excessive noise, having little to say about how a job should be performed, overspecialisation, lack of communication and recognition, and work overload. Personal individual stress factors can also have an effect on an employee's behaviour at work. Refer to Figure 12.3.

Burnout is the most severe stage of distress. Career burnout generally occurs when a person begins questioning his/her own personal values. The person no longer feels what he/she is doing is important, and depression, frustration and a loss

Figure 12.3 Possible causes of stress for the individual employee

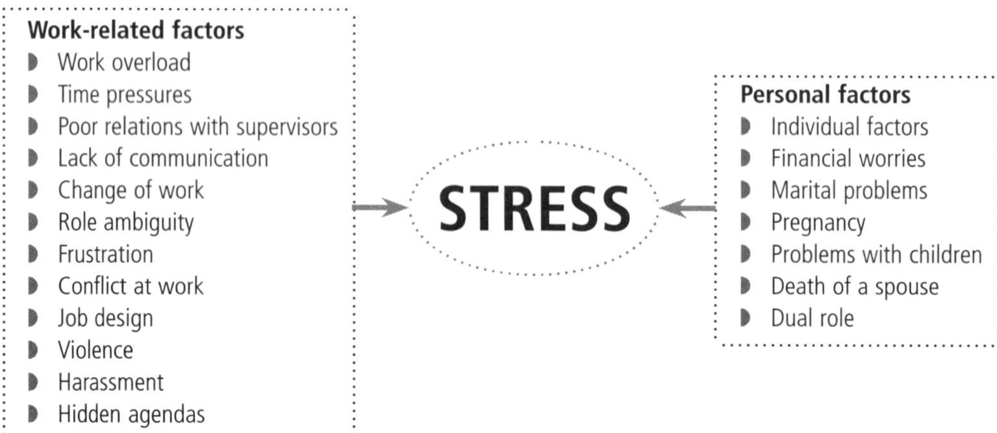

Source: Adapted from Bratton & Gold 2003:170

of productivity are all symptoms of burnout. Sherman et al. (1996:489) are of the opinion that burnout is primarily due to a lack of personal fulfilment in the job or a lack of positive feedback about performance.

Typical symptoms of workplace stress are recognised as tension and anxiety, anger and aggression, chronic worry, uncooperative attitudes, forgetfulness, irritability and boredom, reduced job satisfaction, sleeping problems, inability to relax, high blood pressure, digestive problems, absenteeism, increased accidents, excessive alcohol and/or tobacco use and anti-social behaviour.

Alcohol and drug abuse

The excessive consumption of alcohol is both a health problem and job performance problem in every occupational category, be it manual, white-collar or managerial. Behavioural problems of employees who abuse alcohol range from tardiness, high levels of absenteeism and a greater chance of having accidents than non-alcohol drinkers. The direct and indirect costs of alcohol abuse to employers include lower productivity, poor quality work, bad decisions, the cost of accidents, absenteeism and managers' lost time in dealing with employees with an alcohol problem.

Drug-addicted employees receive less attention than those with an alcohol problem. This could be because it has not assumed the proportions of alcohol abuse, and usually affects employees aged between 20 and 25, who have been employed by the organisation for less than four years. Drug abusers tend to attempt to persuade fellow workers to also take drugs, thus providing management with a reason to terminate their employment (Gerber et al., 1998:248). In the health field the statistics may be different as the staff members, doctors and nurses, who have access to drugs, would be older with a drug abuse problem stretching over a number of years.

Whereas alcoholism was previously regarded as a moral and criminal problem, the modern approach is to regard it as an illness that requires special treatment. The most important components of a programme to control alcoholism include:

- **Policy document**. In this document management declares the organisation's commitment to the programme and allocates responsibility to relevant people, confirming its willingness to assist the affected. It should thus be supportive instead of punitive.
- **Cooperation of trade unions**. For union members, the early involvement of trade unions may play an important role in obtaining the support of the employee's colleagues.
- **Education**. An information and training programme covering all the dimensions of alcoholism and spelling out the extent of the organisation's control programme is desirable.
- **Training**. Supervisors and managers must know their responsibilities regarding the programme and receive preparation in how to handle alcoholism. The supervisor bears the primary responsibility for identifying the problem and handling the individual as an alcoholic (Gerber et al., 1998:248).

Smoking

Smoking is a problem for employees and employers. In a study reported by Dessler (1997:647) it was found that smoking employees are less healthy than non-smokers, are absent more often, make more expensive claims for health and disability benefits and endanger co-workers who breathe in the affected air. Non-smokers have now begun to protect themselves by demanding from smokers and management a smoke-free work environment. In South Africa, legislation has been passed prohibiting smoking in public places and transport, and requires that smoke-free zones be provided in restaurants and social places by the owner of the organisation. Banning smoking from communal working areas, has, however, led to another problem for management, and that is how many smoke breaks and of what duration smokers should be allowed to enjoy per day, as this removes them from their work station and therefore affects their productivity.

Acquired immune deficiency syndrome (AIDS)

AIDS is a disease that undermines the immune system of the body and consequently exposure to common ailments can become fatal complications. Employees in professions directly exposed to AIDS are dentists, dental assistants, nursing staff, medical staff, first aid and trauma practitioners, police officers, laboratory technicians and personnel in the correctional services.

The direct cost of AIDS will impact in organisations in several ways. Medical aid premiums will increase to cover employees against AIDS, medical costs will increase because of AIDS victims who do not have medical insurance and the medical aid burden will increase. The indirect costs will include lost work time, with others having to do their work while they are unavailable. Productivity will suffer if co-workers refuse to work with AIDS-infected employees. It is also known that recruitment and training costs will increase as it is generally accepted that AIDS is a lethal disease at this stage (Gerber et al., 1998:247).

In the workplace, being proactive by giving attention to the dissemination of information about AIDS and the reduction of fear among employees who have to work with colleagues who are HIV infected or who already have AIDS has been found to be helpful in the management of AIDS-related problems. Training should cover aspects such as the nature, means of infection and transmission, and signs and symptoms of the illness and prepare employees emotionally for the time when a fellow-worker contacts this disease. (Also refer to Chapter 9, Management of HIV/AIDS).

Sexual harassment

Although sexual harassment is not always considered a true health and safety issue, it is an occurrence which poisons the atmosphere and relations in the workplace, and it can be said to affect the mental wellbeing of employees and especially women. Sexual harassment must be dealt with by management for two reasons, it has legal and economic consequences.

First, workplace sexual harassment is unlawful, and the courts have increasingly viewed its prevention as the responsibility of the employer. Sexual harassment pertains to the legal concept of 'detriment', it can lead to an employment-related detriment to the female employee and, as such, has serious implications for management. Workplace sexual harassment is considered the most intimate manifestation of employment discrimination faced by women, and legal protection against it is complex and sensitive, considering that women are still disadvantaged because of patriarchal or sexist jurisprudence in many instances (Bratton & Gold, 2003:174). Therefore a policy on sexual harassment should be developed involving representatives from all relevant stakeholders in the work environment, which will serve to inform employees of the nature and context of this particular form of unacceptable behaviour, and in turn will aid the disciplinary process when it is required.

The stress caused by sexual harassment affects the expectations that employees and employers have of one another. The employee's loyalty to the organisation decreases and the intent to leave the organisation increases, thus adversely affecting the psychological contract. A number of negative work outcomes have been identified due to sexual harassment which have economic implications for the employer. They are loss of commitment to work, decreased job satisfaction, increased absenteeism and decreased job performance.

12.5.1.3 Managing health and safety

Senior management's involvement in developing and implementing health and safety policies and programmes is essential and often required by law. Health and safety issues offer management the opportunity to be more proactive than reactive. There are a number of strategies that organisations can use to ensure a healthy and safe work environment for their employees and customers. The strategies are summarised in Figure 12.4. The bases for creating a healthy and safe work place are founded upon

Figure 12.4 Strategies to improve workplace health and safety

1 Design	Safe and healthy systems of work
2 Exhibit	Strong management commitment
3 Inspect	The workplace for health and safety hazards
4 Establish	Procedures and control for dealing with health and safety issues
5 Promote	Safe working behaviours
6 Develop	Training programmes
7 Set up	Health and safety committees
8 Monitor	Health and safety policies
9 Draw up	An action plan and checklist

Source: Bratton & Gold, 2003:175

strong management commitment, safe work systems, policy, procedures and control measures, identification of hazards, training programmes, safe working behaviours, health and safety committees and action plans.

12.5.1.4 Employee assistance programmes (EAPs)

Health includes the psychological and physical components of one's life. While emotional problems, personal crisis, alcoholism and drug abuse are considered to be personal matters, they become organisational problems when they affect behaviour at work and interfere with job performance. Employee Assistance Programmes are job-based programmes operating in an organisation for the purpose of identifying troubled employees, motivating them to resolve their troubles, and providing access to counselling or treatment for those employees who need these services (Bamberger & Meshoulam, 2000:151).

EAPs are aimed at preventing and treating a wide variety of employee behavioural and or medical problems, including not only substance abuse but family disruptions, stress and work-based traumas. Contemporary EAPs are designed to provide organisations with a mechanism to avoid costly disruptions, productivity losses and increased turnover stemming from any of these primarily external sources. In a strictly confidential manner, the EAP provides an assessment of the employee's problems and then refers the individual to the appropriate treatment provider. Typically, such a programme refers employees in need of assistance to in-house counsellors or external professionals.

12.5.2 Quality of work life and productivity

Traditional work designs such as autocracy and bureaucracy may have been productive, but they exacted high human costs. Productivity was emphasised at all costs, status symbols became measures of success, workers were driven to produce in the name of profit, without regard for their needs. The pay cheque was expected to purchase not only labour but loyalty as well. Consequently, job satisfaction was low and turnover high. Realising there must be a better way, organisations began to experiment with work/job designs that could provide high levels of productivity for the employer but also a better quality of work life (QWL) for employees.

12.5.2.1 Quality of work life defined

The QWL refers to the impact the work environment has on the individual and the favourableness or unfavourableness of the work climate as experienced by the employee. The QWL is a concept widely used to refer to a philosophy of management that enhances the dignity of employees, introduces changes in the organisation's culture, and improves employees' physical and/or emotional wellbeing (Ivancevich & Matteson, 1996:240).

In some organisations QWL programmes are intended to increase employee trust, involvement and problem-solving in order to increase both employee satisfaction and organisational effectiveness. Quality of work life relates to teamwork and comes directly from the concept of autonomous working groups, with the twin aims of improving the quality of work life and enhancing productivity (Torrington & Hall, 1998:499). This view is supported by Carrell et al. (2000:423) who indicates that QWL programmes are aimed at improving productivity and quality through greater job satisfaction and cooperative employee-management relationships.

12.5.2.2 Enhancing the quality of work life

Walton, the most widely quoted author on the quality of work life, explains the requirements that constitute a good or desirable quality of working life in terms of eight broad conditions of employment as depicted in Figure 12.5 (Beach, 1985:325–6; Gerber, Nel & van Dyk, 1998:230). The eight conditions are as follows:

(1) **Adequate and fair compensation**. This includes adequate payment and fringe benefits so as to enable the employee to maintain an acceptable standard of living while working in the institution.

(2) **Safe and healthy working conditions**. These apply to both the physical and psychological environment in which the employee functions.

(3) **Opportunity to utilise and develop human capacities**. This means that the employee is granted as much autonomy in his/her work as possible. It also implies that the work content should be made stimulating and interesting by involving the employee in the planning phases of projects, by delegating tasks in their entirety and not just in parts, by delegating tasks that require a number of skills, and by supplying the employee with the necessary information and management perspectives in order for the individual to recognise the value and place of his/her work in the organisation.

(4) **Future opportunity for continued growth and security**. This involves expanding one's capabilities, the opportunity to use new knowledge and skills, promotion opportunities, as well as job and financial security.

(5) **Social interaction**. Opportunities should be created for social interaction among employees and should follow a policy of equal opportunities, disallowing discrimination.

(6) **Constitutionalisation in the work environment**. This includes the right to privacy and freedom of speech in the organisation, as well as the protection of all employee rights in terms of the Labour Relations Act, 1995 (Act 66 of 1995). Employees are to enjoy dignity and respect, and are to be treated like adults in the work environment.

(7) **Work and total life space.** There should be a balanced relationship between an employee's working time and time away from work to spend on family life and recreation.

(8) **Social relevance of the work**. The employee's job must be to the benefit of all in the organisation and in the community, for example maintaining decent standards in the marketing and production of goods.

Dessler (1985:430) adds the following to Walton's list:
- Fair, equitable, and supportive treatment of employees
- Open, trusting communications between all employees
- An opportunity for all employees to take an active role in making important decisions that involve their jobs.

It is clear that the quality of work life involves all facets of the employee's functioning in an institution. Optimal utilisation of an employee and satisfaction in the work environment are essential to the achievement of a high quality of work life. Because of individual differences among people, and because of differences in the opportunities for satisfying needs in different departments, considerable variation in the satisfaction experienced by employees can be expected in the same institution.

Figure 12.5 Walton's eight components of the quality of work life

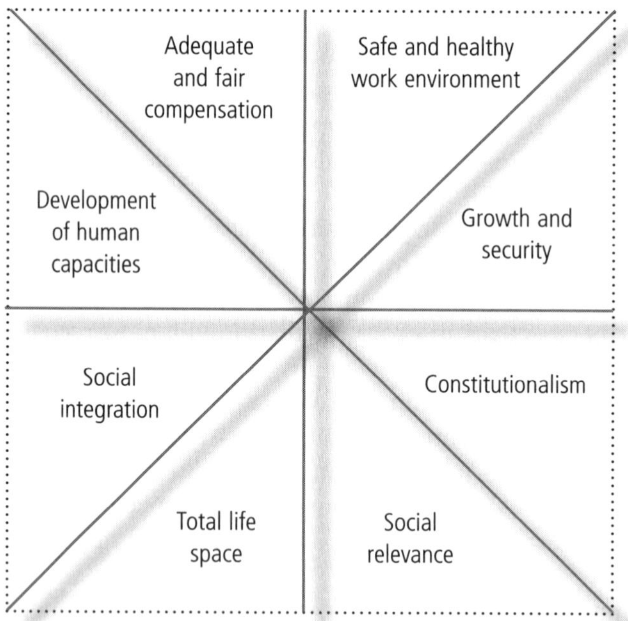

Source: Moorhead & Griffin, 1995:476

12.5.2.3 Strategies to improve the quality of work life

As people mature into adults, they develop needs for independence, broader interests and the power to control their own destinies. An institution that is characterised by autocratic leadership, absence of teamwork, lack of trust, lack of commitment, victimisation, discrimination and discourteous behaviour would obviously not enhance the quality of work life for employees. In order to enhance the quality of work life for employees, an institution has to take into account each employee's needs and values, and the extent to which the values are being conformed to. Institutions will have to become involved in activities aimed at satisfying needs that are regarded by the employees as being important.

For employers to plan and facilitate change with the aim of improving their employees' QWL, they should take note of their employees' personal goals and try to integrate them with the goals of the organisation. Organisations are redesigned in order to improve the environment, while jobs are redesigned to include attributes desired by the employee. This results in employees being afforded opportunities for growth and skills development, as well as chances to contribute individual ideas. Where traditional management systems used people, quality of work life programmes aspire to develop people.

Programmes developed to improve the quality of work life consider topics such as the job tasks, job design and improvement, open communication systems, physical work environment, social environment in the organisation, administrative system, employee security, equitable reward systems and the relationship between life on and off the job. Efforts are related to enriching workers' jobs through skill development, cooperative labour relations and techniques for reducing occupational stress. Methods that may be used to improve the quality of work life are described below.

Participatory management

Both decentralised and participatory management delegate authority from top managers downward to the people who report to them. In doing so, objectives or duties are assigned, authority is granted, and an obligation and responsibility are created by acceptance, the employee is thus accountable for results (Swansburg & Swansburg, 1999:422). Typically, it involves a departmental manager or supervisor conducting meetings with immediate subordinates to make plans and decisions regarding such matters as the staffing of units, distribution of tasks, the handling of problems and working conditions. This process increases employee motivation, generates ideas, and reduces resistance to new methods and processes. It helps to meet the human needs for autonomy, achievement and self-expression.

Management by objectives (MBO)

MBO involves three psychological foundations, namely goal-setting, feedback and participation. It is a process consisting of a series of interdependent and interrelated steps designed to facilitate planning and control, decision-making, and other important management functions. It is also a philosophy of management which reflects a proactive rather than reactive approach to managing. Successful use of MBO depends on the ability of participants to define their objectives in terms of their contributions to the total organisation and to be able to accomplish them. MBO basically consists of the following three steps:

(1) The supervisor and subordinate meet to discuss organisational and departmental goals.
(2) They then jointly establish attainable objectives for the subordinate.

(3) After this, meetings are scheduled for the supervisor and subordinate to meet at predetermined dates to evaluate the subordinate's progress towards meeting the objectives and providing positive feedback.

It is known that employees who have clear goals usually perform better than those who do not. Clear, attainable goals help channel energies in specific directions and let subordinates know the basis on which they will be appraised and rewarded. Employees who receive frequent feedback concerning their performance are usually more highly motivated than those who do not. Feedback that is specific, relevant and timely helps satisfy the need most people have for knowing where they stand and exactly what is expected of them.

Allowing subordinates to genuinely participate in setting their own goals can increase their commitment to those goals and improve their performance and contribution to the organisation. It also improves the attitudes and satisfaction of participants, leads to greater role clarity and makes them feel more involved, and this appeals to their higher-level needs, resulting in a feeling of self-worth and positive contribution.

Quality circles

Quality circles are a participatory management technique that uses statistical analysis of activities to maintain quality products. Quality circles consist of groups of employees who frequently meet with their supervisors to identify production and service problems and recommend plans of action for their solution. The recommendations are submitted to management for approval after which the approved plans are implemented with employee participation.

According to Gerber, Nel and Van Dyk (1998:232), quality circles are a work team approach used in organisations to improve the quality of work life. A circle usually consists of between five to ten specially trained employees who meet with their supervisors for approximately an hour per week to solve problems in their field of work. For the quality circle programme to be effective, clear objectives must be known to the employees, the programme must be supported by top management, the organisational culture must support participative management, participants must receive sufficient training and the programme must be introduced slowly with gradual process, led by a group of enthusiastic and cooperative employees. Employees are trained to identify, analyse and solve problems because they identify with ownership, and as a result of being recognised, employees develop goodwill towards their work and employers.

Job enrichment

Job enrichment is aimed at satisfying the various psychological needs of employees and can be defined as the purposeful restructuring of a job to be more challenging, meaningful and interesting for an employee. This process assumes that the employee is able to do a job at a higher level, carry more responsibility, and that he/she will respond positively for being given the opportunity to function at a higher level. Hackman and Oldham's (1980 in Bratton & Gold, 2003:123) model on job enrichment suggests that five core job characteristics result in the worker experiencing a favourable psychological state, which in turn will lead to positive outcomes (see Figure 12.6). The five core job characteristics are:

(1) **Skill variety**. This refers to the degree to which the employee requires a variety of different activities in carrying out the work, requiring the use of a number of the worker's skills and talent.
(2) **Task identity**. This consists of the degree to which the job requires the completion of a 'whole' and identifiable piece of work.
(3) **Task significance**. This is the degree to which the job has a sustained impact on the lives or work of other people.
(4) **Autonomy**. This is the degree to which the job provides the worker with substantial freedom, independence and discretion in terms of scheduling the work and determining the procedures to be used when carrying it out.
(5) **Feedback**. This is the degree to which the worker possesses information of the actual results of his/her performance.

Job enrichment may be achieved in various ways. First, work groups may be formed where each employee is allocated a specific section or responsibility of the total

Figure 12.6 The job characteristics model of Hackman and Oldham

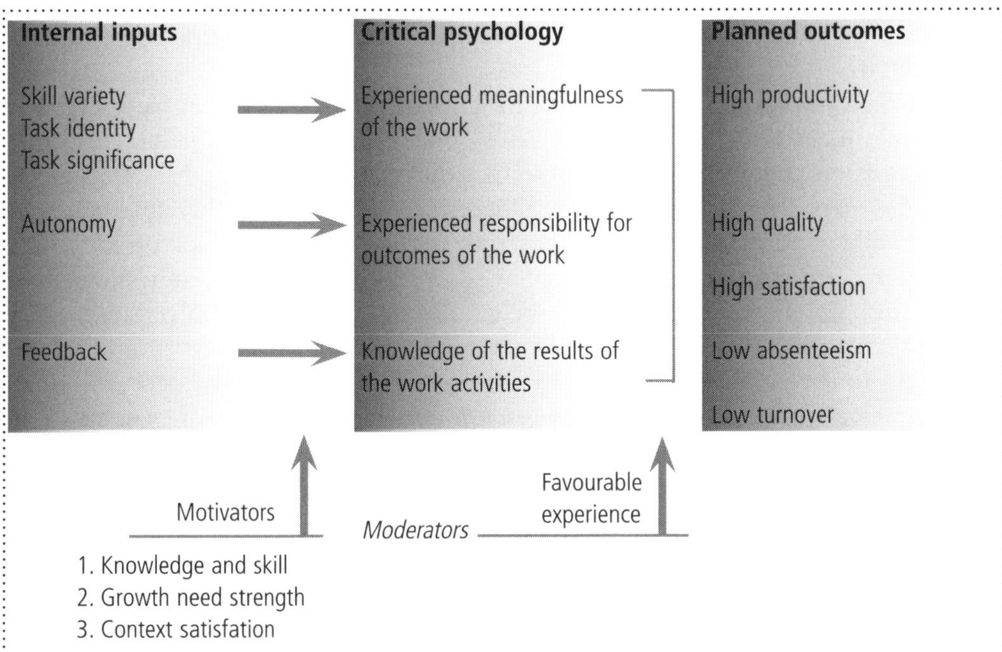

Source: Bratton & Gold, 2003:124

number of tasks that need to be done, they should be able to identify with it. Second, tasks can be combined so that one employee will be responsible for assembling a product or rendering a service from beginning to end. Third, vertical loading may be instituted, which means that employees, rather than someone higher up, will plan and control their own work. Fourth, channels for feedback need to be introduced so that faster and better work methods can be communicated to employees without delay.

It must be noted that job enrichment is not synonymous with job enlargement. **Job enlargement** affects the scope of the job, offering the employee a larger variety of tasks. This could have a negative effect if the new tasks are no more interesting or meaningful than present ones, as employees may feel that they are required to do more tasks without an increase in their salary (Gerber et al., 1998:233).

Career development

Organisations have traditionally engaged in human resource planning and development, which involves charting the moves of large numbers of employees through various positions in an organisation and defining future staffing needs. Career development programmes, with their greater emphasis on the individual, introduce a personalised aspect to the process.

A common approach to establishing a career development programme is to integrate it with existing HR functions and structures in the organisation. Figure 12.7 illustrates how HR structures relate to some of the essential aspects of the career development process. A career development programme should be seen as a dynamic process that strives to meet the needs of managers, their employees and the organisation.

Individual employees are responsible for initiating their own career planning, thus they should identity their knowledge, skills, abilities, interests and values, and seek out information about career options so that they can set goals and develop career plans. Managers should encourage employees to take responsibility for their own careers, while continuously offering assistance in the form of feedback on individual performance, information about the organisation, job information, and information about career opportunities that might be of interest (Sherman, Bohlander & Snell, 1996:264).

To fully utilise people's potential, to help employees realise their career ambitions, and to enhance their feelings of achievement and recognition, management needs to implement a systematic career planning and development programme aimed at guiding and developing subordinates. The principal components of a comprehensive career programme in an institution are (Beach, 1985:328):

- Human resource planning
- Communication of job opportunities and career path information to employees
- Career counselling, both by the supervisor as part of the performance appraisal review and by the human resources department

- Provision for the education and training of employees both in and external to the organisation
- Special broadening and stimulating job assignments and job rotation.

Some institutions also have formal assessment centres to analyse and evaluate the capabilities and potential of personnel.

Figure 12.7 The integration of the career development process with HRM structures and functions

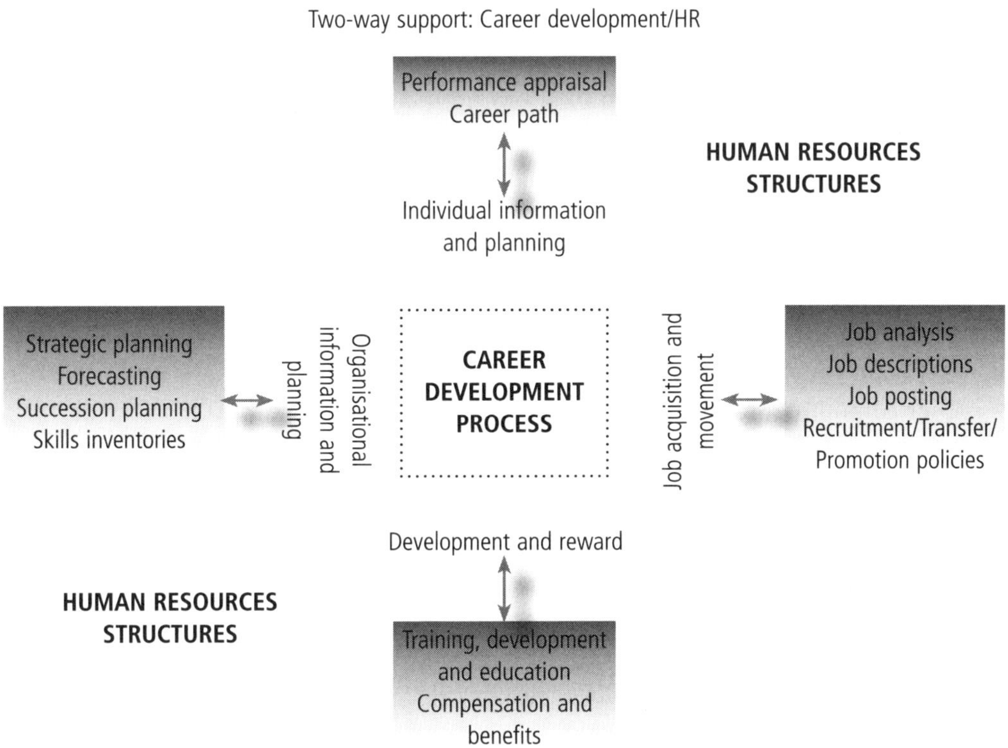

Source: Adapted from Sherman, Bohlander & Snell, 1996:265

Effective leadership and supervisory behaviour

Employees like to work for supervisors who show consideration for them, who are supportive, and who are fair and just in their treatment of others. Supervisors should create an atmosphere of approval in interpersonal relationships with their subordinates, as the latter's perception of the quality of working life is heavily affected by the treatment they receive from their supervisors.

The supervisor must be able to organise and direct people in order to enable them to reach the organisational goal of delivering quality patient care. The supervisor should also possess the technical knowledge and skills required to diagnose difficulties or problems in the working area or unit. Challenging but attainable performance standards should be set, the supervisor should be available when needed, but he/she should leave enough room for independent thought and the use of initiative when subordinates have the potential to be creative and autonomous.

Another important dimension of effective leadership and supervision is the development of teamwork among employees. The supervisor should generate an appropriate degree of participation in day-to-day decisions, so that employees care about their work because they are highly involved.

Alternative work schedules

Employers are continually trying to introduce more flexible work arrangements which will give employees more freedom of choice in their working hours. Such schedules currently appear in three different forms, namely flexi-time, part-time employment/job sharing and shorter work weeks.

- **Flexi-time** is a system in which the workday is divided into core and choice time. The worker is able, within certain predetermined limits, to begin and end his/her workday as it suits the individual. Core time is defined as the predetermined number of hours during which all staff assigned to a shift must be on duty.
- **Part-time employment** is especially attractive to working mothers who have other commitments and do not wish to work a full eight-hour day, every day of the week. The concept of job sharing means that two people share a full-time job. This may be especially useful in times of economic recession where it can prevent people from losing their jobs. And even though they may then be earning a smaller income they still have the advantage of having a job and the quality of work life that accompanies it.
- **Shorter working weeks** involve accomplishing a full week's work in less than five days. In nursing practice 12-hour shifts have become common practice, resulting in a four-day work week with a longer time off duty.

Institutions have to take care of their employees by offering a good quality of work life. Management can purposefully plan and implement certain strategies to enable employees to experience a higher quality of work life, depending on their specific personal needs. Most of the strategies discussed constitute attempts to increase employee satisfaction and performance through intrinsic motivation.

12.6 UNDERLYING DYNAMICS

The underlying dynamics related to the maintenance of HR are closely related to human behaviour, commitment and aspirations. However, management's leadership style, concern and foresight in looking out for the health and safety of their employees are crucial to a stable, contented workforce who experience a high quality of work life. The following determinants affect the maintenance of HR:

- The organisational culture has a definite impact on the wellbeing of employees and leaders help shape the culture by their demonstration of what the organisations's philosophy entails, by their projection of a vision for the future, by setting policies, professing values, creating systems and supporting organisational reward systems. Thus the way in which management values and treats their HR is an important factor in creating a conducive work environment.
- The way employees experience their place of work is exhibited in the organisational climate which could be described by individuals as a formal, relaxed, defensive, cautious, accepting or trusting environment.
- The commitment of staff to the ethics, work standards and vision of an institution are important variables to create loyalty and ensure high levels of productivity.
- Business ethics such as incentives given to management for cost-containment processes related to the curtailment of human resources expenditures has led to ambiguity, distrust and disappointment for both managers and their subordinates.

12.7 CONCLUDING STATEMENTS

The following concluding statements are relevant to the maintenance of human resources in a healthcare organisation:

- Human resource management and the consequential maintenance of the people working in an organisation occur in the legal and professional-ethical context, in accordance with the business ownership of the particular healthcare organisation, with reference to labour-related legislation and ethical codes of the different professions.
- The major role-players in the maintenance of HR are the state by means of legislation, managers, employees, safety representatives and committees, inspectors and organised labour encompassing the employees and their trade unions.
- The purpose of HR maintenance is to ensure the health and safety of employees and visitors to the organisation and to create a work environment that enables the individual employees to experience a high quality of work life which is a requirement for productivity.
- The process of maintaining HR relates mainly to the health and safety of employees, the prevention of risks and hazards in the workplace and the proactive implementation of strategies that would allow an acceptable quality of work life for all employees.
- Employee health and safety should be an important aspect of managing the employment relations, and deserves management's full commitment. The importance of workplace health and safety is related to legal, moral, economic and psychological reasons.
- Government legislation and regulations guide and influence the management of

health and safety in the workplace. Management assumes all responsibilities and liabilities in respect of health and safety issues in the workplace.

- Contemporary health and safety issues are sick building syndrome, stress, alcohol and drug abuse, smoking, AIDS and sexual harassment. Handling of the latter is increasingly being viewed as the responsibility of the employer.
- A number of strategies, such as safe work processes and behaviour, policy, procedures and control measures, training, the identification of hazards and management's commitment can be applied to ensure a safer place of work.
- Employee assistance programmes are aimed at assisting the employee with physical, emotional and behavioural problems that affect work behaviour and performance.
- Quality of work life is a way of thinking about people, work and organisations. Its distinctive elements are a concern about the impact of work on people, as well as on organisational effectiveness, and the idea of participation in organisational problem-solving and decision-making.
- Strategies for improving the quality of work life include participative management, management by objectives and quality circles, which all seek to involve employees more thoroughly in decision-making and activities related to their jobs, resulting in a feeling of participation, commitment, satisfaction, self-actualisation, security and high self-esteem.
- Various underlying dynamics, such as the organisational culture and climate, management and leadership styles, the commitment of staff and business ethics related to the allocation of incentives for management in view of HR cost containment initiatives impact on the wellbeing and loyalty of personnel.

Self-assessment

(1) Explain the role of the HR manager in providing a safe and healthy environment for employees.
(2) Explain the causes and symptoms of stress in the workplace and what an organisation can do to alleviate them.
(3) Explain how training can improve occupational health and safety.
(4) Visit www.aidslink.org.za for information on AIDS and HRM.

13 Utilisation of human resources

KEY CONCEPTS

Communication
Lateral relations
Staffing allocation
Nursing service delivery systems
Absenteeism
Turnover

SPECIFIC OUTCOMES

After studying this chapter, you should be able to:

- Interpret the legal and professional-ethical human resource management **context** in relation to the utilisation of human resources, with reference to public and private (type of business ownership) healthcare organisations and the scope of practice of their relevant healthcare practitioners or clinicians
- Identify and describe the **role-players**, such as the managers/supervisors, employees, statutory bodies and organised labour, and interpret their roles and responsibilities in terms of the utilisation of human resources in a healthcare organisation
- Analyse and debate the **purpose** of the utilisation of human resources in the context of a healthcare organisation
- Analyse and debate the **process** of utilising human resources in the context of a healthcare organisation, with specific reference to communication, lateral relations, staffing allocation, nursing delivery systems, absenteeism and turnover
- Debate the **underlying dynamics** that could impact on the utilisation of human resources of a healthcare organisation, with specific reference to policy and procedures, consistency and fairness in relation to the utilisation of processes and strategies, organisational structure, the flow and effectiveness of communication, problem-solving and shortages.

13.1 INTRODUCTION

Utilisation of human resources focuses on the way staff members are placed and utilised. It is important to involve employees in decisions that affect their direct work environment, by creating the best possible mechanisms for effective communication; such mechanisms make it possible for lateral relationships with other teams and departments to be pleasant and functional. These are important issues if an organisation is to create an environment in which the employee feels safe and secure. This approach also encourages the individual to be loyal and to contribute to the achievement of the goals of the organisation.

If the working environment demonstrates little regard for the employees' quality of work life, and if conflict is allowed to remain unresolved, then people may well withdraw and resort to being away from work as a means of coping with an unsatisfactory situation. This chapter deals with communication and lateral relations, staffing allocation, nursing delivery systems, absenteeism and turnover.

This chapter will highlight the following components (see visual presentation in Figure 13.1):

Figure 13.1 Visual presentation of the utilisation of human resources in a healthcare organisation

Context	◗ All healthcare services ◗ Communication as a means of human interaction ◗ Basic Conditions of Employment Act, 1997 (Act 75 of 1997) ◗ Scope of practice regulations
Purpose	◗ Transference of meaning ◗ Communication affects all human interaction ◗ Effective cooperation with other units/divisions ◗ Proper staff allocation ◗ Prevention of absenteeism and abnormal turnover
Role-players	◗ State ◗ Statutory bodies ◗ Managers and supervisors ◗ Employees ◗ Organised labour
Process	◗ Communication ◗ Lateral relations ◗ Staffing allocation ◗ Nursing delivery systems ◗ Absenteeism and turnover
Underlying dynamics	◗ Policy and procedures ◗ Consistency and fairness ◗ Organisational structure ◗ Communication effectiveness ◗ Problem-solving ◗ Shortages

- The **context** of human resource management in terms of the utilisation of human resources, with reference to the legal and professional-ethical environment.
- The **purpose** of HR utilisation is brought about by effective communication and lateral relations through which the appropriate application of staff is enabled.
- The different **role-players** in HR utilisation, with specific reference to managers/ supervisors, employees, statutory bodies and organised labour.
- The **process** of HR utilisation is divided into communication, lateral relations, staffing allocation, nursing delivery systems, absenteeism and turnover.
- The **underlying dynamics** impacting on human resource management in a healthcare organisation refer to policy and procedures, consistency and fairness in the application of processes, organisational structure, communication, problem-solving and shortages.

13.2 CONTEXT

In order to achieve the mission of an organisation, the goals and objectives have to be communicated down to departmental or unit level so that the functional staff members know what is expected from them. Therefore effective communication is essential in order to get people to cooperate, and to coordinate everybody's contributions to the running of the organisation. In the healthcare industry, communication is instrumental in staffing units, allocating work and dealing with absenteeism and turnover. The scope of practice of different healthcare categories serves as a regulated guideline for the allocation of work to healthcare practitioners. and the Basic Conditions of Service Act, 1997 (Act 75 of 1997) prescribes the maximum number of working hours and leave allocation.

13.3 PURPOSE

No group can exist without communication, that is, without the transference of meaning. It is only through transmitting meaning from one person to another that information and ideas are conveyed among members. Communication is the activity that influences all the other activities and management of any work unit. It forms a crucial part of effective management, as none of the steps of the management process, namely planning, organising, leading and controlling, can be implemented effectively without proper communication. It is thus an essential medium through which relations are built, staff is allocated and absenteeism and turnover can be controlled.

13.4 ROLE-PLAYERS

The role of organisational communication is indispensable as managers spend a vast proportion of their working time on interpersonal communications with their seniors, colleagues, staff, and on interactions with other departments, clients and visitors. The business of managers is communication, as it is an important means of getting things done by others in the work arena. HRM communication programmes and processes are designed to keep employees informed of organisational events, and knowledgeable about policies affecting them, it thus focuses on the internal constituents – the employees.

The most significant role-players in the utilisation of human resources are the managers and supervisors who interact with their subordinates in dealing with work allocation and problem-solving, statutory bodies who regulate the scope of practice of healthcare practitioners, and organised labour who usually have an input in the development of HR-related policies.

13.5 PROCESS

No aspect of HRM is so pervasive as communication. It provides the means for gathering and disseminating information, providing feedback and counselling, negotiating, presenting training and the like. Managers must therefore understand how to manage communication, as well as how to communicate effectively with employees at all levels of the organisation. Refer to Figure 13.2 for a summary of this chapter's content.

Figure 13.2 Outlay of components dealt with under the utilisation of human resources

Communication	• Meaning and scope of communication • Functions of communication • The communication process • Communication fundamentals • Effective employee communication
Lateral relations	
Staffing allocation	• Patient census • Patient acuity classification system • Diagnostic-Related Groups (DRGs) • Staff or skills mix • Productive versus non-productive time • Budgetary provision • Nursing care delivery systems
Absenteeism	• Absenteeism • Turnover

13.5.1 Communication

An idea, no matter how great, is useless until it is transmitted and understood by others. Communication is the heart of leadership. Whether it is a word of praise, a written set of instructions, a frown of displeasure, or an encouraging squeeze of the hand, communication is the means through which interaction and leadership are accomplished. Communication and the channels used for it are essential for the survival of any organisation. The communication methods and channels used in organisations usually determine the effectiveness of communication between the various groups, such as supervisors and subordinates, the employer and employee groups.

13.5.1.1 Meaning and scope of communication

A manager's day is consumed with communicating, with subordinates, other managers, supervisors, consumers, with regulators. Effective managers are effective communicators. Their communication skills can affect the satisfaction of those who work for them, the effectiveness of the work unit, and the subordinates' understanding of their duties. The sharing of information on aspects such as financial performance, strategy, operational measures and organisational difficulties conveys to the employees they are being trusted and valued as members of the organisation.

13.5.1.2 Functions of communication

In a group or organisation, communication serves four major functions: information sharing, control, motivation and emotional expression (Robbins, 1996:378):

- Communication is the conduit for the sharing and distribution of **information**. It facilitates decision-making by providing the information that individuals and groups require to make decisions by transmitting the data to identify and evaluate alternative choices.
- Communication acts to **control** behaviour in several ways. Organisations have formal hierarchal authority structures, policy documents, guidelines, procedures and job descriptions which employees have to follow, and by doing so, communication is performing a controlling function as the means of conveying the message in all circumstances.
- Communication fosters **motivation** by clarifying what it is that employees should be doing, and what can be done to improve performance if it is below standard. The formulation of specific goals, feedback on progress towards goal achievement, and reinforcement of desired behaviour all stimulate motivation and require communication.
- In the workplace, groups are the primary source and setting for interaction. The communication that takes place in the group is a fundamental mechanism by which members show their feelings of satisfaction and frustrations. Communication, therefore, provides a release for **emotional expression** of feelings and for fulfilment of social needs.

Communication scholars have emphasised that, to be effective, organisational communication must take place regularly, it must be a two-way process to provide an opportunity for employees to participate, and it should involve all members of the management team, including first-level supervisors. Researchers, academics and practitioners have also stressed some other key issues related to communication in the workplace, as listed in Figure 13.3 (Bratton & Gold, 2003:366–167).

Figure 13.3 Key issues pertaining to workplace communication

- Communicating is the fundamental process of organising
- Understanding communication provides insights into management strategies
- Senior management should be committed to open communication
- Communication skills are the basis for effective leadership
- Management should take the initiative in devising and maintaining the communication system
- Messages should occur in a form that can be readily understood
- Information should be perceived to be relevant to employees
- Efficacy – desired effect or effectiveness of written versus face-to-face channels of communication
- Messages should be consistent with actions
- Male and female managers communicate differently in the work place
- Cross-cultural communication is an increasing feature of a diverse work organisation
- Training in communication skills increases the effectiveness of the system
- Communication systems should be monitored and evaluated

Source: Bratton & Gold, 2003:366

13.5.1.3 The communication process

Before communication can take place it must have a purpose, which is expressed as the message. The message may be verbal, non-verbal or written in format. Messages have different levels of meaning, including informational, emotional, and relational. The **informational level** contains the facts or information conveyed in the message, it is usually overt, not hidden. The **emotional level** may be partially covert. Emotions are often revealed in the non-verbal portion of the message, sometimes they are obvious, but often they are conveyed subtly. The **relational level** conveys information about the interpersonal relationship between the sender and the receiver (Tappen, 2001:59). Sometimes what is left unsaid in an exchange is the most important message, and like unexpressed complaints, are the difficult ones to deal with.

Communication is an interactive, dynamic and continuous process between people which involves the transfer and interpretation of a message between individuals or groups. It is a two-way process between the sender and the recipient, therefore the skills and perceptions of both the sender and the recipient impact on the understanding and perceptions of complex verbal and non-verbal messages along with other barriers to communication. Refer to Figure 13.4 for an illustration of the communication process.

People can communicate with one another because a broad range of verbal symbols, which stand for objects and abstractions, can be manipulated. For communication to succeed, both the sender and receiver must understand the general meaning of the symbols. However, in the complex world of organisational communication, a variety

Figure 13.4 The communication process

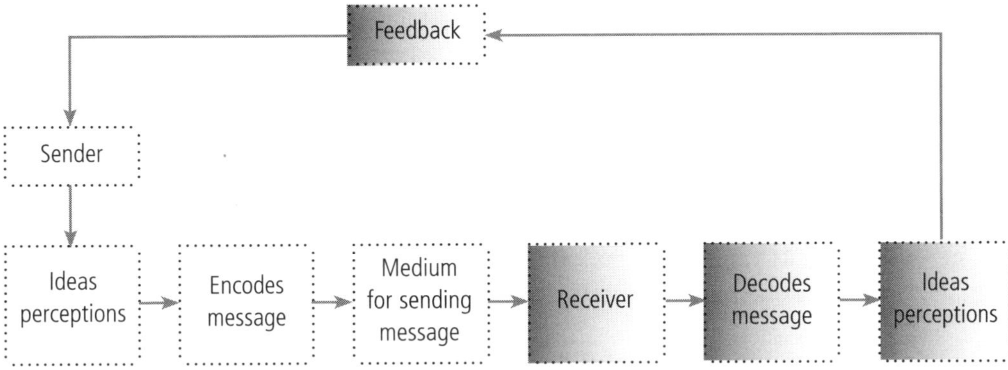

Source: Adapted from Sherman et al., 1996:537

of words can be used to refer to the same object, practice or idea, so the choice of a particular word often implies bias in communicators' evaluations and perceptions. For example, managers may choose to call those who report to them subordinates, workers, colleagues, supervisees, staff, crew, the gang, or my people. Employees will perceive a certain kind of relationship with their supervisors/managers depending on which word is used to describe them. Managers are therefore challenged to choose the right words when communicating with employees, since this choice can have a significant influence on their relationship (Sherman et al., 1996:537).

13.5.1.4 Communication fundamentals

A working knowledge of communication requires an understanding of some fundamental concepts related to communication. Flow patterns of communication, formal versus informal communication networks, the importance of non-verbal communication and the barriers to effective communication (Robbins, 1996:380–390) are described below.

Direction of communication

Communication can flow vertically, which could be downward or upward, and laterally.

- **Downward communication** flows from one level of an organisation or group to a lower level. The assigning of goals and objectives, providing job instructions, informing about policies and procedures, pointing out problems, disciplinary action and feedback on performance are examples of downward communication.
- **Upward communication** flows to a higher level in the organisation or group. Upward communication informs managers about ways things can be improved and enlightens seniors about the way employees feel about matters in general. Examples of upward communication are progress reports about goal achievement, relaying current problems and filing a grievance.

- **Lateral communication** takes place between members of the same group, among members of work groups at the same level, among managers at the same level, or among any horizontally equivalent personnel. Horizontal communications are often necessary to save time and facilitate coordination. Since strict adherence to the formal vertical structure for all communications can impede the efficient and accurate transfer of information, lateral communications can be beneficial. However, they can create dysfunctional situations when the formal vertical channels are breached, when employees go above or around their superiors to get things done, or when managers learn that actions have been taken, or decisions made without their knowledge.

Formal versus informal networks

Communication networks define the channels along which communication flows. The two channels through which communication is transferred can be either formal or informal. **Formal networks** are usually vertical, follow the chain of command, and are focused on task-related communications. **Informal networks**, also known as the grapevine, are free to move in any direction, regardless of authority levels, and take place to satisfy the social needs of workers in the work environment.

Formal communication

Management has a responsibility to be effective communicators, in addition, they are often responsible for developing effective communication systems for the organisation, most of which are designed to convey information from management to employees. This type of communication is referred to as formal or downward communication. Organisations who realise the importance of effective communication systems and methods frequently develop strong policies that encourage management to communicate with employees openly, regularly and in a transparent way. These policies emanate from general philosophies of how employees should be treated and the ideal relationship that should exist between employee and management. Examples of formal communication are employee handbooks and policy manuals, organisational newspapers, bulletin boards, videos, meetings, memos and circulars.

The grapevine

The grapevine can convey messages upward, laterally, and externally, and it can foster employee motivation, encourage commitment, and create job and organisational satisfaction. Unfortunately it can also distort information, cause resentment, and work against management plans and objectives (Sherman et al., 1996:551). Recent advances in communication technology have added to the speed with which the grapevine functions, and the extensive impact it can have in a very short time span. The grapevine has three main characteristics. First, it is not controlled by management; second, it is perceived by most employees as being more believable and reliable than formal communiques issued by top management; and third, it is largely used to serve the self-interests of those people who are affected by the circulating information. Evidence indicates that about 75% of what is carried in the grapevine is accurate (Robbins, 1996:383). But what conditions foster an active grapevine, in other words, what gets the rumours rolling? It has been shown that rumours emerge as a response to situations which are important to people, where there is ambiguity, and under conditions that arouse anxiety. These three conditions are common in work situations due to proposed changes, the appointment of new managers, transformation, proposed retrenchment and the like.

Rumours do not usually start because they make interesting gossip, rumours have at least four purposes. They aim to structure and reduce anxiety, to make sense of limited or fragmented information, to serve as a medium by which group members can be organised into coalitions, and to signal a sender's status or power.

The grapevine is an important part of any group or organisation's communication network and rumours cannot be stopped as a matter of rule. However, management should minimise the negative consequences of rumours by their range and impact.

This can be achieved by:
- Announcing timetables for making important decisions
- Explaining decisions and behaviours that may appear inconsistent or secretive
- Emphasising the downside, as well as the upside of current decisions and future plans
- Openly discussing worst case possibilities, it is almost never as anxiety provoking as the unspoken fantasy.

Non-verbal communication

Non-verbal communication includes body movements, the intonations or emphases given to words, facial expression, gestures, posture, position and distance relative to other, clothing and grooming. Non-verbal communication is usually congruent with the verbal message sent and serves to support the verbal communique. A body position or movement does not in itself have a precise or universal meaning, but when it is linked with the spoken word, it gives fuller meaning to a sender's message. However, body language often complicates verbal communication as it is sometimes in contrast to the words uttered. When this is the case, the receiver has difficulty in truly understanding the message, and is often confused, uncertain or taken aback when confronted with such a duel message.

Interpreting non-verbal communication is complicated in a multi-cultural society, as gestures and posture can mean different things in different cultures. It should therefore be kept in mind that non-verbal clues should not only be interpreted according to a person's own frame of reference, but that the sender or receiver's culture should be accommodated.

Effective listening

Effective listening is possible through active listening, the latter being necessary to pick up all three levels of meaning in communication. Inattention or surface listening frequently leads to misunderstandings. Listening should not be confused with hearing, hearing is merely picking up sound vibrations, while listening is making sense of what is heard. It can thus be deduced that listening requires paying attention, interpreting and remembering sound stimuli.

The following eight behaviours are associated with effective listening skills, and can be used as guidelines for self-improvement:

(1) Make eye contact to acknowledge that you are listening
(2) Exhibit affirmative head nods and appropriate facial expressions to show interest
(3) Avoid distracting actions and gestures like looking at your watch or shuffling papers
(4) Ask questions as a means of analysing what has been heard
(5) Paraphrase, as it is a way of checking whether you are listening carefully
(6) Avoid interrupting the speaker by guessing what the speaker's thought would be
(7) Don't talk unnecessarily or too much, as one can't talk and listen at the same time
(8) Make smooth transitions between the roles of speaker and listener by concentrating on what the other person is saying, and only formulate your response once the sender pauses.

Barriers to effective communication

The section on the fundamentals of communication is concluded with a discussion of the more prominent barriers to effective communication. The grouping of people into a complex organisation imposes conditions affecting human relations that may become potential barriers to communication. In order for communication to be effective, it is essential for managers to recognise these potential barriers and to plan communication so that these barriers may be eliminated or at least minimised.

- **Filtering** refers to a sender manipulating information so that it will be perceived more favourably by the receiver. The major determinant of filtering is the number of levels in an organisation's structure. The more vertical levels in the hierarchy, the more opportunities for filtering.
- **Selective perception**. One result of prior experiences is that each employee brings to the job a unique way of looking at things, because of their personal frame of reference. Receivers in the communication process electively see and hear the message based on their needs, motivations, experience, background and other personal characteristics. Receivers also project their interests and expectations into communication as they decode them.
- **Emotions**. How the receiver feels at the time of receipt of a communication message will influence how he/she interprets it. The same message received

when one is angry or distraught is likely to be interpreted differently from when one is in a neutral position.

- **Language and semantics**. Words, like gestures, can be interpreted in various ways, thus creating a barrier to communication. A person's age, education and cultural background are three obvious variables that influence the language a person uses and the definitions he/she gives to words. In most organisations employees usually come from diverse backgrounds and therefore have different patterns of speech.
- **False assumptions.** The perceptions of communicators are based on certain assumptions people have of one another, about the situation, and about other persons and places they have in common. Whenever senders and receivers have conflicting assumptions, the quality of their communication deteriorates. A method used to minimise the problems of false assumptions is to separate the facts from inferences. A fact is a verifiable statement to which many people can agree, while an inference is a conclusion that is based on a non-fact but depends on the assumptions that are made.
- **Bias**. Bias may be a barrier in face-to-face as well as any form of written communication, such as letters, speeches, statements or reports. When the sender or receiver has judgemental ideas about the other person, or about the topic under discussion, many unjust assumptions can be made, which may lead to misunderstandings. Personal values, such as the way in which a person regards certain aspects as right or wrong can also influence the person's interpretation of a message. Both the sender and the receiver can overtly or subtly express their bias in relation to many variables concerning the message or even the two parties communicating with one another.
- **Hastiness**. Being in a hurry causes the receiver not to always take the time or interest to listen carefully to a given message, resulting in incomplete communication, or a confusing message.
- **Lack of feedback**. When there is a lack of feedback from the recipient, after receiving the message, the sender is never sure whether the message was received clearly and correctly, as intended.
- **Vague messages**. When vague or unclear messages are sent, it becomes very difficult for the receiver to ascertain what the true message was intended to be. This can be due to the sender not having thought about the formulation of his/her message carefully before submitting it. Or, it could also be the result of over-talking, when the sender rambles on, including a lot of additional information which confuses the receiver in identifying the essence of the message.
- **Noise and interruptions**. Noise makes it difficult for the physiological proses of hearing to take place, while interruptions cause a temporary breakdown in the communication process, making it difficult for both the sender and the receiver to adhere to the line of thought and concentrate on the real message being transmitted.

When employees speak a common language such as English, the usage of that language is far from uniform. The problem is that members of the organisation usually do not know how others with whom they interact have coded the language. Senders tend to assume that the terms and words they use mean the same to the receiver as they do to them. This is often not so, especially in a diverse community, thus creating communication difficulties.

13.5.1.5 Effective employee communication

It has become the trend for companies to restructure and downsize in terms of structure and human resources, in order to reduce costs and improve competitiveness. In times of transformation, the company's effectiveness in communication is a crucial factor in managing change. The factors described below have been identified as important guidelines for better communication in times of major organisational change (Robbins, 1996:390–393).

- **The CEO must be committed to the importance of communication.** The most significant factor in a successful employee-communications programme is the chief executive's leadership. He/she must be philosophically and behaviourlly committed to the notion that communicating with all employees is essential to the achievement of the organisation's goals. If the senior executive is committed to communication through his/her words and actions, it flows down to the rest of the organisation. The CEO should be a visible communicator by delivering key messages, conveying their vision to the company, talking to employees, responding to questions and listening to comments. By personally championing the cause of good communication, the CEO lessens employee fears about changes that are being implemented and thus sets the precedent for other managers to follow.
- **Managers match actions with words**. Employees will listen to what management has to say regarding changes being made and where the company is going, provided these words are backed up by matching actions. It is known that actions speak louder than words. When the implicit messages that managers send contradict the official communications, the managers loose credibility with employees.
- **Commitment to two-way communication**. Successful programmes balance downward and upward communication, while ineffective programmes are dominated by downward communication. Ways of promoting upward communication are interactive television broadcasts and electronic e-mail messaging, which allow employees to call in questions and get responses from top management. Company publications with question-and-answer columns, grievance procedure which processes complaints quickly, and feedback techniques are other examples of enabling upwards communication allowing management to hear the views of employees.
- **Emphasis on face-to-face communication**. Major restructuring efforts are fraught with uncertainty, fears and concerns. Employees struggle with non-

routine and ambiguous issues such as job security, the acquisition of new skills, and possible abandonment of certain units. The maximum amount of information can be transmitted through face-to-face conversation. Candid, open face-to-face communication with employees presents executives as living, breathing people who understand the needs and concerns of their employees.

- **Shared responsibility for employee communications.** Top management provides the big picture of where the company is going and what the implications will be. Supervisors then link the big picture to their work group and to individual employees. Every manager has some responsibility for ensuring that employees are well informed, with the implications for change becoming more specific as they flow down the organisational hierarchy. This requires management to keep middle and lower level managers fully informed of planned changes, and the latter to share the information with their work groups as soon as possible and comprehensively so that ambiguity is minimised.
- **Dealing with bad news.** All organisations will, at times, have product failures, delivery delays, customer complaints or might have to consider retrenchments. The issue is how comfortable people are communicating these problems. When bad news is candidly reported, a climate is created in which people aren't afraid to be truthful and good news gains increased credibility.
- **The message is shaped for its intended audience**. Different people in the organisation have different information needs. What is important to middle managers may not be so for all divisions at functional level. What information do employees have to and want to know? When do they need to know and in what form (newsletter, e-mail, team meeting or at home) will it be appropriate to convey the message? Managers need to recognise these questions and design their communication programme accordingly.
- **Treat communication as an ongoing process**. Successful companies view employee communication as a critical management process, which is illustrated by five common activities pertaining to communication:
  (1) Convey the rationale underlying decisions
  (2) Timeliness is vital
  (3) Communicate continually
  (4) Link the big picture with the circumstances of the employees
  (5) Don't dictate the way people should feel about the news.
- **Feedback**. It is the perceptions of the receivers of a message that to a large extent determine the effectiveness of communication. If they do not understand the message they will not be able to receive it as intended. It is more effective if the manager or sender of a message focuses on the aspirations, values and needs of the receiver when conveying a message, rather than concentrating solely on what he/she wants to get across. By giving feedback to employees, the communication cycle is completed, making it two-way communication. The latter can only truly be effective in an atmosphere of mutual respect and confidence.

Feedback should be a planned endeavour, identifying the topic on which feedback should be given, and in addition, contemplating what it is about the topic that is to be conveyed. Is it deficiencies, successes, problems or acknowledgement that are to be transmitted? Having received feedback the receiver should be able to fully understand the situation and what he/she is expected to do about it.

13.5.2 Lateral relations

Lateral communication usually follows the pattern of work flow in an organisation, occurring between members of work groups, between one work group and another, between members of different departments, and between line and staff management. The main purpose of lateral communication is to provide a direct channel for organisational coordination and problem-solving.

Because of the growing complexity of modern healthcare service organisations, and the need for fiscal management, interdepartmental relations can become complicated. The various departments and sections all serve to contribute to patient care. As the nursing department normally acts as the main coordinator of services for patients, it is important to establish healthy relations between the nursing service and other departments. Interdepartmental discussions between heads of departments are essential and problems must be discussed so that a mutual understanding about the problems can come about. The official heading the hospital or healthcare service should regard such meetings as a necessary, routine measure.

Apart from nurses and doctors, there are other members of the multi-disciplinary health team (e.g. pharmacists, physiotherapists, radiographers, social workers and occupational therapists) who are actively involved in patient care and therapeutic activities. Other categories, such as the purchasing department, house keeping, linen, catering, central sterilising and service and maintenance departments do not directly deal with patient care but provide a safe and clean environment in which patients and staff can interrelate. However, the well-being of the patient should remain the central focus for all parties concerned in any healthcare service.

Cooperation, mutual support and respect should be the aim of all parties concerned, regardless of the circumstances. Managers in healthcare services should set an example by ensuring that this kind of cooperation exists at all times. For this reason, healthcare workers should be aware of the aims and contributions of other departments involved in patient care and the maintenance of the environment.

There are three requirements for healthy interdepartmental relations:

(1) The functions of every department and its contribution to the overall effort regarding patient care must be clearly defined and recognised.
(2) Delivery times and deadlines must be strictly observed. Non-observance of fixed time schedules can create disruption and frustration, and these are major causes of interdepartmental friction.
(3) All employees in the various departments, and not just the heads of departments,

must realise that good relations should be maintained at all levels of interaction. Courtesy and consideration cost nothing, but can achieve a great deal.

13.5.3 Staffing allocation

Staffing refers to the allocation of HR to service units. If management means to get work done through others, a primary managerial function is to staff the different units or departments with sufficient, appropriately trained and experienced members of staff from the different required categories.

Nurses form the largest component of healthcare workers and it is they who apply the required care for each patient, depending on their level of training, experience and qualifications. The essence of nursing rests in how nurses care for patients, and the way in which they provide services revolves around issues such as care delivery, staffing, scheduling, patient classification and organisation culture (Sullivan & Decker, 1992:61).

Despite the wide variety of healthcare personnel functioning in organisations today, nurses remain the core staff of any healthcare facility. Not only do they tend to the patients' needs around the clock, they also constitute the facility's early warning system, alerting physicians when a problem arises and intervening rapidly to prevent injury and often death for many of their patients. Without registered nurses, healthcare facilities, as they are today, cannot exist. Yet many questions remain about optimal staffing numbers and the effectiveness of various scheduling methods.

The issue of staffing and scheduling is complex as healthcare service managers are responsible for providing sufficient numbers of qualified nursing personnel to ensure adequate, safe nursing care for all patients 24 hours a day, seven days a week, every week of the year. According to Tappen (2001:253–266) the major factors that should be considered in making staffing decisions are patient census, patient acuity and classification systems, skills mix, allowing for non-productive time, and the adequacy of the budget. Delivery systems as a means of providing nursing care is another variable that should be noted in the staffing process. Using this information allows healthcare service managers to best meet staffing needs.

13.5.3.1 Patient census

Average daily hospital census is roughly the product of the average admission rate and the average length of stay. The number of patients to be cared for is obviously a major factor affecting staffing decisions. The census of any unit can fluctuate in a given shift and from one day to the next. Concomitant variations in admission rate and length of stay could maintain a constant census, while allowing work volume to change markedly, for example a change in patient population could cause an increased nursing workload. Generally, more nursing care is required to admit, provide total care and discharge a patient in a single day than it takes to adjust care from total to intermediate to rehabilitative measures over several days, as is customary with long-term, in-patient care (Gillies, 1994:222).

The healthcare services manager is expected to avoid both understaffing and overstaffing as the unit census fluctuates. If nursing staff are sent home early because of a decreased census, a sudden influx of admissions can create a severe shortage as the shift progresses. Adjusting for staffing levels by census assumes that managers can forecast census accurately. If the census fluctuates in an unpredictable manner, efforts to match staff levels will be thwarted. Percentage of occupancy is one way of assessing staffing needs based on unit census, knowing the average occupancy rate allows for more accurate predictions about the number of staff needed.

13.5.3.2 Patient acuity classification system

In predicting nursing workload, the manager must calculate not only the total number of patients to be cared for, but also the proportion in each category of care needs, such as self-care, minimal care, full care or intensive care. To quantify workload, patient care needs must be quantified. This means the total care needs for each patient are the sum of the patient's needs for direct hands-on-care, for indirect or administrative care, and for health teaching (Gillies, 1994:224). In many countries norms have been developed for a classification of patient care needs, known as an *acuity index*.

The patient can be assigned to an acuity or complexity category to estimate how many hours of nursing care will be needed during a particular shift. When this information is collected in the unit for every patient, for every shift during the day, the total number of hours of care required will provide an indication of the number and type of nursing staff required on that unit for a particular 24-hour period.

Clearly, different patients with the same medical diagnosis require different amounts of nursing care. To account for these differences, patient classification systems were developed. Patient classification is defined as '... the categorization or grouping of patients according to an assessment of their nursing care requirements over a specific period of time' (Hilliard & Marrelli, 1997 in Tappen, 2001:255). In other words, patients are classified based on the projected number of nursing hours required to provide care. A valid and reliable patient acuity classification instrument is an ideal tool for determining the cost of nursing care.

13.5.3.3 Diagnostic-Related Groups (DRGs)

In contrast to the acuity and complexity approach, the prospective payment system, which is a form of managed care, informs the hospital what amount of money they will be reimbursed with for a patient with a particular diagnosis. DRGs are based on the medical diagnosis of a patient and the established categories are consistent across settings and hospitals. The amount of money a facility is reimbursed for a particular DRG has to cover the cost of all supplies, equipment, tests, procedures, and staff needed to care for the patient during the entire stay.

The primary aim of DRGs and managed care is to control costs, but this system does not take into account the patient's actual self-care deficits or nursing needs. They do not consider, for example, what kinds of disabilities the patients come in with, what psychological factors may interfere with their learning abilities to care for themselves, or other problems that are not indicated by their DRG allocation, but which impact on the number and kinds of nursing needs. Some examples of such differences not indicated in the DRG classification are:

- Self-feeding versus total assistance with feeding
- Emotionally stable versus panic-stricken patient
- Oral medication versus intravenous medication
- Partial isolation versus complete isolation
- Simple wound dressing versus complex wound care
- Alert and oriented versus confused and disoriented
- Vital signs every four hours versus every 15 minutes.

13.5.3.4 Staff or skills mix

Once the number of patients and the patients' acuity levels are known, a third factor is the mix of staff members assigned to care for the patients. Which category of nursing staff would be the most suitable and best equipped to care for the needs of a particular patient, or group of patients?

In South Africa, the training of nurses and the quality of care provided are regulated by the South African Nursing Council (SANC). The scope of practice regulations for the different categories of nursing personnel stipulate the type and level of tasks that nurses are allowed to perform, depending on their qualifications and whether they form part of the registered or enrolled categories of nursing staff with the SANC. The type of supervision required for non-professional categories of nursing staff is also indicated in these regulations.

Different views are held about the staff mix required in patient care units. In some institutions, non-professional staff were eliminated and replaced by a lesser number of professionally prepared staff. The argument for this was that registered nurses (RNs) can provide more complex care than either staff nurses (SNs) or nursing auxiliaries (NAs), and so can be assigned to meet all of the patients' needs. In other situations it was argued that professional staff are expensive and their skills can be used more efficiently if the non-professional tasks are done by ancillary personnel. In this case, fewer RNs are available to care for patients and relatively more SNs and auxiliary nurses are used to do routine basic nursing care activities.

Both of these approaches have disadvantages, and healthcare service managers need to assess the impact of these changes on their individual units and the patients. The use of an acuity index may help in determining the proper staff mix. The unit with a high acuity or complexity index may be able to make the most efficient use of a high proportion of RN staff, and a few ancillary staff who can assist with basic routine tasks, like for instance an intensive care unit. In contrast, if the acuity levels of patients indicate that they have a high proportion of chronic care needs requiring considerable help with the basic activities of living, then the unit may operate more efficiently with relatively more non-professional staff, with fewer RNs needed to plan and manage care, carrying out higher level assessment and complex interventions, and develop appropriate discharge plans.

13.5.3.5 Productive versus non-productive time

During the process of staff planning, the healthcare service manager also needs to identify the number of full-time equivalents (FTEs) needed to run the unit. A full-time equivalent is an employee who works full-time, 40 hours per week, or 2 080 hours per year. This figure includes the productive time as well as the non-productive time which all employees are entitled to, such as vacation, sick, compassionate and educational leave. Although the organisation pays the employee for 2 080 hours of work, the employee does not actually work those hours.

Consideration must also be given to time spent on necessary activities, but which are not directly associated with patient care, these could be staff development programmes, performance appraisals, counting narcotics, waiting for elevators, getting supplies and travelling for home visits, or activities related to the institution's organisation of support services like the transport of patients, collecting medicine from the pharmacy, or the layout of nursing stations.

Some types of non-productive time can be predicted and planned for while others cannot. For example, if a 30-bed unit can be adequately staffed by a combination of 12 nurses from different categories, more than 12 staff members are actually required to cover the unit for days off, sick days and vacational leave of the 12 nurses.

13.5.3.6 Budgetary provision

It is advised that the healthcare service manager is involved in developing the unit budget, as these managers have the dual responsibility to ensure that a sufficient number of staff are available for the safe care of patients, while being mindful of the costs pertaining to the unit budget.

The staffing budget is often determined by financial administrators and is based upon the previous year's census and productivity levels. Greater flexibility in adjusting staffing to existing needs is accommodated by allocations in the budget for overtime, temporary staff, changes in salary scales and unexpected increases in census or patient referrals.

13.5.3.7 Nursing care delivery systems

Before they can specify the overall staffing programme, healthcare service managers must decide what method of personnel assignment is to be used in each unit, as this will influence the type and number of nurses required from the different categories. Once the decision is made on the type of modality to be used in this particular service, a committee can develop policies and procedures for implementation of this modality.

As curative healthcare services provide a 24-hour service, it is necessary to cover the service adequately with appropriate staff from different categories to not only take care of patient requirements, but also to man the supporting services such as radiology, laboratories, blood services, kitchen, porter service and so forth. Thus, shift work is essential in hospitals and 24-hour comprehensive healthcare services. Shift work can bring about several problems for both management and the employees having to do the shift work, such as difficult adjustments between night and day duty sessions, and the payment of night duty allowances, and additional remuneration for working on weekends and public holidays, which impacts on the HR budget.

Several modalities or methods of nursing practice have evolved during the past fifty years, including functional nursing, team nursing, primary nursing, case method, joint practice, and case management (Swansburg & Swansburg, 1999:278–283; Tappen, 2001:243–253), as described below.

Functional nursing

The functional method can best be described as a task-oriented method in which a particular nursing function is assigned to each staff member. For example, one registered nurse is responsible for administration of medication, one for dressings and treatments, one for managing fluid intake and output, another is responsible for admission and discharges, while someone else is responsible for bed baths and making beds. No nurse is responsible for the total care of a patient, but is responsible to the unit manager for the specific tasks allocated to him/her. The functional method is efficient and the best system for a nursing staff confronted with a large patient load and a shortage of professional nurses.

The advantage of functional nursing is that:

- It accomplishes the most work in the shortest amount of time

But there are several disadvantages which include:

- Fragmentation of nursing care
- No one takes responsibility or accountability for a particular patient's well-being
- It is difficult to establish a nurse-client relationship as a nurse does not tend to all the needs of a particular patient
- It gives professional nursing low status in terms of responsibility for patient care.

Team nursing

Under the leadership of a professional nurse, a group of nurses from different categories work together to fulfil the full functions of professional nurses. The team leader has the responsibility for coordinating the total care of a block of patients and is the leadership figure. Several elements are considered necessary for this approach to be effective:

- The team leader is delegated the authority to make assignments for team members and guide the work of the team.
- The leader is expected to use a democratic or participative style in interactions with team members.

- The team is responsible for the total care given to an assigned group of patients.
- Communication among team members is essential for success, and includes written patient care assignments, nursing care plans, reports to, and from the team leader, team conferences and frequent feedback among team members.

The advantages of team nursing are that:

- It involves all team members in planning patients' nursing care through team conferences and written nursing care plans.
- It provides the best care at the lowest cost.

Disadvantages of team nursing include the following:

- It can lead to fragmentation of care if the concept is not implemented properly.
- It can be difficult to find time for team conferences and care plans.
- It results in the RN, who is the team leader, to have the only significant responsibility and authority.

The disadvantages of team nursing can be overcome by educating competent team leaders in the principles of nursing team leadership.

Primary nursing

As a means of decentralisation of authority, the primary nurse (in the person of a professional nurse) is assigned to care for the patient's total needs for the duration of the hospital stay. Responsibility covers a 24-hour period, with associate nurses providing care when the primary nurse is not available. The care is planned and prescribed totally by the primary nurse, thus focusing the responsibility on one, instead of several nurses. The following characteristics are relevant to the primary nursing modality:

- The primary nurse has full responsibility for the nursing care of a patient 24 hours a day, from admission through to discharge.
- Assessment of nursing care needs, collaboration with the patient and other healthcare professionals, and the resulting formulation of a care plan for the patient are all in the hands of the primary nurse.
- Execution of the nursing care plan is delegated by the primary nurse to a secondary nurse during other shifts.
- The primary nurse consults with nurse managers.
- Authority, accountability and autonomy rest with the primary nurse.

It is noted that this modality of nursing care has many positive results, such as reduced hospital stay of patients, fewer nursing hours and less salary expense per patient. It thus saves money, but also increases job satisfaction, group adhesion, patient satisfaction, and decreased costs of overtime and sick leave.

Advantages of primary nursing are:

- It provides for increased autonomy on the part of the RN, thus increasing responsibility, accountability and motivation.
- It assures better continuity of care as the primary nurse directs care throughout the hospitalisation.
- Because the primary nurse does the history and physical assessment, develops the care plan and acts as liaison between the patient and other healthcare workers, it makes available increased knowledge of the patient's psychological and physical needs.
- It leads to increased rapport and trust between nurse and patient that will allow the formation of a therapeutic relationship.
- It improves communication of information to physicians and other healthcare personnel.
- It eliminates nursing aids from the administration of direct patient care.
- It frees the charge nurse to assume the role of operational manger to deal with staff problems and assignments, and to motivate and support staff.

The main disadvantage of primary nursing is said to require that the entire staff be RNs, which increases staffing costs. This can be overcome by delegating all non-nursing duties to be performed by other categories of personnel.

Case method

The case method involves the assignment of one registered nurse to the total care of one or more patients, also known as the term 'specialing' among the nursing community. The assigned nurse is responsible for providing all the nursing care that is needed. The work of the private duty nurse is an example of the case method. Community health agencies often use this method to assign cases to individual nurses, and intensive care units use a modified version of this method for delivering nursing care.

Advantages of the case method are that:

- The care given is comprehensive, continuous and usually holistic
- It is simple and direct in comparison with other delivery methods
- It has clear and short lines of responsibility.

Disadvantages of the case method are:

- It is less efficient than some of the other methods because it uses highly skilled, higher paid professionals to do work, of which some could be done by less skilled, lower-paid personnel.
- In most instances, the case method cannot be used to assign patients to ancillary staff due to the level of activities required by the patient.

Case management

Case management is more than a modality of nursing. It has been described as a clinical system that focuses on the accountability of an identified individual or group for conditioning a patient's care.

Nursing case management is the set of activities undertaken by a single nurse to mobilise, monitor, and evaluate all resources used by a patient during the total course of illness. Simply stated, case management is a process of coordinating services, and the case manager is the person who does the coordination. When a patient is admitted to a healthcare institution, a nurse from one unit where the patient will receive care is designated the patient's case manager. The case manager has the responsibility and authority for planning, implementing, coordinating and evaluating care for the patient throughout the entire episode of illness, regardless of the patient's movement among various units and services, such as the emergency room, surgical unit, operating room, recovery unit and surgical clinic.

The objectives of nursing case management are:

- Establishing and achieving a set of standardised patient care outcomes for each patient
- Facilitating early patient discharge, or within an appropriate length of stay
- Using the fewest possible appropriate healthcare resources to meet the expected patient care outcomes
- Facilitating the continuity of patient care through collaborative practice of diverse healthcare professionals
- Enhancing nurses' professional development and job satisfaction
- Facilitating the transfer of knowledge of expert clinical staff to novice staff (Gillies, 1994:218).

Several methods of delivering nursing care have been discussed, no method is perfect in all situations, and differing personnel demands are relevant to each modality. Healthcare service managers are urged to carefully consider the characteristics, needs and demands of their own services, before adopting a delivery method.

13.5.4 Absenteeism and turnover

Absenteeism and turnover are work-related behaviours which result in withdrawal from the work environment. It is obviously difficult for an organisation to operate smoothly and to attain its objectives if employees fail to report for work. The work flow is disrupted, and often important decisions have to be delayed. Absenteeism levels beyond the normal range in any organisation have a direct impact on the organisation's effectiveness and efficiency.

13.5.4.1 Absenteeism

Absenteeism occurs when an individual does not show up for work. The cause may be legitimate, such as illness or a crisis at home, or, it could be feigned, meaning that it is reported as legitimate but is in actual fact just an excuse not to come to work. High absenteeism may also be a symptom of other problems such as job dissatisfaction, tension at work and low morale. No matter for what reason, absenteeism is a costly and disruptive problem facing managers.

When an employee is absent, it disrupts the workflow because it requires that schedules have to be adjusted or modified, or, the employee's work does not get done at all, or a substitute must be hired to do it. In each case, the quantity and quality of actual output is likely to decline. In any organisation, some absenteeism is expected, but the major concern of organisations are to minimise feigned absenteeism and reduce legitimate absences as much as possible.

Torrington and Hall (1998:136) suggests three main approaches to quantify absence, which can be applied on an individual or aggregate workforce basis:

(1) **Absence rate** is the number of days absent of all employees (who should have attended work).
(2) **Absence percentage rate** is the absence figure divided by the total number of actual working days for all employees over a year, multiplied by 100. This simple percentage calculation is the one most often used, and enables the organisation's absence level to be compared with national figures, or other organisations in the same sector.
(3) **Absence frequency rate** is the number of spells of absence over a period, usually a year. Comparing this and the absence percentage rate gives critical information about the type of absence problem the organisation is experiencing.

The costing of absence needs to have a wider focus than just the pay of the absent individual. Other relevant costs include:

- The manager's cost in finding a temporary replacement or rescheduling work
- The actual costs of the temporary employee
- The costs of orienting the new employee as to what is expected from him/her
- The costs associated with a slower work rate or more errors from a temporary employee
- The costs of work/contracts not completed on time.

Employees go to work because they are motivated to do so, the level of motivation will remain high if an individual feels that attendance will lead to more valued rewards and fewer negative consequences than alternative behaviours. Unfortunately, it is also a known fact that the commitment of some employees to their work and employer is lacking, resulting in frequent illegal spells of absence from work. Managers can have some influence over attendance behaviour through their ability to take disciplinary action, establish bonus systems and allow employee participation in developing relevant plans.

13.5.4.2 Turnover

Turnover occurs when an employee quits his/her job. An organisation usually incurs costs in replacing persons who have resigned from their jobs, but turnover that involves especially skilled or productive employees are even more costly. Turnover is not always a negative occurrence, in times of downsizing, turnover can facilitate natural attrition, or when troublesome employees resign, it may well be accepted with relief. The turnover cost is calculated by adding the Separation costs + Replacement cost + Training costs (Sherman et al., 1996:736).

Turnover seems to result from a number of factors including aspects related to the job, the organisation, the individual, the labour market and family influences. In general, a poor person-to-job-fit is likely to be a cause of turnover (Moorhead & Griffin, 1995:69–70).

Bevan (1991 in Bratton & Gold, 2003:198–199) provides a guide to some of the reasons for high staff turnover. Significantly, but not unexpectedly, pay was not the only issue. Among the main factors identified were:

- The job not matching new employees' expectations
- A lack of attention from line managers and a lack of training
- A lack of autonomy, responsibility, challenge and variety in the work
- Disappointment with the promotion and development opportunities
- Standards of management, including unapproachability, uncaring and distant behaviour and a failure to consult.

Ideally, if managers could develop reward systems that retained the best performers and caused poor performers to leave, the overall effectiveness of an organisation would improve. To approach this ideal, an equitable and favourably compared reward system must exist which has an external orientation. The comparison with external equivalent organisations is important because quitting most often means that a person leaves one organisation for a better alternative elsewhere.

A merit-based reward system should encourage most of the better performers to remain with the organisation. There should also be some differential in the reward system that discriminates between high and low performers, the point being that high performers should receive significantly more intrinsic and extrinsic rewards than their fellow low performers.

13.6 UNDERLYING DYNAMICS

The underlying dynamics affecting the utilisation of human resources are strongly related to the effectiveness of communication, behaviour and commitment from both management and employees. The following aspects are particularly relevant when considering staffing and work allocation:

- Policy and procedure availability and application, especially if consistent and fair process and strategy application is desired

- Organisational structure with reference to the provision, organisation and utilisation of human resources
- The means, channels and willingness to communicate openly and effectively with all levels of staff
- Staff shortages related to professional healthcare practitioners can undermine the best planned staffing strategies and processes, resulting in a deterioration of quality in service provision
- Management's commitment to identify, investigate and successfully handle absenteeism problems with the legal framework
- Communication effectiveness.

13.7 CONCLUDING STATEMENTS

The following concluding statements are relevant to the utilisation of human resources:

- The utilisation of human resources occurs in the legal and professional-ethical context, in accordance with the business ownership of the particular healthcare organisation, and is affected by labour-related legislation such as the Basic Conditions of Employment Act and the Scope of Practice regulations.
- The major role-players in the utilisation of human resources are the state, statutory bodies, managers and supervisors, employees and their trade unions.
- The purpose of HR utilisation is brought about by effective communication and lateral relations through which the appropriate application of staff is enabled.
- The process of HR utilisation relates to communication, lateral relations and staffing allocation, as well as absenteeism and turnover.
- Without communication, an enterprise would not exist, let alone survive. Communication is the essence of an organisation, both as an entity (organisation) and as a process (i.e. the way in which activities are organised).
- An organisation's entire way of life incorporating the mission statement, philosophy, strategies, policies and procedures, the organisational chart, the balance sheet, the budget, training manuals, job descriptions, appraisal forms, plans, forecasts, memoranda, briefings, contracts, statement of objectives, electronic mail, computer conferencing, presentations, meetings and interviews, all depend upon one activity, which is communication. It is communication which holds everything together and makes things happen.
- Communication basically has four functions: to control, to motivate, emotional expression, and the gathering and distribution of information.
- In order to best apply and utilise communication, it is necessary to understand the fundamental concepts of communication. These include the direction of communication, formal versus informal networks, non-verbal communication, barriers to effective communication, and elements for effective employee communication.
- To accomplish work through others' efforts, the healthcare services manager

must assemble appropriate types and numbers of personnel to administer the level of care demanded by patients.

- To predict nursing workload, the manager must determine the number of each type of patient (medical diagnoses, severity and acuity group) to be cared for, the expected treatment measures and care needs and the expected length of stay.
- To calculate the number of employees in each job category to fulfil the anticipated needs, the manager must weigh employee's knowledge and skills, the method of nursing care delivery, optimum mix of personnel, annual work hours and patterns of employee work schedules.
- Absenteeism is defined as any time away from work. Absence could be due to legitimate reasons of ill health or other emergencies, or could be feigned to avoid work for other reasons.
- Turnover applies to staff resigning from the employment of a specific employer. This could be due to better job offers or as a result of difficult, unpleasant work circumstances.
- Various underlying dynamics, such as policy and procedures, consistency in the application of processes, organisational structure, the effectiveness of communication, staff shortages and a willingness to solve problems affect the utilisation of human resources.

Self-assessment

(1) Describe the functions that communication provides in a group or organisation, and give an example of each.
(2) List four specific problems related to language difficulties in cross-cultural communication.
(3) How might managers use the grapevine to their benefit?
(4) Go to www.acas.org.uk/publications/pub_ab_absenceturnover.html. The booklet contained at this address provides assistance to organisations that have labour turnover and absenteeism problems.

14 Performance management and development of human resources

KEY CONCEPTS

Performance appraisal process
Performance appraisal principles
Performance appraisal methods
Performance appraisal review session
Human resource development
Quality process in education and training
Motivation
Career management
Supervision
Job design

SPECIFIC OUTCOMES

After studying this chapter, you should be able to:

- Interpret the legal and professional-ethical human resource management **context** with reference to public and private (type of business ownership) healthcare organisations in relation to performance management and development of human resources in terms of the following legislation and structures:
  - Labour Relations Act, 1995 (Act 66 of 1995)
  - Skills Development Act, 1998 (Act 97 of 1998)
  - Skills Development Levies Act, 1999 (Act 9 of 1999)
  - South African Qualifications Authority (SAQA)
- Identify and describe the **role-players**, such as the state, employers, employees and organised labour and interpret their roles and responsibilities in the assessment and development of human resources in a healthcare organisation
- Analyse and debate the **purpose** of human resources assessment and development in the context of a healthcare organisation
- Analyse and debate the **process** of human resource management in the context of a healthcare organisation, with specific reference to performance appraisal and management, human resource development, career management, supervision and motivation

- Debate the **underlying dynamics** that could impact on the assessment and development of human resources of a healthcare organisation, with specific reference to systems and processes in place, skills of assessors and knowledge of employees, feedback and remedial action.

14.1 INTRODUCTION

Of all the activities comprising human resource management, performance appraisal is the most contentious. Managers do not like doing the appraisals and the employees face them with a sense of apprehension. Yet, it is accepted that there should be a means by which performance can be measured, monitored and controlled. This is called performance management. Performance appraisal is an important technique for developing an effective workforce in order to achieve the organisational goals. The performance appraisal process is guided by a number of principles but is also affected by certain pitfalls. Selection of the most appropriate methods and instruments can limit the negative outcomes of a biased assessment process, enabling guidance and remedial action after proper feedback has been given during the review process.

South Africa faces the challenge of high unemployment among unskilled individuals, and on the other hand a shortage of skilled employees. Organisations have a crucial role to play in building a nation's skills levels, as only a small part of a country's skills are acquired through formal educational qualifications. The larger part of skills development takes place at the workplace, thus emphasising the important role of training and development at organisational level. It is therefore essential to devise a strategy for human resource development, implement the process of training and development and assist employees with their career planning. In order to implement appropriate training and development activities, skilled supervisors who know their staff, must be present at all levels to identify training needs and motivate their colleagues.

This chapter will highlight the following components (see visual presentation in Figure 14.1):

- The **context** of human resource management in terms of assessment and development of human resources with reference to the legal and professional-ethical environment.
- The **purpose** of performance appraisal is to monitor, measure and evaluate performance so that the necessary remedial steps can be taken. The development of HR is based on a needs analysis after which the appropriate training can be activated.
- The different **role-players** in the assessment and development of HR are the state, employers, supervisors, employees and organised labour.
- The **process** of HR assessment and development deals with performance

management, HR development, motivation, career management, supervision and job design.

- The **underlying dynamics** impacting on the assessment and development of human resources in a healthcare organisation refer to the systems and processes in place, integrity of assessors, feedback and remedial action.

Figure 14.1 Visual presentation of the assessment and development of human resources in a healthcare organisation

Context	- Labour Relations Act, 1995 (Act 66 of 1995) - Skills Development Act, 1998 (Act 97 of 1998) - Skills Development Levies Act, 1999 (Act 9 of 1999) - South African Qualifications Authority (SAQA)
Purpose	- Monitor, measure and evaluate employee performance - Take remedial action if necessary - Ensure optimal utilisation of HR - Undertake developmental needs analysis - Provide appropriate training
Role-players	- State - Employers - Supervisors - Employees - Organised labour
Process	- Performance appraisal and management - Human resources development - Motivation - Career management - Supervision - Job design
Underlying dynamics	- Systems and processes in place - Integrity of assessors - Knowledge of employees - Feedback - Remedial action

14.2 CONTEXT

The major human capital development challenge in South Africa is to ensure that the requirements of the organisation, the requirements of the component parts of the organisation, and the requirements of the staff are closely aligned, if the nurturing and retention of good staff, the optimism of commercial opportunity, and exponential growth in the market place are to be realised (SPA, 2001:1).

South Africa's human resources have been identified as the prime determining factor for the country's future progress and prosperity. The high rate of illiteracy, the shortage of skilled human resources and low levels of work ethic are some of the human resource problems that managers are faced with. Further, South Africa needs to prepare its workforce for the new requirements originating from the globally changing work environment.

Healthcare professions have historically enjoyed the status of self-regulation, and for many decades the parameters for assuring quality and standards of specific professions were determined by esteemed members of the professions. The alignment of healthcare professional education to the requirements set by the South African Qualifications Authority Act, 1995 (Act 58 of 1995) should not be seen as undermining any self-regulatory mechanism, but should instead be viewed as a means to further improving and enhancing the quality and standard of professional education (Subedar in Vasuthevan & Viljoen, 2003:vii).

Under the South African Qualifications Authority (SAQA), a National Qualifications Framework (NQF) was developed to facilitate the transformation of the education system in South Africa in order to redress social and educational imbalances. The primary aim of the NQF is to ensure that education is accessible to all in this country. Additionally, through the establishment of National Standards Bodies (NSBs), professional regulatory bodies, known as Education and Training Quality Assurance Bodies (ETQAs), the NQF is further assisted to ensure that professional qualifications are developed and arrived at through a process that facilitates the alignment of professional qualifications with the overall educational system.

The legislation and structures that pertain to the training and development of employees over a broad sphere of educational possibilities (Vasuthevan & Viljoen, 2003:4) are described below. See also Figure 14.2, which illustrates the relationships between the different structures in the SAQA quality process.

The South African Qualifications Authority (SAQA)

The SAQA was established through the SAQA Act (Act 58 of 1995) to oversee the development and implementation of the NQF. SAQA is established through the appointment of 29 members by the Minister of Education, in consultation with the Minister of Labour, for a three-year period. The SAQA members represent the country's major stakeholders in education and training, including representatives from government, business and labour.

SAQA's vision is to develop an education and training system that reflects the objectives of the NQF. The mission is to ensure the development and implementation of a NQF which contributes to the full development of each learner and to the social and economic development of the nation at large. The **National Qualifications Framework (NQF)** is a framework of qualifications, representing a national effort at integrating education and training into a unified structure of recognised qualifications. The NQF contains a set of principles and guidelines by which records of learner achievement are registered to enable national recognition of acquired skills and knowledge, thereby ensuring an integrated system that encourages life-long learning.

SAQA has the following structures through which its responsibilities are effected:

- **National Standards Bodies (NSBs)** are one of SAQA's institutional pillars, with one NSB established per field and registered by SAQA for a period of three years. NSBs are responsible for establishing education and training qualifications and/or standards, and they have specific functions relating to the registration of national qualifications and/or standards. The NSBs were disbanded in 2005 and are being replaced by consultative panels which are assembled on an ad hoc basis.
- **Standard Generating Bodies (SGBs)** are registered bodies responsible for the generation of qualifications and standards. The recognition or establishment of an SGB occurs in the framework of a SAQA-accepted subfield as described by the NSB. The NSB for a specific field, such as Health and Welfare, establishes relevant SGBs in the framework of specific subfields and ensures that the work of the SGB meets SAQA requirements.
- **Education and Training Quality Assurance Bodies (ETQAs)**. An organisation or group of organisations may seek accreditation from SAQA as an ETQA in either the social, economic or education and training sectors. ETQAs are established by SAQA in each of these sectors in order to monitor and audit achievements in terms of national qualifications and/or standards. An ETQA must abide by relevant regulations, and it may delegate selected functions to a provider or other body with the prior approval of SAQA.

Each SETA has a responsibility to perform the quality assurance function for education and training in the sector for which it is responsible. For the first time, individuals will be given credit for existing skills and knowledge, which may have been acquired

Figure 14.2 The SAQA quality structure

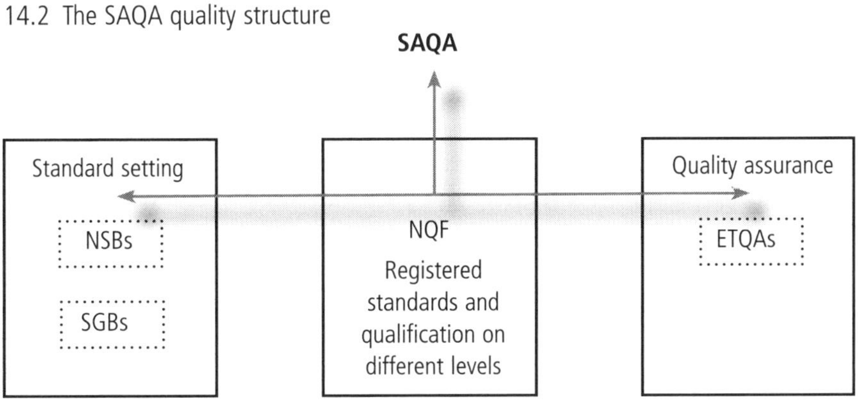

Source: Vasuthevan & Viljoen, 2003:6

by other means than formal education through Recognition of Prior Learning (RPL). In the case of the Health and Welfare SETA, professional councils, such as the South African Nursing Council and Health Profession's Council, will perform this ETQA function.

In terms of the **Higher Education Act, 1997 (Act 101 of 1997)**, the **Council on Higher Education (CHE)** was established in May 1998. The mandate of the CHE is to advise the Minister of Education on all matters of higher education so that the system is characterised by equity, quality, responsiveness to economic and social developmental needs, effective and efficient provision and management, and contributes to the public good. The Higher Education Act makes provision for the establishment of a **Higher Education Quality Committee (HEQC)** as a permanent committee of the CHE.

The HEQC has a statutory responsibility for quality assurance in the higher education sector (NQF levels 5 to 8), its primary purpose with regard to quality is to ensure that providers effectively deliver education, training, research and community service which are of a higher quality and which produce socially useful and enriching knowledge, as well as a relevant range of graduate skills and competencies necessary for social and economic progress.

The **General and Further Education and Training Council (GENFETQA)** was established by the **General and Further Education and Training Quality Assurance Act, 2001 (Act 58 of 2001)** to give expression to quality assurance of the NQF in the General and Further Education and Training Bands (NQF levels 1–4). It is an accredited quality assurance body of SAQA, and serves providers in the General and Further Education and Training Bands, thus functioning as a building block of the NQF. This organisation is now referred to as AMALUZI, a Xhosa word meaning 'shepherd'.

The **Skills Development Act, 1998 (Act 97 of 1998)** is the primary legislation that seeks to restructure the country's national education and training system. It is supported in law by the **Skills Development Levies Act, 1999 (Act 9 of 1999)**. These Acts were promulgated to develop and improve the skills of the South African workforce. Based on international experience, South Africa has adopted an approach emphasising a decentralised mode. This allows for public and private participation in governance structures that are market and demand driven and responsive to the needs of the sectors they serve.

Two structures were established to facilitate the achievement of the objectives of the Skills Development Act, namely the National Skills Authority (NSA) and the Sector Education and Training Authorities (SETAs):

- The **National Skills Authority (NSA)** was established to advise the Minister of Labour on the development of national skills policy and strategy, to liaise with Sector Education and Training Authorities, to report on the implementation of the National Skills Development Strategy (NSDS), and to allocate funding available through the National Skills Fund (NSF).

- Twenty-five **Sector Education and Training Authorities (SETAs)** were established by the Minister of Labour in March 2000 to serve the interests of different sectors of the nation's economy. Each SETA comprises members representing organised employers, organised labour and the relevant government departments. The most important function for each SETA, in a process of stakeholder participation, was to develop a Sector Skills Plan (SSP), which would be used as a framework for the implementation of workplace education and training in a sector. SETAs are also required to accredit learnerships, ensure quality in the provision of education and training, collect levies and pay grants. The Health and Welfare SETA (HWSETA) was established as SETA No 11 to cover areas of public and private health and social development services.
- **Levies**. A payroll levy was imposed on employers with effect from 1 April 2000 at 0.5% of an organisation's payroll expenditure, increasing one year later to 1.0% of the payroll. The payroll levy is based on remuneration paid by an employer to all its employees. The flow of levies and funds is prescribed in Regulations to the Skills Development Levies Act, 1999 (Act 9 of 1999). Employers are required to pay the levy annually to the South African Revenue Service (SARS). SARS in turn, pays 20% of the collected levies to the NSF and the remaining 80% to the SETA to which the employer belongs. A maximum of 10% of the levy may be used to cover the SETA's administrative costs. Employers can then claim back from the SETA for training that has met the requirements of the SETA.
- **Learnerships** are one of the most significant innovations of the Skills Development Act, 1998 (Act 97 of 1998). A learnership combines a structured learning component and practical work experience which leads to a qualification that is nationally recognised. For a learnership agreement to exist, there must be an agreement between the learner, the employer, and an accredited training provider. Refer to Figure 14.3. The employer is then committed to provide

Figure 14.3 Learnership agreement of the Hospital Association of South Africa

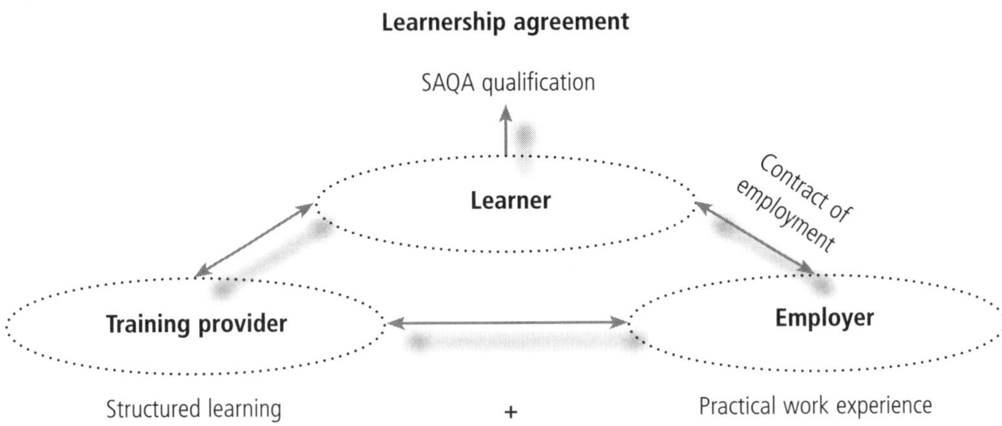

Source: Vasuthevan & Viljoen 2003:31

training facilities, support the learner and ensure proper implementation of the learning programme, pay the learner, keep records and apply workplace procedures consistent with workplace practices. In exchange the employer has the right to benefit from the employee's work.

- **Skills planning**. A process is determined for skills planning, to participate in the process, in addition to complying with the levy payments, the Regulations to the Skills Development Act require an employer to have the following in place:
  - **Skills Development Facilitator (SDF)**, who is appointed by the employer to assist and advise the employer and employees in developing a Workplace Skills Plan and submitting it to the SETA, drafting the Annual Training Report, quality assurance, and acting as the contact person between the employer and the SETA.
  - The **Workplace Skills Plan (WSP)** is a critical component of the annual process to plan for the education and training that will take place in the workplace. Refer to Figure 14.4 for an example of the workplace skills planning process developed by the Hospital Association of South Africa.
  - **Annual Training Report (ATR)**. Each employer is required to submit an Annual Training Report which details the training that took place in the workplace during the period under review. Only once this ATR has been approved will the employer receive grants for training.
  - **Workplace consultation**. All of the processes of the Act require consultation with the workforce. This is in line with the new labour legislation, which supports initiatives to democratise the workplace. A training committee and representative of the workforce must be established for organisations employing more than 50 employees.

Figure 14.4 Workplace skills planning process (Hospital Association of South Africa)

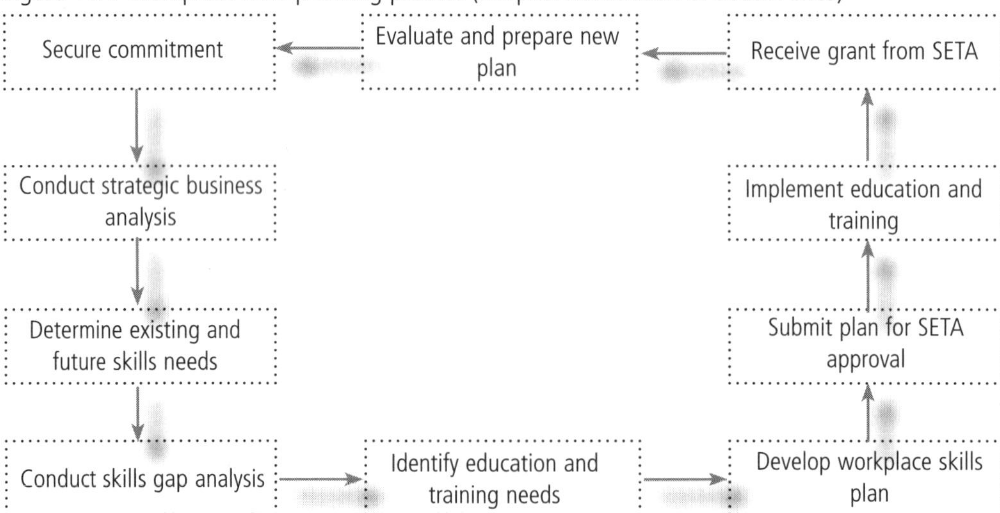

Source: Vasuthevan & Viljoen, 2003:33

This brings to a close a brief discussion of the legislative framework in which education and training should take place in South Africa, affecting as much the workplace as institutions of learning.

14.3 PURPOSE

There are several reasons to appraise performance in a work environment. It creates an opportunity to review the employee's work-related behaviour, enabling plans for correcting deficiencies and to reinforce employee strengths, provides information upon which salary decisions can be made, and is central to career planning processes. But there are also a variety of other purposes and desired benefits of performance appraisal (Bratton & Gold, 2003:251):

- Setting goals and targets in the form of performance standards
- Clarifying expectations and reducing ambiguity about desired performance
- Improving communication
- Improving motivation and morale
- Determining rewards
- Selecting people for promotion
- Managing careers
- Identifying opportunities for training and development
- Planning remedial actions
- Counselling
- Discipline.

Vision and values directly affect crucial decisions relating to investment and the deployment of the organisation's resources, including people. Human resources development (HRD) strategy of any kind relies on the presence of a vision of the organisation which sees a well-trained and continuously developing workforce as essential to its success. Employee socialisation, training and development are an organisation's intentional efforts to improve current and future performance by increasing capabilities of the workforce. In providing assistance to employees to become effective in their jobs, modifying their attitudes and adjusting their behaviour in line with organisational goals, the organisation gains quality labour inputs.

14.4 ROLE-PLAYERS

The state is involved as a role-player by means of the legislation and structures put in place, of particular relevance in the processes of assessment and development are the following:

- Labour Relations Act, 1995 (Act 66 of 1995)
- Skills Development Act, 1998 (Act 97 of 1998)
- Skills Development Levies Act, 1999 (Act 9 of 1999)
- South African Qualifications Authority (SAQA).

The immediate supervisor should do the actual appraisal. Therefore the supervisor must be familiar with the basic appraisal techniques, have sufficient contact with the employees in relation to work inputs and general work performance, understand the problems that can negatively affect the appraisal, and be able to conduct the appraisal fairly. The HR department serves a policy-making and advisory role. It concentrates on accurate assessment of performance through the development and application of assessment systems such as rating scales, and the training of managers/supervisors to effectively use the performance appraisal interview as a tool for constructive feedback that will reinforce good performance and motivate employee development.

The other group of role-players is the employees who need to be assessed. They must know what is expected from them in relation to job requirements, which is usually documented in the job description, containing the key performance areas and their weighting. The employees should be informed about the assessment tool and be allowed to clarify uncertainties in this regard. Because work is an important part of one's identity, people are very sensitive to opinions about how they perform. When applied fairly and correctly, performance appraisal can enhance motivation and thus increase retention and productivity. However, inexperienced raters or unfair treatment during the appraisal process and feedback session can discourage and demotivate staff.

Marquis and Huston (1996:403) stipulate the leadership roles and management functions inherent in performance appraisal as the following:

- **Leadership roles**. A leader does the following:
  - Uses the appraisal process to motivate and promote growth
  - Applies techniques to reduce the anxiety inherent in the appraisal process
  - Involves employees in all aspects of the performance appraisal process
  - Is aware of own biases and prejudices
  - Develops trust by being honest and fair when evaluating performance
  - Encourages peer review among professional staff
  - Uses appraisal interviews to facilitate two-way communication
  - Provides ongoing support to employees attempting to correct performance deficiencies
  - Uses coaching techniques that facilitate employee growth in work performance.

- **Management functions**. A manager does the following:
  - Uses a formalised system of performance appraisal
  - Gathers data for performance appraisals that are objective and fair
  - Uses the appraisal process to determine staff education and training needs
  - Bases performance appraisal on documented standards
  - Attempts to be as objective as possible during the process
  - Maintains appropriate and complete documentation of the appraisal process

- Follows up on identified performance deficiencies
- Conducts the appraisal interview in a manner that promotes a positive outcome
- Provides frequent informal feedback on work performance.

In relation to HRD, a comprehensive set of legislation sets the scene in which the employer creates opportunities and provides assistance for employees at all levels to strive for life-long learning. Socialisation, education, training and development are all important in the process of facilitating adjustment and improved performance in any institution. For purposes of clarification these concepts are briefly defined even though they form part of an integrated system (Jackson & Schuler, 2000:350–351; Amos, Ristow & Ristow, 2004:89):

- **Socialisation** refers to teaching employees the corporate culture and philosophies about how the specific organisation functions. Upon entry into a new job or a new organisation, all employees initially need to 'learn the ropes', through socialisation, they learn how things are done in the new environment, including things they can't find written in any policy or procedure manual.
- **Education** is a process that provides basic knowledge, skills, moral values and understanding required in the normal course of life and is focused on building for the future.
- **Training** refers to an attempt at altering or changing knowledge, skills and behaviour in such a way that organisational objectives are achieved, thus improving competencies required at present in the workplace.
- **Development** refers to a longer-term organisational process that provides learning opportunities, thus enabling learning in the organisation, improving competencies over the long term.

Socialisation, training and development serve many strategic purposes, of which the most important may be considered to be the creation of shared experiences and understanding among employees with many different backgrounds. This helps to speed up the development of organisational cohesiveness and employee commitment, while arming employees with the competencies they need in order to perform well in both their current and future positions.

14.5 PROCESS

The process in this chapter entails two broad interrelated sections, first that of performance measurement and second, the training and development of employees. Refer to Figure 14.5 for a summary of this chapter's content.

The appraisal process begins with the establishment of performance standards in line with the strategic goals of the organisation. These standards need to be communicated to employees so that they know what is expected from them. The third step in the appraisal process is measurement of performance after which the

Figure 14.5 Outlay of components dealt with wider performance management and development of human resources

Performance appraisal and management	◗ Factors affecting performance ◗ Principles of performance appraisal ◗ Common pitfalls of performance assessment ◗ Types of performance criteria ◗ Appraisal methods and instruments ◗ The appraisal interview
Human resources development	◗ Strategy and human resources development ◗ The training and development process
Career management	
Supervision	◗ Criteria for selection of supervisors ◗ Skills and qualities of a supervisor
Motivation	◗ Factors influencing motivation ◗ Motivational approach to job design

performance is compared with the actual performance standards. The final step in the appraisal is identification of corrective action where necessary.

14.5.1 Performance appraisal and management

Performance management is basically concerned with measuring, monitoring and evaluating performance, and then initiating steps to improve performance where it is warranted (Abedian, Strachan & Ajam, 2001:81). The main instrument used to control the human resources of an organisation is performance management. Performance management refers to the entire group of tools which management can apply to guide, control and improve the performance of their employees. Relevant tools are job descriptions, standards, the performance appraisal process, a reward system, job design, training and developmental efforts and leadership approaches. From a control point of view, the performance of individuals and groups is assessed and compared with predetermined standards, as illustrated in Figure 14.6.

Specifically, performance evaluations should address developmental and documentation concerns. Development refers to those areas that could be better if some effort was expended to enhance the employee's performance. As far as the issue of documentation is concerned, a performance evaluation system would be remiss if it did not concern itself with the legal aspects of employee performance. HRM must make the effort to ensure that the evaluation systems used support the legal needs and responsibilities of the organisation.

Figure 14.6 The performance management process for human resources

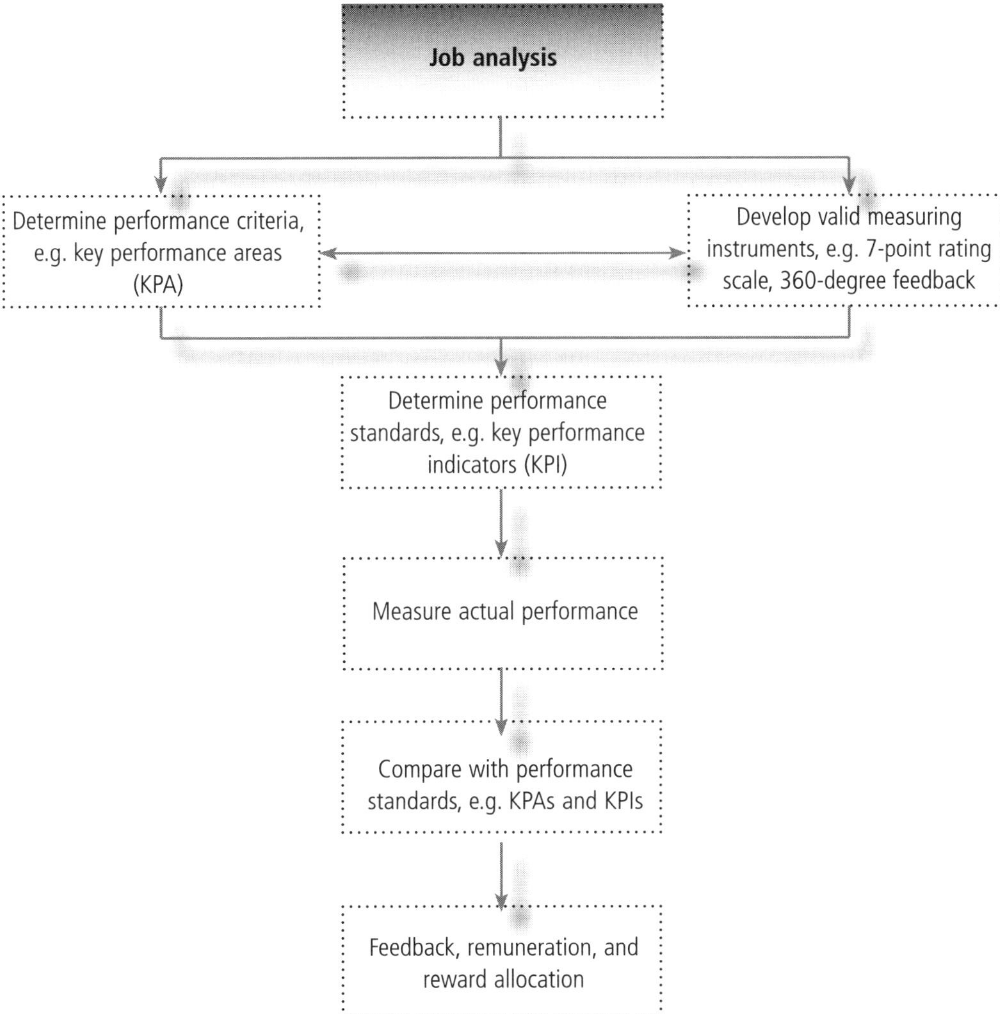

Source: Adapted from Smit & Cronjé, 2002:405

Performance management:

- Is a means of getting better results from the organisation, team, and individuals in an agreed framework of goals and standards
- Serves to clarify goals and in doing so, motivates people to perform well
- Is a way of translating corporate goals into achievable objectives that cascade down the organisation to produce optimum results
- Aims at improving strategic focus and organisational effectiveness by continuously securing improvements in the performance of individuals and teams.

Figure 14.7 Goals of performance appraisal

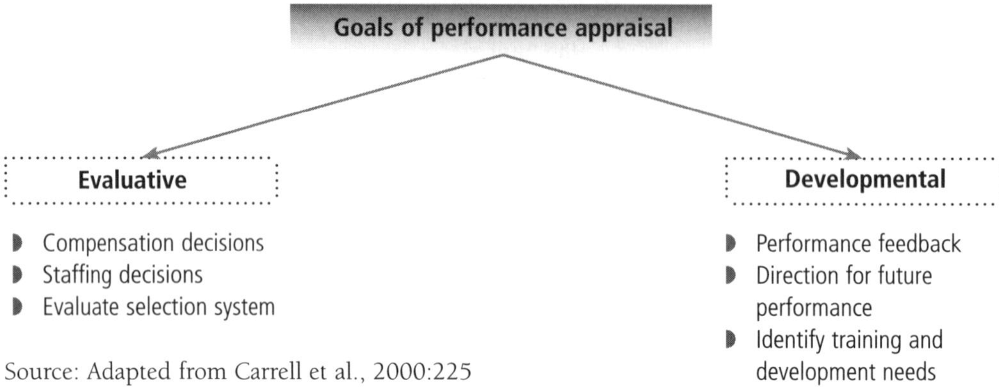

Source: Adapted from Carrell et al., 2000:225

The two core goals of performance appraisal are judging and guiding (as illustrated in Figure 14.7) and are evident in practice as evaluation and development. If the performance appraisal system can fulfil its objective of evaluating performance fairly and can also honour its purpose of guiding and improving the employee's performance, then the appraisal system is effective (Carrell et al., 2000:225).

14.5.1.1 Factors affecting performance

Individuals can only perform well if managers foster an environment that is challenging and conducive to producing a high standard of work. Within the individual and the surroundings there are three factors in particular which may influence an employee's performance:

- **Opportunity** is determined by the specific situation in which a person works. Work environments differ and restrictions may be present that are beyond the control of the employee, thus preventing growth advancement.
- **Capacity** is the ability to do the work. It involves physical and mental abilities, such as knowledge, intelligence, skills, age, health, stamina and energy levels.
- **Willingness** to do the work involves the employee's emotional characteristics. Such emotions influence personality, attitudes, values, needs, role expectations, job involvement, motivation, job satisfaction, anxiety and self-image.

An individual's work performance thus depends upon his/her personal job-related opportunities, ability to make the most of a situation, and the willingness to work and strive for higher goals in view of personal growth and organisational goal achievement.

14.5.1.2 Principles of performance appraisal

Principles of performance appraisal can be referred to as a set of recommended actions for developing and implementing a legally defensible appraisal system. Possible legal ramifications exist whenever management is not consistent in its performance appraisal systems. Nonetheless, it should be remembered that even though human endeavours are mostly legal, they are not always ethical. Yet ethics should form the bases of a performance appraisal, in which an honest assessment of performance is coupled with fair and objective feedback. The following principles are relevant:

- A job analysis to ascertain important duties and tasks before development of a performance appraisal system should be conducted.
- The performance appraisal system should be standardised and formal.
- Specific performance standards related to the job description should be developed and communicated to employees and raters in advance of the appraisal period.
- Objective and uncontaminated data should be used based on the general performance of the individual.
- Information, such as anecdotal notes, should be written down, as and when they occur, and not be trusted to memory.
- Ratings on traits such as dependability, drive, loyalty, honesty and attitude should be avoided or operationalised in observable and measurable behavioural terms.
- Employees should be evaluated on specific work dimensions, such as key performance areas, rather than on a single global or overall measure.
- If work-related behaviours rather than outcomes are to be evaluated, the rater should have ample opportunity to observe the employee's performance.
- A representative sample of the employee's performance should be monitored as the norm, in contrast to isolated cases of unusually good or bad performance.
- Whenever possible, more than one rater should conduct the appraisal and conduct all such appraisals independently in order to eliminate individual error and biases.
- Behavioural documentation should be prepared for extreme ratings.
- Employees should be given sufficient opportunity to review their appraisals.
- Formal appeal mechanisms and review of ratings should be utilised by upper-level personnel.
- Raters should be trained to use the rating instruments properly, to prevent discrimination and to evaluate performance consistently.
- Evaluations and reasons for actions taken should be documented carefully in order to substantiate decisions.
- Feedback should be provided as soon as possible after the appraisal, focusing on the positive aspects, and where appropriate, guidance should be provided to assist poor performers in improving their performance.
- Attainable, measurable and realistic goals should be set by both the rater and employee within reasonable time frames for reassessment of deficiencies identified.
- The direct supervisor must be responsible for doing the appraisals of subordinates (Booyens, 1998:153–155; Schuler & Jackson, 1996:348).

14.5.1.3 Common pitfalls of performance assessment

Accurate ratings reflect the employees' actual job performance levels. However, employment decisions that are based on inaccurate ratings are not valid and would thus be difficult to justify if legally challenged. The appraiser needs to guard against the common problems associated with performance appraisal. An appraisal system can fail its original goals if heed is not taken of the following factors which may adversely affect the outcome of a performance assessment:

- **Supervisory bias** could be conscious or unconscious and is not related to the job performance but may stem from personal characteristics such as age, gender, disability or race, or from organisational-related characteristics such as seniority, membership of the organisations' sports team, or friendship with top managers (Carrell et al., 2000:236).
- **The halo effect** occurs when the appraiser allows positive aspects or characteristics of the employee's behaviour or assessment to influence all other aspects of the employee's performance. This problem often occurs with employees who are especially friendly towards the supervisor.
- **The horns effect** takes place when the appraiser allows some negative aspects of the employee's performance to influence the assessment to such an extent that other levels of job performance are not accurately recorded.
- **Leniency** and **severity error**s are evident when raters provide ratings that are unduly high, while severity error occurs when ratings are unduly low.
- **Central tendency** implies that the assessor is hesitant to risk true assessment by avoiding giving extreme ratings as warranted and therefore rates all employees as average.
- **Recency error** occurs when a rater may be unable to recall all the employee's pertinent behaviours that have taken place during the rating period, and then the ratings are heavily influenced by recent events that are more easily remembered.

Appraisers should not only become aware of these rater errors but should receive appropriate training and information to conscientiously minimise the errors. During training it must be emphasised that performance appraisal should be truthful, candid but constructive, and not malicious (Carrell et al., 2000:227). There are at least three ways to reduce the impact of appraisal problems. First, be aware of the problems, understanding the problem can aid in avoiding it. Second, choose the appropriate assessment tool which will reduce the particular error, and third, train supervisors to eliminate rating errors such as halo, leniency and central tendency.

14.5.1.4 Types of performance criteria

Once the important job duties and tasks have been established, performance standards and criteria should be developed. Criteria are dimensions against which the performance of an incumbent, a team, or a work unit can be evaluated. Criteria are the performance expectations individuals and teams strive for in order to achieve the goals of the organisation.

According to Schuler and Jackson (1996:350–351), three basic types of performance criteria have been identified:

- **Trait-based criteria** focus on the personal characteristics of an employee. This type of criteria concentrates on what a person is, and not on what a person does or accomplishes on the job. Loyalty, dependability, communication abilities and leadership skills are examples of traits often assessed during the appraisal process. The link between traits and performance is often difficult to establish as traits are not easy to define and might mean different things to different people.
- **Behaviour-based criteria** focus on how work is performed. These criteria are especially important in jobs that involve interpersonal contact, such as most healthcare institutions require. With behaviours clearly defined, an employee is more likely to exhibit the acts that lead to peak performance. Examples of behavioural criteria could be attendance and punctuality, and that the employee exhibits safe practices in work performance, promotes team work and action, does task right the first time and uses personal initiative.
- **Outcome-based criteria** are becoming more relevant due to the increased emphasis on productivity and competitiveness. These criteria focus on what was accomplished or produced rather than on how it was accomplished, for example, the number of cases handled by a doctor or a count of the word processing errors an administrative staff member makes during a given time.

14.5.1.5 Appraisal methods and instruments

To meet the standards and criteria set for the specific job, an appropriate and effective rating system and form must be used. The methods chosen and the instruments used to implement these methods are critical in determining whether the organisation manages its performance successfully. Performance appraisal methods and instruments should transmit the operational goals and objectives to individuals, groups and the organisation at large. HR experts have developed a variety of methods and instruments for appraisal purposes, of which a number will be briefly introduced (Carrell et al., 2000:229–236; Kleiman, 2000:216–224). Refer to Figure 14.8 for types of performance appraisal systems.

Rating scales

- The **Graphic Rating Scale** rates the employee on some standard or attribute of work. Traditionally, the focus was on personal traits such as friendliness and cooperation, but in recent times, work behaviour and outcomes, such as whether the employee does the task correctly and in time with the first attempt, or whether the employee deals effectively with a certain number of clients have

Figure 14.8 Types of performance appraisal systems

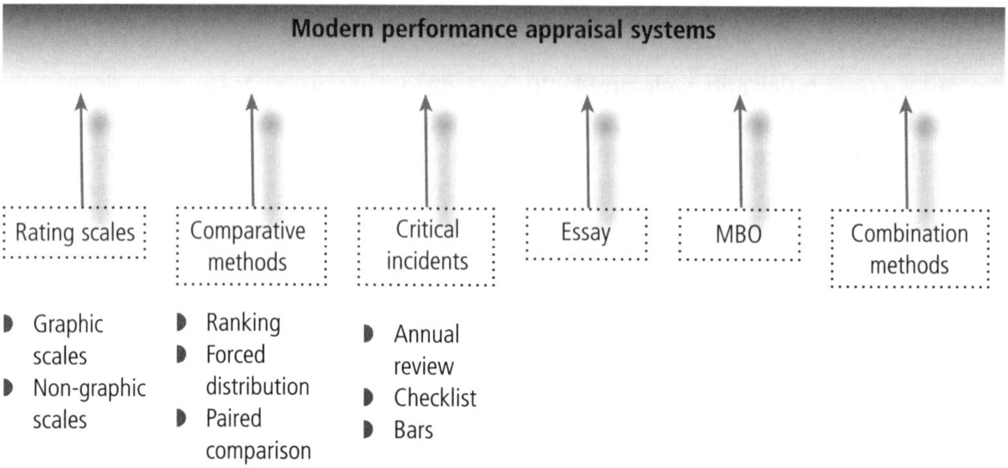

Source: Adapted from Carrell et al., 2000:229

become the criteria at stake. However, the criteria are only listed and not described. The rating is often done on a 1–5 point Likert-type scale.

- The **Non-Graphic Rating Scale** contains an overall description of each trait, ability or characteristic, and then describes the criteria at different positions on the 5-point scale. The rater can give a more accurate description of the employee's behaviour on a particular attribute because a description clarifies each level of the rating scale. For example, the trait 'accuracy' implies the correctness of work duties performed. On the scale the following five options appear:
  (1) Careless; makes recurrent errors
  (2) Makes frequent errors
  (3) Usually accurate; makes only average number of mistakes
  (4) Requires little supervision; is exact and precise most of the time
  (5) Requires absolute minimum of supervision; is almost always accurate.

This is thus a more valid instrument than the Graphic Rating Scale.

Comparative methods

Supervisors often do not differentiate sufficiently between employees even though real differences in performance are evident. Comparative methods can be used to sort out differences between employees by providing direct comparisons.

- **Ranking** employees from the most effective to the least effective forces differentiation between individuals. This differentiation rating is applicable to the total job performance. This is a fast and easy method, however, it seldom provides feedback on developmental needs.

- **Forced distribution** requires that supervisors spread their employee evaluations in a prescribed distribution, placing them in categories ranging from poor (10% of employees), below average (20% of employees), average (40% of employees), above average (20% of employees) and excellent (10% of employees).
- **Paired comparison** requires that a chart be made of all possible pairs of employees. Comparison of two staff members in a unit is made in relation to identified dimensions such as 'accuracy' or 'job knowledge'. This method is fairly easy to use if only a few employees are being rated, but very time-consuming with large numbers of employees.

Critical incident

The critical incident method of appraisal uses specific examples of job behaviour that have been collected by both the supervisor and the employees. A list of actual job experiences involving extraordinary good or bad employee performances is composed throughout the time span between assessments. Normal procedures or average work performance cannot be considered critical incidents, the focus is on outstanding or poor job performance that separates employees into excellent, average, and poor performers.

- **Annual review file or calender** is a way in which the supervisor keeps an ongoing record of his/her employee's critical incidents contemporaneously during the period of appraisal. The appraiser then reviews this record before preparing for the performance appraisal. The advantage of the annual review is that it is usually very job specific. With precise dates and incidents included in the appraisal, the supervisor is less affected by bias. Employees who have little or no record during the year are usually doing their jobs satisfactorily.
- **Checklist of critical incidents** may have 20 to 30 critical traits or dimensions for a specific job. The rater then simply checks whether the employee has performed in a superior manner in any one of the critical dimensions. Outstanding individuals would receive many marks as a consequence of good performance during the appraisal period in numerous dimensions, while average employees would only receive a few checks because they succeeded to perform better than average in only a few dimensions. The critical traits/dimensions could be weighted giving different weights to different items in the checklist to indicate their importance above others.
- **Behaviourally anchored rating scale (BARS)** uses critical incidents (in the form of traits or dimensions) in combination with a rating scale. The typical BARS includes seven or eight dimensions, each anchored by a seven- or nine-point scale. Rather than using numbers or adjectives, a BARS anchors each trait with examples of specific behaviour that reflect varying levels of performance. The BARS technique requires that a separate rating form be developed for each job classification.

Essay method
In this method of performance appraisal, the supervisor is required to write an essay, in narrative style, describing the employee's performance, specifying examples of strengths and weaknesses. Supervisory bias is reduced in this method as the focus is on specific examples, but it is a very time-consuming method. Essays are also not very useful for evaluative purposes as their description of different employees' performance cannot easily be compared as there is no common standard.

Management by objectives
Management by objectives (MBO) is a management system designed to achieve organisational effectiveness by steering each employee's behaviour towards the organisation's mission. The MBO process includes goal setting, planning and evaluation, as illustrated in Figure 14.9.

Goal-setting is initiated by top management with the establishment of the organisational mission and strategic goals. The goal-setting process then cascades down the hierarchy of the organisation to the level of the individual employee. An employee's goals should represent outcomes that, when achieved, would contribute to the attainment of the organisation's strategic goals. In most instances, individual's goals are mutually set by employees and their supervisors, during which time performance management standards are set and time frames determined.

As they **plan**, employees and supervisors work together to identify potential obstacles to reaching goals, and devise strategies to overcome these obstacles. Regular meetings between the supervisor and employee take place to discuss the employee's progress to date and to identify any changes in goals necessitated by organisational circumstances.

In the final phase, the employee's success at meeting goals is **evaluated** against prior agreed-upon performance standards. The final evaluation, usually occurring annually, serves as a measure of the employee's performance effectiveness. MBO improves job performance by monitoring and directing behaviour as it serves as an effective feedback device which informs people of what is expected from them so that they can focus on achieving their goals.

The weaknesses of MBO are briefly summarised as the following:
- Although it focuses the employee's attention on goals, it does not specify the behaviours required to reach them.
- It tends to focus on short-term goals, which may be at the expense of long-term goals.
- The successful achievement of MBO goals my be partly dependent on factors outside the control of the employee.
- Employee standards vary from employee to employee, thus MBO provides no common basis for comparison.

Figure 14.9 Performance appraisal under the MBO programme

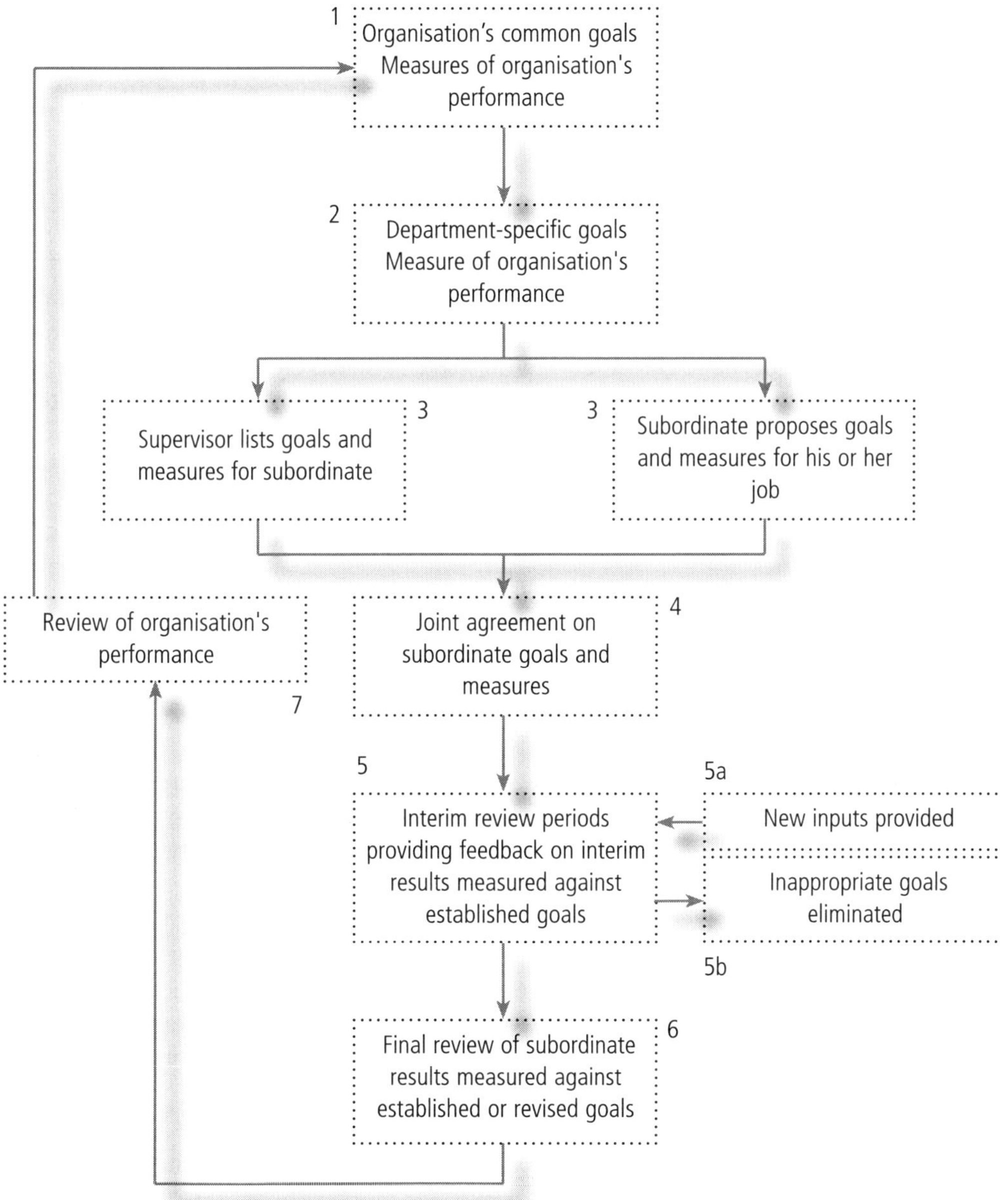

Source: Adapted from Sherman et al., 1966:325

- MBO often fails to gain user acceptance, as managers may feel it robs them of their authority, and employees dislike the performance pressures it places on them.

It is evident that many performance appraisal methods and tools can be applied when measuring the performance of employees, and the choice of instrument or method will depend upon the individual circumstances. It is accepted, however, that performance review should be developed using the employee's job description as the standard of measurement.

14.5.1.6 The appraisal interview

The most accurate and thorough appraisal will fail to produce growth in employees if the information gathered is not used appropriately. Therefore, one of the most important steps in the performance appraisal process is to discuss the appraisal with the individual during the appraisal interview. Many appraisal interviews have negative outcomes because the interview is used to focus only on the weaknesses, rather than looking at the strengths as well. Both parties in the appraisal process tend to be anxious before the interview, thus the appraisal interview is often an emotionally charged event as the supervisor finds it difficult to convey constructive criticism, and most people feel threatened and defensive in view of any form of criticism. The handling of such an interview should thus be well planned and managed to refrain from traumatising the individual employee.

The following guidelines have proven to work towards a situation where a fair and calm discussion of outcomes and expectations can take place. The given sequence of events leads to an easy progression of the feedback process (Kleiman, 2000:232–233; Marquis & Huston, 1996:414–417):

- **Inform employees** well in advance of the standards against which their performance will be measured and provide a copy of the performance appraisal instrument. Inform employees about the review interview a few days in advance and ask them to do a self-appraisal and to think about how well they have done and which problems they face.
- **Arrange a time and place** convenient to both parties, in a private comfortable place where there will be no interruptions, and be mentally and emotionally prepared for the discussion. Plan a seating arrangement that reflects collegiality rather than a power position and make every effort to make employees feel comfortable.
- **Start the interview** by greeting the employee warmly on a pleasant and informal note, but create the impression that you consider the interview discussion to be very important and that you have a sincere interest in his/her growth. Also make sure employees know precisely what the appraisal is used for and what the consequences are.
- **Review information** by starting off with the job requirements in the employee's job description. Ask the employee to comment on his/her progress since the last performance appraisal and allow ample opportunity for employees to discuss their performance, raise questions about the facts raised, and to add their own data and perceptions. Then review the ratings you have given the person by using a coaching approach throughout the process. Be prepared to state the

reasons for rating the employee as you did, and make use of documented evidence where possible.

- **Discuss the employee's performance** by starting with something positive and show the person you appreciate his/her successes. If the overall performance has not been satisfactory, due to new or long-standing problems, do not overwhelm him/her at the review session. If there are too many problems to be addressed, select the major ones. Conduct the interview in a non-directive and participatory manner, soliciting input from the employee throughout the process. Focus on the employee's performance and not on his/her personal characteristics.

  Rather than starting by stating the ratings you allocated to the employee, ask them for their own perceptions and personal ratings, these can then be discussed and adjusted if necessary to balance with the rater's assessment. Positive as well as negative feedback helps employees to gain a better understanding of their performance. Avoid generalities, either be positive or negative and provide explicit examples. Be straightforward and state concerns directly, otherwise the employee may be unsure of the significance of the supervisor's message.

  When giving negative feedback, do so in unemotional terms, be direct, never threaten, intimidate, or use status in any manner. The appraiser should not threaten the self-esteem of the employee as this will prevent the nurturing of a meaningful and constructive relationship between the supervisor and employee. Let the employee know that the appraiser is aware of his/her uniqueness, special interests and valuable contributions to the unit. Use a language and terminology understandable to both parties, without talking down to employees.
- **Discuss implications** by asking the employee to summarise what has been discussed in the meeting and then indicate how the performance appraisal results will affect employment decisions such as pay and promotion.
- **Set goals for improvement** by mutually discussing the problem areas and get the employee to set improvement goals, and the steps he/she needs to take to improve performance. Decide on how goals will be accomplished and evaluated, and what support is required. Set a follow-up date for the purpose of determining the employee's progress in meeting these goals. If specific long-term coaching needs have been identified, the supervisor should develop a follow-up plan to ensure that coaching takes place. Document the goals for further development that have been agreed upon by both parties.
- **End the interview** by indicating your availability for employees should they wish to further discuss the appraisal review at a later stage, especially if the review did not go well for them. Both the supervisor and employee need to sign the appraisal form even though this does not mean that the employee agrees with the assessment ratings. End the interview in a pleasant manner.

The performance appraisal review session is an important feedback tool, which is often difficult to handle but which is essential to complete the appraisal process.

Through the feedback provided on positive and negative aspects of an employee's performance, credit can be given where due and areas for development are identified enabling remedial action, support and guidance. Emphasis will now be given to the development of human resources.

14.5.2 Human resource development (HRD)

Human resource development comprises the procedures and processes that purposefully seek to provide learning activities to enhance the skills, knowledge and capabilities of people, teams and the organisation so that there is a change in action to achieve the desired outcomes.

HRD is an organisation's investment in the learning of its people, and acts as a powerful tool of its intentions. First, HRD implies that learning will be a strategic consideration in the organisation, focusing on longer-term benefits for both the employee and the organisation. Second, HRD acts as a triggering mechanism for the progression of other HRM policies that are aimed at recruiting, retaining and rewarding employees. As an investment in employee learning, HRD creates a primary internal market, and policies are aimed at progressively upgrading skills, thus reducing an organisation's dependency on external sources for skills. Third, if an organisation is seeking to engender the conditions whereby loyalty and commitment towards an organisation's aims can be encouraged, HRD carries the prospect of unleashing the potential that lies within all people, allowing employees to contribute to, and indeed, transform the strategy (Bratton & Gold, 2003:317).

14.5.2.1 Strategy and human resource development

A strong framework of HRM policy and systems is essential to the development and implementation of a HRD strategy. As many organisations find themselves suffering from overcapacity and competition in a stagnant market, the need arises to develop a strategy driven by restructuring, high investment in new technology, research and a cost-reduction target. In order to achieve the overall goals of a flexible, efficient and high-quality workforce, the following **components** and guidelines need to be considered in the development of an HRD strategy (Harrison, 1997:35–360):

- Continuous reduction in unit labour costs
- Elimination of demarcation barriers, improved rewards for employees, and complete harmonisation in terms of pay, terms and conditions of service
- New forms of work organisation to improve the work flow processes.

This HR strategy implies three **priorities** which should be considered when developing a HRD policy:

(1) To achieve a lean, high-quality and efficient workforce
(2) To ensure the workforce has the skills needed to operate the new technology
(3) To develop a workforce with high added value.

The HRD **goals** derived from these priorities could be to:
- Assist employees to achieve and apply the competencies required to operate more efficiently, and to adapt to the new culture necessary to meet the challenges of change
- Encourage and enable employees to work more effectively in teams
- Develop supervisors and managers who can manage teams effectively.

From these goals the following components could be contained in the subsequent HRD **strategy**:
- **Building an enhanced quality of basic skills in the workplace**. Employees who are willing and have the capability for learning the new skills would be offered the relevant training. Those unable, or who do not wish to do so, may be offered the opportunity to retire early.
- **Training for all geared to business needs**. Every employee should be given the opportunity to learn a new skill every year over the following number of years, and a reward system in addition to the annual pay negotiations should be devised.
- **Encouraging team work**. The aim should be to develop a new breed of supervisors who would operate differently from the way they had before and who could adapt quickly to new situations and challenges while meeting the targets of productivity and quality.

The goals and strategy for HRD formulated at corporate level focus on both short- and longer-term organisational needs. Taking into consideration the extent, complexity and changing nature of public issues and consequent challenges facing managers, management training and development are extremely important. Therefore a major HRD goal prioritises management development, as the organisation needs adaptable, flexible and innovative managers who can provide vision and leadership that will ensure full motivation and understanding in the rest of the workforce. Its imperative that managers learn quickly from experience, be sensitive to the external environment, be strategically minded and keen to discover new trends, challenges and information that will be relevant to the organisation's future course of action.

14.5.2.2 The training and development process

A formal training process is necessary to ensure appropriate and orderly training and development. Figure 14.10 illustrates the different steps in such a process. Training and development are the most common means of acquiring organisational knowledge and skills.

In order for training to be focused and appropriate, a needs analysis should be done at the organisational, job and individual levels to ascertain the real needs for training and development.

Figure 14.10 The basic training and development process

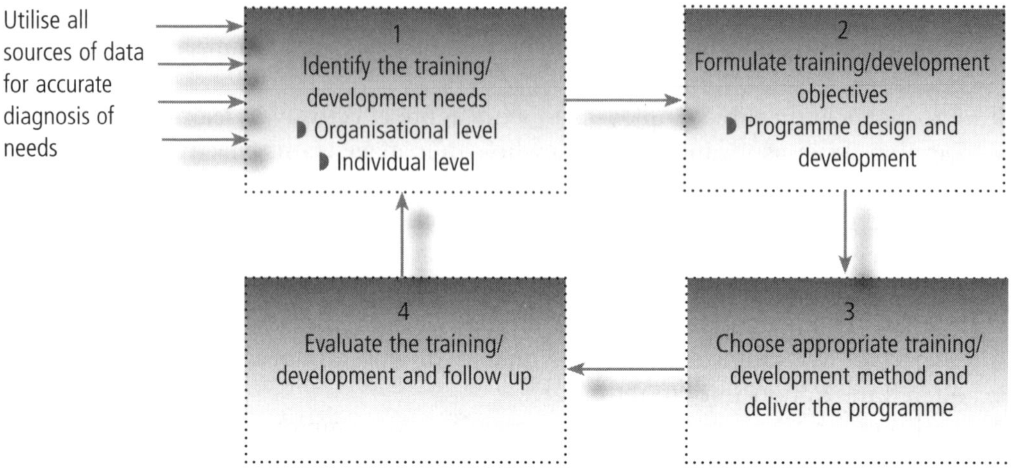

Source: Adapted from Amos et al., 2004:89

Identify training and developmental needs

A needs analysis can be done at different levels, using a variety of techniques such as questionnaires, interviews, performance appraisal, attitude surveys, observation or even complaints received from clients, delays in output, excessive maintenance costs or a high accident rate.

- **Organisational level**. The organisational needs analysis should translate the organisation's strategic goals into an accurate estimate of the demand for human resources, stipulating the knowledge, skills and abilities the organisation will need in future based on the strategic plan.
- **Job level**. The specific content of present or anticipated jobs is examined by means of the job analysis, taking into consideration deficiencies in knowledge and skills (job specification) to execute the tasks and responsibilities encompassed in the job description, at the minimum acceptable standards gleaned from the performance appraisal (Jackson & Schuler, 2000:359).
- **Individual level**. The common mechanism for identifying the learning needs of individual staff members is performance appraisal information, identifying any performance gaps which could be dealt with by relevant training and development.

Formulate training and developmental objectives

Training should always be done as a means to an end. Thus, formulation of clear measurable objectives, specifying the expected change in behaviour that the learning programme is supposed to bring about, are essential to overcome the performance gap of individual staff members. These outcomes should be formulated in terms of knowledge, skills behaviours and attitudes that need to be acquired for effective performance, enabling the assessment of the programme's effectiveness (Amos et al., 2004:91).

Select the appropriate method of training and development

The method of teaching is dependent on what to teach. Training and development can be offered either on-the-job by the supervisor, or off-the-job by in-house trainers or experts from outside the organisation. The manager must be aware of the various courses and programmes available in order to select or recommend the training that would best meet the training needs and objectives that have been identified and set. Herewith some examples of different types of training and development modes:

- **Lecture** is a structured presentation aimed at a group of learners and could be supplemented by videos, learning instruments or role-plays.
- **Tutorial** is a one-on-one structured instructional experience, building skills by demonstrating a procedure or utilisation of a piece of equipment.
- **Case study** is usually a written description of a real-life or fictitious situation prepared for instruction purposes.
- **Mentoring** enables the novice to work as an understudy to an experienced employee, who serves as a role-model but also looks out for the learner.
- **Role-play** assigns parts to trainees to play in a dramatised version of a case study or problem situation.
- **Apprenticeship training** provides an employee the opportunity to serve an apprenticeship for a specific trade, learning specific knowledge and skills in a structured manner.
- **In-basket training** is where the employee is presented with a number of documents typically found in his/her in-basket, and asked to deal with them.
- **Learning instruments** usually are in the form of a questionnaire or checklist used to create an awareness through identifying a learner's current level of skill or knowledge pertaining to a specific variable.
- **Buzz groups** consist of a small group of people, assembled to identify a problem(s), and to consider and select alternative solutions.
- **Simulation** attempts to create a real situation, in which the learner must deal with a matter or procedure typical of the simulated environment.
- **Panel discussions** consist of a structured or unstructured presentation on a topic, problem or issue by a group of three to ten people.
- **Videotape** is the use of a televised presentation to provide instruction, often in a form that mixes instruction with entertainment.
- **Computer-based instruction** takes on the form of an individualised programme through which the learner must progress at his/her own pace.
- **Private training consultants** provide training in different forms as mentioned above, but often utilise workshops to enhance an interactive milieu in which participation is encouraged (Amos et al., 2004:91–93; Gerber et al., 1998:456).

Evaluate the implemented programme

Assessment of the training programme is necessary to determine whether the training or development has been successful in meeting the set objectives. This can be achieved by asking the trainees for their opinion on the effectiveness of the intervention once the programme has been completed, by doing an analysis of the knowledge and skills acquired by attending the training session, or by assessing whether the individual's behaviour on the job has changed or improved as a result of the intervention.

14.5.3 Career management

Arnold (1997 in Bratton & Gold, 2003:214) views a career as the '... sequence of employment-related positions, roles, activities and experiences encountered by a person'. In the past, employees could look forward to a path of promotion that signified the development of their careers. However, many employees encountered obstacles to their visualised careers, such as lack of opportunities and support, and cultural and structural prejudices to career progress referred to as the glass ceiling.

At the beginning of the twenty-first century, globalisation, enhanced communication methods, transformation, downsizing, affirmative action and the subsequent decrease in loyalty all have an influence on how people see their career paths in the current labour market. The effect of these factors has been that especially younger people, and members of previously disadvantaged groups, do not see their careers in an appointment at a particular organisation, but rather as a constant endeavour searching for better opportunities, the wider world becoming their target/stage. For many people there has been a growing realisation to accept responsibility for their career development through the skills of employability and lifelong learning. Over a course of a person's working life, an individual might expect to work for a variety of different organisations in a variety of positions, so each person will need a range of skills, learning new ones, as and when they are required.

Career management is the process by which organisational career planning is implemented. Organisations have a vested interest in the careers of their employees as career planning and development programmes not only develop the individual but also enhance the person's job performance and thus the overall effectiveness of the organisation. Thus, each supervisor and manager in the organisation plays an important role in making the organisation's career planning programme work to the benefit of the institution and its employees. Career planning entails the steps of planning one's working life and contemplating the direction one wishes to take in being an employed person for the whole of one's employable life period. It involves evaluating abilities and interests, considering alternative career opportunities, establishing career goals, and planning practical development activities.

Specific systems, funding and guidelines for skills development have been established by legislation as noted earlier in this chapter, however, individuals and organisations can benefit from the following four career management skills (Ball, 1997 in Bratton & Gold, 2003:215):

- First is **optimising the situation**, through which circumstances are created that support career advances. This requires setting broad goals while anticipating future changes in the organisation's and one's life, as well as being in a position to respond. Mentoring and networking opportunities should be cultivated.
- Second is the process of **career planning**. In view of probable changes in work, individuals will need to learn how to review their skills and determine future learning requirements. This process may well be repeated a number of times during one's working life.
- By **engaging in personal development**, people will become life-long learners. This requires a measure of self-awareness, and self-evaluation, and taking into account one's transferable skills so that arising development opportunities can be fully utilised.
- Finally, there should be a **balance between work and personal time** as illustrated in Figure 14.11.

Figure 14.11 A model for career competencies

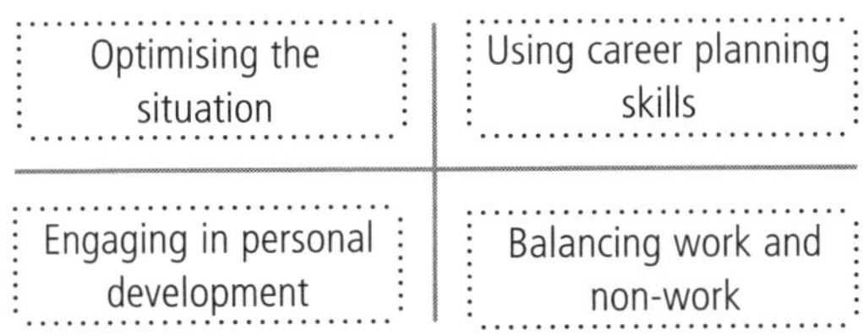

Source: Bratton & Gold, 2003:215

14.5.4 Supervision

Supervisory training is essential for first line managers to function to their maximum potential, especially if a good functional worker has been promoted to the level of supervisor without management experience. Apart from the technical skills, supervisors also require skills and knowledge to manage people effectively.

A supervisor is a person who has the authority to hire, direct, transfer, suspend, lay off, recall, promote, discharge, reward or discipline other employees (Gillies, 1994:602). The tasks of a supervisor entail inspecting another's work, providing guidance, support and feedback, evaluating performance and approving or correcting performance. The supervisor as a leader should direct the work of his/her personnel towards attaining the unit or departmental objectives. This includes planning, coordinating, instructing, guiding and regulating their activities. The work of subordinates should be monitored and they should be encouraged towards attaining the set standards of performance in all activities they perform.

In participatory management, supervision is facilitative rather than directive, as a knowledgeable supervisor inspects work in progress and acts timeously to correct inadequate performance before serious consequences develop. Supervisors and leaders are responsible for the implementation of management decisions and have legal obligations when getting work done through the efforts of others, they may, in fact, be liable for the negligence of others to whom they have delegated certain duties.

14.5.4.1 Criteria for selection of supervisors

According to Humphrey and Halse (1991 in Booyens, 2001:293), the criteria for selecting good supervisors are:

- A genuine liking for other people and an ability to recognise their strengths and weaknesses
- An ability to see mistakes as problems requiring solution rather than as reasons for apportioning blame
- Acceptance that workers probably know more about the functional processes than they themselves do
- An ability to counsel rather than to punish
- The ability to keep a unit on target without arousing resentment and antagonism
- A high degree of self-confidence
- A desire to develop personally and an ability to cope with change
- A marked ability to communicate fluently and clearly.

14.5.4.2 Skills and qualities of a supervisor

As the task of supervision relates to people, good interpersonal relations are a prerequisite for good working interaction, and it can therefore be expected that supervisors should have the following qualities and skills:

- Communicate effectively both laterally and vertically
- Set attainable standards
- Create and lead an effective work team, thus building team spirit and group cohesiveness
- Inspire a sense of responsibility and accountability in subordinates
- Consult employees and listen to what they have to say
- Be fair and objective, avoid bias and prejudice
- Help subordinates to achieve the desired goals, both work related and professionally
- Exhibit sound decision-making and problem-solving skills
- Investigate, identify and solve work problems using a participative management style
- Make logical decisions and be able to plan work and explain the underlying reasons for the decisions and plans
- Acknowledge good work and give credit and praise where its due
- Motivate the team to improve their productivity and quality of work
- Be caring, loyal and radiate mutual respect towards colleagues and subordinates
- Have integrity and be patient in nature
- Show sound, up-to-date knowledge and skills in the field of work being supervised.

The first-line supervisor is a valuable link in the participative management process, as he/she can truly provide day-to-day support and leadership to the subordinates in their communal quest for quality service delivery.

14.5.5 Motivation

Lower productivity, unsatisfactory output, stifled creativity, lost opportunities, and employees who are indifferent to their jobs are just a few of the symptoms of unmotivated people (Carrell et al., 2000:127). How to turn apathetic members of staff around, make people aware of quality again, and encourage innovative thinking are frequent challenges of line managers and motivated employees.

Motivation is a concept used to describe both the extrinsic conditions that stimulate certain behaviour and the intrinsic responses that make human beings the way they are. Intrinsic responses are sustained by sources of energy, termed motives, also described as needs, wants and drives. All living people have motives and their motivation is measured by observable or recorded behaviour. Unsatisfied needs encourage people to seek ways and means to meet these needs.

Different things motivate different people. Even though everybody in a group may behave in the same way, the individuals in the group may have different motives for their behaviour. When one considers the reasons why people work, it is obvious that the primary need is to earn a living and maintain a certain standard of living for themselves and their dependants. However, they also want (thus have a motive) to acquire self-esteem and identity, to achieve some status in a particular community, to associate with certain other people, and to experience a sense of competence, success, power, control and pride.

There are a number of motivational theories, these are categorised into two groups: **content theories** that focus on the factors that motivate people, and **process theories** that focus on the process of motivation. According to Herzberg's Two-Factor theory of motivation, the motivation of subordinates can be increased by modifying each job in order to increase people's demand for responsibility, autonomy and professional growth (Gillies, 1994:354).

14.5.5.1 Factors influencing motivation

It is expected that leaders should maximise subordinates' performance by enhancing their work motivation. Motivation is the force that energises behaviour, gives direction and tends to make people persist in their quest to meet their needs, even in the face of obstacles. Motivators are, to a large extent, specific to the individual.

Hellriegel and Slocum (1989:427) stipulate three sets of factors that influence motivation, namely individual traits, attributes of the job, and attributes of the job environment (organisational features). (These factors are reflected in Figure 14.12.)

- **Individual traits** refer to all the needs, values, attitudes and other factors that influence an employee's work.

Figure 14.12 Interaction between motivational factors

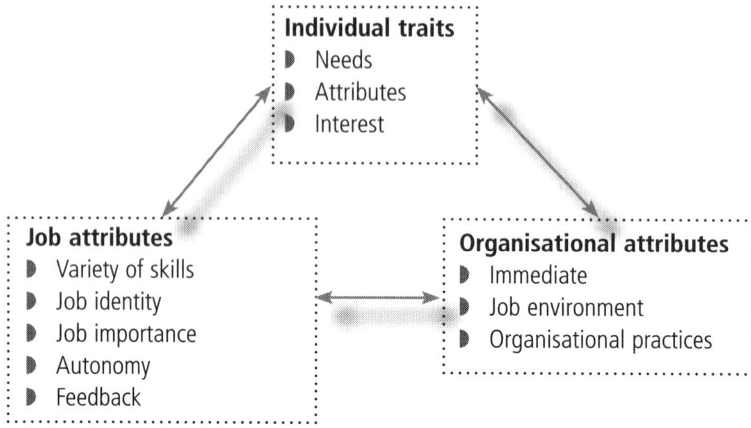

Source: Hellriegel & Slocum, 1989:429

- **Job attributes** encompass aspects such as autonomy, variety of skills, the significance of the job and the feedback that employees receive.
- **Organisational attributes** consist of the rules and regulations, staff policy, management practices, leadership style and remuneration system. The latter will motivate employees only if it is applied fairly and based on true performance measurement.

In order to motivate an employee as much as possible, the manager must know which needs the employee strives to satisfy through his/her job. It is assumed that an individual's **attitude** toward his/her job, and the variables related to the job, are related to work **motivation**. An attitude is a constant mental position or feeling about some event or environmental stimulus, while a motive is a need or desire that incites and directs an individual's actions. For example, a nurse with a strong need for belonging, would probably prefer team nursing (which entails working in close collaboration with other nurses), to primary nursing, which would require more independent, self-directed behaviour.

Several factors can be used by management to improve the motivation levels of healthcare employees, among others vision, goal setting, reinforcing quality work, appropriate awards, development programmes, career planning, delegating authority, flexible working hour schedules, sharing information, and participatory management. Job design is another aspect to be considered and will be briefly explained.

14.5.5.2 Motivational approach to job design

Job design is the process of combining tasks and responsibilities to form complete jobs and their relationships in an organisation. Job design determines the characteristics and qualities that make up the job. Should nurses at a hospital work rotating shifts, or is it always better to have the same staff on night duty? What happens after retrenchments, will the remaining personnel be expected to work harder in order to absorb the additional tasks? How can everybody work smarter? In view of the advanced communication technology, is it necessary for all employees to work from an office in the organisation? Questions such as these raise the issue of job design. Since existing jobs in most organisations have already been designed, either intentionally or spontaneously, the re-design of jobs becomes relevant (Jackson & Schuler, 2000:152) in the motivation of staff.

Job design is the manipulation of content, functions and relationships of jobs in a way that both accomplishes the organisational goals and personal needs of the individual. According to Carrell et al., (2000:133), modern management has established that the increased costs of employee absenteeism and turn-over, as well as decreased productivity and quality, may outweigh the advantages of highly specialised jobs. The challenge is therefore to balance the employee's human needs and the employer's economic goals.

In the motivational approach to job design, the purpose of job design is the application of motivational theories to the structure of work in order to improve satisfaction and productivity. The Hackman-Oldham theory is a well-established framework for designing jobs which people will find motivating and is called the **Job characteristics model** (as illustrated in Figure 14.13). This theory postulates that **three critical psychological states** are required to create high levels of motivation in the work place, they are:

(1) **Experienced meaningfulness** refers to whether employees perceive their work as being valuable and worthwhile.

Figure 14.13 The Hackman-Oldham job characteristics model

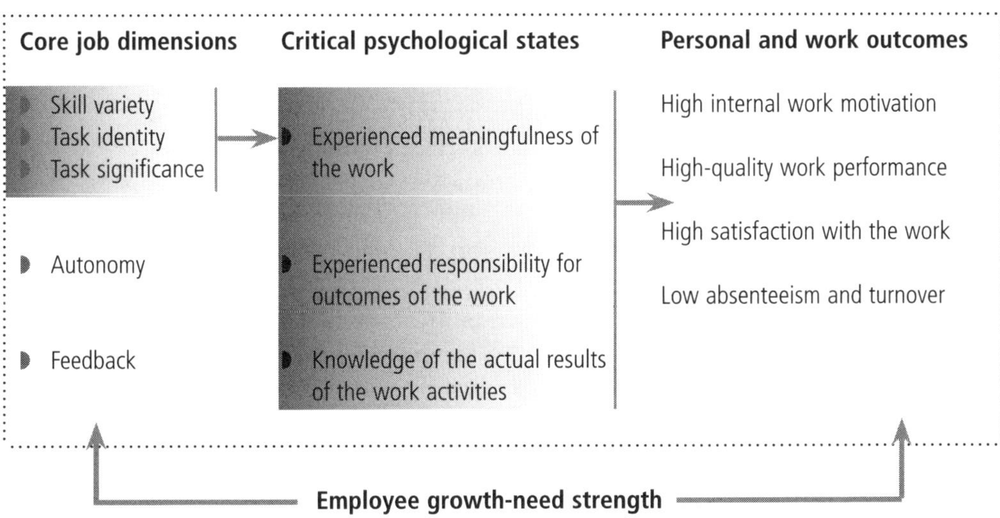

Source: Daft, 2000:554

(2) **Experienced responsibility** relates to whether employees feel personally responsible for the quantity and quality of their work.
(3) **Knowledge of results** pertains to the extent to which employees receive feedback about their work performance. (Jackson & Schuler, 2000:154–155)

These psychological states are affected by five **key job characteristics**:
(1) **Task identity** involves completing an identifiable section of work from beginning to end.
(2) **Task significance** is determined by the impact the job has on the goals or work of others in the organisation.
(3) **Skills variety** entails the many different work activities, skills and talents required by the job.
(4) **Feedback** is successful when the results provide the employee with clear and direct information on work performance.
(5) **Autonomy** is present when the job allows the job incumbent substantial freedom, independence and discretion in determining work procedures and scheduling.

Individuals with strong growth needs, which are evident in a desire for personal challenges, and a sense of accomplishment and learning, are more likely to respond positively to enriched jobs, than employees with weak growth needs.

Several different approaches can be used for designing jobs with a motivational core, they are generally classified as follows:

- **Job rotation** systematically moves employees from one job to another. Employees take turns in carrying out certain jobs, it makes provision for more flexible job allocations, reduces monotony and boredom, and makes it possible to distribute unpleasant jobs. Job rotation is often used as a training technique for new, inexperienced employees, and at higher organisational levels, rotation helps managerial generalists as it exposes them to several different positions.
- **Job enlargement** combines a series of tasks into a new, broader meaningful job to alleviate employee dissatisfaction with oversimplified jobs. Job enlargement provides job variety and a greater challenge for employees as it strives to create a 'whole' job for the employee to perform and complete. When a job is enlarged, either the tasks being performed are enlarged or several short tasks are given to one person. It does not increase the depth of the job, but enlarges it horizontally.
- **Job enrichment** incorporates high-level motivators into the work, such as job responsibility, recognition, opportunities for growth, learning and achievement. The responsibility of employees is increased by giving them more autonomy and control. In an enriched job, employees have control over the resources required for doing the job, make decisions on how the work should be done, experience personal growth, and set their own work pace. The enrichment takes place on a vertical plane.

Motivation implies at least the assessment of external and internal factors impacting on the individual, and necessitates an analysis of theory and strategy in an attempt to activate the individual to higher levels of motivation.

14.6 UNDERLYING DYNAMICS

During the processes of assessment and development of employees, several factors can have an impact on the outcomes envisaged. Although many of these factors are related to the organisation, the attitude and commitment of employees also play an important role. Some of the relevant issues are:

- The validity, credibility and trustworthiness of systems and processes in place, whether they provide consistent, fair and just appraisals
- The integrity, transparency and honesty of assessors and employees
- Whether feedback that is provided is constructive and guiding in nature
- The type of remedial action taken and subsequent follow-up procedures.

14.7 CONCLUDING STATEMENTS

The following concluding statements are relevant to performance management and human resources development:

- Performance management and HR development occur in the legal and professional-ethical context, in accordance with the business ownership of the particular healthcare organisation, with reference to the labour-related legislation, skills development and ethical codes of the different professions.
- The major role-players in the assessment and development of HR are the state, employers, supervisors, the employees and organised labour.
- The purpose of assessment and development of HR is to monitor, measure and evaluate individual performance in order to reward exceptional performance and to take remedial action if deficiencies are evident. This can be augmented by appropriate training and development as a means of achieving the organisational goals and simultaneously contribute to the personal and professional development of an individual employee.
- The process of assessment and development of HR encompasses the following: performance appraisal, training and development, career management, supervision and motivation.
- The employee performance appraisal is a sensitive and important part of the management process, requiring skill and confidence.
- Performance appraisals are used to determine how well employees are performing their jobs, using the job description as a standard of measurement from which specific criteria for assessment are developed.
- The performance appraisal process is guided by a number of principles but is also adversely affected by human errors made by the raters.

- There are many different types of appraisal tools, all of which have advantages and disadvantages.
- The employee must participate in the appraisal process and must view the appraisal as accurate and fair to serve the best purpose.
- MBO has the potential to increase productivity and commitment, but can also have a negative impact on both the employee and supervisor.
- Conducting the performance appraisal interview entails asking for self-assessment, inviting participation, expressing appreciation, minimising criticism, changing behaviour and not the person, focusing on solving problems, being supportive, establishing goals and regular follow-up.
- Showing genuine interest in the employee's growth and seeking his/her input during the interview will increase the likelihood of a positive outcome from the appraisal process.
- Human resource development implies that learning will be a strategic consideration in the organisation, focusing on longer-term benefits for both the employee and the organisation.
- The training and development process entails the steps of doing an assessment of learning needs, formulating training objectives, selecting the most appropriate method and finally evaluating the training programme for effectiveness in reaching the set objectives.
- Although organisations assist individuals with career planning and development, the responsibility for personal career planning and preparation has shifted towards the individual as employees tend to change jobs more frequently than in the previous century.
- Supervision is the process of striving for quality outputs in a work team and is achieved by means of monitoring, guiding and supporting staff in the quest for goal accomplishment.
- Motivational ideas are illustrated in job design which can include approaches such as job rotation, job enlargement and job enrichment. Managers can change the structure of work to meet employees' high-level needs and aspirations.
- Various underlying dynamics, such as the validity of the systems and processes in place, the integrity of assessors and employees, the knowledge of employees, feedback, remedial action and follow-up are relevant.

« Self-assessment

(1) Develop six observable and measurable performance standards suitable to your position in the organisation where you are employed.
(2) Discuss the guidelines that performance appraisals should meet in order to be legally defensible and identify those that are difficult to implement.
(3) Do you think employees should have a greater say in appraising themselves and one another?
(4) Visit www.balancedscorecard.org/ to ascertain how the Balanced Score Card can be implemented as a performance measurement framework.
(5) Access the South African Board for Personnel Practice (SABPP) at www.sabpp.co.za for a list of consultants registered as practitioners with the SABPP and their specialities.
(6) Examine the HRM web link www.uea.ac.uk/ccen/employability/welcome.htm and make a list of activities you can embark upon to make yourself more employable, also determine what the skills are of life-long learning.
(7) A survey of teachers found that two of the most important rewards were the belief that their work was important and a feeling of accomplishment. Is this consistent with the Hackman-Oldham's job characteristics model?

15 Fair labour practice

KEY CONCEPTS

Approaches to labour relations
Participants to the labour relationship
Communication and joint consultation
Participation and involvement
Collective bargaining
Industrial action
Dispute resolution
Policies, procedures and practices
Negotiation
Grievances and disputes
Discipline
Retrenchment

SPECIFIC OUTCOMES

After studying this chapter, you should be able to:

- Interpret the legal and professional-ethical **context** of fair labour practice with reference to public and private (type of business ownership) healthcare organisations and their relevant healthcare practitioners or clinicians in terms of the following legislation:
  - Constitution of the Republic of South Africa, 1996 (Act 108 of 1996)
  - Labour Relations Act, 1995 (Act 66 of 1995)
  - Basic Conditions of Employment Act, 1997 (Act 75 of 1997)
  - Occupational Health and Safety Act, 1993 (Act 85 of 1993)
  - Skills Development Act, 1998 (Act 97 of 1998)
  - Skills Development Levies Act, 1999 (Act 9 of 1999)
  - Employment Equity Act, 1998 (Act 55 of 1998)
  - The Compensation for Occupational Injuries and Diseases Act, 1993 (Act 130 of 1993)
  - Unemployment Insurance Act, 2001 (Act 63 of 2001)
- Identify and describe the **role-players**, such as the state, employers, employees and organised labour, and interpret their roles and responsibilities relating to labour relations in a healthcare organisation

- Analyse and debate the **purpose** of fair labour practice in the context of a healthcare organisation
- Analyse and debate the **process** of human resources management in the context of a healthcare organisation, with specific reference to the applicable labour-related perspectives, processes and practices
- Debate the **underlying dynamics** that could impact on the labour relations in a healthcare organisation, with specific reference to management's role and integrity, policies and procedures, the commitment of employees, and the objectives of trade union officials.

15.1 INTRODUCTION

The term labour relations refers to the relationship between people who work and those for whom they work, and thus pertains to the institution of job regulation. Labour relations are a set of human resource practices that seek to secure commitment and compliance with organisational goals and standards through the consideration and involvement of employees in decision-making and by managerial disciplinary action (Bratton & Gold, 2003:357).

The context of labour relations is regulated by specific labour-related legislation, which affects all parties in the tripartite relationship of the three main role-players. Perspectives affect the way both the employer and employees view the labour situation, and important aspects to consider in this regard are the approaches to labour relations, concepts and values, individualism versus collectivism, rights and responsibilities, as well as integrity and trust. Labour relations processes are influenced by concepts such as communication and consultation, participation and involvement, collective bargaining, industrial action and dispute resolution. One of the fundamental issues in labour relations is that both sides will come to the bargaining table to negotiate. In fact, it is mandated by law in South Africa, and both unions and management are required to negotiate in good faith during collective bargaining endeavours.

Workplace practices are best regulated by written and communicated policies and procedures that convey consistent and fair guidelines for performance and behaviour. This is especially appropriate for the handling of grievances, disputes, discipline and retrenchment for operational reasons.

This chapter will highlight the following components (see visual presentation in Figure 15.1):

- The **context** of labour relations management refers to the legal and professional-ethical environment.
- The **purpose** of sound labour relations is to deal with employees in such a way that they feel comfortable and committed to work towards achieving the goals of the organisation.
- The different **role-players** in labour relations have specific reference to the state, employers, employees and organised labour.

- The **process** of fair labour practice is divided into the perspectives, processes and practices of labour relations.
- The **underlying dynamics** impacting on fair labour practice in a healthcare organisation refer to management's role and fair administration of policy and procedures, the employees' commitment, as well as the objectives of the trade unions.

Figure 15.1 Visual presentation of labour relations in a healthcare organisation

Context	Constitution of the Republic of South Africa, 1996 (Act 108 of 1996) Labour Relations Act, 1995 (Act 66 of 1995) Basic Conditions of Employment Act, 1997 (Act 75 of 1997) Occupational Health and Safety Act, 1993 (Act 85 of 1993) Skills Development Act, 1998 (Act 97 of 1998) Skills Development Levies Act, 1999 (Act 9 of 1999) Employment Equity Act, 1998 (Act 55 of 1998) The Compensation for Occupational Injuries and Diseases Act, 1993 (Act 130 of 1993) Unemployment Insurance Act, 2001 (Act 63 of 2001)
Purpose	Management to consult with employees and their representatives Set relevant policies and procedures Ensure fair and consistent treatment of all employees Deal with labour-related problems timeously Encourage transparent behaviour by all parties
Role-players	State Employers Employees Organised labour
Process	Perspectives on labour relations Processes Practices
Underlying dynamics	Availability of labour-related policies and procedures Management's role and integrity in dealing with HR Employee's commitment to adhere to rules Objectives of trade unions

15.2 CONTEXT

Employment relations have undergone major changes over the past two decades. An adversarial race-based dualistic system evolved from labour legislation in 1924 excluding trade union rights for black people. Inclusive bargaining councils were fostered through the Labour Relations Act, 1995 (Act 66 of 1995) and black unions grew to over 3 million members in 2001, from less than 10% of the formal labour sector workforce in the late 1970s (Kamoche et al., 2004:6). The largest unions are affiliated to union federations such as the Congress of South African Trade Unions (COSATU) and the National Council of Unions (NACTU).

The Constitution of South Africa, 1996 (Act 108 of 1996) stipulates that employees have the right to fair labour practice and spells out various rights of workers, employers, trade unions and employers' organisations (Rautenbach & Malherbe, 1998:17).

The Labour Relations Act, 1995 (Act 66 of 1995) (LRA) sought to bring employment law in line with the Constitution (Act 108 of 1996) and ratified Conventions of the International Labour Organisation in doing so. The Act strives to give constitutional rights, allowing freedom of association, permitting employees to form unions, the right to fair labour practices and the right to strike for collective bargaining purposes. It further seeks to promote employee participation in decision-making through workplace forums and employee consultation and joint decision-making on certain issues. This Act established labour and labour appeal courts, and the Commission for Conciliation, Mediation and Arbitration (CCMA). (Refer to Figure 15.2 for an illustration of South Africa's labour relations system guided by the LRA.) The CCMA handles both procedural and distributive or substantive justice in considering the fairness of a wide range of matters related to labour relations.

Several other Acts also contribute to the regulation of the employment relationship and situation:

- The **Basic Conditions of Employment Act, 1997 (Act 75 of 1997)** provides for establishing minimum standards of employment. These conditions cover areas such as the designated working hours, leave, employment and remuneration particulars to termination regulations.
- The new **Unemployment Insurance Act, 2001 (Act 63 of 2001)** and the **Unemployment Insurance Contributions Act, 2002 (Act 4 of 2002)** have brought sweeping changes to the statutory scheme of unemployment insurance. More workers are now covered by this legislation, the method of collecting contributions and calculating benefits has changed, the consequences of non-compliance with these Acts are more severe, and a new dispute resolution system has been introduced.
- The **Occupational Health and Safety Act, 1993 (Act 85 of 1993) (OHSA)** covers almost all areas of employment and the use of machinery. The OHSA does not aim only to cover the health and safety of employees, but also regulates for members of the general public who may be affected.
- The **Compensation for Occupational Injuries and Diseases Act, 1993 (Act 130 of 1993) (COIDA)** provides for the compensation of employees who are injured in accidents that occur during their normal course of employment or who contract occupational diseases. Benefits are paid in three categories, namely temporary disability, permanent disability and to dependants of employees who have died as a result of their injuries or illness.

Figure 15.2 South Africa's labour relations system

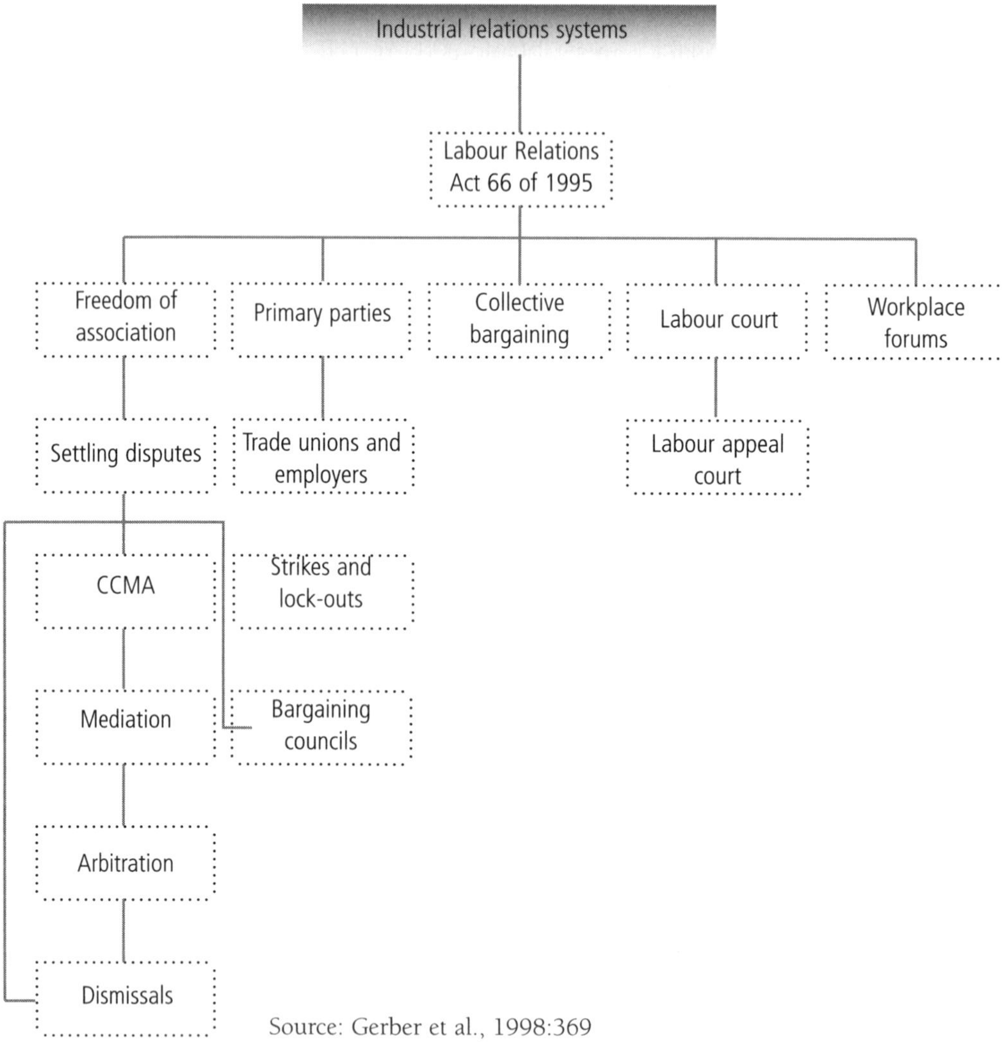

Source: Gerber et al., 1998:369

- The purpose of the **Employment Equity Act, 1998 (Act 55 of 1998) (EEA)** is to achieve equity in the workplace by promoting equal employment opportunity and fair treatment in employment through the elimination of unfair discrimination, and by implementing affirmative action measures by designated employers.

A key challenge in employment relations is the need to move from a legacy of adversarial relationships to workplace cooperation in order to compete successfully in the market place. There is increasingly an unclear distinction between employment relations and HRM. According to Kamoche, Debrah, Horwitz & Muuka (2004:7) the new agenda extends beyond the traditional collective bargaining items and adversarial dismissal disputes, to organisational transformation, performance improvement, human resources development and employee benefits. Trade unions have become more willing to engage employers around these issues. Finding an acceptable balance between equity and workplace justice imperatives on the one hand, and HR and employment strategies enhancing competitiveness on the other, is a vital challenge for managers and unions.

15.3 PURPOSE

In order to ensure sound labour relations, and to minimise any disruption of service delivery, management needs to be proactive in creating timeous opportunities for employee representatives and themselves to negotiate and develop the necessary policies and procedures to guide the management of human resources and labour-related issues in their place of work. In doing so, agreement is reached on how both parties will handle specific aspects/issues when they arise, what communication channels to follow and what measures can be afforded to deal with the conflict that is inevitable in any relationship. Commonality and conflict constitute the two poles of interaction in the labour relationship. Thus, the parties can either cooperate and engage in participative processes or rely on the use of power and collective bargaining, although these processes are not mutually exclusive. Also, the attention may continually shift between the individual and collective group. The manner of interaction will be largely determined by the interactive effect of custom and tradition, legal determination, mutual agreement and ethical considerations, among the most important are integrity, trust and concepts of fairness (Bendix, 1996:2).

15.4 ROLE-PLAYERS

The labour relationship is considered an open system and has been known to consist of three role-players, namely the state, employers and employees, with an interplay between employment relations and other forces and variables such as social, economic, political and technological systems (see Figure 15.3). Nel (2002:10–12) is of the opinion that customers and competitors should also be brought into the equation as no organisation can exist without the necessary support from customers making use of its services or products. Similarly, competitors play a significant role, if they can deliver new or alternative products preferred by the customers, this will impact on the employer and employee role players.

- The **state** provides a statutory controlled framework by means of its legislation and policies, in which the relative power of employers and employees is balanced, enhancing constructive interaction. The overall aim of government is to encourage societal justice, institutionalise conflict and facilitate cooperation and labour's participation in a democratic society in order to ensure prosperity for the country's people.

Figure 15.3 Parties to the labour relationship

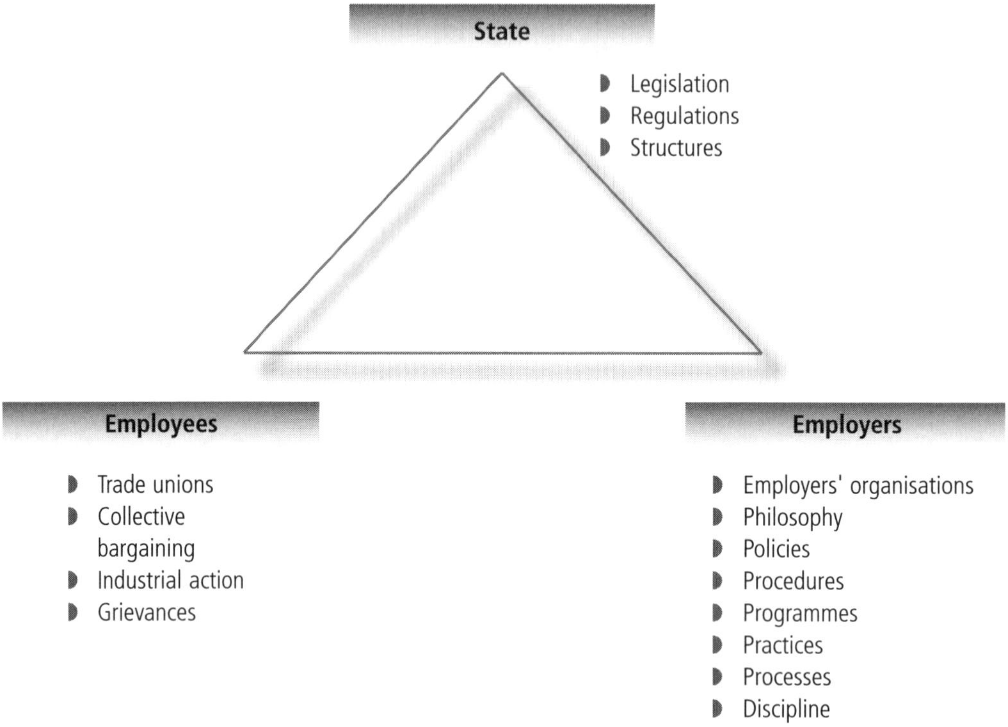

The government is promoting a form of societal corporatism through structures such as the National Economic Development and Labour Council (NEDLAC), which serve as a means whereby the state, employers and employees can coordinate their interests through agreements. The purpose is to transform the employment relationship from an adversarial relationship, where employers and their employees tend to constantly be in conflict, to a more cooperative, democratic relationship in which both parties can work together as partners to achieve common objectives (Amos et al., 2004:293).

- The **employer** is represented by management. The latter is responsible for protecting the interests of the employer or owners of the organisation. Managers are given the authority and responsibility to manage the organisation in such a way that the needs of customers are met and consequently, the owners receive the required return on their investments.

  Employers in similar industries can join forces to be represented by employers' associations. The creation of Business South Africa aims to combine the majority of employer associations into a single umbrella federation in order to represent employer interest at macro-level. An example of an employer association is the South African National Security Employers' Association (SANSEA), which operates in the security industry.

- The **employees** are often represented by trade unions, as a means of balancing the power between the employer and employees. A **trade union** is a collection of employees in a particular organisation, profession, industry, or trade who are united for the purpose of representing their interest both in the workplace and society. Trade unions are legally instituted by the Labour Relations Act, 1995 (Act 66 of 1995) and strive to protect their members by improving their conditions of service through collective bargaining. They also provide a means to express their members' views on societal matters outside the limits of the work environment.

  Salamon (1992:314) identifies the following three major functions of trade union activity:
  (1) **Mutual insurance** includes the provision of friendly society benefits in the event of sickness, unemployment, industrial action and so forth.
  (2) **Collective bargaining** entails the negotiation of terms and conditions of employment direct with employers on behalf of their members.
  (3) **Legal enactment** pertains to the lobbying for legislation supportive to their members' interests.

According to Barker (2003:321), trade unions in South Africa are probably no longer seen as a vehicle for liberation and a weapon against oppression, and even though they will remain politicised, they will most certainly focus more on workplace and socio-economic issues in future. Challenges facing trade unions include lower membership growth rates, the loss of leadership to national and local government, the plight of unemployment versus demands for higher wages, global economy issues, and protecting job security in the face of transformation, downsizing and restructuring (Amos et al., 2004:296).

15.5 PROCESS

Organisations are composed of sectional groups that have different and divergent interests, and whose expectations, perceptions and attitudes are the product of both social and organisational factors and differences. Any consensus between the participating groups in respect of their need to establish and maintain institutions, processes and rules to regulate their relationship requires all the parties to be prepared to cooperate and compromise in resolving problems and issues between them. The management of labour relations is based on certain perspectives, values and interactive processes that facilitate participation and shared decision-making. Following is an outlay of the components dealt with in this chapter (refer to Figure 15.4).

15.5.1 Perspectives

The subject matter of labour relations may be presented in many different ways. It is apparent, however, that this field of study has a multi-disciplinary nature and encompasses complex relationships. The different perspectives introduce a range of

Figure 15.4 Visual respresentation of components relevant to fair labour practice

Perspectives	◗ Approaches to labour relations ◗ Concepts and values in labour relations
Labour relations processes	◗ Communication and joint consultation ◗ Employee participation and involvement ◗ Collective bargaining ◗ Industrial action ◗ Dispute resolution
Labour-related practices	◗ Policies, procedures and practices ◗ Negotiation ◗ Grievances ◗ Discipline

concepts and approaches that are central to understanding the true meaning of labour relations and the management thereof.

15.5.1.1 Approaches to labour relations

Labour relations refer to a specialist area of organisational management which is concerned with a particular set of phenomena associated with regulating the human activity of employment. The way in which both management and the employees perceive this field as frame of reference determines to a large extent how specific labour-related issues are approached and analysed and how others are expected to behave and what means are adopted to modify their behaviour.

There are basically three major approaches to employment relations (Salamon, 1992:30–31):

(1) The **unitary perspective** emphasises the organisation as a coherent and integrated team which is unified by a common purpose, values, interests and objectives shared by all members of the organisation. Management's role in the unitary perspective can encompass either an authoritarian or paternalistic style. Management's prerogative is regarded as legitimate, rational and accepted, and any opposition to it is considered to be irrational. The underlying assumption of this approach is therefore that the organisational system is in harmony, and conflict is perceived unnecessary and unusual. Trade unions are regarded as an intrusion into the organisation from outside which competes with management for the loyalty of employees.

(2) The **pluralistic perspective** views the organisation as an amalgamation of separate, homogeneous groups, with divergent interests, objectives and leaders, over which management attempts to maintain some kind of dynamic equilibrium. The pluralistic perspective acknowledges the existence of conflict in all relationships, but emphasises cooperation between the parties. The inherent assumption is

that the organisation is in a permanent state of dynamic tension resulting from the inherent conflict of interests between the different groups and requires to be managed through a variety of roles, institutions and processes. Conflict is seen as both rational and inevitable but it is realised that destructive conflict should be avoided to ensure the continued existence of the organisation. There has to be acceptance of the need for shared decision-making between management and employee representatives. The pluralistic perspective acknowledges that it is legitimate for employees to combine in formal organisations such as trade unions in order to influence management and achieve their objectives.

(3) The **Marxist perspective** concentrates on the nature of society surrounding the organisation and considers group/class conflict as a source of societal change. Group conflict arises due to the disparity in the distribution of and access to economic power in the society. The nature of society's social and political institutions is derived from this economic disparity and reinforces the dominant position of the establishment group. Social and political conflict in whatever form is an expression of the underlying economic conflict in the society. The Marxist perspective views the growth of trade unionism as an inevitable employee response to capitalism.

15.5.1.2 Concepts and values in labour relations

It is argued that the most important issues and debates in labour relations centre not only on the conflicting relationship of the participants, but also focus on concepts such as fairness versus equity, power versus authority, trust versus integrity, and individualism versus collectivism. The differing perceptions of concepts such as what is good or bad and right or wrong provide the underlying tension in the scope of industrial relations, bringing about much uncertainty and misunderstanding. Salamon (1992:58–73) clarifies the concepts described below to enable a better understanding of their role in labour relations.

Fairness and equity

The concepts of fairness and equality are linked, as anything that causes or sustains inequality may be considered to be unfair. Fairness is a relative and variable concept with which to question the conduct of human relationships. Application of fairness can be construed as that there should be reasonable reciprocity or balance between the parties concerned during an exchange. Fairness can suggest that a particular exchange is consistent with other similar exchanges, or it could imply equality of treatment and consideration in the conduct of different relationships, or the same relationship over time.

Power and authority

Power, and the imbalance of power, plays a central role in labour relations. The concepts of power and authority are inextricably linked in practice, as authority is achieved through power and the reverse is also true. Power is the ability to control or impose a situation or persons by directing and regulating the circumstances. Power is also the ability to influence and thereby secure some modification in another party's decision or action. Power is used for a purpose but is exercised over people, the sources of power should thus be identified in the employment relationship.

- **Legitimate power** is derived from the individual's position in the organisation's hierarchical structure, this position is formally designated as containing superior direction or regulation of others.
- **Reward power** is derived from having influence or control over rewards sought by employees, such as promotion, desired assignments or formal acknowledgement of accomplishments.
- **Coercive power** entails having the ability and authority to inflict some punitive measure against another. This could be in the form of disciplinary action or withholding certain privileges.
- **Expert power** is derived from an individual's knowledge, skills and information that is considered to be superior to those of others, it could be linked to the employment role occupied by the person or their personal attributes.
- **Referent power** is based on a person's attractiveness or appeal influencing others to defer in their decisions and opinions in accordance with the power figure's views.

Individualism and collectivism

The freedom of the individual to choose and make decisions in respect of his/her conduct and life is considered a fundamental right in a democratic society. However, there is no such thing as total freedom to do as one wishes. Individualism and the consequent freedom a person has, can only be acceptable if it is expressed within the bounds of responsibility, and does not interfere with the rights and freedom of others. An important issue to consider is whether or not the act of joining an organisation voluntarily relinquishes the individual's freedom.

A collective basis to the employment relationship exists because it meets certain needs of both management and employees. Management plans, organises and implements procedures and strategies while each employee fits in this systemised arrangement of tasks, roles and operations. The fact that the individual is a member of a group, which is subject to the same conditions of employment and controls, means that for most, any improvement in their personal situation can only be achieved by improving the group's situation – thus individualism has to be replaced by collectivism.

Rights and responsibilities

A right is defined as a just or legal claim or title, or as that which a person is entitled to due to the law, tradition or nature, such as a right to freedom of speech. However, such freedom may not impinge on the rights or freedom of others. A fundamental rights issue in labour relations is management's prerogative (exclusive right or privilege) to manage the organisation.

The term responsibility is explained as the duty, obligation, burden or control over something, thus requiring the employee to be accountable in terms of the given responsibility. It must be noted that a responsibility may either be generated internally from within the individual's own personal perceptions and beliefs, or it may arise from the external expectations of others.

Integrity and trust

The conduct of the personal relations which underpin labour relations is very much concerned with the values of integrity and trust, whether it is between employer and employee, employee and supervisor, between shop steward and member, full-time official or manager or between negotiators.

Integrity must be defined in terms of the individual acting in accordance with his/her personal values and beliefs (such as Marxism or capitalism) rather than in terms of the individual acting according to some universally accepted code of conduct. The essential quality of integrity (honesty) is that the individual's words and actions should be seen by others to coincide and express a consistent set of values. If personal integrity is compromised then the trust and respect of others will be lost.

Trust is established between people and not organisations. Interpersonal trust exists where the individuals have confidence in, and feel able to rely on, one another, and not to seek to harm one another, either in an active or passive manner. In labour relations, trust does not require that individuals be totally open and frank with one another because of the adversarial relationship in which it is perceived that each person seeks to gain the maximum in a situation where they are competing for resources. Instead, the establishment of trust requires the individual not to subvert the other's position or relationship with third parties, to keep his/her word and agreements, to keep confidences or off-the-record information as such, and especially, to accept the legitimacy of the other's role and objectives. It should be acknowledged that trust is difficult to establish but easy to lose, and because it is based on interpersonal relationships between individuals it is not easy to transfer from one role incumbent to another.

15.5.2 Labour relations processes

Labour relations are of special importance to human resource managers, as they are often the people who have to ensure that the appropriate policy, procedures and processes are put in place. Communication is considered the conveying of information between people and is clearly an essential and continuous element of labour relations. It is central to processes such as joint consultation and collective bargaining, but is also essential for the establishment of policies, strategies and decisions during which employee participation and involvement play an important part in determining ways to deal with, among others, dispute resolution and industrial action.

Figure 15.5 The labour relations process

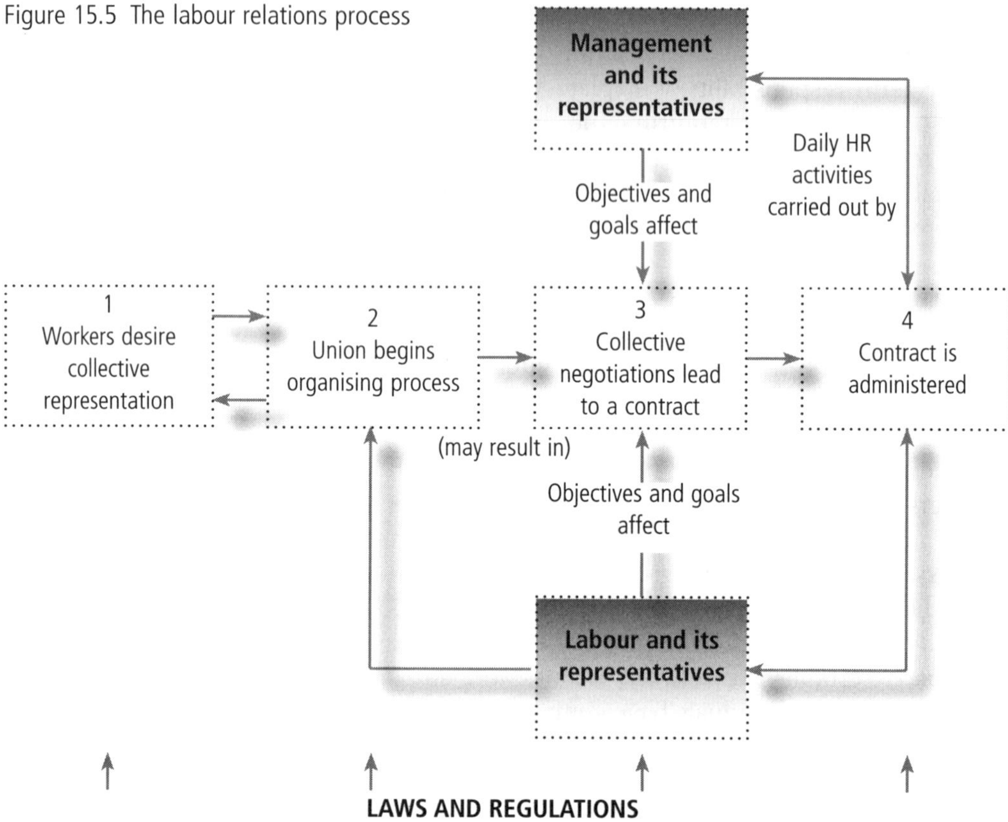

Source: Amended from Sherman, Bohlander & Snell, 1996:616

Individually, employees may be able to exercise relatively little power in their relations with the employer. The treatment and benefits employees receive depend in large part on how their employers view their worth in the organisation. If they feel they have been treated unfairly they could either quit or organise and bargain with the employer, collectively initiating the labour relations process. Figure 15.5 illustrates the logical sequence of four events in this process, namely, workers' desire for collective representation, an organising campaign by the union takes off, collective negotiations lead to an agreement in the form of a contract and eventually the contract is administered.

15.5.2.1 Communication and joint consultation

While **communication** is an inherent facet of all aspects of labour relations, it is specifically applied in the direct conveying of information from management to the union or employees, and vice versa, about arrangements for joint consultation and collective bargaining.

It is important that organisations should create an adequate system of internal communication. However, the two parties in the work environment have different views about the purpose of communication. Whereas management strives to provide information so that employees are informed about the organisation's goals, problems and position on certain matters, trade unions regard the acquiring of information as a means of strengthening their position in respect of the processes of collective bargaining and joint decision-making in the organisation (Salamon, 1992:283).

Problems in the work environment are sometimes attributed to poor or inadequate communication between the different parties. However, it should be noted that the significance of communication as the cause of problems and disagreements between management and employees is sometimes overrated, as communication cannot in itself remove conflict of interest and values.

Joint consultation can be defined as the process upon which management bases its identification of issues about which it is willing to seek the opinion of its employees, but retains the right to make the final decision. Marchington et al., 1992 (in Nel, 1997:32) consider joint decision-making as '... a mechanism for managers and employee representatives to meet on a regular basis, in order to exchange views, to utilise members' knowledge and expertise, and to deal with matters of common interest which are not the subject of collective bargaining'. Important characteristics of joint consultation should be management's sincerity in considering the criticisms and proposals of the employees, to earnestly consider their own proposals before finalising decisions or implementation, and that they should provide reasons for not accepting the views and proposals made by the employee representatives.

The purposes of joint consultation can be listed as follows:
- A means to improve efficiency in the organisation
- The creation of labour harmony between management and employees
- An avenue towards labour democracy in the organisation
- A grievance forum (Salamon, 2002:297–299).

15.5.2.2 Employee participation and involvement

A distinction is made between employee participation and involvement even though both concepts seek to accommodate and utilise the knowledge and skills of employees. Figure 15.6 indicates the different dimensions of employee involvement.

Anstey (1997:30) defines **worker participation** as a process that recognises the right of employees individually and collectively to be involved with management in areas of organisational decision-making beyond those usually associated with collective bargaining. It thus builds on a management philosophy and style that recognise the need and rights of employees to influence and be involved in work-related decisions that affect them. Decision-making during the participative process is affected by three interrelated elements, namely influence, interaction and information sharing. For employee participation to be meaningful, all the relevant information

Figure 15.6 Dimensions of employee involvement

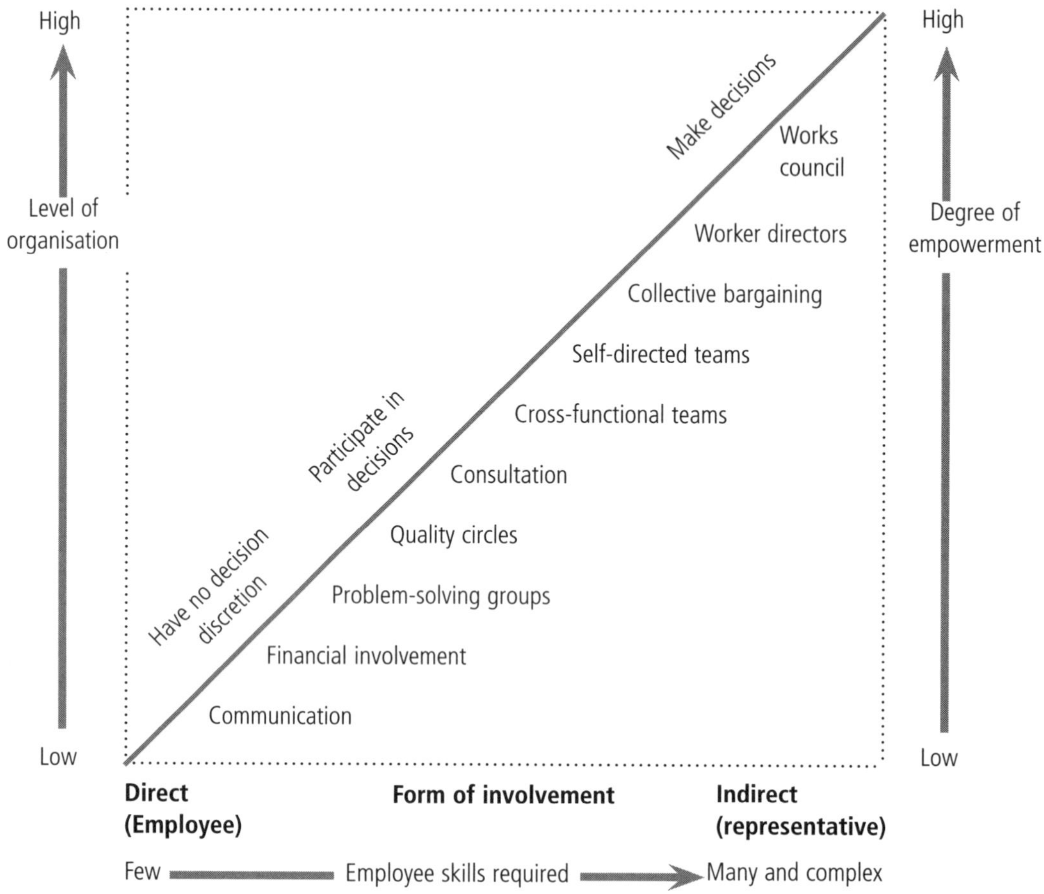

Source: Bratton & Gold, 2003:362

must be available, consultation about changes should occur and personal involvement in the decision-making process is required (Nel, 2002:219).

Employee involvement is considered the means used to acquire the co-operation and commitment of the workforce pertaining to the common interests they share with management. Salamon (1992:342) defines employee involvement as '... measures introduced by management intended to optimise the utilisation of labour and at the same time secure the employee's identification with the aims and needs of the organisation'.

Ways of enhancing employee participation and involvement include:

- **Job enrichment programmes**, where the employee is provided with the opportunity to extend the depth and width of his/her work tasks
- **Work place forums** instituted by the Labour Relations Act, 1995 (Act 66 of

1995), are structures comprising representatives of employees to promote the interests of all employees in the workplace

- **Employee representation** on departmental or management boards, supervisory committees or work councils in addition to their functional responsibilities
- **Quality circles** are workers' discussion groups, consisting of six to ten employees from the same section in the organisation. They meet regularly to identify, analyse, investigate, evaluate and consider issues pertaining to the outputs of their section and make recommendations for improvement
- **Joint consultation committees** usually consist of a number of experienced managers and employees who are elected to represent the other employees on relevant matters (see Figure 15.6 for a more extensive illustration of ways to involve employees).

15.5.2.3 Collective bargaining

Collective bargaining is a form of joint regulation that has institutionalised conflict and enables trade unions to represent employees to bargain on their behalf with representatives of the employer about all aspects of the employment contract. Salamon (1992:309) defines collective bargaining as a method of determining terms and conditions of employment that utilises the process of negotiation and agreement between representatives of management and employees. It is thus a formal channel through which the differing interests of management and employees may be resolved on a collective basis.

The essential characteristic of collective bargaining is that employees do not bargain individually and on their own behalf, but do so through their representatives for the collective good of the employee group. This requires that employees must be able to identify a commonality of purpose, and organise and act in unison, while the employer, in the form of management, must be prepared to recognise their organisation and accept the fact that they now deal with the employees collectively and no longer on an individual basis with regard to certain matters.

The right to collective bargaining is protected by the Labour Relations Act, 1995 (Act 66 of 1995), and in particular provision is made for sectoral level collective bargaining as the desired method of setting wages and conditions of employment.

15.5.2.4 Industrial action

During the conduct of labour relations, sanctions can be imposed by either party to illustrate its discontent with goals, intentions or actions of the other side, or to force the other party to relinquish its position during the negotiation process and move closer to that of the party imposing the sanction.

Industrial action can be described as any temporary suspension of normal working activities which is initiated unilaterally by either the employees, usually by means of their trade unions, or management with the aim of exerting pressure in the collective bargaining relationship. The use or threat of industrial action is a controversial issue, yet it plays a critical role in the display of power by influencing the employer-employee relationship and the outcome of any specific negotiation process. Industrial action is the ultimate power of trade union officials and their rank and file members to disrupt production, or service delivery, thus, by the withdrawal of labour, management is prevented from ignoring their requests.

Sanctions may be of an individual or collective nature. An employer imposes individual sanctions when an employee is disciplined or dismissed, whereas a collective sanction could be the introduction of unilateral rules, policy or conditions relating to the employees' conditions of service. During the negotiation process, collective sanctions are imposed by the employer's mass dismissal of employees, by a decision to close the organisation, or by locking out the employees. On the other hand, employees may impose individual sanctions by repeated absenteeism, by resigning from their positions, or by industrial sabotage. Collective sanctions by employees and unions may be in the form of strike action, work-to-rule, go-slow, a ban on overtime and community or international pressure.

Due to the imbalance of power in the individual labour relationship, a single employee is less likely to benefit from an individual sanction than that of an individual employer, therefore, employees through their unions engage in the imposition of collective sanctions more readily than would an individual employer. Thus, strike action is viewed as the main form of collective sanction (Bendix, 1996:521). Figure 15.7 illustrates the variables pertaining to organised collective action in the work environment and its relationship with collective bargaining.

15.5.2.5 Dispute resolution

Disputes are a natural occurrence in the employment relationship. Discontent handled by the grievance procedure and negotiations does not always end in agreement, and in addition, to the unsatisfactory outcome, fundamental disagreements may have occurred during the interchange, giving rise to the declaration of a dispute. This occurs when the parties to the negotiation process fail to determine a solution on their own, they thus reach an impasse with no further prospect of movement by either side, and generally, with no further levels of joint negotiating opportunities to which the issue may be referred. A dispute can perhaps best be defined as a formal expression of individual or collective employee dissatisfaction at the organisational level resulting from either a prior failure to resolve a grievance or a failure to agree on a matter of interest in the negotiation process.

Disputes

Two kinds of disputes exist, namely disputes of right and disputes of interest. It is important to distinguish between them as the way in which they are handled in order to reach a settlement differs.

- **Disputes of right** pertain to a right that has already been acquired by means of the law, a contract, agreement or common practice. Disputes of right are not

Figure 15.7 Organised collective action in the workplace

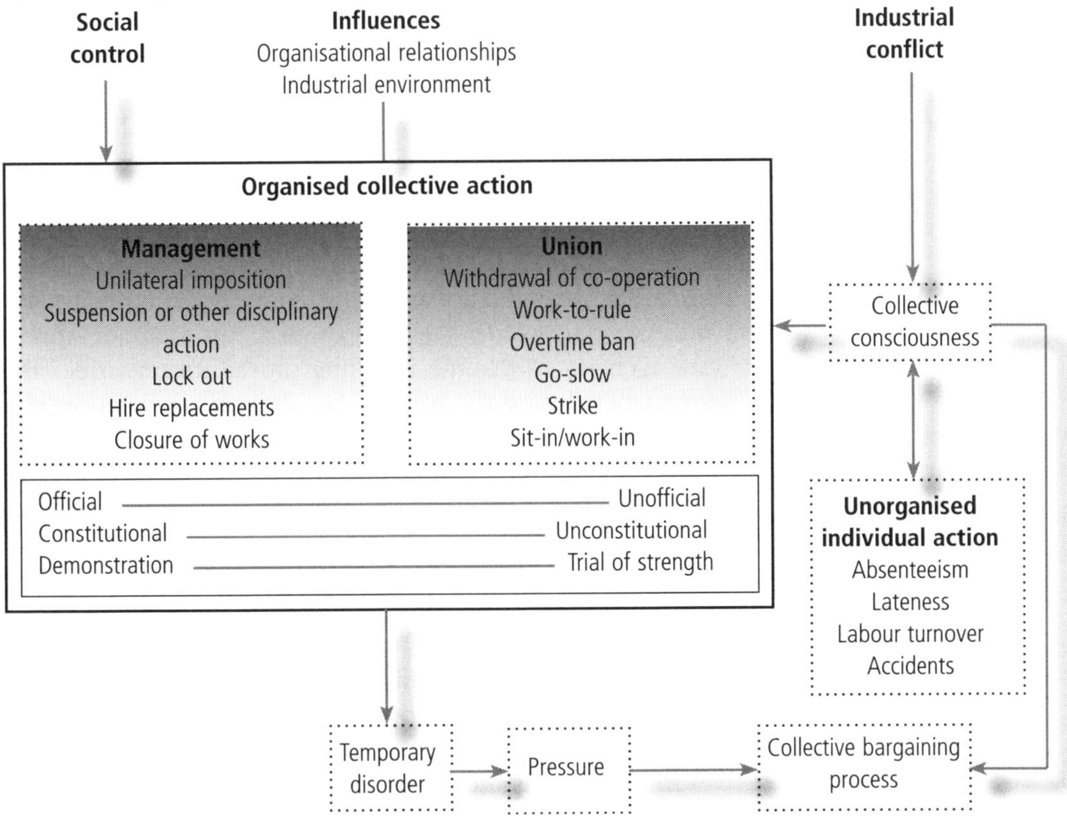

Source: Amended from Salamon, 1992:376

subject to negotiation for their resolution. The achievement or creation of rights may have been affected by negotiation but once a right has been established, its transgression constitutes an offence and may lead to civil and other legal remedies. The failure to implement the terms of a legally enforceable agreement serves as an example.

- **Disputes of interest** centre on the creation of a new right or the variation of an existing right. An interest is that to which a party is not yet entitled but wishes to be entitled to. Thus, disputes of interest are subject to collective bargaining or negotiation. Once agreement has been reached, the interest sought may become a right. When disputes of interest arise, the conflict is of such a nature that it cannot be resolved by the normal means of negotiation, or either party could have refused to negotiate. The immediate reaction is usually to resort to coercive power, often in the form of strike or lock-out. However, industrial action is always detrimental to both parties and the labour relationship, therefore it is advisable to attempt settlement by other means before reverting to industrial action, hence the institution and use of dispute settlement procedures established by the Labour Relations Act of 1995.

Dispute settlement

Dispute settlement procedures may be agreed upon between the parties themselves, known as in-house procedures, or the statutory mechanisms and processes provided for by the LRA can be utilised. The aim of labour legislation is that disputes be resolved internally, or as close to the level at which the conflict actually took place. If this proves impossible, disputes can then be referred to the appropriate dispute resolution institution such as an accredited bargaining council, Commission for Conciliation, Mediation and Arbitration (CCMA), the Labour Court, Labour Appeal Court or accredited private agencies. A dispute handling procedure prescribes the action to be taken by both parties during the interval between the declaration of a dispute and possible industrial action such as work stoppage or strike action.

- **Bargaining councils**. The duty of a bargaining council is to maintain industrial peace between employers and employees under its jurisdiction. Once it has been accredited by the CCMA, it can proceed to resolve disputes.
- **The Commission for Conciliation, Mediation and Arbitration**. The CCMA is an independent body with jurisdiction in all the provinces of South Africa, of which the head office is in Johannesburg, but the CCMA is required to maintain an office in each province and as many local offices as it considers necessary. The CCMA attempts to resolve, through conciliation, any dispute referred to it in terms of the LRA. It can also arbitrate the dispute if the Act requires arbitration or if it remains unresolved after conciliation, or if either party has requested that the dispute be resolved through arbitration.

  Conciliation, mediation and arbitration have come to be regarded as the best methods of settling labour disputes (Bendix, 1996:484–489):
  - **Conciliation** is the act of procuring renewed goodwill, allowing both parties to cool off and to approach each other in a friendlier manner in order to seriously attempt settlement before industrial action can be undertaken. This is done by establishing a forum in which the parties in conflict, or who have failed to reach agreement, can come together once again and attempt to settle their differences. A third party may be present, to act as chairperson during the conduct of the meetings, but will not play an active role in the negotiation process. Conciliation extends the negotiation process and allows for settlement between parties, but in this case, conciliation forms part of the dispute settlement procedure, and failure to conciliate may lead to industrial action or to further steps in the dispute-handling process.
  - **Mediation** involves the active intervention of an objective third party, for the purpose of inducing a settlement. The mediator plays an active part in the process by advising both sides, acts as intermediary and suggests possible solutions in an attempt to bring about a settlement. However, a mediator acts

only in an advisory and conciliatory capacity, he/she has no decision-making powers and cannot impose a settlement on either party.

- **Arbitration** entails the appointment of a third party to act as adjudicator in a dispute and to decide on the terms of the settlement. In the case of arbitration the continuation of negotiation is permitted, as is the case in conciliation and mediation. The arbitrator takes on the role of the decision-maker, listens to, and investigates the demands and counter-demands on both sides, then decides on a final settlement, which is binding on both parties.
- **Labour Court**. This is a court of law and a superior court with authority, inherent powers and standing equal to a court of a provincial division of the Supreme Court and has jurisdiction in all the provinces of the Republic. Under certain circumstances the Labour Court can adjudicate a dispute, and under certain circumstances only the Labour Court is entitled to resolve a dispute, such as in the case of unfair labour practices or appeals against CCMA arbitration decisions.
- **Labour Appeal Court**. This is the final court of appeal in respect of all judgments and orders made by the Labour Court. The Labour Appeal Court is a superior court and is equal to the Appellate Division of the Supreme Court.

15.5.3 Labour-related practices

This section examines a number of labour relations activities undertaken at organisational level. If a conducive climate for healthy labour relations and good management practices is to be cultivated, it is essential to have the necessary policies, procedures and practices in place so that both management and employees know what is expected of them in the performance of their normal duties, but also if a grievance or disciplinary transgression should take place. The act of negotiation is often called upon in the work environment but especially so during collective bargaining and when major changes, such as retrenchment, are being considered.

15.5.3.1 Policies, procedures and practices

Management and employees have different interests, needs and goals, it is therefore essential that there should be written documentation in the form of policy to regulate communication and interaction between them. As policies, procedures and established practices serve as guidelines for performance and behaviour in the work environment, their formulation and consistent implementation require careful consideration.

- A **policy** may be defined as a statement of objectives and the strategy for their achievement. It provides proof of commitment and of preparedness to declare views and attitudes and it sets limits for behaviour. Organisational policy forms the basis upon which all other policies and procedures in the organisation are compiled. The formulation of the labour relations policy is the end product of corporate planning and strategy formulation, it is therefore a responsibility of top management.

The labour relations policy of an organisation is the expression of top management's philosophy towards the human resources of the institution. It is a declaration of the fundamental values, beliefs, standards and principles that underlie the behaviour of the organisation, but it contains sufficient detail to provide specific guidelines for the relationship between the people of the organisation (Gerber et al., 1998:342).

- **Managerial principles** such as the right to manage and make operational decisions
- **The relationship** between management and employees, for instance recognition of the value of employees as an asset of the organisation
- **The determination** of terms and conditions of employment like the intention to be bound, and to expect employees and trade unions to be bound, by agreements reached in any recognised collective bargaining process
- **The approach** to employment being adopted incorporating, among others, an adequate level of trained and experienced employees for the organisation's needs, consistent with maintaining security of employment for individual employees
- **The role of procedures**, for example in resolving problems speedily in a mutually accepted manner.

Once a policy is formulated and accepted it is important to put it in writing and make it public by communicating it to all the relevant levels in the organisation:

- A **procedure** may be defined as an operational stipulation which details and regulates the manner in which a specified issue is to be handled. It provides the means for the implementation of policy and the objectives contained within. In the event of such procedures being determined by negotiation between management and unions as representatives of employees, they also represent an important part of the system of joint regulation by providing a body of rules that defines the extent and manner in which both management and trade union power is to be exercised in the organisation (Salamon, 1992:453).
- A **practice** is explained as a set of decisions or actions made in response to a given problem or situation. Where these actions and decisions are made in the framework of an existing policy they may be regarded as a process of policy interpretation and application, signalling the custom and practice in the organisation. The application of policy through the practices of management provides evidence of the precise meaning and effect of the policy, but more importantly, management's intention both to implement and to be constrained by the policy.

15.5.3.2 Negotiation

The process of negotiation is considered a deliberate interaction of two or more persons or social units attempting to redefine the terms of their interrelationship. The representatives of the parties interact in an explicit attempt to reach a jointly acceptable position on one or more divisive issues. In the labour relations context it is usually the representatives of management and the employees respectively, who, through an intense interpersonal process, attempt to resolve their differences and reach agreement on particular matters.

It must be emphasised that negotiation and collective bargaining are not synonymous, however, negotiation forms part of the collective bargaining process. Collective bargaining emphasises the institutional arrangements of labour relations and encompasses the parties, goals, environments and content, as well as the processes utilised in resolving the conflict of interest between management and employees (Salamon, 1992:509). Negotiation represents the interaction between the parties during which an attempt is made to convince the other party to comply with their wishes.

15.5.3.3 Grievances

To distinguish between employee complaints and grievances is not a simple matter as they both stem from employee dissatisfaction with some aspect of their terms and conditions of employment. Torrington and Chapman, 1983 (in Salamon, 1992:567) make the following differentiation: a complaint is a dissatisfaction that is being expressed, but not in a procedural way, while a grievance is a complaint being presented formally and which triggers the procedural machinery, it carries with it the perception that the complaint has been ignored or unfairly treated, or there is a difference in the interpretation of working rules.

A grievance can thus be described as a formal expression of individual or collective employee dissatisfaction primarily, but not exclusively, in respect of the application or non-application of collective agreements, managerial policies and actions or customs and practice.

The purpose of a grievance policy should be to establish the organisational climate, objectives and manner in which managers will be expected to respond to a grievance presented. The grievance procedure provides the formal process for the identification and resolution of any formal complaint that employees or their unions have lodged. Employers are required to inform employees on employment about the grievance procedure and who they should approach to seek redress for any grievance relating to their employment. Both managers and employees should receive in-service training on the application of the grievance procedure, so that they are prepared should the need arise, providing them with the necessary confidence, knowledge and skills to apply the procedure timeously, effectively and fairly.

The grievance procedure commences when the employee lodges a grievance with the direct supervisor and should end at the highest authority in the organisation

Figure 15.8 Grievance procedure

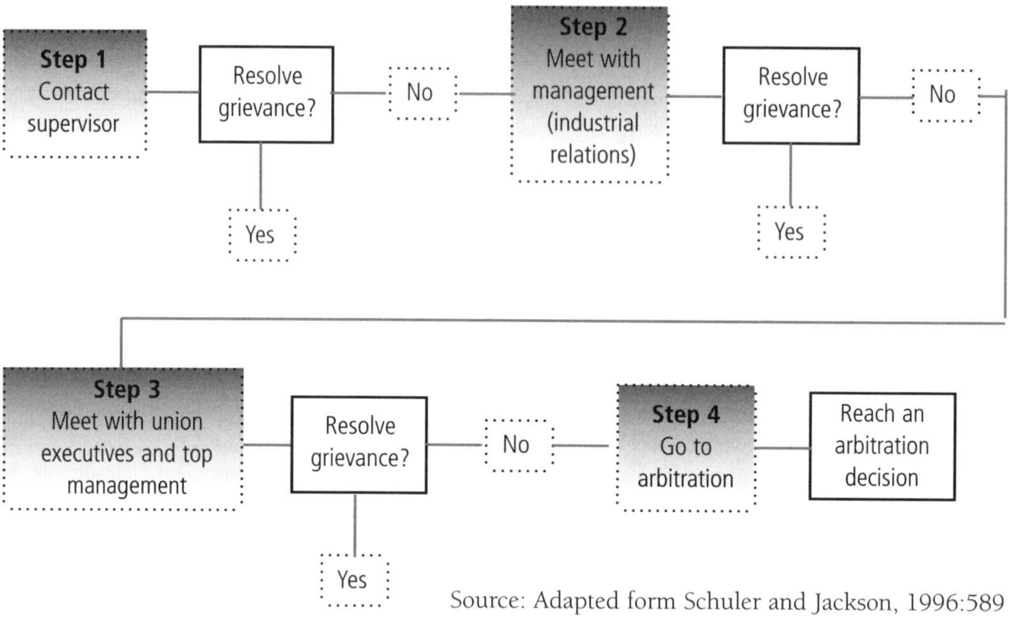

Source: Adapted form Schuler and Jackson, 1996:589

(refer to Figure 15.8 for an example of a grievance procedure). The roles and responsibilities of the different role-players should be clearly stated, time limits for responses by management should be specified, and records of the proceedings should be kept. Prompt action by management is absolutely essential to avoid complicating the matter further. It is the duty of the human resources department to monitor the process and to provide advice and guidance if required.

The prevention of grievances is important, and proactive management of potential problem areas is essential to maintain a calm and productive work environment. Being sensitive to potential causes of dissatisfaction and taking steps to alleviate or prevent them will remove the need to apply the grievance procedure, which unavoidably brings about strained relations.

15.5.3.4 Discipline

Discipline is the process of maintaining compliance with the rules that regulate employment in order to produce a controlled and effective performance. Disciplinary action is defined as the action taken by management against an individual or group who have failed to conform to the rules established by management in the organisation.

Disciplinary action taken against employees must be for justifiable reasons, and there must be effective policies and procedures to govern its use. Such policies and procedures serve to assist those responsible for taking disciplinary action and help to ensure that employees will receive fair and constructive treatment. In addition, and equally important, is the fact that these guidelines help to prevent disciplinary action from being voided or from being reversed through the appeal system. Disciplinary codes and procedures are necessary for promoting order in the work environment, but also to ensure fair and consistent treatment of individuals by supervisors and managers. Rules and codes set standards of conduct and performance in the workplace, whereas procedures aim to ensure that the standards are adhered to by providing a method for dealing with transgressions in a fair and consistent manner. Figure 15.9 presents a disciplinary model that illustrates the areas where provisions should be established, it also indicates the natural sequence in which disciplinary steps must be carried out to ensure enforceable decisions.

Purpose of discipline

The purpose of discipline is as follows:

- **To serve as a deterrent for unacceptable behaviour**. Information, education and training are provided to let employees know what is considered acceptable behaviour and performance, and also to inform them of the offences they should avoid.
- **To bring about improvement**. The disciplinary process is seen as one of counselling the disobedient employee back to acceptable behaviour.
- **To act as punishment**. The disciplinary process applies penalties where they are due, as a means of eliminating negative behaviour in future.

In creating order in the work environment by means of proper disciplinary measures, all employees are informed of their personal responsibility pertaining to quality work performance and envisaged behaviour, taking into account the goals of the organisation and the wellbeing of colleagues. Hence, it is the employer's right and duty to ensure that employees adhere to reasonable standards of efficiency and conduct.

According to Bratton and Gold (2003:384), corrective discipline refers to management action that follows the infraction of a rule and should be guided by

Figure 15.9 Components of the disciplinary process

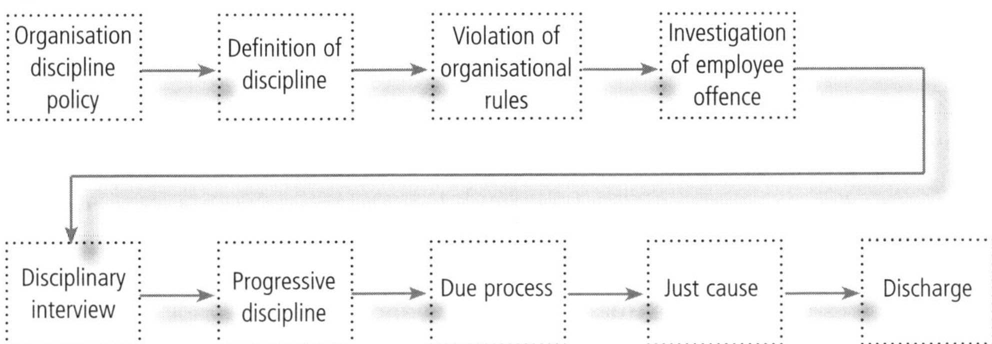

the 'hot-stove-rule' principle, which implies that the individual should receive the same penalty as when knowingly touching a hot stove. This states that discipline should be with warning, immediate, consistent and impersonal. Employees should know the consequences of violating the rule, so that it has preventive value. It is advised that progressive discipline be applied in cases where the transgression does not require summary dismissal. Progressive discipline entails that the employer notifies individuals of unacceptable conduct and provides them with adequate opportunity to correct their behaviour according to the severity of the transgression. Progressive sanctions include a first written warning, second written warning, third and final written warnings and dismissal accompanied by a disciplinary inquiry as the severity of transgressions increase and before dismissal can be considered (see Figure 15.10).

Figure 15.10 Procedural steps of progressive discipline

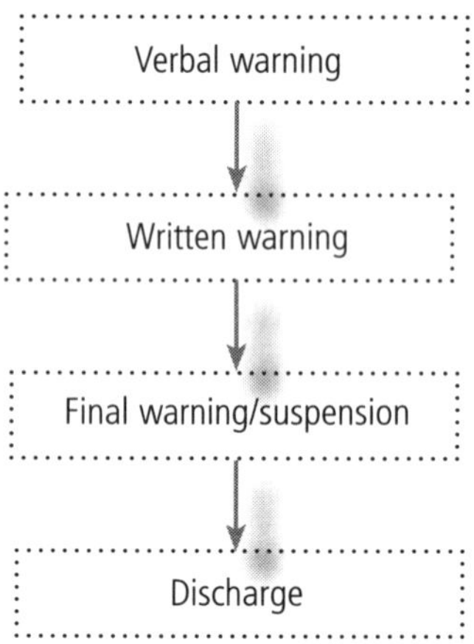

The disciplinary process should incorporate the requirements of natural justice, which are that employees should be informed in advance of any alleged misconduct or disciplinary hearing or be given the right to challenge the alleged evidence, have the right to representation and translation, to have witnesses, and be given the right to appeal against any decision taken by management, as illustrated in Figure 15.11.

Organisational rules and codes

The setting of organisational rules is the foundation for an effective disciplinary system, as these rules govern the type of behaviour expected of employees. It is important to realise that these rules determine permissible behaviour for all employees in the particular organisation, the rules should therefore be applied consistently to all employees regardless of their level of functioning or position held. Different sets of rules are required in the work place, for instance, rules pertaining to work procedures and tasks, rules relevant to conditions of service, and disciplinary rules, more often known as the disciplinary code.

Figure 15.11 Requirements of fair disciplinary procedures

- Be in writing
- Specify to whom they apply
- Be non-discriminatory
- Provide for matters to be dealt with without undue delay
- Provide for proceedings, witness statements and records to be kept confidential
- Indicate the disciplinary actions which may be taken
- Specify the levels of management which have the authority to take the various forms of disciplinary action
- Provide workers with an opportunity to state their case before decisions are reached
- Provide workers with the right to be accompanied (by a co-worker or trade union official)
- Ensure that, except for gross misconduct, no employee is dismissed for a first breach of discipline
- Ensure that disciplinary action is not taken until the case has been carefully investigated
- Ensure that workers are given an explanation for any penalty imposed
- Provide a right of appeal – normally to a more senior manager – and specify the procedure to be followed

Source: Selwyn, 2000 in Bratton & Gold, 2003:387

In compiling the disciplinary code or code of conduct, it is helpful to group the problems into the following four categories, namely minor offences, serious offences, very serious offences and dismissible offences with the first transgression. The appropriate and progressive sanctions can then be allocated to each of the four categories, providing specific guidelines for supervisors and thus ensuring consistent implementation.

Dismissal

Schedule 8 of the LRA provides for a code of conduct that should be followed whenever dismissal of an employee is contemplated. This Act recognises three grounds on which the termination of employment might be legitimate, they are based on the conduct of the employee, the capacity of an employee, and the operational requirements of the organisation.

(1) **Misconduct**. Transgression of the organisational rules or code of conduct is known as misconduct. Formal procedures do not have to be invoked every time a rule is broken, informal advice and counselling are usually the first action taken by the employer (in the form of management or supervisor) when minor violations have taken place. Repeated misconduct warrants warnings as indicated in the progressive disciplinary process. Transgression of a more serious nature may call for a final warning or action short of dismissal.

Generally it is not appropriate to dismiss an employee for a first offence, however, if the misconduct is serious and of such gravity that it makes a continued employment relationship intolerable, then dismissal is seriously considered. Examples of dismissible offences are gross dishonesty or insubordination, or wilful damage to the property of the employer, a fellow employee, client or customer, incitement and intimidation.

Apart from applying a fair procedure when dismissal is considered, the employer should take note of factors such as the employee's circumstances including length of service, previous disciplinary record and personal circumstances, the nature of the job and the circumstances of the infringement itself.

(2) **Incapacity: Poor work performance.** Incapacity may be for two reasons, firstly due to poor work performance, and secondly due to ill health or injury. Newly hired employees are often placed on probation for a specific period during which the new employee should be given the necessary instruction, training, guidance or counselling in order to render satisfactory service. Dismissal during the probationary period should be preceded by an opportunity for the employee to state a case in view of his/her performance.

After the probationary period, an employee should not be dismissed unless the appropriate guidance, training, instruction and evaluation had been given, and after a reasonable period of time, the employee continues to perform unsatisfactorily. The procedure leading to dismissal should include an investigation as to the reasons for the unsatisfactory performance, and the employee should be allowed to be heard and may be assisted by a fellow employee or trade union representative.

(3) **Incapacity: Ill health or injury.** Incapacity on the grounds of ill health could be temporary or permanent in nature. If the incapacity is temporary, the employer should investigate all the possible alternatives short of dismissal. In cases where the incapacity is permanent, the employer should ascertain the possibility of securing alternative employment, or adapting the duties or work circumstances of the employee to accommodate the employee's disability.

The degree of incapacity is relevant to the fairness of the dismissal, so should the cause for the incapacity be taken into account when considering alternatives to dismissal.

Operational reasons: Retrenchment and redundancy

Two similar terms are used to terminate the services of employees for operational reasons. **Retrenchment** refers to the termination of the employment contract of an employee or group of employees because of factors beyond their control, but which are directly related to financial losses experienced by the employer. Reasons for this could be loss in sales, seasonal changes, economic fluctuation or production delays, obliging the employer to reduce the organisation's labour force. **Redundancy** applies to the termination of the employment contract due to technological changes, automation or reorganisation of the organisation making the specific job held by the employee superfluous. In the case of retrenchment, the jobs may be reinstated if economic circumstances improve, while in the case of redundancy, the loss of jobs is usually permanent. The LRA does not distinguish between the handling of these two concepts, and simply defines the reason for dismissal as for operational reasons. The emergence of constitutional labour rights has changed retrenchment practices dramatically, since employers can no longer claim that retrenchment or redundancy is entirely a managerial prerogative that can be applied on an ad hoc basis. Retrenchment is a delicate and very difficult process which needs to be handled with sympathy and great circumspection. Those managers who use reorganisation and subsequent redundancies as an excuse to rid themselves of unwanted employees may find themselves facing serious charges (Nel, 2002:261).

Handling retrenchment. As in all other aspects of labour relations that require a specific method of management, it is important for management and employee representatives to develop a policy and procedure for dismissing employees for operational reasons. Trade unions may not always be willing to participate in such a process as their agreement to a retrenchment policy and procedure will imply their acceptance of the need for retrenchment and a weakening of any opposition they may wish to make when the need for retrenchment arises.

The LRA provides guidelines as to what fair retrenchment ought to be. The Act specifically sets out the process of consultation that is required when planning for retrenchments. During this process the employer and employee representatives must attempt to reach consensus about certain matters. In the handling of dismissals for operational reasons, three main phases are appropriate (Salamon, 1992:640–641).

The **preliminary discussion** phase requires the two parties to consult and attempt reaching agreement on the following aspects:

- Ways to avoid the retrenchments
- Means to reduce the number of people to be retrenched
- Ways to limit the harsh effects of retrenchment
- The method for selecting the employees to be retrenched
- The number of employees to be dismissed and the period of time over which the reduction in the labour force is to be achieved
- The calculation of severance pay.

The LRA further determines in relation to retrenchment, that the employer must:

- Provide all the relevant information relating to the proposed retrenchments
- Pay a retrenched employee severance pay in terms of the negotiated agreement
- Select the employees to be dismissed according to criteria agreed upon by the consulting parties, and if such criteria were not established, then selection should take place according to criteria that are objective and fair (Gerber et al., 1998:363).

Figure 15.12 Common disciplinary problems

Attendance problems
- Late coming
- Unexpected absenteeism
- Unexcused/excessive tardiness
- Leaving without permission

Dishonesty and related problems
- Theft
- Falsifying employment application
- Willfully damaging organisational property
- Punching another employee's time card
- Falsifying work records

Work performance problems
- Failure to complete work assignments
- Producing substandard products or services
- Failure to meet established production requirements

On-the-job behaviour problems
- Intoxication at work
- Insubordination
- Horseplay
- Smoking in unauthorised places
- Fighting
- Gambling
- Failure to use safety devices
- Failure to report injuries
- Carelessness
- Sleeping on the job
- Using abusive or threatening language with supervisors
- Possession of narcotics or alcohol
- Possession of firearms or other weapons
- Sexual harassment

The **main procedural application phase** is concerned with the implementation of the previously determined retrenchment policy or procedure, especially in respect of:

- The selection of employees to be retrenched
- The level of compensation to be paid
- The provision of assistance to the retrenched employees

The **individual employee phase** involves the notification and counselling of the individual employees to be retrenched.

Results of inaction

Figure 15.12 lists the more common disciplinary problems identified by managers. Failure to take disciplinary action in any of these areas only serves to aggravate a problem that eventually must be resolved. The result of inaction is that it implies that the performance or behaviour of the concerned employee was satisfactory and acceptable. When disciplinary action eventually needs to be taken, the possibility exists that the action might be appealed as it was permitted to continue before, while management was aware of the problem. Such contradictions in practice can only aid employees in successfully challenging management's corrective actions and thus further undermining their authority.

15.6 UNDERLYING DYNAMICS

The underlying dynamics in the labour relations sphere are closely related to organisational structures, managerial integrity and human behaviour. The following determinants more specifically affect the process of fair labour practice:

- The availability of mutually agreed upon policies and procedures regarding HR issues pertaining to appointment, promotion, grievances, discipline and retrenchment
- Management's commitment and integrity to apply the set policies and procedures in a fair and just manner
- Transparency, good faith and equal treatment of all subordinates
- Management's relationship with representative trade unions and their officials
- Trade union objectives in a specific organisation.

15.7 CONCLUDING STATEMENTS

The following concluding statements are relevant to labour relations and the quest to be fair in one's interactions in the workplace:

- Fair labour practice occurs in the legal and professional-ethical context, in accordance with the business ownership of the particular healthcare organisation, with reference to the Constitution, labour-related legislation and codes of conduct.
- The major role-players in fair labour practice are the state, employers, employees, and organised labour.
- The purpose of healthy labour relations is for management to consult with employees and their representatives, set relevant policies and procedures, be fair and consistent in the treatment of all employees, deal with labour-related problems timeously, and transparency in the behaviour of all parties.

- The process of labour relations is broadly divided into three sections, namely perspectives, processes and practices.
- Perceptions of labour relations are individual and value laden. Perceptions are based primarily on a belief of what is right with respect to fairness and the exercise of power and authority.
- The strength of a trade union depends on the collective consciousness of its membership and the preparedness of the individual to subordinate his/her personal aspirations to those of the group.
- Management strategies in labour relations are the result of constrained rational choices, which are always aimed at maintaining managerial security in the organisation's decision-making processes.
- The task of the employers' association is to represent and coordinate its members' activities at the organisational level.
- Improved communication between management and employees/unions will not, in itself, solve problems, it can only provide a means for them to gain a better understanding of one another.
- Collective bargaining is a voluntary, bipartite process, of which the character is determined by management's and the employees' perception of the nature of their mutual interdependence.
- The most effective structure of employee participation in an organisation is one that combines direct employee involvement in decisions relating to their immediate work situation with indirect participation at the board level on major organisational decisions, whilst not undermining the representational role of established trade unions.
- Industrial action is primarily an institutionalised means for employees and unions to exert power in the collective bargaining relationship through the temporary introduction of disorder into the economic and authority relationship of the organisation.
- Organised collective industrial action requires the development of a collective consciousness among the employees concerned.
- Conciliation, mediation and arbitration provide channels through which management and unions may seek to resolve their differences by introducing a third party, the availability or use of such processes does not automatically mean an avoidance or reduction in the use of industrial action.
- To achieve an orderly and consistent labour relations system, management needs to adopt an integrated approach to policy development, planning and decision-making.
- Decision-making by management on labour relations matters is not the sole province of either labour relations specialists or line management, but a collective responsibility requiring the involvement and commitment of all parties involved.
- Negotiation is a process that allows the representatives of different interest

groups to reach a mutually acceptable settlement of an issue, whilst at the same time seeking to maximise the advantage to be gained for their interest groups.

- The grievance and dispute process is an integral part of the system of collective bargaining at the organisational level, and as such, is concerned with the determination of rules, as well as their interpretation and application. The effectiveness of formal procedures is largely dependent upon employee and union acceptance of their integrity and usefulness in resolving their dissatisfaction.
- Whilst the formal disciplinary process is a management-oriented control process intended to 'penalise' employees whose performance or behaviour does not meet management's expectations, the disciplinary procedure affords an opportunity for employees to grow and improve their conduct and performance by means of progressive discipline.
- Management's goals in any retrenchment situation are to reduce its labour force whilst maintaining the morale and goodwill of its remaining employees, whereas the union aims to resist, or minimise the extent of the retrenchment and to secure the best possible financial compensation for those who are to be dismissed.
- Various underlying dynamics, such as the availability of labour-related policies and procedures, management's role and integrity in dealing with HR, employees' commitment to adhere to rules and the objectives of trade unions affect the management of human resources in terms of labour relations.

Self-assessment

(1) Obtain a copy of the LRA from the Internet at http://polity.org.za/govdocs/legislation/1995/act95-066.html
(2) Access the CCMA website at www.ccma.org.za to acquire the forms necessary for lodging a request for (a) conciliation, and (b) for arbitration.
(3) Do you think employee involvement in decision-making leads to higher quality decisions?
(4) Develop a labour relations policy for your organisation and include specific stipulations regarding grievances and discipline.

16 Leadership in healthcare service management

KEY CONCEPTS

Nature of leadership
Leadership theories
Leadership styles
Power
Leadership in teams
Leadership and cultural issues
Leadership communication
Empowerment
Transactional and transformational leadership

SPECIFIC OUTCOMES

After studying this chapter, you should be able to:

- Interpret the legal, professional-ethical and healthcare **context**, with reference to the role of the leader in the healthcare environment
- Analyse and debate the **purpose** of leadership in promoting effective healthcare delivery
- Identify the **role-players** and interpret their roles and responsibilities in the leader-follower relationship
- Describe and apply the **process** of leadership, with reference to leadership styles, utilisation of power, leadership in teams, effective leadership communication, and empowerment of followers
- Debate the **underlying dynamics** that could impact on the leadership process in a healthcare environment.

16.1 INTRODUCTION

> The nature of leadership is about enabling ordinary people to produce extraordinary things in the face of challenge and change, and to constantly turn in superior performance to the long-term benefit of all concerned (Charlton, 2000:30).

Leadership is an influential relationship among people; involving the leaders and followers who intend real changes that reflect their shared goals. The influence emanating from the relationship between the leader and follower is multidirectional and non-coercive. In a relationship the superior, for example the director of the healthcare service, influences subordinates, namely the heads of the different departments in the healthcare service. By interacting, subordinates can influence their leaders. Leadership involves changes that lead to the attainment of goals shared by leaders and followers. Both leaders and followers in the healthcare setting desire a shared purpose of quality healthcare delivery that motivates them towards achieving it in future. Therefore, committed healthcare professionals take personal responsibility to achieve the desired outcome in future.

Leadership has its roots in a joining of the arts, humanities and sciences (Apps, 1994:8).We are constantly moving between leadership perspectives. We leave a perspective that we are acquainted with and move towards a new perspective that is appearing on the horizon. When we move in a new direction, the most fundamental characteristics of what we believe and value often change to some extent. On the other hand, some elements of the older perspective of leadership nonetheless remain and continue to guide our actions. We can never cut all ties with a previous perspective in favour of the new. New kinds of leaders will emerge to lead in ways different from those that we have known in the past. The reason for the latter is that different times and different conditions demand different approaches.

16.2 CONCEPTUAL FRAMEWORK

What is leadership? Leadership is an influencial relationship among leaders and followers who intend real changes that reflect their shared purposes (Daft, 1999:5–6). The key elements in defining the term leadership are briefly described below.

Influence refers to an active relationship among people that is multidirectional and non-coercive. Leaders influence followers, but followers also influence their leaders. Leadership is therefore a *people* activity, a relationship among people. The people involved in the relationship want substantive *changes*, and do not want to maintain the status quo. The changes are not dictated by leaders but reflect the *purposes* shared by leaders and followers. Change is towards a future-oriented outcome, that motivates them in obtaining their desirable future. Leaders and followers therefore take *personal responsibility* for their own role in their honest intention to be actively involved in striving to obtain their shared purpose.

Jooste (2003:viii–ix) gives her interpretation of the important concepts involved in leadership in healthcare services management. It involves departure from the *theoretical background* and assessment of leadership towards leadership in the *future*. In the leadership journey the steps of *planning for excellence, implementation* of effective leadership *strategies* and *evaluation* of leadership outcomes are essential.

The following conceptual framework (Figure 16.1) thus highlights the important elements of leadership.

Figure 16.1 Elements of leadership

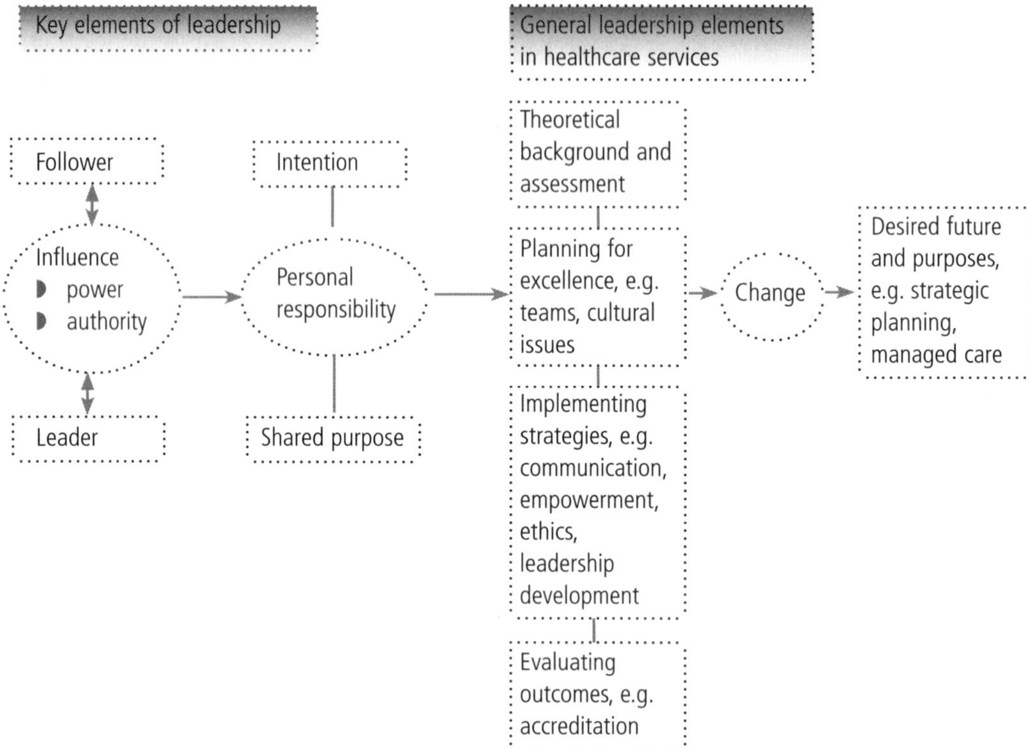

16.3 CONTEXT

'Leadership is a complex process by which a person influences others to accomplish a mission, task or objective and directs the organisation in a way that makes it more cohesive and coherent' (Bennis, 2002:1). In healthcare institutions, a person (or persons) carries out this process by applying his/her leadership attributes (beliefs, values, ethics, character, knowledge and skills). Your position in a healthcare facility as a manager or a supervisor gives you the authority to accomplish certain tasks and objectives in the hospital, clinic or healthcare centre. This power does not make you a good leader. Good leaders are made not born; they are developed through a never-ending process of self-study, education, training and experience. The basis of good leadership is a honourable character and selfless service to your organisation (Bennis, 2002:2). Leadership should be viewed in the context of early towards contemporary leadership theories (see Table 16.1). These theories are comprehensively discussed by Bezuidenhoudt in Jooste (2003:45–85).

Table 16.1 Leadership theories

Early leadership theories	
Trait theories • Asserts that leadership could be learned and certain traits make an effective leader	Great man theory • Acceptance of the leader-ruler, the 'hero-leader' who leads an organisation into a successful future
Behavioural theories • Anyone who adopts the appropriate behaviour can be a good leader	Leadership styles (Lewin, Lippitt and White) • Authoritarian leaders (restrictive) • Democratic leaders (teamwork) • Laissez-faire leaders (without direction) • Participative leadership (retains control) Leader behaviour descriptions (Hemphill, Halpin and Winer) • Effective leader initiating structure through task-related functions and considering relationship-oriented functions Task versus relationship orientation (Blake and Mouton)
Early management theories	
Scientific management	Human relations (Taylor, Gantt and Mayo)
Contemporary leadership theories	
Motivational theories • Internal and external forces arouse enthusiasm to pursue a certain course of action	Content theories (need-based theories) • Hierarchy of needs theory (Maslow) • ERG theory (Alderfer) • The acquired needs theory (McCelland) • Two-factor theory (Herzberg) Theories X and Y (McGregor) Process theories • Equity theory (Adams) • Expectancy theory (Vroom) • Management by objectives • Reinforcement theory (Skinner)
Situational theories • It explores the context in which leadership occurs • A person may be a leader in one situation and a follower in another	Contingency theory (Fiedler) Situational theory (Hersey and Blanchard) Path-goal theory (House)

➜

Environmental theories • A positive environment may influence a leader positively	
Interactional theories • Focus on the qualities of a leader as a ruler and the achievement of the goals of the group	Elements of leader situation (Hollander) Leader-group interaction (Schreisheim, Mowby and Stogdill) Complex man and organisations (Schein)
Changing leadership theories	Transactional leadership • An exchange of e.g. information to satisfy the needs of both the leader and follower, who have separate but related purposes Charismatic leadership theory • One may overcome obstacles not thought possible Transformational leadership • Create new visions that give a sense of meaning and purpose • Develop trusting repationships between leader and follower • Promote a commitment to organisational and professional visions and goals with the effect that followers are empowered

16.4 THE PURPOSE OF LEADERSHIP

Leadership is an *influence relationship* among the leaders and followers who intend real changes that reflect their shared goals. Effective leadership leads to competent, motivated healthcare practitioners who are the most valuable assets of any healthcare system. Healthcare professions of the world must be developed to their optimal potential.

Leadership in all healthcare professions is a crucial element in the development of the type of healthcare practitioner that the world needs. They are the prime agents for change and leadership must therefore ensure *change* takes place and provide the *motivation* to excel (Searle & Pera, 1995:425–6). Healthcare services as a system forms part of the broader social system, constantly affected by change. Issues facing healthcare services are the characteristics of this constant change process. Leadership involves change and people for change, the leader thus needs to have the theoretical knowledge of change theories and view change as a challenge. The people aspect involves a *team*, especially in a multi-disciplinary set-up. Leadership is the *art* of how we relate to people – usually those people on whom we depend to make our institution successful. Leaders understand the value of *self*-management and self-motivation. This is the sort of thinking that is absolutely necessary if we are going to motivate the workforce – not the workforce of the future, but the workforce that is standing at our front door right now. The real issue is how to release the brainpower, the intelligent curiosity, the know-how, of our greatest asset – our people, the people we work with every day. Leadership is important because leaders have followers. Leaders *empower and inspire*. Leaders set *directions* and then empower and enable their team to make their own decisions and solve their own problems. Leaders know how to do. It is therefore important that a leader, as the head of a department, has the ability to take a standpoint, to negotiate, convince and persuade team-members.

The *quality of leadership* practised/exercised at all levels in healthcare service management influences the quality of healthcare practices in a healthcare service organisation. Quality leadership is especially essential to support the individual practitioner in her/his pursuit of providing quality healthcare services. Leadership determines the quality of service and therefore, also the acceptance of different professions as a profession (Jooste, 2003:42).

In discussing the purpose of leadership, it is also important to make a distinction between the terms management and leadership. The difference may be summarised as activities of communication and coordination among people, which facilitate effectiveness as a leader, versus activities of controlling resources, and mastering procedures and routines, which facilitate efficiency as a manager. The main differences between the two concepts are summarised by Jooste (2003:27) as follows:

- Managers have employees, leaders have followers.
- Managers command and control, leaders empire and inspire.
- Management can be taught, leadership must be experienced to be learned.
- Managers seek stability, leaders seek flexibility.
- Managers make decisions and solve problems. Leaders set directions and then empower and enable their team to make their own decisions and solve their own problems.
- Managers accept the organisational structure and culture. Leaders look for a better way.
- Managers think incrementally. Leaders think radically (Pascale, 1990:65). This means that managers do things by the book and follow policies. Leaders follow their intuition, which may be of more benefit to the company.
- Managers control. Leaders let vision, strategies, goals and values be the guidepost for action behaviour (Predpall, 1994:30–1).
- A manager must be obeyed and may only have obtained his/her position of authority through time and loyalty given to him/her by the institution. A leader is someone who people naturally follow through their own choice.

16.5 ROLE-PLAYERS

Healthcare professionals should constantly invent and reinvent new leadership approaches. They should become continual, reflective, self-directed practitioners who critically examine the healthcare environment in which they work and make adjustments in what they do on the basis of their evaluations of their circumstances.

Leadership attributes, qualities and skills

The modern nurse leaders should have a variety of qualities and principles to follow. The following are some of the crucial attributes needed in the rapidly changing healthcare environment of today:

- **A clear vision**. Leaders should be proactive and see the present as a springboard to achieve future aims.
- **Strategic thinking abilities**. They should have a strategic attitude and accept that there is more than one way to do something, be willing to take risks and move towards more participation.
- **Change management skills.** Skill management is also essential in assessing competencies and skills of followers to determine and plan for changes in individual and team performances.
- **Strength and courage**. It is never too late to become a leader and one should have the courage to change and do things differently. One should use the full capabilities of the organisation. By developing a team spirit, a person will be able to employ the organisation, department, section, etc. to its fullest capabilities. Standing firm in the face of criticism, and having the courage to admit when they are wrong are hallmarks of courageous leaders.
- **Confidence**. Every healthcare professional should keep the leader in her/him alive and should believe that there is a way to be the leader she/he wants to be.
- **Negotiation skills**. Leaders should make sound and timely decisions by using good problem-solving, decision-making and planning tools.
- **Knowledge management skills**. These skills should be applied by capturing and communicating information to those who seek it or who need it, thus providing information to the right person at the right time. People should be informed and should know how to communicate with people, seniors and other key people in the organisation.
- **A willingness to form strategic alliances**. Strategic actions should focus on building trust through behaviour that represents openness, acceptance and appreciation. The team leadership style moves the focus away from the leader towards the team as a unit.
- **Emotional intelligence**. Negative emotions should be managed cognitively and the focus should be on people rather than principles. Leaders should use principle-centred leadership carefully with fairness and kindness.
- **Respect**. This refers to protecting and supporting the important relationship between caregivers and their patients, as well as honouring the individual needs of people.
- **Caring**. The leader should value individual emotional and spiritual needs, respect individual preferences, prize good communication skills, and focus on

multidisciplinary team approaches to care. Leaders should know human nature and the importance of sincerely caring for your followers.

- **Advocacy and honesty**. Leaders should make sure that relevant individuals have all the information they need, to understand how their healthcare and career plan works. They should set the example and be a good role-model for followers.
- **Self-knowledge**. In order to know oneself, one should have to understand one's own being. Seeking self-improvement means continually strengthening your attributes. This can be accomplished through reading, self-study, classes, etc.
- **Technical proficiency.** As a leader, one must know the job and have a solid familiarity with employees' jobs. Leaders should ensure that tasks are understood, supervised and accomplished. Communication is the key to this responsibility.
- **Responsibility**. Leaders should search for ways to guide the organisation to new heights. They should analyse situations, take corrective action, and move on to the next challenge. All leaders should develop good character traits in followers that will help them carry out their professional responsibilities and train followers as a team.
- **Focus**. Effective leaders stay focused on the outcomes they wish to create, and emphasise the mission, vision and strategic goals of their organisation and at the same time building the capacity of their organisations to achieve them.
- **Authenticity**. Leaderships who are authentic attract followers, even leaders who are viewed as being highly driven and difficult to work for. Authenticity provides the leader with the currency to obtain 'buy-in' from key stakeholders, because it builds and maintains trust.
- **People management skills**. Effective leaders know how to listen empathetically, thus legitimising others' input. By doing so, they promote consensus building, and build strong teams. They coach others to do the same, and so create a culture of inclusiveness.

Types of leadership styles

A nurse leader is a person who works not only *with* human beings but *for* human beings, because the effective care of those in need of healthcare and support is his/her objective. A leadership style is the approach that she/he follows to provide direction, implement plans and to motivate people. There are many different classifications of leadership styles, namely (authoritarian/autocratic), (democratic/participative), (bureaucratic), (delegative/free-reign), (permissive/laissez-faire), to name a few.

Jooste describes four main types of leaders that are often encountered in nursing (Booyens). The *team-builder (democrat)* is a person who maintains a continuously high level of production. The *maternal* type of leader is behind everything and she protects her workers against everything. She turns her workers into 'dependent children'. The *driver* type of leader (authoritarian) gives the impression of being a good leader and a wise manager because she manages to get a great deal of work done. She is, however, so afraid that her image of an economic, effective, top-level supervisor will suffer, that she considers only the work and neglects the people who have to do the job. On the other hand, the *'stupor-visor'* is the type of person who fosters a climate in which each employee tends to rise to his/her level of incompetence! This type of nurse manager was probably promoted to the position on the grounds of seniority or because she held the necessary qualification without having proved herself in practice. She is not a member of the team, let alone its leader, because she is unsure and ineffective.

In Booyens (2001:158–160) different leadership styles are outlined (see Table 16.2).

Table 16.2 Leadership styles

Team-builder (Participative style)
Leadership actions She consults employees before makings decisions. She establishes attainable standards in cooperation with employees, ascertaining what the desirable standards should be and how these should be attained. She ensures that the work is understood, encourages suggestions in regard to the work and gives credit for work well done. *Follower's reactions and feelings* Staff members, in her absence, carry on with the same high level of care. The team is able to handle emergencies expeditiously. They are loyal to her. Such a person finds the recruitment of personnel relatively easy for the service is given a good name by the existing staff members. Employees experience a feeling of belonging. They feel that they are accomplishing something worthwhile. Their willingness to accept responsibility and their worth is recognised, and they tend to feel more confident, for they know they will be given a chance to develop.

Driver type (Authoritative style)
Leadership actions She adopts the attitude 'obey orders – or else'. She watches her employees all the time, is quick to blame and slow to praise. She seldom considers other people's ideas and suggestions, continually finds fault with the work of her employees, and is always difficult to approach, although she pretends that her door is open to all. *Follower's reactions and feelings* Production always drops when she is away. Her employees are irritable, insecure and tense. Employees tend to compete for her favour. They become experts at 'passing the buck'. Her employees do not display initiative but tend rather to shirk responsibility. They are eager to be transferred and there is always a high staff turnover. She is freely discussed in private. They do not feel they belong in a team and feel they are just numbers. They feel they are expendable because their future depends on the supervisor's whims and fancies. They are frustrated because they feel they are always being driven, and this results in indifference or aggressiveness.

➜

→ **Maternal type (Parental style)**

Leadership actions

She involves herself in all her employees' problems instead of helping them to solve them themselves. She is as interested in details as in results. She sets all the work standards herself and at a level that challenges her employees. She tends to adopt an attitude of martyrdom. Employees tend to call her their 'mother'.

Follower's reactions and feelings

The work output is generally fairly high but the organisation is unduly upset by any emergency. No one grows or develops. Subordinates do not want to assume responsibility and tend to check everything with their direct heads. As time goes on they become more and more dependent and, after a time, they make no decisions in her absence.

Employees feel completely dependent. Although they feel secure under her protection and have some sense of belonging, after a time frustration sets in and staff turnover accelerates.

Stupor-visor (Bureaucratic style)

Leadership actions

She buries herself in administrative detail and paperwork. She does not mix with her personnel and blames failures in the organisation on the members of her team. She does not know how to set goals or organise by objectives and cannot make decisions.

Follower's reactions and feelings

Work is often of a low standard and the finding of scape-goats abounds. Personnel absenteeism is high. The housekeeping in general is slack. There is a noticeable lack of respect for her and personnel are frequently irritable, tense or even desperate.

They are uncertain about what to do and the future is as uncertain as the present. Nothing new is tackled and a persistent sense of insecurity pervades the scene.

There is little interest in the work and a lack of loyalty is evident.

16.6 PROCESS

The process of leadership is dependent on a specific setting in which leadership takes place. It is an interactive and dynamic process in which three dimensions are involved; the leader, the follower and the situation (Booyens, 1998:418). The process of leadership entails different aspects that will be addressed as set out in Table 16.3.

Authority, influence and sources of power

The essential components that are needed to lead healthcare professionals are authority, power and influence. Formal authority is one type of power that is based on the recognition of the legitimacy or lawfulness of the attempt/right to exert influence. This right arises from the formal position (legitimate power) in the organisation. The formal basis of authority is that management has a right to give lawful orders and

Table 16.3 Important components of the leadership process

- Authority, influence and sources of power
- Leadership development in healthcare services
- Executive leadership in the complex healthcare situation
- Leadership in teams
- Leadership and cultural issues
- Effective leadership communication
- Empowerment and leadership.

followers have an obligation to obey. *Line authority* is the standard chain of command, from top-level managers, middle-level managers to functional-level managers and healthcare professionals that deliver basic nursing care activities. *Staff authority* is given to individuals with a staff function to assist line managers with expertise and advice to improve the quality of services rendered.

Influence can be thought of as the ability to affect the perceptions, attitudes, or behaviours of others. Nurse leaders could use three basic categories of influence to create an environment supporting culturally appropriate care namely 1) to model by example, 2) to build caring relationships, and 3) to mentor by instruction. How effectively a person affects the behaviour of others through influence ultimately determines whether he/she is really a leader.

Power is the capacity to ensure outcomes one wishes and to prevent those one does not want (Swansburg, 1993:283). It is important to note that the old hierarchy, where power was at the centre, is making room for an organisational network with shared power. Several *sources of power* could be described based on either the basis for acquiring power, or whether the basis for power is due to personal characteristics (*personal power*) or derived from a position (positional power) (Bezuidenhoudt in Jooste, 2003:119–121).

Leadership development in healthcare services

Development refers to the sustainment or improvement of behaviours. Leadership development is defined as the expansion of a healthcare practitioner's capacity to be effective in leadership roles and processes. Leadership roles and processes are those that enable groups of healthcare practitioners to work together in productive and meaningful ways. Leadership development or education is seen as a requirement for the healthcare professions if leaders are to emerge. The process of planning, implementing and evaluation of leadership development in a healthcare facility could encompass the following structure:

- The drafting of a **conceptual framework/model tailored to meet the needs of a specific healthcare service**
- The launching of a **situational analysis**, assessing and reviewing the organisation and management structures and specific needs

Table 16.4 Sources of positional and personal power

Positional power This power Is granted in accordance with the managerial position in the organisation. It resides in the position, regardless of the person holding the job. Positional power is thus similar to authority. Thus, legitimate, reward and coercive power are all forms of position power used by managers to change employee behaviour. The manager with positional power cannot order or control activities that fall outside his/her sphere of power.	
Reward power	This power is the authority to bestow rewards that are valued by another. Leaders can use rewards to influence followers' behaviour. Leaders may have access to formal rewards, such as pay increases or promotions; they also have at their disposal non-material rewards, such as acceptance, praise, attention and recognition.
Coercive power	The opposite of reward is coercive power. It refers to the authority to punish or recommend punishment. Coercive power exists when someone has the ability to physically or psychologically harm another person. Managers have coercive power when they have the right to fire or demote employees or withdraw pay increases. In addition, berating, criticising and belittling employees in front of others are more subtle forms of coercive power.
Personal power This power comes from internal qualities, capabilities, experiences, and wisdom of the individual. It resides in the person, and entails a person's special knowledge or personality characteristics, and it is evident regardless of his/her position in the organisation. Meticulous attention to appearance and communication serve to enhance personal power. Followers follow a leader because of respect, admiration or caring they feel for the leader as an individual and his/her ideas. Two types of personal power are expert and referent power.	
Expert power	This power is influence exercised as a result of a person's expertise, special skills, or knowledge of a specific subject area. When the leader is a true expert, followers go along with recommendations because of his/her superior knowledge. Leaders at supervisory level often have experience in the production process or in service delivery, which gains them promotion. However, at top management levels, leaders may lack expert power because followers often have more up-to-date knowledge about technical details than they do (Daft, 2000:505).

➜

Referent power	Referent power is enabled through identification with a person who has desirable resources or personal traits. Like expert power, referent power does not always correlate with formal organisational authority. In some ways, referent power is similar to the concept of charisma in that it often involves trust, similarity, acceptance, affection, willingness to follow, and emotional involvement. When followers admire a supervisor because of the way he/she deals with them, the influence is based on referent power.

- The **development/design** and **implementation** of a selection of training and development programmes, targeted to meet the needs of specific managers and individuals exhibiting management and leadership potential
- The **evaluation** of the leadership development strategy implemented in the healthcare organisation.

These steps in leadership development are discussed in the book *Leadership in health services management* by Jooste (2003).

Executive leadership in the complex healthcare situation

The nurse executive is an increasingly essential member of the administrative team by acting as a liaison and mediator between nursing personnel and the administrative departments. The role of an executive leader can be described by using active, assertive verbs such as: lead, create, develop, define, participate, represent, initiate and support. In the executive leadership role, the need for multiple intelligences exists, of which emotional intelligence is one of them. It is not only knowledge that drives one's behaviour, but also the traits centred on the emotional centre of the brain which lends power to actions. For greater success and satisfaction there is thus a need to also manage the emotional quotient (EQ). The latter measures the ability to focus and direct emotions towards success instead of having feelings that hold the individual back (Du Randt in Jooste, 2003:139).

During the past decade there has been an increasing interest in the **diversity of the workforce** and its implications. This has expanded into the fact that this diversity is also a cultural one that affects the way in which we respond to situations, messages, etc. This diversity can affect the values of individuals, their perceptions of themselves and of others, as well as the workplace. One of the key issues is to encourage acceptance of diversity, through a supportive culture of leadership and coaching. This leadership is described as:

- Mentoring skills from the people providing opportunities for diversity
- Having a vision of diversity opportunities and benefits

- Communicating this creatively and understandably
- Inspiring and earning trust in the process, developing trust in the leader, and having trusting followers
- Having the ability as leader to be congruent in word and deed
- Creating an empowering environment.

The above leadership skills should be applied at four levels simultaneously, namely at the intra-personal, inter-personal (coaching), team and organisational levels (Du Randt in Jooste, 2003:143).

Leadership in teams

Team members are fully committed to common goals and a mission they developed themselves. Leadership in teams is characteristic of a specific team vision or purpose that exists. In this scenario members are mutually accountable to one another, trust one another and form a collaborative culture. Members thus all share in leadership.The advantages of teamwork are summarised by Roos and Pilane in Jooste (2003:158–159) as:

- The right combination of skills provides more creative ideas and can manage more complex situations than individuals could do on their own.
- Teamwork requires coordination and team members communicating with one another to prevent duplication or contradictory actions or guidance.
- Team members are stimulated into a highly motivated group of people through the synergic effect of the combination of energies to complete a task.
- The combination of talents of team members puts the team in a position to handle a greater variety of situations competently and flexibly.
- Effective teams provide emotional support to fellow team members and can help manage stress and tension build-up in organisations.
- Team members participating in the objective setting and the planning process are usually more committed to the set objectives. Team synergy and support reinforce this commitment.
- The quality of performance of team members is usually more obvious in a team. Team members serve as a valuable source of feedback.
- Team members can expand their knowledge and skills through the opportunity they have to work closely together.
- It is to the advantage of the organisation when the collective expertise of the team is available when problems occur.

The stages of team development are forming, storming, norming, performing and adjourning. Each of these stages are characterised by specific individual and group tasks, as well as specific climate and behaviour and leadership. An outline of each stage with its most important characteristics is given in *Leadership in health services management* by Jooste (2003).

Leadership and cultural issues

According to Monareng in Jooste (2003:185–186) the leader should acknowledge the importance of the following cultural skills in the healthcare environment:

- An essential step is to develop effective working relationships among people. One should have knowledge of both your own cultural patterns and those of other cultures.
- Recognise that people of the same culture may not necessarily be the same or alike.
- Interpret behaviour of a different culture on the basis of its meaning to the other person and that person's culture.
- Increase one's cultural awareness by watching ways in which people from different cultural groups interact when greeting, maintenance of space and distance, eye contact, use of hands and both ways of verbal and non-verbal expressions.
- Facilitate communication and working relationships by adjusting one's own cultural patterns, and also try to reduce the difference between one's own and other people's patterns.
- Distinguish between behaviour that needs to be changed and that behaviour that needs to be accommodated. Some behaviours can be changed, for example that on the observance of time. Expressions of African time and Western time may cause disruption in the effective running of the organisation as employees may be expected to report on time to work, and hence African time practice will have to change.
- Create cultural awareness by conducting workshops, seminars, role-playing and skills building to increase cross-cultural understanding.
- Encourage formation of informal support systems and networks.
- Promote fairness and prohibit discrimination by ensuring that affirmative action programmes are well run and implemented, e.g. equal employment opportunities.

Effective leadership communication

Leaders who engage in frank, open, two-way communication and whose non-verbal communication reinforces the verbal communication are seen as informative communicators. Communication is even more enhanced when the leader listens carefully and is sensitive to others. Successful leaders are able to persuade others and enlist their support (Jooste 2003:200–201).

Communication is described as the matrix of thought and relationships between persons, as well as the generation and transmission of meaning. Thus, communication is based on the transfer of symbols. Verbal communication in healthcare services is primarily associated with the spoken word. Verbal communication requires psychological and cognitive mechanisms that facilitate speech production and reception. Non-verbal communication consists of all forms of communication that do not involve the spoken or written word. Public leadership is one of the most dynamic and visible forms of social influence to attempt to modify the attitudes and behaviors of mass audiences. The delivery of an effective public speech enhances the audience's perception of one's personal power and leadership potential.

A message from a credible leader can change attitudes and behaviour and is remembered long after the messenger is forgotten. All healthcare professionals should take the lead and work on their own credibility by the following:

- Making and keeping eye contact when communicating with others
- Using positive and spontaneous gestures to add emphasis to the statements and facts you are pointing out
- Maintaining an open, relaxed posture when talking with others. Leaning forward and smiling when answering a question should establish rapport
- Striving to sound positive and confident, and using a conversational speaking style with variation in rate, pitch and volume
- Dressing in appropriate and suitable clothes.

It is believed that *charisma* is the product of communication. Charismatic leaders could be viewed as relationship builders who are skilled at linking with others. These relationships with followers are characterised by strong feelings of excitement, loyalty and devotion. *Charismatic healthcare leaders* can raise the consciousness of other healthcare professionals about new possibilities and motivate them to transcend their own interests for the sake of the healthcare team, healthcare department or healthcare organisation.

Empowerment and leadership

Empowerment refers to a dynamic process of interaction between the follower and leader (with personal characteristics and leader skills) during motivation, power-sharing and participative decision-making, both working in a management and leadership structure, with the aim of accomplishing a power balance in the healthcare service. The leader and follower, as healthcare professionals, are in interaction and both have responsibilities with regard to empowerment.

Empowerment as a process means more than merely giving consent to an individual to exercise control over her/his tasks. It refers to the use of a person's potential and competencies, the discovery of new expertise and the creation of new opportunities to apply such competencies. The health leader, with unique *characteristics* and skills, is in interaction with her/his environment, which includes the management and organisational structures, as well as followers in the healthcare organisation. The leader attempts through management *structures* by means of *motivational strategies* and *participative decision-making*, to empower followers in the healthcare service and to improve her/his own expertise in empowerment.

Jooste (2003:218) describes the model of empowerment that could be implemented in a healthcare environment. The following provides a brief overview of the model:

) **The contribution of management structures in a healthcare service towards the empowerment of followers**. When there is decentralised management in organisational structures, a process of change takes place resulting in the process of power being distributed to lower-level staff members. The organisational structure also enables open channels of communication that provide nurses with essential information to function effectively in their work situation. Flatter organisations offer a new set of management actions; more teamwork, less bureaucracy, better communication, opportunities for professional development and greater satisfaction. A discussion climate for members of the healthcare team is reflected by an open climate for discussions and dialogue. Decentralisation creates opportunities for innovation in the work situation by providing followers with more opportunities to develop their specific areas of expertise, which is not the case in centralised management. Two-way interaction and information ensure that followers have ready access to information. The flow of information facilitates decision-making in the practice.

(2) **Power sharing in the empowerment of followers**. Followers experience a fair distribution of power to all levels if they have a say in, for example, the financial management of their divisions, and by being part of the decision-making process of, for example, prioritising budgetary needs. The empowering leader should see that decentralised distribution of power to the lowest possible level in the service occurs and in this way improves the job satisfaction of followers. An empowering leader should, however, not be afraid that his/her power base would be undermined when expert followers are allowed to make decisions in their scope of practice.

(3) **Participative decision-making in the empowerment of followers**. Participative decision-making demands the establishment of a positive work climate with team spirit, participation of all involved parties in decision-making, effective conflict management, and the delegation of authority. Unnecessary grievances and conflict should be avoided in the workplace and participation of followers in decisions that affect them directly is a necessary process. In an empowering environment authority is discreetly delegated to promote independent decision-making. The follower should possess the necessary authority to identify and solve problems in a section, for example the handling of staff absenteeism.

(4) **Motivation and reward strategies that contribute to empowerment**. There are five systems that motivate and reward followers (Jooste 1997:181–5). The own role system (self-motivation system) focuses on followers who want to deliver quality work. Followers, who, for example, exceed expectations by formulating healthcare standards and criteria when they are off-duty, should be compensated financially (for example in the form of bonuses). This will strengthen their self-motivation. An acknowledgement system is a system in which outstanding followers are identified and promoted. Through this, sustained work performance is achieved. An incentive system is one, which has financial and other rewards

for staff motivation. For example, funds are allocated for staff members to attend symposia. Followers can also be motivated through a constructive feedback system. Their self-worth is strengthened through emotional support.

(5) **The skills and responsibilities of the leader in daily task design**. The existence of a vision and mission in a healthcare service is important. Followers should be involved in the planning of projects and during the setting of objectives for better productivity leaders should ascertain that room is left for followers to attend to their personal objectives. The empowering leader creates a climate of trust, in which followers design their tasks in such a way to promote their independent empowered behaviour. Feedback from the leader should be a positive learning situation and appropriate supervision and control are necessary in the workplace.

(6) **Attributes that are characteristic of an empowering leader**. The empowering leader:

- Acts as a role-model by behaving in a way similar to what is expected from followers
- Reveals her/his fairness in the equal opportunities she/he gives each follower to reach her/his fullest potential
- Shows her/his expertise in her/his consulting role concerning healthcare issues, which is her/his responsibility, encouraging lower-level followers to handle healthcare management issues themselves before consulting the leader
- Plans her/his daily management tasks taking into account the times that nurses would normally approach her/him
- Exhibits her/his trustworthiness through her/his honest interactions with her/his followers
- Should be dedicated in the performance of her/his own daily tasks and through this reach the highest position in her/his career
- Is a hardworking and credible individual who works on her/his own self-development by applying the appropriate strategies for career progression
- Cares for followers, and as a leader is aware of expectations in providing them with problem-solving solutions, keeping appointments with them, opening dialogue with them, and where necessary, assisting them with their problems
- Promotes two-way communication between followers and their supervisors which creates a platform for exchange of opinions and openness to criticism.

Transactional and transformational leadership

Transactional leadership is the best approach to the problem of purchasing motivation from individuals knowing their individual goals and preferences according to a logic of give and take.

Transactional leadership is mostly defined with the enumeration of the following properties:

- Subordinates' behaviour is contingently rewarded
- Management seeks out deviations from demanded performance and corrects them.

The advantage of transformational leadership has been identified as the effective fostering of adaptive expectations among employees.

Transformational leadership is defined by enumeration of the following features:

- Motivation occurs through personal identification with the organisation or group. The leader acts as a role-model for followers and communicates through vision and symbols to strengthen efforts.
- Trust building takes place by 'walking the talk', meaning that leaders produce norms concerning behaviour and attitude by example and role-modeling.
- The feeling of honesty concerning membership is further supported by the individual treatment invested in followers by the leader. The individual treatment involves communication by feedback and revealing a concern for individual developmental needs.
- Followers are encouraged to experiment and challenge existent constraints, possibly by taking risks concerning the organisation and individuals' position in them.
- Continuous learning is stimulated and old beliefs and values should be addressed (Torpman, 2004:895).

16.7 UNDERLYING DYNAMICS

In the scenarios of, for example strikes or lack of resources, these situations become very complex, as top-level leaders have moral obligations towards their professional practices and of the management practices of the institution at heart. Ethical dilemmas are thus related to the use of human and financial resources, as well as dilemmas in clinical practice and leadership.

All healthcare organisations have to adapt to an increasing level of change, as they are becoming part of a global village with potential customers and competitors. The political, economical, social and technological changes of the past decade have challenged the ability of healthcare leaders to become strategic change agents.

16.8 CONCLUDING STATEMENTS

- Leadership involves changes that lead to the attainment of goals shared by leaders and followers.
- Essential key and general elements and processes contribute to successful leadership.

- Leadership should be viewed in the context of early towards contemporary leadership theories.
- The modern nurse leaders should have a variety of attributes, qualities, skills and principles to follow.
- A leadership style is the approach to be followed to provide direction, implement plans and to motivate people.
- The essential components that are needed to direct healthcare professionals are authority, power and influence.
- Leadership development is essential to expand the healthcare practitioner's capacity to be effective in leadership roles and processes.
- An executive leader has a major responsibility in dealing with diversity of the workforce, that affects the values of individuals, their perceptions of themselves and of others, as well as the workplace.
- Leadership in teams is characteristic of a specific team vision/purpose that exists.
- The leader should promote a cultural awareness among members of the multidisciplinary team.
- Communication is basic to effective leadership and successful leaders are able to persuade others and enlist their support towards a common goal.
- An empowering leader motivates followers to strive towards excellence in their performances.

Self-assessment

Case study

A new project team is appointed on an ad hoc basis to market a new type of service to be rendered by their hospital. The team members spend a lot of time exploring, shaping and agreeing on the purpose and end up with a statement of purpose that they seem to be committed to. After one month the team cannot submit a progress report on their activities and the Director of the hospital informs them that no progress has been made on the project. The team members should indicate what the core problem is by answering the following questions:

- Why do we exist as a team?
- What do we do as a team?
- Who are our direct and immediate customers?
- How do we add value to our customers?
- How is our team different and unique from other teams in the organisation?

By answering the above questions the project team would get back on track.

Activity

Write a narrative sketch on how you experience the different leadership roles and problems surrounding the issue of male and female leaders or followers in your healthcare organisation. After writing your story, study the solutions offered to address the gap between gender issues in your service.

The gap between gender leadership should be narrowed. There is no one strategy that spells out the solution but the following ideas could be helpful in addressing the dilemma:

- Change perceptions
- Lure more women for leadership positions
- Break down gender segregation by occupation
- Use objective performance criteria
- Develop mentor programmes
- Communicate competences – women must develop communication skills if they want to emerge as organisational leaders, and superiors must recognise that women possess these skills.

Questions

(1) Which attributes are crucial for the future leader in healthcare organisations? Give reasons for your choice of attributes.

(2) Identify themes that you would like to make part of a leadership development programme in your organisation.

(3) Considering the job you currently hold, does your supervisor have the authority to direct your work? Why does he/she have this authority?

(4) How does leadership play a role in managing diversity in the workplace?

(5) Consider the team-building initiatives in your organisation. What barriers exist that undermine team-building initiatives?

(6) What is the role of each and every healthcare professional in promoting healthy communication with colleagues and patients in the healthcare sector?

(7) How would you go about minimising the effects of negative beliefs on the part of individuals involved in a change programme?

17 Financial management of a healthcare organisation

KEY CONCEPTS

Financial management
Budgeting
Expenditure control
Financial risk management

SPECIFIC OUTCOMES

After studying this chapter, you should be able to:

- Interpret the legal and professional-ethical financial management **context**, with reference to the Constitution, the National Health Act, Corporate Governance, Public Finance Management Act, and public and private (type of business ownership) healthcare organisations
- Identify the **role-players** and interpret their roles and responsibilities in financial management in a healthcare organisation: funder, financing intermediary or purchasing agent, accountant and financial manager
- Analyse and debate the **purpose** of financial management in the context of a healthcare organisation
- Describe and apply the **process** of financial management in the context of a healthcare organisation, with specific reference to the fundamental principles of financial management, budgeting, expenditure control, and financial risk management in a healthcare organisation, as well as the public service financial cycle and process framework
- Debate the **underlying dynamics** that could impact on the financial management of a healthcare organisation, with specific reference to economic and institutional determinants, as well as business ethics.

17.1 INTRODUCTION

Politicians and board directors respond to the needs of the people/clients by compiling a strategy/strategic plan in accordance with the vision and mission statement and core values of the relevant organisation/company. The strategy and strategic plans are translated into objectives, appropriate organisational structure to accommodate the plan, operational/action plans, policies and subsequent performance indicators/

outcomes. In strategic management, the performance of the organisation is measured by the extent to which the performance indicators and outcomes have been achieved (refer to Chapter 2, Strategic management in a healthcare organisation). Financial management is therefore closely linked to the strategic management process of an organisation: strategic objectives are translated into operational plans, followed by the process of budgeting and subsequent execution of the plans, applicable monitoring, reporting, analysis and feedback, and ultimate determination of compliance with the performance indicators. The interface between financial management and strategic management is depicted in Figure 17.1.

Figure 17.1 Interface between budgeting and the strategic management process

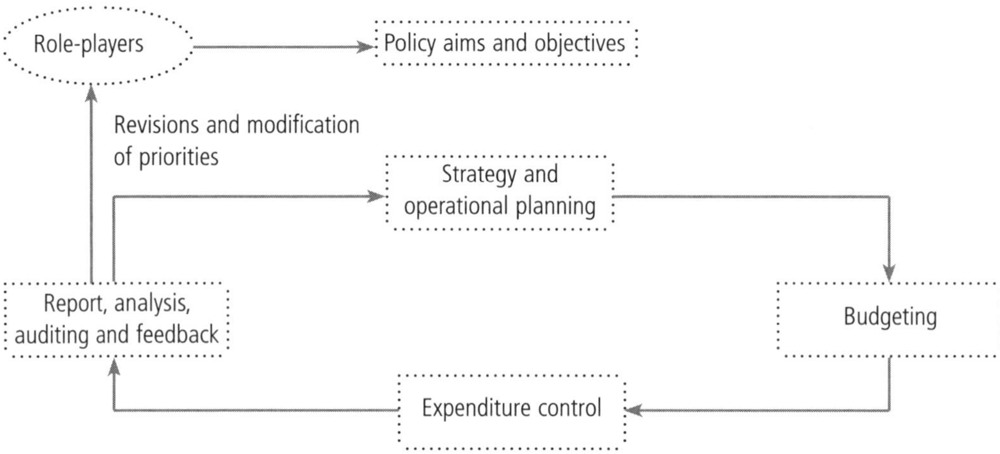

Financial management is described as budgeting, expenditure control and financial risk management (Abedian, Strachan & Ajam, 2001:6–7; Correia, Flynn, Uliana & Wormald, 2003:1:5–7; Marx, De Swardt, Beaumont-Smith, Naicker & Erasmus, 2004:2–4).

17.2 CONTEXT

Financial management occurs in the context of a specific national and international economy and is therefore practised in a dynamic economic and healthcare environment, in accordance with the specified form of business ownership. The form of ownership has numerous socio-political, legal and tax implications that will affect the financial management process and subsequent decisions. There is a variety of ownership forms, for example non-profit public or non-governmental healthcare organisations, or those having a profit-making objective, such as the sole proprietor, the partnership, the private company, the close corporation and a limited liability company (Correia et al., 2003:1:7–8). Due to legislation-specific requirements, the legal context in this chapter is described in accordance with the South African financial legal and professional-ethical framework.

Figure 17.2 Visual presentation of financial management in a healthcare organisation

Context	Constitution Medical schemes-related legislation Health Act Companies Act Corporate governance Organisational context Public Finance Management Act
Role-players	Funding source or funder Financing intermediary or purchasing agent Accountant Financial manager
Purpose	Value for money Optimal utilisation of resources Maximisation of specified variable in accordance with the business ownership context
Process	Budgeting ◗ costing approaches ◗ presentation Expenditure control ◗ principles ◗ monitoring ◗ reporting ◗ cost containment Financial risk managment ◗ responsibility and framework ◗ internal audit ◗ integrated sustainability reporting ◗ accounting and auditing ◗ portfolio management ◗ business continuity management
Underlying dynamics	Economic determinants Institutional determinants Business ethics

The healthcare context is first and foremost determined by the National Health Act, 2003 (Act 61 of 2003), as stipulated in Chapter 1. Financial management in a public healthcare organisation in South Africa is governed by the Constitution of the Republic of South Africa, 1996 (Act 108 of 1996), the Public Finance Management

Act, 1999 (Act 1 of 1999), as well as the generic principles of Corporate Governance (refer to Chapter 1). Private healthcare organisations are regulated by the Companies Act, 1973 (Act 61 of 1973), the Medical Schemes Act, 1998 (Act 131 of 1998), the Council for Medical Schemes Levies Act, 2000 (Act 58 of 2000), as well as the principles of corporate governance related to financial management. The context with reference to the financial management of a healthcare organisation in South Africa therefore relates to at least the following:

- The Constitution of the Republic of South Africa, 1996 (Act 108 of 1996)
- The National Health Act, 2003 (Act 61 of 2003)
- Corporate governance
- Public-specific legislation on financial management
- Private-specific legislation on financial management.
- Organisational context.

17.2.1 The Constitution

Chapter 13 of the Constitution of the Republic of South Africa, 1996 (Act 108 of 1996) deals with the underlying financial constitutional principles that aim at a financial system that is fair, equitable, transparent, competitive and cost-effective. The different sub-sections focus on the following:

- National Revenue Fund
- Equitable shares and allocations of revenue
- National, provincial and municipal budgets
- Treasury control
- Procurement
- Government guarantees
- Remuneration of persons holding public office
- Financial and Fiscal Commission
- Central Bank
- Provincial and local financial matters.

17.2.2 National Health Act

The National Health Act, 2003 (Act 61 of 2003) provides a framework for a structured healthcare system in the Republic of South Africa, taking into account the obligations imposed by the Constitution and other laws on the national, provincial and local governments with regard to healthcare services and to provide for matters connected therewith. This Act delineates the functions at national, provincial and district health system levels, as well as the regulation of health establishments. The level and context of healthcare service delivery therefore determines the context of financial management.

17.2.3 Corporate governance

The principles of corporate governance are described in what is referred to as the King II Report. These principles are applicable in accordance with the business ownership type. The principles of risk management are described in section two of the King II Report (refer to Chapter 18, Risk management in a healthcare organisation). Companies/organisations need to comply, among others, with the principles of internal auditing, integrated sustainability reporting, as well as accounting and auditing (King Committee on Corporate Governance, 2002).

17.2.4 Public Finance Management Act

The object of the Public Finance Management Act, 1999 (Act 1 of 1999) is to secure transparency, accountability and sound management of the revenue, expenditure, assets and liabilities of the institutions to which this Act applies. This Act applies to constitutional institutions (as listed in Schedule 1 of the Act), major public entities (as listed in Schedule 2 of the Act), as well as other public entities, such as national public entities and national government business enterprises (as listed in Schedule 3 of the Act). This Act aims to modernise and improve financial management in the public sector. The Act focuses on a performance-oriented approach to management coupled with strong reporting and accountability requirements. It promotes greater clarity of the responsibilities of accounting officers and their political heads and lays the foundations for the evolution of improved government accounting standards. The Act delineates the legal framework of the following:

- National treasury and national revenue fund
- National budgets
- Departments and constitutional institutions
- Public entities
- Executive authorities
- Loans, guarantees and other commitments
- General treasury matters
- Financial misconduct
- Accounting Standards Board.

Guidelines resulting from the Act are published with reference to the macro-budget accounting format (i.e. for reporting at provincial level by Accounting Officers) for current and capital expenditure and revenue. The guidelines serve as a macro-framework towards performance budgeting based on outcomes/outputs and incorporating performance measures. It therefore provides the framework for the integration of strategic management and financial management principles. Development of strategic plans and their integration into the budget process is an interactive exercise. Strategic planning and prioritisation is the starting point for preparation of the departmental budget submission, as it guides departmental reprioritisation in medium-term baseline allocations and provides the rationale for policy options regarding changes to baseline allocations over the strategic period (three years). Integrating strategic planning, budgeting and monitoring of service delivery performance, coupled with effective financial information and advice, will enhance the link between the services that departments provide and the benefits and costs of such services (South African Treasury, 2002, MTEF Guidelines).

17.2.5 Medical Schemes Act

The Medical Schemes Act, 1998 (Act 131 of 1998) aims to protect the interests of members of medical schemes by setting out guidelines on the terms and conditions for membership of schemes. The Act stipulates that premiums must be based only on income and/or the number of dependants, and not on any other grounds, such as the age, gender or medical history of an applicant. All medical schemes are obliged to offer a compulsory minimum benefits package. This Act also makes provision for the establishment of a Council for Medical Schemes.

The principles of Managed Health Care have been developed to curtail private healthcare costs. Healthcare organisations continue to be challenged to reduce costs while providing high-quality care. Cost-reduction methods that healthcare organisations can use successfully include cost data analysis, interdisciplinary approaches, benchmarking, clinical pathways, physician profiling, and case management. Cost reduction can also be achieved through the application of performance improvement strategies (refer to Chapter 4, Dimensions of functional management).

17.2.6 Council for Medical Schemes Levies Act

The Council for Medical Schemes Levies Act, 2000 (Act 58 of 2000) provides for the imposition of levies by the Council for Medical Schemes, and to provide for matters incidental thereto.

17.2.7 Companies Act

The Companies Act, 1973 (Act 52 of 1973, as amended) regulates, among others, the financial management of private organisations registered in accordance with this legislation.

17.2.8 Organisational context

The organisational context is based on the type of business ownership (public, private or mixed) and subsequent legislative and service delivery framework, the nature and size of the organisation, and other related internal determinants.

17.3 ROLE-PLAYERS

The following role-players in financial management will be briefly described: the funding source (funder), the financing intermediary (purchasing agent), the accountant and the financial manager.

17.3.1 Funding source (insurer/funder)

Healthcare is funded by means of different sources, i.e. the government, employers, households (contributions to medical schemes and premiums for other forms of private health insurance or directly 'out of pocket' payment), and donors (including non-governmental organisations). The funder (source of finance) therefore plays a major role in finance management, in accordance with the legislated business ownership context (Van Rensburg, 2004:35–40).

17.3.2 The financing intermediary (purchasing agent)

Funds that are raised from a source will flow through one or more purchasing agents – or financing intermediaries – before being passed on to a healthcare provider. These financing intermediaries could be the public healthcare sector (national, provincial and district), the private healthcare sector, medical schemes, household, or other governmental departments, such as Correctional Services, Defence, Education and Safety and Security. There are various mixes of public-private collaboration in healthcare financing and provisioning (Van Rensburg, 2004:37). These public-private collaboration types are reflected in Figure 17.3.

Figure 17.3 Mixes of public-private collaboration in healthcare financing and provisioning

FINANCING \ PROVISION	Public	Private
Public	◗ Government funding and provision ◗ Carefree point of service ◗ National health service	◗ Services contracted to private providers ◗ Government subsidy to mission hospitals
Private	◗ Supplementary direct user charges ◗ Private beds in public hospitals ◗ Procurement of services from private providers	◗ Private healthcare funded by private insurance ◗ Health maintenance organisations ◗ Services by non-governmental organisations

17.3.4 Accountant

The following two responsibilities related to the accountant as a role-player are highlighted (Marx et al., 2004:35–36):

- The accountant's primary functions are to develop/collect and provide data for measuring the performance of the healthcare organisation, to assess its financial position and to see to the compliance of legal financial obligations.
- The accountant complies with the Generally Accepted Accounting Practice

(GAAP) determined by the accounting profession – such as the meaningful description of the accounting entity, money measurement, conservatism, consistency concept, materiality, going-concern concept and accrual principles.

17.3.5 Financial manager

The financial manager is a pivotal role-player in the financial management of the healthcare organisation, in accordance with the business ownership context and subsequent corporate, legal and professional-ethical responsibilities. The financial managers have to locate the financial management function in the context of the strategic management process of the organisation and the devolved organisational responsibility (directorate, district, hospital, business unit or cost centre). For the financial system programme managers, this involves having clearly defined objectives and outcomes to fit the budget programme framework. For district, institution, business unit and cost centre managers it involves having clearly defined activities and outputs which fit into the budget programme framework. These objectives, activities and outputs need to have been informed by the organisational strategic plan. The budget is the resourcing of the strategic plan. Mandatory/legal responsibility for financial management, the general responsibilities of the financial manager, as well as the role of the financial manager in a private organisation, are briefly described.

17.3.5.1 Mandatory/legal responsibility for financial management

Prudent and effective financial management is a legal obligation of each 'accounting officer'. In accordance with the Financial Management Act, 1999 (Act 1 of 1999), the designated accounting officer (i.e. provincial treasury), is responsible for at least the following:

- Preparation of the budget in accordance with the legal/regulatory guidelines
- Exercising control over the implementation of the budget (expenditure control)
- Promoting and enforcing transparent and effective management of revenue, expenditure, assets and liabilities, public entities
- Ensuring that fiscal policies do not materially and unreasonably prejudice national economic policies.

The Financial Management Act of 1999 also provides a devolved and enabling framework which makes management accountable for organisational performance and therefore budget performance. The policy, legislative and economic environment provides obligatory conditions for management to the lowest appropriate level.

17.3.5.2 Responsibilities of the financial manager

The following responsibilities are summarised (Abedian, Strachan & Ajam, 2001:22–38; Correia et al., 2003:1:11–13; Marx et al., 2004:3–7):

- Interpret the economic, legal and professional-ethical context of the healthcare organisation in accordance with the applicable type of business ownership
- Identify/locate the financial management function in the context of the

healthcare organisation's strategic management process and devolved organisational responsibility (directorate/national, provincial/regional, local/ district, hospital, business unit or cost centre)

- Establish and sustain the appropriate financial management systems, policies and procedures/processes to accommodate the organisational, legal and ethical (corporate governance) requirements in accordance with the type of business ownership
- Ensure timely execution of the financial management principles and processes (budgeting and expenditure control) in accordance with the organisational, legal, professional-ethical and corporate governance requirements
- Ensure that money is spent in relation to the budget for the defined output and service delivery
- Provide appropriate financial risk and portfolio management in accordance with the strategic decisions and business ownership context
- Formulate clearly defined objectives and outcomes to fit the budget framework of the organisation, in accordance with the organisation's strategic plan
- Develop clearly defined activities and outputs which fit into the budget framework, in accordance with the organisation's strategic plan
- Synthesise the dimensions of management, inputs and service delivery with reference to budgeting, expenditure control and financial risk management
- Provide continuous evaluation of the most cost-effective forms of delivery and improvement of efficiency and resource utilisation
- Make financing decisions
- Ensure a positive cash flow – that cash inflow exceeds cash outflow
- Comply with the legal and general best practice principles, standards and code of conduct with reference to financial management.

17.3.5.3 The role of the financial manager in a private organisation

The first role of the financial manager in the private context is to pursue wealth-creating investment opportunities (Correia et al., 2003:1:11–13):

- Such opportunities are then evaluated in order to establish whether they are profitable by determining whether they are likely to increase the value of the business. Needless to say, there are often numerous possible opportunities available from which to select.
- The financial manager is required to evaluate the possibilities and rank them in order of potential profitability. This may seem to be a relatively straightforward procedure, however, when it is considered that such evaluation is based on predicted outcomes and that different opportunities have different levels of risk attached to them, it becomes apparent that selection from among competing investment opportunities requires consideration of many interacting factors. Investment opportunities can be broadly classified in two categories, namely investment in operating assets and investment in financial assets.

Having identified investment opportunities with wealth-creating potential, the second major role of the financial manager is to raise funds in order to finance the investment (Correia et al., 2003:1:11–13):

- The objective when canvassing financing alternatives would be to obtain funds at the lowest cost. The cost of finance from the viewpoint of the investor will usually be determined by the risk which is seen to be associated with the investment. This in turn depends on the type of projects being undertaken, the length of time for which the funds are provided, and the legal standing of the finance in the event of liquidation of the company.
- Finance is usually obtained in one of four ways – by going to the capital markets and attracting long-term finance, by making use of suppliers' credit, by going to the money markets and using short-term finance, or by retaining profits which could otherwise be paid to shareholders in the form of dividends.
- Investment decisions must be made.
- Profitability must be ensured – that income exceeds expenses.
- The organisation's liquidity and solvency must be maintained.

17.4 PURPOSE OF FINANCIAL MANAGEMENT

Although there are commonalities between the public and private sector with regard to the purpose of financial management of healthcare organisations, there is obviously a difference of focus. The appropriate allocation and utilisation of resources is the ultimate objective of the public sector budgeting system. This means not only that best practice financial management standards are adhered to, but that resources are allocated in line with the socio-political preferences of the society as pronounced by the government of the day. As such, 'control' is not only a mechanism ensuring that resources are not misappropriated, but also for ensuring that public funds are placed at the service of social welfare through a sound and credible management system.

The fundamental objectives of financial management in a healthcare organisation are to facilitate (Correia et al., 2003:1:9–10; Abedian et al., 2001:3–5; 82–87; Marx et al., 2004:4–5):

- Value for money (efficiency, effectiveness and quality)
- Optimal utilisation of resources (the allocation of scarce resources in the most appropriate manner)
- Maximisation of a specified variable in accordance with the business ownership context of the healthcare organisation (i.e. national/public interest with reference to specific healthcare indicators, profit, share price, investors' wealth and company growth).

17.5 FINANCIAL MANAGEMENT PROCESS

Financial management relates to the processes by which management allocates money and other resources to realise objectives/outcomes and performance indicators of the organisation. Financial management is described as a process of budgeting, expenditure control and financial risk management. Whilst budgeting is concerned with the allocation targets and anticipated results, expenditure control focuses mainly on the detail of implementing the budget. This process is summarised in Figure 17.4.

Figure 17.4 Summarised process of financial management

Budgeting	**Expenditure control**	**Risk management**
Costing • incremental • zero-based • programme-based • performance-based Presentation • Line item • Programme-based	Principles of expenditure control Financial management monitoring Financial management reporting Cost containment	Responsibility & framework Internal audit Integrated sustainability reporting Accounting and auditing Portfolio management Business continuity management

The financial management process is described in accordance with the following framework:

- Description of concepts (refer also to the glossary at the end of the chapter)
- The fundamental principles of financial management
- Budgeting system as a prerequisite
- Budgeting (costing and presentation)
- Expenditure control
- Financial risk management.

17.5.1 Description of concepts

Budget

The healthcare budget deals with income and expenses. It is the combination of expenditure plans and revenue generation plans for the coming year.

Budgeting

Budgeting refers to the resourcing of the healthcare organisation's strategy, that is, what inputs are needed to undertake defined activities for specified objectives – the processes by which management allocates the money and other resources to realise outcome objectives/results. Budgeting entails compiling a plan for acquiring resources (planned revenue) and deploying them in pursuit of policy objectives (planned expenditure). Budgeting is thus concerned with translating policy priorities into resource allocations – and is essentially a strategic exercise. Strategic objectives are unlikely to be achieved without the requisite resources. Because the budget indicates policy preferences, budgeting also becomes a political exercise. Yet, budgeting should not be divorced from strategic management objectives (Abedian et al., 2001:5–7).

Budgeting is therefore defined as the resourcing of the organisation's strategy by compiling a plan for acquiring resources (planned revenue) and the deployment of resources in pursuit of the organisation's objectives (planned expenditure) according to the type of business ownership, and the legal, professional-ethical and organisational management framework of the healthcare organisation.

Expenditure control

Expenditure control refers to the operational management of the approved budget with reference to the fundamental principles, monitoring and reporting, as well as cost containment.

Financial risk management

The word risk usually refers to a potential hazard or the possibility of an unfortunate outcome resulting from a given action – the chance of a bad consequence. In financial management, the term indicates that there is an expectation that the actual outcome of a project may differ from the expected outcome. The magnitude of the possible difference reflects the magnitude of the risk. Risk implies that it is possible to attach financial probabilities to identified expected financial outcomes (Correia et al., 2003:3:2–3). A business risk results from the nature of the business itself, and the type of business ownership. It includes all the uncertainty that surrounds the industry in which the business operates (Correia et al., 2003:3:3). Financial risk management is based on the following: responsibility and framework, internal audit, integrated sustainability reporting, accounting and auditing, portfolio management and business continuity management.

17.5.2 Fundamental principles of financial management

Financial management is based on the fundamental principles of cost-benefit, risk-return and time-value-of money (Marx et al., 2004:8–9), as detailed below.

Cost-benefit principle

Decision-making that is based on the cost of resources only will not necessarily lead to the most economical use of resources. Sound financial decision-making requires analysis of the total cost and the total benefits. As far as possible, the benefits should be greater than the cost of any decision. The process of cost-benefit analysis should therefore focus on at least the following: clarification of the objective(s) to be attained; identification and analysis of different alternatives in which the objective(s) could be attained; calculation of the costs and the benefits of each alternative; determining the effectiveness of the benefits, followed by informed decision-making.

Risk-return principle

Risk is an inseparable characteristic of any decision. Risk is the probability that the actual result of a decision may deviate from the planned end result and may entail an associated financial loss or waste of funds. Risk should be measurable by means of probabilities. The risk-return principle is a trade-off between risk and return – the higher the risk, the higher the required rate of return. As far as possible, the return should exceed the risk involved in any business decision. Risk should always be minimised or managed.

Time-value-of-money principle

The time-value-of-money principle means that a person could increase the value of an amount of money by earning interest. If the amount is invested in equipment, vehicles or other assets, the amount could not earn interest. The financial manager should therefore consider the time-for-value principle when making financial decisions.

17.5.3 Budgeting system as a prerequisite

Effective financial management is dependent upon a trustworthy budgeting system, in accordance with the type of business ownership of the healthcare organisation and the legal, professional-ethical context of healthcare service delivery. The following budgeting principles are highlighted (Abedian et al., 2001:66):

- Budgeting systems provide a planning framework.
- Having a planning framework encourages managers to think ahead (to forecast), identify targets and establish the levels and types of resources needed to achieve those targets.
- Budgeting systems enable a financial control and monitoring framework to be established by drawing up cash flow (expenditure) patterns and forecast which monitor progress on a timely basis and enable corrective action to be taken.
- Since proper budgeting requires targets and resources to be decided upon, a budget can provide a yardstick for measuring performance once operations are up and running. This performance measurement aspect of budgeting is particularly well suited to measuring efficiency and effectiveness. It also helps with the measurement of performance-related reward systems.
- Well-developed budgets allow for devolved authority and accountability, and enable managers to take responsibility for their own performance. Such a budgeting structure is essential to ensuring successful decentralisation.
- Participative preparation of budgets encourages ownership of budgets, thereby increasing motivation and a manager's sense of responsibility.

17.5.4 Budgeting

The process of budgeting is briefly described with reference to the objectives of the budget, basic principles of budgeting, approaches to costing, as well as the different methods of presentation. The South African annual public service budget cycle is also presented.

Objectives of the budget

The objectives of the budget are summarised as follows:

- To determine priorities and to allocate financial and other resources to them
- To provide a detailed plan of revenue and expenditure for which spending departments/business units can be held responsible
- To provide a system of accountability and controls over organisational officials and agencies, setting limits on their activities and safeguarding against corruption.

Basic principles of budgeting

The following principles are highlighted (Abedian, 2001:111–112; Correia et al., 2003:1:11–15):

- Aggregate fiscal/financial discipline: budget totals should be the result of explicit decisions; they should not merely accommodate spending demands. These totals should be set before spending decisions are made and should be sustainable over the medium term and beyond.
- Costing therefore follows decisions on types of services to be delivered, the standard of services to be provided and the quality of services rendered.
- Allocative efficiency and effectiveness: expenditure should be based on organisational priorities and on effectiveness of healthcare programmes. The budget system should spur re-allocation from lesser to higher priorities and from less to more effective programmes. The principle of *option appraisal* is applied when determining priorities (such as financing options, sourcing options, contracting and provision versus production options). Costing and budgeting are inevitably about making choices and dealing with trade-offs. Options have to be weighed up and hard decisions need to be made. Optional appraisal therefore is an important part of good budgeting (Abedian et al., 2001:118).
- An organisational environment that fosters organisational performance and better service delivery – this means having clear strategic and operational objectives and outcomes that are implemented.
- A reliable, accurate and integrated Financial Management Information System is necessary.
- A thorough understanding is required of how to use existing systems to monitor and control expenditure and resource inputs. This implies that financial managers understand the financial information.
- A developing management commitment is understanding and managing the stated outputs and performance indicators as opposed to the administration of the budget without concern for the impact thereof.
- An organisational structure that fosters alignment of managerial and financial accountability – managers should be accountable and thus able to control the finances allocated to their area of responsibility.
- Have effective financial auditing before moving to performance auditing, i.e. use

the Financial Management Information System well and be able to audit inputs before moving on to audit inputs in relation to output.

- Be able to adopt and implement predictable budgets before moving to managing performance and the efficiency of resource utilisation. Where the budget bottom line is constantly changing, managers cannot be expected to manage.

Costing approaches

Costing refers to the process of determining in monetary terms the value of the inputs that are required to generate a particular service or programme. Costing therefore involves estimating the quantity of inputs required by a particular activity in pursuit of the organisational objectives, as well as their associated monetary value. The bulk of costing is concerned with estimating operational (recurrent) expenses. Costing of items with a life-span of more than one year is referred to as capital costing (Abedian, 2001:111). There are different approaches to costing. A brief description of the following costing approaches is given: incremental, zero-based, programme-based and performance budgeting.

Incremental costing

Incremental costing is a very simple and unsophisticated approach to budgeting – it assumes that the existing budget is the best basis for estimating the budget for the year ahead. Therefore, it uses the current year's estimates for the various components of expenditure and projects forward to arrive at the budget estimates. Clearly, this method of costing presupposes that the objectives and activities of the department under consideration are optimal and there is no need to reconsider them. It follows that via incremental costing, no policy shift would occur. Nor would there be any changes in the financing approaches in service delivery (Abedian, 2001:110). This approach takes the previous year's budget and adds a pre-determined increment. This increment is usually related to the inflation rate, as well as other internal organisational variables (expansion of services) and external factors (demographic changes, stakeholder demands, etc).

Zero-based costing

The zero-based approach to costing involves costing each programme from activity level upwards for each budget cycle. This means assuming the budget for each input or programme is zero and then compiling the budget in the light of the current priorities and the most efficient methods of service delivery. The expenditure for each item has to be justified again annually. There is a common appeal in this method – the re-examining of expenditure items every year presupposes that there is real scope for changing expenditure patterns from year to year (Abedian, 2001:110–111).

Programme-based costing

Programme (Abedian et al., 2001:56–57) costing focuses on the objectives that emerged from the strategic planning and policy-making process. Programme budgeting begins with the objectives of an organisation and determines which activities contribute to the outcomes of the objectives. In essence, this entails looking at each existing and proposed activity and inputs sub-programme and programme in terms of the following: is the programme going to be delivered next year? At what level/quality is the programme going to be delivered? What resources are needed to deliver the programme in the most efficient manner? As goals and priorities change, some programmes are phased out and others are introduced (Abedian, 2001:110).

Performance budgeting

Performance budgeting (budgeting for service delivery outputs and health status outcomes) links budgeting, strategic planning, financial management and reporting, as well as performance management, with one another. Performance budgeting integrates resource and financial management into the management process. The main purpose of performance budgeting is to enable managers to analyse and allocate resources in terms of purposes to be achieved and to relate resources to results – in other words to relate inputs to outputs and outcomes in a complex organisational context. A performance budget places emphasis both on outputs and on outcomes in managing performance (Abedian et al., 2001:68–69). The process of performance budgeting is summarised in eight steps (refer also to Chapter 4, Dimensions of functional management):

Step one: *Establishing objectives and programmes*

Performance budgeting aims to set up a hierarchy of objectives which reflects the strategic plan of the organisation/department. The core and supportive objectives that are identified become the framework for the programme structure. Structure programmes and sub-programmes form the strategic aims and outcome objectives of the department/organisation. The programme structure needs to be comprehensive, taking into account all activities required to reach the conceptual and organisational goals. The programme structure should enable strategic budget analysis and enhance management synergy between different objectives. Programmes should also be structured according to the organisational structure and accountability chain of the programme, directorate or business unit. This strategic function involves the programme managers and chief/senior executive officers.

Step two: *Define and quantify outputs*

Define and quantify outputs or service rendering results that contribute towards the outcomes. Outputs are defined according to how the goals or objectives of the programme will be realised. The quantification of the service delivery outputs is done by estimating the coverage for the target group receiving the service (i.e. for immunisation coverage it will be necessary to estimate the number of children who need immunisation in a given population).This is a task for programme, business unit and activity managers. In the management structure of the public sector, this task involves programme, sub-programme, objective and responsibility managers.

Step three: *Identify and define activities*
Identify and define activities that result in the outputs. Activities are the actual provision of goods and services in each programme of the healthcare organisation. Activities are the actions required to result in the planned outcomes in order to achieve the defined objectives of the organisation. Activities take inputs (i.e. staff, transport, drugs and equipment) and translate them into physical outputs (i.e. patients treated, women screened and children immunised) to realise broad objectives. This operational function involves programme, business unit and activity managers. In the management structure of the public sector, this task involves programme, sub-programme, objective and responsibility managers.

Step four: *Develop performance measures and indicators*
Develop performance measures (outputs) and performance indicators (outcomes). Again, this is the task of the activity manager in consultation with the programme/business unit and activity managers. In the management structure of the public sector, this task involves programme, sub-programme, objective and responsibility managers.

Step five: *Identify inputs and cost the resources*
Identify inputs and cost the resources required in these activities. This implies compiling the project budget (activity-based programme budgeting), by identifying the inputs, quantifying the inputs needed for each activity and costing each input and activity – assigning a money value to each input and activity. This is the task of the activity and financial managers.

Step six: *Project and schedule cash flow*
Project and schedule the cash flow, by applying the basic principles of budgeting. This is the task of the financial manager.

Step seven: *Develop a multi-year budget*
Develop a multi-year budget and make budget adjustments, in accordance with the legal and organisational financial policy framework. This is the task of the financial manager in consultation with programme and activity managers. In the case of the public sector, this task involves programme, sub-programme, objective and responsibility managers.

Step eight: *Performance management*
Integrate performance budgeting with performance management (refer to Chapter 4, Dimensions of functional management). Various performance-improvement

strategies could be integrated in performance budgeting in a healthcare organisation, such as case management, physician/healthcare practitioner profiling, credentialing and resource utilisation review.

Presentation of the budget

Broadly speaking, there are two main methods of presenting expenditure information in budgets. These are line-item and programme formats.

Line-item format presentation

The line-item presentation refers to a budget where the expenditure information is presented according to a set of standard items or categories. The items or categories in effect capture and compile all the separate items of a budget according to type. Typical examples of line-item categories are:

- Personnel expenditure: salaries, skills development, etc.
- Administrative expenditure
- Stocks and supplies
- Equipment
- Land and buildings
- Professional and special services
- Miscellaneous expenditure, etc. All the budgets in a particular organisation are presented in this format – from national to operational/business unit level.

The weaknesses of a line-item budget are as follows:

- It does not reflect how money was actually used to realise programme objectives
- It does not differentiate between managerial, administrative and operational staff
- It does not differentiate between different inputs in different programmes
- It gives little indication of the actual utilisation of funds in a programme or sub-programme.

Programme budget format presentation

In a programme budget the expenditure information is presented according to programme and sub-programme and the line items correspond to the actual inputs required to meet the objectives of the programme. This means that while certain line-items, like management and administration, may be the same across all programmes, others will differ. Examples of inputs would be: personnel, general administration, stores and equipment, transport, security, land and buildings, etc. The logic underlying a programme budget is that it reflects exactly what resources are allocated to the implementation of a particular programme and how those resources are to be spent. As such, programme budgets tend to present far more detailed information. Programme budgeting is useful when it comes to:

- Determining whether the allocation of resources actually reflects priorities
- Planning the delivery of different services

- Monitoring the use of resources
- Ensuring that value for money is being realised in each programme
- Identifying areas in the budget where savings can be realised or where more funds are needed to ensure effective delivery.

Public service budgeting cycle and process

A distinguishing feature of government budget preparation is the long and complex process that is involved. Commonly, the budget cycle could be as long as 18 months. Given the enormity of the budget exercise, it is inevitable that a great deal of interdepartmental, intradepartmental, and intergovernmental co-ordination has to take place on an annual basis so as to ensure a timely enactment of the budget. The public service annual budget cycle consists of nine steps, as reflected in Figure 17.5.

Figure 17.5 Public service annual budget cycle

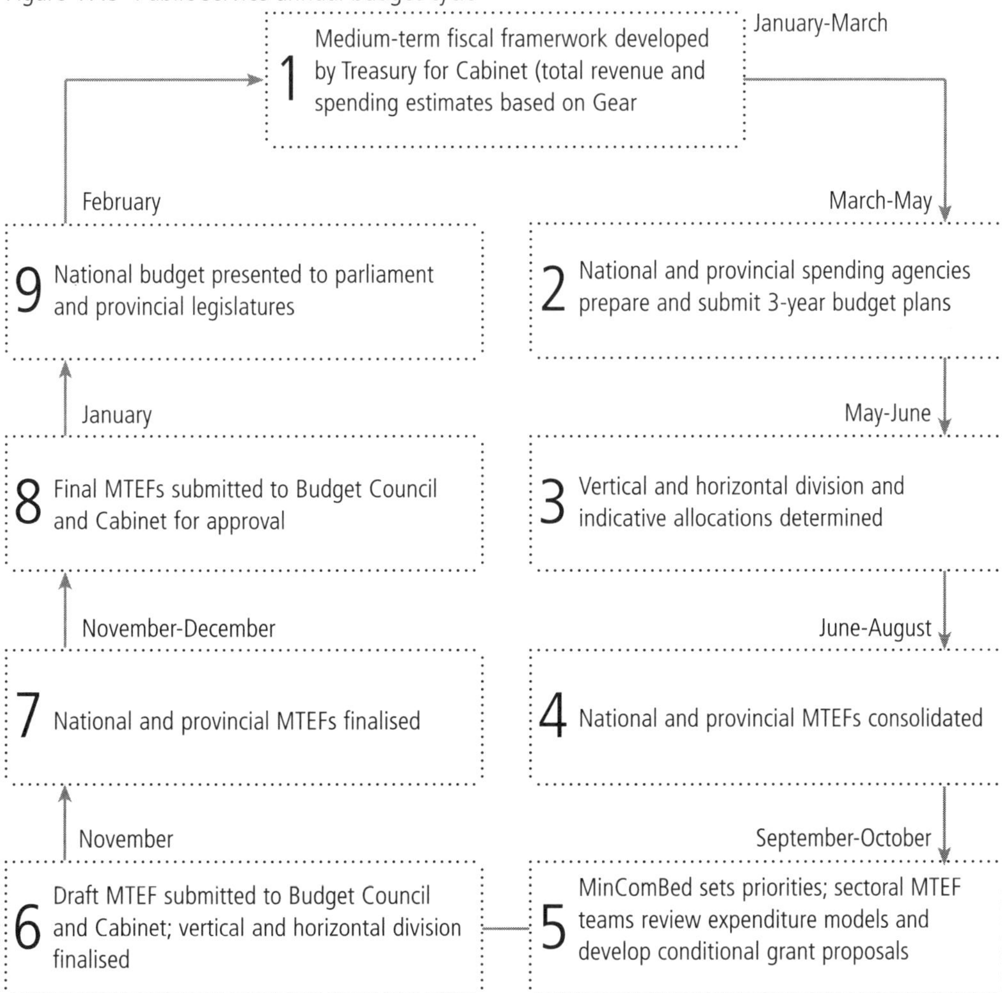

The budget format outlines policy developments, legislation and other factors affecting expenditure alongside spending plans. Details of national departmental outputs and service delivery indicators take another step forward towards setting measurable objectives in line with the Public Finance Management Act, 199 (Act 1 of 1999). Such measurable objectives, linked to departmental performance targets and annual reporting to Parliament and provincial legislatures, is a formal requirement of the budget for national and provincial departments. The format allows departments to build the necessary capacity to develop, implement and track service delivery indicators and performance measures. In general, the budget process involves three distinct types of interactions (Abedian et al., 2001:38–39):

- **Intradepartmental actions**. These involve setting priorities, costing programmes, projects, activities and considering optimal financing options.
- **Interdepartmental activities**. These are related to either collaboration with other departments with mutual interests, or with the Department of Finance on the budgetary and financing issues.
- **Interaction with politicians**. This takes two forms – first is the ongoing interface with the political head of the department (i.e. the MEC or premier), and second is the engagement of Parliament or the provincial legislature via the standing committees.

There are key stages in the public sector budgeting process, in accordance with the Public Finance Management Act, 1999 (Act 1 of 1999). Unpacking the budget process is simplified by viewing it as a series of decision stages that form the building blocks in preparing the budget. This process comprises six overlapping stages that correspond to the critical decision nodal points:

(1) **Prioritisation phase.** The financial executive focuses on the broad medium-term policy and spending priorities associated with the Government's social, economic and developmental priorities, usually between April to September.

(2) **Preparation and review of the Medium Term Expenditure Framework (MTEF) budget**. Submissions of national departments and Medium Term Expenditure Forum (MTEF) budgets at the provincial sphere take place between April to August.

(3) **Review of the macroeconomic and fiscal framework and the Division of Revenue**. These take place between the three spheres of government, are the subject of technical analyses and consultation between July to August, and are considered by the extended Cabinet in September.

(4) **The Medium-Term Allocation Process – Recommendation Stage**. This is initiated by and during the Medium Term Expenditure Committee hearings and discussions at the national and provincial level between September and October.

(5) **Medium-Term Budget Policy Statement**. Government's broad medium-term policy and spending plans are considered by Cabinet and tabled before Parliament in the October Medium Term Budget Policy Statement.

(6) **Medium-Term Allocation Process – Decision Stage**. November to February sees national departments and provincial treasuries work closely with the National Treasury to prepare the budget and documentation that is tabled before Parliament and before provincial legislatures.

At provincial level, the provincial treasuries and departments prepare and submit their annual budgets in accordance with the Public Finance Act, 1999 (Act 1 of 1999, section 27). This budget should be in accordance with a format as prescribed, and should contain at least the following:

- Estimates of all revenues to be raised during the financial year to which the budget relates
- Estimates of expenditure per vote and per main division with the vote
- Estimates of interest and debt servicing charges and repayments of debt
- Estimates of capital expenditure per vote and main division in a vote for that financial year and the projected financial implications of that expenditure for future financial year
- Estimates of revenue excluded for that financial year
- Estimates of all direct charges against the Revenue Fund and standing appropriations for that financial year
- An indication of intentions regarding the borrowing and other forms of public liability that will increase public debt during that and future financial years
- The projected review of the previous financial year; expenditure per vote and main division in the vote for the previous financial year; borrowing for the previous financial year; any information as may be prescribed, including any multi-year budgets.

The provincial budgets are submitted in accordance with the prescribed format, comprising three budget statements: budget overview, departmental estimates and capital works:

Budget Statement No 1: *Budget Overview*
This budget statement will provide a provincial summary of the main budget aggregates, including strategic policy directions, the MTEF process, expenditure and revenue trends aggregates and trends.

Budget Statement No 2: *Departmental Estimates*
This budget statement is an overview of each department's mission and strategic directions in the vote and will include a review of the key budget and programme outcomes for each Department in a province.

Budget Statement No 3: *Capital Works*
An overview of a province's capital works and endeavours to indicate whether the

expanding of a province's infrastructure has promoted economic development and employment and assisted in meeting the GEAR's social objectives (see Glossary at the end of this book) by ensuring that government services be delivered effectively and efficiently.

17.5.5 Expenditure control

Expenditure control is the second dimension of financial management and relates to the implementation and control of the approved budget. Expenditure control is described with reference to the **principles** of expenditure control, financial management **monitoring** and financial management **reporting**.

Principles of expenditure control

The principles of expenditure control are summarised as follows (Abedian et al., 2001:139–150):

- Cash management: manage requisitions, pay salaries, allocate transport, pay claims and advances, manage cheques, manage suppliers, link orders and requisitions to credit payments, interface with creditors, etc.
- Ensuring efficient procurement management: ordering, payment of debtors, management of the efficient and effective provision of resources (i.e. timely delivery of drugs)
- Enabling and monitoring expenditure (cash flow) in line with budget and in relation to planned output
- Monitoring best use of resources to achieve a given output
- Applying appropriate accounting practices, such as cash accounting, accrual accounting, as well as commitment accounting
- Monthly, quarterly and annual reporting on expenditure and resource utilisation
- Taking responsible and appropriate action on any of the above when necessary
- Internal and external auditing.

Financial management monitoring

The primary tool for financial management monitoring is a well-established and trustworthy Financial Management Information System (FMIS). This system should consist of an interrelated set of sub-systems that plan, process and report upon resources, quantifying them in financial terms. The basic sub-systems may be accounting, cash management, budgeting, debt management and other related internal controls. Procurement and personnel information should interface with the financial information management system. The financial information management system should be a reliable set of commonly shared, reliable and valid data bases to and from which all data expressed in financial terms flows. The financial information system should then link to other service delivery systems which use financial resources for their operations. The criteria for an effective financial management information system are as follows (Abedian et al., 2001:155–156):

- Integrate with other resource (personnel, equipment, etc.) and management information systems
- Provide accurate and timely information in a framework of use for management decision-making
- Be linked to reflect service delivery activities and therefore budget outputs.

Financial management monitoring also relates to the basic principles of expenditure control, as well as the fundamental principles of financial management as described.

Financial management reporting

Management should identify and define financial reporting requirements in accordance with the strategic and management objectives. The different types of reporting, frequency (monthly, quarterly and annually), as well as the level of reporting, should be deliniated. A brief description of commonly used reporting types is given.

(a) *Expenditure control report*

- Actual and budgeted expenditure. These reports (financial statements: balance sheet, income statement and cash flow statement) detail line-item and standard expenditure across the whole department/cost centre, by activity and programme.
- Expenditure variance report. This type of report shows the degree of deviation between the budgeted and actual spending at various levels.
- Committed expenditure, actual expenditure and remaining budget. This report could reflect money not spent but for which requisitions have been authorised, and for which budget may be already committed in contracts, statutory expenditures or regular standardised/projected expenditure such as electricity.

(b) *Expenditure management report*

- Expenditure by output report. These reports detail expenditure by standard item and by output per activity, in accordance with the strategic objectives and subsequent programmes.
- Cash flow report. These reports detail monthly cash flow per activity and programme or sub-programme.
- Delivery schedule report. These reports detail monthly delivery schedule per activity and programme or sub-programme.

(c) *Performance measurement report*

These reports enable management to evaluate financial and service delivery performance through key measures. The types of reports that can be generated here are numerous and depend very much on management imperative. Examples of performance measurement reports are:

- Actual and planned delivery of services

- Comparative efficiency reports in the form of cost per patient for clinic or activity, nursing staffing levels per unit/clinic/hospital, cost per patient day for hospitals, occupancy rates, and average length of stay in hospitals.

(d) *Financial statement analysis: Audit report*
At the end of every financial year, the directors of each company are obliged to produce annual financial statements and to lay them before an annual general meeting in terms of the Companies Act, 1973 (Act 52 of 1973, as amended). These financial statements must, in conformity with generally accepted accounting practice, fairly present the state of the affairs of the company and the results of operations for the financial year (Correia, 2003:5–1). The audit report should be submitted, in accordance with corporate governance or legislative requirements (usually three months after closure of the organisation's financial year). This report reflects the monetary organisational performance.

Levels of reporting
The integrated financial information management system should be able to generate reports for different management and decision-making levels, such as geographical, institutional, programme-based or activity breakdown.

Cost containment
Cost containment refers to the measures put into place to manage expenditure. Selected cost containment methods in the healthcare organisation are briefly highlighted.

Financial policies and procedures
The organisation's financial resources are vital to the success and sustainability of the organisation. There should be financial policies and procedures in place on at least the following:

- The budgeting process and aspects related to the various dimensions, such as the annual budget, cash-flow budget and capital budget
- Short-, medium- and long-term finance policies
- Purchasing/procurement of equipment, stocks and supplies, etc. (including tender management)
- The management of debtors: credit policy, credit terms, collection policy, etc.
- The management of stocks and supplies and subsequent risk mitigation strategies
- Human resources: a system that makes provision for the determination of staffing levels, posts, exceeding of normal salary levels, etc. (refer to the chapters on human resource management).

Management of physical resources

An organisation's physical resources are its tangible assets, such as clinical equipment, buildings, vehicles, stocks and supplies. Control systems for these resources involve utilisation policies and procedures, periodic inspections and stocktaking (which often fall in the ambit of the internal audit), condemning and replacement of equipment, tender management, utilisation review practices, inventory control, maintenance, logistics management, etc. The following principles are emphasised:

- There are organisational policies and procedures on the management of physical resources, such as inventory, condemning and replacement, maintenance, periodic inspections (also form part of risk management) and utilisation review.
- A tender management policy and procedure is in place in accordance with the type of business ownership and subsequent legislative and regulatory guidelines.
- The principles of logistics management are applied.
- National, provincial, regional or local sharing of expensive medical equipment.

Management of stocks and supplies

The management of stocks and supplies (materials required for service delivery) is an overarching organisational concept embracing purchasing management and 'warehousing', as well as certain operational functions such as the transfer of stocks and supplies through the transformation (service delivery) process. It is an effort to combine demand and supply principles in the most cost-effective and efficient manner. Medical stocks and supplies need to be managed due to the cost thereof and the expiry dates involved. The following measures are important:

- There are organisational policies and procedures on the management of medical/clinical and non-clinical stocks and supplies
- Risk management strategies are in place to mitigate medico-legal risks with regard to stocks and supplies (i.e. storing and checking of expiry dates)
- The principles of Supply Chain Management (SCM) are applied, in accordance with the nature and scope of clinical service delivery: a reliable system of determining the needs (benchmarks) and the timely supply thereof
- The principle of Economic Ordering Quantity (EOQ) is utilised: based on the replenishing of inventory/stock levels by ordering the most economic quantity in accordance with demand and supply calculations (topping-up system)
- A Material Requirement Planning (MRP) system is utilised: an estimate is made of the demand for stocks and supplies, and the components necessary to render the planned service (i.e. MRP is applied to the determination of medicine required for a one month period in the primary healthcare clinic)
- The just-in-time (JIT) is a refinement of the MRP system: JIT is based on the premise that actual orders for stocks and supplies are converted into orders for new stocks and supplies, which arrive just in time for service delivery purposes
- The principles of Managed Health Care are also applied in the private healthcare industry, in accordance with the Medical Aid requirements.

Maintenance

The maintenance of physical resources also forms part of the risk management process in the healthcare service. It is important to ensure that a maintenance policy and procedure are in place. A maintenance department could also be centralised in a province or region, in accordance with the corporate or national policies.

Knowledge management

Knowledge management is the process of identifying, collecting, storing, and transforming data and information into an intellectual asset that is available to staff members or line managers. It aims to develop a solid base of intellectual capital by gathering and sharing the knowledge of individual staff members. It increases workplace efficiency, saves time, reduces costs, and facilitates the exchange and re-utilisation of knowledge.

Managed healthcare

Managed healthcare refers to the regulated process of cost containment in the context of private medical insurance (according to the medical aid/insurance legislative framework), to facilitate affordability without compromising access and quality of service delivery. Managed healthcare is regulated by means of, among others, the following methods: preferred service providers (i.e. Health Maintenance Organisation, accredited by the insurer), the involvement of an intermediate clinical agent/assessor – to determine whether the patient requires that type and scope of treatment, with the subsequent authorisation (or denial thereof) of treatment and care prior to the commencement thereof, case management and care mapping in accordance with the optimal clinical guidelines, drug utilisation reviews, negotiated medical aid tariffs, etc.

17.5.6 Financial risk management

The old adage that you shouldn't place all your eggs in one basket reveals a general approach to risks. Because virtually all future outcomes are uncertain, it would be folly for an investor to place all available funds in one investment. It is therefore sensible to diversify into a number of investments in the expectation that those which are profitable will at least compensate for the loss which may be sustained from those that are not (Correia et al., 2003:4:1). The principle of portfolio management therefore becomes important. The sources of risks could be as follows: general economic risks, inflation and disinflation risks, as well as organisation-specific risks (business, financial and issue/programme-specific (Marx et al., 2004:86–87).

Financial risk management principles are deliniated in the King II Report, (King Committee on Corporate Governance, 2002: section 2), focusing on the risk management responsibility and framework, internal auditing, integrated sustainability reporting, as well as accounting and auditing. The principles of Business Continuity Management (BCM) are also important; especially with regard to private healthcare organisations (refer to Chapter 18, Risk management in a healthcare organisation). A brief description of the dimensions of financial risk management is given.

Risk management: Responsibility and framework

The Board is responsible for the total process of risk management. The healthcare organisation's management is accountable to the board for designing, implementing and monitoring the process of risk management with reference to the development of a risk strategy and subsequent policies, determination of the organisation's tolerance for risk, application of recognised risk management practices, such as internal control, documentation, application and reporting (refer to Chapter 4, Risk management in a healthcare organisation). The Board is responsible to ensure that a formal risk assessment is undertaken at least annually, for its public statement, which also acknowledges its responsibility. A system would yield at least the following (Cruywagen, 2004:3):

- A register with key financial risks
- Significant loss costs
- Reconciliation between risk profile and risk costs
- Material losses and reduction in earnings/cash flows
- Material changes to the risk profile
- Details of risk finance arrangements
- Due diligence activities
- The risk-bearing capacity of the business.

Internal audit

The status and role, as well as the scope of internal auditing, are described in the King II report. A mandatory Audit Committee is recommended. Organisations should reflect and demonstrate a trustworthy system of internal auditing, compliant with regulated requirements and general best practices (King Committee on Corporate Governance, 2002).

Integrated sustainability reporting

Integrated sustainability reporting focuses on two dimensions: sustainability reporting and organisational integrity/code of ethics. Reporting requirements focus on the nature and extent of its social, transformation, ethical, safety, health and environmental management policies and practices, as well as an integrated stakeholder reporting system. The organisational integrity/code of ethics dimension focuses on stakeholder engagement and the principles of ethical behaviour in an organisation (King Committee on Corporate Governance, 2002).

Accounting and auditing

The responsibilities of the Audit Committee are deliniated in the King II Report to ensure sound financial auditing practices. The reporting of financial and non-financial information is also stipulated. Lastly, the appointment of regulatory measures with reference to the Audit Committee are described.

Portfolio management

Portfolio management refers to the diversification of investments – of investing in more than a single investment. Portfolio management focuses on the investment principles used by both individual and corporate investors. This is relevant to financial management of private healthcare organisations, since the objective is to create wealth through effective business operations (Correia et al., 2003:4:1–2; Marx et al., 2004:92–94).

Business continuity management

Business Continuity Management (BCM) is a holistic management process that identifies potential impacts that threaten an organisation and provides a framework for building resilience and the capability for an effective response which safeguards the interests of its key stakeholders, reputation, brand and value creating activities (Business Continuity Institute (BCI), 2001). The following attributes relate to Business Continuity Management (see also Chapter 18, Risk management in a healthcare organisation):

- Business Continuity Management is the planning and implementation for events that occur despite risk management.
- Business Continuity Planning may also be the outcome of risk management where risk reduction strategies do not or cannot effectively control the hazard. Hazards that originate outside an organisation, risk reduction measures that are too costly, or high probability organisational risks that, despite controls, may result in critical or terminal disruptions, may best be addressed through business continuity.
- Business Continuity Management consists of disaster recovery, contingency planning and crisis management.
- A disaster recovery plan needs to be compiled.

17.6 UNDERLYING DYNAMICS

There are various underlying dynamics that could impact on the quality of financial management in a healthcare organisation. These, among others, could be the economic determinants, the institutional determinants, as well as the principles of business ethics.

17.6.1 Economic determinants

A few economic determinants are highlighted:

- Among the most powerful extraneous determinants are the prevailing economic climate, the economic system of the country, and specific economic factors.
- A country's particular modes of economic production, distribution and

consumption, as well as its patterns of ownership, economic control and the distribution of resources and wealth, directly affect the healthcare organisations and traditions in the healthcare system.

- Obviously a country's economic ability, economic prosperity, levels of economic development and industrialisation, economic growth and dependence on international economic aid, as well as the national and international economic trends and crises, have a pronounced effect on the national healthcare system and the quality of financial management in the healthcare system and organisations.

17.6.2 Institutional determinants

There are various institutional determinants impacting on the quality of financial management in a healthcare organisation:

- The economic support system, the nature and scope of resources available, the type of healthcare programmes and level of service delivery, the leadership and management framework, as well as cultural determinants, impact on the quality of financial management.
- An organisational culture and environment that fosters organisational performance and better service delivery should have a positive impact on the quality of financial management. This means having clear strategic and operational objectives that are implemented.
- A reliable and accurate accounting system is required – to ensure optimal utilisation of the financial management system.
- Competence with regard to financial management is required: a good understanding of how to use existing systems to monitor and control expenditure and resource inputs.
- A management commitment to understanding and managing outputs is necessary – this requires a shift from old management practices which administered the budget without concern for impact.
- Organisational structure which fosters an alignment of managerial and financial accountability – managers must be accountable and thus able to control the finances allocated to their area of responsibility.
- Practise effective financial auditing before moving to performance auditing – use the financial management system well and be able to audit inputs before moving on to audit inputs in relation to outputs.
- Be able to adopt and implement predictable budgets before moving to managing performance and the efficiency of resource utilisation. Where the budget bottom line is constantly changing, managers cannot be expected to manage.
- Human resources capacity with regard to financial management is essential.

17.6.3 Business ethics

Business ethics relates to the ethical dimensions of economic activity. This ethical aspect is constituted by the impact of economic activity on individuals, society, and the natural environment. Ethics is concerned with what is good or right in human interaction. Consequently it revolves around three basic concepts, namely the good, the self and the other. Ethical behaviour is being conceived of as behaviour that not only considers what is good for oneself, but also what is good for others. Business ethics therefore relates to the impact of ethical behaviour on economic activity (Rossouw, 2004:2–3). The King II Report (King Committee on Corporate Governance, 2002) requires that every organisation should demonstrate its commitment to organisational integrity by codifying its standards in a code of ethics. The principle of integrity is also important. Integrity is derived from the word 'integer', meaning wholeness. Systems with integrity are balanced, in step, and working for a common goal. The signs of integrity are: reliability and dependability, openness and transparency, responsibility, competence, consistency, confidence and optimism. Business ethics – or lack thereof – can therefore also impact on the quality of financial management.

17.7 CONCLUDING STATEMENTS

The following concluding statements are made:

- Financial management occurs in the legal and professional-ethical context, in accordance with the business ownership of the healthcare organisation, with reference to the Constitution, the Health Act, the principles of Corporate Governance, as well as the public or private specific legislation on financial management.
- The most important role-players in financial management are the insurers and funders, the financing intermediaries or purchasing agents, the accountant and the financial managers.
- The purpose of financial management is to secure value for money, optimal utilisation of resources and maximisation of a specified variable in accordance with the business ownership context of the healthcare organisation.
- The process of financial management relates mainly to budgeting, expenditure control and risk management.
- This process of financial management is determined by the legislative context and subsequent principles and guidelines.
- There are various underlying dynamics impacting on the quality of financial management, such as economic and institutional determinants, as well as business ethics.

Self-assessment

(1) Interpret the financial legal framework that impacts on your healthcare organisation.
   (1.1) Compile a job description for this financial manager, with due regard to the contextual dynamics of this healthcare organisation (apply the principles of compiling a job description as described in Chapter 13, Utilisation of human resources).
   (1.2) Compile a skills development programme for this financial manager in accordance with the expected job requirements and responsibilities (in accordance with the principles of skills development as described in Chapter 14, Performance management and development of human resources).

(2) Differentiate between the public and private sector budgeting processes in a healthcare organisation.

(3) Compile a performance-based budget for a healthcare organisation of your choice, in accordance with the strategic plan of this healthcare organisation.

(4) Write an essay on the concept and principles of whistle-blowing as a method to pro-actively avoid or mitigate financial corruption in an organisation.

18 Risk management in a healthcare organisation

The prudent see danger and take refuge, but the foolish keep going and suffer for it. (Prov 27:12)

KEY CONCEPTS

Risk management
Business continuity management
Disaster management
Environmental management
Adverse event management

SPECIFIC OUTCOMES

After studying this chapter, you should be able to:

- Interpret the legal and professional-ethical risk management **context**, with reference to the Constitutional requirements, the National Health Act, corporate governance, professional, ethical and legal framework of healthcare practitioners, and various risk-related legislation, public and private (type of business ownership) healthcare organisations
- Describe and apply the **process** of risk management (strategy analysis, strategy development, strategy execution and strategy review), with reference to the different dimensions of risk management: corporate governance, business continuity management, disaster management, occupational health and safety, environmental management, as well as adverse event management in the context of a healthcare organisation
- Analyse and debate the **purpose** of risk management in the context of a healthcare organisation
- Identify the **role-players** and interpret their roles and responsibilities in risk management in a healthcare organisation
- Debate the **underlying dynamics** that could impact on risk management of a healthcare organisation, with specific reference to institutional determinants, business ethics and stakeholders/community engagement.

18.1 INTRODUCTION

The well-known historical 'risk managers' in healthcare – Ignaz Philipp Semmelweis (1847) and Florence Nightingale (1863) – set the scene for risk management in healthcare. Semmelweis required students and doctors to clean their hands with a chlorinated lime solution when entering the labour room, in particular when moving from the autopsy to the labour room. Nightingale's *Notes on hospitals*, published in 1863, stated some risk management principles, such as: 'the very first requirement in a hospital is that it should do the sick no harm'. We learnt the basic principles of risk management from these historical risk managers in healthcare: recognise, explain and act (Pittet, 2005). The management of a healthcare organisation cannot be expected to deal in a confident, structured and planned manner with unexpected catastrophic events if these events were not identified and assessed, if there are no plans to deal with the events and if no provision is made to deal with the effects of the events. There are various types of risks, such as financial risks, occupational health and safety risks, nosocomial infections, internal disasters (fires, power failure in the healthcare organisation, etc.), external disasters (natural or human-induced). Risk management is described as follows (Cruywagen, 2004:2):

- The total set of interventions in diverse matters: organisation, ethics, recruitment criteria, key financial, operation and other processes and chosen indicators of desired performance, etc.
- The process of dealing with risks: to avoid, control, transfer or accept/tolerate
- The identification and evaluation of actual and potential risk areas as they pertain to the organisation/company as a total entity, followed by a process of either termination, transfer, acceptance (tolerance) or mitigation
- The process entails the planning, arranging, and controlling of activities and resources to minimise the impacts of all risks, to levels that can be tolerated by shareowners and other stakeholders.

Risk management is therefore defined as strategy analysis (risk assessment), strategy development (the designing of a risk management plan (RMP)), strategy execution (implementation of the risk management plan) and strategy review (continuous evaluation of the RMP):

- Risk assessment involves the identification and assessment of actual and potential internal risks (physical, clinical, operational, occupational/human resources, technology, business continuity and disaster recovery), as well as external risks (environmental, social, natural or artificial/synthetic, credit, market and compliance risks).
- Designing of a risk management plan involves planning, establishing institutional risk management capacity and cooperative arrangements, prevention and mitigation of risks, handling of risks, disaster recovery and business continuity.

- Implementation of the risk management plan involves establishment of structures, development of policies and processes, education and training.
- Continuous evaluation of the effectiveness of the risk management plan involves evaluation, monitoring and improvement.

The **context** is elucidated, focusing on the Constitutional requirements, the Health Act, corporate governance, the healthcare organisation in accordance with the type of business ownership, professional, ethical and legal framework of healthcare practitioners, and various risk-related legislation. The **purpose** of risk management is to safeguard the patient, employees and the public during healthcare provision, and to safeguard the healthcare organisation/establishment. The **process** of risk management is divided into the following dimensions: corporate governance, business continuity management, disaster management, occupational health and safety, as well as adverse event management in a healthcare organisation. The main **role-players** involved in risk management focus on the Board of Directors, managers, risk management officers, professional healthcare practitioners, government officials, occupational health and safety officers, occupational healthcare practitioners, stakeholders/ community representatives and volunteers. The **underlying dynamics**, with reference to institutional determinants, business ethics and stakeholder/community engagement, are briefly highlighted. Figure 18.1 reflects the visual presentation of risk management in a healthcare organisation.

18.2 CONTEXT

Risk management is described in the context of a healthcare organisation, with specific reference to the Constitution, the National Health Act, corporate governance, healthcare organisation business ownership, the professional, ethical and legal framework of the healthcare practitioners, as well as risk management-related legislation.

18.2.1 Constitution

Every South African citizen has the right to life, as well as the right to an environment that is not harmful to their health or well-being (South Africa, 1996:section 36). This implies that the principles of risk management need to be practised at all spheres of healthcare service delivery, based on the principles of cooperative government and corporate governance.

18.2.2 National Health Act

The National Health Act of a country provides the legal framework for healthcare service delivery and, among others, the protection of the constitutional and healthcare rights of the citizens of the country. The South African National Health Act, 2003 (Act 61 of 2003) therefore makes provision for risk management by means of the

Figure 18.1 Visual presentation of risk management in a healthcare organisation

Context	Constitution Corporate governance Healthcare organisation Legislation: Disaster management, occupational health and safety, and environmental management Other risk management-related legislation
Purpose	To safeguard the patient, employees and the public during healthcare provision To safeguard the healthcare organisation/establishment against actual and potential risks: sustained service delivery/productivity/functional capacity
Process	Strategy analysis Strategy development Strategy execution Strategy review
Dimensions	Corporate governance Business continuity management (BCM) Disaster management Occupational health and safety Environmental management Adverse event management
Role-players	Board of Directors Healthcare organisation managers Professional healthcare practitioners Government officials Risk management officers Occupational health and safety officers Occupational health practitioners Stakeholders/community representatives Volunteers
Underlying dynamics	Institutional determinants Business ethics Stakeholders/community engagement

regulation of healthcare service delivery. Legislative requirements related to informed consent by the user, user/patient confidentiality, participation in decision-making by the user, as well as the healthcare organisation's obligation to keep patient records, the prevention of spread of communicable diseases, are also regulated by the National Health Act.

Various subsequent health-related legislation (such as Occupational Health and Safety and Human Tissues, etc.) also focuses on the protection of the citizens. Various legal structures, such as Councils (i.e. the National Health Research Ethics Council), are also involved in various specialised dimensions of risk management.

18.2.3 Corporate governance

Risk management is identified as a core component in the code of corporate practices and conduct, in terms of the King Report on Corporate Governance (2002:30–34).

18.2.4 Healthcare organisation: Business ownership

Risk management takes place in the legal, professional-ethical and management framework of the particular healthcare organisation/establishment, in accordance with the type of business ownership – public or private – (refer to Chapter 17, Financial management in a healthcare organisation), and the level of healthcare service delivery and management (local, regional, provincial or national), in accordance with the National Health Act of 2003).

18.2.5 Professional, ethical and legal framework: Healthcare practitioners

Clinical practice by healthcare practitioners is governed by the respective professional, ethical and legal frameworks. Risk management should focus on the mitigation of clinical adverse events, competence to perform a clinical act, and compliance with applicable laws, regulations and supervisory requirements. Various mitigation strategies could be utilised, such as credentialing of healthcare practitioners and clinical auditing (refer to Chapter 20, Continuous quality improvement in a healthcare organisation).

18.2.6 Risk management-related legislation

Disaster management legislation (South Africa, 2002) and subsequent Guiding Framework for Disaster Management in South Africa (2004), National Environmental Management Act, 1998 (Act 107 of 1998), as well as the Occupational Health and Safety Act, 1993 (Act 85 of 1993, as amended) and subsequent regulations, are important regulatory measures in risk management. Refer to the process of risk management for a brief description of selected regulatory measures.

18.3 PURPOSE OF RISK MANAGEMENT

The purpose of risk management is summarised as follows:

- To safeguard the patient, employees and the public against actual and potential risks
- To safeguard the healthcare organisation/establishment against actual or potential risks: sustained service delivery/productivity/functional capacity.

18.4 PROCESS AND DIMENSIONS OF RISK MANAGEMENT

Risk management is broadly defined as risk strategy analysis, development, execution and review (see Figure 18.2).

Figure 18.2 Risk management process

This chapter covers the following dimensions of risk management: corporate governance, business continuity management, disaster management, occupational health and safety, as well as adverse event management.

18.4.1 Corporate governance

The principles of corporate governance are applicable to any organisation. The principles outlined in the King Report on Corporate Governance (Institute of Directors, 2002) are, however, mandatory to all JSE-listed private organisations (such as listed private healthcare organisations), as well as to public sector healthcare organisations that fall under the Public Finance Management Act (refer to Chapter 1, Management of a healthcare organisation and Chapter 17, Financial management in a healthcare organisation). The risk management principles, in accordance with the requirements of corporate governance, are summarised as follows (Institute of Directors, 2002):

- The Board should make use of generally recognised risk management models and frameworks, to maintain a sound system of risk management and internal controls to:
  - safeguard the company's assets and investments
  - support business objectives and sustainability
  - support business sustainability under normal as well as adverse operating conditions
  - behave responsibly towards all stakeholders having a legitimate interest in the company.
- Risk analysis/assessment should be be conducted with reference to the core business (operational practice risks), human resource risks, technology risks, business continuity and disaster recovery, market risks and compliance risks.
- A risk management strategy/plan (model/framework and process) should be developed to mitigate the risks.

18.4.2 Business continuity management (BCM)

Business continuity management (BCM) is a holistic management process that identifies potential impacts that threaten an organisation and provides a framework for building resilience and the capability for an effective response which safeguards the interests of its key stakeholders, reputation, brand and value-creating activities (Business Continuity Institute (BCI), 2001). The following attributes relate to business continuity management:

- Business continuity management is the planning and implementation for events that occur despite risk management.
- Business continuity planning may also be the outcome of risk management where risk reduction strategies do not or cannot effectively control the hazard(s). Hazards that originate outside an organisation, risk reduction measures that are too costly, or high-probability organisational risks that, despite controls, may result in critical or terminal disruptions, may best be addressed through business continuity.
- Business continuity management also includes disaster recovery.

Disaster recovery is a dimension of risk management, pertaining to the mechanisms activated to mitigate or handle the impact of the disaster on humans, infrastructures, technology, environment, etc., and to restore normal service delivery or core business functionality. A disaster recovery plan (DRP) needs to be developed, in accordance with the identified actual and potential risks. This could include making provision for temporary disruptions, such as strike action, by means of a human resources contingency plan. Medical disaster recovery is obviously an important dimension and consists of at least the following principles (De Beer, 2004:1):

- Emergency treatment and evacuation of injured people, in accordance with the medical disaster recovery plan
- Rehabilitation of people to restore functionality, with reference to physical, psychological and social consequences of the disaster
- Reasonable accommodation of affected people in the workplace, that is, disability management by means of transitional work, adjusted or alternative work
- Treatment of psychological dysfunction, such as post-traumatic stress disorder, anxiety, phobias or depressive mood disorders
- Management of the community and the environment (social responsibility).

The principles of BCM could therefore be applied in any healthcare organisation – as part of risk management – to contribute to the sustainability of the organisation, in the interest of the community and relevant stakeholders.

18.4.3 Disaster management

A disaster is a natural or human-caused event, occurring with or without warning, causing or threatening death, injury or disease, and damage to property, infrastructure or the environment, which exceeds the ability of those affected by the disaster to cope with its effects using only their own resources (South Africa, 2002:89). Disasters can be classified as internal (in the healthcare organisation) or external disasters, dependent on the cause of the disaster, that is natural or induced disasters.

Disaster management is a collective term encompassing all aspects of planning for and responding to significant events and events classified as disasters. Disaster management refers to a continuous and integrated multi-sectoral, multi-disciplinary process of planning and implementation of measures aimed at (South Africa, 2002):

- Preventing or reducing the risk of disasters
- Mitigating the severity or consequences of disasters
- Emergency preparedness
- A rapid and effective response to disasters
- Post-disaster recovery and rehabilitation.

Every healthcare organisation requires a disaster management plan (DMP) to make provision for both internal and external disasters. The following **standards** are applicable:

- There is a written internal disaster management plan/programme in accordance with the risk assessment, with appropriate evacuation management practices.
- There is an external disaster management plan/programme, in accordance with the risk assessment and the local government and community engagement framework.
- There is a reliable internal and external communication strategy, including early warning principles, systems and procedures.
- The disaster management plan/programme makes provision for an organisational and medical disaster recovery plan.
- The internal and external disaster plans/programmes are continuously rehearsed.
- The internal and external disaster plans/programmes are evaluated after occurrence of any internal or external disaster, with subsequent amendment of the plan/programme to improve the quality of disaster management in the healthcare organisation.

Disaster management is also regulated by the Disaster Management Act, 2002 (Act 57 of 2002) and the subsequent Guiding Framework for Disaster Management in South Africa (South Africa, 2004).

Disaster Management Act

The Disaster Management Act, 2002 (Act 57 of 2002) provides for:

- An integrated and coordinated disaster management policy that focuses on

preventing or reducing the risk of disasters, mitigating the severity of disasters, emergency preparedness, rapid and effective response to disasters, and post-disaster recovery
- The establishment of national, provincial and municipal disaster management centres
- Disaster management volunteers
- Matters relating to these issues.

The Act recognises the wide-ranging opportunities in South Africa to avoid and reduce disaster losses through the concerted energies and efforts of all spheres of government, civil society and the private sector. However, it also acknowledges the crucial need for uniformity in the approach taken by such a diversity of role-players and partners.

Guiding Framework for Disaster Management

The Guiding Framework for Disaster Management in South Africa is the legal instrument specified by the South African Disaster Management Act, 2002 (Act 57 of 2002:section 7(1)) to address such needs for consistency across multiple interest groups, by providing a coherent, transparent and inclusive policy on disaster management appropriate for the country. In this context, Guiding Framework for Disaster Management recognises a diversity of risks and disasters that occur in southern Africa, and gives priority to developmental measures that reduce the vulnerability of disaster-prone areas, communities and households. Also, in keeping with international best practice, the Guiding Framework for Disaster Management places explicit emphasis on the disaster risk reduction concepts of disaster prevention and mitigation as the core principles to guide disaster management in South Africa. The Guiding Framework for Disaster Management also informs the subsequent development of provincial and municipal disaster management frameworks and plans, which are required to guide action in all spheres of government.

The Guiding Framework for Disaster Management was published in May 2004 for public comment and input (South Africa, 2004). This framework comprises six key performance areas (KPAs). Each KPA is informed by specified objectives and, as required by the Act, key performance indicators (KPIs) to guide and monitor its implementation. These KPAs are briefly summarised (South Africa, 2004:11–12) below.

Key performance area 1: *Establishing institutional arrangements*

KPA 1 focuses on establishing the necessary institutional arrangements for implementing disaster management in the national, provincial and municipal spheres of government and describes some of the mechanisms for funding disaster management. It specifically addresses the application of the principles of cooperative governance for the purposes of disaster management. It also includes the following: involvement of stakeholders, the processes and mechanisms for establishing cooperative arrangements, and it outlines the institutional arrangements for establishing the disaster management information system.

Key performance area 2: *Risk assessment and priorities*
KPA 2 addresses the need for disaster risk assessment and monitoring in order to set priorities, guide risk reduction action and monitor the effectiveness thereof.

Key performance area 3: *Disaster management planning and implementation*
KPA 3 introduces disaster management planning and implementation to inform developmentally oriented approaches, plans, programmes and projects that reduce disaster risks. Particular attention is given to the planning for and integration of the core risk reduction principles of prevention and mitigation into ongoing programmes and initiatives.

Key performance area 4: *Disaster response and recovery and rehabilitation*
This KPA presents implementing priorities concerned with disaster response and recovery and rehabilitation, to make provision for an integrated and coordinated policy that focuses on rapid and effective response to disasters and post-disaster recovery.

- **Key performance area 5**: *Public awareness, education, training and research*

KPA 5 addresses disaster management priorities in public awareness, education, training and research. It makes provision for the development of accredited and non-accredited education and training for disaster management and associated professions, as well as the development of a coherent and collaborative disaster risk research agenda.

- **Key performance area 6**: *Evaluation, monitoring and improvement*

The processes for the evaluation, monitoring and improvement of disaster management are presented in this KPA. A range of mechanisms for measuring and evaluating compliance with the national disaster management framework and the Act (such as performance audits, self-assessments and peer reviews) are introduced.

18.4.4 Occupational Health and Safety Management Act

Occupational health and safety are regulated by means of legislation (South Africa, 1993, as amended) and subsequent regulations. The Occupational Health and Safety Act, 1993 (Act 85 of 1993) aims to provide for the health and safety of persons at work and for the health and safety of persons in connection with the use of plant and machinery, as well as the protection of persons other than persons at work against hazards to health and safety arising out of or in connection with the activities of persons at work. The general duties of employers to their employees are elucidated in the Act (South Africa, 1993, as amended, section 8), and boils down to the provision, as far as is reasonably practicable, of a working environment that is safe and without risk to the health of the employees and to persons other than their employees. This includes: to provide and maintain a safe and healthy working environment; to ensure workers' health and safety by providing information, instructions, training and supervision, the duty to inform the employees of (made conversant with) the hazards and safety-related incidents. The general duties, and where applicable the functions and/or powers, of the following role-players are also described in the Act:

- Employees at work
- The chief executive officer charged with certain duties
- Health and safety representatives
- Health and safety committees
- Government officials, i.e. occupational health and safety inspectors.

Occupational health and safety can be summarised in the following three key issues:
(1) Occupational hygiene: anticipate, recognise, evaluate and control
(2) Occupational health: prevention, diagnosis and treatment
(3) Safety: free from hazard or as low as possible.

The statutory requirements relate to the following:

- To provide and maintain a workplace that is safe – without risk to the health of the employees
- The appointment of relevant staff members and health and safety representatives
- The appointment of a Health and Safety Committee, whose responsibilities are summarised in the following key words: initiating, developing, promoting, maintaining and reviewing.

Healthcare organisation managers therefore have a legal obligation to provide a safe, functional and supportive facility for patients, families, employees and visitors. The following dimensions should be reflected in the healthcare organisation's occupational health and safety management programme (COHSASA, 2004):

- Occupational health and safety programmes in accordance with legal requirements
- Fire safety certification and maintenance in accordance with local legal requirements
- Maintenance programme (facilities, plant and machinery) to ensure the provision of safe and effective healthcare service delivery, in accordance with legal requirements: maintenance (including proactive replacement programmes), inspections and testing, emergency preparedness (water and electrical disruptions), gas and vacuum provision
- Critical site management: theatres and emergency facilities, medical equipment, medical/contaminated waste

- Internal and external disaster programmes in accordance with the local disaster management framework and the healthcare organisation's engagement in this regard
- The management of hazardous materials, in accordance with legal requirements, i.e. handling, storage and use of radioactive, flammable and other materials, as well as medical waste management
- Security management to protect the occupants and property from harm or loss.

18.4.5 Environmental management

Organisations have a social responsibility to ensure that the principles of environmental management are executed: to minimise harmful effects on the environment caused by its core business activities, and to continually improve its environmental performance. Healthcare organisations are no exception – they have a responsibility to protect the environment, such as the management of clinical waste and nuclear medicine practices. National and international standards organisations are beginning to introduce formalised standards for environmental management systems. The British Standards Institute (BSI) first started the process by producing the BS Specification for Environmental Management Systems in 1992. The South African Bureau of Standards followed not long after with a Code of Practice for Environmental Management Systems in 1993. The International Standards Organisation (ISO) produced an environmental management systems standard in 1996 (ISO 14001), which dovetails with the ISO 9000 quality system series. This ISO standard was amended in 2004. An Environmental Management System (EMS) is an organised approach to improving the environmental performance of organisations – private or public, small or large. The idea is to integrate responsibilities and practices into an overall management system to increase efficiency and reduce environmental impacts. The EMS should accomplish core goals of pollution prevention and environmental compliance and integrate with existing systems for quality, health and safety. The ISO 14001 EMS consists of the following, applied to the organisation in accordance with the business ownership and core business activities:

- Environmental policy on the organisation's commitment to the environment
- Environmental aspects and impacts related to the core business delivery of the organisation
- Legal and other requirements
- Objectives and targets
- Environmental management programme
- Structure and responsibility
- Training, awareness and competence
- Communication
- EMS documentation
- Document control
- Operational control

- Emergency preparedness and response
- Monitoring and measuring
- Non-conformance and corrective/preventive action
- Records of EMS performance
- EMS audit
- Management review of the EMS.

The King II Report (2002) requires companies to report on environmental corporate governance. This should be compliant with current South African law by the application of the 'Best Practicable Environmental Option' standard – defined as that option that has most benefit, or causes the least damage to the environment at a cost acceptable to society in the long term as well as in the short term (PricewaterhouseCoopers, 2003:85). Environmental management is South Africa is regulated by the National Environmental Management Act, 1998 (Act 107 of 1998). Regulatory requirements are summarised as follows:

- National environmental management principles
- National structures and coordination (National Environmental Advisory Forum and Committee for Environmental Coordination)
- Procedures for cooperative governance: environmental implementation plans and management plans, and the content thereof
- Fair decision-making and conflict management
- Integrated environmental management
- International obligations and agreements
- Enforcement measures and general administration.

Application to healthcare organisations

In addition to the management of occupational health and safety in general, the healthcare organisation has to attend to hazardous materials: the handling, storage and use of radioactive, flammable and other material and hazardous waste is safely disposed of. This implies at least the following:

- There is an environmental management plan, based on the assessment of hazardous materials related to the core business practice of the healthcare organisation (i.e. nuclear medicine).
- There is a plan for the handling, storage and disposal of clinical and other waste, in accordance with national and international best practice guidelines.
- Nuclear medicine is practised in accordance with the national and provincial regulatory framework and subsequent standards.
- Radiation safety programmes are complied with, and policies and procedures guide staff in the application of safety measures: provision of protective clothing and dosimeters, other appropriate safety devices, the monitoring of contamination, etc.
- The monitoring and maintenance of related clinical equipment is in accordance with best practice.

- Relevant and specialised skills development programmes are in place.
- Environmental management is reflected in the total quality management system in the healthcare organisation.
- General environmental management principles are practised in the healthcare organisation.

18.4.6 Adverse event management

Adverse events (also referred to as sentinel events) are defined as any event or circumstance arising during a patient's stay in a healthcare organisation that leads to unintended or unexpected physical or psychological harm, injury, disease, suffering, disability or death not related to the natural cause of the patient's illness, underlying condition or treatment (Pittet, 2005; Timmons, 2005). An adverse event is therefore an event that results in unintended harm to the patient by an act of commission or omission rather than by the underlying disease or condition of the patient.

Research evidence indicates that in Western healthcare clinical errors being associated with 10% of hospital admissions, are the third most potent cause of mortality and in the UK account for some 32 000 deaths. Initial evidence suggests that in hospital care in developing countries this figure may be significantly higher (and certainly not lower), and constitutes a major public health issue. Given the budgetary constraints, the impact of HIV and AIDS, a brain drain of doctors and nurses to better-paid international climes and the delay in providing legal tools to implement the transformation in healthcare services, hospitals are battling to deliver quality care to all patients, particularly in the poor, rural areas of the country (Vincent & Corbett-Nolan, 2003:12). More Americans die from medical errors each year than from breast cancer, AIDS or car accidents (Timmons, 2005:9).

The National Patient Safety Agency (NPSA) of the United Kingdom is a special health authority charged with reducing the epidemic of clinical errors in the UK. Key to achieving this has been the development of a national adverse events reporting system that can be accessed both by professionals and the public. The system was piloted in 2002 and could possibly be transferred and adopted by the Council for Health Service Accreditation of Southern Africa (COHSASA) to utilise in the accreditation system.

The World Health Organisation (WHO) has identified the need for a concerted international effort, in which it plays a proactive leadership role, with a broad system perspective of patient safety as a major challenge of quality improvement and enhancing provider performance. The WHO World Alliance for Patient Safety launched the Africa project in Durban (RSA) on the 19th of January 2005. At this conference, it was emphasised that healthcare errors could be the following (Timmons, 2005:7–8):

- Failure to diagnose
- Incorrect diagnosis
- Failure to utilise or act on a diagnostic test

- Use of inappropriate or outmoded diagnostic test or procedure
- Failure to provide follow-up
- Medication error or adverse drug event
- Wrong-site surgery or surgical error
- Transfusion error
- Nosocomial infections.

The causes of adverse events can therefore be summarised as follows: problems in practice, products, procedures and systems. Adverse Event Management (AEM) is briefly described with reference to root cause analysis, mitigation strategy (Timmons, 2005), as well as infection control.

Root cause analysis

Root cause analysis is a thorough and credible analysis related to the cause of the adverse/sentinel event. This could assist the healthcare organisation to identify where in its process the error might have occurred. The organisation should then use the results of its root cause analysis to make improvements to prevent a recurrence of the event (Timmons, 2005:28). The quality of a root cause analysis is dependent on leadership and organisational structure, as well as a credible process of analysis (Timmons, 2005:29–33).

(a) *Leadership and organisational structure*

A formalised system in the healthcare organisation is required. This implies at least the following:

- A commitment from leadership/management to purposefully manage sentinel/ adverse events
- Creating a safe environment with adequate mitigation strategies, such as utilising humans as 'hidden cameras', empowerment of patients, adequate and constant supervision, regular clinical in-service education, and multi-disciplinary cooperation and respect
- Establishment of a formalised structure (i.e. Root Cause Analysis Committee) in the healthcare organisation, consisting of the quality improvement role-players, as well as hands-on professionals
- Development of a non-punitive patient safety paradigm focusing on at least the following: systems are the root cause, a culture of openness asking 'why', responsible reporting, quality circles, making lessons accessible to all, zero tolerance to negligence, identification and elimination of hazards in the design phase, applicable patient safety alert processes and projects, and celebrating successes.

(b) *Thorough and credible process of analysis*

A thorough and credible root cause analysis process consists of at least the following (Timmons, 2005:29–32):

- Collect and identify the facts of the sentinel/adverse event case: who? what? where? when?
- Describe the process(es) as designed, as usually performed and as performed in this case
- Describe the system(s) involved
- Compare with good/best standards of practice
- Drill down to the root cause(s): keep asking 'why?'; resist the temptation to stop drilling; don't mistake obvious causes for root causes
- Analyse the underlying process(es) and systems (i.e. poor communication, inadequate orientation of staff, inadequate competency/credentialing, inadequate staffing levels, faulty alarm systems, availability of information/data, physical environment, procedural compliance)
- Suggest potential improvements in systems and process(es)
- Develop an action plan to mitigate future potential hazards
- Develop a strategy for measuring effectiveness
- Ensure internal consistency (reliability) of root cause analysis
- Ensure trustworthy participation of applicable role-players.

Mitigation (remedial action) strategy

The purpose of the mitigation (remedial action) strategy is to avoid a recurrence of the sentinel/adverse event. The data and other information from the root cause analysis or Sentinel Event Database are utilised to identify recommendations to prevent a specific type of adverse event in future. These recommendations are used in the Skills Development Programme and/or published in a newsletter such as a Sentinel Event Alert online newsletter (refer to the American Joint Commission on Accreditation of Healthcare Organisations website for an example of a Sentinel Event Alert publication). A mitigation (remedial action) strategy complies with at least the following (Pittet, 2005:44; Timmons, 2005:16–17):

- Adequate leadership and administrative support for the management of sentinel/ adverse events is reflected.
- The legal requirements with regard to informed consent by the user, confidentiality, record keeping and access to information are adhered to.
- All significant errors/adverse events are identified.
- There is thorough and credible root cause analysis of adverse events.
- There is evidence of trustworthy compilation of data about adverse event frequencies and root causes.
- There is evidence of appropriate dissemination of derived information to permit redesign of systems and processes.
- There is adequate and appropriate systems change in accordance with the database.
- There is adequate and appropriate process (and behaviour) change.
- A non-punitive culture of safety is established.

- There is widespread shared acceptance of responsibility and accountability for risk reduction.
- There is a trustworthy (valid and reliable) system of data collection, reporting and dissemination, performance management, including awareness or alert campaigns.
- There is acknowledgement of the high-risk, error-prone nature of healthcare delivery.
- There is open communication about safety concerns in a non-punitive environment – therefore freedom of fear of reporting problems.
- The reporting of errors and safety concerns is facilitated.
- All role-players learn from errors and are involved in redesigning safer systems and processes.
- It ensures that the organisational structure, processes, goals and rewards are aligned with improving patient safety.
- There is appropriate education, on evidence-based best practice, of all healthcare workers concerned.
- There is evidence of periodic assessment of effectiveness of risk reduction efforts.

Infection control

The prevention and control of infections is one of the key risk management responsibilities of all the role-players concerned in a healthcare organisation/establishment. The goal of a healthcare organisation's infection control programme is to identify and reduce the risks of acquiring and/or transmitting infections among patients, professional health practitioners, support staff, contract workers, volunteers, students and visitors. The infection control programme may differ from organisation to organisation, depending on the focus/type of clinical service delivery, patient population, human resource capacity and other relevant institutional determinants. The following standards are applicable (adapted from COHSASA, 2003):

(a) There is a formalised infection control structure reflecting at least the following:

- Infection control committee
- Infection control officer/manager with appropriate qualifications and abilities
- Multi-professional and multi-disciplinary involvement of key role-players
- A credible and appropriate infection control information management system.

(b) There is a formalised infection control/management programme to reduce the risks of nosocomial infections in patients and healthcare workers, reflecting at least the following:

- The organisation identifies the processes/procedures associated with the risk of infection and implements mitigation strategies accordingly, with due regard of national and global best practices.
- The programme addresses those epidemiologically important infections,

infection sites and associated devices that will provide the focus of efforts to prevent and reduce the incidence of nosocomial infections with reference to respiratory tract, urinary tract, intravascular invasive devices and surgical wounds, etc.
- The management of infectious and communicable diseases is in accordance with legal requirements and national/global best practices.
- There are appropriate infection control policies and procedures.
- Applicable epidemiological and medical surveillance strategies are implemented, in accordance with risk identification and reported nosocomial infections.
- There are appropriate infection control strategies implemented with reference to at least the following: soiled laundry/linen management, disposal of infectious waste, disposal of clinical waste (including the disposal of blood and blood components), catering/food preparation, housekeeping services, etc.

(c) Infection control is reflected as an integrated dimension of adverse event management in the organisation's quality management programme:
- The organisation tracks infection risks, infection rates and trends in nosocomial infections on at least a quarterly basis.
- Monitoring includes using indicators related to infection issues that are epidemiologically important to the organisation.
- The organisation uses risk, rate and trend information to design or modify systems, processes/procedures to reduce nosocomial infections to the lowest possible levels.
- Infection rates are compared with those of other similar healthcare organisations through comparative databases.
- The results of infection monitoring in the organisation are regularly communicated to professional healthcare practitioners and other relevant staff in the organisation.
- The organisation reports information on infections to appropriate external public and formalised healthcare agencies.
- Indicators are utilised for local, regional, national and international comparisons.

(d) The principles of infection control are part of the organisation's in-service training and skills development programmes:
- The infection control management programme is part of the induction and orientation programme of newly appointed employees.
- There is an appropriate in-service education programme, based on the quarterly and annual surveillance and infection monitoring results.
- The infection control officer/manager is exposed to national and global best practice programmes/conferences.

18.5 ROLE-PLAYERS

There are various role-players involved in risk management. This chapter will focus on the following selected role-players only: Board of Directors, healthcare service managers, risk management officers, professional healthcare practitioners, government officials in the case of disaster management, occupational health and safety officers, occupational health and safety practitioners, stakeholder/community representatives and volunteers.

18.5.1 Board of Directors

The King Report on Corporate Governance (2002:30–34) identifies the Board of Directors as key role-players in risk management, focusing on the responsibilities, application and reporting.

Responsibilities

- The Board is responsible for the total process of risk management, as well as for forming its own opinion on the effectiveness of the process. Management is accountable to the Board for designing, implementing and monitoring the process of risk management and integrating it into the day-to-day activities of the company.
- The Board should set the risk strategy policies in liaison with the executive directors and senior management. These policies should be clearly communicated to all employees to ensure that the risk strategy is incorporated into the language and culture of the company.
- The Board must decide the company's tolerance for risk – those risks it will take and those it will not take in the pursuit of its goals and objectives. The Board has the responsibility to ensure that the company/organisation has implemented an effective ongoing process to identify risk, to measure its potential impact against a broad set of assumptions, and to activate what is necessary to proactively manage these risks.
- The Board should apply generally recognised risk management and internal control models/frameworks in order to maintain a sound system of risk management and internal control to provide reasonable assurance regarding the achievement of organisational objectives with respect to the effectiveness and efficiency of operations, safeguarding of assets, compliance with applicable laws, regulations and supervisory requirements, supporting business sustainability under normal as well as adverse operating conditions, reliability of reporting and behaving responsibly towards all stakeholders.
- The Board is responsible for ensuring that a systematic, documented and trustworthy risk assessment is conducted with reference to at least the following: physical and operational risks, human resources risks, technology risks, business continuity and disaster recovery, credit and market risks, as well as compliance risks.

- A Board Committee should be appointed to assist the Board in reviewing the risk management process and the significant risks facing the company/organisation.
- Risk management and internal control should be practised throughout the organisation/company by all staff and should be embedded in day-to-day activities.
- In addition to the company/organisation's compliance and enforcement activities, the Board should also consider the need for a confidential reporting process ('whistleblowing') covering fraud and other risks.

Application and reporting

- A comprehensive system of control should be established by the Board to ensure that risks are mitigated and that the company's objectives are attained. The control environment should set the tone and cover ethical values, management's philosophy and the competence of employees.
- Risks should be assessed on an on-going basis and control activities should be designed to respond to risks throughout the company/organisation.
- A system of risk management and internal control should be developed, demonstrating that the company's key risks are being managed. The system should incorporate mechanisms to deliver at least the following: dynamic risk identification, a commitment by management to the process, risk mitigation activities, a system of documented risk communications, a system of documenting the costs of non-compliance, a documented system of internal control and risk management, an alignment of assurance of efforts to the risk profile, as well as a register of key risks that could affect shareowner and relevant stakeholder interests.
- The Board must identify key risk areas and key performance indicators of the company/organisation, and monitor these factors as part of a regular review of processes and procedures to ensure the effectiveness of its internal systems of control, to maintain quality decision-making and the accuracy of its reporting.
- The Board is responsible for disclosures in relation to risk management.

In addition to the above responsibilities, it is important to note that the individual Director also has a responsibility: 'It is any director's legal duty to act in the best interests of the company at all times, and as such h/she must adopt the necessary skill, care and diligence to safeguard the company's assets and ability to operate. Any director who fails to timeously identify all the risks and threats facing the company and ensuring that they are adequately and appropriately managed, may find it extremely difficult to justify that h/she acted in the best interest of the company' (Cruywagen, 2004:3).

18.5.2 Healthcare organisation managers

The healthcare organisation managers are accountable for risk management in the healthcare organisation, in accordance with legislative requirements and the type of business ownership. The responsibilities of risk management (internal and external) can be delegated to line managers and risk management officers, provided there are clear job descriptions and designated lines of reporting/authority. The manager of the healthcare organisation is responsible for the risk management of the organisation with reference to the appropriate risk assessments (strategy analysis), designing of the risk management plan (strategy development), implementation and evaluation of the risk management strategy (strategy execution) and continuous evaluation of the risk management plan, based on mock-rehearsals and actual events (strategy review).

18.5.3 Risk management officer

The management or Board of Directors may decide to appoint a risk management officer and subsequent risk management committee(s). There are specialised risk management officers (such as the infection control officer) in healthcare organisations. The risk management officer could be responsible for the facilitation and coordination of the risk management functions:

- Development of the risk management strategy
- Establishment of the structure(s) and formalising of respective responsibilities accordingly
- Risk assessments
- Risk mitigation
- Risk evaluation
- Reporting
- Integration
- Compliance auditing.

The risk management officer reports to management, who remains accountable to the Board of Directors, or in accordance with the organisational structure of the respective healthcare organisation/establishment and related legislative requirements.

18.5.4 Professional healthcare practitioners

Professional healthcare practitioners are independently (in accordance with their specific professional legislation) and collectively responsible and accountable for compliance with regulatory and best practice requirements, as well as for the execution of the healthcare organisation's policies and procedures, in accordance with the specified risk management strategies. Professional healthcare practitioners have an ethical and legal responsibility to acquaint themselves with the latest infection control reports and subsequent quality management (prevention and mitigation) strategies.

18.5.5 Government officials

The responsibilities of the various government officials at national, provincial and local/municipal levels, with reference to health establishment, occupational health and safety and disaster management, are in accordance with the National Health Act, 2003 (Act 61 of 2003), the Occupational Health and Safety Act, 1993 (Act 85 of 1993), the Disaster Management Act, 2002 (Act 57 of 2002) and the Guiding Framework for Disaster Management in South Africa (South Africa, 2004).

18.5.6 Occupational health and safety officers

Occupational health and safety officers are specialised risk management officers, with designated responsibilities in accordance with the occupational health and safety legislative requirements. The manager in charge of the healthcare organisation is, however, still legally accountable for compliance with the legislative requirements.

18.5.7 Occupational health practitioners

The occupational health practitioner holds a professional occupational health and safety nursing or medical qualification. The occupational health and safety medical practitioner is a medical practitioner as defined in the Medical, Dental and Supplementary Health Service Professions Act, who holds a qualification in occupational medicine (South Africa, 1993). The occupational health practitioners are responsible for the organisation's occupational health, in accordance with their respective legal scope of authority, with reference to medical surveillance monitoring, recommendations related to employee placements, and even the boarding of employees due to health-related incapacity.

18.5.8 Stakeholder/community representatives

Various stakeholders and community representatives play a role in risk management, based on their shareholder engagement and interest in business continuity management. Designated community representatives also play an important role in disaster management, in accordance with the disaster management legislation and subsequent framework.

18.5.9 Volunteers

Volunteers are utilised during disaster management and play an important role by means of community forums and structures, community disaster management committees, disaster management-related training and education, including awareness campaigns, etc. The principles of community engagement are included in the Guiding Framework for Disaster Management in South Africa (South Africa, 2004) and the Disaster Management Act, 2002 (Act 57 of 2002).

18.6 UNDERLYING DYNAMICS

The success of risk management is related to the institutional determinants, business ethics and stakeholders/community engagement.

18.6.1 Institutional determinants

Institutional leadership plays a key role with regard to risk management in a healthcare organisation, reflecting at least the following:

- Responsibility of leadership to create an environment that is conducive to risk management
- Development of a culture of safety and an environment that encourages risk management, error identification and mitigation strategies/remedial steps to reduce risk of future recurrences, and minimises individual blame or retribution for the involved staff and for the reporter
- Shared acceptance of responsibility for collaborative and co-operative risk management
- Organisational engagement in proactive systems analysis as an error prevention strategy
- Training at all levels that addresses teamwork and error identification, analysis and prevention
- Importance of effective communication in the service/care delivery process
- Use of knowledge-based information
- Encouragement of open communication about safety concerns in a non-punitive environment, freedom of fear of reporting problems
- Facilitates reporting of errors and safety concerns
- Learns from errors and redesigns safer systems
- Embraces accountability for risk management and patient safety
- Ensures that organisational structure, processes, goals and rewards are aligned with improving patient safety.

18.6.2 Business ethics

Credible business ethics related to risk management is crucial. Every healthcare organisation's leadership should demonstrate its commitment to organisational integrity with regard to risk management, especially patient safety and the protection of patient rights. Inter-professional relationships between all the professional healthcare practitioners also play a role in business ethics related to risk management. The various healthcare professions have their ethical codes of conduct and subsequent professional regulatory systems to deal with professional errors and misconduct. The healthcare organisation should, however, institute formal structures to analyse negative outcomes in the healthcare organisation/establishment. A few examples are highlighted:

- Peer review committee (refer to Chapter 20, Continuous quality improvement in a healthcare organisation)

- Mortality committee
- Patient safety committee
- Infection control committee
- Occupational health and safety committee
- Corporate risk management committee
- Ethics committee.

18.6.3 Stakeholders/community engagement

The principle of public accountability by means of stakeholders/community engagement should be adhered to. The community and – where applicable – the shareholders, have the right to credible/trustworthy information with regard to risk management. The principle of corporate governance with reference to disclosure of risk management strategies should be adhered to.

18.7 CONCLUDING STATEMENTS

The following concluding statements are made:

- Risk management is a process of strategy analysis, strategy development, strategy execution and strategy review.
- Risk management entails risk assessment (internal and external environment), the designing of a risk management plan (RMP), implementation of the RMP and continuous evaluation of the effectiveness of the RMP.
- Risk management occurs in the context of the Constitution, the principles of corporate governance, the type and location of the business ownership (public or private), as well as the legislation related to occupational health and safety, environmental management and disaster management.
- The dimensions of risk management in a healthcare organisation are divided into the following: corporate governance, business continuity management, occupational health and safety, environmental management and adverse event management.
- The purpose of risk management in a healthcare organisation is to safeguard the patient, employees and the public during healthcare provision and to safeguard the healthcare organisation/establishment to ensure sustained service delivery, productivity and functional capacity.
- There are many role-players, in accordance with the dimension of risk management and related legislation: the board of directors, healthcare organisation managers, professional healthcare practitioners, government officials, risk management officers, occupational health and safety officers, occupational healthcare practitioners, stakeholders/community representatives and volunteers.
- The underlying dynamics in risk management are complex, with special reference to the institutional determinants related to responsibility of the leadership to create a culture of safety and shared acceptance of responsibility

for collaborative and co-operative risk management. Business ethics and stakeholders/community engagement also play an important role.

Self-assessment

(1) Conduct a risk assessment of a healthcare organisation of your choice. Use any instrument/checklist downloaded from the Internet.
(2) Compile a business continuity plan for your healthcare organisation, based on the principles of business continuity management.
(3) Compile a business contingency plan for your healthcare organisation (www.contingenz.com).
(4) Compile a terms of reference for the occupational health and safety committee.
(5) Compile standards of professional competence and business ethics in the provision and maintenance of business continuity management and services www.thebci.org.
(6) Compile a disaster recovery plan for your healthcare organisation. Use the disaster recovery toolkit that can be downloaded from Internet: www.eBRP.net; www.itilsurvival.com.
(7) Apply the key performance areas, as listed in the Guiding Framework for Disaster Management in South Africa (2004) in the development of an institutional disaster management plan/strategy.
(8) Initiate a project on creative environmental management with the community.

19 Quality improvement models in a healthcare organisation

KEY CONCEPTS

Quality improvement models
International Standardisation Organisation (ISO)
Business excellence
Balanced Scorecard
Accreditation

SPECIFIC OUTCOMES

After studying this chapter, you should be able to:

- Interpret the **context** that determines and impacts on the selection and application of quality improvement models in healthcare organisations, with specific reference to the global context, the constitution of the country, national health-related legislation and subsequent licensing regulations, professional-ethical legislation on the training, practice and licensing of professional clinicians and practitioners, human resource management legislation, patient/consumer-related expectations and charters, the type of business ownership and the subsequent delivery legislation/policies impacting on service delivery, as well as the corporate governance context
- Analyse and debate the **purpose** of applying quality improvement models in a healthcare organisation with reference to improving the quality of service delivery, to reduce or mitigate the risks involved in healthcare service delivery, and to positively impact on the healthcare indicators of the country
- Identify the main **role-players** involved in the application or implementation of quality improvement models in healthcare organisations, with specific reference to the following: accountable authority and subsequent Board of Directors, the healthcare managers, the clinical practitioners or clinicians, non-clinical managers, the various types of quality coordinator in a healthcare organisation, the patients or consumers (including relevant consumer unions), professional institutes and regulatory bodies, healthcare insurance funders, as well as the facilitators and surveyors involved in accreditation assessment

- Analyse and debate the following **quality improvement models**: ISO, business excellence, the Balanced Scorecard and accreditation, with reference to their background, purpose and respective dimensions
- Identify and debate the **underlying dynamics** that impact on the success or failures in the implementation of quality improvement models in a healthcare organisation, with reference to the external and institutional determinants.

19.1 INTRODUCTION

Modernising and improving healthcare organisations and subsequent systems lie at the heart of efforts by the national governments and the international development community to assist countries to reach their 2015 Millennium Development Goals (MDGs) – with their promise of vastly improved human and economic welfare. Despite broad agreement on the urgency of such an overhaul, the practical difficulties involved in grappling with the complex and multi-disciplinary nature of healthcare delivery models and systems, and resolving widespread concerns about their quality, cannot be underestimated. It is widely recognised that good governance is required in the healthcare sector. The general public, organisations of patients and disabled persons, and third party payers/funders want to have more objective assessments of the quality of service delivery. Countries have taken different approaches to maintaining quality and improving standards. In some countries, professional organisations and provider associations try to exercise quality control over members to improve standards of care, often without input from government or society. In other countries, the state exercises rigid control over the healthcare sector, leaving almost no scope for professional judgement – resulting in defensive medicine. The challenge is to balance the roles of healthcare professionals, government policymakers, members of the public, and other stakeholders in enhancing the quality of and setting the standards for the healthcare sector (Shaw, 2004:foreword by the Director Health, Nutrition and Population Network, World Bank).

There are obviously different quality improvement models in healthcare organisations. This chapter will highlight the ISO, business excellence and accreditation models, including the Balanced Scorecard. Figure 19.1 illustrates the conceptual framework.

19.2 CONTEXT

Refer to Chapter 1, Management of a healthcare organisation, for a detailed description of the context in which healthcare organisations operate. A brief description is given in relation to quality improvement models in a healthcare organisation:

- Global context
- Constitution
- National health-related legislation and subsequent licensure standards and regulations

Figure 19.1 Visual presentation of quality models in a healthcare organisation

Context	Global context Constitution National Health Act/legislation Professional-ethical legislation on the training, practice and licensing of professional clinicians and practitioners Human resource management legislation Patient/consumer-related expectations and charters Business ownership and service delivery legislation/policies Corporate governance
Purpose	To improve the quality of service delivery To reduce or mitigate risks involved in healthcare service delivery To positively impact on the healthcare indicators/outcomes of the country
Role-players	Accountable authority (private/public/agencies) and subsequent board of directors where applicable Healthcare managers Clinical practitioners/clinicians Non-clinical managers Quality coordinators Patients/consumers or representative bodies/unions Professional institutes and professional regulatory bodies Health insurance funders Facilitators and surveyors Quality improvement models
Quality improvement models	ISO: International Standardisation Organisation Business excellence models Balanced Scorecard Accreditation
Underlying dynamics	External determinants Institutional determinants

- Professional-ethical legislation and subsequent regulations related to the healthcare practitioners/clinicians
- Human resource management-related legislation
- Patient/consumer-related expectations and values reflected in charters or service delivery legislation/policies
- The type/nature/scope and level of clinical service delivery
- The type/nature of the healthcare organisation and subsequent business ownership and related management practices.

19.2.1 Global context

The International Society of Health Care was established in 1989 and has been holding an annual congress ever since. This has influenced the formalised quality improvement move in healthcare organisations, focusing mainly on certification of compliance with standards (ISO model), implementation (and modification) of the business excellence models in healthcare services, as well as the accreditation of healthcare services (Shaw, 2003).

19.2.2 Constitution

The constitution of the country (refer to Chapter 1, Management of a healthcare organisation), stipulates the health-related rights of the citizens. The Constitution of the Republic of South Africa, 1996 (Act 108 of 1996) stipulates, among others, the right to life, the right to bodily and psychological integrity, the right to an environment that is not harmful to their health or well-being. In addition to these health-related rights, section 27 stipulates the right to have access to healthcare services, including reproductive healthcare and emergency medical treatment. The state therefore has an obligation to take reasonable steps to protect these rights. Specific health-related rights are also stipulated in section 28 with regard to children.

19.2.3 National health legislation

The quality of service delivery in a healthcare organisation is first and foremost regulated by the healthcare legislation of the particular country and other health-related legislation and subsequent regulations. Nationally regulated licensure standards for healthcare organisations serve to define the quality level required for the safe delivery of patient care, or of healthcare services, such as drug dispensing. They also define the capabilities required for a healthcare organisation to be entitled to advertise to its public that it is a hospital or a healthcare centre/establishment. For example, the licensure standards of a particular jurisdiction might require a healthcare facility to provide surgery, radiology testing, round-the-clock service delivery (i.e. nursing care) for patients, pharmacy services and laboratory services, in order to be classified as a hospital. Licensure in accordance with national legislation is therefore by definition mandatory. The types and levels of healthcare service delivery are delineated in the national health legislation. The national directorate for quality in a country develops a national strategy for quality care and quality improvement, with the necessary devolution of authority in accordance with the levels of service delivery and types of business ownership. The National Health Act, 2003 (Act 61 of 2003) is applicable in South Africa.

19.2.4 Professional-ethical legislation

The quality of clinical service delivery is regulated by the particular healthcare practitioners' legislation, with specific reference to education, practice and licensing, including the disciplinary measures that can be taken when there is evidence of transgression or non-compliance (refer to Chapters 10–15 on Human resource management).

19.2.5 Human resource management legislation

Human resource-related legislation and regulations will also be applicable, as described in Chapters 10–15 on Human resource management.

19.2.6 Patient/consumer expectations and service delivery legislation

The Patient Charter, if available in a country, is also applicable and impacts on the quality improvement models and service delivery foci. In addition to the Patient Charter, other service delivery legislation/policies (such as the South African Batho Pele policy/regulation), could also determine the context of quality improvement models in healthcare (refer to Chapter 1, Management of a healthcare organisation). When selecting and implementing a quality improvement model in the healthcare organisation, these principles need to be taken into consideration.

19.2.7 Type of business ownership and related service delivery legislation policies

The utilisation and application of quality improvement models in the healthcare organisation are very much based on the type of business ownership (public, private or mixed), and the subsequent regulatory framework and policies.

19.2.8 Corporate governance

As a healthcare organisation could also be seen as a business enterprise, the general principles of business excellence and corporate governance are also taken into consideration. International and national best practice principles related to the management of a healthcare organisation and clinical governance are also applicable (refer to Chapter 1, Management of a healthcare organisation).

19.3 PURPOSE

The overall purpose of quality improvement models applied to healthcare service delivery is to:

- Improve the quality of service delivery
- Reduce/mitigate the risks involved in healthcare service delivery
- Positively impact on the healthcare indicators and outcomes of a country.

19.4 ROLE-PLAYERS

This chapter focuses on the models of quality improvement in healthcare. The different role-players in quality improvement are therefore just briefly highlighted:

- The accountable legal/ownership authority with reference to the state (ministry), private owners/agencies (Board of Directors) has a legal responsibility to regulate the service delivery and to account for the quality of services rendered.
- Healthcare managers are accountable for the quality of service delivery in the

healthcare organisation, in accordance with the designated scope of practice/authority and organisational reporting structures.

- Clinical practitioners are all accountable for quality clinical service delivery in accordance with the regulated scope of practice/authority and subsequent clinical guidelines, indicators and benchmarks, critical/clinical pathways, etc.
- There are many non-clinical managers (such as support and hotel services). They are responsible for the quality of non-clinical service delivery, in accordance with the standards determined.
- Different types of quality coordinators can be appointed (i.e. infection control officer, divisional quality coordinator, etc.), in accordance with a designated scope of authority and organisational reporting structure. These coordinators are usually responsible for the development/coordination of the quality improvement strategies (refer to Chapter 20, Continuous quality improvement in a healthcare organisation) in the healthcare organisation.
- Patients/consumers are the core role-players. Their expectations and rights should impact on the quality improvement models utilised in the healthcare organisation.
- Professional institutes and professional regulatory bodies also play an important role in the setting of standards and determination of benchmarks.
- Health insurance funding systems should benefit by quality service delivery and should provide financial benefits/incentives to those healthcare organisations complying with the standards and reflecting a positive impact on healthcare indicators in a country.
- Facilitators and surveyors in the case of external peer group assessment (i.e. accreditation) are contracted by the agency. The agency will also have a group of decision-makers in accordance with the formalised structure and authority.

19.5 QUALITY IMPROVEMENT MODELS

A brief description of the following quality improvement models is given: the International Standard Organisation (ISO), business excellence, with specific reference to the Malcolm Baldrige model for quality management and the South African Excellence Model (SAEM), the Balanced Scorecard (BSC) and accreditation, with specific reference to the Southern African healthcare accreditation model developed by the Council for Health Service Accreditation of Southern Africa (COHSASA).

19.5.1 International Standardisation Organisation (ISO)

Background

The International Standardisation Organisation (ISO) (lately also referred to as the International Organisation for Standardisation) is a network of the national standards institutes of approximately 148 countries, with a Central Secretariat in Geneva, Switzerland, that coordinates the system. ISO is a non-governmental organisation and was established in 1947.The well-known ISO 9000 standards were developed and accepted in 1987, focusing on the promotion and maintenance of quality in connection with commodities and subsequent service delivery (www.iso.org). This system provides standards against which organisations or functions may be certificated by accredited certification bodies or organisations. Although originally designed for the manufacturing industry, these standards are now applied to healthcare – in particular to radiology and laboratory systems – and more generally, to quality systems in hospitals and clinical departments. A country-specific Standards Act usually regulates the promotion and maintenance of standardisation and quality with reference to commodities and the rendering of services. A regulatory body (i.e. the South African Bureau of Standards) acts as the national institution/council for the promotion and maintenance of standardisation and the control thereof. In South Africa the Standards Act, 1993 (Act 29 of 1993) regulates the promotion and maintenance of standardisation and quality in connection with commodities and the rendering of related services (Shaw, 2004:8).

The ISO 9000 standards were revised in 1994, with other subsequent revisions and variations to accommodate different types of service delivery. The ISO 9000 and ISO 14000 standards are among ISO's most widely known standards. ISO 9000 is concerned with quality management – what the organisation does to enhance customer satisfaction by meeting customer and applicable regulatory requirements and to continually improve its performance in this regard. ISO 14000 is primarily concerned with environmental management, assisting organisations to meet their environmental challenges – this means what the organisation does to minimise harmful effects on the environment caused by its activities, and to continually improve its environmental performance. The Quality Management Systems Standard was developed in 2000. Any business/organisation could therefore register with the International Standard Organisation and be certified on compliance with the ISO 9001:2000 Quality Management System Standard (www.iso.org).

Purpose

The purpose of ISO is summarised as follows:

- To improve the quality of production/manufactured commodities in accordance with regulatory requirements
- To improve service delivery and enhance customer satisfaction by means of quality management
- To improve environmental management/performance.

Dimensions of the ISO 9001:2000 Quality Management System Standard

The ISO 9001:2000 standards focus on the following dimensions (www.iso.org/iso/en/iso9000–14000/):

Principle 1 *Customer focus*
Organisations depend on their customers and therefore should understand current and future customer needs, should meet customer requirements and strive to exceed customer expectations.

Principle 2 *Leadership*
Leaders establish unity of purpose and direction of the organisation. They should create and maintain the internal environment in which people can become fully involved in achieving the organisation's objectives.

Principle 3 *Involvement of people*
People at all levels are the essence of an organisation and their full involvement enables their abilities to be used for the organisation's benefit.

Principle 4 *Process approach*
A desired result is achieved more efficiently when activities and related resources are managed as a process.

Principle 5 *System approach to management*
Identifying, understanding and managing interrelated processes as a system contributes to the organisation's effectiveness and efficiency in achieving its objectives.

Principle 6 *Continual improvement*
Continual improvement of the organisation's overall performance should be a permanent objective of the organisation.

Principle 7 *Factual approach to decision-making*
Effective decisions are based on the analysis of data and information.

Principle 8 *Mutually beneficial supplier relationships*
An organisation and its suppliers are interdependent and a mutually beneficial relationship enhances the ability of both to create value.

19.5.2 Business Excellence

Background
The principle and subsequent model of business excellence was initiated by the United States Malcolm Baldridge National Quality Awards (www.as.org/abtquality/awards/baldrige.html), followed by the European Excellence Awards (www.efqm.org) and others such as Australia (Shaw, 2004:8). The South African Excellence Foundation (SAEF) developed a South African Excellence Model (see Figure 19.2) by integrating both ISO and business scorecard principles. This chapter focuses on the South African Excellence Model (Botha, 2005) with reference to business excellence.

Purpose

The purpose of the business excellence model is to facilitate business excellence in accordance with the business ownership and expected results by applying the underlying principles of the model.

Dimensions of the South African Excellence Model (SAEM)

The SAEM reflects an integration of the ISO 9001 quality principles with certain enablers (leadership and processes) and business results, resulting in a cyclic continuous improvement principle (see Figure 19.2).

Figure 19.2 South African Excellence Model

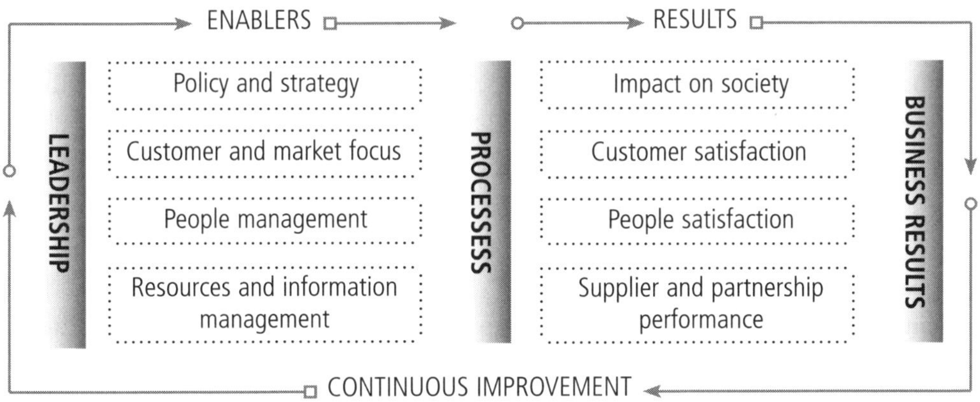

Source: Botha, 2005:8

The first fundamental principle focuses on the following: people are utilised to perform the business-related processes ending in results. RADAR sits at the heart of the model. Its logic states that an organisation needs to determine the **R**esults aimed for as part of its policy and strategy developing process. Plan and develop an integrated set of sound **A**pproaches to deliver the results. **D**eploy the approaches in a systematic way to ensure full implementation. **A**ssess and **R**eview the approaches (Botha, 2005:20–21). The South African Excellence Model focuses on the following underlying assumptions and principles (Botha, 2005:9–19).

Leadership

Excellent leaders develop and enrich an organisation's culture and inspire the effective and efficient utilisation of the resources and efforts of the organisation in its pursuit of excellence. They facilitate the achievement of the organisation's vision and mission and during periods of change they retain a constancy of purpose. When required, such leaders are able to change the direction of the organisation and inspire others to follow.

Policy and strategy

Excellent organisations consider how the goal of the excellence and the need for continuous improvement can be addressed in developing vision, strategies, objectives, policies and values and how these can be translated to action.

Customer and market focus

Excellent organisations define their immediate customers and all other customers in the chain of distribution of their product and services right through to the final customer or 'end user'. The customer is the final arbiter of product and service quality and customer satisfaction, and those issues that influence customer loyalty are also measured and analysed.

People management

Excellent organisations release the full potential of their people at an individual, team-based and organisation level. They promote fairness, equality, shared values and a culture of trust and empowerment for all. This is supported by opportunities to learn and develop skills in a way that motivates staff and builds commitment. The satisfaction of staff is continually monitored and improved.

Resources and information management

Excellent organisations continuously strive to maximise the use of all resources, including financial and information resources, materials, buildings, equipment and even intellectual property. External suppliers and partners and internal resources should be managed in such a way that they support policy and strategy and the effective operation of processes. The current and future needs of the organisation, the community and the environment need to be balanced.

Processes

Excellent organisations design, manage and improve processes in order to fully satisfy and generate increasing value for customers (both external and internal) and other stakeholders.

Impact on society

Excellent organisations comprehensively measure and achieve outstanding results with respect to society. This includes involvement in the local community and economy and efforts in areas such as the preservation of the environment, energy conservation and recycling.

Customer and stakeholder satisfaction

Excellent organisations comprehensively measure and achieve outstanding results with respect to their customers.

People satisfaction
Excellent organisations comprehensively measure and achieve outstanding results with respect to their people.

Supplier and partnership performance
Excellent organisations comprehensively measure the performance of their suppliers and partners in areas of continuous improvement, innovation, cost reduction, improved productivity, enhancement of knowledge and response to organisational needs.

Organisational results
Excellent organisations comprehensively measure and achieve outstanding results with respect to the key elements of their policy and strategy.

19.5.3 Balanced Scorecard

Background
The Balanced Scorecard (BSC) is an integrative approach to performance evaluation. It is a logical strategic framework organised across four key perspectives (financial perspective, customer perspective, internal perspective, and learning and growth perspective), which enables an organisation to articulate its strategy into a set of focused, strategic objectives and measures. The Balanced Scorecard was developed by Robert Kapland and David Norton (1996) as a way of addressing performance measurement limitations in an organisation – it was developed to address the following needs (Chang & Morgan, 2000:xv–xvi):

- A demand for timely, easy-to-understand information. Performance scorecards provide a concise summary of critical measures needed for updates and decisions.
- A desire to see a graphic depiction of the performance of key measures. Performance scorecards allow the manager to monitor performance against targets, business goals and competitive benchmarks.
- A need for timely information on the measures that matter. The scorecards contain indicators that directly relate to decision-making and business results.

In addition to strict financial outcomes, healthcare financial managers should assess intangible assets that affect the organisation's bottom line, such as clinical processes, staff skills, patient satisfaction and loyalty. The Balanced Scorecard, coupled with data-warehousing capabilities, offers a way to measure an organisation's performance against its strategic objectives while focusing on building capabilities to achieve these objectives. It is designed to communicate and assess strategic performance – to test the validity of the strategy – and to monitor the organisation's performance against its delivery on a regular and frequent basis. Priorities for today are deduced from where we need to be tomorrow. The Balanced Scorecard examines performance related to the four key perspectives, based on the following premises:

- Planning outputs become coaching inputs
- Coaching outputs become evaluating inputs
- Evaluating outputs become planning inputs.

Because the Balanced Scorecard requires substantial amounts of data, it is a necessity to establish an organisational data warehouse of clinical, operational and financial data that can be used in decision support. Because it presents indicators that managers and staff can influence directly by their actions, the Balanced Scorecard approach to quality improvement and performance measurement encourages behavioural changes aimed at achieving corporate strategies. Traditional financial management systems measure the tangible and financial assets of the healthcare organisation. But healthcare financial managers also need to measure and respond to intangible assets of value to the organisation, such as best-practice clinical processes, skilled staff and satisfied and loyal patients, because of their substantial effect on the bottom line.

Purpose

The purpose of the Balanced Scorecard is to (Chang & Morgan, 2000:xvi):

- Drive achievement toward business goals
- Provide focus on business strategies
- Align employees' efforts toward objectives (performance management)
- Sustain improved business performance
- Guide shifts in business direction
- Achieve balanced results across stakeholder groups.

Dimensions of the Balanced Scorecard

Kaplan and Nortan (1996) state that organisations can more effectively manage results with a balance of measures in four categories – also known as the four perspectives: the financial perspective, the customer perspective, the internal processes perspective, and the learning and growth perspective. When developed, the Balanced Scorecard becomes an instrument for aligning organisational performance with strategy.

Figure on 19.3 reflects the application of the BSC in business excellence (Botha, 2005:25).

Underlying perspectives

The following underlying perspectives related to the BSC are briefly highlighted: financial, customer, internal process and learning/growth perspectives, in relation to the vision and strategy of the organisation.

- **Financial perspective**. This includes the financial objectives, measures, targets and initiatives (to succeed financially, how should we appear to our shareholders?).
- **Customer perspective**. This includes the customer-related objectives, measures, targets and initiatives (to achieve our vision, how should we appear to our customers?).

Figure 19.3 Application of BSC in business excellence

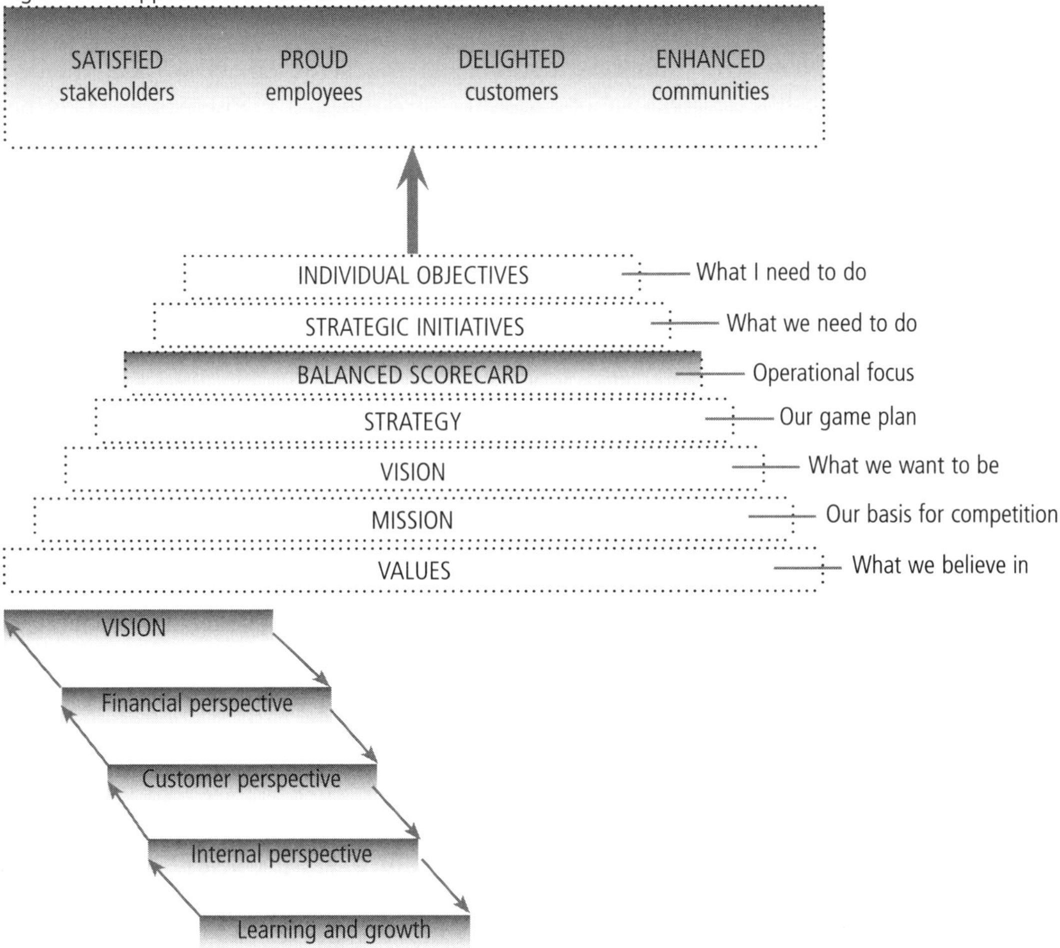

- **Internal processes perspective**. This consists of the objectives, measures, targets, initiatives (to satisfy our shareholders and customers, and what business processes we must excel at).
- **Learning and growth perspective**. This includes the learning and growth objectives, measures, targets and initiatives (to achieve our vision, how will we sustain our ability to change and improve?).

Concluding statements

- A Balanced Scorecard is a selected set of measures that provides a balanced and timely view of business performance specific to an area of responsibility.
- The BSC focuses on four perspectives: financial, customer, internal processes and learning and growth.

19.5.4 Accreditation of healthcare organisations

Background

Accreditation refers to a public recognition of the achievement of accreditation standards by a healthcare organisation, demonstrated through an independent external peer assessment of that organisation's level of performance in relation to the pre-determined standards. These independent, voluntary programmes, which began with a focus on training, have developed into multi-disciplinary assessments of healthcare functions, organisations and networks. Unlike ISO standards, the programmes used to assess healthcare facilities for accreditation have been developed specifically for healthcare. They began in the Anglo-Saxon countries, but spread into Latin America, Africa and South East Asia during the 1990s. Mandatory programmes have recently been adopted in France, Italy and Scotland. Less than a decade ago, accreditation was still waiting to be included in the agendas of many countries and healthcare institutions. In 2002, accreditation systems were clearly defined in approximately 40 countries. The past ten years have therefore been marked by a significant increase in national healthcare accreditation programmes (Shaw, 2004:8).

Accreditation is a formalised process whereby national standards are set and compliance with them is evaluated by means of a sequential process comprising internal evaluation by the healthcare service staff themselves during the preparatory phase, followed by an external evaluation by peers during the survey phase. A computerised calculation of results is done, followed by the validation of these results by a specialised committee, usually referred to as the Technical Committee. On compliance with the standards, the accreditation status is awarded to the healthcare service by the Accreditation Board of the accrediting agent/organisation, such as the Council for Health Service Accreditation of Southern Africa (COHSASA). Accreditation certificates are usually valid for one to three years and in some countries for five years.

The Council for Health Service Accreditation of Southern Africa (COHSASA), was established in 1995, and registered with the Companies Act, 1973 (Act 61 of 1973, as amended) as a 'not-for-gain' company. COHSASA was accredited by the International Society for Quality in Health in 2003. COHSASA offers a facilitated or a non-facilitated process of accreditation.

Purpose

The purpose of accreditation is summarised as follows (Shaw, 2004:12):

- To improve the quality of healthcare service delivery at all levels, by establishing optimal achievement goals in meeting standards for healthcare organisations
- To stimulate and improve the integration and management of healthcare services
- To empower all role-players in the context of healthcare service delivery to attain excellence
- To facilitate team work in the healthcare organisation, especially among the managers and leaders of different professional, clinical, administrative and support service departments

- To justify accountability to the community, healthcare funders and service providers, with regard to the quality of healthcare service delivery
- To strengthen the public's confidence in the quality of healthcare service delivery
- To provide a basis for the comparison of performance outcomes in a competitive or non-competitive market, which can meet selected structure, process and outcome standards or criteria
- To provide the basis for negotiation with the funders and/or management to improve facilities, equipment and general conditions
- To determine the viability, cost-effectiveness and efficiency of the healthcare service – therefore the measurement of healthcare service performance
- To reduce risks associated with injury and infections for patients and staff.

Dimensions of the accreditation process

The dimensions of the accreditation process with reference to the following, as recommended by ISQua (Shaw, 2004), are briefly highlighted:

- Requirements pertaining to the accreditation agency/body
- Purpose of accreditation
- Regulation of accreditation
- Incentives for uptake
- Stakeholder engagement
- Configuration of the programme
- Governance structure of the accreditation agency
- Accountability and culture
- Management of accreditation
- Core accreditation elements
- Process of accreditation
- Resources for accreditation.

Requirements pertaining to the accreditation agency/body

The accreditation agency requires a formal constitution and clear operating procedures. The International Society for Quality in Health Care (ISQua) has developed minimum standards for healthcare accreditation agencies/organisations by means of the international ALPHA standards on corporate governance and strategic directions. The relevant accreditation agency/body should comply with the following accreditation agency elements (Shaw, 2004:29):

- Mission, vision and values
- Strategic planning
- Operational planning
- Leadership
- Effective governance
- External relations.

Purpose of accreditation

The purpose of accreditation should be described by the accreditation body/agency, reflecting the potential impact on healthcare service delivery, such as clinical effectiveness, consumer empowerment and decision-making, health system governance, professional and personal development, management development, the development of quality systems, increased team work and internal cohesion, revision of policies and procedures, integration of the quality agenda, external networking, marketing and publicity, achievement of standards, etc. (Shaw, 2004:13–14).

Regulation of accreditation

The role of the government needs to be clarified, with reference to at least the following (Shaw, 2004:16):

- Activating government-driven or accepting independent accreditation programmes
- Initiating legislation/policy pertaining to voluntary or mandatory accreditation
- Enabling the accreditation process, for example through policy decisions, avoiding conflict, reciprocal recognition of assessments and the joint development of standards
- Providing leverage, for example by according preference to accredited facilities, such as in reimbursement tariffs and payment procedures
- Using accreditation as a criterion in its own purchasing decisions, for example in defining preferred providers and contract monitoring
- Regulating individuals and institutions, for example by ensuring consistency and the distinction between licensing and accreditation
- Providing financial support, such as the establishment of the programme and the funding of continuing development of the programme.

In addition to the role of the government, public-private partnerships in quality improvement need to be established. The need for active collaboration between public and private agencies in order to reconcile the conflict between top-down regulation and bottom-up development has been emphasised by means of independent reviews.

Incentives for uptake

What both consumers and regulators of accreditation in any state or institution aspire to, is having every healthcare provider participate in a standards-based assessment process – whether it is mandatory or not. Participants need to see, however, the business value with reference to financial, social and professional aspects. The incentives/benefits of accreditation therefore need to be clarified and justified (Shaw, 2004:19–20).

Stakeholder engagement

Associated with each aim or potential impact of accreditation, there is a population of stakeholders that includes those who stand to gain from accreditation, and those who might gain by undermining it. How these stakeholders are defined, and how their expectations are reconciled, varies in and between countries. Traditional profession-driven programmes have tended to build links with regulators and consumers, thus becoming more accountable and transparent. Stakeholders could include professional associations, private insurers, health ministries, university departments, voluntary membership societies and health service charities (Shaw, 2004:21–22).

Configuration of the programme

The accreditation programme could focus on selected priorities (such as hospital accreditation), or may provide a variety of accreditation focus areas, in accordance with the needs of the community and the country's healthcare service provision system. Services are mostly offered to both public and private facilities. Larger countries are in a position to achieve economies of scale, offering a full spectrum of accreditation options (Shaw, 2004:23–24).

Governance structure of the accreditation agency

The governance structure of the accreditation agency needs to take the following into consideration (Shaw, 2004:29–30):

- Authority should be vested in a national or a decentralised regional structure.
- Corporate governance and representation. A non-governmental agency should have a Board of Directors, consisting of and accountable to the various stakeholders. Appropriate representation is therefore crucial.
- Typically, independent boards include representatives of professional associations, funding agencies, consumer councils, statutory bodies and governmental legislatures.

Accountability and culture

Accreditation programmes which have succeeded in effecting improvement in organisations have generally done so by stimulating internal motivation and commitment to self-assessment and change. This requires a culture of transparency and acceptance of personal and corporate responsibility among management, clinical and non-clinical staff. The scope of responsibility and authority of healthcare managers for quality and accreditation, and the mechanisms for their accountability to the public, should be explicitly set out at all levels and types of healthcare service delivery facilities/systems (Shaw, 2004:30–31).

Management of accreditation

The management of accreditation needs to comply with the following international best practice principles (Shaw, 2004:32–40):

- National standards, based on the scope of standards determined by the ISQua ALPHA initiative (refer to the core accreditation elements). The development,

local adaptation, validation and revision of standards are in accordance with the international best practice principles.
- Surveyor selection, development and deployment including requirements, recruitment, selection, contracting, training and evaluation of surveyors should follow a credible process, in accordance with national expectations and lessons learnt from other countries.
- Survey management. The process of accreditation entails at least the following with reference to survey management: engagement with the institution, survey planning, self-assessment by means of a baseline survey, the development of clinical and organisational indicators and the collection of evidence-based data in this regard, a process of facilitation to implement the standards, and the external survey.

Core accreditation elements

The national healthcare accreditation agency/body should make provision for national standards focusing on at least the following (Shaw, 2004:32):
- To identify the rights of patients to choice, dignity and information
- To promote accountability and internal quality improvement mechanisms
- To focus on improving performance and safety in available resources
- To be oriented to continuity and to adopt the 'patient's pathway' through the system
- To seek research evidence and operate in consultation with stakeholders.

Process of accreditation

The accreditation body/agency maintains a system for the determination, awarding and maintenance of accreditation that ensures the integrity of the process. This system should facilitate (Shaw, 2004:37):
- Transparency
- Consistency of decision-making and the basis for accreditation awards
- Trustworthiness – reflecting the truth value of the accreditation outcome
- Decisions based on the compliance with standards
- Determination of the impact of non-compliance in relation to patient safety and legal considerations, efficiency
- Reasonableness/fairness as to the duration or timescale for accreditation decisions to be made
- The duration and maintenance of accreditation awards: the duration commonly ranges from one (conditional, with reservations) to three years (full accreditation with commendations), and are usually subject to continuing monitoring and mid-term or random reviews
- A non-adversarial process for appeals
- Publication of results: the extent and methods of public disclosure of survey findings and accreditation awards must be agreed in advance by the accrediting body and the various stakeholders

- Programme evaluation of the accreditation agency, in accordance with the ISQua standards and process.

A combined quantitative and qualitative accreditation strategy should therefore be followed in accordance with the formalised accreditation process as developed and implemented by a particular accreditation agency/organisation (such as the Council for Health Service Accreditation of Southern Africa (COHSASA)), consisting of at least the following: a baseline survey, followed by an internal and external evaluation survey, the process of decision-making and finally the accreditation status award.

The accreditation process follows a sequential and formalised process:

- A healthcare service entering into a contractual agreement with the accrediting agency/body (such as COHSASA) on a voluntary basis
- A preparatory phase with a baseline self-evaluation
- A facilitated (optional) process during the preparatory phase
- Followed by the external survey phase
- The process of decision-making
- In the case of non-conformance with certain standards, a focus survey is conducted once the necessary remedial actions have been taken by the hospital/healthcare management to verify compliance with the standards
- Finally, the accreditation status award or denial thereof.

The COHSASA process of accreditation is reflected in Figure 19.4.

Figure 19.4 Visual presentation of COHSASA accreditation process

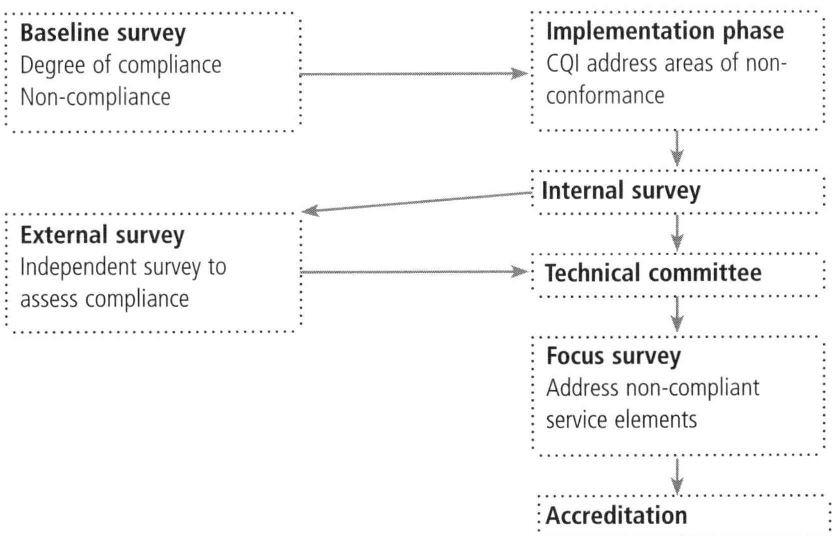

Resources for accreditation

In addition to a supportive environment, sustainable accreditation programmes require targeted resources to develop and operate an accreditation system. This relates to at least the following (Shaw, 2004:42–53):

- Adequate and competent staff, usually structured into functional units such as survey planning and management (facilitation), standards research, development and revision, surveyor recruitment, selection, development and deployment
- Information Technology System in accordance with the ISQua standard
- Education services to meet quality standards and client needs
- Adequate time for the development and establishment of the accreditation system, the development of the standards and the assessment process, selection and training of facilitators and surveyors, pilot testing, sustainability, as well as the maintenance of accredited facilities
- Generation of income by means of facilitation and survey fees
- Financial management system in accordance with best practice requirements (refer to Chapter 17, Financial management in a healthcare organisation).

19.6 UNDERLYING DYNAMICS

The following underlying dynamics impacting on the application of the selected quality improvement models in healthcare organisations are briefly discussed, with specific reference to the following: external determinants and institutional determinants.

19.6.1 External determinants

The following external determinants are important:

- The type of business ownership (public, private or mixed ownership) and subsequent legislative and strategic direction by the external stakeholders and role-players. This will determine whether there is primarily an external or internal motivator to select and implement a quality improvement model in the healthcare organisation.
- Mandatory or voluntary external peer review legislation or government directives. This will impact on the internal motivation of all the healthcare organisation's role-players.
- External incentives are crucial, such as preference from private insurers to deal with facilities whose clinical and management processes have been independently verified; they may also make reimbursement simpler and faster to the certified/accredited organisation. Reduction of liability insurance costs could also be considered – premiums reflect a reduced risk rating. Exemptions from regulatory inspections by the licensing body is another example of an external incentive (Shaw, 2004:20).
- There are also ethical challenges that could impact on the success of accreditation programmes, for example should accreditation results and outcomes be made public?

19.6.2 Institutional determinants

The following success factors are highlighted:

- Designated leadership, accountability, supervision, monitoring and communication of quality at all the levels of service delivery
- Ownership and accountability at operational level by the relevant role-players
- Public accountability via the reporting of quality improvement systems through objective external assessment by independent bodies
- Dissemination of quality information to civic groups with a particular interest in health, such as women's groups, health educators, legislators and the mass media
- Coordination of multi-disciplinary quality improvement projects to impact on the overall outcome of the projects
- Regular, systematic feedback of data on important process and outcome measures to individuals, organisational units and organisations
- Disincentives, such as the cost in terms of time, human resources capacity, management, money and fears of the outcome.

19.7 CONCLUDING STATEMENTS

The following concluding statements are relevant:

- The selection and application of a quality improvement model are influenced by the international directives and the internal **contextual** dynamics, such as national legislation, patient/consumer expectations and related charters, the type and nature of business ownership (public or private), as well as the principles of corporate governance and accountability.
- The **purpose** of selecting and implementing a quality improvement model is to improve the quality of healthcare service delivery in the organisation, to reduce or mitigate the risks involved in healthcare service delivery, and to positively impact on the healthcare indicators of the country.
- Various **role-players** are involved in the selection and implementation of a quality improvement model, depending on the business ownership and resultant accountable authority. The managers – both clinical and non-clinical – play an important role. Various types of quality coordinators and facilitators are also involved.
- The background, purpose and respective dimensions of the following **quality improvement models** were presented: ISO, business excellence, the Balanced Scorecard and accreditation.
- Selected external and institutional **underlying dynamics** that impact on the implementation of quality improvement models were highlighted, focusing mainly on mandatory or voluntary directives, external incentives available and ethical challenges, and institutional success factors.

Self-assessment

(1) Download the ISO 9001:2000 Quality Management Principles (www.iso.org). Debate the application value of these principles in your healthcare organisation.
(2) Download the ISQua toolkit for accreditation programmes. Assess the national and/or regional/local accreditation programme in accordance with the Self-Assessment Tool – Key Factors in Accreditation (www.isqua.org/isquaPages/Accreditation.html).
(3) Compare the ISO, business excellence and accreditation quality improvement models with one another. Give a critical reflection of the suitability/transferability of each in your own healthcare organisation.

20 Continuous quality improvement in a healthcare organisation

KEY CONCEPTS

Quality
Continuous quality improvement
Quality improvement cycle
Standards
Monitoring, assessment and evaluation
Remedial action
Clinical governance
Total quality management

SPECIFIC OUTCOMES

After studying this chapter, you should be able to:

- Interpret the legal, professional-ethical and healthcare continuous quality improvement (CQI) **context**, with reference to global, national, provincial and local, professional-ethical legislative framework, human resources management legislation, patient/consumer expectations and service delivery framework, business ownership and corporate governance
- Analyse and debate the **purpose** of CQI with reference to general management practice, functional and specialised management practice (including clinical governance), benchmarking, marketing and public accountability
- Identify the **role-players** and interpret their roles and responsibilities in CQI
- Describe and apply the **process** and various dimensions of CQI in a healthcare organisation: pre-requisites for CQI, the CQI cycle, clinical governance, consumer satisfaction and involvement programmes, and total quality management (TQM)
- Debate the **underlying dynamics** that could impact on the success or failure of CQI in a healthcare organisation.

20.1 INTRODUCTION

Quality improvement refers to a formal process whereby standards are set, work performance is measured and evaluated against the set of pre-determined standards, and remedial steps/actions are taken to solve or counteract problems in order to improve the quality of service delivery and performance outcomes. Organisational managers are accountable for the quality of services delivered. Accountability requires proven evidence that quality services have indeed been delivered. It is often said: one cannot improve what one cannot measure and one cannot measure what one cannot define. It is therefore important to develop continuous quality improvement (CQI) programmes in a healthcare organisation. Quality service delivery in healthcare is associated with the following principles:

- **Accessibility**. This means that the services are not compromised by undue restrictions in time or distance, and refers to the ease with which patients can obtain the care that they need when they need it.
- **Relevance and appropriateness**. This means that the service delivery interventions are relevant and appropriate, based on the needs of the community and healthcare consumers, and in accordance with the core business and strategic direction of the healthcare organisation. It applies to the degree to which the correct care is provided, given the current state of the art.
- **Continuity of care**. This indicates the degree to which the care needed by patients is coordinated among practitioners and across organisations and time.
- **Patient perspective**. This pertains to the degree to which patients (and their families) are involved in the decision-making processes in matters pertaining to their health, and the degree to which they are satisfied with their care.
- **Safety of the care environment**. This refers to the degree to which the environment is free from hazard and danger.
- **Timeliness of care**. This pertains to the degree to which care is provided to patients when it is needed.
- **Effectiveness and efficiency**. This relates to value for money in the context of health and means getting acceptable quality services to people who need them and making people as healthy as possible with given resources. To obtain value for money, healthcare spending must be effective and efficient:
  - *Effective* pertains to whether the organisation is pursuing those interventions that will have maximum impact on the health status of its patients. Will it achieve the intended benefit? Is there reasonable accommodation of consumer expectations? Are the right things being done? What is the degree to which care is provided in the correct manner – without error – given the current state of the art?
  - Efficient pertains to whether the organisation is delivering the maximum number of services given the resources at its disposal. Are things being done correctly? What is the degree to which the care received has the desired effect with a minimum of effort, expense and waste?

The conceptual framework of this chapter on quality improvement in a healthcare organisation is reflected in Figure 20.1.

Figure 20.1 Visual presentation of continuous quality improvement in a healthcare organisation

Context	Global context National context Provincial and local context Professional-ethical legislative framework Organisational context Human resources management legislation Patient/consumer expectations and service delivery-related legislation Business ownership context Corporate governance context
Purpose	*Continuous quality improvement:* • General management practice • Functional and specialised management practice, including clinical governance • Benchmarking • Marketing • Public accountability
Role-players	Legislative authorities Board of directors Managers (general and functional) Healthcare practitioners (clinical and non-clinical) Community Recognised trade unions Quality coordinator
Process	CQI strategy analysis, development, execution and review CQI cycle: standard setting, monitoring, assessment and evaluation, and remedial or corrective action Clinical governance Consumer satisfaction and involvement programmes Total quality management
Underlying dynamics	Institutional capacity Leadership Organisational culture Skills development and CPD Performance management

20.2 CONTEXT

The context description of quality improvement in healthcare organisations includes the following: the global context, the national, provincial and local context, the professional-ethical legislative framework, patient/consumer expectations and service delivery-related legislation, the organisation itself in terms of the type of business ownership, as well as the principles of corporate governance.

20.2.1 Global context

The World Health Organisation (WHO) provides the international leadership on quality promotion and improvement. The WHO is the United Nations specialised agency for health. It was established on the 7th of April 1948. WHO's objective, as set out in its Constitution, is the attainment by all peoples of the highest possible level of health. Health is defined in the WHO's constitution as a state of complete physical, mental and social well-being and not merely the absence of disease or infirmity. WHO is governed by 192 Member States through the World Health Assembly. The Health Assembly is composed of representatives from the WHO's Member States. The main tasks of the World Health Assembly are to approve the WHO programme and the budget for the following biennium and to decide major policy questions (www.who.org). They render a comprehensive global service by means of policy development, consultations, research, and many guidelines on quality improvement.

In addition to the WHO, there are many other organisations that promote quality – not only related to clinical service delivery, but to all spheres of healthcare service delivery (i.e. USAID and the Centre for Disease Control). There are also many quality improvement models (refer to Chapter 19, Quality improvement models in a healthcare organisation) offered through international agencies, such as ISO certification, business excellence and various accreditation services.

20.2.2 National context

Quality improvement in healthcare services are primarily regulated and directed by the national Department of Health, in accordance with its mandate and legislative framework (South Africa, 2003). Quality guidelines are developed for almost every cluster of public healthcare service delivery. A few examples of quality directives are as follows:

- Essential Drugs Programme: standard treatment guidelines and essential drugs list
- Protocols for the management of a person with a sexually transmitted disease
- The South African Tuberculosis Control Programme Practical Guidelines
- National Guideline on home-based and community-based care
- Saving mothers: policy and management guidelines for common causes of maternal deaths
- Hospital Strategy Project
- District Hospital Service Package for South Africa
- Strategic priorities for the national health system 2004–2009 (Department of Health, 2004)
- National Policy on Quality and subsequent proposal of a National Institute for Health Care Quality (NIHCQ)
- The Primary Health Care Package
- Norms and Standards for Primary Health Care Service delivery
- Antiretroviral roll-out guidelines.

The private healthcare sector (including the not-for-profit and state-aided services) also develops national guidelines and quality directives, in accordance with the nature and type of business ownership and national corporate governance set-up.

20.2.3 Provincial and local context

The provincial and local legislative frameworks (related to public healthcare service delivery) provide direction to quality improvement by means of quality structures, quality policies/directives, etc.

20.2.4 Organisational context

The organisational context is based on the type of business ownership (public or private or mixed) and subsequent legislative and service delivery framework, the nature and size of the organisation, and other related internal determinants.

20.2.5 Professional-ethical legislative framework

The quality of clinical service delivery is regulated by the particular healthcare practitioners' legislation, with specific reference to education, practice and licensing, including the disciplinary measures that can be taken when there is evidence of transgression or non-compliance (refer to Chapters 10–15 on Human resources management).

20.2.6 Human resources management legislation

Human resources-related legislation and regulations will also be applicable, as described in Chapters 10–15 on Human resources management.

20.2.7 Patient/consumer expectations and service delivery-related legislation

The Patient Charter, if available in a country, is also applicable and impacts on the quality improvement models and service delivery foci. In addition to the Patient Charter, other service delivery legislation/policies (such as the South African Batho Pele policy/regulation), could also determine the context of quality improvement models in healthcare (refer to Chapter 1, Management of a healthcare organisation). When selecting and implementing a quality improvement model in the healthcare organisation, these principles need to be taken into consideration.

20.2.8 Type of business ownership and related service delivery legislation and policy framework

The utilisation and application of quality improvement models in the healthcare organisation are very much based on the type of business ownership (public or private), and the subsequent regulatory framework and policies.

20.2.9 Corporate governance

As a healthcare organisation could also be seen as a business enterprise, the general principles of business excellence and corporate governance are also taken into consideration. International and national best practice principles related to the management of a healthcare organisation and clinical governance, are also applicable (refer to Chapter 1, Management of a healthcare organisation).

20.3 PURPOSE

The purpose of formalised continuous quality improvement in healthcare organisations is summarised as follows:

- To improve the quality of general management practice
- To improve the quality of functional (i.e. financial management) and specialised management practice, including clinical governance
- To benchmark (internal and external), that is comparing results of departments' and organisations' evaluations to the results of other interventions, programmes or organisations, and examining processes against those of others recognised as excellent, as a means of making improvements
- To market: the reputation of the healthcare organisation is based on the quality of care rendered, as reflected in CQI outputs and outcomes
- To ensure public accountability at national, provincial/regional and local levels: the quality of service delivery is determined through internal and/or external assessments, reported and justified.

20.4 ROLE-PLAYERS

There are many role-players involved in the rendering of quality services in the healthcare organisation, as reflected in Chapter 1: legislative authorities, Board of Directors, managers (general and functional), healthcare practitioners (clinical and non-clinical) community, recognised trade unions and other stakeholders. In addition to these role-players, quality specialists or quality coordinators are also appointed in a designated post, mainly to coordinate the different quality activities and to supply the necessary leadership in this regard.

20.5 CONTINUOUS QUALITY IMPROVEMENT PROCESS AND DIMENSIONS

20.5.1 Process description

The continuous quality improvement process entails: CQI strategy analysis, strategy development, strategy execution and strategy review (see Figure 20.2).

- **Strategy analysis**. This involves assessing the patient profile, in accordance with the specific core business (type of healthcare service delivery), with regard to the high-volume interactions, the high-risk interactions/interventions and the problem-prone interactions. This analysis is based on document analysis and existing patient outcomes.

- **Strategy development**. This relates to the nature and scope of CQI programmes that should be in place based on the strategy analyses data. This includes the organisational design and structure required for clinical governance in the healthcare organisation.
- **Strategy execution**. This entails the implementation of the CQI cycle – the development of standards, monitoring and evaluation of actual performance against these standards and subsequent remedial action.
- **Strategy review**. This entails the evaluation of the CQI strategy with reference to output, outcome, effectiveness and efficiency.

Figure 20.2 Continuous quality improvement process

The execution of the continuous quality improvement (CQI) strategy is described, with reference to the following dimensions: the pre-requisites for CQI, the CQI cycle (standard setting, monitoring, assessment and evaluation, and remedial action). In addition to the CQI process, brief descriptions on clinical governance, consumer satisfaction and involvement programmes, and total quality management (Shaw, 2003), are also given.

20.5.2 Prerequisites for continuous quality improvement

Quality is everyone's concern. Various quality improvement models were presented in the previous chapter, illustrating the complexity of quality improvement in healthcare service delivery. The prerequisites for quality improvement in healthcare organisations are summarised as follows:

- The principles of accessibility, relevance and appropriateness, continuity of care, patient perspective, safety of the care environment, timeliness of care, as well as effectiveness and efficiency of healthcare service delivery, are adhered to, in accordance with the community profile and national, provincial, local and organisational directives.
- The five levels of leadership – as recommended by Jim Collins (2001) – are reflected in the organisation:

- *Level 1: Highly capable individual* makes productive contributions through talent, knowledge, skills and good work habits
- *Level 2: Contributing team member* contributes individual capabilities to the achievement of group objectives and works effectively with others in a group setting
- *Level 3: Competent manager* organises people and resources toward the effective and efficient pursuit of excellence and predetermined objectives and outcomes
- *Level 4: Effective leader* catalyses commitment to and vigorous pursuit of a clear and compelling vision, stimulating higher performance standards
- *Level 5: Executive* builds enduring greatness through a paradoxical blend of personal humility and professional will.

- CQI programmes are developed in all the spheres of healthcare service delivery in the organisation, reflecting the principles of TQM, that is general and functional management dimensions, clinical service delivery, support services, hotel services, etc. (refer to Chapter 19, Quality improvement models in a healthcare organisation, with reference to the requirements laid down by the International Society for Quality in Health).
- The development of a CQI Programme is based on a CQI profile analysis:
  - profile analysis of the population involved (i.e. surgical patients and staff members)
  - analysis of the high-volume, high-risk and problem-prone duties, tasks and responsibilities (DTRs) and subsequent intervention activities related to the particular area of core business practice in the organisation are also identified.
- The CQI programmes are compliant with best practice principles, with reference to at least the following: validity of standards, trustworthiness of the monitoring and evaluation system, production of reliable results (reflecting truth value), reporting and feedback, and purpose-driven remedial action or corrective measures to continuously improve the quality of service delivery.
- CQI programmes are continuously reviewed with reference to system-related problems, efficiency and effectiveness.
- Purpose-driven skills development and continuous professional development programmes for staff imply that the non-compliant results/outcome of CQI programmes are addressed in the skills development programmes of the healthcare organisation.
- Stakeholder uptake (both internal and external stakeholders involved in the process and principles of continuous quality improvement) reflects the necessary ownership and accountability by all level managers and practitioners. There is evidence of a CQI culture in the organisation.
- It is essential that a passion and drive for CQI is visible in the thinking, behaviour and action of employees and management.

- There is an information management system to accommodate the principles of CQI, compliant with at least the following:
  - validity and reliability (trustworthiness)
  - the ability to capture and collate the key performance areas and quality indicators (both clinical and non-clinical)
  - the ability to accommodate the necessary clinical pathways measuring mechanisms.
- There is a stakeholder-based organisation structure/design and subsequent formalised total continuous quality management strategy.
- CQI is owned by the operational practitioners and line managers – not by the quality specialist or coordinator.

20.5.3 Continuous quality improvement cycle

Continuous quality improvement (CQI) is a formalised process of setting standards, monitoring, analysing and evaluating compliance with these standards, and taking remedial action/steps to maintain the standards, improve existing performance and output, and to facilitate change by means of capacity building. It is a cyclic process. Quality improvement is analogous to the systems approach: input, throughput and output (see Figure 20.3).

Figure 20.3 Quality improvement cycle

The quality improvement process therefore consists of inputs (i.e. human resources), throughput by utilising and applying the inputs to achieve certain results (outputs and/or outcomes). The quality improvement process should ultimately impact on the outcome (i.e. health indicators in a region, province or country). The quality improvement process can be simplified as follows:

- The setting/formulation of standards
- Monitoring, assessment and evaluation of compliance with these standards
- Responding by means of adequate remedial actions and continuous capacity improvement and empowerment to ensure the achievement of quality-related goals and objectives.

Standards

A standard is a written description or statement of the expected level of performance with reference to structure, process and outcome; a standard is a desired and achievable level of performance against which actual performance is measured. Standards should comply with at least the following:

- Reflect a systems framework (input, throughput/process and output)
- Address the full scope of core business in the healthcare organisation: the general and functional managerial functions, including clinical and non-clinical functions of a healthcare organisation
- Focus on the patient in the context of their family and the community
- Reflect a balance of structure, process and outcome standards
- Set optimal, achievable expectations
- Set measurable expectations.

A brief description of standard setting is presented, based on the following themes:
- Classification of standards
- Scope of standards
- Setting of standards
- Assessment of clinical guidelines and indicators
- Format presentation of clinical guidelines and clinical indicators
- AGREE instrument for the assessment of clinical guidelines and clinical indicators.

Classification of standards

Three types of standards are classified:

(1) **Structure standards.** These describe the resources required to be able to facilitate quality service delivery, such as infrastructure, systems (i.e. information management system), human, physical and financial resources.

(2) **Process standards**. These describe how the act or intervention is performed Process standards relate to all the managerial, clinical and non-clinical processes, interactions or interventions.

(3) **Outcome standards**. These are a description of the end results, outcomes or performance indicators.

Scope of standards

There are many examples of standards, such as policies, procedures and clinical guidelines.

- **Policies**. These are written statements (structure standards) that act as guidelines and reflect the position and values of the organisation on a given core business activity, that is, patient admission policy, patient discharge policy, corporate policy on continuous quality improvement, financial policy, policy on the maintenance and replacement of equipment.
- **Procedures**. These are written statements and instructions conveying the approved and recommended steps for a particular interaction or intervention – how it should be executed (process standards).
- **Clinical guidelines**. These guidelines are systematically developed statements – derived from evidence-based clinical practice – to assist the clinical practitioner in

making decisions about appropriate healthcare interventions for specific clinical circumstances (i.e. the management of hypertension). Their purpose is to make explicit recommendations with a definite intent to influence what clinicians do.

- **Algorithms or clinical pathway**. An algorithm or clinical pathway is an interdisciplinary approach of standardised patient care and treatment to improve the quality and efficiency of care/treatment for a select patient population. The goal of clinical pathways is to provide a 'map' of care for certain conditions to standardise the care/treatment and to reduce costs.
- **Performance indicator**. This is the exact, absolute, measurable output (result) and/or outcome (impact) associated with a defined key performance area (i.e. financial management, clinical indicators, such as infection rate).
- **Clinical indicator**. This indicates the exact, absolute, measurable output (result) and/or outcome (impact) associated with a defined clinical dimension (i.e. infection control) or clinical intervention. Examples of clinical indicators are nosocomial infection rate and the rate of unplanned re-admission of patients.

Setting of standards

Standards could be developed in-house (at operational, middle and corporate levels), or for national and global purposes. Standard setting is divided into the following phases or steps: getting a project group together, literature review, drafting of the standards, validation and field testing, ratification, publication, implementation and promotion, revision and updating.

(a) *Project group*

Constitute a project group/team. The members should reflect credibility as experts in the field. It is also advisable to formalise the project committee by means of a Charter or Terms of Reference (see Chapter 1, Management of a healthcare organisation, with reference to committee structures).

(b) *Literature review*

Access sources related to the standards, that is, existing standards at national or international levels, consensus between practitioners, professions, stakeholders on what constitutes 'best practice', research-based evidence, national, provincial or local policies and directives, and legislation.

(c) *Drafting of the standards*

The standards are drafted, based on the following principles:

- Define the purpose and scope of the standards.
- Use the literature review and subsequent theoretical framework as point of departure for the writing of the statements.
- In the case of clinical guidelines/indicators, the principles of clinical logic should be applied: assess epidemiology and natural history of disease or condition,

identify the main interventions at each step that can favourably influence disease progression, determine which interventions are evidence-based, for interventions with solid evidence of effectiveness and benefit, determine if intervention is likely to be cost-effective.
- Determine what you want to measure: the data element construction and the availability of such data.
- Use the correct layout format (i.e. title, rationale/purpose, definition of terms, content of the standards and criteria).
- Write the standards in affirmation format: positive behavioural/conduct statements in present tense.

(d) *Validation of the draft standards*
The draft standards should be validated by the various stakeholders. This could be a simplified once-off process (for in-house standards) by means of critical debate and consensus decision-making, or by means of a rigorous research method. In the case of clinical guidelines or the development of clinical indicators, the process of validation should follow a rigorous process of critical debate, refinement and lastly, a process of quantitative validation – by determining the content validity index (CVI) of each standard. This entails the identification of validation criteria, such as:
- Relevance or applicability, with reference to the current reality in the healthcare organisation
- Professional-ethical and legal alignment, in accordance with the national, provincial or local framework
- Potential impact on quality – consider the contribution of the standards towards efficiency and effectiveness of the core business activities in the organisation
- Feasibility – consider the practical implementation value and/or affordability
- Clarity, whether the formulation of the standards is clear and unambiguous.

A Lickert rating scale can be utilised for the determination of the CVI (see the AGREE instrument: www.agreecollaboration.org.instrument). The stakeholder group members rate each standard (based on the chosen Lickert Scale) according to the selection validation/appraisal criteria. The average CVI for each standard is determined. Non-discriminant standards are rejected. In the case of clinical guidelines and clinical indicators, the professional bodies (societies/associations and regulatory boards or councils) should also form part of the stakeholder group involved in the validation of the standards.

(e) *Field testing*
The standards should be piloted for relevance, legal alignment, impact, feasibility and clarity, etc. Amendment of the standards is recommended to the Project Group for consideration, followed by the refinement and/or modification of the standards in the case of problems detected.

(f) *Formal ratification of standards*
The standards should be ratified by the various level managers and relevant business ownership-related authorities. In the case of clinical guidelines and clinical indicators, expert group(s), preferably the professional association and/or the professional regulatory body/council, should also ratify the standards to enhance the credibility and possible enforcement value thereof.

(g) *Publication, implementation and promotion of the standards*
The standards are published and promoted as 'best practice' guidelines in the organisation. Various promotion methods could be used, for example websites and handy pocket guides. The implementation of the standards should be facilitated by means of the following:

- Skills development programmes
- Integration in the performance management system (reflected as key performance areas), including integration in the individual Balanced Scorecard performance system
- Enforcement by means of policies at all management levels
- Support by the relevant authorities, including the professional societies/ associations and the professional regulatory boards/councils.

(h) *Revision and update of the standards*
The standards are continuously revised and updated, in accordance with the predicted 'lifespan' of the standards and transformation dynamics involved. Litigation could occur if out-dated standards are practised, resulting in adverse events.

Assessment of clinical guidelines and indicators
Clinical practice guidelines and indicators are being developed and used in many countries throughout the world to improve and standardise the quality of patient care. Principles of evidence-based medicine dominate current clinical guideline programmes. Medical practitioners generally fanatically protect their professional independence and 'freedom of practice' in clinical decision-making. They tend to resist the principle of conforming to clinical guidelines that direct (or regulate) their independent accountability and subsequent professional practice. Clinical guidelines therefore have to reflect evidence-based validity and credibility. This demands a rigorous research and developmental process to ensure evidence-based validity – and subsequent ownership – of the guidelines. The more common priority areas are as follows:

- Management of hypertension
- Management of diabetes mellitus
- Acute myocardial infarction
- Congestive heart failure
- Pneumonia

- Pregnancy and related conditions
- Surgical procedures and complications.

Format presentation of clinical guidelines and clinical indicators

Clinical guidelines are usually presented and published in the following format:

- Title of the clinical guidelines
- Scope, rationale and purpose of the guidelines
- Definition of terms
- Content of guidelines
- Reference to the process methodology.

Clinical indicators are usually presented and printed in the following format:

- **Indicator statement**. This is also referred to as the title.
- **Definition of terms**. Define the terms contained in the indicator that need further explanation for data-collection purposes.
- **Type of guideline/indicator**. This includes the structure, process or outcome; or specific identification, i.e. rate-based, sentinel (adverse event).
- **Rationale**. This is the justification for existence, potential benefit and impact on outcome, and present supportive research-based references.
- **Description of indicator population**. This includes:
  - the denominator, the full population, i.e. total intubated patients on ventilators in the given monitoring time frame
  - the numerator, the episodes or events (i.e. unplanned extubations).
- Indicator data collection logic. This involves:
  - listing the elements and corresponding data sources from which data elements may be retrieved
  - describing the sequence of data element aggregation through which the numerator events and denominator events are identified by the indicator.
- **Underlying factors**. The factors that may explain variation in indicator data and thereby direct quality activities are listed.

AGREE instrument for the assessment of clinical guidelines and clinical indicators

The quality of clinical guidelines and indicators can be assessed by utilising the AGREE instrument. AGREE refers to the **A**ppraisal of **G**uidelines **R**esearch **E**valuation. It originated through the international collaboration of researchers and policy makers who work together to improve the quality and effectiveness of clinical practice guidelines through collaborative research efforts. This research collaboration commenced in 1998 and developed the AGREE research methodology instrument (www.agreecollaboration.org.instrument). This instrument (AGREE Collaboration, 2001) provides a framework for assessing the quality of clinical guidelines – the confidence that the potential biases of guideline development have been addressed adequately and that the recommendations are both internally and externally valid, and are feasible for practice. This process involves taking into account the benefits, harms and costs of the recommendations, as well as the practical issues attached to them. Therefore, the assessment includes judgements about the methods used for developing the guidelines, the content of the final recommendations and the factors linked to their uptake. The AGREE instrument assesses both the quality of the reporting, and the quality of some aspects of recommendations. It provides an assessment of the predicted validity of a guideline – that is the likelihood that it will achieve its intended outcome. It does not assess the impact of a guideline on patients' outcomes. The AGREE instrument presents a quantitative assessment of the guidelines with reference to the following:

- Scope and purpose of the guidelines
- Stakeholder involvement
- Rigour of development
- Clarity and presentation
- Applicability
- Editorial independence.

Monitoring, analysis and evaluation

Monitoring, analysis and evaluation is the process related to the measuring of actual performance against the set standards. This entails at least the following: review strategies, data-collection design, data-collection strategies, instrument development, data management, data analysis and interpretation, and the reporting of findings.

Review strategies

Quality review can be conducted by the person him-/herself or by means of self-assessment and peer review.

(a) *Self-assessment*

Self-assessment refers to the individual practitioner's (clinical and non-clinical practitioners) own critical assessment of performance, based on the set standards, the individual KPA, as integrated in the individual balanced performance scorecard, aligned with the unit/area, departmental and organisational strategies in this regard.

(b) *Peer review*

Peer review refers to the assessment by peers – those practitioners with an equal level of expertise as reflected by qualifications, experience, abilities (knowledge, skills, attitudes and values). Peer review can be conducted internally or externally and the nature thereof can be informal or formal. A few examples are highlighted:

- **Continuous assessment**. This refers to the internal (and usually informal) daily supervision by peers and line managers. Continuous assessment entails the assessment of performance and compliance with standards during the daily

execution of duties, tasks and responsibilities (DTRs), with resultant immediate empowerment and correction of deviations when and where applicable. The principles of direct and indirect observation, as well as continuous document analysis, are some of the strategies used during continuous assessment by peers.
- **Internal formal assessment.** This is done by peers during internal quality surveys and audits, in accordance with the organisational CQI programme. Examples could include clinical auditing, the auditing of documents, competency evaluation (i.e. resuscitation abilities), adverse event monitoring and evaluation, clinical ethical conduct and mortality meetings.
- **External peer review**. This is the formal assessment of organisational performance by external peers, that is, national, provincial or local quality audit teams or surveyors, or by contracted independent accreditation or certification agencies (refer to Chapter 19, Quality improvement models in a healthcare organisation).

Data-collection design

The data-collection design refers to the development and execution of quality review and data-collection methods and subsequent instruments – in accordance with the set standards and performance indicators. The data-collection design should make provision for the corporate dimensions of management (general and functional), as well as for the management of clinical care, also referred to as clinical governance. A trustworthy (valid and reliable) data-collection design should therefore be in place, to counteract the following: the information you have is not what you want, the information you want is not what you need, the information you need cannot be obtained. The following dimensions should be considered:
- The information management system required
- The type of monitoring and evaluation strategies and subsequent data-collection instruments to be used
- The type of performance measures involved: the data source, the frequency of data-collection, the frequency of data reporting and review, etc.

Data-collection strategies

There are many data-collection strategies that should be used in combination to reflect the quality of service delivery (true picture or truth value) in the healthcare organisation. The principles of TQM should be executed. This implies that a quality review should be conducted in all the general and specialised/functional management areas. The most commonly used strategies are briefly highlighted:
- **Continuous informal quality assessment**. This requires daily proactive quality assessment and supervision, by means of coincidental/casual or purposeful random selection of activities, events, patients, clinical rounds/reviews at 'bed-side', etc. Continuous informal quality assessment is conducted by means of indirect or direct/participative observation.

- **Management quality review**. The quality of management, as applied to all the general and functional (specialised) management levels and areas, should be assessed. Examples are the quality of:
  - nursing service management
  - nursing unit management
  - operating theatre management
  - financial management
  - risk management
  - dietetic and food service management
  - maintenance and equipment management.
- **Auditing of records**. This is the continuous or retrospective auditing of records, in accordance with the CQI auditing programme of the organisation. Both clinical and non-clinical records should be audited.
- **Document analysis**. The healthcare organisation has many types of records, i.e. patient records, strategic plan, policies and procedures. The purpose of document analysis is to ascertain the quality of documentation, as well as the alignment in the organisational, departmental and operational management levels.
- **Clinical auditing**. Clinical auditing refers to the assessment of clinical performance against the pre-determined standards (i.e. clinical guidelines and clinical procedures) and compliance with clinical indicators (patient outcomes and impact of clinical care).
- **Adverse event monitoring**. This is the monitoring of an unexpected occurrence involving serious physical or psychological injury (or risk thereof) or an unexpected death. Adverse event monitoring is conducted in accordance with the organisational, departmental and operational unit/area analyses of potential and actual risks (refer to Chapter 18, Risk management in a healthcare organisation). Examples of adverse event monitoring are nosocomial infection rates, medication errors and patient injuries.
- **Patient Satisfaction Index (PSI)**. This includes formalised patient satisfaction surveys on completion of care (i.e. discharge). Continuous internal comparative analysis of PSI is assessed, with subsequent analysis of any deviations. In addition to these formal surveys and determination of the PSI, the daily management of patient complaints is executed.
- **Other stakeholder satisfaction surveys**. These include formal or informal assessment of the quality of service delivery, i.e. community representatives and staff satisfaction rates.

Instrument development

The data-collection instrument should be developed to suit the type of data-collection strategy. The following principles are important:

- Instrument development is exposed to a rigorous research-based process to ensure validity, reliability and feasibility.

- Validity of the instrument means that it measures what it purports to measure. The predetermined standards are reflected as the main items in the instrument, with the integration of the subsequent criteria. Validity is confirmed by means of accepted (best practice) methods and scope of validity determination.
- Reliability means that the accuracy of measurement is facilitated by using the most appropriate measurement scales:
  - Checklist: yes/no
  - Compliant, partial compliance or non-compliance
  - Descriptive performance scales: poor, average, excellent, etc.
  - Lickert rating scales.
- The reliability of the instrument is tested and confirmed by means of accepted (best practice) methods and scope of reliability determination.
- The layout of the instrument facilitates accurate data-capturing and allocation of ratings, as well as the writing of commendations/recommendation, and when appropriate, the written justification on non-compliant ratings.

Data management

Once the data has been collected, it should be managed, preferably by means of an electronic data management system. Data could be collected on a daily, weekly and monthly basis, but the collation and interpretation of such data are done on a quarterly basis. The data therefore needs to be 'stored' until it is collated and interpreted. A few principles are highlighted:

- Data management is regulated by means of policies and procedures at the appropriate level of management.
- Access to data is managed in accordance with organisational polices and related legal framework (i.e. access to information legislation).
- Ethical standards on the management of information are in place.

Data analysis and interpretation

Data analysis and interpretation entail at least the following:

- Data-analysis and interpretation are done in accordance with 'best practice' guidelines, according to the type of audience, nature and scope of the practitioners involved in the specific CQI programme (i.e. financial managers and clinicians).
- The data-analysis and interpretation reflect the principles of trustworthiness.
- The data is reflected in the most suitable presentation format, i.e. tables, figures, histograms or other graphs.
- Collated data is reflected in a quality report, in a suitable format, according to the preference of the level managers and the policy of the organisation.

Reporting of findings

The development and implementation of a CQI strategy is indeed a very labour-intensive and often stressful event. It is therefore important to report the findings to the relevant role-players and stakeholders.

- Quality reports are submitted to the various role-players, stakeholders and accountable managers/authorities, in accordance with the CQI strategy of the organisation and the regulatory framework(s).
- The CQI report(s) serve(s) at the various decision-making structures for consideration and subsequent follow-up decisions.
- The annual report of the organisation reflects the quality review outcomes, in the interest of public accountability.

Remedial action

Remedial action refers to corrective measures taken to improve the quality of service delivery, with specific reference to the non-compliant elements. Remedial action could relate to the improvement of systems (organisational structures, communication channels and information management system), abilities (knowledge, skills, attitudes and values) and performance/behavioural problems (i.e. resistance, conflict and insubordination). Remedial action strategies include the following: CQI governance, organisational development, project management, change management, skills development, project management, change management, skills development and continuous professional development.

CQI governance

The CQI governance design (refer to Chapter 1, Management of a healthcare organisation) should facilitate the management of CQI, by means of a corporate CQI Committee system and subsequent alignment with the various functional departments and units/areas of service delivery. A corporate CQI policy and strategy should be in place to give the necessary direction and a purpose-driven united effort in this regard. The principles of performance management (see Chapter 4, Dimensions of functional management, with reference to performance management) should obviously be linked to quality-related KPAs and related indicators and outcomes.

Organisational development

Address the capacity limitations with reference to resources and – very importantly – to change the systems when appropriate (i.e. the CQI system and revision of standards and indicators when appropriate, risk management system). In the case of an independent external quality review by COHSASA, a facilitative organisational development programme could be negotiated, with follow-up focus surveys to determine progress or compliance with the standards.

Project management

Different projects can be initiated, for example the development of clinical guidelines, amendment or adaptation of data-collecting methods and instruments, holding a Quality Awareness week and launching of a quality award strategy.

Change management

Apply the principles of change management, based on the CQI results and the justification of evidence-based practice. Behavioural change, organisational change and diversity management strategies could be initiated.

Skills development and continuous professional development

The skills development and continuous professional development (CPD) programmes should reflect the necessary corrective measures required based on the results and outcomes of the CQI programmes.

20.5.4 Clinical governance

Clinical governance refers to all the collective CQI activities and principles related to clinical care, such as the means by which organisations ensure the provision of quality clinical care by making individuals accountable for setting, maintaining and monitoring performance standards. A formalised system is required through which management can prove accountability for continuously improving the quality of the healthcare service delivery and safeguarding high standards of care by creating an environment in which clinical excellence can flourish. Clinical governance reflects at least the following: clinical governance and organisational design, policy and procedures, appropriate clinical risk management and clinical CQI programmes.

Clinical governance organisational design

Apply the principle of functional management (refer to Chapter 1, Management of a healthcare organisation) by making provision for a functional clinical management structure, in accordance with the nature, size and type of core business and business ownership. This implies the following:

- A clinical specialist is accountable for the clinical governance in the healthcare organisation, as reflected in the organogram of the organisation.
- The organisational design makes provision for a decentralised clinical governance structure (i.e. Clinical Manager Obstetric and Maternity services).
- There is evidence of operational clinical governance accountability.

Clinical governance policy and procedures

This refers to the formalisation of clinical governance by means of organisational policies and procedures, stating the minimum requirements of departmental and operational CQI programmes.

Appropriate clinical risk management

Refer to Chapter 18, Risk management in a healthcare organisation, with reference to adverse event management and infection control management systems.

Clinical CQI programmes

This refers to the development, execution and review of appropriate clinical continuous quality improvement programmes, in accordance with the national, provincial and local policies and directives, as well as the general global principles of clinical best practice and evidenced-based clinical care. The clinical CQI programmes should reflect at least the following:

- Clinical auditing
- The development of clinical indicators and assessment of compliance thereof
- The principles of clinical benchmarking (at national, provincial, local and organisational levels) are executed and taken into consideration when clinical governance or clinical CQI programmes are reviewed
- There is a system of credentialing and privileging of clinical medical staff, in accordance with national, provincial, local and organisational policy frameworks.

20.5.5 Consumer satisfaction and involvement programmes

The following examples of consumer/community involvement are listed:

- Systematic analysis to form a basis for planning and evaluation services or the re-certification/accreditation of services. This type of survey would normally include criteria for the evaluation of primary healthcare, covering issues related to accessibility, effectiveness of care, etc.
- Provision of a Certificate of Need by private healthcare providers. This would include a consumer needs analysis and satisfaction survey.
- Internal and external patient satisfaction surveys are often managed by the Public Relation's manager. The intention of these surveys is to also create community awareness of their rights and the standards of excellence expected by the service provider. The patient satisfaction survey is also reflected as the Patient Satisfaction Index.
- Local registering of complaints and compliments includes systematic encouragement of patient feedback, analysis and reporting of results.
- Appeals to national complaints authority, including investigation and arbitration.
- Involvement in the analysis of an appeal by the health services ombudsman and the subsequent national publication when applicable.
- Monitoring of Patient Charter indicators includes collection and publication of measures such as waiting times for appointments and admissions.
- Consumer/community representatives should be included in internal clinical auditing teams and external certification/accreditation panels.

20.5.6 Total quality management

Total quality management (TQM) is a management philosophy – a method of thinking and doing – by making quality everybody's business, especially those at operational level. It involves the devolution of authority to facilitate responsible and quick decision-making and problem-solving at operational level. TQM has developed into a sophisticated, integrated and coordinated management approach. It makes provision for the integration of corporate, middle and operational management strategies, and the integrated execution of the organisation's CQI strategy across all these management levels. The introduction of the Balanced Scorecard is in fact a modification of the TQM model. The COHSASA standards for hospitals and healthcare facilities also reflect the principles of TQM. The pre-determined dimensions of quality are assessed at the hospital/facility management level, as well as at functional clinical and non-clinical levels. These dimensions are:

- Management and leadership
- Human resources management
- Administrative support
- Access to care
- Patient and family rights
- Management of information
- Health and safety
- Quality management and improvement
- Prevention and control of infections.

20.6 UNDERLYING DYNAMICS

Many underlying dynamics and critical success factors have an impact on the CQI in a healthcare organisation. The following critical success factors are highlighted:

- **Institutional capacity**. This refers to the organisational CQI structure, information management system and resources (physical, financial, equipment and staff).
- **Leadership**. This includes abilities, support and commitment towards excellence in healthcare service delivery at all levels in the organisation. The levels are as follows:
  - *Level 1: Highly capable individual* makes productive contributions to CQI through talent, knowledge, skills, and good work habits
  - *Level 2: Contributing team member* contributes individual capabilities to the achievement of CQI group objectives and works effectively with others in a group setting
  - *Level 3: Competent manager* organises people and resources toward the effective and efficient pursuit of excellence and pre-determined objectives and outcomes
  - *Level 4: Effective leader* catalyses commitment to and vigorous pursuit of a

clear and compelling vision, stimulating higher performance standards
- *Level 5: Executive* builds enduring greatness through a paradoxical blend of personal humility and professional will.

- **Organisational culture**. This refers to the shared acceptance of responsibility and accountability for collaborative and cooperative CQI management at all levels of management and operational activities.
- **Skills development and CPD**. This entails a high-level investment in skills development and continuous professional development of all staff, with reference to the knowledge and skills required for developing and implementing CQI programmes.
- **Performance management**. This refers to the necessary reward system, based on the principles of performance management, to facilitate active purpose-driven CQI engagement of staff.

20.7 CONCLUDING STATEMENTS

The following concluding statements are relevant:

- Quality healthcare service delivery is associated with accessibility of care, relevance and appropriateness of care, continuity of care, compliance with patient perspectives, safety of the care environment and timeliness of service delivery.
- The continuous quality improvement (CQI) process refers to the CQI strategy analysis, development, execution and review.
- A CQI programme refers to the formalised process of standard setting, monitoring and measuring actual performance with these standards, and taking the appropriate remedial actions steps to counteract problems and to facilitate the quality of service delivery in the healthcare organisation.
- CQI is practised in the relevant business ownership context, influenced by global, national, provincial and local quality directives. The various legislative frameworks are taken into consideration.
- The purpose of CQI is to facilitate quality management practice at all management levels in the healthcare organisation, in accordance with the clinical and non-clinical best practice guidelines.
- There are certain prerequisites for the successful development and execution of CQI programmes related to leadership and management, CQI structures and systems, and best practice principles with regard to the development, implementation and review of CQI programmes and activities.
- Standards are classified into structure, process and outcome.
- Many types of standards are used in healthcare services: policies and procedures, clinical guidelines, clinical indicators, as well as general performance indicators.
- The setting of standards is a formalised process that reflects a credible process of drafting, validation, testing, ratification, publication and implementation, as well as the revision and updating thereof.

- Many clinical guidelines and clinical indicators are available. The transferability of these guidelines and indicators can be assessed by utilising the AGREE instrument.
- The monitoring, analysis and evaluation of performance is based on the selection of review strategies, the data-collection design and subsequent strategies required, instrument development, data management, data analysis and interpretation, as well as the reporting of findings.
- Remedial action is the third step in the CQI cycle. The strategies that can be employed to counteract negative CQI results and subsequent outcomes are improvement of CQI governance, organisational development, project management, change management, skills development and CPD.
- It is important to ensure that the principle of clinical governance is adequately formalised in the healthcare organisation, such as an appropriate organisational design, corporate policies and procedures, adequate clinical risk management strategies and relevant CQI programmes that include clinical auditing.
- The healthcare organisation should also invest in relevant consumer satisfaction and involvement programmes.

Quality healthcare service delivery is based on the principles of Total Quality Management (TQM). The dimensions of TQM are reflected in this book – from the first to the last chapter. TQM relates to the following:

- Quality management of the healthcare organisation, based on planning, organising, leading and control
- Appropriate strategic management of the organisation, with reference to strategy analysis, strategy development, strategy execution and strategy review
- The application of appropriate management models in the organisation, such as participative management and utilisation of specialised management systems (i.e. systems approach)
- The appropriate utilisation and application of various functional management skills, such as decision-making and problem-solving, project management and performance management
- Appropriate change and transformation management
- Adequate communication in the healthcare service, including the principles of information management, knowledge management and the management of patient records
- Appropriate marketing of the healthcare organisation
- The management of HIV and AIDS with reference to workplace programmes and clinical governance
- Quality management of human resources in the organisation
- Quality leadership practice in the organisation
- Quality financial management in the organisation
- Appropriate risk management in the organisation

- Selection and implementation of the most suitable quality improvement model(s)
- The formalisation of CQI in the healthcare organisation.

Self-assessment

(1) Compile a CQI strategy for your healthcare organisation.
(2) Compile a CQI programme for any clinical or non-clinical intervention/activity.
(3) Select any international published clinical guidelines. Use the AGREE instrument to assess the transferability of the clinical guideline to your organisational situation/context.

Glossary

Absenteeism Failure to be present at the workplace during normal working hours on a given day.

Absenteeism rate Number of worker days lost through job absence during a period divided by the average number of employees times the number of workdays, multiplied by 100.

Access The ability of clients or potential clients to obtain required or available services when needed within an appropriate time limit.

Accountability Being answerable for responsibilities and subsequent outcomes. The obligation to account for responsibility conferred to the appropriate line manager or legislative authority. The manager should therefore account for the intention, objectives and strategies, the cost of the strategies and the actual results and outcomes.

Accounting Accounting is concerned with recording and reporting financial information.

Accreditation A public recognition of the achievement of accreditation standards by a healthcare organisation, demonstrated through an independent external peer assessment of that organisation's level of performance in relation to the standards.

Accreditation agency/body The organisation responsible for the accreditation programme and the granting of accreditation status.

Accrual accounting The accrual system of accounting recognises revenue and expenses as they are earned and incurred – not as money is received or paid. Operationally this means that revenue is taken to mean that invoices have been issued; costs are incurred when services are received.

Achievement tests Measures of what a person knows or can do at a point in time.

Action plan A description/listing of the organisational goals and relevant key priorities/key performance areas, related objectives for each KPA, activities required to achieve the goals and objectives, assignment of accountability and subsequent duties, tasks and responsibilities (DTRs) and finally, the due dates of execution or performance.

Active listening Process of trying to understand what the speaker is saying by paying close attention and focusing responses on what is said.

Adverse event An adverse event is an unexpected occurrence involving death or serious physical or psychological injury, or the risk thereof. (Serious = the loss of limb or function; Risk thereof = any process variation for which a recurrence would carry a significant chance of a serious adverse outcome). Adverse events are also referred to as sentinel events in selected literature.

Affective change A short-term change in emotional condition or state.

Affirmative action A policy requiring employers to take positive steps to guarantee equal employment opportunities for people within protected groups.

AIDS Acquired Immune Deficiency Syndrome – a syndrome that results from infection with HIV.

Antibodies Substances produced by cells in the immune system of the human body in response to foreign substances that have entered the body.

Application form A device for collecting information about an applicant's education, previous job experience, and other background characteristics.

Apprenticeship training System of training in which a worker entering the skills trades is given thorough instruction and experience, both on and off the job, in the practical and theoretical aspects of the work.

Appropriateness The degree to which a service is consistent with a client's expressed requirements and is provided in accordance with current best practice.

Aptitude tests Measures of a person's capabilities to learn or acquire skills.

Arbitration award A final and binding award issued by an arbitrator in a labour dispute.

Arbitrator Neutral third party who resolves a labour dispute by issuing a final decision in the disagreement.

ARV Antiretroviral therapy: medicinal treatment to mitigate and control HIV and AIDS.

Assessment A process by which the characteristics and needs of clients, groups or situations are evaluated or determined. The assessment forms the basis of a plan for services or action.

Assessment centre A technique for selecting individuals with high managerial potential based on their performance in a series of simulated managerial tasks. It is a process by which individuals are evaluated as they participate in a series of situations that resemble what they might be called upon to handle on the job.

Attitude An internal, emotional opinion a person has towards people, things, actions, behaviours, etc.

Audit A systematic independent examination and review to determine whether actual activities and results comply with planned arrangements or predetermined standards and criteria.

Auditing An analysis of financial practices and may be internal or external. Internal auditing is the internal analysis of the organisation's management and financial practices to ensure adherence to management policies and directives, to safeguard assets, to ensure trustworthiness of systems and practices and to effect compliance with statutory requirements. The external audit is an independent analysis/assessment and an expression of opinion by an external party in relation to the adequacy of internal control systems, the compliance with statutory, regulatory and contractual requirements, economy, efficiency and effectiveness of resource utilisation (value for money auditing) and environmental practices.

Authority Authority refers to the right to command or to take a decision. Authority is the power that has been legitimised by the organisation (via the accountable line manager). It includes the right to take action to compel the performance of duties and to punish default or negligence. Formal authority is passed down from above by means of delegation.

Behaviour modification Technique that operates on the principle that behaviour which is rewarded, or positively reinforced, will be exhibited more frequently in the future, whereas behaviour that is penalised, or is left unrewarded, will decrease in frequency.

Behaviour observation scale A behavioural approach to performance appraisal that measures the frequency of observed behaviour.

Behaviourilly anchored rating scale (BARS) A behavioural approach to performance appraisal that consists of a series of vertical scales, one for each important dimension of job performance.

Benchmarking Comparing results of organisations' evaluations to the results of other interventions, programmes or organisations, and examining processes against those of others recognised as excellent, as a means of making improvements.

Best practicable environmental option The option that provides the most benefit or causes the least damage to the environment as a whole, at a cost acceptable to society, in the long term as well as in the short term (South Africa, 1998).

Best practice Best practice is an approach that has been shown to produce superior results, selected by a systematic process and judged as exemplary, or demonstrated as successful. It is then adapted to fit a particular organisation.

Boycott A union tactic to encourage others to refuse to patronise an employer or service.

Brainstorming A decision-making technique in which group members present spontaneous suggestions for problem solution, regardless of their likelihood of implementation, in order to promote freer, more creative thinking within the group.

Burnout Most severe stage of distress, manifesting itself in depression, frustration and loss of productivity.

Business ethics The conduct of business that reflects generally morally accepted values, norms and standards. The person's judgement of what is inherently right or wrong in his/her business interaction with others.

Business plan The current action plan for achieving organisational goals, capacities, abilities, resources, assets, and strengths of groups or individuals to deal with situations and meet their needs.

Care Steps taken to promote a person's well-being through physical, medical, psychosocial, spiritual and other means.

Career counselling Process of discussing with employees their current job activities and performance, their personal job and career goals, their skills and suitable career development objectives.

Career paths Lines of advancement within an organisation in an occupational field.

Cash accounting Cash inflows (income) and cash outflows (purchases) are recognised as they occur. Sales are only recognised when cash is received (so there are no debtors); purchases are only recognised when cash is paid (so there are no creditors).

Centralisation The decision-making authority is located in management, who make all the important decisions.

Change A process resulting in a difference of varying magnitude and/or nature in the state and/or condition of a given organisation – whether a phenomenon, situation, person and/or object.

Change management A catch-all phrase for all organisational practices relating to change and premised on the common yet presumptuous belief that change is amenable to management, i.e. change can be planned/designed, introduced/ implemented, facilitated, coordinated and controlled to the point of producing the desired outcomes.

Change paradigm Very powerful schemata, worldviews or frameworks that determine how we see, construe and make sense of change within organisations.

Chaos Deterministically random behaviour, i.e. behaviour that appears random but on closer inspection reveals underlying patterns of order.

Chaotic change Also referred to as complex change or catastrophic change. A rapidly unfolding form of comprehensive change, triggered by an insignificant incident, with unpredictably catastrophic outcomes.

Clinical governance Clinical governance is a collective phrase that refers to all the quality improvement strategies and methods used to facilitate the highest level of quality in clinical service delivery.

Clinical guidelines Descriptive standards (mainly clinical process standards) to guide clinical practices. Clinical guidelines are based on scientific evidence with expert opinion.

Clinical pathways A clinical pathway is an interdisciplinary approach of standardised patient care and treatment to improve the quality and efficiency of care/treatment for a select patient population. The goal of clinical pathways is to provide a 'map' of care for certain conditions to standardise the care/treatment and to reduce costs (also referred to as clinical algorithms).

Code of ethics A formal statement of the organisation's values regarding ethics and social issues.

Code of practice Guidelines to direct management and behaviour, in this case related to the management of HIV and AIDS.

Collective bargaining process Process of negotiating a labour agreement, including the use of economic pressures by both parties.

Commitment accounting Predicted/expected income and expenditure are reflected before the income/expenditure has been incurred (e.g. service fees and electricity).

Communication Communication is a two-way process whereby information (the message) is sent from one person (sender) through a mode or channel to another (the receiver or recipient) who in turn reacts by interpreting the message and responding, with due regard of many communication barriers: the sender – also referred to as the communicator, addresser, transmitter, source or encoder) is the person who initiates the communication activity and formulates the message. The sender usually sends a message because of a need to convey information, express feelings, obtain feedback or satisfy needs. The success of the communication depends mainly on the sender's ability to speak, write, reason and listen competently. The sender formulates thoughts into a message, using a code which the receiver can understand. This code could be any set of symbols such as language, figures, pictures or sign language which both the sender and receiver understand. The message is the information which is conveyed during the process of communication. The receiver (also referred to as the recipient, the addressee, respondent, destination or decoder) is the person to whom the sender directs the message. The receiver takes an active part in the communication process and is responsible for making sense of, interpreting and reacting to the message – the receiver decodes the code in order to understand it. The channel is the way in which the message is sent from sender to receiver and feedback is sent from receiver to sender. The channel is informal or formal. There is a wide range of formal and informal channels to choose from: verbal (voice, intercom, telephone, interview, meeting, fax, letter, advertisement, memorandum, report, radio or television), or non-verbal channels of communication, such as body language, pictures, music, etc. Feedback (also referred to as reaction or response) is the message the receiver sends in response to the sender's message. It is the receiver's reaction. Feedback can be verbal or non-verbal and is often an indication that communication has taken place successfully. Feedback also reflects whether the message was understood correctly. A communication barrier is also referred to as noise or interference. During the communication process something may prevent communication from taking place successfully. This could be any physical (pathological), structural, system-based obstruction/interference which causes communication breakdown or prevents the receiver from receiving the message (Van Staden, Marx & Erasmus-Kritzinger, 2002:12–14).

Communication competency A manager's skill in speaking and writing effectively, including the ability to select the proper medium for communication.

Community Collection of individuals, families, groups and organisations that interact with one another, cooperate in common activities, solve mutual concerns, usually in a geographic locality or environment.

Community engagement The purposeful and deliberate consultation and involvement of the community (by means of formalised representative structures) in the management of healthcare service delivery (from the planning phase to the control or evaluation phase).

Competence The guarantee that an individual's abilities (knowledge, skills, values and attitudes) are appropriate to the selected service provision and the assurance that these abilities are regularly updated in accordance with science development.

Complexity The mixture of a sizeable number of variables, a high degree of interdependence, as well as a high degree of interaction among these variables. In organisational terms, complexity commences when three or more variables are interdependent and interact on a consistent basis (i.e. a variation in one results in variation in the other).

Compulsory binding arbitration Binding method of resolving collective bargaining deadlocks by a neutral third party.

Confidentiality Right of a person, employee or job applicant to have their medical status and medical information, including HIV status, kept private. Disclosure may only be done based on informed consent by the affected person.

Conflict Incompatibility arising from opposing demands or impulses. Discrepancy between the ways things are supposed to be and what we perceive or see now within reality.

Consideration A cluster of leadership behaviours manifesting mutual trust, respect and rapport between the superior and the group.

Consumerism The social force that protects the consumer by exerting legal, moral, economic and even political pressure on management.

Continuous quality improvement (CQI) Continuous quality improvement refers to the formalised system of continuous quality improvement in the healthcare organisation, reflected in the CQI strategy at corporate, middle and operational levels of service delivery. The CQI programme reflects the full cycle of quality improvement: standard setting, measuring compliance of actual performance with the predetermined standards and remedial/corrective actions to improve the quality of service delivery.

Continuous reinforcement schedule A schedule in which every occurrence of the desired behaviour is reinforced.

Control Proactive, continuous and reactive control by means of: setting standards, measuring actual performance against the standards, evaluating deviations (performance gap) and rectifying deviations.

Controlling The management function concerned with monitoring employees' activities, keeping the organisation on track towards its goals, and making corrections as needed.

Coordination The quality of collaboration across departments.

Coordination costs The time and energy needed to coordinate the activities of a team to enable it to perform its tasks.

Core skills Skills considered critical for an employee's success in the workplace.

Cost-benefit analysis (CBA) A way of presenting information to assist in the selection and appraisal of projects.

Cost centre Cost centres are units in the budget structure in terms of which managers may conduct resource allocation and exercise control over finance and resource utilisation. Cost centres may be designed in terms of institutions, functions, line-items, client groups, speciality or diagnostic-related groups.

Cost data Cost data refers to data on expenses and revenue, as well as clinical information, such as the number and types of procedures performed, length of patient stay in hospitals, patient outcomes and diagnostic data.

Costing The process whereby the cost associated with an activity or programme is determined.

Counselling Process involving a dynamic relationship between two parties in which one is free to discuss needs, feelings and problems of concern for the purpose of obtaining help.

CQI data-collection design The CQI data-collection design refers to the development and execution of data-collection methods and subsequent instruments – in accordance with the set standards and performance indicators – followed by the collection of the data, the analysis and interpretation (evaluation) of the data and reporting on the results in the formalised quality structural design of the healthcare organisation. The data-collection design should make provision for the corporate dimensions of management (general and functional), as well as for the management of clinical care, also referred to as clinical governance.

Craft unions Unions that represent skilled craft workers.

Credentialing The process of assessing and attesting to an individual's abilities (knowledge, skills, attitudes and values) and their compliance with specific requirements to practice.

Creditors Creditors refer to the expenses – certain liabilities representing goods/services that have been received but have yet to be paid for. These items are usually listed on the balance sheet as accounts payable.

Criteria Steps/activities to be taken to achieve a standard. Sub-divisions of a standard.

Critical incident Unusual event that denotes superior or inferior employee performance in some part of the job.

Cultural appropriateness The design and delivery of services consistent with the cultural beliefs and values of clients who use them.

Culture The set of key values, beliefs, understandings and norms that members of a societyor an organisation share.

Current reality The truth of how things are right now: stable, turbulent, comfortable, etc.

Danger Anything which may cause injury or damage to persons or property (South Africa, 1993).

Data Unorganised facts from which information can be generated.

Debtors Debtors refer to the income resulting from the service delivery on credit for which the actual cash payment has not yet been received and appear on the financial statements as accounts receivable.

Decentralisation The devolution of decision-making authority at operational levels where the core business of the organisation is executed.

Delegation The downward passing or devolution of duties, tasks and responsibilities (DTRs) by a supervisor to the subordinate. The process managers use to transfer authority and responsibility to positions below them in the hierarchy.

Depreciation The loss of value of an asset through usage over time.

Diagonal formal communication Diagonal formal communication takes place across the different levels of authority, mainly in the form of an advisory peer group consultation.

Dialogue A group communication process aimed at creating a culture based on collaboration, fluidity, trust and commitment to shared goals.

Dignity A quality of being worthy, honourable or esteemed which is not dependent on social standing, status, wealth, power, abilities or achievement.

Disaster A progressive or sudden, widespread or localised, natural or human-caused occurrence which:

(a) causes or threatens to cause:
- death, injury or disease;
- damage to property, infrastructure or the environment; or
- disruption of the life of a community; and

(b) is of a magnitude that exceeds the ability of those affected by the disaster to cope with its effects using only their own measures (South Africa, 2002).

Disaster management A continuous and integrated multi-sectoral, multi-disciplinary process of planning and implementation of measures aimed at:
- preventing or reducing the risk of disasters
- mitigating the severity or consequences of disasters
- emergency preparedness
- a rapid and effective response to disasters
- post-disaster recovery and rehabilitation (South Africa, 2002).

Discipline Treatment that punishes, aims at orderly behaviour in an organisational setting, and is training that moulds and strengthens desirable conduct, and develops self-control.

Discrimination The hiring or promoting of applicants based on criteria that are not job related.

Distress Harmful stress characterised by a loss of feelings of security and adequacy.

Diversity awareness training Special training designed to make people aware of their own prejudices and stereotypes.

Downward communication Messages sent from top management down to subordinates.

Economic forces Forces that affect the availability, production and distribution of a society's resources among competing users.

Effective and efficient Value for money in the context of health means getting acceptable quality services to people who need them and making people as healthy as possible with given resources. To obtain value for money, public health spending must be effective and efficient.
Effective. Is the organisation pursuing those interventions that will have maximum impact on the health status of its patients? Doing the right things.
Efficient. Is the organisation delivering the maximum amount of services given the resources at its disposal? Doing things right.

Effectiveness The degree to which the stated goals are achieved.

Efficiency The use of minimal resources, such as raw material, money and HR to produce a desired volume of output.

Emergency preparedness A state of readiness which enables organs of state and other institutions involved in disaster management, the private sector, communities and individuals to mobilise, organise, and provide relief measures to deal with an impending or current disaster or the effects of a disaster (South Africa, 2002).

Employee assistance programme (EAP) Service provided by employers to help workers cope with a wide variety of problems that interfere with the way they perform their jobs.

Employee rights Guarantees of fair treatment from employers, particularly regarding an employee's right to privacy.

Encode To select symbols with which to compose a message.

Environment The conditions, circumstances, and influences that affect the organisations' ability to achieve its objectives. The surroundings within which humans exist and that are made up of:

- the land, water and atmosphere of the earth
- micro-organisms, plant and animal life
- the physical, chemical, aesthetic and cultural properties and conditions of the foregoing that influence human health and well-being (South Africa, 1998).

Environmental comfort zone The place or environment in which we feel comfortable; the kind of environmental conditions to which we have become accustomed, which enables the individual or group to function without fear or uneasiness. This feeling of comfort will not create energy or dissonance for change.

Environmental scanning Environmental scanning refers to the process of monitoring, assessment, measurement, forecasting/projection and evaluation of change in the different environmental variables impacting on the management of the organisation.

Epidemic The disease, usually infectious, that spreads through a population.

Equity A situation that exists when the ratio of one person's outcomes to inputs equals that of another's.

Ethics The code of moral principles and values that governs the behaviours of a person or group with respect to what is right and what is wrong.

Eustress Positive stress that accompanies achievement and exhilaration.

Evaluating Designing the procedures and processes that measure, evaluate and communicate the value-added component of HR practices and the entire HR system to the organisation.

Evaluation Assessment of the degree of compliance with predetermined standards. Assessment of the degree of success in meeting the goals and expected results, outputs and outcomes.

Evidence Data and information used to make decisions. Evidence can be derived from research, experiential learning, indicator data and evaluations. Evidence is used in a systematic way to evaluate options and make decisions.

Expatriates Employees who live and work in a country other than their own.

Feedback A response by the receiver to the sender's communication.

Final-offer arbitration Method of resolving collective bargaining deadlocks whereby the arbitrator has no power to compromise but must select one or the other of the final offers submitted by the two parties.

Financial management system (FMS) The computerised information system used by governments and organisations to manage their finances.

Financial statements Financial statements consist of at least the following: a balance sheet, an income statement, a cash-flow statement, any other statements that may be prescribed, and any note to these statements (South Africa, 1999:8).

First-line manager A manager who is at the first management level and is directly responsible for the production of goods and services.

Flexitime Flexible working hours that permit employees the option of choosing daily starting and quitting times, provided that they work a set number of hours per day or week.

Formal communication channel A communication channel that flows within the chain of command or task responsibility defined by the organisation.

Fruitless and wasteful expenditure Expenditure that was made in vain and would have been avoided had reasonable care been exercised (South Africa, 1999:8).

Functional management Functional management refers to specialised management requiring general management abilities, as well as the appropriate specialised management abilities (knowledge, skills, attitudes and values), i.e. marketing management, operating theatre management.

GEAR The Growth, Employment and Redistribution strategy is the ANC's macro-economic plan for attaining a growth rate of 6% per annum and a job creation of 400 000 per annum.

Generally recognised accounting practice An accounting practice complying in material respects with standards issued by the Accounting Standards Board (South Africa, 1999:8).

General management General management refers to the application of the general management activities with reference to planning, organising, leading and control.

Gestalt The theory of wholeness and completeness. The drive to get things back into order – by making the pictures (sub-units) match; putting the bits and pieces together to reflect the complete picture.

Glass ceiling The invisible, yet real or perceived, attitudinal or organisational barriers that serve to limit the advancement opportunities of minorities and women.

Globalisation The standardisation of product design and advertising strategies throughout the world.

Goals Written statements that describe the expected/desired end-results, achievements, outputs or outcomes within a given period of time. Goals provide direction for the day-to-day decisions and activities. Goals support the mission of the organisation.

Governance The function of determining the organisation's direction, setting objectives and developing policies to guide the organisation in achieving its mission, and monitoring the achievement of those objectives and the implementation of policy, in the interest of the stakeholders and quality outcomes.

Grapevine An informal, person-to-person communication network of employees that is not officially sanctioned by the organisation.

Graphic rating scale method A trait approach to performance appraisal whereby each employee is rated according to a scale of characteristics.

Grievance Complaint or objection, originating from an employee.

Grievance mediation A process where a neutral party assists in the resolution of an employee grievance.

Grievance procedure Formal procedure that provides for the union to represent members and non-members in processing a grievance.

Halo effect An overall impression of a person or situation based on one favourable attribute.

Halo error A type of rating error that occurs when an employee receives the same rating on all dimensions regardless of his/her performance on individual dimensions.

Hazard The source of or exposure to danger (South Africa, 1993).

Healthcare expenditure This refers to the way in which healthcare funds are actually used, e.g. on different healthcare providers, on different types of inputs, such as personnel and drugs, and on different geographic areas.

Health status Health status refers to the standard of health or the level of ill-health of the population concerned. Traditionally, health status is pre-eminently indicated by morbidity and mortality date, and by extension life expectancy. In addition, health status also reflects in disability, invalidity, nutritional status, disturbed social functionality and general health complaints.

Hierarchy of needs theory A content theory that proposes that people are motivated by five categories of needs: physiological, safety, belonging, esteem, and self-actualisation, that exist in a hierarchical order.

HIV Human Immunodeficiency Virus – the name of the virus which weakens the immune system and leads to AIDS.

HIV testing A form designed to identify the HIV status of a person, including blood tests, saliva tests and medical questionnaires.

Horizontal communication The lateral or diagonal exchange of messages among peers and co-workers.

Horizontal formal communication Horizontal formal communication takes place across departments/units between people who are on the same level of authority or organisational structure.

Hot-stove-rule Rule of discipline that can be compared with touching a hot stove in that it gives a warning, is effective immediately, is enforced consistently, and applies to all employees in an impersonal and unbiased way.

Human relations movement A movement in management thinking and practice that emphasises satisfaction of employee's basic needs as the key to increased worker productivity.

Human resource development Analysing learning requirements to ensure that employees possess the knowledge and skills to perform satisfactorily in their jobs or to advance in the organisation. Performance appraisal is one method to identify employees' key skills and competencies as well as their developmental needs.

Human resource management Activities undertaken to attract, develop, and maintain an effective workforce withing an organisation.

Human resource planning Preparing forecasts of future HR needs in the light of the organisation's environment, mission and objectives, strategies, and internal strengths and weaknesses, including its structure, culture, technology and leadership.

Immune system A complex system of cells and cell substances that protects the body from infection and disease.
Incapacity Inability to perform a specific job for reasons such as inability or disability.
Incidence of HIV The number of new cases of HIV in a given time period, often expressed as a percentage of the susceptible population.
Indicator An indicator refers to the numerical presentation of information that quantifies input, output, dimensions of processes and outcomes. A performance measurement tool, screen or flag that is used as a guide to monitor, evaluate and improve the quality of services. Indicators relate to structure, process and outcomes, in accordance with the core business of the organisation.
Individual change A gradual and progressive form of human change which encapsulates both cognitive and affective change and is viewed as attempts at coming to terms on an intrapersonal level with environmental changes that impact on the person.
Industrial unions Unions that represent all workers; skilled, semi-skilled and unskilled, employed along industry lines.
Informal communication channel A communication channel that exists outside formally authorised channels without regard for the organisation's hierarchy of authority.
Information Data that has been converted into a meaningful and useful context for the receiver.
Information reporting system A system that organises information in the form of pre-specified reports that managers use in day-to-day decision-making processes.
Information technology The hardware, software, telecommunications, database management, and other technologies used to store, process and distribute information.
Irregular expenditure Expenditure other than unauthorised expenditure, incurred in contravention of or that is not in accordance with a requirement of applicable legislation (South Africa, 1999:8).

Job A group of related activities and duties.
Job description Statement of the tasks, duties and responsibilities of a job to be performed.
Job design Outgrowth of job analysis that improves jobs through technological and human considerations in order to enhance organisational efficiency and employee job satisfaction.
Job enrichment Enhancing a job by adding more meaningful tasks and duties to make the work more rewarding and satisfying.

Job evaluation The process of determining the value of jobs within an organisation through an examination of job content.
Job progression Hierarchy of jobs a new employee might experience, ranging from a starting job to successive jobs that require more knowledge and/or skills.

Knowledge management Knowledge management is the process of identifying, collecting, storing and transforming data and information into an intellectual asset that is available to all staff members. It consists of the following steps: identify existing knowledge, reflect on existing knowledge, redistribute and apply the knowledge.

Labour market The people available for hire by an organisation.
Labour relations This is a key strategic issue for organisations because the nature of the relationship between the employer and employees can have a significant impact on morale, motivation, and productivity. Proper, mutually accepted policies and procedures are thus paramount.
Labour relations process Logical sequence of four events; workers desire collective representation, union begins its organising campaign, collective negotiations lead to a contract, and the contract is administered.
Leadership Leadership is an influencing relationship among leaders and followers who intend real changes that reflect their shared purposes.
Leading The purposeful and deliberate influencing of followers to facilitate the attainment of organisational goals, outputs and outcomes, in the interest of stakeholders, role-players and the organisation.
Learning A change in behaviour or performance as a result of experience.
Licensure A process by which a government/legislative authority grants permission to an individual practitioner or healthcare organisation to operate or to engage in an occupation of profession.
Line authority A form of authority in which individuals in management positions have the formal power to direct and control immediate subordinates. The line of authority indicates the direction of accountability (line authority) and the line of consultation/advisory relationship (staff authority) in relation to the different post-levels within the organisation.
Liquidity This is the organisation's ability to satisfy its short-term obligations as they become due.
Listening The skill of receiving messages accurately so that facts and feelings are interpreted as they were genuinely meant.
Lockout Strategy by which the employer denies employees the opportunity to work by closing its operations.
Locus of control The need of a person to be in charge of his/her own destiny. People with a strong internal locus of control believe that the outcome of an event is determined by their own actions. Luck or change of fate is therefore

of little importance. Problems and obstructive barriers are converted into challenges – to make the best of the situation.

Maintaining human resources The administration and monitoring of workplace safety, health and welfare policies to retain a competent workforce and comply with the statutory standards and regulations.

Management The process whereby human, financial, physical and information resources are deployed to facilitate attainment of the organisational goals, objectives and outcomes, by applying the fundamental management activities of planning, organising, leading and control.

Management by objectives Philosophy of management that rates performance on the basis of employee achievement of goals set by mutual agreement of the employee and manager.

Management information system (MIS) A computer-based system that provides information and support for effective managerial decision-making.

Managing change This involves communicating the vision, helping others envision the future, setting clear expectations for performance, and developing the capability to reorganise people and reallocate resources in view of the planned change.

Managing relationships Encompasses a range of employee involvement or participation schemes in both unionised and non-unionised workplaces. Striving to enhance employee decision-making in areas that affect their work directly. Where unions are involved, this includes negotiating contracts and administering the collective agreement to the satisfaction of both parties.

Matrix organisational design The matrix organisational structure makes provision for an equal distribution of authority by the project manager and functional project experts to expedite decision-making.

Mediator Third party in a labour dispute who meets with one party and then the other in order to suggest compromise solutions or to recommend concessions from each side that will lead to an agreement.

Medical surveillance A planned programme of periodic examinations (which may include clinical examinations, biological monitoring or medical tests) of employees by an occupational health practitioner, or, in prescribed cases, by an occupational medicine practitioner (South Africa, 1993).

Mentoring functions Functions concerned with the career advancement and psychological aspects of the person being mentored.

Mentors Managers who coach, advise and encourage individuals in lesser positions.

Mission The mission is the statement of core business-related service delivery to concretise the vision of the organisation – what we believe we can do.

Mitigate To reduce, lessen or moderate the effect of something.

Motivating This is effected by the design and administration of recognition and reward systems. HR practices include job evaluation, performance appraisal, pay and benefits which are aimed at activating employees to enhance their performance and productivity.

Nepotism A preference for hiring relatives of current employees.
Network A system that links together people and departments within or among organisations for the purpose of sharing information resources.
Non-verbal communication Communication by means of appearance, attitude, facial expression and gestures (body language). Transmitted through actions and behaviours rather than through words.

Occupational health Includes occupational hygiene, occupational medicine and biological monitoring.
Occupational medicine practitioner A medical practitioner as defined in the Medical, Dental and Supplementary Health Service Professions Act, who holds a qualification in occupational medicine (South Africa, 1993).
Office automation system Systems such as word processors, desktop publishing and e-mail that transform manual procedures to electronic media.
On-the-job training Method by which employees are given hands-on experience with instructions from their supervisor or another trainer.
Open communication Sharing all types of information throughout the organisation, across functional and hierarchical levels.
Opportunistic infections Infections that occur because a person's immune system is so weak that it cannot fight the infections.
Organisation A social entity that is goal directed and deliberately structured.
Organisational culture The beliefs and values shared by people in a business/organisation.
Organisational profile A description of the organisation's profile related to the following: financial profile, nature and extent of the core business, management performance, research contribution, human resource profile and strategic management performance profile.
Organisation structure The framework in which the organisation defines how tasks are divided, resources are deployed, and departments are coordinated.
Organising The logical and orderly distribution of the core business by means of organisational structure design, designing of posts, assigning of responsibilities and authority, establishing a command structure and coordinating systems.
Organogram The visual graphic illustration of the logical distribution and grouping of the core business of the organisation, the subsequent organisational structural design, the related managerial posts, as well as the lines of authority (line and staff authority).
Outcomes The ultimate impact on broader society of a programme/project, e.g. an

immunisation programme's desired outcome is the reduction of the number of cases of a particular disease.

Output The results of an intervention. The consequences of a service. The goods or services produced under a particular programme/project which requires various inputs, e.g. the output of the immunisation programme is the number of vaccinations.

Participative management A system of management that enables employees to participate in decisions relating to their work and employment conditions, thereby creating a psychological partnership between management and employees. It is a process of dynamic interactive decision-making and problem-solving, shared governance, ownership and accountability, organisational transformation and empowerment, as well as applicable communication.

Pattern bargaining Bargaining in which unions negotiate provisions covering wages and other benefits that are similar to those provided in other agreements existing in the industry or region.

Peer appraisal Performance appraisal done by one's fellow employees, generally on forms that are compiled into a single profile for use in the performance interview by the employee's manager.

Peer assessment A process whereby the performance of individuals, groups and organisations are evaluated by members of similar organisations, or the same profession or discipline and equal status and abilities of those delivering the service.

Performance The way we act in reality; an act or behaviour of any kind.

Performance appraisal The process of observing and evaluating an employee's performance, recording the assessment, and providing feedback to the employee.

Performance gap A disparity between existing and desired performance levels.

Performance indicators Assessment tools used to monitor and evaluate the quality of important governance, management, clinical and support functions that affect outcomes.

Performance management This is concerned with the measuring, monitoring and evaluating performance, and then initiating steps to improve performance where this is warranted.

Performance review The continuous process by which a manager appraises and reviews a staff member's performance against set performance goals and evaluates his/her progress towards these goals.

Planning The management function concerned with determining the mission and goals of the healthcare organisation, the development of implementation strategies and action plans, and the development of strategies to assess the attainment of goals and outcomes. Thus the act of determining the organisation's goals and the means of achieving them.

PLWA People living with AIDS.

Policy A written document reflecting the position and practices on an issue, i.e. HIV and AIDS.

Prevalence The number of people affected or infected at a given point in time, usually expressed as a percentage of the total population.

Prevention programme A programme designed to prevent HIV transmission, including components such as awareness, education and training, condom distribution, treatment of sexually transmitted infections, occupational infection control, peer group education, etc.

Privileging Privileging refers to the granting of permission or right to a clinical practitioner to practise a specific clinical profession in a particular healthcare organisation. The decision is based on a formalised process of assessment and justification of the practitioner's qualifications, experience (including past clinical performance) and abilities (knowledge, skills, attitudes and values) that are required. Renewal of privileges is also based of clinical performance by the practitioner, in accordance with the CQI programme and clinical indicators that have been determined in the healthcare organisation.

Probationary Describes a trial period.

Profitability This relates to the organisation's ability to generate revenues that will exceed total costs by using the assets for productive purposes.

Progressive discipline Application of corrective measures by increasing degrees.

Provider/Physician profiling Provider profiling relates to the collection, collation and analysis of data to develop provider-specific profiles. Provider/Physician profiling is a process of analysing and comparing physician/healthcare practitioner 'case-management' of patients with peer-practice-based norms/benchmarks or community standards of practice. These include: diagnostic services/tests, treatment/care regimes, services/resource utilisation, patient outcomes. Provider profiles can be used for producing provider feedback reports, assist providers to modify their own service delivery/behaviour, recruiting providers into the network and choosing which providers may be the right fit for the managed healthcare philosophy and goals. Provider profiling facilitates focused utilisation management.

Quality The degree of excellence, extent to which an organisation meets clients' needs and exceeds their expectations. Also generally defined as:
- doing the right thing, right, the first time
- doing it better next time.

Quality assessment Planned and systematic collection and analysis of data about a service, usually focused on service content and delivery specifications and client outcomes.

Quality assurance Quality assurance is a guarantee of compliance with predetermined standards and usually relates to legal requirements.

Quality circles (QC) A group of 6 to 12 volunteer employees who meet regularly to discuss and solve problems affecting the quality of their work.

Quality control The monitoring of output to check if it conforms to specifications or requirements and action taken to rectify the output. It ensures safety, transfer of accurate information, accuracy of procedures and responsibility.

Quality improvement Quality improvement is a formal process whereby standards are set, work performance is measured/evaluated against these set standards, and remedial steps/actions are taken to solve or counteract problems in order to improve performance outcomes.

Quality improvement activities Activities that measure performance, identify opportunities for improvement in the delivery of service and include action and follow-up.

Quality of work life (QWL) The extent to which work is rewarding, meaningful, and free of anxieties and stresses.

Reasonably practicable Practicable having regard to:

- the severity and scope of the hazard or risk concerned
- the state of knowledge reasonably available concerning that hazard or risk and of any means of removing or mitigating that hazard or risk
- the availability and suitability of means to remove or mitigate that hazard or risk
- the cost of removing or mitigating that hazard or risk in relation to the benefits deriving therefrom (South Africa, 1993).

Recruiting The activities or practices that define the desired characteristics of applicants for specific jobs.

Reinforcement Anything that strengthens the trainee's response.

Reliability The extent to which results are consistent through repeated measures by different measurers, or at different times by the same measurer, when what is measured has not changed in the interval between measurements. Reliability reflects the truth value of the results.

Remedial action Remedial action is the formal process to address the quality an empoyee's performance.

Reserved rights Concept that management's authority is supreme in all matters except those it has expressly conceded to the union in the collective agreement.

Resilience The inner strength to face and recover from setbacks; ability to bounce back in the face of adversity.

Responsibility Responsibility is a particular obligation or commitment on the part of the managers and – to a more limited degree, their subordinates – to carry out tasks that have been assigned (by means of job descriptions) or delegated to them, or in accordance with the policies and directives they have received.

Retrenchment The termination of service of an employee for business reasons, e.g. when the business goes bankrupt or restructures.

Reverse discrimination Act of giving preference to members of protected classes to the extent that unprotected individuals believe they are suffering discrimination.

Rights Something that can be claimed as justly, fairly, legally, or morally one's own. A formal description of the services that clients can expect and demand from an organisation.

Rights arbitration Arbitration on the interpretation of the meaning of contract terms or employee work grievances.

Risk Chance or possibility of danger, loss or injury. This can relate to the health and well-being of patients, staff, the public, property, reputation, environment, organisational functioning, financial stability, market share and other things of value to the organisation.

Risk assessment Identification of factors that may make a particular workforce, workplace or surrounding communities more vulnerable to infection with HIV.

Root cause analysis A process for identifying the basic or causal factors that underlie variation in performance, including the occurrence or possible occurrence of a sentinel/adverse event (Timmons, 2005:27).

Sanction A means of controlling behaviour, e.g. a penalty or reward.

Schemata A schema is a cognitive structure of substantial scale that is constructed from abstract and generic knowledge that will remain applicable or relevant across different situations and contexts. Structures of meaning (due to learning) – that will provide a framework for interpreting new or incoming information. Schemata (structures of meaning) will influence the way a person evaluates a situation and makes a judgement about the situation, object, behaviours, etc.

Scope of services The range and type of services offered by the organisation and any conditions or limits to service coverage.

Selection The process of choosing individuals who have relevant qualifications to fill existing or projected job openings.

Self-appraisal Performance appraisal done by the employee being evaluated, generally on the accepted appraisal form, prior to the performance interview.

Self-regulation Adhering to and following an internal standard; control from within. We are a self-regulating mechanism as we keep checking and correcting our performance against standards of our belief.

SENCER The Science Education for New Civic Engagements and Responsibilities model. A model utilised in the education of sensitive social issues, such as HIV and AIDS.

Sexual harassment Unwelcome advances, requests for sexual favours, and other verbal or physical conduct of a sexual nature in the working environment.

Skills inventories Files of education, experience, interests and skills that allow managers to quickly match job openings with employee backgrounds.

Solvency This is the extent to which the organisation's assets exceed its liabilities – the excess of total assets over total liabilities.

Span of command or control The number of subordinates supervised by a manager, based on the nature (complexity/type) of service delivery, the competencies/abilities of the subordinates and the competencies/abilities of the manager, to facilitate quality of service delivery and attainment of organisational goals and outputs.

Staffing Obtaining people with the appropriate skills, abilities, knowledge and experience to fill jobs in the work organisation. Key practices are human resource planning, job analysis, recruitment, selection and placement.

Stakeholder Individuals, organisations or groups that have an interest or share in services.

Standards A standard is a written description or statement of the expected level of performance with reference to structure, process and outcome. A desired and achievable level of performance against which actual performance is measured.

STIs Sexually transmitted infections.

Strategic goals Broad statements of where the organisation wants to be in the future. These goals pertain to the organisation as a whole rather than to specific divisions or departments.

Strategic management Strategic management is the continuous positioning or repositioning of the organisation, based on strategy analysis (external and internal environmental assessment), strategy development (determination of the organisation's mission, vision, values, goals and related strategic actions required to achieve the goals), strategy execution (the implementation or deployment of the strategy by translating the corporate goals and strategy into achievable objectives and action plans that cascade down to departmental, unit/area and individual levels), and strategy review (evaluation of organisational, departmental, unit/area and individual performance in accordance with the outcomes and indicators determined).

Strategy The plan of action that prescribes resource allocation and other activities for dealing with the environment and helping the organisation attain its goals.

Strategy analysis Strategy analysis consists of the internal (organisational profile analysis) and external environmental (scanning, monitoring, forecasting and assessing) analyses.

Strategy development Strategy development is a process of:

- Strategy assessment results: description of the organisational profile and the external environmental scan, as well as the strategic choices based on these results
- Formulation of the vision, mission and value statements
- Formulation of strategic goals
- Development of key priorities (Key Performance Areas) and subsequent action plans

- Master strategy
- Integration with the Balanced Scorecard.

Strategy execution Strategy execution refers to the implementation or deployment of the strategy/strategic plan.

Strategy review Strategy review is the process of strategic control, by which management ensures that the organisation's strategic goals are accomplished and/or that actual performance compares favourably with the predetermined performance standards. This process comprises four steps: setting of standards, measuring actual performance against these standards, evaluating deviations that might occur, and taking steps to rectify deviations.

Structured interview An interview in which a set of standardised questions having an established set of answers is used.

Substantive Describes a tangible reason or action, something that can be quantified, or a confirmed state or condition.

Surveyor External peer assessment which measures the performance of the organisation against an agreed set of standards.

Susceptibility Factors determining the rate at which the HIV pandemic is propagated at an individual, group or societal level.

Symbol An object, act, or event that conveys meaning to others.

Task analysis Process of determining what the content of a training programme should be on the basis of a study of the tasks or duties involved in the job.

Team appraisal Performance appraisal, based on TQM concepts, that recognises team accomplishment rather than individual performance.

Total quality management (TQM) Refers to an integrated and coordinated management approach that makes provision for the corporate, middle and operational management and execution of the organisation's CQI strategy. The CQI strategy is reflected in the key performance areas (KPAs) of the overall strategic plan of the healthcare organisation, focusing on both general corporate governance as well as specialised clinical governance.

Transfer of training Effective application of principles learned to what is required on the job.

Transgression Breaking of a rule or law.

Treatment Steps taken to care and manage an illness.

Tripartite Consisting of three parties.

Trustworthiness Trustworthiness refers to the validity and reliability of a system. This means that the results or outcomes reflected are credible and can be confirmed when a similar investigation is done in the same circumstances (internal and external variables impacting on the result/outcome remain stagnant). Trustworthiness implies the following:

- Truth value: the assessor has faith in the findings – they are accurate and correct

- Relevance: the findings relate to the purpose, intention and content of the assessment
- Consistency: the same findings or results will be obtained when the same data sources are used – the assessor will allocate the same rating if the process is repeated. This implies that the results are saturated – the sample is representative of the whole
- Neutrality: the findings are based on objective judgement and are not influenced by the assessor's bias or self-interest.

Turnover rate Number of separations during a month divided by the total number of employees at mid-month times 100.

Ubuntu This is a metaphor that describes the significance of group solidarity, on survival issues, that is central to the survival of African communities.

Unauthorised expenditure Overspending of a vote or a main division within a vote; expenditure not in accordance with the purpose of a vote or the purpose of a main division (South Africa, 1999:10).

Unfair discrimination An employee is treated differently due to their real or perceived HIV status, in a way that impairs their fundamental dignity. Discrimination is not unfair if it is based on the inherent requirements of the job.

Unfair labour practice Specific employer and union illegal practices that operate to deny employees their rights and benefits under labour law.

Union shop Provision of the labour agreement that requires employees to join the union as a requirement for their employment.

Union steward Employee who as a non-paid union official represents the interests of members in their relations with management.

Upward communication Messages transmitted from the lower to higher levels in the organisational hierarchy.

Validity The extent to which a measure truly measures only what it is intended to measure.

VCT Voluntary counselling and testing programmes, to determine the HIV status of a person.

Vertical formal communication Vertical communication takes place between the practitioners and management at different levels, according to the organisational design of the healthcare organisation, with reference to general and functional management.

Vision A dream, aspiration or idea as to what the future should be or look like.

Votes In the public sector budget framework, the vote describes the entire budget of each department that is brought before Parliament and provincial legislators. Each department then has a vote on its budget.

Vulnerability External factors that place a person at risk of HIV infection. Vulnerability factors includes for example, age, gender and income level.

Waive Not to insist, to give up or forgo.

Wellness programme A programme designed to promote the physical and mental well-being of employees, including components such as counselling, support groups, nutritional supplements, provision of treatment for opportunistic infections, provision of antiretroviral therapy, etc.

World of work The operational, intra-organisational or micro-dimension of economic activity.

Worker's compensation insurance State-mandated insurance provided to workers to defray the loss of income and cost of treatment due to work-related injuries or illness.

Workplace programme A formalised and structured programme to mitigate and manage HIV and AIDS in the workplace, focusing on dimensions related to the leadership and management framework, prevention and awareness programmes, as well as care support programmes.

Work specialisation The degree to which organisational tasks are sub-divided into individual jobs; so-called division of labour.

Work team A job involvement technique whereby jobs are structured for groups rather than for individuals, and team members are given discretion in matters traditionally considered management prerogatives, such as work scheduling, individual work assignments and/or performance reviews.

References

Abedian, I., Strachan, B. & Ajam, T. 1998. *Transformation in action. Budgeting for health service delivery*. Rondebosch: University of Cape Town Press.

Abedian, I., Strachan, B. & Ajam, T. 2001. *Transformation in action: Budgeting for health service delivery*. Rondebosch: University of Cape Town Press.

Alderslade, R. & Hunter, D.J. 1994. Commissioning and public health. *Journal of Management in Medicine*, 8(6):20–31.

Amos, T., Ristow, A. & Ristow, L. 2004. *Human resource management*. Second edition. Lansdowne: Juta.

Anstey, M. (ed). 1997. *Employee participation and workplace forums*. Kenwyn: Juta.

Apps, J.W. 1994. *Leadership for the emerging age*. San Francisco: Jossey-Bass.

Bamberger, P. & Meshoulam, I. 2000. *Human resource strategy*. Thousand Oaks: Sage.

Barker, F. 2003. *The South African labour market*. Fourth edition. Pretoria: Van Schaik.

Beach, D.S. 1985. *Personnel: The management of people at work*. Fifth edition. New York: Macmillan.

Bechtold, B.L. 2004. Chaos theory as a model for strategy development. *Empowerment In Organizations*, 5 (4), 2004:93–201.

Belohlav, J. & LaVan, H. 1989. The impact of corporate restructuring on human resource management functions. *International Journal of Manpower*, 10(3). (Http://miranda.emerladinsight.com).

Bendell, J. 2003. *Waking up to risk. Corporate responses to HIV/AIDS in the workplace*. Geneva: United Nations Research Institute for Social Development.

Bendix, S. 1996. *Industrial relations in the new South Africa*. Third edition. Kenwyn: Juta.

Bennett, A.R. 1994. Business planning: Can the health service move from strategy into action? *Journal of Management in Medicine*, 8(2):24–33.

Bezuidenhout, M.C., Garbers, C.J. & Potgieter, S. 1998. *Managing for healthy labour relations. A practical guide for health services in Southern Africa*. Pretoria: Van Schaik.

Booyens, S.W. (ed). 1998. *Dimensions of nursing management*. Second edition. Lansdowne: Juta.

Booyens, S.W. (ed). 2001. *Introduction to health services management.* Second edition. Kenwyn: Juta.
Botha, L. 2005. Moving from plan, sing, hope and forget (PSHF) to plan, do, check and act (PDCA). Unpublished paper delivered at the 11th Annual ISO Symposium 15–17 February 2005, Sandton, South Africa.
Bratton, J. & Gold, J. 2003. *Human resource management theory and practice.* Third edition. New York: Palgrave.
Brownlie, D. 1999. Benchmarketing your marketing process. *Long Range Planning,* 32(1):88–95.
Buys, L. 2004. Disaster management: Early warning systems. Unpublished paper delivered at the International Risk Control Conference Johannesburg 27–28 July 2004.
Byers, J.F. 2001. Marketing: A nursing leadership imperative. *Nursing Economics,* 19(3):94–99.

Carrell, M.R., Elbert, N.F. & Hatfield, R.D. 2000. *Human resource management. Strategies for managing a diverse and global workforce.* Sixth edition. Sydney: The Dryden Press.
Chang, R.Y. & Morgan, M.W. 2000. *Performance scorecards. Measuring the right things in the real world.* San Francisco: Jossey-Bass.
Charlton, G. 2000. *Human habits of highly effective organisations. The human race.* Cape Town: Van Schaik.
Chase, R. 1997. Knowledge management benchmarks. *Journal of Knowledge Management,* 1(1): 83–92.
Collins, J. 2001. *Good to Great.* London: Random House Business Books.
Corporate Governance Series 2003. *Being a director. Duties and responsibilities – King II.* Johannesburg: PricewaterhouseCoopers.
Correia, C., Flynn, D., Uliana, E. & Wormald, M. 2003. *Financial management.* Fifth edition. Lansdowne: Juta.
Council for Health Service Accreditation of Southern Africa (COHSASA). 2004. *Standards for hospitals, Service element 6: Information management.* COHSASA: Pinelands.
Cruywagen, G. 2004. Risk and disaster management as part of corporate governance: Leading to best business practice. Unpublished paper delivered at the International Risk Control Conference Johannesburg 27–28 July 2004.

Daft, R.L. 1999. *Leadership. Theory and practice.* Orlando: Harcourt Brace College.
Daft, R.L. 2000. *Management.* Fifth edition. Fort Worth: Dryden Press.
De Beer, C. 2004. The health impact during a disaster. Unpublished paper delivered at the International Risk Control Conference Johannesburg 27–28 July.
De Bruyn, H.E.C. (editor). 2003. *Strategic Management. A South African Perspective.* Fourth edition. Johannesburg: Entepro Publishers.

De J. Cronjé, G.J., Du Toit, G.S., Motlatla, M.D.C. & De K. Marais, A. (eds). 2004. *Introduction to business management*. 6th edition. Southern Africa: Oxford University Press.

Department of Health. 1999. *A patients' rights charter*. Pretoria: Department of Health.

Department of Health. 2000. *HIV/AIDS & STD strategic plan for South Africa 2000–2005*. Pretoria: Department of Health.

Department of Health. 2002. *Strategic priorities for the national health system 2004–2009*. Pretoria: Department of Health.

Department of Labour. (undated). *HIV/AIDS technical assistance guidelines*. Cape Town: Department of Labour.

Dessler, G. 1985. *Management fundamentals*. Fourth edition. Englewood Cliffs, NJ: Prentice Hall.

Dessler, G. 1997. *Human resource management*. Seventh edition. London: Prentice Hall.

Dienemann, J.A. 1998. *Nursing administration. Managing patient care*. Second edition. Stamford: Appleton & Lange.

Dolan, S.L. & Schuler, R.S. 1996: *Personnel and human resource management in Canada*. St Paul: West Publishing.

Ehlers, V.J., Oosthuizen, M.J., Bezuidenhout, M.C., Monareng, L.V. & Jooste, K. 2003. Post-basic nursing students' perceptions of the emigration of nurses from the Republic of South Africa. *Health SA Gesondheid*, 8(4):24–37.

Fiang, P. 2000. Segment-based mass customerisation: An exploration of a new conceptual marketing framework. Internet research: Electronic networking applications and policy, 10(3):215–226.

Galbraith, P. 2003. Chaos mini-theme: Organisational leadership and chaos theory. Let's be careful. *Journal of Educational Administration*, 42 (1), 2003:1,9–28.

Gauld, R. 2003. The inpact on officials of public sector restructuring. *The International Journal of Public Sector Management*, 16(4):303–119.

Gerber, P.D., Nel, P.S. & Van Dyk, P.S. 1998: *Human resource management*. Fourth edition. Johannesburg: Thomson.

Gido, J. & Clements, J.P. 2003. *Successful Project Management*. Second edition. United States: Thomson South-Western.

Gillies, D.A. 1994. *Nursing management a systems approach*. Third edition. Philadelphia: W.B. Saunders.

Handy, L., Barham, K., Panter, S. & Winhard, A. 1989. Beyond the personnel function: The strategic management of human resources. *Journal of European Industrial Training*, 13(1). (Http://miranda.emeraldinsight.com)

Harrison, R. 1997: *Employee development*. Wiltshire: Cromwell.

Hellriegel, D. & Slocum, J.W. 1898: *Management*. Fifth edition. Menlo park, NJ: Addison Wesley.

Hill, J., McGowan, P. & Maclaran, P. 1998. Developing marketing planning skills. Combining theory and practice. *Journal of Marketing Practice: Applied Marketing Science*, 4(3):69–84.

Institute of Directors. 2002. *King report on corporate governance for South Africa 2002. Executive Summary*. Johannesburg: Institute of Directors.

International Labour Organisation. 2001. *Code of practice: HIV/AIDS in the world of work*. Geneva: ILO.

International Labour Organisation. 2004. *HIV/AIDS and work: Global estimates, impact and response*. Geneva: ILO.

Ivancevich, J.M. & Matteson, J.M. 1996. *Organizational behavior and management*. Fourth edition. Chicago, Ill: Irwin.

Jackson, S. Skills required for health commissioning. *Health Manpower Planning*, 24(1):40–43.

Jackson, S.E. & Schuler, R.S. 2000. *Managing human resources: A partnership perspective*. Seventh edition. Cincinnati: South-Western College Publishing.

Johnson, D.M. 2004. Adaptation of organizational change models to the implementation of quality standard requirements. *International Journal of Quality & Reliability Management*, 21(2):154–174.

Jooste, K. (ed). 2003. *Leadership in health services management*. Cape Town: Juta.

Kamoche, K.N., Debrah, Y.A., Horwitz, F.M. & Muuka, G.N. 2004. *Managing human resources in Africa*. London: Routledge.

Kaplan, R.S. & Norton, D.P. 1996. *The balanced scorecard*. Harvard Business School.

Kaplan, R. 2000. The balanced scorecard. Making strategy happen. Workshop presentation 8 May 2000. Midrand South Africa.

Karami, A., Analoui, F. & Cusworh, J. 2004. Strategic human resource management and resource-based approach: The evidence from the British manufacturing industry. *Management Research News*, 27(6):50–68.

Keating, M. & Thompson, K. 2004. International human resource management: Overcoming disciplinary sectarianism. *Employee Relations*, 26(6):595–612.

King Committee on Corporate Governance. 2002. *King report on corporate governance for South Africa (Executive summary)*. Parktown: Institute of Directors in Southern Africa.

Kleiman, L.S. 2000. *Human resource management*. Second edition. Cincinnati: South-Western College Publishing.

Koekemoer, L. (ed). 2001. *Promotional strategy. Marketing communications in practice*. Kenwyn: Juta.

Laing, A.W. & McKee, L. 1998. Structuring the marketing function in complex professional service organisations. *European Journal of Marketing*, 34(5/6):576–597.

Lamb, C.W., Hair, J.F. & McDaniel, C. 2004. *Marketing*. Australia: Thomson.

Lewin, K. 1951. *Field theory in social science*. New York: Harper & Row.

Marquis, B.L. & Huston, C.J. 1996: *Leadership roles and management functions in nursing, theory and application*. Second edition. Philadelphia: Lippincott.

Marriner-Tomey, A. 1996. *Guide to nursing management and leadership*. St Louis: Mosby.

Marx, J., De Swardt, C., Beaumont-Smith, M., Naicker, B. & Erasmus, P. 2004. *Financial management in southern Africa*. Second edition. Cape Town: Pearson Education.

Mbigi, L. 1992. UNHU or UBUNTU the basis for effective HR management. *People Dynamics*, October 1992:20–25.

Mbigi, L. Maree, J. 1995. *UBUNTU the spirit of African transformation management*. Randburg: Knowledge Resources.

McCourt, W. & Eldrige, D. 2003. *Global human resource management. Managing people in developing and transitional countries*. Cheltenham, UK: Edward Elgar.

Mintzberg, H. 1987. The nature of managerial work. In J.H. Donnely, J.C. Gibson & J.M. Ivancevich, *Fundamentals of Management*. Texas: Business Publications.

Mondy, R.W. & Noe, R.M. 1993. *Human resource management*. Fifth edition. Boston: Allyn and Bacon.

Moorhead, G. & Griffin, R.W. 1995: *Organizational behavior*. Fourth edition. Geneva: Houghton Mifflin.

Morgan, R.E. 1996. Conceptual foundation of marketing and marketing theory. *Management Decision*, 34(10:19–26.

Muller, M.E. 2002. *Nursing dynamics*. Third edition. Sandown: Heinemann.

Nel, P.S. (ed). 2002. *South African employment relations theory and practice*. Third edition. Pretoria: Van Schaik.

Nicholas, R. 2004: Knowledge management impacts on decision making process. *Journal of Knowledge Management*, 8(1): 20–31.

Norton, D. 1999. *The balanced scorecard. Translating strategy to action (Workbook 2nd annual forum)*. Rosebank: Institute for International Research.

Pascale, R. 1990. *Managing on the edge*. London: Penguin Books.

Pennington, S. 2001. What's happening out here? In *Human capital strategies for the 21st centuary*. Rivonia: SPA Publications.

Pittet, D. 2005. *Global patient safety challenge 2005–2006*. Paper delivered at the WHO World Alliance for Patient Safety, Durban RSA 19 January 2005. (www.who.int/patientsafety/en).

Predpall, D.F. 1994. Developing quality improvement processes in consulting engineering firms. *Journal of Management in Engineering*, May & June edition, 30–31.

PricewaterhouseCoopers & Institute of Directors. 2003. *Being a director. Duties and responsibilities*. Corporate Governance Series. Johannesburg. Institute of Directors.

Rautenbach, I.M. & Malherbe, E.F.J. 1998. *What does the constitution SAY?* Pretoria: Van Schaik.

Robbins, S.P. 1996. *Oganizational behavior.* Seventh edition. Englewood Cliffs: Prentice Hall.

Robbins, D. 2004. Importance of crisis management. Unpublished paper delivered at the International Risk Control Conference Johannesburg 27–28 July 2004.

Rossouw, D. 2002. *Business ethics in Africa*. Second edition. Oxford: Oxford University Press.

Salamon, M. 1992. *Industrial relations theory and practice*. Second edition. New York: Prentice Hall.

Schuler, R.S. & Jackson, S.E. 1996. *Human resource management positioning for the 21st century*. Sixth edition. Los Angeles: West Publishing.

Searle, C. & Pera, S. 1995. *Professional practice. A Southern African perspective.* Durban: Butterworths.

Shaw, C.D. 2003. *Quality and accreditation in health care services: A global review.* Geneva: WHO/ISQua.

Shaw, C.D. 2004. *Toolkit for accreditation programs.* The International Society for Quality in Health Care (ISQua): Australia (www.isqua.org).

Sherman, A., Bohlander, G. & Snell, S. 1996. *Managing human resources*. Tenth edition. Cincinnati: South-Western College Publishing.

Siddiqui, J. & Kleiner, B.H. 1998. Human resource management in the health care industry. *Health Manpower Management*, 24(4):143–147.

Smit, P.J. & De J. Cronjé, G.J. 2002. *Management principles: A contemporary edition for Africa*. Third edition. Lansdowne: Juta.

South Africa (Republic). 1973. *Companies Act, No 52 of 1973*. Pretoria: Government Printers.

South Africa (Republic). 1993. *Compensation for Occupational Injuries and Diseases Act, No 130 of 1993*. Pretoria: Government Printers.

South Africa (Republic). 1993. *Standards Act, No 29 of 1993*. Pretoria: Government Printers.

South Africa (Republic). 1996. *Basic Conditions of Employment Act, No 75 of 1997*. Pretoria: Government Printers.

South Africa (Republic). 1996: *Constitution of the Republic of South Africa, No 108 of 1996*. Pretoria: Government Printers.

South Africa (Republic). 1996. *Employment Equity Act, No 55 of 1998*. Pretoria: Government Printers.
South Africa (Republic). 1996. *Labour Relations Act, No 66 of 1995*. Pretoria: Government Printers.
South Africa (Republic). 1996. *Occupational Health and Safety Act, No 85 of 1993*. Pretoria: Government Printers.
South Africa (Republic). 1996. *Skills Development Act, No 97 of 1998*. Pretoria: Government Printers.
South Africa (Republic). 1996. *Skills Development Levies Act, No 9 of 1999*. Pretoria: Government Printers.
South Africa (Republic). 1996. *Unemployment Insurance Act, No 63 of 2001*. Pretoria: Government Printers.
South Africa (Republic). 1997. *White Paper on Transforming Public Service Delivery. Batho Pele White Paper, No 18340 of 1997*. Pretoria: Government Printers.
South Africa (Republic). 1998. *Medical Schemes Act, No 131 of 1998*. Pretoria: Government Printers.
South Africa (Republic). 1998. *Municipal Structures Act, No 117 of 1998*. Pretoria: Government Printers.
South Africa (Republic). 1998. *National Environmental Management Act, No 107 of 1998*. Pretoria: Government Printers.
South Africa (Republic). 1998. *South African Quality Assurance Act, No 58 of 1998*. Pretoria: Government Printers.
South Africa (Republic). 1999. *Financial Management Act, No 1 of 1999*. Pretoria: Government Printers.
South Africa (Republic). 1999. *Public Finance Management Act, No 1 of 1999*. Pretoria: Government Printers.
South Africa (Republic). 2000. *Council for Medical Schemes Levies Act, No 58 of 2000*. Pretoria: Government Printers.
South Africa (Republic). 2000. *Municipal Systems Act, No 32 of 2000*. Pretoria: Government Printers.
South Africa (Republic). 2000. *Promotion of Access to Information Act, No 2 of 2000*. Pretoria: Government Printers.
South Africa (Republic). 2001. *Unemployment Insurance Act, No 63 of 2001*. Pretoria: Government Printers.
South Africa (Republic). 2002. *Disaster Management Act, 57 of 2002*. Pretoria: Government Printers.
South Africa (Republic). 2003. *National Health Act, No 61, of 2003*. Pretoria: Government Printers.
South African Treasury. 2002. *MTEF Budget Guidelines*. Pretoria: Government Printers.
SPA Publications. 2001. *Human capital strategies for the 21st century*. Rivonia: SPA.

Stacey, R.D., Griffen, D. & Shaw, P. 2000. *Compexity and emergence in organizations.* New York: Routledge.
Stanton, W.J., Etzel, M.J. & Walker, B.J. 1994. *Fundamentals of marketing*. Tenth edition. New York: McGraw-Hill.
Sullivan, E.J. & Decker, P.J. 1992. *Effective management in nursing*. New York: Addison-Wesley.
Sullivan T.J. 2003. The viability of using various system theories to describe organizational change. *Journal of Educational Administration*, 42(1)2003:43–54.
Swansburg, R.C. 1993. *Introductory management and leadership for clinical nurses*. Boston: Jones and Bartlett.
Swansburg, R.C. 1996. *Management and leadership for nurse managers*. Second edition. Boston: Jones & Bartlett.
Swansberg, R.C. & Swansburg, R.J. 1999: *Introductory management and leadership for nurses*. Second edition. Boston: Jones and Bartlett.

Tappen, R.M. 2001. *Nursing leadership and management concepts and practice*. Fourth edition. Philadelphia: FA Davis.
Timmons, K. 2005. Fundamentals of patient safety. Paper delivered at the WHO World Alliance for Patient Safety, Durban RSA 19 January 2005. [www.who.int/patientsafety/en]
Torpman, J. 2004. The differentiating function of modern forms of leadership. *Management Decision*, 42(7):892–906.
Torrington, D. & Hall, L. 1998. *Human resource management*. Fourth edition. London: Prentice Hall.

UNICEF. 2003. *Fighting HIV/AIDS strategies for success 2002–2005*. New York: UNICEF.
United Nations General Assembly Special Session (UNGASS). 2001. Declaration of Commitment of HIV/AIDS: 'Global Crisis – Global Action'. United Nations General Assembly Special Session on HIV/AIDS, 2 August. (www.unaids.org/whatsnew/others/unspecial/Declaration2706_en.htm).
United Nations Programme on HIV/AIDS (UNAIDS). 2003. *Waking up to risk. Corporate responses to HIV/AIDS in the workplace*. Geneva: UNRISD.

Van der Waldt, G. & Du Toit, D.F.P. 1999. *Managing for excellence in the public sector*. Second edition. Kenwyn: Juta.
Van Rensburg, H.C.J. (ed). 2004. *Health and health care in South Africa*. Pretoria: Van Schaik Publishers.
Van Staden, E., Marx. S. & Erasmus-Kritzinger, L. 2002. *Corporate communication. Getting the message across in business*. Pretoria: Van Schaik.
Van Tonder, C.L. 2004. *Organisational change. Theory and practice*. Pretoria: Van Schaik.

Varey, R.J. & Lewis, B.R. 1998. A broader conception of internal marketing. *European Journal of Marketing*, 33(9/10):926–944.
Vasuthevan, S. & Viljoen, M. 2003. *Educating for better health: A handbook for healthcare professionals*. Lansdowne: Juta.
Verwey, S. & Du Plooy-Cilliers, F. 2003. *Strategic organizational communication. Paradigms and paradoxes.* Cape Town: Heinemann.
Vincent, C. & Corbett-Nolan, A. 2003. Adverse event reporting in store for South Africa. *Quality Healthcare*, 1(1) 2003:12.

Whittaker, S. 2005. *COHSASA Executive Unit Report May 2005.* Pinelands: COHSASA (unpublished).

Websites

AGREE Instrument: (www.agreecollaboration.org.instrument).

Bennis, W. 2002. (http://www.nwlink.com/-donclark/leader/leadled.html)

International Society for Quality in Health Care. (www.isqua.org).
International Standardisation Organisation (ISO). 2003. *AIDS management standard 16001:2003*. (www.iso.org).
International Standardization Organization (ISO). 2005. Introduction. (www.iso.org).
International Standardization Organization (ISO). 2005. *Quality management principles*. (www.iso.org).

Knowledge management: www.knowledgemanagementnetwork.com/whatis.htm.
(http://www.duke.edu/-mccann/m-nature.htlm)

Malcom Baldridge Awards (www.asq.org/abtquality/awards/baldrige.html).

SENCER. 2002. Science Education for New Civic Engagements and Responsibilities. Washington: Association of American Colleges and Universities. (http://www.aacu.org/SENCER).

Wolf, L.E. & Bernard, L. 2001. Ethical dimensions of HIV/AIDS. HIV InSite. (www.hivinsite.ucsf.edu/InSite.jsp).
World Health Organisation: (www.who.org).

Index